KT-368-493

Social Psychology and Everyday Life

Darrin Hodgetts
Associate Professor, University of Waikato

Neil Drew
Dean, University of Notre Dame, Australia

Christopher Sonn
Senior Lecturer, Victoria University, Australia

Ottilie Stolte
Lecturer, University of Waikato

Linda Waimarie Nikora
Senior Lecturer, University of Waikato

Cate Curtis
Lecturer, University of Waikato

palgrave
macmillan

© Darrin Hodgetts, Neil Drew, Christopher Sonn, Ottilie Stolte, Linda Waimarie Nikora, Cate Curtis 2010

All rights reserved. No reproduction, copy or transmission of this publication may be made without written permission.

No portion of this publication may be reproduced, copied or transmitted save with written permission or in accordance with the provisions of the Copyright, Designs and Patents Act 1988, or under the terms of any licence permitting limited copying issued by the Copyright Licensing Agency, Saffron House, 6-10 Kirby Street, London EC1N 8TS.

Any person who does any unauthorized act in relation to this publication may be liable to criminal prosecution and civil claims for damages.

The authors have asserted their rights to be identified as the authors of this work in accordance with the Copyright, Designs and Patents Act 1988.

First published 2010 by
PALGRAVE MACMILLAN

Palgrave Macmillan in the UK is an imprint of Macmillan Publishers Limited, registered in England, company number 785998, of Houndmills, Basingstoke, Hampshire RG21 6XS.

Palgrave Macmillan in the US is a division of St Martin's Press LLC, 175 Fifth Avenue, New York, NY 10010.

Palgrave Macmillan is the global academic imprint of the above companies and has companies and representatives throughout the world.

Palgrave® and Macmillan® are registered trademarks in the United States, the United Kingdom, Europe and other countries.

ISBN: 978–0–230–21795–9

This book is printed on paper suitable for recycling and made from fully managed and sustained forest sources. Logging, pulping and manufacturing processes are expected to conform to the environmental regulations of the country of origin.

A catalogue record for this book is available from the British Library.

A catalog record for this book is available from the Library of Congress.

10 9 8 7 6 5 4 3 2 1
19 18 17 16 15 14 13 12 11 10

Printed in China

WEST SUFFOLK HOSPITALS
CLINICAL RESOURCE CENTRE
AND LIBRARY

DATE 2 . 9 . 10 .

VENDOR: Tomlinsons

CLASSMARK Hm 251 /to D

PRICE £ 28 . 50

Contents

Acknowledgements vi

About the authors vii

1 Introduction to the social psychology of everyday life 1

2 A history of social psychology 21

3 Contemporary social psychology and the focus on everyday life 51

4 Making sense of everyday knowledge 77

5 Indigenous psychologies and the social psychology of everyday life................................. 113

6 Social psychology and place 149

7 Immigration, acculturation and settlement 181

8 Understanding health and illness 217

9 Social justice in everyday life 253

10 Pro-social behaviour and critical humanism 287

11 Media and daily practice... 321

12 Towards social psychologies of everyday life... 357

References.. 373

Author Index 413

Subject Index...419

Acknowledgements

The authors would like to acknowledge that many discussions with colleagues have helped to shape ideas for this book. Particular colleagues include Andrea Hodgetts, Alan Radley, Caroline Howarth, David Snell, Dawn Darlaston Jones, Doug Boer, Kerry Chamberlain, Lutfiye Ali, Mariolga Reyes Cruz, Mohi Rua, Romana Morda, Sarla Sujan, Sharon McCarthy, Shiloh Groot, Wen Li and Wilf Holt. Thanks to Jamie Joseph from Palgrave Macmillan for supporting the project. The time and effort of the anonymous reviewers is appreciated, and their comments were particularly helpful in extending the scope of this book. We are grateful to John Dixon for allowing us to reproduce photos he has produced in his research. We would also like to acknowledge the ideas and enthusiasm of our artists, James Foley and Marian Stolte de Vletter. Thanks also to Rob Bakker for technical assistance with illustrations.

About the authors

Associate Professor Darrin Hodgetts
Darrin Hodgetts is currently a reader in Social Psychology in the Faculty of Arts and Social Sciences at the University of Waikato. Prior to this appointment, Darrin held posts in Community Health at Memorial University in Canada and in Psychology and Media and Communications at the London School of Economics and Political Science. Darrin has more than ten years' experience working in a range of community settings. His research spans the media, health, homelessness, social inequalities, place and civic engagement.

Professor Neil Drew
Neil Drew is Head of Behavioural Science and Dean of Arts and Sciences at the University of Notre Dame Australia (UNDA). He is a social psychologist with more than twenty-five years' experience working with a range of communities and groups. He has worked with Aboriginal and Torres Strait Islander communities since beginning his career as a volunteer at the Aboriginal and Torres Strait Islander Medical Service in far north Queensland. He was a psychologist for the Department of Family Services in Queensland. Prior to joining UNDA, he was Director of the University of Western Australia Institute for Regional Development. At UNDA he is the programme head and cofounder of the Aboriginal Youth and Community Wellbeing Program in East Kimberley, established in 2006. The programme is funded by the Gelganyem Aboriginal Trust. It promotes wellness and suicide prevention among young people in East Kimberley Aboriginal communities.

Dr Christopher Sonn
Christopher Sonn is a lecturer at Victoria University in Community and Cultural Psychology and Qualitative Research Methods, Australia. His research is into sense of community, intergroup relations and community cultural development. Christopher is an associate editor for the *Journal of Community and Applied Social Psychology* and co-editor of *Psychology of Liberation*.

Dr Ottilie Stolte

Ottilie Stolte has pursued research in the areas of community development, the not-for-profit sector, policy frameworks and grassroots responses to social and environmental issues. Currently, Ottilie holds an academic position in the Psychology Department at the University of Waikato, where she teaches in Applied Social and Community Psychology and co-manages a project researching the lifeworlds of homeless people.

Associate Professor Linda Waimarie Nikora

Linda Waimarie Nikora is Director of the Maori and Psychology Research Unit at the University of Waikato, New Zealand. Her training is in social, community and ethnocultural psychology. As a Maori person she has pursued her commitment to her own indigenous group through extensive Maori community research. She is currently working on a project that explores the changing nature of Maori ways of death and death rituals.

Dr Cate Curtis

Cate Curtis is a lecturer at Waikato University. She has previously managed a large university research unit and has a senior consultant for a private research organisation; she is the co-author of a text on research. Her current interests are in the field of youth health, particularly the ways risk, resilience and recovery are conceptualized and the implications of these concepts for policy and practice.

1 Introduction to the social psychology of everyday life

Core questions to consider while reading this chapter

- What would it mean for you to get on the bus and become a social psychologist?
- What is action research?
- Why is social transformation important to social psychologists?
- What contributions have social psychologists made to society?
- What does 'praxis' mean, and how does is relate to 'reflexivity'?
- What do we mean by 'social transformation'?

Chapter scenario: Getting on the bus by James Ritchie, March 2008

It is 1960 and the South of the United States is seething with the consequences of racial desegregation. Following the stand by Rosa Parks in Alabama to refuse to sit in the segregated back of a rural bus, challenges were arising wherever racial discrimination was practised. The rhetoric of Martin Luther King and Malcolm X was shaking the South and school desegregation was not far ahead. The challenges in the courts were out on the streets and change was inevitable and hard.

I was at Harvard at the time. Why Harvard? Why not! I was beginning a career in social and cultural psychology. Harvard was loaded with repute and with names, and I wanted to meet the real people whose books I had read. Social psychology was on its great modern wave. Gordon Allport was there. His *The Nature of Prejudice* had joined Theodor Adorno's *Authoritarian Personality*, Kurt Lewin's *Resolving Social Conflicts* and many others, had shaken the bounded limits of orthodox psychology and captured the excitement of the times. Notably, these were voices calling for a psychology that spoke to the issues of the day, calling for political, social and indeed personal commitment.

How could psychologists possibly ignore this? Well, many, even at Harvard, did, but not so Allport's students. They issued the challenge and for several weeks ran training seminars in nonviolent action and organized buses to drive down over weekends to Selma and other places in the Deep South, where they staged sit-ins in segregated bars. They knew that they would be confronted by angry citizens, moved on by the police, subjected to hostility and terror, but they went. The risk of getting your head bashed in was real.

This was the psychology of action that Kurt Lewin had called for in his book twelve years before. The alternative campus excitements of dropping acid with Timothy Leary at Palfrey House or of teaching rats to press bars or pigeons to peck with Skinner at Memorial Hall could not compete with a psychology of the real. Even the clinicians were entering the arena of social understandings because the real client, beyond the individual, was society, and mental health could never be achieved unless social change supported personal change. Social issues moved to the centre of the discipline, where they remain.

We begin with this firsthand account because it raises a number of issues central to this book and the approach to social psychology that we adopt. It highlights how social psychology has been around for some time as an applied area of the human sciences that attempts to meet the needs of people in society. James Ritchie describes a situation in which a group of psychologists are responding to events in the world, and acting in an overtly political manner to help shape the direction of a society. Ritchie was present when psychology rediscovered its conscience.

The scenario also highlights how exciting the world can be. Social psychology can also be exciting, particularly when we involve ourselves in events in the world. Social psychologists have a long history of getting involved in social issues. Through this scenario we can see how social psychology and those contributing to its development can be influenced by, and influence, circumstance. Events in our lives and our experiences permeate our work. Examples of such links are explored in Chapter 2, such as Kurt Lewin fleeing persecution in Nazi Germany and subsequently advocating the need for psychological work to resolve social conflicts (Farr, 1991). For the authors of this book, this is reflected in Linda's and Neil's work on indigenous land rights; Chris's work with immigrant groups; Cate's responses to the needs of young people who self-harm; and Darrin's and Ottilie's efforts to improve the lives of homeless people.

Review exercise

Put yourselves now in the place of those students in 1960 featured in the chapter scenario.

■   Would you be on the bus or off the bus?

■   How would you decide?

Chapter overview

This chapter provides an introduction to the orientation of this book, the importance of research that addresses everyday realities, and the subsequent chapters. The first section briefly introduces our stance regarding the socially and culturally located nature of social psychology and how this informs the book. The second section explores the importance of an action research and social transformation orientation to the social psychology of everyday life. The final section provides an overview of the book. In summary, this chapter emphasizes:

■   The social and cultural embeddedness of social psychology and this book

■   The centrality of action research and social transformation in social psychology

■   The contributions of each chapter to a psychology of everyday life

A socially and culturally embedded orientation to social psychology

This book encourages readers to think of social psychology as a historically and culturally embedded, relevant and socially responsive discipline. We would like you to consider getting on the bus and engaging in the broader project of social justice that is central to the discipline.

Social psychology is maturing. The discipline is increasingly reaching beyond notions of psychology as science and deeper into the social sciences and humanities. Many social psychologists find themselves working unashamedly as value-oriented and engaged individuals pursuing socially just outcomes through research and practice. James Ritchie certainly got on the bus and contributed four decades of work that improved the lives of many Maori, the indigenous people of New Zealand (Ritchie, 1992). Similarly, Gordon Allport (1968, 1985) extended his work on prejudice as a result of his experiences, to develop a social psychology that was relevant to bettering people's lives. Such work requires an acknowledgement of the social influences on human life, both academic and private. No approach to social psychology is value-free, and all approaches reflect aspects of the social, historical and political climate in which they are developed (Tajfel, 1981). This is why multiple perspectives are valuable.

Social psychology is replete with references to the importance of situations and contexts for understanding human thought, actions and relationships (Montero, 2007; Parker, 2005). Discussions of seminal experimental studies into obedience to authority (Milgram, 1965), which you were probably introduced to in introductory psychology courses, often invoke the events of Nazi Germany. These studies attempted to explain why, given specific circumstances, citizens might participate in the systematic extermination of their neighbours. Such studies, which respond to historical events in society, are crucial for the development of a social psychology that is relevant and can contribute to promoting peaceful relations. Needless to say, it was impossible for researchers actually to conduct such a study on local populations, so a series of experimental simulations were appropriate. Yet the reduction of complex social processes to simulations comes at a cost, and it has not gone without criticism. As noted in Chapter 2, in the late 1960s and early 1970s the dominance of experimental methods and reduced engagements with actual events as they occurred in society led to some disciplinary soul searching. Many social psychologists began to reflect openly on the orientation and limitations of the discipline (Gergen, 1973; Parker, 1989). Questions included, What can we know? How do we collect information? What should we do with the knowledge generated through research?

In this book we apply insights both from a social psychology modelled on the physical sciences and from social psychologies that draw more from the social sciences and humanities. This constitutes an attempt to acknowledge the limitations of the discipline while informing our trips on the bus and our efforts to winding roads of research and practice.

All social psychologists need to consider the context of their own interests and work (Montero, 2007; Parker, 2005). However, it seems that many social psychologists are somewhat reticent about their investments in, and motivations for, research. Many scholars feel unable to be open about the ways in which their own backgrounds and experiences influence the focus and direction of their work. This is because such disclosures might be seen as a kind of bias that undermines the 'objectivity' of the work. Other psychologists are less concerned about accusations of bias. As the Liberation Psychologist Martín-Baró (1994) notes:

There is an assumption that taking a stand represents an abdication of scientific objectivity, but this assumption confuses bias with objectivity. The fact that something is biased does not necessarily mean it is subjective; bias can be the consequence of interests, more or less conscious, but it can also be the result of ethical choice. (p. 29)

Many social psychologists still take their direction from physical scientists and seek objectivity, or detachment from the subject matter being studied, in an attempt to remove bias from the research process. This is reflected in the widespread use of experimental methods in psychology. What is useful in this orientation is the emphasis on careful planning and the systematic conduct of research. Science-inspired work is part of the picture that is social psychology and provides useful insights into the human condition. However, we need to supplement such work and do more. For some time now social psychologists have embraced the relationship between their personal histories, research interests and efforts to work with people to ensure that social psychology remains relevant to the complexities of social life.

In this book we do not assume that forgoing claims to objectivity and science will necessarily result in biased and subjective research. The pragmatic stance adopted in this book, and which is advocated by figures such as Martín-Baró, is informed by a return to the early work of William James, Gustave Le Bon, and scholars in the late eighteenth century (Billig, 2008; Farr, 1991, 1996). This work has been extended over the years by figures such as James Dewey, Marie Jahoda and Gordon Allport. As we will show in Chapter 2, these social psychologists engaged directly with people and communities in their attempts to make the world a better place, and it is from such work that we take our lead in this book.

Central to this book is the idea that social psychology has much to offer in developing an understanding of everyday life and the challenges of living in increasingly diverse societies. We seek rapprochement in the interests of a deeper understanding of social psychology in everyday settings. When discussing nothing less than the nature of people as social beings we must expect controversy. Some sectors of the discipline have been accused of being so focused on the technicalities of experimental control that they are no longer engaged with the issues of our times. They might respond, as noted above, with accusations of bias and political involvement. It is not our intention to overly simplify the complex philosophical debates regarding the nature of reality and knowledge produced in research (Chapter 4), which lie at the heart of the so-called crisis in social psychology (Chapter 2) (Gergen, 1973; Lubek & Apfelbaum, 2000; Parker, 1989). Our aim is to be pragmatic and to explore insights from a range of traditions and sources and how these can help us understand and improve social life, particularly for the economically and socially marginalized citizens in our midst. The decades of work by social psychologists committed to working with particular social problems in context is our focus, rather than the robust defence of whatever approach is preferred during any given historical period. A complex world deserves and demands complex understandings and solutions. No one approach or orientation to social psychology holds the key to all of these. Consider yourselves invited to participate in a critical conversation about a discipline that has contributed much and has even more to offer the world of understanding and meaning in our lives.

We will explore what social psychology can tell us about the interactions and social situations people experience as they develop, establish social relations and participate in social life. Of course, human relations are forged somewhere, and thus we also need to explore wider historical, institutional, cultural and sociopolitical contexts shaping everyday life (Highmore, 2000a, 2000b; Montero, 2007; Parker, 2005). We cover the core topics educational institutions have come to expect in a social psychology textbook. These include the self and identity, socialization, group dynamics, social cognition and public understanding, conflict resolution, interpersonal influences, media and resilience. These concepts can shed light (or at least cast an eerie glow) on human experience and action. Our engagements with these topics are informed by multiple perspectives, including experimental studies and more critical and qualitative work. What makes the book different is that we have integrated notions of culture, indigeneity and other dimensions of *difference* throughout the chapters, rather than treating these simply as isolated topics. This is because these notions are central to many people's lived experiences. We also consider the potential of a social psychological approach for addressing problems such as intergroup conflict and discrimination and which seeks to improve the lives of people. This reflects the ethical and political commitment that we share with other social psychologists to contribute towards building more equitable, inclusive, just and psychologically healthy societies.

Practicalities in combining theory, research and action

Everyday life is a complex, frequently rewarding and often problematic place. It contains conflict, dislocation and contradiction, as well as support, love and belonging. Consequently, the research process through which social psychologists attempt to understand, document and improve the world is also complex and at times problematic. Psychology has a long history of informing our engagements with the world, and the peoples who inhabit it, through research. Research and broader engagements have enabled us to make significant contributions to the world (Apfelbaum, 2000; Zimbardo, 2004). These have not always been as positive for the groups we were working with as many of us might have hoped. However, psychologists have worked to improve group decision-making processes, challenge discrimination and promote health. In providing a synthesis of insights from these diverse efforts, this book emphasizes the relationship between theory, research and action. It is important to note that not all studies have all three of these components. Some research is purely inquisitive in nature and not linked to immediate courses of action. As a discipline, social psychology exhibits all three elements through a range of quantitative and qualitative research methods, the findings of which have been applied in a range of settings. In this section, we briefly draw on literature that covers praxis, action research and social transformation to outline the practicalities of doing theoretically informed research that contributes to society.

We propose that an ideal within social psychology is the use of research both to address social issues and to generate broader theoretical understandings of pertinent socioeconomic processes shaping such issues. This approach is often referred to as 'action research' (Lewin, 1946/1948) and involves a cyclical process of theorizing, planning, conducting, gaining feedback on, implementing, evaluating and revising a research project in dialogue with a range of stakeholders from the beginning to the end of a project (Figure 1.1).

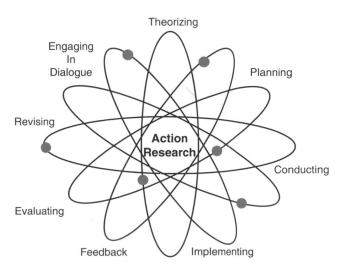

Figure 1.1. The action research process

Figure 1.1 reflects a process of doing research *with* rather than *on* people (Jovchelovitch, 2007), which is expanded in Chapter 4. Here stakeholders do not simply implement the results. They participate in the direction and planning of the project and the production of practical applications. Evaluation strategies enhance our ability to assess and steer the project through dialogue with end-user project partners who have a say in the direction of the research and its implementation. This action research orientation provides for adaptability and enables us to ensure the relevance of research findings to organizations that are also evolving to meet the needs of the people concerned. This orientation allows social psychologists to enact commitments to self-determination (Chapter 5), community partnerships (Chapter 6), social inclusion (Chapter 7) and social justice (Chapter 9). It allows us to transcend artificial and often unhelpful barriers between those who conduct studies and those who are studied (Chapters 4 and 10).

For us, social transformation spans large-scale change in the very societal structures that shape our lives, involving governments and economics and more micro-level processes in the home and workplace. Social transformation is associated with events such as the dismantling of oppressive systems like Apartheid in South Africa or the communist system in Eastern Europe. It is also about ensuring equity, safety and fairness in everyday life settings such as schools, workplaces and homes. Clearly, as we will show in Chapter 3, these levels of social transformation are interwoven.

Central to social transformation is an action orientation in research that draws on notions of praxis and reflexivity regardless of whether one is employing experimental or ethnographic methods. After all, social psychology is about developing understandings of and improving social life (see Chapters 2 and 3). To be effective, we need to be aware of how and why we go about producing such work in specific ways and what other options might be available to us (Box 1.1).

One central concern for many social psychologists is the transformation of oppressive social realities (Martín-Baró, 1994). The impetus for research and action is often derived from the everyday life problems confronting people. Theoretical concerns are not the only motivations for many social psychologists. This often means that methodological choices are pragmatic and eclectic, combining what have become conventional techniques (e.g. surveys, experiments) and re-emerging techniques (testimony, performance). For example, Sapene-Chapellín (2009) used a research design that Montero (2006) referred to as *participatory experimental intervention* to challenge destructive reactions that people often develop in the context of political polarization. Sapene-Chapellín was concerned with political polarization employed by an authoritarian political regime that uses

BOX 1.1   Useful and interconnected concepts

In the nineteenth century, the philosopher Karl Marx stated, "philosophers have only interpreted the world in various ways; the point is to change it". The integration of theory and research in concrete actions to promote *social transformation* is often referred to as *praxis*. Praxis is a synthesis of theory and practice so that each has a function in informing the other. Paulo Freire (1970/1993) proposed that theory, research and action should be mutually informing. In this context, *reflexivity* is about self-awareness in terms of how one's theory, research and actions are affecting others. Reflexivity is about making one's assumptions and motives and the implications of interventions transparent to those involved. Reflexivity is central to a cyclical process of developing a theory, engaging with events or what is at stake in everyday life, refining the theory and engaging in new applications. Reflexivity requires dialogue with stakeholders and feedback. The concept is used to invoke the multidirectional relationship between theorizing, conducting research, reporting findings, gaining feedback and modifying one's theoretical assumptions. It allows psychologists to monitor the impact of the application of theory and the conduct of research, and to modify our theories and research strategies in accordance with the lessons learned in practice. This is where action research comes in as a mode of social transformation. Students *getting on the bus* in the scenario at the beginning of this chapter were engaged in social transformation. Along with their academic mentors, they went on to engage in action research as a means of putting the theories they developed out of their experiences into practice (praxis) and revising these. Action research works best where there is a long-term commitment to a relationship between psychologists and the groups being assisted. It is about engaging in a process of dialogue that can benefit both the investigators and other partners in the research. Action research is an attempt to restore the relationship between researchers and researched, and to avoid extractive data-gathering that furthers researchers' careers and interests but does little for those who were the subject of the research. Because of this inclusive orientation it can take years to build up the necessary trust and relationships for such research.

strategies geared towards social division, creating two poles of political opposition – those who support the government and the opposition. This researcher was particularly interested in addressing the emotional reactions among children (e.g. fear, aggression, anxiety) that resulted from political polarization. Such emotions tend to concentrate attention in one direction, which reduces people's appreciation of social complexities at play. One of the interventions involved designing a quasi-experimental situation that reflected political polarization, typically in a classroom situation. This was combined with a reflection–action–reflection process that allowed participants to reflect on their experiences and life situation. This type of design is not aimed at *controlling* what participants do; instead, it is aimed at creating conditions in which the process of problematization that is central to consciousness-raising is enabled. Thus, experimental designs can be part of our repertoire for engaging in transformative processes, as in this case quasi-experimental methods were used alongside qualitative techniques to address the effects of particular repressive social realities.

Given the orientation of much social psychology to social transition, it is not surprising that this book emphasizes everyday life. It is crucial that psychologists attend to the daily practices of, and realities experienced by, those we are working with if we want to foster social transformation. Such transformation is unlikely to occur from the top down. We need two-way communication, and action research facilitates a dialogue (see Chapters 4 and 5). This is why social psychologists increasingly do research *with* rather than *on* people (Jovchelovitch, 2007).

Paulo Freire (1970/1993) noted that daily practices are sites for the reproduction of social injustices, and therefore need to be considered in developing collective responses to injustice. He engaged in a process of consciousness-raising and dialogue with oppressed groups as a basis for building trust and a commitment to working collaboratively towards social transformation through collective action and ongoing reflection. His work on critical consciousness-raising and community-based action research approaches to social transformation focused on fostering the intelligence, autonomy, creativity, freedom and choices available to illiterate peasants living under repressive regimes in South America. Freire developed an approach that shifted power relations in education from a sermon-type approach to a conversational approach involving the mutual exploration of topics. This egalitarian orientation conceives insights and knowledge as being the products of joint introspection and exploration fostered through dialogue between researchers and participants. This reflects a belief in people's insights into their own experiences, and in their ability to grow and act autonomously. Rather than research always being an abstract process driven by experts, simple strategies such as drawing exercises can be used to open dialogue about social psychological phenomena and possible solutions. The key concern is to find ways to allow people to speak about their issues more holistically and appropriately. Such dialogue is seen by psychologists as a basis for building awareness, reflection and dialogue with those in positions of power who can facilitate the provision of resources for change that will benefit less powerful people (Carlson, Engebretson & Chamberlain, 2006; Montenegro, 2002; Montero, 2007). Freire emphasized that social change requires a combination of insights from actual experiences and daily life along with more abstract academic understandings of the social processes shaping such lives. This work has a long tradition in humanistic psychology (see Chapter 10), where the arts are used as a medium for encouraging dialogue, reflection and conflict resolution (Estrella & Forinash, 2007).

In brief, the orientation towards social psychology foregrounded in this book emphasizes the collective level in relation to issues of social cohesion, inclusion, support and action. Our approach is based on the proposition that all human beings and communities have dignity and the right to equitable chances in life. Psychologists can work in a dignified manner to ensure that the dignity of others is respected and that barriers to people living a dignified existence are removed.

Overview of the book

This book is written primarily for undergraduate students new to social psychology who are attending universities in developed nations such as the United States, the United Kingdom, Singapore, Australia, South Africa and New Zealand. In providing a text on social psychology and everyday life for students from these contexts we have assumed certain things. First, students have access to spaces such as shopping malls, schools and pubs and the virtual spaces offered by media technologies. Second, students are familiar with events that occur in such settings of daily life. Third, students want to engage in a social psychology that is relevant to the world in which they live.

Correspondingly, the book is structured somewhat differently than many social psychology textbooks. Rather than list topics on social cognition, crowds and interpersonal relations we have focused on descriptions of situations from everyday life that can be built upon in a manner that demonstrates the applicability of research findings and interventions from social psychology.

The general structure of each chapter comprises a scenario of an everyday situation, which is unpacked through the chapter by drawing on insights from social psychology. In unpacking the scenario we consider:

- Why such situations occur
- Why it is important to study them
- What we know about such situations
- What it is like for the people involved and what the implications are for their lives
- The strengths and weaknesses of the groups involved
- What can be done to address problems and build upon opportunities

We have chosen this approach in order to bring social psychology to life. We also acknowledge that each reader brings a personal interpretive frame to the enterprise of understanding social life that is based on his or her unique experiences. In our experience as lecturers, the extent to which this frame accords with the insights from research and practice in social psychology will determine the engagement with the material. So we invite you to join a conversation about what is going on in the world. We invite you to bring your experiences to the scenarios we develop and to explore them systematically through the lenses offered by social psychology.

Before reviewing the content of each chapter, we offer a general scenario regarding the plight of an Aboriginal family in Australia. This scenario is presented in order to show how many, but not all, such families can face a raft of issues and experiences, and with these a range of both positive and negative social psychological phenomena. This scenario also provides a way for us to demonstrate the interrelated nature of the topics social psychologists investigate and to offer a sneak preview of the way the content of this book and the ideas behind it are interlinked.

Everyday reality for an Aboriginal family in Australia

Colin and Maria have four children and live in the far north of Western Australia. They run an extremely successful cultural tourism company. For more than a decade they have offered camping tours through the traditional country of their ancestors. They have a longstanding partnership with an Australian university and have conducted cultural immersion camps with more than 1,000 American study-abroad students. They also conduct spirituality tours and have a regular gig taking geologists into the wilderness in far northern Australia to study the beautiful and unique mountain ranges of the region. Colin and Maria's children are all successful in their own right. Colleen works in the local diamond mine as a manager of travel services, Ronald also works at the mine as a process manager, Beck works for a film company and Mark works with Colin and Maria as a travel guide.

Recently, Colin and Maria moved back to Colin's family's traditional lands, where they own a large block just outside the port town of Wyndham with several buildings and a workshop for the maintenance and repair of the company vehicles. Maria is the co-chair of an Aboriginal trust organization that manages the distribution of funds provided under a royalty agreement with the local diamond mine.

Colin was born in Oombulgurri. Oombulgurri is a small remote Aboriginal community about one hour by boat, twenty minutes by light aircraft, or fourteen hours (and two flat tyres and perhaps a broken axle) by four-wheel drive from Wyndham. Colin was born in Oombulgurri because his mother was stolen from her family by the child welfare authorities early last century and taken to the Forrest River Mission (which was renamed Oombulgurri) when she was just a child. She was one of thousands of children removed from their families and placed in missions as part of the Australian government policy of forced removal of indigenous children from their families that began in the 1920s and continued through to the late 1960s. Most of these children never saw their families again and were subjected to harsh, often inhumane, lives of servitude in pursuit of 'civilizing' them into white society. Colin's mother was one of the very few lucky ones to be reunited in late life with her mother. In the mission the benevolent dictatorship of the Church controlled almost every aspect of community life. The forced removal and placement of children in Oombulgurri brought together hugely disparate groups of desert and saltwater people and systematically eradicated their connection to family, culture and country. Resistance was futile. On the escarpment overlooking the community of Oombulgurri is a shrine, a simple cross made from fencing iron. The cross is embedded in the ground with dirt containing the remains of the forty or so men, women and children who were killed and whose bodies were burned in the Forrest River Massacre. The massacre occurred as retaliation for the killing of a white man by an Aboriginal man who was by all accounts simply defending his family from abuse.

There was not much to do in Oombulgurri. There still isn't. Most men of working age today are forced to participate in the Community Development Employment Program (CDEP) or 'work for the dole'. This scheme was introduced by the Australian government as part of its obligation towards Indigenous Australians. Four of Colin's brothers still live in Oombulgurri, where they have become respected community leaders. Many community members regularly fly the short trip to Wyndham to shop, drink or meet family members and friends.

In Oombulgurri, as in many remote communities, there is very little adequate housing, power supplies are irregular and the standards of health care for residents are far below those enjoyed by non-indigenous Australians. Although there is a school, engagement of young children in schooling is poor, and basic services are virtually nonexistent. Over the years, there has been a palpable rise in the sense of hopelessness and despair that characterizes the lives of people stolen from their loved ones and raised in remote areas often shunned and ignored by government and society. Widespread binge drinking became endemic. Violence also became commonplace, particularly intimate partner violence. Accusations of child sexual abuse were rife. By 2007 the community was in crisis. In the previous eighteen months, six young people had taken their own lives in a community of fewer than 200 people. The community elders were at their wits' end. They were expected to support their community while they and the community were in a cycle of unrelenting grief and loss.

Colin and Maria are highly respected members of their community. But they are regularly stopped by the police on their way to town. Colin's brothers have been arrested several times and held in custody for offences for which the brothers vehemently proclaim their innocence. On every occasion to date they have been released without conviction after several weeks in custody, only to be re-arrested some time later and have the pattern repeated. They believe their only crime is their determination to be strong leaders who challenge the dominance of white structures and authority.

In the state capital of Perth a series of stories about Oombulgurri have appeared over several months. Invariably, the stories focus on the negative aspects of the community, often accompanied by photographs. When confronted about the unrelenting negativity about the community, despite the efforts of many determined and compassionate people, one journalist replied cynically, "That's not the story we are telling at the moment." One man in the community was heard to say, "When I walk down the street not only am I seen as a blackfella, now I'm also seen as a blackfella who is abusing his kids!"

This scenario is a true story recounting the experiences of real people whom one of the authors has worked with for several years on a youth suicide prevention programme. The scenario represents the kinds of situations and circumstances that ought to be grist for the mill of social psychology. Although social psychologists have a history of researching and responding to such situations (see Chapters 2 and 3), our solutions and reflections often seem, paradoxically, both too simplistic and too complex (see Chapter 5). Our attempts to reduce human behaviour to cause-and-effect relations have led to the nagging belief that it is all too hard. And yet it ought not to be so. This scenario provides an authentic setting within which we can see the relationship between complex social psychological phenomena as it is played out in everyday life.

Collectivist streams in social psychology have responded to the issues of poverty and discrimination faced by the family in this scenario. Chapter 2 reconsiders some of this early work. It provides an extended account of the importance of historical events and socio-political contexts for the development of social psychology and for understanding the issues faced by such families. The chapter begins with an introduction to social psychology, the topics social psychologists are interested in and some of the tensions in psychology. Particular attention is given to crucial historical points of development of the discipline and to the links between classic and contemporary subject matter. We discuss theoretical, political and conceptual issues regarding the cultural location of social psychology and the re-emergence of overtly historically and culturally embedded social psychologies. We consider how this more contextually and politically oriented tradition fell out of favour following the Second World War, to be replaced by a more individual-focused approach that is modelled on the physical sciences and has taken centre stage in some countries. As a result, although psychologists have worked to assist people in situations such as the one outlined in the scenario above, social psychologists have in recent decades often responded in a manner that has not been as effective as it could have been. This book resurrects the importance early social psychologists gave to historical events and sociopolitical contexts for the development of social psychology. In sum, Chapter 2 provides a contextualized history of social psychology that substantiates the relevance of engaging with the complexities of social psychological issues and societal problems as these occur within historical and cultural contexts. We can, and must, seek to learn from the variety of voices in our pursuit of understanding.

Chapter 3 outlines a contemporary orientation for the social psychology of everyday life. Of core concern is what social psychology has to offer in developing an understanding of the challenges of living in increasingly complex and diverse societies. The issues faced by the family in our scenario are played out within specific social psychological contexts. To be responsive to the needs of such people and to develop informed ways of understanding the issues and how to help, social psychology needs to be oriented towards everyday life. This chapter explores social psychology today as a vibrant and interdisciplinary field. It draws on research conducted from a social cognitive perspective into everyday experiences, attitudes, influences and relationships. Attention is paid to what we mean by everyday life and how people such as Colin and Maria develop a sense of self though daily practices. An orientation towards the self as a socially, historically and culturally embedded being is also introduced. In line with the broader orientation of the book, the importance of the material world and places, as well as cognitions and thoughts, in understanding social psychological phenomena is introduced.

Whether collectivist or more individually oriented, social psychologists assume certain things such as common understandings of the world between us and the people with whom we work. Chapter 4 extends this notion to discuss in depth the ways in which we come to know the world and understand the plight of people such as Colin and Maria. When human beings make sense of the world around them and behave, they do not do so in a social vacuum. Others have already rendered the world meaningful, and we must grapple with the societal narratives and power relations already in play, many of which may contain stereotypes and prejudices, as well as empathy and understanding. Thus, when we think about knowledge production it is important to note that we are born into a world that is already rendered meaningful by others. Shared understandings, norms and ways of doing things are negotiated within social groups and primary settings for socialization, such as the family. Colin and Maria and their family make sense of themselves as part of the shared meanings in society that are sociopolitical, cultural narratives constructed purposely towards some end. They come to be whom they believe themselves to be (and, importantly, whom others believe them to be) in a complex and dynamic interplay. Chapter 4 considers how knowledge is constructed in everyday settings and how this relates to the research and practice undertaken by social psychologists. We explore different perspectives on specific situations such as those experienced by Colin, Maria, their family and their community and how this can lead to intergroup tensions. This chapter includes a discussion of key issues and literature across the social sciences, as well as specifically from social psychology, such as the nature of knowledge and the social construction of knowledge and beliefs.

Extending the discussion of Western social psychology from Chapters 2 and 3, Chapter 5 provides an account of indigenous social psychologies. These psychologies offer broad and distinct orientations to the social world and our places in it, and for conceptualizing social relations. They legitimate the voices of people such as Colin and Maria. Chapter 5 explores what indigenous psychologies can contribute to developing more pluralistic, flexible and relevant understandings of people in social settings. After all, what it means to be a person in societies that are increasingly diverse can be different for different people in different circumstances. Different cultures have different perspectives on the nature of individuals and groups and the extent to which people and environments influence us. In fact, the very notion of a separation of individuals and environments is a particularly

Western one. This is exemplified by the people of Oombulgurri. To make sense of the situation the family find themselves in and how we might respond, we need to understand processes of colonization. The associated forced removal of people from their traditional lands and culture has been the cause of pain and deep feelings of alienation and loss that many non-indigenous people simply cannot fully grasp. The case of mental health assessment will be used to illustrate the importance of cultural competence as a precursor to insight into, and understanding of, people from different cultural backgrounds. This chapter illustrates how there is not just one legitimate approach to social psychology or understanding for the people involved in our scenario. It includes an account of the interconnected self, which explores what it means to be a person in societies that are increasingly diverse. We also address processes of socialization, acculturation and enculturation through which we come to understand ourselves and others in the context of everyday life.

A sense of place in a home, club or social networking site is central to social relations and our sense of belonging. When people talk about themselves they often tell us where they are from. The family in our scenario often refer to Oombulgurri in this context. When we meet new people we also often make judgements about them on the basis of where they are from or live. Oombulgurri is associated with stigma, which taints the people who come from and live there. Chapter 6 explores how the cultivation of place-based identities can increase social participation and have positive benefits for the health of communities. Central to the chapter are the social psychological processes through which places are imputed with meanings or textured through use. We consider also how a sense of belonging somewhere can be ruptured and what consequences this can have for communities. As is illustrated in the scenario, our access to places is determined by our socioeconomic and in-group or out-group status, and by whether we conform to particular social codes. Consequently, place has a particular importance for many indigenous people. Attention is given to how social psychologists can work to support opportunities for repairing social relations in such places as a means of supporting the health of people who live there.

Explorations of indigenous psychologies and place bring us directly to consideration of people who have experienced dislocation, fracture, displacement and change in their lives. Throughout human history groups of people (such as the family in our scenario) have been displaced, losing a sense of belonging, and have often had to adapt to the social settings and norms of other groups. Chapter 7 explores the issue of human displacement and what happens to groups of people when they are uprooted and displaced. What can we learn from the experiences of refugees and immigrant groups that can help us assist people on the move? What can issues around land rights and tenure among indigenous people whose connection to place is ruptured tell us about contemporary social and health disparities? We document research and theoretical notions central to understanding acculturation experiences and the different ways in which immigrants and refugees respond to dislocation and relocation. The chapter uses scenarios to extend acculturation models in two ways. First, it highlights the political nature of intergroup relations and the need to understand the multiple social and cultural resources that people draw on to remake their lives in new places. This includes a discussion of the importance of history and collective memory in the reconstruction of community and social identities. Second, emphasis is given to a more interconnected conceptualization of intergroup relations that will bring in to focus the responses of receiving communities. That is, how do receiving communities respond? What are the social, cultural and political processes of privilege protection that the receiving communities develop? Chapter 7 emphasizes the need for a dynamic and political reading of the processes of immigration and settlement.

Chapter 8 picks up the issue of disruption in everyday life with a focus on the social influences on health and illness. This chapter provides an account of the ways social psychological processes can either enhance and preserve our health or contribute to the incidence of illness. We draw on the work of social psychologists who propose that health is both physical and relational. The chapter includes a criticism of common rhetoric promoted by some social psychologists that endorses the idea that health and illness are the products of personal lifestyle choices. Associated health promotion initiatives propose a moral obligation to make the 'right' decisions to ensure one's well-being. This neglects that fact that many people, such as the family in the scenario, do not have control over many factors in their environments that contribute to illness. Their health is shaped by social structures and inequalities, as well as by personal choices and actions. In the scenario, Nicky, a young mother, attempts to make healthy choices for her family in the supermarket but faces a number of challenges and situations that make it less realistic for her to meet the expectations of wellness campaigns. The chapter explores notions of personal responsibility for health in relation to lifestyle choices, encompassing the roles of social influences, theories of conformity and normative practices, and the impact of social and economic policies on these choices. On the basis of the scenario, the options available to Nicky are discussed, such as the availability of safe options for physical exercise.

Issues raised in Chapters 1 to 8 bring us to what, in many ways, is the passionate and compassionate heart of the book. The experiences of Colin and Maria and their friends are quintessentially issues of justice, or more precisely injustice. Chapter 9 continues the focus on intergroup relations and explores social justice and inclusion in the context of differential power relations and efforts at influence and persuasion. Perspectives of justice have permeated our social world, yet for most people justice is poorly understood at the coalface of everyday life. Whereas philosophical ideas of justice address the standards of justice that ought to pertain, the social psychology of justice explores everyday experiences of, and reactions to, justice and, more pertinently, injustice. The chapter provides a framework or lens to understand more fully inclusion (exclusion), power and the creation of discourses in the media (in all its forms) that marginalize, disenfranchise and oppress. Chapter 9 begins with an exploration of the complex and contestable nature of justice. The search for a comprehensive definition of social justice will conclude with the following anonymous observation that 'justice is like a greased pig; it squeals loudly but is hard to catch' – which is probably as good a definition as any currently available. The chapter reviews the theoretical threads in the literature: distributive justice, procedural justice, the scope of justice and retributive justice. What is presented is a particular lens on social justice through which to explore not only the experiences of marginalized groups but also the everyday experience of people in society. The scenario guiding the chapter raises possibilities for encounters with many groups and provides an opportunity to deconstruct taken-for-granted and stereotypical views from a justice perspective.

The individuals and families in the Oombulgurri scenario may seem to be facing some fairly dire circumstances. The tragedy is that this scenario is based on the experiences of real people facing injustice. What is particularly remarkable about human beings is that many people facing such difficulties do more than just survive: they also continue to love, support and grow. As we emphasized earlier in this chapter, social psychology does not focus simply on problems or the negative side of life. It is also important to explore positive processes through which social life can enhance our lives. However, it is in Chapter 10 that we focus directly on strengths and humanistic dimensions of social psychology such as altruism, social support and agency. Despite the hardships they face, the family from Oombulgurri is still altruistic towards other members of the community. Brought to the fore in this chapter is the idea that human beings are social beings who need each other. Mostly, our behaviour towards others is pro-social and conditioned by the norms and expectations of our social contexts. Pro-social behaviour – being polite and considerate of others, helping others out, doing favours – has its returns. We get something out of it, and so do others. This chapter begins with a consideration of positive-focused traditions in social psychology and how these can be combined, repoliticized and extended into a critical humanism. Chapter 10 covers the literature on social exchange and reciprocity, social support, solidarity and collective agency, with particular attention to what we get from doing these things. Emphasis will be placed on the importance of critical humanism for understanding community resilience.

Chapters 1 through 10 focus primarily on face-to-face interactions as these occur in everyday daily life. It is, however, important to note that aspects of our identities, relationships and understandings of events and situations in our lives are also constructed with resources obtained at a physical distance via various media technologies. Many people spend considerable time reading the newspaper, listening to the radio, checking their email and posting material on social networking sights. They might learn about the events in Oombulgurri from news reports and might even respond by writing a blog. Chapter 11 explores the centrality of media to everyday life and social psychology. We ask whether we can have a relevant social psychology today that does not engage with media processes. Most Australian do not know Colin, Maria or the people of Oombulgurri yet feel they have come to know them through the various media constructions and representations of Aboriginal people. The chapter explores classic concerns and current knowledge regarding what media do to people, what people do with media, and the general and increasing role of media devices in daily life. The chapter also explores ways in which psychologists have produced various forms of media content to support educational initiatives and have worked to facilitate access to a 'voice' in the media for socially marginalized groups. An important consideration is how media provide spaces within which human interaction can occur and people can dwell, often for considerable periods of time. These representational spaces overlap in everyday life with offline spaces, such as the bedroom. The interweaving of online and offline places raises a range of issues regarding time and place that are of central concern to many social psychologists.

In the final chapter of the book, we provide a review of content from across the chapters. However, we do not try to tidy up the field too much or give the impression that somehow the social psychology of everyday life comprises a coherent whole. Chapter 12 elaborates the 'social psychology of everyday life' by providing a synthesis of the scenarios offered in the previous chapters. We restate the importance of reconfiguring social psychology in a way that is engaged with people and events occurring in the world around us. Social psychology is therefore located once again at the heart of everyday understandings of the social, cultural and political world in a way that makes it accessible and relevant for students. The chapter explores what we can do, what we have to offer society and what we do not know, which leaves the field open for students to develop their own research agendas. We finish the book by emphasizing that more work needs to be done to address social psychological issues in everyday life. In this way, the book ends by offering you, the reader, a seat on the bus, and a say in where we are headed to the future (Box 1.2).

BOX 1.2   Key themes from the book

1. One key thread is the complex and interconnected nature of self, which manifests inside heads/bodies and human relations and in places and objects. This gets us beyond the limiting and dated notion of an enclosed independent individual who reasons and behaves in predictable ways. It also allows us to present a socially, politically and economically situated vision of people.
2. The importance of history and culture in shaping and orienting social psychology is also threaded throughout the book. This thread allows us to include many social cognitive and humanist ideas as useful insights for the times in which these were formulated (and within the historical and cultural restraints).
3. Another key thread is the importance placed on taking research insights into action. Each chapter presents practical suggestions on how social psychologists can get involved and improve the human condition.

Review exercise

What are some of the ways in which psychologists get involved in social events? (We are not asking about parties.) In answering this question you might do a web search using the term 'giving psychology away'.

2 A history of social psychology

Core questions to consider while reading this chapter

- ■ Why are social psychologists interested in groups?
- ■ What do social psychologists mean by the term 'socialization'?
- ■ Which prominent experimental social psychologists also worked in applied settings?
- ■ In what context did liberation social psychology emerge?
- ■ What is the Society for the Psychological Study of Social Issues?
- ■ What is the crisis in social psychology?
- ■ What is bystander apathy?

Chapter scenario

Mary is nineteen years old and is the first person in her family to attend university. She was raised by her father and grandmother, both of whom work two jobs to support Mary and her younger siblings. Mary grew up early by taking responsibility for looking after her younger siblings. The family emphasized the importance of education, and as a result Mary is enrolled in an undergraduate course in social psychology. She took the course because of her interest in the consequences of the poverty and social exclusion that exist in her local community. Mary's interests are not solely the social problems often associated with lower socioeconomic status groups and neighbourhoods. She is also interested in the sense of belonging and support that she feels in the neighbourhood. For Mary, social psychology is a subject that she hopes she can draw on to make sense of her own life and to inform her efforts to make a positive contribution to her family and community.

We had students such as Mary in mind while writing this book. Like Mary, we all come to social psychology with interests and questions from our experiences and everyday lives:

- What makes a healthy community?
- Why do some people devote their lives to helping others?
- What role do mass media have in setting public agendas?
- How might immigration laws be made less discriminatory?

Such questions can help us understand the world around us and how to make it a better place for a greater number of people.

This chapter continues our introduction to the field of social psychology, with an account of the discipline's history and focus. Particular attention is given to the importance of the social dimensions of everyday life. We consider conceptual, research and political issues within social psychology in an effort to paint a portrait of a discipline that can address Mary's interests. A one-size-fits-all approach to social psychology is certainly inadequate in the face of the complexities of social life today. As you read this chapter, we invite you to consider your own interests and how these might be elaborated and understood through the lens provided by social psychology.

Our account of the history and focus of social psychology should be seen as an attempt to highlight aspects of where we have been as a discipline, in order to understand what social psychology does today and what it might become in the future. Of necessity, our account of the history and focus of social psychology is, like any other history, incomplete. As Billig (2008) notes, "The past is never finished. As new intellectual challenges arise, so our views of the past change" (p. 2). The development of social psychology has varied around the world and has not simply involved the accumulation of knowledge through scientific investigations (Harris, 1983). The development has been a messy (some would argue haphazard) process influenced by broader social shifts and political events, including economic depressions, wars and witch hunts (Billig, 2008; Farr, 1996; Lubek & Apfelbaum, 2000). It has also been influenced by tensions within the discipline between different ideas about what social psychology is, how research should be conducted, what we should focus on and whether social action is necessary.

This chapter emphasizes how a considerable amount of effort has shifted historically between two primary streams of social psychology. The dynamics of these shifts continue to shape many aspects of the discipline. The first (collectivist)[1] stream is located overtly in social and political life and seeks civic participation and the construction of more just societies. The second (individualist) stream is modelled on the physical sciences and seeks detachment from objects of study and an understanding of behaviour and experience among individuals under specific conditions. Of course, these streams intersect in broader waterways, and we will show that throughout the history of the discipline scholars (e.g. Kurt Lewin) have drawn on both streams, depending on the topic of concern. Both streams have much to offer our understanding of everyday life.

This chapter foregrounds examples of historical shifts primarily in the US and European contexts because these shifts have had implications globally due to the dominance of these countries over publication and education in psychology (Moghaddam, 1987). We do, however, raise points of comparison between what might be termed Western social psychology and social psychologies emerging in different cultural contexts in this and subsequent chapters. These comparisons are dealt with in more detail in Chapter 5, where we explore

Chapter overview

In the first section, we explore the emergence of modern social psychology in the late eighteenth and early nineteenth centuries and the stream of research focused on social contexts and change. The second section explores key developments in the emergence of the individualistic stream, which is modelled on the physical sciences. The third section considers the period of growth and rise to dominance of the focus on individuals and the use of experimental methods from the 1940s onwards. It is in the fourth section that we turn to the re-emphasis on social relevance and action during the 1960s and 1970s, often referred to as the crisis in social psychology. In the fifth section we reconsider bystander research in light of insights resulting from the crisis in social psychology. The chapter ends with a brief summary linking the core ideas expressed in the chapter. In summary, this chapter:

- Focuses on the origins of collectivist and individual-oriented streams in social psychology
- Considers the historical influences on the development of the discipline

the history and recent re-emergence of indigenous psychologies around the world. It is also important to note that there is considerable diversity even within Western social psychology, including in non-Anglophone Western contexts (Montero, 2007).

An early focus on social life in psychology

Social psychology has a long past and a short history (Farr, 1991). The long past relates to the history of psychology as a branch of philosophy in the West and to indigenous philosophies around the world that constitute forms of social psychology in their own right (Moghaddam, 1987; Yang, 2006).[2] All human cultures have speculated about the psyche, mind, soul (Chapter 5). Buddhism provides a classic example of an approach to self, mind, human action, ethics and interaction (Mikulas, 2007). In India theories of the self were developed over millennia (Paranjpe, 1998). In the Western world, interest in the social nature of people goes back to the ancient Greek philosophers, whose work remains influential today (Billig, 2008). For example, Plato emphasized the flexibility of human beings and the centrality of social influences to our development. The word 'psychology' is widely attributed to the German philosopher Rudolf Goclenius. The term combines the Greek word *psyche*, meaning 'soul', with *-ology*, for the 'study' of the soul.

The short history is often dated from Wilhelm Wundt and the establishment of the psychological laboratory in Leipzig in 1879. It was not until the late nineteenth century that psychology emerged from philosophy as a distinct discipline. A distinctly social orientation to psychology emerged with the work of William James and his *Principles of Psychology* (1890). We will touch on this work throughout this book, and in particular the influence of James on the work of later psychologists such as Charles Horton Cooley and George Herbert Mead, who refined his ideas regarding the self or person.

The long past and the short history overlap in terms of a focus on the relationships between people and social contexts. Before the modern Western discipline of psychology emerged, philosophers considered the social character of human beings (Billig, 2008). The resulting emphasis on links between individuals and society remains a core focus for social psychology today. This focus is often sourced to Auguste Comte (1798–1857), who asked how individuals can be both the "cause and consequence of society" (Allport, 1985, p. 8). Comte proposed that individuals are both the products and producers of the social environments within which they are intermeshed. Adopting Comte's question as central, the field of social psychology expanded in the United States from 1902 with such books as Charles Horton Cooley's *Human Nature and the Social Order*, in which he proposed that self and society are twin born (Musolf, 2003). Cooley introduced the concept of a 'looking-glass self' to illustrate that it is through interactions with other people that we develop and come to know ourselves. From interactions with people around us (especially those in our primary groups, such as family, neighbourhoods, and colleagues) we learn how others may see us. In the process, we develop complex understandings of ourselves, our situations and relationships. In the early 1900s most social interactions were face-to-face or via postal services. If websites or electronic media had been available, Cooley would likely have also identified chat rooms and electronic communities as domains for social interaction. He could barely have imagined the possibilities offered by the Internet, and how virtual social interactions allow people to present various versions of themselves online (see Chapters 7 and 11).

George Herbert Mead (1934) drew on the work of earlier social psychologists to conceptualize social psychology as *the investigation of the behaviour of individuals within the context of social processes.*[3] The individual was conceptualized as being the product of interactions between people and, therefore, as being fundamentally social in character. Emphasis was placed on the idea that there is no individual outside of the social contexts in which that individual lives, because we are all born into a world with existing meanings, shared practices, institutions and traditions through which we become socialized (Box 2.1). Such conceptualizations of the social nature of the self

BOX 2.1   Socialization

Human beings are born without the personal, social or cultural competence to function in the world. People need to learn how to live in their communities. 'Socialization' refers to the processes through which human beings learn what is expected of them and how to function within particular groups. It involves the acquisition of habits, repertoires, skills, norms, values, understandings, and symbols that enable a person to adopt roles as daughters, sons, fathers, mothers, workers, friends and citizens. Through socialization people learn what it means to be a member of a particular ethnic group, social class, and gender. Socialization often involves a combination of learning centred around family and peers and learning from institutions such as schools and media. Socialization is not a passive process. People actively engage in their socialization and increasingly come to be socialized into a number of communities, with varying degrees of success. During the 1920s and 1930s socialization emerged as a core interest for Charles Cooley, George Mead and other psychologists associated with the Chicago School (Clausen, 1968).

More recently the term 'resocialization' has been used to capture how people can move beyond their socialized patterns of being in a particular group and become socialized into a new community by adopting new patterns of being (Berry, Poortinga, Seggall & Dasen, 2002). Resocialization can occur throughout a person's life. Mary (in the opening scenario) is resocialized through university-based interactions with people from backgrounds different from her own. Resocialization is increasingly prevalent in societies made up of a range of cultures and communities. In Chapter 4, we develop this idea further in our discussion of social representations and interpretive communities, and in Chapter 7 we explore resocialization in relation to immigration and resettlement.

and what it means to be human inform later sections of this chapter and are developed throughout the book. The situated self is a major unifying theme in social psychology.

A 19th CENTURY SOCIAL PSYCHOLOGIST RESEARCHING THE ISSUES OF THE DAY

Along with the focus on individuals in social contexts, psychologists have studied and been involved in addressing a range of social problems at least since the Industrial Revolution. For example, Apfelbaum (1986, 2000) recounts the tradition of social psychologists researching alcoholism, epidemics, prostitution and pauperism during the nineteenth century. The work of early scholars focused on links between individual lives and social circumstances. This work reflects how social psychology has developed as a direct response to broader social transformations.

In the second half of the 1800s in Europe, new societal structures were being generated amid drastic rises in urban populations. Social psychology emerged out of philosophy at this time as a distinct discipline in the context of increased urbanization and fears about revolution and social upheaval (Lubek & Apfelbaum, 2000). These developments were linked to new social formations in crowds, unions, police forces, communes, political parties, and emancipated slave groups. Scholars were rethinking traditional assumptions about the influence of social systems such as the Church and government on the lives of citizens, indentured servants, slaves and wage-earners (Lubek, 2000). This is the context in which Le Bon (1895/1977) wrote his early account of crowd psychology. In doing so he sought to address topics that have become central to the social psychology of intergroup relations, social transformation and popular culture.

LE BON JOVI,
EXPERT IN CROWD PSYCHOLOGY

In the midst of the turmoil and rapidly changing social structures of the late eighteenth century, many early social psychologists came to understand the interwoven nature of who people are and the social environments in which they live and engage with others. As a result, they saw the need to enhance the social context so as to best enable individuals to reach their full potential. This emphasis was reflected, for example, in the work of John Dewey and colleagues in the late eighteenth and early nineteenth centuries. These scholars emphasized the application of psychological knowledge to address social problems and foster social renewal (Collier, Minton & Reynolds, 1991). Such efforts took Dewey and colleagues to Hull House, where they ran education and literacy programmes, while also working to address the primary, personal, social and financial needs of new immigrants to Chicago. These early social psychologists advocated an interdisciplinary (Box 2.2) and humanistic approach (Chapter 10), and proposed that social psychological knowledge could be applied to problems through a process of systematic problem solving similar to action research. This involved a form of 'reflexive intelligence' in which alternative courses of action could be identified and assessed through an ongoing process of criticism, evaluation, dialogue and revision (see Chapter 1). These early articulations of the importance of dialogue, actions, reflection and social transformation are at the heart of the social psychology of everyday life developed throughout this book. This type of work continues today, with many services for migrant and homeless people, including Hull House (Box 2.3), working to assist and guide people in need so they can operate as citizens who participate fully in social and economic life.

The crash of global stock markets and the Depression during the 1930s intensified the study of social problems by psychologists and their efforts to improve the social situations of people experiencing poverty, prejudice and social exclusion. Many psychologists were not prepared to sit by and observe from afar as the Great Depression unfolded. In Europe, the likes of Marie Jahoda (Box 2.4), Paul Lazarsfeld and Hans Zeisel (1933/1971) continued their work from the 1920s by leading teams of psychologists working in community settings. They sought to identify community needs while also developing strategies to improve the living conditions and life chances of their fellow citizens (Fryer, 2008). These psychologists

---

BOX 2.2   Interdisciplinarity

'Interdisciplinary' is a term referring to the spanning of boundaries between academic disciplines in order to draw on a broader range of insights, and thus advance knowledge of a particular phenomenon. It involves integrating insights from various fields in order to grapple with complex topics that no single discipline has the scope to handle. Examples include health, employment and intergroup relations. Different perspectives on a problem can generate different insights that can be shared to build a more complex picture of what is going on in people's lives. Interdisciplinarity also provides a mechanism for dialogue between groups of professionals and addresses issues of excessive specialization, where each discipline comes to work on a narrow band of social issues from a narrow perspective. We elaborate this further in Chapter 4 in our discussion of interpretive communities. Unfortunately, many academic disciplines foster exclusive interpretive communities that stymie attempts at interdisciplinary collaboration. This book promotes an interdisciplinary approach to social psychology advocated by Allport (1968, 1985), because a lot of good social psychology is being produced in sociology, geography and other academic disciplines.

BOX 2.3   Hull House

Jane Addams and Ellen Gates Starr founded Hull House (an early resettlement service) in Chicago in 1899. The house was eventually expanded to include thirteen buildings offering a range of free educational, arts-based social programmes (Chapter 6 contains a contemporary example of one such programme) and clubs for working-class people and recent immigrants (Johnson, 2004). The environment was designed to be welcoming and open. The organization was founded on the notion that all people possess fundamental human dignity (see Chapter 10) regardless of origin, gender or ethnicity. Emphasis was placed on fairness in opportunities and the need for neighbours to help neighbours as a basis for cultivating civic responsibility and social inclusion. Hull House provided a focal point for scholars working towards social and legislative reforms in child labour, occupational safety, prostitution, women's rights, immigration policy, healthcare and social welfare at local, state and national levels. John Dewey and George Herbert Mead worked in collaboration with the leaders of Hull House. This involvement shaped the pragmatic orientation of what was to become known as the Chicago School at the University of Chicago. Involvement at Hull House exposed these social psychologists to the need to promote civic participation for all citizens in order to build an inclusive and healthy society. The Hull House tradition continues today, and further information can be found at http://www.hullhouse.org/.

were eclectic and interdisciplinary in their approach, using whatever theory or methods were available from the social sciences to generate insights that could be used to improve people's lives. Their work gave us concepts such as hardiness, social support and situated studies of individuals and interpersonal relations that considered the broader sociopolitical and economic contexts of everyday life.

BOX 2.4   Marie Jahoda

Marie Jahoda (1907–2001) was born and grew up in Austria, where she witnessed economic hardship and oppression. These experiences shaped her life and work. In 1933, Jahoda earned a PhD from the University of Vienna and co-wrote a classic book on the social consequences of unemployment on a small industrialized community with her husband of the time, Paul Lazarsfeld, and Hans Zeisel (1933/1971). After experiencing the hospitality of the Nazis for nine months in 1937, Jahoda left Germany and spent the Second World War in England. In 1946, she travelled to the United States and taught at New York and Columbia universities. In 1958 Jahoda returned to England and taught at Brunel and then Sussex University. Jahoda researched a range of topics, from the consequences of unemployment, the authoritarian personality, race relations, prejudice, mental health and well-being, to competition and the global environment (Connell & Russo, 1990). Coherence was brought to this broad range of interests through an attempt to document and understand everyday life experiences. Jahoda emphasized the idea that to be relevant to everyday life social psychology must draw its themes from the social problems facing society. In addressing social problems, she proposed that psychologists must not lose sight of the fact that these emerge and are experienced in social contexts. Jahoda argued that things that count cannot always be counted. Therefore, qualitative methods have a place alongside quantitative methods in psychology. Social problems, and not disciplinary preferences for specific methods, should drive the conduct of research.

Jahoda and colleagues conducted studies of suicide and illness rates and located causes for these phenomena in social and economic deprivation. Other key concerns were how socioeconomic conditions shaped character, learning, mental and physical health, and the interactions between individuals, groups and institutions (Fryer, 2008). The Depression was associated with reduced social participation and the disintegration of family and community structures. The consequences of the Depression were found to be mitigated by the strength of existing community ties and social support systems, or community resilience (see Chapter 10). By demonstrating the origins of individual and group hardship in social inequities and mediating factors, these social psychologists were able to advocate for social reforms that would better protect citizens from adversity (Collier, Minton & Reynolds, 1991). This was an orientation taken up in psychology through the formation of the Society for the Psychological Study of Social Issues (Box 2.5).

The course we have charted through the early decades of the short history of social psychology emphasizes social and political aspects of the discipline. As we will show in the following section, another and often overlapping stream in social psychology that emphasizes individual and small group factors also emerged. This second stream came to dominate the discipline in the latter half of the twentieth century and increasingly distanced itself from direct political and social action aimed at social transformation. Lubek and Apfelbaum

---

BOX 2.5   Society for the Psychological Study of Social Issues

The 1930s saw the formation of the Society for the Psychological Study of Social Issues (SPSSI) in the United States. Goodwin Watson, who had been mentored by John Dewey, brought together a group of psychologists to form the SPSSI as an organization affiliated to the American Psychological Association (APA) (Harris, 1986). The organization later became a division of the APA. It exemplified the emphasis being placed by many social psychologists at the time on exploring the societal origins of interrelated social problems such as poverty, conflict and prejudice. "Economic problems brought on by the depression were seen as at least partially responsible for racial prejudice, anti-Semitism, and growing world tension" (Collier, Minton & Reynolds, 1991, p. 144). One core focus was the impact of economic inequalities on the lives of many social groups. Collective efforts and cooperation, or the need to all pull together, were promoted as a way to address problems such as social unrest, crime and unemployment. As in Europe at the time, the emphasis was on the systematic collection of research evidence with a view to instigating practical efforts to address the needs of communities.

(2000) provide resources for learning about the rise of behaviourism and individualized versions of psychology in the 1920s. The following section provides a brief account of the development of the physical science orientation and then, in a subsequent section, we explore the increased centrality of this approach in social psychology from the 1950s onward.

A short history of experimental social psychology

In this chapter we emphasize the applied and collectivist stream in social psychology. However, it is important to note that key figures such as William James, Kurt Lewin and Frederic Charles Bartlett (see Chapter 4) engaged in both applied fieldwork and projects in the experimentalist tradition. Wilhelm Wundt (Box 2.6) is widely credited as the founder of psychology as a laboratory-based science conducted through the use of experimental designs adapted from the physical sciences. A key moment in this development was the establishment of a laboratory in Leipzig, Germany, in 1879, and the associated quantitative methods designed to control the research situation have been widely used in social psychology (Mandler, 2007). This approach focuses primarily on the thoughts and behaviour of individuals as independent beings who can be separated from their environments (see Chapter 4).

Central to the development of experimental social psychology was the establishment of laboratories in both Europe and the United States

BOX 2.6   Wilhelm Wundt

Wilhelm Wundt was born in Neckarau, Baden, on 16 August 1832 and died on 31 August 1920. He combined methodologies such as philosophical introspection with laboratory experiments borrowed from his training in physiology. From 1851 to 1856 he studied in Heidelberg and Berlin. After graduating from the University of Heidelberg in medicine, he gained employment as a research physiologist and wrote *Contributions to the Theory of Sense Perception* (1862). Wundt also developed a course in scientific psychology that emphasized the use of experimental methods from the natural sciences. Lectures from this course were published as *Lectures on the Mind of Humans and Animals* (1863). It was in 1864 that Wundt was promoted to Assistant Professor of Physiology. As his career progressed, Wundt studied human consciousness, feelings, sensations and ideas. In 1875 Wundt moved to the University of Leipzig and established his psychological laboratory. Over his career, Wundt supervised almost 200 doctorial dissertations across a range of disciplines, and his work has had a clear impact on the later development of experimental psychology and an individual-oriented stream of the discipline (Brock, 2006). Prior to his death in 1920, Wundt completed a ten-volume series on social psychology.

For more information on the work of Wundt and how it relates to figures such as William James, see Mandler (2007).

in the late nineteenth and early twentieth centuries (Mandler, 2007). For example, Edward Titchener studied with Wundt and colleagues at the University of Leipzig and subsequently established what some believe to be the first laboratory at Cornell University, in 1892. This was followed by the addition of a growing number of facilities at other universities in the United States. Similar facilities were established in other countries. For instance, after a visit to Wundt's laboratory, John Smyth set up his own facility in Melbourne, Australia, in 1903 (Taft & Day, 1988). These early facilities used both experimental and introspective or more qualitative methods to study consciousness, memory and various mental events.

In the British context a crucial figure for the development of experimental psychology was Frederic Charles Bartlett (Box 2.7). Bartlett was particularly notable in that he conducted both experiments and applied field research, as well as working interdisciplinarily by drawing together insights from psychology, anthropology and sociology. Bartlett emphasized the importance of culture for understanding the transfer of knowledge, social memory, human thought and action (Wagoner, Gillespie & Duveen, 2007). Like Mary from the opening scenario, Bartlett was interested in unravelling issues of culture and human understanding.

Another area of historical note in the experimental stream of social psychology is behaviourism. Behaviourism is often referred to as a learning perspective. It is based on the idea that everything that a person or animal does, including our actions, thoughts and feelings,

BOX 2.7 Frederic Charles Bartlett

Frederic Charles Bartlett was born on 20 October 1886 in Gloucestershire. Bartlett took a distance course with the University Correspondence College and developed an interest in experimental social psychology and politics. Bartlett obtained a degree in philosophy in 1909 and became a tutor at the correspondence college. He completed a masters degree in sociology and ethics from the University of London in 1911. Subsequently, Bartlett embarked on undergraduate study at Cambridge University in order to follow his interest in anthropology and experimental work. He graduated with distinction and a degree in moral science with a solid grounding in German psychology inspired by Wundt (Bartlett, 1956). Bartlett became increasingly interested in how people use their memories in transforming cultural forms and completed a PhD in this area in 1917 (Bartlett, 1958). From 1924 to 1948 Bartlett edited the *British Journal of Psychology*, and he was awarded a chair in experimental psychology at Cambridge University in 1931.

Bartlett is particularly noted for his work on schema theory and memory structures, which are discussed in Chapter 4. Bartlett became increasingly interested in applied psychology and worked as a consultant for the armed forces on personnel research. During the Second World War he was given various awards, including a CBE, for his work. In the applied arena, Bartlett established the National Institute of Industrial Psychology. Despite the social and applied nature of much of his work, Bartlett retained the view that psychology was at its core a physical science. This resulted in an emphasis on rigorous research design and the systematic use of experiments, field observations, and participant self-reports. Bartlett retired in 1952.

For a more detailed account of Bartlett and his work, see the comprehensive review written by Alberto Rosa: http://www.ppsis.cam.ac.uk/bartlett/Bartlett%20The%20Person.htm.

can be regarded as a learned behaviour (Skinner, 1945/1984). Such behaviours are to be explored through the use of experimental methods in terms of direct observation. Behaviourism epitomizes the idea that psychology is a branch of the natural, rather than the human, sciences (Baum, 2004). Arguably the most famous proponent of behaviourism was Burrhus F. Skinner, who conducted experimental investigations primarily of animal behaviour from the 1930s to the 1950s. Skinner dismissed the earlier idea of John B. Watson that mental events could not be studied scientifically. Skinner emphasized the importance of mental states and developed his own brand of radical behaviourism and the field of the experimental analysis of behaviour. From this perspective, mental events are not seen as causes of behaviour. Rather, mental events are seen as preconditioned behaviours in their own right. According to radical behaviourists, human action is not determined by free will, but is conditioned by previous interactions of individuals with their environments (Baum, 2004). The organism (read 'person') is conditioned over time to adopt particular strategies and ways of interacting with the world.

Skinner and colleagues developed a compartmentalized approach to behaviour in which human action and mental events could be broken down into constituent parts. This enabled researchers to explore the influence of specific biological and cultural factors in condition-ing behaviour in controlled settings (Box 2.8).

It should be noted that internal tensions remain rife within the broad church advocating the adoption of an approach to psychology modelled on the physical sciences. This stream is actually a cluster-ing of experimentally oriented traditions. For instance, figures such as Frederic Bartlett (1927) wrote early criticisms of behaviourism and the work of John B. Watson (1925). Bartlett and others promoted the focus on internal cognitive events and not just observable behaviours. Behaviourism was largely displaced from the core of social psychology by the cognitive revolution (Box 2.9) and the development of human-istic psychology (Schneider, Bugental & Pierson, 2001). Both of these psychologies seek to enrich social psychology with notions of human thought, meaning, agency and spirit (see Chapters 4 and 10).

In brief, the adoption of experimentalism offered the promise of scientific rigour and legitimacy to the new discipline of psychology (Mandler, 2007). It provided a means of controlling factors interacting

---

BOX 2.8   Behavioural analysis today

Today, applications of the philosophy of behaviourism are often referred to as 'behaviour analysis'. This work is coordinated internationally through the Association for Behavior Analysis. The association encompasses a wide range of interests, including education, disability, mental health, organizations and forensic settings such as prisons. The approach has inspired the use of several practical techniques for modifying the behav-iour of individuals. This is particularly evident in hospital and correctional facilities or controlled and dynamic social environments. For instance, Martin and Pear (2003) defined a token economy as a "program in which a group of individuals can earn tokens for a variety of desirable behaviours, and can exchange tokens earned for backup reinforcers" (p. 306). Token economies were initially formulated by Ayllón and Azrin in the late 1960s to increase socially desirable behaviours on the ward by psychiatric patients living in hospital. Essentially, the token economy increased socially appropriate behaviour, including in patient–patient interactions and staff–patient interactions. Interestingly, Ayllón and Azrin (1968) found that patients would work harder (save more tokens) for social reinforcers (e.g. going for walks with the staff or visitors) than for chocolate bars or cigarettes. Token economies are still used today, but usually in modified and personalized forms – discussing certain goals with clients and agreeing on a level system to attain those goals. For example, if a client living in residential care enjoys going for an escorted lunch with friends on the weekend, she may agree to decrease her swearing at staff in order to earn check marks on a recording sheet: five days of no swearing at staff could earn her the opportunity for lunch out with her friends. Probably the most interesting aspect of token econ-omy systems is that such programmes show how important it is to have a good therapeutic relationship with one's client and also to agree on attainable goals. The client, then, becomes in charge of gaining extra privileges. A token economy based on good faith, rather than primarily punishment and control, generally results in better social skills, better adherence to all programme standards, improved personal hygiene and quicker discharge to the community.

For more information on behaviour analysis, see http://www.abainternational.org/.

BOX 2.9   The cognitive revolution

The cognitive revolution that occurred in psychology in the 1950s presented a direct challenge to behaviourism by repositioning the core of experimental psychology (Bruner, 1990). It was assumed that by developing computer technology and looking at how machines solved problems we would be able to reverse engineer these processes and extend our understandings of what was going on in the minds of individuals. This emerging cognitive approach also sought to establish meaning, rather than behaviour, as the central subject matter of psychology. The focus turned to how individuals make sense of the world around them and the underlying mental processes. We explore aspects of the social cognitive approach to social psychology in Chapters 3, 4 and 8. This approach explores human thinking processes, language use, remembering, knowing, attending and understanding. From a cognitive perspective people do not simply act in particular ways because they are preconditioned to do so; rather, people also take specific courses of action because they think and are inquisitive. People respond to the world not just from the lessons they may have learned in the past, but also according to novel ideas and imagination.

in the formation of human thought and action. 'Experimentalism' is a term used today to refer to an approach to social psychological research that models itself on the methods of the physical sciences and is associated with calls for objectivity in research. It is assumed that experimenters can remove people from the social, cultural and historical contexts in which they are embedded and place them in controlled conditions in order validly and reliably to measure their reactions to specific stimuli. Such research seeks to uncover universal processes shaping social psychological phenomena. Assumptions underlying experimentalism have been questioned by many social psychologists, including those established in this tradition (Billig, 2008; Tajfel, 1972). The stance taken in this book is that experiments can provide valuable insights into social psychological phenomena. However, social psychology has much more to offer, and we also need to engage in fieldwork and focus on social psychological phenomena in the contexts in which events take place. What we advocate is the need for readers to become critical consumers of all research, especially research presented as being value free. Psychologists need to consider historical and cultural contexts for research and the very phenomena being analysed.

Influences on the rise of experimentation and individualism

Social psychologists were active during the Second World War, when considerable resources were devoted to psychological studies of propaganda and leadership and the consequences of wartime experiences on individuals, families and communities. For instance, despite having won an Iron Cross fighting for Germany in the First World War, Kurt Lewin worked with colleagues in the United Kingdom and the United States, busying himself applying psychological knowledge of group dynamics, leadership, persuasion, morale, learning, attitudes and personality (Lewin, 1935, 1946/48, 1948). These psychologists worked to improve the functioning of the militaries of the allied forces and to streamline the transition of civilians into suitable military roles (Farr, 1991). The work exemplifies the way in which many social psychologists sought to respond to societal and historical events, to make sense of horrors, and to try to prevent them from recurring (Box 2.10).

Following the Second World War, social psychology expanded considerably. In terms of the influence of the war on the growth of social psychology, it has been proposed that the most influential person was Adolf Hitler (Cartwright, 1979). The actions of this man and the other Nazis contributed to a focus on issues of social conformity, persuasion, power and prejudice, as researchers sought to understand the horrors of the Holocaust (Milgram, 1974). The expansion of social psychology was associated with a sense of confidence and direction for many. Kurt Lewin, among others, had laid the groundwork for this expansion during the war. Lewin is often cited as the founder of modern experimental social psychology in the United States. He envisioned a social science directed towards solving social problems, including anti-Semitism and demonstrating the virtues of democracy over autocracy. Clearly, these interests were linked to his experiences as a soldier during the First World War and as a German Jew in the 1930s and 1940s. One of Lewin's first papers was a phenomenological analysis of the experiences of combat soldiers, in which he drew on his own experiences as a combatant. The paper introduced later themes of his work, such as the focus on democratic leadership and group behaviour. Lewin maintained that fieldwork was just as important as laboratory research. Unfortunately, the balance he maintained throughout his career between laboratory-based research and fieldwork was lost by many of his colleagues and students after his death in 1947 (Farr, 1991). The experimental approach came to dominate social psychology, along with a focus on individuals and small groups, and the emphasis on application and social transformation was reduced (Collier, Minton & Reynolds, 1991; Farr, 1996).

The turn to experimentalism was not simply the product of the Second World War. It was also influenced by useful insights into group behaviour gained from experimental studies in the 1930s. Let us consider for a moment a setting for a classic early experimental investigation of intergroup relations. Imagine that you are an adolescent who has come to a holiday camp. You join a group of nine other boys and begin to make friends. There is another group of boys in the camp with whom your group comes into conflict. Arguments

---

BOX 2.10   The APA and the sanctioning of torture under 'certain conditions'

It is important to assert here that the involvement of psychologists in social events and in particular wars is not always a positive practice and can be controversial. For instance, since 2004 there have been reports in newspapers such as the *New York Times* of US psychologists being involved in interrogations at the Guantánamo Bay prison (Zimbardo, 2007). Psychologists had agreed to assist the US military with interrogations, whereas psychiatrists were prohibited from doing so by the American Medical Association (AMA) and the oath to do no harm. The APA stance was clarified as being that under certain circumstances psychologists could be involved in interrogations. This raised considerable controversy. For example, many psychologists staged a protest outside an annual meeting of the APA, and several prominent members resigned from the APA and handed back their prestigious citations. Others withheld their membership dues. Subsequently, the APA leadership relented and held a referendum in which 60 per cent of participating members voted to ban the involvement of psychologists in interrogations.

The fundamental issue here is an ethical one. Psychologists should not use their knowledge to harm others. We are a helping and not a harming profession. We have learned from the early prison dilemma studies how corrupting prison environments can be for those in positions of power (Zimbardo, 2007).

The response rate for the referendum of 60 per cent opposing involvement is strong, but not overwhelming, indicating that a significant minority did not oppose the use of coercive techniques to obtain information. What do *you* think?

---

and fights develop with members of the other group. It is not until your two groups are forced to work together that you begin to forge friendships and that hostilities between the groups decline.

The situation we have just described is based on three experiments with boys aged eleven to twelve years in camp settings (see Sherif, 1966). There were three phases to the work. The first involved group building. Here two groups of ten boys lived together and were encouraged to develop a group structure. The second involved group conflict. Here tasks such as a tug of war were used to promote competition and negative aspects of intergroup attitudes and behaviour. Tensions and rivalry promoted through competitive relations between the groups were allowed to deteriorate into further forms of open conflict. The third phase involved a reduction of conflict. Here the researchers evaluated the situation and intervened to reduce conflict and improve intergroup relations. This was done by having the groups work together to achieve shared goals such as pulling on a rope together to start a truck that was needed to obtain food for both groups. Within days hostility reduced and friendships emerged across groups. These studies exemplify the emphasis Lewin placed on the need to draw on observations of events in society and to theorize these and design research to extend our understandings and interventions to address the issues (Box 2.11).

It is customary when reporting experiments to talk only about the experimental groups or conditions; in the case of the Sherif studies, these are the two groups of boys in the camp. This custom neglects

> **BOX 2.11   Relevance of experimenter background to topic selection**
>
> What becomes apparent when reviewing such studies and placing them into a history of social psychology is that the backgrounds of researchers and the social and historical contexts in which they were working shaped their investigations. For example, Muzafer Sherif immigrated to the United States from Turkey, where he had spent time in prison as punishment for speaking out against the pro-Nazi actions of the Turkish government of the time. His interest in group processes, norms and social problems came from his experiences of the societal shift from the Ottoman Empire to the modern Turkish republic (Gorman, 1981). Muzafer and his wife Carolyn were very aware of the socially and culturally related nature of their research on intergroup relations in the boys camps. In a 1976 textbook, Carolyn Sherif (née Wood) emphasized how research is a process of social engagement. She discussed the historical and culturally located nature of social psychology.

the fact that experiments are particular social situations that reflect broader social norms and relationships between groups. These are evident in the relationships established between 'experimenters' and 'subjects'. For instance, Billig (1976) reappraised the Sherif studies from the perspective of his interest in the ways in which dominant social groups can subordinate minority groups through false consciousness.[4] Billig identified three rather than two groups interacting in the summer camp studies. There were the two groups of boys, and the third group comprised the experimenters and camp staff. The situation involved the group of experimenters setting up the two groups of boys and the conditions for their interactions. The experimenters defined the social reality for the two groups of boys. The experiment was a culturally located microcosm of the broader society in which dominant groups exercise authority to influence the lives of minority groups. Billig points out that the boys did not see the experimenters as the source of their hostilities. This is often the case for minority groups who perhaps fail to see the influence of colonizing groups in their own intergroup rivalries (see Chapter 5). Thus, we can reinterpret the classic camp studies as illustrations of the function of social power relationships between groups in society.

The influence of the social and political climate on the shift to experimentation in North American social psychology has been attributed in part to some psychologists striving to legitimate psychology as a scientific discipline (Farr, 1996), and to the rise of anti-communist sentiment and McCarthyism in the United States (Lubek & Apfelbaum, 2000).[5] What we see during this period is a shift in focus from the social psychology of responding to the needs of oppressed groups to instead reacting to the needs of the state and industry. Social psychologists were encouraged to shift from being political activists, as they had been during previous decades, and instead to become neutral intermediaries between government interests and labour and cultural movements. In addition, many psychologists moved away from studying groups and social psychological processes as they occurred in actuality to studying topics such as conformity and group influence in laboratory settings:

Many social psychologists dropped the study of real-life groups and political attitudes and voting behaviours, for example, as the terms "social", "group", and "collective" were sometimes given politically surplus meanings and linked to notions of Comradeship, "socialism", or a career-disruptive tendency toward "premature anti-fascism". (Lubek & Apfelbaum, 2000, p. 423)

During this period members of the Society for the Psychological Study of Social Issues were targeted in anti-communist crusades. Those who lost their academic posts as a result of communist witch-hunts were provided social and financial support by the SPSSI (Collier, Minton & Reynolds, 1991).

The laboratory provided refuge from social engagement for many social psychologists in the 1950s, even those interested in socially embedded group processes such as conformity (Box 2.12). Psychologists could preoccupy themselves with increasingly sophisticated experimental modelling behind the supposed neutrality of a white lab coat. Unfortunately, the move from the street to the laboratory contributed in some ways to an increasing narrowness of focus on subjects that could be studied in laboratory conditions (Lubek & Apfelbaum, 2000). The focus for some social psychologists became the particularities of research design and getting the study right, rather than the ecological validity of relating the topic to how it works in people's everyday lives. Some commentators have proposed that social psychology began to study more and more about less and less (Gergen, 1978; Lubek, 2000).

BOX 2.12   Studying group pressure and conformity in the 1950s

A topic particularly pertinent to everyday life is social influence, or how the feelings, thoughts and behaviours of others affect us. Underlying social psychological processes associated with social influence are thought to be strongest in the context of social groups. A particularly notable form of social influence is conformity, or the tendency of individuals to think like other people in their social groups. Such conformity is thought to relate to the status of self and others, group size, unanimity, levels of cohesion in the group and one's commitment to the group.

Consider for a moment that you are a social psychologist in the 1950s and you want to explore the impact of group pressure on personal conformity. How might you go about such as a study?

Asch (1956) conducted a series of eloquently simple experiments that are widely cited as being groundbreaking in terms of providing new insights into conformity. One experiment included six *confederates*, who gave incorrect responses to a series of exercises in which they judged the length of lines of string, and one real participant who also took part in the exercises. All participants were seated around a table so that the real participant was second to last, and all gave their judgements verbally. In early exercises the actors matched lines of comparative length with the target line. In later exercises the actors made uniformly incorrect matches. Asch wanted to know whether the real participant would conform to these incorrect judgements. On average four to five incorrect judgements were in fact made by these real participants in the twelve exercise trials. Around 30 per cent of real participants made incorrect judgements that conformed to the judgements of the actors and were against their own true judgements at least once. Such studies provide a means of continuing investigations of group processes when faced with a sociopolitical environment that discourages more field-based studies. They also demonstrate the utility of experimental methods for generating knowledge of social psychological processes.

For a recent example of research in this area that explores how power can insulate people from the influence of a situation, see Galinsky, Magee, Gruenfeld, Whitson, and Liljenquist (2008).

The experimental approach did not become so dominant in all parts of the world. For example, liberation psychology and liberation social psychology (LSP), reviewed by Burton and Kagan (2009), exemplify the political commitment to social justice and social transformation by social psychologists. This approach was developed in the context of Latin American societies with histories of colonization, endemic poverty and socioeconomic exclusions (which often affect the majority of people living in such countries) and had its roots in liberation theology. In response, LSP developed as a collectivist-oriented social psychology to address the needs of the majority of the population in these countries to overcome economic and political oppression and marginalization. Contexts for this work have included repression and civil war in El Salvador; the aftermath of dictatorships in Chile, Argentina and other countries; and the experience of poor, marginalized and migrant communities in Venezuela, Puerto Rico, Costa Rica and Brazil (Burton & Kagan, 2005; Flores-Osario, 2009;

Montero, 2007). Getting involved in such work can be dangerous. Leading advocates for LSP have been murdered. Martín-Baró, a key figure, was assassinated in El Salvador in 1989 because of his efforts to support positive social transformation (Box 2.13). It is arguably less life threatening to support social justice in countries such as the United States, although as mentioned above psychologists have lost their jobs for their political activities and needed to be supported by colleagues.

To recap, the period from 1945 to 1970 is often referred to as the golden age in social psychology (Apfelbaum, 2000). Psychologists were busy building research areas and formulating theories to be tested primarily in laboratory settings. They were feeling pretty confident at the time. Unfortunately, this period also witnessed a shift in emphasis away from direct action and the political orientation of social psychology. As discussed, tensions between social psychologists as political activists and as detached scientists occurred from the 1920s onwards. As the dominance of the experimental approach increased, direct attempts to address social problems declined throughout the 1950s and 1960s. Disillusionment and cynicism grew among many social psychologists. It was in the 1970s that concerns regarding such shifts were again brought to the fore. More cynical views reviewed in the following section came into view and have contributed to a rebalancing of the discipline to emphasize both qualitative and quantitative methods, and both laboratory-based and action-based orientations to research.

BOX 2.13   Ignacio Martín-Baró

One of the early champions of liberation psychology was a Jesuit priest, Ignacio Martín-Baró (1996), who was influenced by the work of Paulo Freire (see Chapter 1). Jiménez-Doménguez (2009) writes of how Martín-Baró developed a situated social psychology in partnership with the oppressed masses, and a version of the discipline that used social sciences to unmask repressive practices of the power elites. The focus for these psychologists is thus on social transformation through collaborative participation between psychologists and local people. LSP addresses the needs of people facing oppression by working locally to foster societal transformation (Martín-Baró, 1994). The adoption of this approach in Western social psychology has been hampered by the language barrier. Aron and Corne (1994) edited a volume titled *Writings for a Liberation Psychology: Ignacio Martín-Baró,* which introduces key ideas around liberation psychology and liberation social psychology. Venezuelan scholar Martiza Montero (2006, 2007) has also been a key proponent of liberation psychology and liberation social psychology. LSP is an approach in keeping with the emphasis placed in this book on social justice and transformation and processes of inclusion. LSP is about getting on the bus.

A crisis in confidence and re-emphasis on social relevance

An early reflection on the growing focus in social psychology on individuals and small group behaviour in laboratory settings was provided by Solomon Asch. Asch (1952) noted that the use of experimental methods from the natural sciences, including his own work, was resulting in the production of a caricature of human beings and social life, rather than a portrait. He recognized a danger in the tendency of some social psychologists to become preoccupied with methodological details and lose sight of events in the social world (see also Allport, 1968). Such reservations are even more significant when it is acknowledged that Wilhelm Wundt was opposed to the use of experiments to research topics in social psychology. Wundt felt that psychology was only partially a natural science and was also partially a social science rightly located in the arts (Farr, 1991, 1996). Wundt proposed that it was overly restraining to study thinking and complex cognitive processes using laboratory experiments because thinking involved language, myth, custom and culture and was anchored in more naturalistic settings. This was the domain of the social sciences and humanities (Danzinger, 1990).

Review exercise

Think about the Asch experiment described earlier. Briefly note some factors that may have influenced or changed the results.

■ How well does this experimental situation emulate situations outside the laboratory in which we might feel pressure to conform?

The 1960s and 1970s saw the re-emergence of questions regarding the overreliance on experimental methods and whether such practices reduced the relevance of social psychology to the realities of everyday life. What is widely termed the crisis in social psychology (Box 2.14) was experienced in North America and Europe, but also acutely in Latin America, Asia and Australasia (Parker, 1989, 2007). According to Rosnow (1981), social psychology had succumbed to Kaplan's law of the instrument – once the experiment had been adopted as the preeminent method for research, it was easy to find that everything needed experimentation. Kenneth Gergen (1973) argued that social psychology cannot be solely a physical science, because many of its findings are culturally and historically located. A similar point was made by Tajfel (1972). The physical sciences rely on the notion that events

BOX 2.14   The crisis in social psychology

The crisis in social psychology occurred in the context of liberation movements of the 1960s to 1970s, and amid calls for a social psychology of relevance to the realities of daily life, particularly of oppressed groups. Social psychology needed to address the pressing social inequalities and problems of the time in the context of broader sociopolitical structures shaping local circumstances. It was felt that the overreliance on experimental methods hampered the engagement with the needs of marginalized groups. This crisis can be summarized in terms of three issues with experimental social psychology:

■ *Social irrelevance*: social psychology regularly does not produce practical knowledge with which to address social problems.

■ *Universal validity*: social psychology often relies on studies of undergraduate students in artificial or experimental settings. Despite this, researchers infer that general social psychological principles identified in these specific settings can be applied to other people in different settings.

■ *Presentation of scientific neutrality*: social psychology often denies the moral and political dimensions of its research while pretending to be value free and unbiased.

occur naturally and underlying processes do not change. Therefore, researchers can discover the underlying laws of physics and chemistry. However, social psychology deals with events and processes that are historically and culturally situated and subject to change. Further, the very publishing of the findings of social psychological research can influence the processes being studied. For example, educating people about the processes of manipulation central to propaganda can inoculate them from such manipulation (Pratkanis & Aronson, 1991) and thus change the course of human history.

Needless to say not everyone agreed with these criticisms. Zajonc (1989) was particularly critical of what he called an 'anti-scientific' attitude being expressed towards experimentation. He too argued that critics were misapprehending the nature of experimental research. For Zajonc the issue is the extent to which a research strategy reflects or reproduces social reality. The question is whether the experimental procedures employed can provide insights into the essence of phenomena central to social psychological processes.

Proponents of the experimental tradition maintained that arguments against the experiment are the wrong arguments (Elms, 1975; Shaw, 1974). The experiment, from this perspective, fails the test of external validity because it is not trying to pass that test. Experiments are not designed to emulate the so-called real world. They are designed to do something quite different. Experiments are used to test theories (Shaw, 1974). Rather than being diminished by emerging criticisms, experimentation in psychology went from strength to strength, culminating in 1982 with acceptance of the

International Union of Psychological Science as a full member of the International Council of Scientific Unions (ICSU).

A careful reading of the literature suggests that the opposing camps were not that far apart. Gergen (1994, 1978) suggested that the experiments should not be abandoned; rather, experiments should be recast as consciousness-raising tools (see Chapter 1). To illustrate the point, he cited the classic early studies of prominent social psychologists, including Asch and Milgram, as serving that purpose. Gergen also advocated using experiments as part of a broader constellation of methods. Other social psychologists made the point that the experiment may be of reduced utility as a method for understanding the complexity of social phenomena when used in isolation (Toulmin & Leary, 1985).

Such debates constitute a form of disciplinary soul searching or reflexivity through which we can better understand the underlying assumptions and functions of social psychological research. Figures such as Gergen (1973) and Tajfel (1972) were seeking increased reflexive awareness among psychologists regarding the history and impact of our discipline (Billig, 2008). Such reflection is evident among leading experimental social psychologists, as is illustrated in the emphasis Sherif and colleagues (1976) placed on the socially located nature of research and in Asch's (1952) questioning of the caricature or portrait of human beings produced via research in social psychology. It is a sign of a healthy discipline. Recounting internal criticisms such as those raised during the crisis in social psychology is important because they can drive innovation and change in social psychology (Lubek & Apfelbaum, 2000). Self-criticisms have had an impact in leading to a return to more qualitative and politicized approaches, particularly in the Southern Hemisphere and in Europe (Montero, 2007; Parker, 2005). This is evident in journals such as the *British Journal of Social Psychology, Qualitative Research in Psychology, Qualitative Psychology, Journal of Community and Applied Social Psychology, Journal of Health Psychology, Culture and Psychology,* and *American Journal of Community Psychology.* The questioning of the relevance of social psychology has reopened the possibility for socially oriented work that is directly engaged with everyday realities in diverse societies (Box 2.15).

BOX 2.15   Developments in critical psychology

For a discussion of the development of critical psychology in a range of countries, see the *Annual Review of Critical Psychology* number 5, at http://www.discourseunit.com/arcp/5.htm. Attention is given to what we can learn about critical psychologies in different sociocultural contexts, what the traditions are and how psychology can be used to promote positive social change.

Reconsidering bystander research in light of the crisis in social psychology

In approaching social psychology as a historical discipline, scholars (Cherry, 1995; Manning, Levine & Collins, 2007) have reanalysed classic studies. Here we will briefly consider the example of bystander apathy, a topic that has featured regularly in social psychology textbooks over the past four decades. Bystander apathy research also provides a practical example of the socially oriented approach to social psychology that we promote in this book.

In 1964 a young women, Kitty Genovese, was murdered in Queens, New York, by a young African American man. Public controversy erupted around why observers of the incident failed to intervene to help the woman. Two behaviourally oriented social psychologists, Bibb Latane and John Darley, were having dinner a few days after the incident, and, as can happen during such dinners, they began to analyse the events. Those at the dinner had read media reports about the incident and had been talking with others and developing opinions regarding what had happened. They asked questions such as:

- Did you read about that murder?
- Why do you think he did it?
- Why did witnesses fail to help her?

The two social psychologists drew on their disciplinary training to try to explain the events. Rather than assigning causes for the lack of action to the broader context of social norms and practices, these psychologists identified immediate situational factors that might discourage intervention on the part of onlookers. These factors were derived from classic work on crowds (Le Bon, 1897/1977) and included diffusion of responsibility across group members, which inhibits individual action. This explanation provided a core focus for subsequent research into bystander apathy. Studies focused on decisions regarding whether to render assistance in the context of how witnesses assessed the situation and their reactions to other witnesses. The context for individual inaction was limited to situational considerations, such as the impact of group size on individual decisions to act and how individuals, when in larger groups, feel less accountable and become less likely to act (Box 2.16). In many respects a mirror of the early work of Georg Simmel (1903) on the blasé attitude, Latane and Darley (1970) produced *Social Inhibition Theory*, which asserts that urban life can promote social disengagement and the diffusion of social responsibility and can reduce the likelihood of people making sacrifices in order to aid other people.

BOX 2.16   Bystander apathy

Bystander apathy occurs when the likelihood of one person assisting another person who is in danger diminishes as the size of an observing group increases. This effect has been demonstrated in a number of simulations since the 1960s (Latane & Darley, 1970; Moriarty, 1975). Diffusion of responsibility is offered as one explanation for why people in group situations can become less likely to render assistance to those in need. Research suggests that people may simply assume that another person will intervene or is in a better position to offer assistance and thus feel less responsibility to act. People in emergency situations can counteract this effect by identifying a specific person and appealing to them directly for help. An observer who is appealed to directly by a victim may then feel more responsibility to act.

Most research into this phenomenon has been conducted in the United States.

■ Can you think of an alternative explanation for why people may fail to render assistance to others in emergency situations?

The United States has individual liability laws, and part of the reason may be that some people are worried about making a mistake and having a lawsuit brought against them.

Recently, Manning, Levine and Collins (2007) proposed that the Genovese case, which has shaped psychological research on helping or pro-social behaviour and apathy, was based on factual inaccuracies. For example, there were far fewer than the thirty-eight reported witnesses. Of the five witnesses testifying during the trial who observed the event from apartments overlooking the area, only three saw the perpetrator and victim together, and several were not clear about what was happening in the street below. These witnesses did not observe for the whole duration of the incident and were not sure that a murder was taking place, and several telephoned the local police to report the incident. Thus, many of the witnesses observed the event in isolation and at a distance, rather than in a crowd situation in the immediate location, as has been assumed within social psychology texts. These details about what actually happened that day were overlooked at the time. Yet the assumption that witnesses observed the entire incident as a group underlies many textbook accounts of the case and was used to construct a behavioural-oriented explanation for bystander apathy.

Regardless of the inaccuracies in the telling of the Genovese story, Manning, Levine and Collins (2007) note that individual- and group-focused explanations have provided useful insights into human behaviour in certain situations. Subsequent studies also illustrate the utility of field experiments in re-engaging psychology with social issues beyond the laboratory. However, problems with this research remain. The restricted focus on individuals in particular settings can lead to events being stripped of the significance of wider social norms, intergroup conflicts in society and political structures. As Cherry (1995) explains:

The daily experience of violence in people's lives is a story too easily decontextualized by social psychological theories that operate at the individual behavioural level. If we theorize at the level of community, then we begin to consider some groups or communities are more vulnerable to violence than others and have been so historically. By understanding the overlap of racism, sexism and poverty, we can understand both the personal suffering and the political significance of any particular attack. (p. 27)

This loss of context and relevance is evident in the evolution of bystander research. For instance, subsequent simulations have tended to ignore the background issues of racism and economic hardship from which part of the explanation for violence against Kitty Genovese can be derived. Alternative explanations for attacks against women and the possibility of public apathy are warranted. For instance, this murder can be read as the product of US society in the 1960s and the tolerance at the time towards violence against women (Cherry, 1995).

Instead of focusing on broader societal norms the emphasis in bystander research was increasingly placed on more depoliticized scenarios of a person having an epileptic seizure or falling down (Box 2.17). These became favoured stimulus situations to establish the intricacies of conditions under which people were more or less likely to render assistance.

We are not arguing that field experiments such as those discussed above cannot generate useful insights into how people might behave under specific conditions (cf. Manning, Levine & Collins, 2007). However, the dominance of experimental studies of individuals in small group settings has fostered a focus that can seem detached from the realities and needs of many people in diverse societies. Social psychology also needs broader conceptualizations of phenomena such as pro-social behaviour that are informed by the questions

---

BOX 2.17   Example of bystander research

Research into bystander apathy and circumstances for pro-social behaviour (see Chapter 10) has emerged as one of the most prolific areas of social psychological research, spawning many thousands of laboratory and field experiments, some of them quite amusing.

In one study seminarians (trainee priests) attended a group discussion on the parable of the Good Samaritan (Darley & Batson, 1973). At the end of the session they were directed to a nearby building. As they walked to the new location they passed a man (an experimental confederate) slumped in a doorway.

■ Guess what the seminarians did.

The priests did not stop to render assistance to the man.

raised during the crisis in social psychology and that take us beyond individuals and small groups. Studies of pro-social behaviour (see Chapter 10) are increasingly diverse, and include studies that focus on helping in terms of emotional dispositions and levels of empathy felt by the observer towards a person; the existence of relationships with the person; and the influence of social norms of reciprocity, collectivism and moral obligations (Batson & Powell, 2003). This reflects a focus in research beyond a behavioural approach that is concerned primarily with factors in the 'immediate' physical context, and extends into considering even how helping occurs online or at a physical distance via the media (see Chapter 11). Developments of and tensions between explanations of social phenomena reflect how the subject matter of our discipline remains open to further interpretation. Today's explanations are not set in stone. Nor should we conceptualize social psychology as being set in stone in terms of theories, methods and interventions.

Chapter summary

The development of Western social psychology is commonly dated from the late nineteenth century and the growth in the discipline during the decades following the Second World War. Many histories of social psychology present partial and sanitized accounts that neglect the more radical and applied edges in favour of the development of laboratories and insights from experimental studies. We have attempted to balance such accounts. In charting this history, we have undoubtedly ourselves taken some liberties and made omissions. It is difficult to pin down where social psychology begins and where borders might be placed alongside other psychologies and social sciences (see Chapter 3). Further, there is no universal agreement on the definition of social psychology, the core objects of study or 'appropriate' research strategies. This disciplinary murkiness is a healthy sign for an academic field that is still developing. It means that development and growth are still occurring. We might say that social psychology has porous borders in that it lacks a definite starting point and is still evolving its focus and approaches.

At this point we hope that students, including Mary from the opening scenario, are not left thinking, "Well, this history stuff is all well and good, but what does it have to do with me? I want to know about what is going on around me, not what happened a hundred years ago." Our response is that it is useful to look historically to get a sense of what social psychology is about, what it does and what has influenced our focus and actions. After all, history has a tendency to repeat itself. We hope that you have come away from reading this chapter with three core themes in mind:

- First, social psychology has been applied and politically engaged with societal events since its modern beginnings.
- Second, social psychology is a product of sociohistorical contexts, which influence the questions researchers ask, the problems we seek to address and the methods and approaches employed.
- Third, the process of observing, theorizing, researching and acting is a cycle that is central to social psychology, whether using field-based or laboratory-based methods.

By focusing on history repeating itself, in terms of the involvement of social psychologists directly in movements to address social issues, we can highlight the fact that there is work to be done and that it is okay to get on the bus and get involved politically in social life. We have presented social psychology as a sociocultural enterprise that should contribute to bettering the human condition. Surely we have more to offer than simply understandings of social life. Social psychological knowledge and theory also needs to be focused towards transforming social conditions in order to make them as equitable and healthy for people as possible (see Chapter 1). The focus on everyday life, as is outlined in Chapter 3, allows us to develop a social psychology that is relevant and can deal with contradiction and uncertainty. We can engage with the experiences and actions of human beings and diverse groups as and where these occur, and within the broader context of the historical and cultural domains in which we conduct our lives together. In short, social psychology has a lot to tell us about everyday life. But more than that, social psychology has a lot to tell us about how to improve people's everyday lives together.

Review exercise

- Who proposed that *not everything that counts can be counted* and what did he or she mean by that statement?
- What were the core findings of the Sherif studies of the boys camps?
- What are the three primary concerns raised during the crisis in social psychology regarding the prominence of experimentation?

Notes

1. It is misleading to contrast cultures in terms of collectivist and individualist (Billig, 2008). All cultures have individual-oriented and collective-oriented ideas and practices. Further, the term

'Western' refers to a number of distinct cultures and contexts. In pointing to the existence of both collective and individual orientations in Western social psychologies, we are highlighting the dynamic interplay of tensions within the discipline.

2. Many of these traditions have been incorporated into indigenous social psychologies over the past three decades. We explore this issue in Chapter 4.

3. In Chapter 5, we reverse this orientation by considering how groups function within individuals through the notion of the cobweb self.

4. False consciousness refers to our inability to see things as they really are, usually because of the false, or misleading, perceptions created by societal or political structures.

5. McCarthyism refers to the anti-communism crusades in the United States in the 1950s, which were personified in the figure of Senator Joseph McCarthy. These events involved the levelling of accusations towards key public figures that they were communists and therefore untrustworthy. Many lost their jobs as a result of these allegations. Ordinary citizens were also monitored, and they risked being ostracized (and were even in some cases interrogated and imprisoned) if they displayed communist leanings.

3 Contemporary social psychology and the focus on everyday life

Core questions to consider while reading this chapter

- How would you conceptualize social psychology?
- Why did Gordon Allport emphasize interdisciplinarity in social psychology?
- How would you conceptualize everyday life?
- What is meant by the dialogical self?
- Are objects and places part of us?
- Is illness a disruption to everyday life?

Chapter scenario

Mary from the chapter scenario in the previous chapter has done well at university. Five years ago she graduated with a PhD in social psychology, and now she has a tenured position at a university. Mary is a keen observer of everyday life and tries to combine her interests and research where possible. This includes trying to understand intimate relationships and perhaps why she broke up with Trevor after eight years together. The relationship with Trevor ended during Mary's PhD, in part due to the travel involved in his consultancy job and her need to focus on the PhD and supporting her family.

Tonight Mary is going out with Carla and Alice to a speed dating session at the local pub. Carla and Alice have become regulars at such events and fill her in on the process. Alice states, "It'll be fun. You get to meet a whole bunch of guys, and if you don't hit it off it doesn't matter 'cos they don't get your details." Mary has read up on such events and states, "Did you know there's research on speed dating. It's attracting quite a bit of attention in the social relations literature – should be pretty interesting." Carla replies, "As long as you don't lose sight of the real job, and that's finding someone." Alice chimes in, "Still, any tips would be great if I can increase my chances." All three laugh as they enter the bar.

Upon arrival, the girls are given assessment forms and an identification number. The facilitator informs them that they will remain seated while the men rotate during the round robin session. The women take their seats and the event begins. In all, they each meet ten men whom they rate in terms of wanting to date or not wanting to date them. Likewise, each man rates each woman, and if there is a match with both strangers seeking a date then their contact details will be passed on. After two of the four minutes they have little left to say, and Mary cannot help but look around the room at the nine other couples. She spots Albert; he looks over and Mary blushes.

Of all the men Mary met tonight, two are memorable. Mary explains to Carla that "Joseph looked really uncomfortable and just didn't make eye contact with me. When the bell went, things went from bad to worse; we just had nothing to say to each other. He was good looking enough, but he just seems shifty to me. His shirt needs an iron, and how about washing those pants, man." Carla laughs. Mary continues, "Now, Albert was a different story, good looking, well dressed, and he seemed like a real gentleman, with my kind of positive attitude. We had a lot to talk about and we've got lots in common. The time just flew by, so I'm banking on him wanting to see me again." Alice walks over and Carla asks how things went. Carla replies, "No plans here, I'm afraid. I've just got to stop getting so stressed when I talk to a guy. I think I'm putting them off."

Events such as speed dating are woven into the fabric of the everyday lives of many people. They provide a focal point for going out with friends and efforts to forge new relationships. Such events can be exhilarating, rewarding, daunting and depressing, depending on the actual interactions and outcomes. The opening scenario raises a number of topics pertinent to everyday life that are of central interest to social psychologists. These include interpersonal interactions, attraction, relationships, attitudes, the functions of similarity and difference, and people's use of common places such as pubs and material objects. In engaging with such events, social psychologists need to consider the nature of social interactions and the perceptions of others.

Of core concern here is what social psychology has to offer in developing an understanding of everyday life and the challenges of living in increasingly diverse societies. Much of everyday life is about going out for the evening with friends, perhaps to the pub, meeting other people, forming relationships, considering the actions of other people who might be similar to or different from you. It is about being in the social world and partaking in social relationships as these occur in particular social spaces (Highmore, 2000a, 2000b). Social psychology has a lot to say about these topics, and we will consider some of its insights in this chapter.

Chapter overview

The first section provides the general orientation to social psychology taken up in this book, which emphasizes the importance of focusing on everyday life and the relationship between social psychology and everyday knowledge. This focus is extended throughout the chapter; we explore what we mean by everyday life, the nature of human attraction and intimate relations, the socialization of human beings and reproduction of the social systems that shape our lives together, and the importance of places and things to social existence. The chapter ends with a brief summary in which we re-emphasize links between core ideas expressed in the chapter. In summary, this chapter:

- Conceptualizes social psychology today
- Conceptualizes everyday life as a core disciplinary consideration
- Outlines the fundamentally social nature of what it means to be human

Conceptualizing social psychology today

Social psychology is regularly applied to a range of contexts, from social interactions to marketing, health care, the development of government policies, supporting communities, addressing poverty, to broader issues of war, peace and reconciliation (Apfelbaum, 2000; Zimbardo, 2004). Today, social psychologists focus on both the problems that can haunt human lives and the positive relationships and other resources that enable people to avoid, cope with and overcome such problems.

When one considers the range of settings in which people interact and within which social psychologists seek to theorize, study, make sense of and assist human beings, establishing a set definition for social psychology becomes challenging. It is common for authors of textbooks to refer to the study of individual behaviour, mental life and interactions between people. Social psychology is often defined as *the scientific study of the individual in society*. In this vein, Allport (1985) proposed that social psychology attempts to explain the ways in which the thoughts, feelings and behaviour

of individuals are influenced by the actual, imagined, or implied presence of other human beings. The term "implied presence" refers to the many activities the individual carries out because of his [sic] position (role) in a complex social structure and his membership in a cultural group. (p. 5)

This focus on interactions between people and groups has led to investigations of group dynamics, crowd formations, interpersonal relations, pro-social behaviour, stereotypes, power and influence, conformity and prejudice across a range of settings. It allows us to consider social psychological processes that occur face to face in a shopping mall or on the street alongside interactions occurring via the Internet and mobile phones, as devices that allow people to interact at a distance (see Chapter 11). This definition has been associated with the individualistic stream of social psychology modelled on the physical sciences. It needs to be tempered with the emphasis Gordon Allport (Box 3.1) also placed on social interactions, communication,

---

BOX 3.1   Gordon Allport

Gordon Allport (1897–1967) was born in Indiana into a family with a strong Protestant work ethic. Allport emphasized the value of social service throughout his life, involving himself in volunteer work and research of social significance. He served in the First World War and subsequently graduated from Harvard College with a PhD in psychology in 1922. He then studied in both Germany and England before returning to Harvard and Dartmouth College. During his career, Allport published more than 200 articles and twelve books on such broad topics as personality, rumour, religion and prejudice (Bowman, 1995).

Allport emphasized the need for diversity in focuses and approaches in social psychology (Lubek & Apfelbaum, 2000). He proposed that our theories, research and actions need to be tailored to the specific subject matter and the sociocultural contexts of our work. Psychologists need to relate lives to the socio-economic and cultural contexts in which they are situated.

Allport was not locked into one definition of the discipline. He recognized the need for social psychology to evolve in response to the needs of people and society. He was acutely aware that social psychology needs to overlap with other social science disciplines because interesting social psychological work is occurring outside of our discipline. We need to draw on insights produced in history, economics, sociology and anthropology, theology, communication science, geography, literary studies, linguistics, anthropology and so on (cf. Tajfel, 1981). Social psychology "thrives best when cross-cultivated in a rich and diversified intellectual garden" (Allport, 1968, p. 19). We will draw on social psychological material from across the social sciences throughout this book.

habits and routines, occurring as pre-scripted aspects of communal life, which can vary across cultures.

This book extends the customary textbook focus on individuals in local group contexts. For us, social psychology is also about the lives of human beings, our inner experiences and outer interactions with others and how these are woven together across various contexts of everyday life. We seek to understand and improve people's lives. Social psychology involves the study of people's lives together, how we interact and change. This orientation retains a focus on people as they take form and live within material, social, cultural and historical contexts. It draws from a European perspective that seeks to "understand the essential phenomena of social and political-life" (Moscovici, 1970, p. 10) and is informed by indigenous (Chapter 5) and humanistic (Chapter 10) psychologies.

To grapple with the broad spectrum of phenomena invoked by this orientation it is useful to include insights from both experimental and fieldwork orientations within the discipline and beyond. In 1968, George Allport pointed out that skills in conducting experiments and statistical analyses are useful for social psychologists. He also noted that we need to maintain a historical perspective and the willingness and ability to get out there and engage with individuals, groups, communities, institutions and the dilemmas of our age. Political, cultural and historical contexts are central to social life and, thus, to the agenda of social psychology (Chapter 2). Allport proposed that we should also avoid being sidetracked by the particularities of our research designs, be these experimental or discursive in nature, to the point of losing sight of the substance of our interests in terms of the potential for enhancing people's lives. The transformative potential of research is important because social psychology is not simply about observing and theorizing social life. It is also about improving the human condition (Chapter 1).

In considering what psychology is and does, it is important to note that the everyday knowledge of human beings (Chapter 4) or their experiences and understandings is not simply a topic for research (Box 3.2). Everyday knowledge is central to the beginning and end of social psychological research and action (Flick, 2000a). Think back to the Kitty Genovese case outlined in Chapter 2. Reading newspaper reports and discussing the case over dinner contributed to the understandings of two social psychologists and led to the development of a series of experimental studies that shaped a field of research. In this way, our research often derives from direct observations or from our exposure to popular reports. We might then conduct research in an attempt to extend our understandings of the world in which we

BOX 3.2   The relationship between everyday knowledge and social psychological insight

In turning our attention to what happens in the social world, it is useful to reiterate that our interests as social psychologists often overlap with the interests of the people with whom we engage. Because people think about and make sense of situations, relationships and the actions of others we might say that there are as many amateur social psychologists in the world as there are people. In developing his work on interpersonal relations, Heider (1958) noted that people constantly make inferences about others as they seek to make sense of events going on around them and their own actions and the actions of other people. People learn about social psychological processes as they experience life and reflect on events and situations. People speculate about the causes and consequences of poverty and tensions between groups in society, and they voice opinions, even arguing against the opinions of others, as they work through their ideas (Billig, 1993). People have opinions about their neighbours, immigration, graffiti or police efforts to stop graffiti. Social psychologists often interpret the opinions that people actively create for themselves in order to make sense of events occurring around them. We often research the processes by which people reach their understandings, and the resulting practices through which these understandings manifest in daily living (Jovchelovitch, 2007). For example, Jodelet (1991) studied the integration of people living with mental health issues into village homes in a French rural community. Jodelet showed that villagers' understandings of mental illness had been co-opted by their understandings of physical illness and contagion. Their shared understandings were reflected in the social practices through which they (dis)engaged with the mental health clients in their midst. The villagers thought that mental illness was spread much like a cold, and so they washed the clothes and bedding of patients separately from those of their families. In studying these processes, Jodelet contributed to the development of social representations theory (see Chapter 4), which provides an explanation for the social negotiation of common knowledge within communities.

reside. In the process, like Muzafer Sherif and Kurt Lewin, we draw on insights obtained from our training as psychologists and our personal experiences when theorizing social phenomena and interpreting the information generated by research. In the opening scenario, Mary experiences speed dating as a participant and is now contemplating how she might research such events. To this end, Mary consults a methodological primer on speed dating research (Finkel, Eastwick & Matthews, 2007). This reflects a key difference between amateur and professional social psychologists. Professionals, such as Mary, have access to a broader and more systematic field of knowledge and have learned to gather insights systematically when theorizing and testing assumptions.

The relationship between social psychology and everyday life is further complicated by the fact that social psychology theories, concepts and research findings are often introduced back into everyday life. Insights from our work are drawn upon and adapted by people as they make sense of their own lives. People regularly talk about themselves and in doing so use psychological concepts such as stress, anxiety, coping, support and attitudes. In our opening scenario Alice talks about being 'stressed' by the speed dating experience and how it makes her 'anxious'. It has long been noted in social psychology that the adoption of insights from social psychology into common knowledge is not necessarily a problem. In fact, this is to be encouraged; one former APA president, George Miller, during a presidential address, advocated giving psychological knowledge away to the public (Box 3.3).

The advice psychologists provide the public with does not relate solely to addressing existing social problems. Advice is also offered with a more positive orientation on how to enhance one's health, live a fulfilled life and prevent problems from occurring. This raises a crucial point in terms of the picture of social psychology we have been painting in this book. From the history we charted in Chapter 2, it may seem as if social psychology is often a problem- or deficit-focused discipline. This interpretation is appropriate in the sense that we are not just an academic discipline; we are also engaged in a profession that trains people to assist in addressing the needs of various groups of people. Yet, in addressing problems, we often forget also to build upon the strengths of people. There is a growing

BOX 3.3   Giving psychology away

Many psychologists engage in giving psychology away via media appearances in which they share research findings and via websites such as http://psychology.about.com/od/psychology101/tp/applying-psychology. htm. This site offers advice on how readers can use psychology to improve their lives. It provides a free newsletter and other resources and advice on getting motivated to lose weight or stop smoking, develop leadership and communication skills, extend your understanding of others, become more productive and become healthier. The APA also provides a useful website with resources outlining contributions to daily life in nineteen broad content areas ranging from adolescence to sexuality, health, memory, justice, sport, violence and the workplace: http://www.psychologymatters.org. The site showcases research and applications. Zimbardo (2004) also provides an overview of what psychology has contributed to North American society, which emphasizes the importance of giving our knowledge away to the public.

Chapter 4 draws upon the concept of interpretive communities as part of a discussion of the relationship between common knowledge and social psychology. Often, the language of one interpretive community (social psychology) is difficult for another interpretative community to comprehend. One key goal of the APA site and this book is to present social psychology in a language that everyone can make sense of and use. You might want to explore the resources noted above in the context of giving psychology away.

emphasis in psychology in general to be both problem and strengths focused, addressing negative problems and positive strengths (Linley, Joseph, Harrington & Wood, 2006; Schneider, Bugental & Pierson, 2001). Exploring how people can be hopeful, honest, supportive and creative is as important as looking at why at other points in their lives these same people might be pessimistic, dishonest and unsupportive and lack creativity (see Chapter 10). This dual focus in the discipline can contribute to a more holistic understanding of people and the situations in which we find ourselves. As has happened throughout our disciplinary history, by incorporating aspects of humanistic or positive psychologies (as referred to in Chapter 10), social psychologists can learn to work with communities to identify their collective strengths and to overcome the social problems they may be facing (Box 3.4).

To recap, in many respects this book constitutes a case of back to the future. We advocate for a social psychology concerned with social issues, conducted from a range of perspectives, that is committed to action and making the world a better place for everyone. This involves a focus on everyday life, which has been evident in our discipline throughout its development. Everyday life is often complex, contradictory and unpredictable. Social psychologists can tidy up aspects of everyday life into experiments that produce useful insights. Yet social psychology is also about engaging with people within the contexts of their lives and not trying to remove the complexity and contradictory aspects of social life from the research process. The remainder of this chapter explores the interwoven nature of everyday life; interpersonal relations as central elements of everyday life; the socialization of human beings and the

---

BOX 3.4   Retaining a positive focus

It is important to note that a positive focus is a mainstay of social psychology. William James (1902) explored 'healthy mindedness', Carl Rogers (1951) and Abraham Maslow (1968) considered human growth and potential, and Csikszentmihalyi (1997) documented human creativity. Such work comes with the realization that the positive dimensions of social life provide as legitimate a focus for social psychological research as the negative dimensions. This realization is particularly important in the context of this book, as many positive things happen to people during their interactions with others. Mary might meet someone at the pub and fall in love. Psychology needs to contribute to a discussion of such events. As Linley and colleagues (2006) note, "As such, positive psychology shifts the implicit value basis of psychological inquiry from only a deficit-focus to also an asset-focus, and thereby reveals what is often new and fertile ground for investigation" (p. 7). This orientation is woven throughout this book.

construction of self; and the importance of links between people, objects and environments.

Review exercise

Take a moment to note some of the things you do each day.

- Do you listen to the radio as you wake up or when driving somewhere?
- If you catch a bus or train to work or school, whom do you interact with along the way?
- When and where do you spend time with friends?
- Are there places where you feel as if you belong more than other places?
- Who has shaped your growth as a person?

Making these notes will help you relate to the material in the following sections.

Conceptualizing everyday life

We suggest that the way Allport (1985) emphasized human interaction, including that occurring at the pub during a speed dating session, is a core part of psychology. The need to explore human interactions relates directly to the emphasis we place on everyday life in this book. After all, everyday life is where we live our lives and engage with others as a matter of course, often without giving much thought to it. We say hello to the bus driver or smile at the clerk when purchasing a magazine. Burkitt (2004) notes, "Everyday life must relate to *all* daily activities because it is here that our social relations are produced and reproduced" (p. 212). Everyday life is made up of lives that overlap and can be similar as well as different. Social psychology focuses on individuals and groups in society, what we have in common and what makes us different and unique. This is particularly important in our increasingly diverse societies, where many of us come into regular contact with people from different cultures.

Everyday life is a slippery concept to grapple with because what we do each day can, paradoxically, be fluid and unpredictable as well as constant and routine. Our lives and relationships can remain constant in some respects and also change as we grow. We would like to avoid a mechanistic approach that reduces everyday life to discrete and repetitive aspects such as talking, shopping, eating, working, playing sport, hanging out with friends or walking. Instead of treating these events as some kind of social artefacts, we see these actions as part of a human life and as phenomena that we 'live through' (Sheringham, 2006). This allows us to avoid presenting everyday life

---

BOX 3.5   Disruption and change in daily life

To this point, we have focused on the constant and familiar aspects of everyday life. It is important to note that much of social psychology is focused on events and situations that disrupt everyday life (see Chapter 8). From time to time events come along that challenge us and our routines, and encourage us to reassess our lives. We can get sick, fired or mugged. A loved one whom we rely on might pass away, requiring us to seek support elsewhere. Such disruptive instances are not separate from or external to everyday life. Rather, they can be approached as key points of renewal and opportunities for growth and change (Faircloth, Boylstein, Rittman, Young & Gubrium, 2004). As noted in Chapter 7, moving countries with one's family often necessitates changes in everyday life and requires adaptation. After a while most people gain a sense of their lives returning to 'normal'. (Well, at least a different normal.) Worth noting here is how events that invoke the recrafting of one's life are not always negative. One day you might actually graduate or win the lottery.

---

as a stable and blandly immutable object of study made up of lots of disconnected routine practices. Rather, we use the term 'everyday life' as a general catchphrase for the ordinary, what we do each day, the typical, the mundane and shared fabric of social existence. In focusing on everyday life this book considers what happens typically when a person gets up, goes to school, eats, meets and greets others, works and plays. However, we would not want to assume the universal nature of the mundane status of such practices for many people in Western societies. For most people in so-called developed countries watching television, spending time with friends, shopping, eating, walking, talking or working seems unremarkable. For others, finding enough to eat is a daily struggle. Many people are faced with constant disruption and change (Box 3.5).

While in many respects everyday lives in Western societies are similar, it is important to note diversity within and between groups and communities. These differences become apparent when we think about issues of colonization (Chapter 5), immigration (Chapter 7) and social class (Chapter 8). For instance, Mary is increasingly spending time with other women in her profession. These women are the same age as she is. However, most colleagues have more free time than Mary. They are not responsible for siblings and do not have to contribute to the budget of an extended family. Likewise, the lives of Mary and Carla and Alice overlap in that they are all young women living in the same apartment block and working as professionals. Their lives also differ due to family income and circumstances.

Differences between people raise the crucial point that everyday life is not always equitable. Everyday life can bring us into contact with deeper and more troubling aspects of the world such as racism and discrimination. In this regard we need to keep in mind that

[e]veryday life is constrained by the interests and the power of others, by resistant structures, both physical and social. Everyday life is where individuals can be free, creative, but also where they can be exploited, excluded and repressed. (Silverstone, 2007, pp. 108–109)

Some people may experience prejudice and inequities, whereas others may experience inclusion and acceptance (see Chapters 5–7). As a result, we need to conceptualize everyday life in a manner that emphasizes multiple lifeworlds and differences, even for colleagues engaged in the shared activities of practising psychology and speed dating. Such issues of difference are threaded throughout this book.

The focus in social psychology on everyday life can tell us a great deal about the origins and consequences of social inequalities and how social problems can be understood and addressed from different perspectives. In considering these issues, we also need to focus on resources, opportunities and strengths if we are to avoid stigmatizing particular groups in society. Being economically less well off does not mean that the quality of one's daily life is somehow inferior to the quality of daily life of more affluent folk. It is different and in many cases highly rewarding.

Interactions, attractions and relationships

The opening scenario raises issues regarding how people meet, get to know one another and forge relationships with others in everyday life. Speed dating is increasingly evident in cities around the developed world and has become a popular way for many people to initiate intimate relationships (Finkel, Eastwick & Matthews, 2007; Houser, Horan & Furler, 2008). A speed dating night in a pub is a particular venue for meeting other people and one that probably carries a range of expectations for many participants. A negative evaluation might be that this is simply a dance of the desperates. This is perhaps an unfair assertion, as such events reflect changing cultural practices and broader societal shifts. Speed dating is simply a more recent adoption of the cultural practice of organizing social events so that single people might meet, get to know each other and fall in love. Speed dating might be considered a good strategy by those who seek options beyond dating the boy or girl next door or the person standing by the office water cooler.

The speed dating example raises questions regarding the factors that influence whether people participating in such events will like each other and want to get to know each other a little more. This section explores what social psychology can tell us about human relations, attraction and perceptions of others in such settings. These topics are all relevant to making sense of the speed dating example, as are personal attitudes and issues of similarity, where individuals are more likely to be attracted to people who share their attitudes (Box 3.6).

Attraction between two people that leads to a romantic relationship or friendship is referred to as interpersonal attraction. This is a core area of social psychological research, and it involves the study of the ways people come to love, like or even dislike each other. If two people meeting for the first time find each other physically and socially attractive, see similarities in each other and display their attraction to each other, they are more likely to seek further interaction (Eastwick, Finkel, Mochon & Ariely, 2007). A range of factors have been taken into account in research in this area. These include physical attractiveness, proximity, complementarity, familiarity, similarity and exchange (Miller, Perlman & Brehm, 2007). Some of these factors are rather straightforward. For example, proximity relates to the notion that the more we come into contact with another person, the more likelihood there is that he or she may become a partner or friend. Perceived similarity refers to the idea that the more we think we are similar to another person, the more likely we are to forge a relationship with them. Morry (2007) has explored this through the 'attraction-similarity model'. This research suggests that people are attracted to others similar to them in terms of attitudes, background, interests and social skills (Box 3.7).

During speed dating physical attraction is likely to be one of the initial factors that come into play in assessing the viability of a potential partner for a relationship (Houser, Horan & Furler, 2008). Physical attractiveness seems relatively straightforward, in that people are often more likely to seek further interaction with people

---

BOX 3.6   Research into romantic action

Research into romantic relationships gained prominence in experimental social psychology in the 1960s and provided insights into the importance of factors such as similarity and physical attractiveness (discussed below). Initially, studies tended to take place in laboratory settings and to use photographs and other visual stimuli. People tended not actually to meet the targets of their attraction. In the 1980s, researchers focused more on actual and ongoing relationships. Research has also extended to the Internet, and it appears that key insights identified in previous offline research remain valid, such as the importance of similarity and proximity (Kurzban & Weeden, 2007). Recognition of the usefulness of speed dating as a setting for extending research into human attraction led psychologists to develop a methodological primer (Finkel, Eastwick & Matthews, 2007). Research also shows that speed daters make decisions regarding whether they are attracted to a person within thirty seconds (Houser, Horan & Furler, 2007).

BOX 3.7   Interesting study

In a study of the success of nineteen speed dating couples, Wilson, Cousins and Fink (2006) used the compatibility quotient (CQ) to predict the willingness to pursue relationships among nineteen heterosexual couples taking part in speed dating. The CQ is a psychometric instrument (see Chapter 5) used to assess similarities of potential and established couples across a domain of factors known to predict relationship success, including the emphasis individuals place on religion, sex drive, TV viewing and so forth. These authors found that the CQ could predict desire to take things further. This was particularly the case with female participants, who seemed more able to detect similarity than males after the relatively short exposure times offered by speed dating encounters.

---

they find physically attractive. In fact, people perceived to be physically attractive tend also to be rated as being more socially competent (Langlois et al., 2000). Such attraction is also often linked to the inferences people make about a person's character and abilities. Physically attractive people are often credited with positive attributes such as happiness, kindness, intelligence, success and sexual prowess (Zuckerman, Miyake & Elkin, 1995). Clearly, physical attraction is not always enough. Mary is not keen on Joseph because of his lack of eye contact, his display of other nonverbal cues signalling nervousness and his presumed lack of personal grooming. Despite Joseph being reasonably physically attractive, his unkempt look and dirty trousers put Mary off (cf. Houser, Horan & Furler, 2007).

In many respects, proximity is fundamental to interpersonal attraction. People are more likely to form intimate relations if they live or work in close proximity to one another and thus come into contact on a regular basis. People in close proximity are more likely to be familiar to us and to be associated with trust and a sense of safety (Bornstein, 1989). Speed dating in some respects addresses the issue of limited proximity in that it brings people together for the first time and provides an opportunity for some familiarity to be initiated and for similarities to be discovered.

People are often drawn to others whom they perceive to possess similar qualities to their own. Relationships with people similar to ourselves have been found to be more satisfying (Arrindell & Luteijn, 2000). Similarity, also referred to as homophily, in attitudes (Box 3.8) has been explored using the 'law of attraction' (Byrne, 1971). This law proposes that the more consistent attitudes are between people, the greater the likelihood of attraction. How might attitudes relate to attraction? In walking back from the pub, Mary talks to Carla and Alice about Joseph and why she was not attracted to him. "He's good looking enough, but I just don't like his attitude; how could someone believe that sort of rubbish." Mary feels dissimilar to Joseph because she perceives him to have divergent attitudes to her own on key issues such as politics and the role of women in society. Jamieson, Lydon and Zanna (1987) demonstrate that individual evaluations of respect for one another, first impressions and activity preferences are partially predicted by attitude similarities. Similarities in educational level and age have also been shown to predict partner selection (Watson et al., 2004). The issue of proximity is evident here also in that people of similar age and educational level are more likely to come into contact with one another. This shows how factors such as similarity and proximity interact and influence attraction.

Factors such as physical attractiveness, proximity and similarity may increase the chances of two people being attracted to one another and an intimate relationship forming. However, everyday life is complex and contradictory, and there are no guarantees. Readers will likely know of couples who seem to be opposites and who maintain relationships over years. There are also intangible elements of social psychological phenomena such as attraction that we cannot fully account for. This is why approaches to social psychology such as Gestalt and humanism (see Chapter 10) have picked up on philosophical opposition to 'atomization'[1] to argue that the whole is always more than the sum of the parts or individual factors (Schneider, Bugental & Pierson, 2001). It is important not to lose sight of the big picture when exploring human relationships.

Out of events such as speed dating, intimate relationships may evolve that involve more than just liking someone and initial attraction. Such intimate relationships are often characterized by physical and emotional intensity, self-disclosure, a deeper level of

---

BOX 3.8   Studying attitudes

Much attention has been paid to the study of attitudes (see Chapter 4). This research is particularly pertinent to everyday life because it relates to prejudice, intergroup relations and conformity. Attitudes are often defined as the evaluations that a person makes regarding particular objects, people or places that are expressed in positive or negative terms as likes and dislikes (Perloff, 2008). Attitudes are considered to be relatively consistent clusters of feelings, beliefs and predispositions (cf. Billig, 1993). Classic examples would be endorsing a specific political party or being positively disposed towards addressing environmental issues. Social psychologists are interested in the formation, structure and function of attitudes and in changes in attitudes. Today, experimental methods are used to explore the difference between self-reported attitudes and unconscious attitudes. For example, a study using the Implicit Association Test revealed that people can hold biases against particular races of people despite self-reported claims of not being racist (Heider & Skowronski, 2007).

familiarity and commitment. Because of their centrality to human life, intimate relationships have concerned philosophers for millennia (Miller, Perlman & Brehm, 2007). These relationships often address human needs for attachment and support, and reflect the social nature of human beings in that people often spend considerable parts of their lives with a special person (or people). Intimate relationships often involve long-term connections between people and a range of emotions spanning love and hate, like and dislike, that occur across the everyday domains of work, home and leisure. These social interactions comprise a particularly well-developed set of interpersonal relationships, which are characterized by some form of interdependence. Contemporary research investigates intimate relationships in the context of friendship, family and romance and deals with both the positive benefits and the negative and destructive aspects of human relations (Miller, Perlman & Brehm, 2007; Vangelisti & Perlman, 2006). What is clear is that people tend to influence one another through their relationships. James (1892/1984) proposed that human self-concepts are constructed in relation to the enduring others in our lives (Box 3.9). As we will see throughout this book, psychologists are increasingly noting that who we are as human being is fundamentally intertwined with who is a part of our everyday lives. People shape and complete each other (Cooley, 1902; Hermans, 2001). People often define themselves in daily settings through their relationships and how they see others perceiving them (Cooley, 1902).

People are generally motivated to establish supportive interpersonal relations. The absence of such relationships is associated with depression and other negative psychological experiences (Baumeister & Leary, 1995). We often learn to develop these relationships from early childhood, and associated socialization experiences shape how we engage

BOX 3.9   Factors associated with partner selection

In the social psychological literature on romantic relationships, including studies of speed dating, there is a tendency to emphasize positive human attributes such as physical attractiveness, success in life and intelligence as important factors in determining partner selection. These are important factors. It is also important that we do not neglect the importance for *all* citizens to find someone special. Jones (2009) outlines the design of a dating service as part of the ongoing support offered to people living with learning disabilities. Conventional dating agencies are ill equipped to deal with the needs of this population group, and so psychologists have been involved in establishing an alternative service. Mates n Dates organizes monthly social events around the United Kingdom, including speed dating, quiz nights and dances. For further information go to http://www.matesndates.org.uk/.

with others throughout or lives. We will consider relevant theoretical work relating to the nature of human relationships throughout this book in the context of social exchange, equity and social justice. For now, it is worth noting that social exchange theory conceptualizes relationships in terms of personal benefits, rewards or what each individual can gain (Blau, 1964; Crosby & Gonzalez-Intal, 1984; Homans, 1961; Thibaut & Kelley, 1959). Equity theory developed out of a criticism of exchange theory. As a criticism of exchange theory, equity theory claims that many people care about more than just what they can get for themselves out of a relationship, or simply maximizing their personal rewards (Hatfield, Walster & Berscheid, 1976; Walster, Berscheid & Walster, 1973, 1976). Human beings also seek equity, trust and fairness. Equity and exchange theories are not necessarily mutually exclusive; after all, it is only fair that partners take turns in buying the drinks at the pub.

Self and everyday life

Early social psychologists understood that who we are is socially located and worked through as an ongoing project within everyday life (Musolf, 2003). For example, James (1884) understood that who people are depends upon their social location. It is through daily life that we take form as human beings and often play many and varied roles (Burkitt, 2004). Who a person becomes is shaped through interactions with others and is refined and modified in routine practices and rituals. Csikszentmihalyi (1997) notes that "The Greek word 'idiot' originally meant someone who lived by himself; it was assumed that cut off from community interaction such a person would be mentally incompetent" (pp. 80–81). A focus on everyday life and social interactions is crucial for a social psychology that studies more than "idiots" and seeks to grapple with the actions of people and their ways of being as these unfold within and across various social contexts. As Csikszentmihalyi (1997) writes:

Everyday life is defined not only by what we do, but also by who we are with. Our actions and feelings are always influenced by other people, whether they are present or not. Ever since Aristotle it has been known that humans were social animals; both physically and psychologically we depend on the company of others. (p. 13)

In many cultures, who a person is considered to be is determined by whose son or granddaughter he or she. In Confucian philosophy, for example, this concept is referred to as filial piety (Box 3.10) (Yang, 2006). We will say more about the relevance of Chinese notions of the self in Chapter 5.

It is through interactions with others and daily processes of socialization that people develop into human beings (Hermans & Hermans-Konopka, 2009). In community settings, human beings learn about

BOX 3.10   Filial piety

The concept of filial piety in Chinese Confucian philosophy proposes that a child's life is an extension of the parents' rather than a totally autonomous existence as is the case in Western societies (Young et al., 2003). As a result, the child has increased obligations towards the parents. This concept partially reflects how some groups see themselves more in terms of 'we' or 'our', whereas others prefer 'me' or 'I'. We do not wish to imply that these collectivist and individualistic modes of self are always mutually exclusive and relative to different cultures. For all groups, certain contexts require a sense of 'we-ness', and others encourage a 'me-ness'. In this way, as we will discuss throughout this book, our very sense of self can vary with the social context we inhabit. Some theorists have gone so far as to propose that people rely on others to complete the picture they paint of themselves (Goffman, 1982).

life and their place in the world (Christopher & Campbell, 2008). "It would be very difficult, if not impossible, to become a person without community" (Jovchelovitch, 2007, p. 71). The idea that humanity is developed through social interactions is supported by studies of feral children who have been cut off from society (Box 3.11). These children do not develop a 'human nature' that we might recognize. Many cannot obtain language and remain extremely uncomfortable in the presence of other people, even after years of intense training (Candland, 1993).

Through processes of growing up in particular groups people take on shared understandings and habits of engagement with the world (Jovchelovitch, 2007). Acting in concert, individuals learn what it means to be human and how to interact with others. People can cultivate a sense of self out of collectively constructed stories that connect the past, present and future of their primary reference groups (Chapter 2), and this can provide a sense of belonging and structure. As noted by early social psychologists, individuals and social contexts are intermeshed. Shared understandings and practices (see

BOX 3.11   Feral children

Work on feral children was popularized by the case of 'Victor', or 'the wolf boy of Aveyron'. Victor was found at age eleven in 1799. Jean-Marc-Gaspard Itard, who had a background as a medical doctor and had experience working with deaf children, took on the task of socializing Victor. After several years of work (1801–1805), Victor showed signs of basic skills for social interaction and improved cognition. Yet he remained unable to speak. Such cases are rare. They raise fundamental questions about the nature of humanity and how people learn and grow as members of communities. These cases also provide insights into how people acquire language and how poor learning environments can be compensated for. If you are interested in such cases conduct a web search using the term 'feral children'.

Chapters 4 and 5) provide a structural basis for social life, but individuals can revise these and at times give up an invitation to fit in with 'how things are done around here'. What we share is plural and heterogeneous; it grows and evolves over time and with changing circumstances (Christopher & Campbell, 2008). Socialization and the development of self is a dialogical process (Box 3.12).

Research into socialization emphasizes the primary role of parents in the development of children and the formation of their social identities (Wetherell, 2006). Everyday parental influence and the reproduction of cultural practices and histories in the home remain central to contemporary investigations (Muldoon, McLaughlin & Trew, 2007). Renewed emphasis is also placed on socialization involving multiple influences and sources, including institutions such as the broader family, peers, community, schools and media. Research shows that a range of aspects of human life, from one's identity (Trew, 2004), emotional development and social skills acquisition (Denham, Bassett & Wyatt, 2007) to political views and associated activities (Bloemraad & Trost, 2008), are cultivated through social interactions in the family and with institutions such as schools, communities and various media forms (Chapter 11).

In terms of the family, socialization is not necessarily only a process of the transmission of social norms and practices from parents

---

BOX 3.12   Dialogue and the construction of self

The concept of dialogue can be contrasted with that of monologue. Whereas a monologue implies one-way communication, a dialogue suggests two-way communication. Social life and socialization can be said to be dialogical in nature in that it involves ongoing interactions between characters and situations. This dialogical process is thought to shape who a person becomes, in that what the person might say or do is set in dialogue with or in response to something already done or said, or in anticipation of an act or response from another person (Hermans & Hermans-Konopka, 2009). From this perspective, human life is said to be fundamentally relational. Daily life comprises, at least in part, the weaving together of various utterances and actions formed through an ongoing dialogical process. Drawing on the work of William James and Mikhail Bakhtin, Hermans and Hermans-Konopka (2009) combine the concepts of self and dialogue in an effort to foreground the interwoven nature of self and society. The dialogical self thus extends our understanding of how the self leaks out into the external world and how the world seeps into our inner selves through a constant process of interaction central to social life. In this way people's environments are not simply external contexts. Rather, the social world is part of who they are and will become. We discuss these ideas again in Chapters 4–7 in relation to indigenous notions of the interconnected self, place-based identities and notions of culture shock. Such thinking has implications for social psychological research. It is difficult to study social life outside the context in which it is situated and not lose sight of important daily interactions (Chapter 2). Research also engages participants in another set of interactions. In this way, research can be seen as an inherently social process. We will explore some of these ideas in Chapter 4.

to children. For instance, recent research indicates that the children of immigrant families can draw on information resources from school and the Internet and communicate with parents and in the process influence the political views and actions of their parents (Bloemraad & Trost, 2008). This is central to processes of resocialization (see Chapter 2). Research indicates how socialization can be bidirectional and dialogical in nature, in that children also train and transmit information and attitudes to their parents (Wong & Tseng, 2008). It appears that as our relationships evolve within families over time, so too can the direction of socialization. Increasing understanding of the complexities of socialization in contemporary society is leading social psychologists to adopt notions of reciprocal socialization, which spans family settings and broader institutional environments, including those provided by media technologies (Box 3.13). In terms of socialization via media, Hoffman and Thomson (2009) documented how viewing late night satirical television shows such as *The Daily Show* had a positive influence on civic participation and political engagement among young people (see Chapter 11).

The present focus on everyday life, socialization and the development of the self extends to the observation of early social psychologists that individuals and social conditions are 'twin born' (cf. Cooley, 1902). It is through simple acts such as getting to work (whether driving, walking, cycling, getting on the bus or using a train) and the interactions with others that occur along the way that

---

BOX 3.13   Gender socialization

A particularly prominent area of research is the socialization of gender. This work has extended to online environments in which girls and boys can swap genders. In a recent article, Hussain and Griffiths (2008) explored gender swapping in multiplayer online game environments. In these game spaces, players can create and explore their own characters in interactions with others. Players choose the gender, ethnicity, moral persuasion and profession of their characters. Online survey results from 119 participants (eighty-three males, thirty-two females and four unspecified) were analysed. Just over half, or 57 per cent, of gamers indicated that they had swapped the gender of their character. Participants indicated a number of reasons for swapping gender, including to:

- Experiment with aspects of character that were difficult to explore in 'real life'
- Change the ways other characters interacted with them
- Avoid unsolicited approaches from male characters
- Simply see how it felt to interact as another gender

Such research illustrates how people can use media technologies to expand their socialization experiences and opens up new possibilities for research into gender and socialization.

social life and societal structures are reproduced. Participation in social life influences who people become and their subsequent ways of behaving and interacting with others. Individuals learn and adapt and in the process have the capacity to influence the social settings that shape their lives. This is because the actions of human beings are woven into and emerge from social interactions, and these interactions occur within the context of shared narratives and practices and in turn reproduce these narratives and practices (Musolf, 2003). There is a sense of openness and creativity in the conduct of everyday life. Everyday life involves ways of doing and being that often include shared practices. It is not simply a site for reproducing macro-social structures, but for working within these, often agentively (actively and purposefully).

Everyday life occurs somewhere and involves the use of things

From reading social psychology textbooks one can get the impression that people do not live anywhere real, or in a physical world. Human experience is often presented as if it is occurring in a shapeless vacuum lacking physical form. Everyday life does not simply occur in the minds of individuals. People inhabit their lives physically, socially, culturally and psychologically (Hodgetts et al., 2009). This raises issues about where people live, or the physical spaces they inhabit, and the material objects they use during the daily conduct of their lives (Chapter 6). For instance, being physically present in, and walking through, the city, the women in the opening scenario can witness everyday life in all its banal and mundane forms: cooking, eating, drinking, conversing, looking, working, arguing and laughing. Cities are noisy landscapes where these women might also hear the clinking of bottles, the chatter of people, the roar of cars and the clattering of trains. These sounds convey the motion of a chaotic landscape. By listening and looking, Mary, Carla and Alice can witness people going about their lives in a range of settings and see how social contexts and relations influence the meanings associated with particular places and objects. Attending to such environments enables social psychologists to explore how the meaning of the city can differ according to one's relationship to the environment. Furthermore, the presence of some people can change these environmental meanings for others. For example, an executive strolling back to her car after dinner would likely experience the sights, sounds and smells of the city differently than a homeless man. In addition, the presence of the homeless man can change the meaning of the evening for the executive. These phenomena are being increasingly considered in social psychology (Hodgetts et al., 2008, 2009).

In the study of everyday life, social psychologists have considered habits and customs, and the associations between habitual acts, stress reduction and a sense of control or mastery (Musolf, 2003). Other work demonstrates a renewed interest in place and the ways in which human relations are played out in material environments (Dixon, Levine & McAuley, 2006; Hodgetts et al., 2008). As discussed in Chapter 6, human beings are always located somewhere. Human locatedness is central to understanding the social practices through which people inhabit their worlds, materially and socially. This means that geographical spaces provide more than backdrops to social interactions and events. People weave their lives and construct themselves within and across social settings.

It is important to note that everyday life is both located in specific places and evident across locales (Hodgetts et al., 2009). Our lives have movement and are conducted across different locations, from the bedroom in which Mary sleeps, to the street she transits when walking, to the pub, to the supermarket where she shops, to the bus she takes to work and the theatre where she meets her friends. In these places, Mary engages in various activities and relationships that give her life purpose and meaning and allow her to be a friend, sister, colleague, employee and woman. Her sense of self can change across these settings and relationships. We can all be different people in different contexts – at work as a psychologist, at home as a daughter or at the pub as a friend. A journey across a day can weave various spaces and situations together and convey a sense of self and place. The self manifests in the places Mary goes, the practices she engages in and the things she uses there – all are central to Mary's existence and of interest to social psychologists.

Links between places, things and self are not new to social psychology. William James (1892/1984) proposed that human beings respond to places and objects according to the subjective meanings inflected into them. James noted, *"Mental facts cannot be properly studied apart from the physical environment of which they take cognizance.* Mind and world in short have been evolved together, and in consequence are something of a mutual fit" (p. 11). The self theorized by James, and later by Cooley (1902), Mead (1934) and Hermans (2001), included material and social aspects from one's internal voice, the body, clothing and possessions, to habits, friends and family (Musolf, 2003). This self was also multiple and dependent on whom one is interacting with and what one is doing. Objects can become self-extensions interwoven with our self-concepts (Belk, 1988). Our things and the places we go become part of us. Places and things crystallize aspects of who we are and who we want to be (Box 3.14).

BOX 3.14   Subject–object relations

Concern with relationships between people's sense of self, the places they go, the people with whom they interact and material objects (their 'things') has proved to be a long-term preoccupation among social psychologists. This is often referred to as subject–object relations (Jovchelovitch, 2007). Chapter 4 considers how a subject–object dualism (based on the assumption that human meaning and experience resides inside one's head while the outer world contains meaningless objects) has come to prominence in social psychology. Conversely, phenomenologically informed psychologists such as Fuller (1990) propose that human perceptions and actions bind us to objects, psychologically, physically and socially. Chapter 6 documents how there is more to our connections with places and things than the construction of personal mental representations. Objects, places, people, situations are interwoven into a lifeworld. The lifeworld is the unique, everyday and meaningful context for a person's existence that weaves the particular places, people, objects and situations into a sense of self.

A core idea developed throughout this book is that self and world are co-constructed, or, as noted earlier, individual and society are 'twin born' (Cooley, 1902). We know ourselves only through our engagements in the world and with objects (Christopher & Campbell, 2008). In this way, the lifeworld is not separated into the private mind inside the body and the world outside. Both penetrate and grow out of each other, and as a result human beings are seen as profoundly emplaced. People are more than self-enclosed entities residing in physical bodies. Research shows that who we are can span the subject–object dichotomy that is often constructed between self and things in the world outside (Hodgetts et al., 2009). People's things can become part of them (Conner, 2002). From this perspective social psychologists can approach people as more than self-enclosed entities. People are materially and socially located beings who take form through 'interobjective relations' (cf. Jovchelovitch, 2007).

There is increased recognition of the materially and relationally embedded nature of human beings (Geismar & Horst, 2004; Gergen, 1985; Hodgetts, Chamberlain, Scammell et al., 2007; Wetherell, 1996). Our relationships with others are central to interobjective relations, in that through intimate relationships other people become part of us. We explore this issue further in Chapter 5 in relation to Chinese notions of the cobweb self. It is clear to many social psychologists that people may feel that other people are a crucial part of who they are. This can be particularly apparent with elderly couples who have lived together for most of their lives if one of them dies (Aron et al., 2004). Interdependence is increasingly recognized as being central to people's daily lives, growth and very being. Healthy lives appear to rely on the establishment and maintenance of meaningful relationships with others. This is not to say that individuals are totally reducible to their relationships (see Chapter 5). *Interdependence theory* of relationships predicts that people are more likely to be content in and maintain relationships that meet their needs as individuals (Rusbult & Van Lange, 2003).

There is a real sense of physicality that comes with a focus on the everyday because people are embodied beings who engage with and use physical objects across different locations. Our bodies are literally inflected with shared meanings through the adoption of symbols and styles of being that reflect the groups to which we belong and can be read by others. Bodily adornment and performance are central to expressions of community where the body becomes a site for, and display of, the acquisition, articulation and negotiation of identity and unity. Bodies are not meaningful in themselves because they are not self-produced, but are transformed and rendered meaningful within the context of community meaning systems. They become meaningful in comparison to other bodies where some bodies share the symbols of our communities and other bodies do not (Diprose, 2005). Styles of dress, tattoos and forms of dance symbolize membership and belonging to different communities where unique styles of existence express the adoption of values, ideas and identities. The presence of these bodies in daily life raise relational issues of sameness and difference, connection and repulsion, belonging and exclusion, trust and distrust, continuity and disruption, often depending on the viewer's membership status regarding the community in question (Box 3.15).

Work on embodied aspects of daily life is of particular interest to social psychologists engaged in areas such as illness and gender. For instance, social psychologists have devoted considerable effort to understanding how illness can disrupt a person's daily life, rupturing the smooth flow of activity and forcing people to contemplate change (Radley, 1999; Caltabiano, Sarafino & Byrne, 2008). If illness is serious enough it can force people to rethink their lives and the things they take for granted (Frank, 1995). Unexpected illness can bring the often taken-for-granted processes and practices through which we conduct our lives to the fore by forcing us to reconsider the patterning of our everyday lives and those of the people with whom we share our lives. We must re-pattern our daily rituals and sense

---

BOX 3.15   Habitus

Bourdieu (1990) introduced the idea of the embodied nature of personal history and experience through the concept of habitus. Habitus comprises the accumulated understandings and practices that are internalized both psychologically and physically and that become taken for granted as appropriate for particular circumstances. Habitus is developed through interactions with others and often shared within groups. It becomes a marker of attributes associated with a particular class of people (such as working-class or corporate women) in particular places (such as workshops, pubs, sports clubs, libraries and barbershops). Think for a moment about your own interactions with people. What markers of clothing, style and physical presence do you use to determine whether a person is like you or different?

of self in terms of what is practical and how we might manage the situation. In the process, we may re-story who we are or our sense of self (Frank, 1995). Illness can make our lives unfamiliar and demand that we attend to the previously unnoticed features of the everyday that we may now be prevented from engaging in. People can come to understand their everyday life through their illness and the new limitations of their body (Radley, 1999). Illness can make our bodies strange and force us to rethink our physicality and self. The event of illness can force us to incorporate new restraints into a life of coping or to respond to the loss of a loved one. We might have to adapt to the use of such things as needles or inhalers. As a result, illness is woven into the conduct of everyday life and the things we use (Box 3.16).

Re-patterning after illness is not always disruptive and can be facilitated in cultures where the onset of particular illnesses is normalized as part of the life course. For instance, Faircloth and colleagues (2004) explored the experiences of people recovering from a stroke and showed that disruption of everyday life was less pronounced when people constructed the stroke as a normal part of the aging process. Stroke was presented as part and parcel of getting older and to be expected. Such research invokes the importance of exploring wide social contexts when understanding individual illness and recovery in everyday life. Illness is not simply an individual phenomenon. In Chapter 8, further attention is given to the biological, social and relational nature of illness. We also need to note here that chronic illness and adjustment is a normal process in many people's everyday lives. As the population in the Western world ages, we have an increased number of people 'living with' illness and disability, rather than 'suffering from' sickness. This is an important play on language in that illness is often a normal, rather than an abnormal, part of everyday life. It is an aspect of life that often brings to the fore issues of physicality and identity.

BOX 3.16   Illness, bodies and gender

The emphasis we are placing in this section on physicality in everyday life is epitomized by illness, which involves bodily sensations that are often read as symptoms. How we read bodily sensations as being 'just a niggle' or a symptom of something more serious is dependent on a range of age, class, cultural and gender factors. It is a form of habitus (Bourdieu, 1990). In terms of gender, research indicates that women experience more physical symptoms and may be more in tune with their bodies due to traditional feminine roles as caregivers (Lyons & Chamberlain, 2006). Conversely, men often face cultural expectations about not giving in to niggles and the sick role (Hodgetts & Chamberlain, 2003). These broader cultural patterns of gender can influence people's experiences of their bodies and decisions regarding illness and what actions (or lack of action) are appropriate.

Chapter summary

Everyday situations are where people conduct their lives. We are all born into communities where we can be healthy and ill, form relationships with others, forge identities, build understandings and share stories. These situations are both material and social, based on sameness and difference. The purpose of social psychology is to extend out from the level of local idiosyncratic experience and behaviour to consider general trends and broader implications of local events. In 1903, Georg Simmel talked of extracting general arguments about city life out of detailed considerations of specific situations such as having dinner with friends. Such an approach is not simply concerned with practices of eating in themselves, but also with the meanings that surround these events and give them social significance. This raises tensions between the individual and the social, local and general that we will touch upon throughout this book. Our approach to social psychology is dialogical in nature. Each chapter moves out from detailed engagements with daily situations and practices, or individual and group experiences, to wider sociostructural contexts.

Any attempt to define social psychology needs to be broad enough to encompass the range of topics tackled and perspectives employed. One central aspect of the discipline is the nature of human interaction and how our everyday lives take shape in particular social situations. Fundamentally, social psychology is occupied with the study of people's lives together and with how humans interact and change. It is a field of endeavour that both investigates and is the product of the social world. Research is often sparked by events that social psychologists witness in their own lives. The relationship between social psychology and everyday life is complex. Theories and research findings from our discipline are often taken up and applied by members of the public, and in fact many psychologists encourage such use of insights from the discipline. We need to give social psychology away in order to support people in addressing social problems and developing the positive resources of their communities.

Forming relationships with other people is a process central to everyday life. Social psychologists have paid considerable attention to the nature of intimate relationships. As a result, several factors have been found to increase the likelihood of interpersonal attraction and the development of an intimate relationship. These factors include similarities in background and attitudes, physical attractiveness, complementarity, proximity and familiarity. What is clear is that relationships are diverse and dynamic living entities. No one theory can account for all the relevant complexities. What social psychology does offer is insights into general trends in the formation of relationships. This is particularly important as, over time, people in intimate relationships tend to grow into one another and to become increasingly interdependent.

We have begun a discussion in this chapter of the human self as an ongoing project that is fundamentally linked to other people and the places we live and things we use. Central to the development of the self are processes of socialization and resocialization that are fundamentally dialogical in nature. It is crucial for us not to lose sight of the fact that human lives and who individuals and groups become do not simply take place and emerge from the minds of individuals. The world is inhabited psychologically, physically, socially and culturally. Our partners, friends and things and the places we live are part of the self (see Chapters 5 and 6).

In this chapter, we have opened up our engagement with social psychological processes such as socialization, the self, things and places. These processes will be unpacked further in subsequent chapters. From this chapter you should keep three core themes in mind:

- Social psychology ought to be part of the construction of complex understandings of our everyday world. It provides a storehouse of understandings that can augment the commonplace conceptions of experiences in our everyday lives.
- Everyday life is worthy of our attention as a primary site for socialization, human development and the reproduction of social relations and structures.
- Human beings exist both psychologically and materially, and increasingly social psychology is exploring links between the self or psyche and places and objects.

Review exercise

- Who proposed that we should 'give psychology away'?
- What did the word 'idiot' originally mean?
- How does the concept of dialog assist us to understand the complexity of social life?

Write a brief summary of your day and what you did, whom you interacted with, the activities you participated in and where these took place. Keep your summary. We will return to it later in the book.

Note

1. Atomization refers to an approach to scientific research that attempts to break down phenomena into base elements. The assumption is that if we can understand the contributing elements, we can understand the phenomena (see Billig, 2008).

4 Making sense of everyday knowledge

Core questions to consider while reading this chapter

- Why do people use schemas in everyday life?
- What is an attribution?
- What is confirmation bias?
- What is a stereotype?
- What is the distinction between prejudice and discrimination?
- How does the mind–world dualism relate to the social cognitive approach?
- Can you explain social representations theory?
- Why is it often appropriate to do research *with* rather than *on* people?

Chapter scenario

Manuel has been the pride of his community since graduating with top grades from high school and then university. He entered a large national bank straight after his graduation and within five years had worked his way up to branch manager. Manuel had invested a lot of his sense of self in his identity as a banker. He ran the annual golf tournament and was a regular at social events. Manuel did not forget his community, and maintained his commitment to helping fellow immigrants by donating money and his time to the local Filipino society. Then the credit crunch hit. Manuel knew things were not going well when his bank was 'bailed out' by the federal government – though he never expected to be made redundant. It is now two years since Manuel was made redundant, and he has not been able to get another job or come to terms with his current situation. Manuel has had a number of brief clerical posts, but nothing permanent has come his way. He is now doubting his abilities. The family had to sell the house. They are managing, on David's income, to pay the mortgage for a smaller place. David and Manuel have two children.

What has helped Manuel is having a supportive partner and loving children. The Filipino community have also stood by him and involved him in a more hands-on capacity within the society. This provides Manuel with a sense of contribution and belonging. However, regularly Manuel is reminded of his surplus status when visiting the job centre and work expos. Recently, when leaving the job centre, Manuel was abused by a passer-by, who shouted at Manuel, "Hey, you useless immigrant, why don't you go home and stop trying to steal jobs from Americans." So much for diversity and tolerance. Such things really knock Manuel's confidence and sense of belonging. David tries to reassure him that it's just the opinion of an ignorant person, but it still wounds Manuel. What really hurts is the fact that Manuel had assumed that he was an American, and such statements really undermine his sense of belonging. Manuel is increasingly hard on himself and likens his situation to suffering from a chronic disease or being a leper whom nobody wants to touch.

Every day people make sense of the world around them. Like Manuel, people make judgements regarding the actions of others. They make decisions about what route to take to work and what they might do in the evening. In the process, people often rely on their memories and the organization of their thoughts into categories that provide shortcuts to enable them to respond quickly to events in the world (Tajfel, 1981). Human beings also draw upon a range of information sources. These include their own direct observations and the advice of others. A person's thoughts are not simply his or her own. Human beings rely on convention, myth, shared narratives and custom. We are all socialized into knowing how 'this place works', how to fit into our towns or cities and 'how things are done around here'. We have a procedural knowledge of how to live in a society with others.

It is tempting for psychologists to assume that human beings make sense of the world around them independently of one another.

After all, people have the capacity to think for themselves. However, the world around us is not meaningless and waiting for us to impose meaning on it. When social psychologists think about how people make sense of the world, it is important to note that people are born into a world that is already rendered meaningful by others (Chapter `3). Shared understandings, norms and ways of doing things are negotiated within social groups and primary settings for socialization such as the family. Individuals must grapple with these meanings, many of which may contain stereotypes and prejudices, when thinking for themselves.

The chapter scenario raises several issues regarding how people make sense of their daily lives and changes in their circumstances. Changes, such as being made redundant, can rupture a person's account of who he or she is. For example, the story Manuel had for himself was anchored in his occupation as a successful banker. After events such as redundancy or illness, people often reconsider who they are and their place in the world (Chapter 3). Manuel is fortunate in that he can rely on David and the Filipino community to nurture his sense of self. Manuel might work to develop his own understanding of what it means to be unemployed in dialogue with those around him. However, this process can be hampered by prejudicial views in society and the discriminatory actions of a passer-by. These issues of personal understanding and the influence of other people in the world are central to this social psychology of knowledge.

One key issue in social psychology is the manner in which people formulate their ideas about the world. One approach to this issue is social cognition, where the focus is on the functioning of individual minds, which receive, process, structure and store information from the senses as mental representations (Perloff, 2008). Discursive and narrative approaches consider the ways in which information taken up in individual minds has already been constructed by other people. Thus, the information individuals draw on to make sense of the world arises from dialogues that have long cultural and social histories (Billig, 2008). A discursive or narrative approach requires us to explore more than just the processing of information by individual minds. We must also explore the history of ideas and patterns of thought. Attention is given to the collective basis of human knowledge production between people, which might include institutions, groups and artefacts such as web pages (Jovchelovitch, 2007). Broadly speaking, the early sections of this chapter address aspects of the cognitive approach and the later sections address the discursive approach. Both offer insights into the production of knowledge in everyday life.

Chapter overview

This chapter considers how knowledge is constructed in everyday settings. Questions and theories of knowledge have been studied by philosophers for centuries. These questions are also important considerations for the social sciences in general, although different disciplines may focus on different aspects. Adopting a social psychological orientation, this chapter explores how people make sense of themselves and the worlds within which they live and interact with other people. We explore a topic of particular interest to social psychologists, social cognition. We then explore some of the limitations of the social cognitive approach, and subsequently briefly outline more collectively oriented approaches to understanding human thought. This chapter draws on social representations theory to illustrate overlaps between individualistic and collectivist understandings of human thought. We will consider how social psychologists research the knowledge of other people. The chapter has three key themes:

- Common knowledge
- Personal and collective perceptions and understandings
- Researching the knowledge of others

What people know

Knowledge is a complex concept that involves the acquisition of skill, experience and education. Knowledge involves both theoretical and practical understandings of everyday life and more abstract fields of human endeavour such as philosophy. Knowledge includes theoretical understandings developed in social psychology to make sense of people's experiences of situations such as being unemployed (Cullen & Hodgetts, 2001). As a broad concept, knowledge can include science, common sense, religion and superstition. These forms of knowledge can overlap and inform each other. For example, Manuel's experiences can be used to inform the development and refinement of social psychological theories of unemployment.

The field of epistemology is devoted to debates about the nature of human knowledge and its relationship to reality. Philosophers often explore the basis of claims that an idea or understanding constitutes knowledge and is not just a set of unfounded assumptions (Box 4.1). At present, there is no universally agreed definition of knowledge. Some would contest the very notion that Manuel's understandings of his situation should be put in the same category as academic theory. Perhaps they should not. We could not hope to come up with a definitive statement as to the nature of knowledge: philosophers have been working on this topic for millennia. This chapter approaches knowledge as an ongoing process of making sense of, or assigning meaning to, the world. The chapter is foundational to this book because knowledge construction, or making sense of experience, is central to everyday life. In exploring what social psychology can tell us about everyday knowledge, we are not attempting to define knowledge as a state or thing. We advocate exploring knowledge as a process. This is what many social psychologists do when researching how people acquire and apply knowledge in everyday settings, through communication and interpersonal interactions.

For some time, many social psychologists have adopted the scientific method as a means to develop knowledge that is more neutral and considered less tainted by the emotions, biases and politics of the researcher (Chapter 2). Clearly, the scientific method is useful for creating knowledge about many aspects of the physical world and some aspects of human thought. Alternative approaches to studying human thinking are also useful. Psychologists drawing inspiration from the human sciences place more emphasis on all knowledge being socially, historically and culturally situated. Contextualizing human knowledge is important because what it means to be human, and how people see the world, is enmeshed in historical and cultural contexts (Chapter 5).

Discussions of these different approaches to knowledge typically invoke explorations of research paradigms, the nature of reality and how human beings know and perceive the world (Billig, 2008). We

BOX 4.1   Introduction to knowledge

Robinson and Groves (1999) provide an accessible introduction to the field of philosophy and the issues of knowledge, meaning making, dialogue and human thought.

will not rehash these well-trod lines of argument regarding differences between physical and human science-inspired understandings of knowledge (Tuffin, 2004). Such debates are endless and are not readily resolvable. We would assert a broadly social constructionist stance (Box 4.2) that is in keeping with the overall orientation of this book. This approach proposes that knowledge can represent events in the world, but human beings are capable of only imperfect representations. In this way, social psychologists can never obtain an objective and universal truth about the social psychological processes we study. Rather, we can produce contextually located interpretations that are at once useful, uncertain, modifiable and imperfect. Such knowledge does not give us certainty. Instead, it provides the best available explanation (Polkinghorne, 1983). In this sense, we can participate in the creation of *assertoric* knowledge, a knowledge claim we assert to the world based on our reasoning. This knowledge claim is offered as a basis for debate, criticism and refinement.

Social psychologists generally agree that the construction of representations (or understandings) of the world is central to the production of everyday knowledge. Representations are the core fabric of people's realities and lives. Social psychologists agree less on the

---

BOX 4.2 Social constructionism

There is a large body of work that documents the influence of social constructionism on the human sciences. According to Berger and Luckmann (1966), society can be comprehended as consisting of both subjective and objective realities, and these can be understood in terms of three dialogical moments: externalization, objectivation and internalization. These dialogical moments occur simultaneously as human beings participate in the production of social phenomena through shared practices. *Externalization* can be viewed as an act of turning ideas into artefacts or practices. That is, people externalize when they act upon the world, turning ideas into reality. For example, when thinking about Manuel's plight, people may have ideas about how to address unemployment. Officials tasked with defining or addressing unemployment can produce a booklet on the social impact of unemployment. This booklet, and what it states, is then circulated in the social world. Over time, the ideas can become fixed in social policy, for instance, and taken-for-granted. At some point, the ideas are no longer viewed as the product of human thought and interaction. *Objectivation* happens when ideas become seen as something natural, immutable and real that exists independent of people. The notion of *internalization* is reflected in the process of people being socialized into a society where things already exist. People internalize ideas and accounts as part of their consciousness and their ways of being in the world. After a few unsuccessful job interviews, Manuel may come to believe himself to be lacking in ability or initiative as he succumbs to some of the negative typecasting of unemployed people.

A social constructionist perspective offers an explanation for how the world is constructed through social practices, as well as the means by which the world comes to be experienced as a natural and fixed reality.

nature of these representations and where they are located. Some locate representations inside people's heads as mental models. From this stance, Manuel's thoughts about who he is now that he is no longer a banker are generated at the personal level. A social cognitive perspective proposes that people produce knowledge primarily in their heads by processing information. According to this view, thinking can be explained through the metaphor of a computer that searches nodes in a mental network and establishes new links between experiences (Bruner, 1990). The ascendance of computer technologies provided a useful metaphor for explaining aspects of human thought and how people might process and retrieve information.[1] From a social cognitive perspective, the knowledge people produce in their heads is thought to be communicated to, or exchanged with, others through social interactions. Human beings use symbolic systems such as spoken and written language to transmit their thoughts to other people in a kind of inter-psychic exchange. Technologies, including writing and drawing, serve to communicate internal cognitive process beyond specific moments and individuals. This intra-psychic perspective is not accepted by all psychologists. Other social psychologists place more emphasis on knowledge as it exists outside of individual people's heads in language and cultural artefacts (Billig, 2008; Jovchelovitch, 2007). According to this critical approach, it is not just inside our own individual heads that thinking occurs or that representations are located. For example, shared languages contain knowledge, categories and ideas that were constructed before many of us were born. When people use a language, they reproduce this existing and shared knowledge, both consciously and unconsciously.

We will return to this issue later in relation to a discussion of social representations, discourse and narrative theories. For now, let us focus on what the social cognitive approach has to offer our understanding of Manuel's thought processes and how others perceive him. This allows us to explore further a central theme in this book – the dynamic relationship between individual and collective thought.

Knowledge as social cognition: How does Manuel think?

'Social cognition' is a term that refers to a general approach to the study of human knowledge in social psychology. It explores how individuals process information in specific settings. This approach draws on concepts such as schemas to invoke the ways in which people categorize and construct mental representations of objects in the world (Box 4.3). Many psychologists trace the history of social cognition to Wundt's (1897) *Outlines of Psychology*, and even further back to the seventeenth-century philosopher John Locke (Billig, 2008). Wundt considered the study of social cognition to be the main purpose of social psychology. He based his studies on self-observation and introspection. His approach was essentially autobiographical and involved personal reflection and narrative. With the increased prominence of experimental methods (Chapter 2), research on social cognition came to rely increasingly on a combination of laboratory experiments and quantitative fieldwork.

Much of the groundwork for the social cognitive approach was laid in the work of Tajfel (1969) and the importance he placed on social categorization (Tajfel, 1981) and social identity (Tajfel & Turner, 1979). Billig (2002) provides an insightful review of Tajfel's work and the influence of the social climate on his theorizing, the intricacies of which are beyond the present chapter. In Chapter 7 we discuss who Tajfel was and how he applied his ideas to social identity theory. In this area Tajfel emphasized how people take perceptual shortcuts in order to make sense of the world, their place in it and their relationships with other people and groups. People cannot deal with all the information available to them; therefore, in order to bring coherence to the world people must organize information into categories (Tajfel, 1981). Social psychologists have paid much attention to the mistakes in reasoning that can result from human categorization and perceptual shortcuts. In this chapter, we focus more on processes of social categorization, which are central to the social cognitive approach and schema theory (Bartlett, 1932), stereotype theory (Brewer, 1979), attribution theory (Heider, 1958) and social learning theory (Bandura, 1988) (Box 4.4). These theories provide insights into intergroup processes and the ways people think about and act towards each other in daily life.

BOX 4.3   Cognitive psychology

By the 1960s, cognitive psychology was having a major influence on many areas of psychology, including social psychology (Bruner, 1990). This development was, in part, due to the inadequacy of behaviourism as an explanation for human thought and action (Chomsky, 1959). Cognitive psychologists argued that human social behaviour and communication are complex, incorporating the use of symbols and representations and influenced by norms, values, emotions and social contexts. They claimed that many of these processes and experiences occur outside of the limited gaze of behaviourism (Chapter 2). In short, the social cognitive approach has gained prominence in mainstream Western social psychology today as the dominant explanation for human knowledge.

BOX 4.4   A brief account of social learning theory

Bandura's (1988) social learning theory is applied to the ways people make sense of media representations in Chapter 11. The theory is based on the idea that people do not have to do or practise something in order to learn how to do it or to acquire relevant skills (knowledge) for the activity. Thus, it is clear that people can model their future actions on their observations of the actions of other people.

The function of schemas in Manuel's life

To organize and manage the events of his day and the mass of incoming stimuli from the environment, a person such as Manuel develops his mental processing into frameworks or *schemas*. Schemas are coherent memories or structures for organizing people's understandings of daily life. They operate as linked-in networks and function as a kind of shorthand cognitive method for Manuel to understand and respond quickly to specific social situations. Schemas organize knowledge into general repeatable structures that we draw on to guide us in similar situations, but schemas are also drawn on when we process new information as it comes to hand. Langer (1989) draws the useful distinction between *mindfulness* and *mindlessness* to help us understand the way people manage complex cognitive tasks routinely. If Manuel remained mindful of every event and stimulus in his environment he would soon be overwhelmed with information and need to lie down. Thus, Manuel needs to be selective in terms of what he attends to. Schemas allow Manuel to achieve aspects of this task. The crucial issue is what a person in a given situation should remain mindful of and what he or she can safely become mindless about. Box 4.5 provides an example.

Schema theory explains how people can function in everyday situations without paying much conscious attention to what they are doing. Getting to the job centre requires little conscious effort because Manuel has a schema. If he moves to a new city, he will learn how to find another job centre and how to interact with new people. Manuel will simply integrate the knowledge from his existing schema with new information, and quickly adapt to a different environment and different experiences.

Social psychologists are particularly interested in the activation of schemas and in how new information comes to be integrated into existing schemas (Box 4.6). Key factors are attention and selectivity. Information that is inconsistent with a schema tends to be ignored, and this is commonly referred to as *confirmation bias* (Nickerson, 1998). This occurs when a person's schemas comprise stereotypes

BOX 4.5   Using schema to navigate the city

Manuel can find his way to the job centre without consciously thinking about it. He has a mental map or schema of how to get there. Manuel puts on his jacket, picks up his CV and walks out the door. He turns right at the gate, walks down to the bus stop and takes the number thirty-two bus to Bryant Street, where he then walks through the park and over the bridge, before turning right into Nowhere Lane and then left at Somewhere Street. The job centre is on the right, and when he enters the building he knows to get a number and say hi to Roberta, the receptionist, who will try to usher him through to see a case manager as quickly as possible. This schema has been developed over his many visits and includes knowledge of how to navigate a city and engage with people along the way. This is a procedural knowledge, so while travelling to the centre Manuel can focus his conscious attention on other matters. When he hits road works on a particular morning on Nowhere Lane, he must increase his cognitive focus to rethink his journey and take an alternative path down Mark Crescent and along Long Lane, which will take him back onto Somewhere Street.

BOX 4.6   Encoding information

Encoding is an important step in the interpretation of information. People spontaneously translate (encode) information into a format to be stored in their memories (Fiske & Taylor, 1991). Unfortunately, this encoding can lead to people jumping to conclusions, perhaps too quickly. Manuel might see an event – for example, a teenager yelling at a middle-aged man on the street. This activates a schema based on previously encoded material. Manuel then interprets the scene accordingly. The person yelling is doing so because he is having an argument with his father. On the other hand, it could just as easily be that the teenager is yelling because he has just been falsely accused of stealing from the man's shop. The point is that although encoding might be a useful strategy for categorizing information into schemas, it is not always reliable, and the process is linked to the development of stereotypes. Once a schema is encoded and activated as a social category (i.e. teenager), associated stereotypes are also activated (i.e. teenagers are moody and disrespectful of older people).

and the person attends only to information that confirms prejudicial views regarding other people, things or experiences. Congruent information is often absorbed into an existing schema in an economical manner requiring little conscious effort. Incongruent information tends to require much more effort to be integrated into a person's existing knowledge base. This can result in people either actively ignoring incongruent information or having to devote mental energy to revising their assumptions.

Clearly, there is more to schemas than simply finding one's way around a city. Frederic Charles Bartlett (1932) was a psychologist who was particularly influential in the development of schema theory, which he adapted from the earlier work of Henry Head (Box 4.7). Bartlett had in mind a remarkably broad understanding of social cognition that in many respects resembles contemporary narrative approaches. He explored processes by which people develop stories of the world that they construct through experiences of particular situations and then apply to similar situations in the future. Bartlett proposed that schemas influence not only what people recall about a situation, but also how they interpret information in a given situation. This raises the important point that schemas are often activated automatically and can therefore contribute to erroneous and inattentive information processing.

In short, social psychologists propose that there are various forms of task, situation, person, self, group and situation schemas. Task schemas were covered in our discussion of how Manuel navigates his way to the job centre. Situation schemas comprise scripts for how someone should behave in particular social situations, such as how to behave and interact while visiting a job centre. Person schemas are organized understandings of the types of people that exist in the world and their associated attributes. We will discuss attribution theory shortly. For now, we use these schemas to aid us in predicting how certain 'types' of people might act in certain situations. Person schemas can be expanded out to group schemas, which often constitute stereotypes, and these frequently arise when we relate to ethnic groups other than our own.

BOX 4.7   Interesting study

A famous study by Bartlett (1932) on the influence of existing schemas on knowledge production involved having research participants read a Native American folktale and then recall the story on several occasions for a year. As time went by, participants modified the specific details of the story to reflect their own cultural expectations and norms. In other words, the story or schema from another culture was integrated into and modified to fit within the participants' own network of schemas. This type of research identified key processes that are central to the modification of schemas. These include omitting events, changing the sequence of events, shifting the focus, placing emphasis on particular characters and events, and adding factitious information that better fits with one's own cultural norms. Such work also shows how long-term memories are not fixed or static. Although we often rely on familiar schemas (and even stereotypes at times), our knowledge of the world is constantly being challenged and extended in response to our ongoing engagements in the world. A core idea introduced by Bartlett is that people integrate knowledge from other cultures into their own cultural frames or schemas obtained through socialization. This is an important point, as we will see in the later sections on social representations, discourse and narrative theory. Those interested in the work, background and influence of Frederic Charles Bartlett should visit the online archive at http://www.ppsis.cam.ac.uk/bartlett/Bartlett%20The%20Person.htm.

Stereotyping Manuel: The social psychology of prejudice

Oversimplified, exaggerated, preconceived and demeaning assumptions about the character of other people are often referred to as stereotypes. The passer-by in the opening scenario voiced such a stereotype when he asserted that Manuel was an unskilled immigrant who does not belong in the United States. Clearly, this is an erroneous viewpoint given Manuel's citizenship, educational achievements and former occupation as a bank manager. Stereotyping involves assigning characterizations (a collection of assumed and generalized group characteristics) to an individual simply on the basis of his or her membership of a particular group (Brewer, 1979). Because Manuel has a Filipino appearance, he is assumed not to have the same rights or abilities as other US citizens. This can have the effect of undermining the dignity (Chapter 10) and legitimacy (Chapter 7) of stereotyped people. Stereotypes are often used by dominant groups to subordinate minority groups and maintain social control. This is evident in processes of colonization (Chapter 5), in which settler societies often refer to indigenous people as 'childlike' and 'uncultured' and therefore requiring protection (Jost & Banaji, 1994). In this way, stereotypes are associated with prejudice and discrimination (Box 4.8), because they are used as the basis for maintaining perceived distinctions or differences between groups based on religion, ethnicity, social class, gender, sexuality and perceived intelligence.

From a social cognitive perspective, stereotypes are mental categories based on distinctions between the in-group (i.e. the group the observer belongs to) and an out-group (i.e. the group the person being stereotyped belongs to) (Turner et al., 1987). Stereotypes are used to differentiate members of one's own group (with whom

---

BOX 4.8   Prejudice and discrimination

Prejudice refers to negative perceptions of people based on their membership of particular social groups. People are judged simply because of the group(s) they are assumed to belong to, rather than on the basis of their personal actions and abilities. Prejudice can contribute to discrimination, whereby certain groups of people are treated unfairly. Many prejudices and acts of discrimination are based on inaccurate stereotypes. Historically, they comprise key aspects of intergroup relations. In the following chapter, we will consider colonization as a particular intergroup practice that is generally based on stereotypes, prejudice and discrimination. In Chapter 6, we also consider these issues in relation to the segregation of social spaces, and in Chapter 9 we explore how this practice serves morally to exclude people from the right to fair treatment.

one has a sense of belongingness) from members of other groups (who are understood in terms of prototypical group members). It is important not to assume that the effect of stereotypes is always negative for individuals. For instance, if one is a member of a dominant group and is stereotyped as more intelligent and motivated, then being stereotyped can be a more positive experience. However, if one is a minority group member there is a greater risk of being stereotyped as being less intelligent and motivated, and this can result in less positive experiences, including fewer opportunities for advancement at work. Manuel is from a minority group and also faces the threat of internalizing negative stereotypes that some members of the majority culture in which he lives may hold about him (Steele, 1997). His state of unemployment is likely to invoke further racial stereotypes. Manuel is depersonalized by the passer-by, who judges him to be just another dishonest and incompetent immigrant. Such categorization can serve political and ideological functions in justifying this perceiver's anti-immigration attitude (see following section) (Box 4.9). Finally, internalized stereotypes can affect the confidence and performance of members of minority groups by creating apprehension and a sense of learned helplessness. If this does occur, then the stereotype can in turn be perpetuated as somehow accurate and real.

Racial stereotyping is a particular concern for social psychologists because it can affect the opportunities and the rights of minority

BOX 4.9   **Stereotype content**

Fiske, Cuddy, Glick and Xu (2002) proposed a structural account of stereotype content that focuses on the broader material relationships between groups. Their research shows how in some instances out-groups may be looked upon favourably by members of in-groups. This theory departs from the convention in social psychology of stereotypes reflecting a dislike of another group (Allport, 1954). The research by Fiske and colleagues (2002) reflects increasing complexity in the field of stereotype research. They identify two additional dimensions of stereotype content – competence and warmth. These tend to vary in relation to the relative social status of the target group and the perceiver's relationship to that group. Most research concludes that the more differences exist between groups, the more stereotyping and prejudices are likely to arise. Yet Fiske and colleagues demonstrate that there can be more conflict between two groups of a similar social status than between a high-status group and a low-status group. For example, low-status groups (immigrants) may be perceived by other low-status groups (working-class locals) as incompetent and with less warmth, even though they share some common ground. In such situations, the immigrant group is regarded as a disruption and as serving no good function. High-status groups may instead view the low-status immigrant groups with warmth and competence because they provide cheap and reliable labour. The relationship is perceived to be one of cooperation rather than competition. Clearly, it is problematic to assert that high-status and low-status groups are not competing for resources. They are.

group members to interact with other people and frequent particular places (Chapter 6). In many cases, racial stereotyping leads to the stratification of groups and intergroup conflicts (Box 4.10). What we have referred to as stereotypes have been used to construct and legitimate prejudicial ideas about racial inferiority. These erroneous beliefs have been used to justify the colonization and brutal subjugation of indigenous peoples for millennia (Chapter 5). In a fascinating series of papers outlined in Chapter 6, John Dixon, Kevin Durrheim and colleagues explored the ways in which anti-racist policies in South Africa failed to bring to an end to segregation. In fact, local beaches were being re-segregated as a result of stereotypes and prejudices held by white South Africans regarding their indigenous fellow citizens.

Social psychologists have proposed that racism is becoming more subtle (Van Dijk, 1992). There is a shift away from 'old school' overt and direct discrimination to 'new' and more indirect or symbolic forms of racism. Old school racism involves strategies such as overt racial segregation, but new and more subtle forms of racism are apparent in the denial of the continuing existence of discrimination in society. We would argue that both old and new forms of racism are interwoven and functioning today (cf. Augoustinos & Reynolds, 2001; Leach, 2005). Leach (2005) argues that the emphasis on so-called new racism detracts from an understanding

---

BOX 4.10   Racism

Social psychologists conceptualize racism as a particularly prominent form of prejudice and discrimination. Gough and McFadden (2001) identify several approaches to racism in psychology, including social cognitive and group membership approaches. The social cognitive approach stems from Allport's (1954) assertion that prejudice is based on an erroneous mental categorization. If prejudice is based on the inaccurate and overly rigid ideas an individual holds about another group of people, then such ideas can be challenged via education and by increasing the person's exposure to members of the other racial group (Chapter 6). A serious limitation of this approach is that if prejudices are simply the product of faulty information processing, which as we have already established seems innate to human beings, they can almost be excused as something that is unpleasant but unavoidable (Billig, 2002). It might then also be possible to argue that we cannot hold a group accountable for their prejudices, because prejudice is a fact of life (Reicher, 2001). A similar problem underlies the group membership (also structural) explanation for prejudice that stems from the classic Sherif boys camp studies (Chapter 2). If conflict over limited resources naturally leads to intergroup prejudice and discrimination, then prejudice is simply excused as a result of a natural response to scarcity. These arguments ignore different histories and the fact that many groups do not start on an equal playing field (Chapter 5). Many dominating groups have had distinct historical advantages, and some of these advantages have been gained (and maintained) by discriminating against other groups.

of the historical continuity of racism in society. Groups historically subjected to racism such as African Americans and indigenous peoples continue to face both old and new forms of racism. Another influence central to our discussion of racism is the media (Box 4.11).

BOX 4.11   Interesting study

Estacio (2009) considered links between media depictions of Southeast Asian female migrant workers in the United Kingdom and racism in Western societies. The article responds to a stereotypical television representation of a young female as simple-minded and sexually available to her employer. This depiction resulted in considerable controversy in the United Kingdom and triggered discussions regarding appropriate representations of minority groups. Estacio (2009) illustrates how old school and new racism are often interlinked in everyday life. She also opens up a number of complex and contradictory issues regarding links between the media and racism. The clip discussed is offensive and exemplifies how the media can function as a site for racialization (Ratele & Duncan, 2004). However, the television comedy show also brought discriminatory practices and perceptions out into the public domain. The negative reactions that followed the broadcasting of the item operate as challenges to discrimination and highlight how the media can also function as sites for controversy and change. In some cases, this can extend to more enlightened depictions of marginalized people and the situations they face.

In an open commentary on the article by Estacio (2009), Hodgetts and Stolte (2009) note that media technologies constitute a representational space that infiltrates the geographical spaces of the everyday lives of migrant workers, while also contributing to the shaping of their relationships with their first-world employers. As meaning-making institutions, the media are woven into the fabric of our homes and workplaces. Media technologies such as television and networked computers function as portals to wider and often physically distant worlds containing representations of other people. Through our interactions with various media we can learn to despise, or develop concern for the plight of, others at a distance. Such an orientation casts the media as more than simply a racist institution. It highlights how the media are sources of information about other people that we can attend to and integrate into our own schemas. We might also simply ignore and dismiss new information as irrelevant because it clashes with our own experiences. The point is that each time people access media representations they are also accessing the understandings of other people, and therein resides the potential for us to either entrench or change our views of others.

Review exercise

Stereotypes do not exist just in the heads of individuals. They are also evident in art and a range of media. Search the web for cartoons containing racial and gender stereotypes.

- What are the core characteristics being assigned to the groups depicted?
- What do these images say about the societies that produced them?

Attitudes towards Manuel

Attitude research also relates to intergroup relations and issues of difference. As we noted in Chapter 3, attitudes can be defined as the evaluations a person holds regarding particular people or objects in the world. These evaluations are expressed in positive or negative terms (Perloff, 2008). They are relatively consistent clusters of feelings, beliefs and predispositions (cf. Billig, 1996). Much energy has been expended exploring the formation, structure and function of attitudes and changes in attitudes. Today, researchers investigate both explicit (self-reported) and implicit (unconscious) attitudes (Rydell & McConnell, 2006). An explicit attitude against immigrants is expressed openly by the abuse our passer-by directs towards Manuel. Other passers-by may hold similar negative attitudes towards immigrants, but these remain private or implicit, perhaps only given away by them crossing the road to avoid contact with 'such people'. "Explicit attitudes are correlated with the content of verbal and controlled behaviours, whereas implicit attitudes are correlated with nonverbal and uncontrolled behaviours that are displayed while interacting with the attitude object" (Castelli, Zogmaister & Tomelleri, 2009, p. 587). A study using the Implicit Association Test revealed that people can hold biases against particular ethnic groups despite self-reported claims of not being racist (Heider & Skowronski, 2007).

The study of attitudes, how people obtain them and how they can be changed can shed light on intergroup relations and the relationship between Manuel and members of the majority group, such as the passer-by. Bigler and Liben (2007) assign a significant role to adult figures in shaping the attitudes of children by the labels they assign to different groups or the extent to which these children are segregated from children from another group. However, evidence for such a link is not as conclusive as one might think (Box 4.12). It is likely that there is no one source of attitudes, that we obtain these from complex combinations of our family and broader community contexts and institutions such as schools and mass media. (Any parent of a teenager will be well aware of the limited extent to which he or she can influence their child's ideas and beliefs.). It is difficult to establish a causal link between a specific attitude and any of these everyday sources of knowledge and information.

Experimental research suggests that some of our (weakly held) attitudes can be manipulated. Briñol and Petty (2003) asked research participants to move their heads either up and down or from side to side while listening to an editorial played over headphones. The participants were told that the researchers were evaluating how the headphones performed while the wearers moved their heads. In fact,

---

BOX 4.12   Interesting study

Castelli, Zogmaister and Tomelleri (2009) investigated the link between the ethnic attitudes of white parents and their preschool children. These authors assessed the implicit and explicit racial attitudes of parents and the racial attitudes of their children aged three to six years. Their results suggest that parents' explicit attitudes were not related to children's attitudes. However, mothers' implicit attitudes were related to children's attitudes. Fathers' implicit attitudes were not related to children's attitudes. These results suggest that racial attitudes may result through socialization and in particular with mothers, with whom there is strong attachment. This study is significant as it illustrates an attempt to move beyond self-professed attitudes, which can remain undisclosed due to social desirability or lack of awareness among participants. The authors also explored spontaneous attitudinal responses or nonverbal reactions (implicit) to relevant stimuli (in this case pictures of white or black faces). The study suggests that the nonverbal behaviour of mothers may be important in the acquisition of intergroup attitudes among their children.

---

this was an experiment into whether nodding, or conversely shaking one's head, influenced attitudes to the editorial – and the answer was yes. Participants were more likely to agree with the message they were hearing when they were nodding their heads – a movement usually associated with agreement. What happens in an experiment is, however, fairly removed from all the other factors that influence our attitudes and from what happens in everyday life. On the other hand, it may be useful to be aware of these unconscious attitude primers such as socially textured body movements. Imagine if decreasing prejudice was as simple as inducing people to nod their heads while they listened to anti-prejudice broadcasts. Unsurprisingly, changing attitudes is often not that simple.

Attribution theory and the tendency to blame Manuel

Every day people make judgements about one another as we attempt to come to understand each other, what motivates us and what we are likely to do next. Is a person kind and caring or self-interested and disengaged from the needs of others? Many social psychologists propose that such meaning-making processes often involve attributions. Attribution theory considers how people attribute or explain their own behaviour and the behaviour of other individuals or groups (Heider, 1958). These explanations are often focused on specific causes for behaviour. These causes are generally divided into internal (dispositional) and external (situational) factors. Internal factors lie within an individual and include personal predispositions, attitudes, motivation and intelligence. External factors lie outside the individual and include poor housing, a lack of opportunities in life and the weather. Internal factors assign responsibility for a particular behaviour to the individual. Conversely, external factors assign responsibility for the situation to causes that are essentially outside the control of the person.

Attribution errors occur when a person wrongly infers the causes of the behaviour of others. One particular type of attribution bias is the *fundamental attribution error* (Heider, 1958; Ross, 1977; Block & Funder, 1986). This error occurs when observers attribute another person's behaviour solely to internal factors and ignore or downplay the influence of external factors. The same observers will likely justify their own actions with reference to external factors because they are more aware of how these are affecting them and are less willing to direct blame towards themselves. The passer-by in the opening scenario for this chapter is also unemployed. He attributes his own unemployment to government policies that allow immigrant workers to enter the country and take up valuable jobs. Yet he attributes Manuel's unemployment to a lack of skill and a lower work ethic.

Social psychologists have put forward a number of explanations for attribution errors. A lack of background knowledge is a core explanation for attribution errors (Augoustinos & Walker, 1995). Attribution biases often occur due to differences between actors (those doing something) and observers (those watching what the actor is doing). The differences occur because actors and observers tend to view situations differently. An actor can experience his or her own inner thoughts and conflicts when making decisions regarding how to act. In contrast, the observer is not privy to such cognitive events and thus can only rely on information that is external to the actor when assigning cause to a particular act. This is known as the *actor–observer bias* (Jones & Nisbett, 1972). An observer might make assumptions about why Manuel is unemployed, attributing his situation to a lack of motivation. In fact, Manuel was made redundant through no fault of his own. The cause of his unemployment was corporate greed rather than personal failing. Nonetheless, when Manuel goes to the job centre he is advised by his caseworker to read self-help books and to buy a new suit.

When we consider influences on attribution errors, it is important to note cultural variations in such errors. Research suggests that in cultures based on individualistic notions of the self, attribution errors are more likely (Miller, 1984) (Box 4.13). People from more collectivist-oriented cultures tend to pay more attention to external factors. It makes sense that people socialized to emphasize individualism will be more likely to associate other people's behaviour with internal factors.

BOX 4.13   Interesting study

Miller (1984) compared white Americans and Hindus in India in terms of how they are influenced by cultural factors when accounting for deviant and pro-social behaviours. Research participants were asked to describe recent pro-social and deviant acts of someone they knew well. Results showed that school children from the different cultures differed very little in the explanations they gave regarding the acts. Cultural divergence increased with age, with Americans (individualist) giving more dispositional-oriented explanations regarding the type of person. Indian participants (collectivist) gave more situational-oriented explanations, such as poverty.

Attributions are associated with assumptions about fairness and justice. As we will see in Chapter 9, fairness and justice are complex concepts that invoke the complexities of many social relationships across groups. For now, it is useful to consider the proposal by Lerner and Miller (1977) that a key explanation for many of our attributions is the 'just-world' belief, or the contention that we all get what we deserve and deserve what we get (Box 4.14). These authors propose that if behaviour is attributed to individual internal factors (which are changeable) and not to social structures (which may be more difficult to change because they are outside an individual's control), then the world can seem like a fairer place. Holding the belief of a just world is often a strategy to allow us to continue in our own lives by distancing ourselves from the many people who are struggling in much more adverse circumstances. A just world can seem less threatening to us. The downside of this process is that it can lead to victim blaming and moral exclusion. The self-protecting process noted here is often referred to as a *self-serving bias* (Miller & Ross, 1975), which allows people to feel okay about not helping others because these others have brought misfortune upon themselves. Consequently, it is the responsibility of people in need to help themselves (Harper, Wagstaff, Newton & Harrison, 1990).

For social psychologists adopting a cognitive approach, attributions are a core focus. Attribution errors are used to explain situations in which human beings make errors of judgement (Box 4.15). The documenting of such errors raises a number of interesting insights into intergroup relations and how erroneous thinking might be addressed. One simple strategy for reducing the risk of making an attribution error is to say to yourself, "How would I act in that situation?" Another strategy is to try to consider alternative explanations for a person's behaviour. We should also note that patterns of attribution are complex and variable. Recent research suggests that these perceptual processes may depend in part on the nature of the

BOX 4.14   Attribution bias

The concept of attribution bias explains the way that people frequently adopt a self-serving bias. Thus, people tend to give themselves credit for their successes by attributing these to internal factors, whereas they dismiss their failures by attributing them to external factors (Miller & Ross, 1975). You might attribute a good grade on this course to your intelligence, and a low grade to the poor quality of the textbook (or poor-quality lecturer – although as lecturers ourselves we don't want to go there!). This strategy would allow you to maintain your self-esteem (and give ours a battering). Another variant of the self-serving bias is group-serving bias. The difference is that the bias occurs between one's own social group and another. A meta-analysis of 266 studies revealed that this self-serving bias is fairly ubiquitous, except in some Asian cultures (Mezulis, Abramson, Hyde & Hankin, 2004). This bias reflects processes of affiliation, in that people tend to judge others favourably if they perceive them to be similar to themselves on key characteristics (e.g. whether or not they are a 'people person') (McElwee, Dunning, Tan & Hollmann, 2001) as well as the more obvious demographic characteristics, such as ethnicity, gender and age. Self-serving and group-serving biases are also linked to *confirmation bias*, which occurs when people search for evidence to confirm their own preconceptions and to avoid information that might contradict their existing assumptions about another person or group. Unfortunately, attribution errors are often foundational to intergroup relations, often justifying out-group discrimination and thus contributing to a social climate of mistrust. Attribution errors contribute to the homogenizing of other groups and the assumption that 'all those people are the same'. This has been a particular issue for indigenous people and immigrants in many countries.

groups involved, the character of the social interactions between groups over time and the additional groups interacted with. This has led some to question core findings from attribution research such as actor–observer bias as more variable phenomena than has previously been assumed. For example, Bazarova and Walther (2009) note:

Traditional attribution research tended to involve a perceiver who did not interact with the target. In contrast, recent research has incorporated several more interaction-based characteristics, which have had significant effects on attribution patterns. One such factor is having multiple targets for comparisons and how comparisons against base-rate behaviour affect attributions. (p. 144)

Such research more closely reflects actual social interactions, which often involve multiple people from multiple groups. Thus, the perceiver witnesses multiple sources of behaviour and information, which can create a base rate that he or she can use for comparison for any given individual's performance. Having observed multiple people, the perceiver has more information on what might be normal performance. Bazarova and Walther (2009) demonstrate that such factors influence dispositional and situational attributions in an online setting.

In moving out from the social cognitive approach in the remainder of this chapter we are not asserting that insights have not been

---

BOX 4.15   Interesting studies

There have been many studies into the automatic attributions people make in their everyday lives, particularly in regards to racism. Payne (2001) showed white research participants photographs of weapons and tools and asked them to identify these objects as quickly as possible. Each photograph was preceded by a picture of either a white or an African American face. The participants were significantly faster in identifying the weapons when they had been preceded by a picture of an African American face, and faster in identifying a tool when it was preceded by a white face. Judd, Blair and Chapleau (2004) varied Payne's experiment by adding types of pictures – sports equipment (believed to be positively associated with African Americans), fruit (positive but not associated with an ethnic group) and insects (negative and also not associated with an ethnic group) – and removing the pictures of white people. They found that the pictures of African Americans facilitated recognition of the stereotyped objects – both the positive and negative objects (the weapons and the sporting goods) – but not the other objects. The bad news: stereotypical assumptions were found to hold true; the good news: this also included positive stereotypes.

---

provided by the work reviewed above. Our point is that all approaches to social psychology are incomplete and constitute oversimplifications that ultimately contain omissions (cf. Billig, 2002). One particular oversimplification central to the social cognitive approach is the conceptualization of people as enclosed and independent thinkers. Other conceptualizations are being developed in an attempt to extend and add detail to the picture social psychology is painting of people and the social world within which they are enmeshed. These developments are important in ensuring that we avoid reducing complex social events, including conflicts, solely to the sense-making processes of individuals.

Beyond social cognition: Manuel does not think alone

North American social psychologists have themselves identified a tendency in their own culture to make fundamental attribution errors. This tendency involves assigning too much emphasis to internal aspects of individuals while ignoring situational factors and groups. For many people around the world, the idea that the North American-inspired social cognitive approach to social psychology overemphasizes individual cognitions is hardly groundbreaking news. We should not dismiss the insights into personal thought processes that the social cognitive approach has provided out of hand. After all, social cognitive research provides valuable insights into the ways people assign responsibility and often internalize individual blame for issues such as poverty and unemployment. Such insights have established the importance of psychosocial factors for the negative consequences of unemployment. However, we do not subscribe to the view that an individual's thoughts are the private products of a distinct mind interacting with other such distinct minds. Social psychology can provide additional insights beyond the mental representations predominant within the North America cultural context. Social psychology has much to offer our understanding of communal aspects of how people make sense of the world.

Addressing the limitations of the individualistic tendency in the social cognitive approach requires us to reconsider some of the underlying philosophical assumptions of our discipline. For instance, the social cognitive approach relies on a Cartesian mind–world dualism (Box 4.16). This dualism can lead to a sole focus on the production of knowledge in everyday life as an ongoing intra-psychic exchange between isolated individuals and objects in the world (Stam, Lubek & Radtke, 1998). This split between the individual and society is ongoing perennial issue in psychology (Christopher & Hickinbottom, 2008). At its core are assumptions about what people are and how they relate to the world outside of themselves. Jovchelovitch (2007) proposes that the conceptualization of the lonely knower positions the individual "as the core unit of experience in the West: we know alone and solitude can provide a zone of freedom from the mistakes and habits associated with customs and traditions that blur our vision and capacity to reach true knowledge" (p. 23). In this book we will not get bogged down in the specifics of the mind–world dualism (Box 4.16). However, it is worth briefly considering how we might move social psychology beyond the separation of mind and world. This is necessary because human thought involves much more than individual cognitive processes. People live somewhere (Chapter 6) and our very ideas are often based on the norms, values, myths and assumptions of our given cultures and communities (Chapter 5) and institutions such as the mass media (Chapter 11). Our ideas can exist and be refined outside of our heads.

In the last three decades, criticisms of sociocognitive approaches have highlighted a lack of adequate engagement with the complexity and fluidity of human thought as it occurs in everyday life. Researchers argue that sociocognitive approaches are too limited because they reduce human experience to asocial hypothetical constructs isolated inside the heads of individuals (Farr, 1996; Flick, 1998a; Gergen, 1985). This neglects the societal, cultural and historical origins of everyday knowledge. Many social constructionists propose that social categories do not reside solely in the minds of individuals and in fact exist in the world in the very language we draw upon to communicate (Wetherell, 1996). There is also a political reason for

BOX 4.16   Mind–world dualism

Central to the mind–world dualism is anxiety among philosophers such as Descartes regarding how we can be sure that our knowledge of the world actually reflects the world outside of our bodies. This uncertainty contributed to the development of a conceptualization of the self as an enclosed universe. This conceptualization underlies the social cognitive approach to social psychology and contemporary notions of schemas, stereotypes and attributions. The argument is that we cannot doubt the fact that our own minds are engaged in doubting all in the world outside of ourselves. Jovchelovitch (2007) notes that it in the loneliness of the cogito: "I think, therefore I am" Descartes (1641/1989) found certainty.

The mind and the mind alone was the only reality he could not doubt: "I am, I exist," is necessarily true each time it is expressed by me, or conceived in my mind. (Jovchelovitch, 2007, p. 20)

The perspective of the self as an enclosed universe takes knowledge out of community and interaction and places it within individual thinkers. People can think for themselves. However, through interaction and dialogue with others in the world people can test and revise their ideas. Social psychology needs to move aspects of knowledge back out into the community and the world, where knowledge is shared with others (Chapter 5) and manifest in material objects and places (Chapter 6). People construct their knowledge from somewhere, and that somewhere is often everyday life.

focusing beyond the individual mind. An individual focus can lead to victim blaming, which can divert our attention away from situational factors that contribute to the misery of so many people around the world. Rarely does a person choose to live in poverty. Social problems cannot be fully understood or accounted for in relation to individual dispositions and thoughts, as conceived by the early attribution theorists (Box 4.17).

Social psychologists have not adequately resolved the distinction between individual thought and collective knowledge production.

BOX 4.17   Interesting study

In an investigation of lay accounts of poverty, Harper (1996) argues that findings from research conducted within an attribution framework can be extended through research that explores the complex and socially derived character of people's experiences of unemployment. Given the psychosocial focus of recent health inequalities research (Chapter 8) and the emphasis on the link between understanding and social circumstances in determining health, the use of more contextually oriented approaches is appropriate (Cullen & Hodgetts, 2001). These alternative approaches provide a way of moving beyond the investigation of beliefs as individualized cognitions to the investigation of the ways in which human thought is communally produced through social interactions within specific material circumstances. This involves a shift in focus from the internal cognitive structures of individuals to the wider social processes, belief systems and cultural practices through which people construct their thoughts (cf. Flick, 1998b; Furnham, 1988; Moscovici, 1994, 1998).

One perspective is that shared meanings are the aggregate of individual understandings, which are shared through language. Another is that we have collective meaning systems that are reproduced through routine social interactions and practices. Social representations theory (Moscovici, 1981, 1994) constitutes one attempt to bridge the mind–world dualism by proposing that personal thought often derives from broader ideologies and dialogues within communities as people make sense of the world and events together.

Social representations theory

In this book, we argue that the causes of, and blame for, social issues such as unemployment do not lie solely at an individual level. Neither do we suggest that individuals are hapless victims of circumstances that are entirely beyond their control. We want to draw on a more flexible understanding of the human condition that acknowledges both structure and agency, while not elevating agency over structure or vice versa. Consequently, we need theoretical concepts that offer a different understanding of the self, knowledge and society. Social representations theory is one such theory in that it considers knowledge creation to be an ongoing socially embedded and inherently communal process. This is in contrast to seeing knowledge as either something possessed and contained at a discrete individual level or as an ideology imposed by powerful and amorphous structural forces onto the minds of individuals (Flick, 1998a, 2000b). In keeping with a core message in this chapter, social representations theory does not dismiss the existence of cognitions. Rather, the focus is on the social origins and locations of knowledge in everyday life. As we will demonstrate, much of the material on which individual engagements with the world are based is generated by social representations.

Serge Moscovici and colleagues (1972, 1981, 1994) have argued that human understanding and actions are essentially social and, therefore, that psychology needs to explore broader social processes in order to understand human thought and action. This theory of social knowledge is useful as a basis for exploring the continual refinement of human understandings of the world as it occurs within the everyday lives of particular communities (Moscovici, 1994). According to Jovchelovitch (2007), "the theory of social representations belongs to a tradition that I call the phenomenology of everyday life seeking to understand how ordinary people, communities and institutions produce knowledge about themselves, others and the multitude of social objects that are relevant to them" (p. 45). Social representations theory (Box 4.18) engages with the ways ideas and shared understandings cultivated through interactions in a community are taken up by its members and used to make sense of the world and their place in it.

BOX 4.18   Social representations theory

For Moscovici (1981, 1994, 1998), social representations can be conceptualized as the shared understandings that evolve through everyday communication and that provide frameworks for people to use when interpreting their own experiences and the experiences of other people. Thus, social representations are the shared ways of defining, categorizing and understanding topics such as unemployment that are evident in the language, metaphors, images, actions and daily practices of a given social group (Purkhardt, 1993). Social representations are malleable networks of ideas, images, values, practices that people elaborate upon in order to orient themselves within the world over time (Billig, 1993; Moscovici, 1994). According to this theory, social representations provide a basis for a culture. Culture is thought to be created by and through communication, and thus human actions acquire their meaning only relative to those who receive (or perceive) these actions and those who perform them. Social representations thus constitute cultural spheres of interaction between people. These cultural spheres reflect common understandings that help to build solidarity among collectivities. Social representations "have an existence to the extent that they are useful, circulate, take different forms in memory, perceptions, works of art, and so on, while nevertheless always being recognized as identical" (Moscovici, 1998, p. 244). These representations are impersonal because they belong to everyone. In keeping with our earlier discussion of social constructionism, social representations do not simply reflect an external world or reality; they shape and constitute that very world.

The consequence of adopting a social representations approach is that knowledge can be viewed in relation to the broader social, cultural and historical contexts in which it is used and produced. A primary focus for research is how knowledge is produced, used and transformed through ongoing social interactions within and across particular social groups (Box 4.19). Each of us is born into a community and, as noted in Chapters 2 and 3, becomes a human being through formal and informal processes of socialization. We learn to adopt specific rituals, daily practices and ways of seeing the world. We are enculturated in the midst of our daily lives and learn to speak the language and to make sense of the world and the people around us. We hopefully gain a sense of belonging and affiliation that becomes central to our sense of self and place (Chapter 6). Jovchelovitch (2007) states:

At the heart of community thus is the construction of intersubjective spaces that construct not only self but also the set of coordinated interrelations that produce phenomena such as communication and dialogue, social identities, social memory, public life and, linked to all of these, social knowledge. (p. 71)

Shared meaning systems or knowledge frames are part of the glue and connections that bind us into a life together and provide the basis for community. As was also noted in the previous chapter, we have a communal history that dates back to before our births and will continue well beyond our individual life spans. We have shared memories and often tell stories of 'who we are' and 'where we are from', 'what is important to us' and 'to whom we belong' (Chapters 5 and 6). It is often, though not always, reassuring to know where we are from and belong. In a time of crisis, Manuel is able to draw upon an alternative sense of self among fellow Filipino community members. This provides a sense of respect and place and a basis for countering the effects of living in a society containing people who are willing to stigmatize people simply for being unemployed.

Applying the social representations concepts of anchoring and objectification (Box 4.19), we might explain some of the reasons unemployment is often constructed as an illness in the accounts of people such as Manuel and in social psychological theories (Cullen & Hodgetts, 2001). Unemployment is anchored within the sets of meanings constructed in relation to illness. This construction often becomes objectified in government policies and direct interventions designed to address 'the needs' of unemployed people. For instance, Warr (1987) proposes a 'Vitamin Model' to explain the effects of environmental factors on the mental health of unemployed people as being analogous to mechanisms by which vitamins affect physical health. Such work has been instrumental in highlighting the plight of the unemployed and in providing a basis from which to lobby for improvements. However, it also contains the idea that unemployment is an 'abnormal' situation or the result of a deficit within individuals. This logic can be used to justify conservative and punitive public policies.

BOX 4.19   Anchoring and objectification

A key question asked by psychologists interested in social representations is how something unfamiliar gets transformed into the familiar. *Anchoring* and *objectification* are considered to be central to the process of social representation (Flick, 1998a, 2000b). Anchoring is a process of classification, of naming and categorizing strange or new ideas into ordinary categories and images. This resonates with Piaget's (1977) notion of accommodation, the process of taking on new knowledge and connecting it with existing categories, thereby expanding, transforming and reframing those categories. Anchoring is a social process that connects an individual to the social contexts and cultural traditions of his or her group. This mirrors the observation by Bartlett (1932) that when people make sense of fairytales from another culture they alter the details and story structure to fit their existing cultural narratives. The process of anchoring is particularly apparent in children, as they can come up with some very amusing ways of making sense of the adult world around them.

Objectification is the process of making something abstract easier to understand by connecting the idea to a concrete example, which can include images, objects or actions. Thus, in trying to make sense of something a little vague, such as the notion of a work ethic, people tend to look for concrete images, objects or actions that portray its presence or absence. In the absence of full information, we may decide that another person has or does not have a work ethic depending on whether that person has a university degree, maintains his or her employment and dresses conservatively as opposed to having dreadlocks and board shorts. Over time, we might come back to these concrete examples (due to anchoring) and come to see them as an objectified aspect of a person's work ethic or lack of one. Thus, a particular value can be imposed on a group as a characteristic of people belonging to that group. In this way stereotyping can be seen as a process of objectification. These stereotypes are not confined to the thoughts of individuals; they are also manifested in the world in the segregation of ethnic groups in specific neighbourhoods and the activities that occur there (see Chapter 9). These locations in themselves can become stigmatized through being identified with particular minority groups, and on the basis of perceived characteristics of such groups as being socially deviant, violent etc. This is an important point that demonstrates clearly how each of us does not construct our own categories out of thin air. We create these through the assimilation of ideas and knowledge available in the social world. Our ideas are culturally patterned within communities (Billig, 2002), and these categories or characterizations can take material form in the world.

In brief, from a social representations perspective people's knowledge is conceptualised as a reflection of common ways of making sense of events in the world that are evident within particular social groups, rather than simply being the product of cognitive processes. It is important to note that people are not conceptualised as passive 'cultural dupes' who simply parrot communal explanations in a predictable manner. A reciprocal relationship exists between social representations and individual thought (cf. Flick, 1998a). The social mediation of human experience is the result of both socially shared explanations and the innovations made when people reflect upon such explanations and employ them when making sense of the world. In other words, social representations are incomplete communal projects that are worked through as people employ various socially shared explanations to make sense of disputed topics such as unemployment (cf. Flick, 1998b). These representations provide insights into the collective assumptions and attributions held within particular groups of people. Social representations theory provides a framework for taking up the call for psychologists to trace the origins of the views of individuals back into the world. It is through the exploration of such processes that researchers can foreground the contingent, shifting and dialectical character of everyday knowledge and the processes through which it is constructed.

Investigating the knowledge of others: How do we engage with people such as Manuel?

Many social psychologists recognize and value the everyday knowledge produced by the groups with whom they engage as researchers and practitioners. Such knowledge provides rich insights into the complexities of daily life and a raft of social psychological processes. Incorporating knowledge from the everyday lives of people is imperative to developing a relevant and responsive social psychology (Chapters 1 and 5). As we will illustrate in this section, language is clearly important to the study of everyday knowledge (Billig, 2002). However, as we demonstrate in Chapter 6, we need to do more than analyse the verbal or written accounts of people. Research can also explore daily practices and how different groups of people act when they come into contact with each other. As we discussed earlier, this is apparent in the research on the racial re-segregation of beaches in South Africa. The perceptions and prejudices of some racial groups can manifest in particular practices, operating as more subtle influences on who goes to a public beach and who exits the beach when members of another group arrive (Chapter 6). As a result, social psychologists such as Dixon and colleagues (2008) emphasize the importance of exploring actual geographically located and embodied daily practices in order to understand the fluid and flexible nature of racism in society. Such research highlights how perceptions can become objectified in the everyday actions and physical proximity of people in the world.

An exploration of interactions between different groups can also be used to explore how different ways of understanding the world held within these groups can contribute to tensions and shape everyday interactions with other groups. The existence of diversity in terms of knowledge also raises issues of overlaps, comparisons, differences and communication between different forms of knowledge. Just how do we relate the knowledge of the participants in our research to our own theories and interpretations as social psychologists? We might ourselves be from the very groups we study (Box 4.20; Chapter 5). How can we, or indeed should we, separate our own personal views from the knowledge we aspire to create as social psychologists? These are core dilemmas in our discipline.

Different social groups, whether they are heavy metal fans, immigrants or social psychologists, can be conceived of as members of different interpretive communities (Throgmorton, 1991). As is

---

BOX 4.20   **Interesting study**

Snell and Hodgetts (2007) investigated the shared cultural practices, identity and everyday knowledge of a group of heavy metal fans who frequented a local bar. David Snell is a member of the heavy metal community and a regular bar patron. He shares the metaller identity with the research participants, wears the same T-shirts and black jeans and has similar tattoos. Insider status gives Dave access to the community, where he was able to negotiate an agreed research methodology using direct observation, participation in gigs, and photograph production and interview methods. The interviews and photographic exercises enabled participants to organize their experiences and provide coherent reflections on the heavy metal community and associated function of the bar. The analysis needed to look beyond specific photographs, transcripts or depicted instances to make broader observations of the ways in which social situations and relationships are rendered meaningful by participants. This proved difficult initially for Snell because he was so enmeshed in the community and was grappling with the multiple roles of bar patron and social psychologist (see Figure 4.1). As a hybrid researcher/participant, he is both a member of this community who participates in shared practices and an observer trying to document and interpret these practices, and to translate his interpretation into social psychological knowledge. This joint role required a balance between experiential insight and critical distance in the analytic process. Many of the practices and norms of this community are those which he took for granted and found difficult to articulate. Problems with achieving analytical distance were addressed through input from Darrin Hodgetts, who was unfamiliar with the metaller scene. Existing literature on community, media as practice, subcultures and geographies of exclusion was also drawn upon to create the necessary analytical distance to interpret community practices, artefacts and locales. This process is often referred to as defamiliarization and is a useful tool in the study of everyday life.

Figure 4.1. Dave Snell (left) with two research participants in the bar

illustrated in Box 4.20, we can be members of multiple interpretive communities and slide between these and their respective social representations as we conduct our lives and work. Each community has a shared language, conventions, customs, practices and rules through which group members make sense of the world. When members of a particular group encounter members of different interpretive communities, there is the potential for misunderstanding, attribution errors and stereotyping, but there is also a potential for dialogue and mutual respect. Bartlett (1932) identified the processes arising when different interpretive communities come into contact. Communities translate the knowledge of others into their own meaning systems or conceptual frames. As social psychologists, we talk about attribution errors and the prejudicial views of particular groups. Within social psychology there are many different interpretive communities. This book brings some of these communities, including those formed around social cognition, social representations theory, narrative theory and discursive psychology, into dialogue with our own experiences of interacting with people like Manuel or heavy metal fans. These dialectical processes are central to how social psychological knowledge is produced and reframed.

Traditionally, research on social cognition has operated as if it is itself a distinct interpretive community that has only fleeting engagements with 'subjects' from other interpretive communities as it does research 'on them'. This is a practice that is increasingly problematized in social psychology, in part because it constrains our ability to grasp the complexities of social psychological phenomena and respond to the lived realities of the people with whom we are working. Increasing emphasis is being placed on more engaged and dialogically oriented approaches to action research (Chapters 1 and 2). This involves moving away from *experience-distant* research towards more *experience-near* research (Jovchelovitch, 2007). This shift relies more on dialogue with people like Manuel than on assessments of them as a means of working towards common goals (Chapters 1 and 5). The remainder of this section outlines a general orientation towards how social psychologists can take seriously and engage with the knowledge of other people in the contexts in which it is embedded. In doing so, we offer an account of commonalities across contextually oriented theories that can guide such research.

Social psychologists and social scientists have recognized for some time that our investigations are never totally separate from the people and social processes we investigate (Christopher & Hickinbottom, 2008). Our interests and approaches to research arise from the cultural histories of our disciplines and communities. "There is, quite simply, no such thing as a value-neutral, culture-free psychology" (Christopher & Hickinbottom, 2008, p. 565). Such ideas are central to approaches such as liberation social psychology (Chapters 1 and 2) and lead to notions of working *with* rather than doing research *on* people (see Box 4.21; Chapter 10). Research is conducted with people because locals often have implicit knowledge of and theories about what is going on that can inform social psychological investigations (Christopher & Campbell, 2008).

One key aspect of social representations theory, discursive psychology and narrative theory is the emphasis placed on the dialogical relations between person and society and on how insights can be applied to furthering our understandings of, and addressing the needs of, people such as Manuel. Narrative theory provides a useful tool for examining the interwoven nature of individuals and society (Rappaport, 2000). Psychologists have argued that narrative should be the root metaphor for psychologies because stories are central to how people develop a sense of self and belonging (Mishler, 1995; Apfelbaum, 2000). A narrative approach is particularly useful for investigating the processes by which groups of people negotiate meaning commonality, organize themselves, maintain social relationships and take communal action (Rappaport, 2000). We can learn about shared everyday lives by exploring stories of belonging, mattering to others, sharing, togetherness, cooperation, support, reciprocity and inclusion. In Mankowski and Rappaport's (2000) view, "stories organize experience, give coherence and meaning to life events, and provide a sense of continuity, history, and of the future" (p. 481). Rappaport and colleagues suggested that stories can be understood at an individual level as a personal perspective that is generated from communal-level narratives or the accounts of events and common experiences that are held within a social group. A narrative approach provides insights into the function of power in the production and legitimation of knowledge (Mankowski & Rappaport, 2000). Those in powerful positions in a society often hold the resources to produce

BOX 4.21   Doing research with people

Research participants in social psychology are often positioned as the subjects of observation and inspection. In this context, research participants usually occupy a severely disempowered role – characterized by passivity and compliance. The label 'research subject' is still commonly used by social psychologists to describe the people they study, yet this label betrays assumptions about the passivity of the prescribed role. The social psychologist decides what questions to ask and where, when and how to ask them. The research data flow one way, from the participant to the researcher (indeed, a flow of information in the other direction is often regarded as methodologically problematic). Conversely, in some areas of social psychology, researchers may wish to reduce their power relative to the participant. This involves doing research *with* rather than *on* people.

dominant narratives, which can work to marginalize groups such as Manuel's immigrant community. Narratives that characterize immigrants as parasites stealing the jobs of true Americans have material implications in terms of de-legitimating the citizenship of people such as Manuel and legitimizing discriminatory practices that favour dominant social groups. These dominant narratives can be reproduced in the stories that people tell about themselves. That is, people can internalize the negative or positive stories that are told about them. Manuel starts to question his place in society and to become increasingly anxious about his abilities and whether he belongs. Rappaport (2000) illustrates how the negative expectations that teachers and others hold of African American students in school can in fact be internalized and act as narratives of terror. These 'tales of terror' can be challenged by local 'tales of joy'. These latter stories reflect the communal knowledge or social representations of minority groups. Manuel needs to re-story his situation and self in order to restore narrative integrity to his life. He can do so by tapping into his cultural identity and community. There is more to Manuel than his former role as a banker.

Another prominent approach within contemporary social psychology research into everyday knowledge is discourse analysis. This approach draws insights from a range of disciplines across the social sciences and humanities. Discursive psychology refers to several distinct approaches that share a focus on deconstructing shared meaning systems in society that are often manifest in written and spoken language and visual texts. The focus is on how social and political power relations are reproduced through discourse, and on how some people have more access than others to discursive resources that shape understanding and institutions in society. Critical discourse analysis is associated with the work of social psychologists such as Ian Parker (1992) who are influenced by the work of Michel Foucault and his book *The Archaeology of Knowledge*. More formalist and perhaps, to an extent, conversation-oriented discourse analysis is associated with the work of Jonathon Potter and Margaret Wetherell (1987). Common to discursive approaches is the view of language use as a key form of social practice and knowledge production in daily life. Discursive psychology developed, in part, as an alternative to social cognition and the focus on internal experiences such as attitudes and memories. It was argued that human thinking can be researched as an interactive process occurring in daily life through social interactions and language use (Box 4.22). Important to this perspective is that language is not viewed as an objective set of labels; rather, languages (including symbols, myths, customs) are systems that shape and organize how we experience things and make meaning of the world.

BOX 4.22 Need to focus beyond language to other daily practices

Some prominent variants of discourse analysis can lead to the reduction of social life to language use. Language is an important focus for research into everyday life. However, as many discursive psychologists would readily concede, we do not exist simply as speakers in a linguistic space. As important as language-based interactions are to social life, we also need to look beyond the talk and text. Discourse analysis often ignores material aspects of life and the role of objects and places in our daily existence. As was noted above, social psychologists need also to focus on material aspects of embodiment, objects and places if we are to understand human subjectivity, action and social life (cf. Stam, Lubek & Radtke, 1998).

To recap, it is through the functioning of interpretive communities and the interactions between these communities that societies think and produce collective ideas. This is where approaches in social psychology such as social representations theory, narrative theory and discursive theory come into their own. Such approaches focus on how different communities draw on different historically located cultural frameworks to make sense of the world. Researching these frameworks provides a means of understanding different communities, the things they value and the norms shaping their actions in everyday life. In the stories people tell we can witness their social knowledge, identities and ways of doing things 'around here', and how 'we' might differ from 'those other' folk (Rappaport, 2000). Within social psychology there is increasing acknowledgement of the difficulty of disconnecting knowledge from the interpersonal, social and cultural worlds in which it is produced (Jovchelovitch, 2007). This leads to a focus on the essential complexities that surround people and how these are woven into our lives and very being. These factors cannot be controlled for as they constitute fluid and changing processes. The approach to engaging with everyday knowledge we advocate requires a broadly humanistic perspective (Chapter 10) that values the legitimacy of everyday knowledge and the intelligence and creativity of the groups producing such knowledge.

Chapter summary

When going about daily life, people have to make sense of the world around them. This sense-making process is central to the production of knowledge and in turn shapes the nature of events in particular communities and historical periods. The range of sense-making processes people engage in spans navigating one's city or town, making judgements about other people and perhaps engaging with social psychologists in a research project. These processes also span individual thought processes and communal understandings, norms, values and cultural practices. In this chapter, we have reviewed some core ideas from social psychology that can inform our understanding of everyday knowledge. This is an important point, because central to social psychology is an effort to understand the understandings and social practices of other people.

It has been important for us to acknowledge the complex, slippery and contested nature of knowledge as a core concept in social psychology. We have provided an overview of an approach to knowledge that is communal in character and that allows us to avoid focusing solely on the intra-psychic experiences of individuals. Knowledge is produced in daily life, and our interpretations of it need to take circumstances into account. We also need to consider how different forms of knowledge from science, common sense, religion and superstition are woven together as people make sense of their worlds. We have not explored this issue as much as we might have because it raises a number of philosophical debates that require more sophisticated elaboration than we can undertake in this book. What we would signal is the need for you to read more about the philosophy and social psychology of knowledge. What you have been provided with in this chapter is simply an introduction to the topic. It is the best possible explanation that we could come up with at this point in time. We expect that as social psychologists of everyday life you will challenge, reflect and elaborate as you seek to understand your social world and the worlds of others.

We have noted that the dominant approach to studying everyday knowledge in social psychology has provided a range of insights into schemas and the ways in which new information is incorporated into existing knowledge structures. We have discussed how people make judgements and attributions and construct stereotypes of people different from themselves. Such issues are grist to the mill of contemporary social psychology and inform our work on social justice and inclusion in later chapters. According to the social cognitive approach, stereotypes, attitudes and attributions are a core focus for social psychology and for understanding intergroup relations. It is, for example, by making attributions that people assign causes to the behaviour of others. We have, however, discussed the limitations of the social cognitive views of the past few decades on knowledge as individualized information processing. The result of this disciplinary tendency has been that the cultural, historical and geographical location of communal knowledge in everyday life is often neglected. There is more to knowledge production and use than information processing. We do not sit outside, and make sense, of society as external observers. If we accept this premise, then it is time to move beyond the Cartesian mind–world dualism and to explore the production of knowledge in daily life.

While not wanting to dismiss the valuable contributions made by social psychologists adopting the social cognitive approach, we have provided alternative perspectives that attempt to move beyond the focus on individuals' heads to 'resocialize' everyday knowledge as also existing 'out there' in the world. By referring to social representations theory, discursive theory and narrative theory, we have illustrated how the production and application of everyday knowledge can be approached as a communal, and not just an individual, process. Yet there is also a sense of change within social cognitive research as narrative and discursive approaches have brought back into sight the dialogical nature of people's lives and the ways in which people are woven into and developed within the world.

We are tied into the world and gain a sense of belonging and self through the use of shared meaning systems. These communal narratives can give us a sense of history and commitment to others that provides the basis of so much that is valuable and rewarding in life. These narratives are central to understanding the production of not only knowledge, but also people as human beings in everyday life. Foundational to our disciplinary engagements with the knowledge of interpretive communities out there in everyday life is the valuing of diversity and the recognition that our thoughts (and social psychologies) are only one way of making sense of the world. In the following chapter, we pick up on this issue in relation to the re-emergence of indigenous social psychologies and how these relate to the discipline as a whole.

In this book we advocate a broad strategic approach linking knowledge, research and action, which is reflected in each of the subsequent chapters. This approach involves:

1. Exploring relationships between people, communities, places and societies
2. Promoting the application of social psychological insights as a means of preserving and enhancing human dignity and social justice
3. Facilitating self-determination among oppressed groups and the development of effective strategies that ensure collective wellness

This approach requires methodological pluralism that may include experiments, but also a range of other research strategies to reflect the uncertain and provisional nature of our knowledge of the world and the social psychological processes we study. Social psychologists of everyday life need to acknowledge the enmeshed nature of our research within cultural, historical and material climates within which people conduct their daily lives together.

Review exercise

Think back to when you enrolled in your first psychology course. You may have already had some idea of what psychology is.

- Where did you get these ideas?
- How accurate were they?
- Was your representation of psychology based on a stereotype of a typical psychologist?
- If there were inaccuracies, how did they occur?

Note

1. We need to remember that the computer analogy is just a metaphor and does not mean that people actually make meaning like a machine.

5 Indigenous psychologies and the social psychology of everyday life

Core questions to consider while reading this chapter

- What makes a person indigenous?
- Why is culture important in social psychology?
- What is acculturation?
- Can you explain the process of enculturation?
- Why are processes of colonization important for the social psychology of everyday life?
- What is the difference between etic and emic approaches to knowledge production?
- What is minority group influence?
- Can you explain the cobweb self?

Chapter scenario

Sue and William are in their mid-thirties and live in a tribal housing project in Localville. The city of 200,000 people stands on the traditional lands of their ancestors. They are happy to be raising Mike (aged eleven) and Anna (aged ten) in this place. This morning, the family is visiting the indigenous health centre across the road. The centre has been running for three years. It was set up with compensation funds that the tribe received from the government as the result of a long-standing legal battle over the theft of the land that Localville is built on. Tribal leaders have been investing in health care, education programmes and local business ventures. Sue comments to William, "It's good that we can come here and get the kids checked out. We could have done with this place when we were children." William: "Yeah, seeing our people helping each other is a really good thing for them. Uncle Bob is coming today, and the nurse wants us to help out with managing his diabetes." Sue: "Makes sense; if we want his diet to change then we probably all need to think about supporting him and changing as well." William: "As long as I still get pork ribs on Saturdays, I'm down with that." As they enter the car park, Mike recognizes his cousin Nigel, and Anna runs off to play with the girls from the cultural group. Sue and William enter the building knowing that the kids are happy playing with family until it is their turn to be seen by the doctor. There are plenty of children playing outside, as the local total immersion school is located on the same premises. Bob is their oldest living relative, at seventy-five years of age. "How's that boy of ours, William?" asks Bob. "Good he's out there with Nigel throwing a ball around," William replies. Bob: "Good mates those two, hey." "How are you feeling Bob?" asks Sue. Bob replies, "A lot better now that I'm seeing the doc here. That boy actually understands me, and it makes such a difference to be able to speak in your own language." Bob then recounts how the clinic staff have asked him to help out with a mentoring programme for local youth. "I'm getting a real kick out of helping. This place really shows what we can do for our people when we have the opportunity." Ronald (the doctor) comes out to meet them all. Ronald is a cousin of Sue's, and his son Nigel attends the school with Mike and Anna. The children are called in, and the consultation continues with the doctor, a traditional healer, a nurse and the family.

This scenario invokes a young family's relationship with a local indigenous health centre in the context of a tribal community that has been severely impacted by colonization. The clinic is linked with the family members as individual users of the service and as people who have complex interconnected relationships within the broader indigenous community. As community spaces, the clinic, school and housing facility reflect the interconnectedness of aspects of indigenous people's lives. Efforts to promote health (see Chapter 8) are enhanced at a community level through the creation of such spaces for interaction and caring. The existence of these spaces highlights the tribe's progressive orientation in providing immediate healthcare alongside education and cultural development. The emphasis on the interconnections between aspects of people's lives, relationships and places sets the stage for the exploration of indigenous world views, indigenous selves and optimistic futures.

The scenario invokes core themes explored in this chapter in terms of colonization, decolonization and the preservation of indigenous knowledges, practices and identities. We will focus on both the consequences of colonization for indigenous peoples and their resilience and ability to respond, preserve their heritage and maintain a sense of self and place (Chapters 6 and 10). The broad focus on and recognition of links between indigenous lives, colonization and health are crucial for developing a responsive social psychology of relevance to the daily lives of such people. After all, as a result of colonization, local indigenous people die on average seven years younger than members of settler societies, and indigenous citizens are more likely to suffer from a range of contagious and chronic diseases, violence, poverty and homelessness (Hanselmann, 2001; Waldram, Herring & Kue Young, 2006). As will be discussed in Chapter 8, health inequalities are not reducible to the individual health-related behaviour patterns of indigenous peoples. They relate more directly to social determinants of health, including social stratification.

Many processes affecting the lives of indigenous peoples, despite having political and economic dimensions, are fundamentally psychological in nature. These include processes of colonization and decolonization, mainstreaming and domination, discrimination and prejudice, adaption and culture change, and connectedness. Social psychologists have often responded to the concerns of indigenous people in a manner that has not been as effective as it could have been. Indeed, some actions have contributed to the continued colonization of indigenous peoples. Effectiveness has been limited, in part, because we have assumed certain things, such as a common understanding of the nature of self, and that this common understanding is shared between social psychologists and the people with whom we work. Sometimes it is, but more often than not understandings diverge across our own interpretive communities (Chapter 4). Different cultures have different perspectives on the nature of individuals and groups and on the extent to which people and environments influence us. In fact, the very notion of a separation of individuals and environments is a particularly Western and historically recent one (Chapters 2 and 3).

This chapter illustrates that there is not just one legitimate approach to social psychology or to understanding the people involved in our scenario. Extending the discussion of Western social psychology, the chapter provides an account of indigenous psychologies. These psychologies offer broad orientations to the social world, the place of different people in it and frameworks for conceptualizing social relations. This chapter does not constitute an attempt simply to appropriate knowledge from indigenous communities into social psychology. Rather, our goal is to expand the possibilities in the discipline to include different ways of thinking about, understanding and approaching social psychological phenomena. The chapter is about valuing and including capacities from new world and Asian contexts in order to increase the inclusiveness and relevance of social psychology. This is important because indigenous psychologies remain marginalized in the broader discipline of psychology. The omission of insights from indigenous psychologists from many texts constitutes a missed opportunity. In short, indigenous psychologies offer a means for broadening social psychological engagements with how people think and act in various cultural and historical contexts every day.

Chapter overview

The first section considers what it means to be indigenous. We cannot escape a discussion of processes of colonization as being central to the lives of indigenous peoples. The second section explores processes of colonization and draws upon the voices of indigenous scholars and leaders. The third section considers indigenous cosmology and acculturation. The fourth section discusses the place of indigenous voices in psychology. What is crucial at this point is a discussion of the process of indigenization as a means of developing local psychologies. The fifth section examines the relationship between emerging indigenous psychologies and the global discipline of psychology. The sixth section relates processes of colonization to the need to decolonize psychology, and in doing so draws on the example of psychological testing and culturally appropriate assessment. The seventh section explores issues of the self and the ways in which many indigenous notions of the interconnected self are compatible with concepts emanating from the collectivist stream of Western social psychology, such as the dialogical self. The chapter is completed with a brief summary section. The three key themes of this chapter are:

- The origins and nature of indigenous psychology (psychologies)
- The need to decolonize psychology
- The importance of the interconnected self (selves)

Indigenous peoples

Indigenous communities, peoples and nations are those which, having a historical continuity with pre-invasion and pre-colonial societies that developed on their territories, consider themselves distinct from other sectors of the societies now prevailing in those territories, or parts of them. They form at present non-dominant sectors of society and are determined to preserve, develop and transmit to future generations their ancestral territories, and their ethnic identity, as the basis of their continued existence as peoples, in accordance with their own cultural patterns, social institutions and legal systems. (Martinez, 1995, p. 86)

Two prominent narratives characterize the histories of indigenous peoples and Martinez's (1995) effort to conceptualize the term 'indigenous peoples'. The first, reflected in the first part of the quotation, tells of how indigenous peoples, their territories, environments, ways of life and worldviews have been impacted by invading or colonizing groups. For those whose voices have not been forever silenced by the resulting trauma and discrimination, the second narrative tells of struggle, survival, adaption, resilience and self-determination in the face of invasion and globalization. This is an important aspect of the latter part of the extract from Martinez (1995). Continuity of a connection to land and sustaining ecologies and ways of life remain important and are, in many instances, critical to the survival of indigenous peoples. Indigenous people are resilient (Chapter 10) – frequently surprisingly so in light of the destruction of food sources and social systems, and in some cases mass slaughter, oppression, poverty and persistent ill health. This resilience is dependent on a capacity to change, to make adaptations, to harness new technologies and to remain self-determining. The health clinic in the opening scenario is a manifestation of such community resilience.

Nobody knows exactly how many indigenous societies there are in the world. Some suggest around 7,000 (Hughes, 2003); others as few as 5,000 (International Labour Organization, 2009, p. 9). Estimates depend on whether the figures include subgroups or enumerate only those groups that fall within the official working definitions of various governments. Worldwide there are at least 350 million people considered to be indigenous, including the forest peoples of the Amazon, the tribal peoples of India, the Inuit of the Arctic and the Aboriginal peoples in Australia. One key point to recognize is the mobility of indigenous peoples, as they can remain indigenous to the areas in which their cultures and languages were developed even when residing away from those areas. This is an important point because many indigenous peoples have been forced to leave their own lands. The term 'indigenous' includes those who self-identify as being indigenous and whose claims of belonging are recognized by other groups. Criteria used to describe indigenous people include place, history, ethnicity and culture. Many indigenous people live in fourth world contexts (e.g. in New Zealand, Australia, the United States and Norway) (Box 5.1).

BOX 5.1   Fourth world

'Fourth world' is a term used to refer to a subgroup of a population that faces social exclusion. The term is often associated with nomadic and hunter–gatherer peoples living outside advanced capitalist economic systems, even when they reside in nation-states with such systems. 'Fourth world' refers to marginalized or stateless peoples. It refers to non-recognized nations that exist without states. People in these contexts are characterized by having remained 'in place' for centuries; having their own unique cosmologies, worldviews, cultural life ways; and actively identifying as indigenous peoples. In addition, their worlds are in continued interaction with and reaction to the nation-states in which they are embedded and that have resulted from the process of colonization (Manuel & Posluns, 1974).

Claims to, and the affirmation of, cultural identities and rights to particular places by indigenous peoples are common responses to colonial experiences of oppression. Claims to indigenous identities can be interpreted as a form of 'strategic essentialism' and efforts to regain sovereignty over one's sense of self and place in the face of ongoing pressure by a settler society (cf. Dudgeon & Fielder, 2006; Martin, 2003; Moreton-Robinson, 2003). These identity claims are tied to political projects aimed at achieving social justice (Chapter 9) within a broader social and historical context of colonialism and ongoing oppressive race relations. These claims are strategic and offer a form of authenticity, a sense of belonging and the basis for gaining human rights (Smith, 1999).

Colonization and the consequences for indigenous peoples

Processes of colonization remain central to the lives of many indigenous peoples and are of direct relevance to social psychology. Colonization involves the invasion of an area by some new group leading to the subjugation and displacement, both 'in' and 'out' of place, of the existing indigenous peoples (Box 5.2). It often occurs when a nation-state seeks to extend its sovereignty and does so by establishing colonies that expand to exploit the resources of an invaded area. Resources include land, minerals, forests and fisheries. The term 'colonization' also refers to situations where the population of an area is subjugated by a new group. This can occur through confining people within a particular geographical area or reservations. The process can also involve the displacement of existing indigenous groups who are moved and assimilated into the rules and practices of the settler society.

BOX 5.2   Colonization

Colonization is often associated with genocide, which usually results from the actions of authoritarian governments or groups who dehumanize and seek to exterminate indigenous groups. This occurred in Tasmania in Australia in the nineteenth century when the indigenous people were hunted and killed by British settlers (McPherson & Manuta Tunapee, 2005). Colonization is also associated with segregation (Chapter 6). This involves the separation of different groups in activities of daily life, such as eating in a restaurant, drinking from a drinking fountain, using a rest room, attending school and going to the movies, or in the rental or purchase of a home.

In developing a local liberation psychology in response to ongoing processes of colonization, the Filipino indigenous psychologist Enriquez (1995) proposed that colonization involves six stages of cultural domination (cf. Dueck, Ting and Cutiongco, 2007):

1. The colonizer denies the existence of a local culture and dismisses the legitimacy of indigenous legal and education systems, while also promoting the settler culture and institutions. Local languages are suppressed and the language of the colonizer is imposed on indigenous groups.
2. The colonizer destroys local cultural artefacts and desecrates sacred sites. The culture is further decimated.
3. The colonizer marginalizes and denigrates local peoples. Traditional cultural practices are dismissed as being primitive.
4. Traditional cultural practices are tolerated in a limited manner in that some dance forms and songs are assimilated into the settler society and in the process are redefined.
5. The settler society draws selectively on elements of the indigenous culture (e.g. medicines and healing practices).
6. The settler society exploits aspects of the indigenous culture for commercial gain.

Colonization is not a new process; it is one that has occurred throughout human history. The ancient Roman and Chinese empires were founded on conquest and colonization. The city of London was a key site for this process, being founded by the Romans as the city of Londinium. From the time of Christ onwards, and over a 400-year period, parts of England were subjected to colonization by the Romans. Centuries later, the English were to engage in extensive processes of colonization in establishing the British Empire. All such histories of colonization reveal how power relations between different ethnic groups are complex and often contradictory. For example, English people engaged in a campaign of highland clearances in which Scottish clans were gathered up, forced to the coast and exported from their home territories to the British colonies. These expulsions occurred between the eighteenth and nineteenth centuries, as part of a process that sought the disarmament of the clans, the depopulation of traditional rural areas and the enculturation of clans-folk into the newly formed agricultural sector and British economic system (Prebble, 1963). Members of these clans were in turn pro-actively involved in the colonization of countries such the Americas, South Africa, New Zealand and Australia (Box 5.3).

The impact of colonization is still felt by indigenous peoples today in locations in Africa, the Americas, Asia and the Pacific, and its history can be traced to the expansion of European powers from the 1800s onwards. Despite diversity in location and culture, common experiences and issues stemming from colonization are evident across different indigenous groups. Colonization often involves the loss of language and culture, rights, identity and

BOX 5.3   Consequences of colonization

Many indigenous societies have been significantly affected by processes of colonization. These are often processes of cultural, social and economic domination and assimilation. Moane (2009) analysed colonialism and identified six mechanisms in the establishment of domination. These mechanisms have significant implications for social psychological functioning and are:

- Violence involving force, conquest invasion and occupation of territory
- Political exclusion from voting and representation, and restrictions of assembly
- Economic exploitation, which includes low-paid labour, taxes, seizure of land and restrictions on trade
- Sexual exploitation, which includes prostitution, rape, sexual slavery and control of women's sexuality
- The control of culture, including restrictions on using and expressing indigenous languages, art, systems of representation, stereotyping, othering and denial of voice
- Fragmentation of community and division along ethnic, religious and linguistic lines

resources. In this regard, it is an ongoing process for future generations, who have often been dislocated from their history and home territories through forced migration and 'education'. In colonial settings, colonization is associated with the disruption of place-based identities (Chapter 6), sense of control and self-efficacy. It involves the treatment of indigenous people as ethnic minorities by the settler society and the loss of sovereignty. Core challenges faced by many indigenous peoples include reducing discrimination, poverty and disparities in health (Chapter 8) and improving education. Indigenous groups must work to overcome oppression and social exclusion, to dispel stereotypes and to gain autonomy and access to resources. The scenario at the beginning of this chapter reflects the progressive possibilities of efforts by indigenous groups to respond to the legacies of colonization and to remake their lives together.

Despite commonalities of process, colonization can be experienced differently by different peoples and in different places. It is possible to separate processes of colonization into two phases: colonization in the 'old world' and in the 'new world' (http://www.un.org/WCAR/e-kit/indigenous.htm). If a point in time were to be established between old and new world acts of colonization, then 1492, the year that Christopher Columbus reached the islands of the 'new world', would mark that point. The old world is the world that Christopher Columbus sailed from, a world with knowledge of Europe, Asia and Africa and a long history of encounters between peoples, resources, lands and markets. The new world was the one that Columbus and subsequent 'discoverers' set sail to. For the old world, exposure to the new world held the promise of more prosperous and powerful empires. For the new world, it inevitably meant long-term subjugation, exploitation, dispossession and domination by some more powerful old world nations. An account of such experience by a Hawaiian scholar (Box 5.4) raises the importance of history and cosmology to understanding indigenous peoples and the situations they often find themselves in today.

Like people in many other new world nation-states, readers in the United States are often taught to celebrate the settling of the country and not to think of themselves as living within a colonial nation. For this reason we have included inserts from prominent indigenous

---

BOX 5.4 Importance of history in understanding indigenous peoples

Geologists tell us that the Hawaiian archipelago was created by volcanic activity and natural erosion over the millennia. Anthropologists tell us that the Kānaka Maoli (meaning true or real humans and used to refer to all Hawaiians today) are descendents of early Polynesians who migrated out of Southeast Asia and Malaysia, and eventually settled in Hawai'i about 2,000 years ago. However, our kūpuna (ancestors) have a different account of our existence. They tell us that the islands of Hawai'i-nui-ākea (the great and vast Hawai'i) were born of the gods – Papa-hānau-moku (mother earth) and Wākea (sky father) – and that all Kānaka Maoli share a common genealogical lineage to Hāloa – the first human. And because of this, our kūpuna were part and parcel of the 'āina (land) that nurtured them, of the kai moana (ocean) that surrounded them, and of the lewa (space) that embraced them.

We contemporary Kānaka Maoli are direct descendants of ancient Kānaka Maoli who inhabited the islands of Hawai'i for nearly 2,000 years. Although we are no longer biologically and socio-culturally homogenous as were our kūpuna, we still maintain the traditional values and beliefs that connect us to our 'āina and our mo'okū'auhau (ancestral lineage). We continue to hold fast to our unique identity and way of life as a distinct ethno-cultural group amidst a multi-ethnic society that now comprises Hawai'i. And, like our kūpuna, we continue to believe that our physical, emotional, and spiritual wellbeing are directly tied to our 'āina, kai moana, and lewa. As were our kūpuna, we are the younger siblings of Hawai'i. We are Kānaka Maoli. Huli Aku, Huli Mai: Change Was Not for the Better

Lawe li'ili'i ka make a ka Hawai'i, lawe nui ka make a ka haole
Death by Hawaiians takes a few at a time; death by foreigners takes many.

The Kānaka Maoli world, as our kūpuna understood it to be, was forever altered in the year 1778 – the year Kānaka Maoli were fortuitously introduced to the western world. This was the year Captain James Cook haphazardly came across the Hawaiian archipelago. The writings of Cook and his crew shed some light on the health and social status of our kūpuna at the beginning of contact between these two worlds. They observed that the inhabitants of the islands of Hawai'i were "above middle size, strong, well made and of a dark copper color, and…a fine handsome set of people" (Beaglehole, 1967, p. 1178). On a socio-psychological note, these fair-skin strangers also observed that Kānaka Maoli were "truly good natured, social, friendly, and humane, possessing much liveliness and…good humour" (Beaglehole, 1967, p. 1181). By these first-hand accounts, it is clear that our kūpuna at the dawn of western contact were physically and emotionally healthy.

By healthy, I mean the absence or very low prevalence of chronic medical (e.g., obesity and diabetes), psychological (e.g., depression), and social (e.g., poverty and marginalization) diseases (for a review of the pre-western contact health status of Kānaka Maoli see Blaisdell, 1993). This is in sharp contrast to the poor health status of contemporary Kānaka Maoli.

Current United States (US) and State of Hawai'i health data indicate that we Kānaka Maoli, as an ethnic group, have the worst health and social status compared to all other ethnic groups in Hawai'i and most other ethnic groups in the US (for a review of the health status of contemporary Kānaka Maoli see Johnson, Oyama, LeMarchand & Wilkens, 2004). We are among the most impoverished, undereducated, and socially disadvantaged people in our own homeland (Marsella, Oliveira, Plummer & Crabbe, 1995). We have the highest rates of chronic medical diseases such as diabetes, heart disease, and certain types of cancers of most ethnic groups in the continental US and Hawai'i. We have the poorest health behaviors as reflected in the high prevalence of cigarette smoking, drug and alcohol use, and obesity (State of Hawai'i Behavioral Risk Factor Surveillance System [BRFSS], 2003). It is suspected that we Kānaka Maoli also suffer from high rates of emotional distress (Crabbe, 1999; Marsella et al., 1995). Consequently, our overall mortality and morbidity rates far exceed those of most other US ethnic groups. Indeed, the poor health condition of contemporary Kānaka Maoli is a far cry from the excellent health condition our kūpuna enjoyed before the arrival of foreigners to Hawai'i. What has happened to us Kānaka Maoli to create such an ominous circumstance?

Source: Extracted reproduced with permission from: Kaholokula, J.K. (2007). Colonialism, acculturation, and depression among Kanaka Maoli of Hawai'i. In P. Culbertson, M.N. Agee & C.O. Makasiale (Eds.), *Penina Uliuli: Contemporary Challenges in Mental Health for Pacific Peoples* (pp. 180–195). Honolulu: University of Hawaii Press. See original publication for the details of references cited herein.

scholars (Box 5.4) and leaders (Box 5.5) from within the US jurisdiction. Later, we will refer to work emerging out of the Philippines (Box 5.8), a country with a long history of oppression as a colony of Spain and more recently the United States. When Filipinos refused to submit to the United States following the Spanish American war, more than 100,000 people paid with their lives (Dueck, Ting & Cutiongco, 2007).

BOX 5.5   An account of the situation of the Navajo People in the USA

The Navajo People believe in President Obama's call for change in our country. His inspiring statement of belief conveys the same thought taught to generations of Navajos that there are no impossibilities in life. Our grandparents have always told us "T'áá hó ájít'éegó," and President Obama's election shows how true that teaching is and remains. It speaks to Native nations in our determination to do for ourselves, to regain the independence that was lost so long ago, and to hold on to our beloved homelands, languages, sacred songs, ceremonies, and ways of life. With this renewed sense of hope, we have worked hard in the hope of taking advantage of the $825 billion economic and infrastructure stimulus package that President Obama has proposed for the country.

We have prepared and submitted a $2.9 billion stimulus package on behalf of the Navajo Nation. I thank the members of the Intergovernmental Relations Committee for their valued input and approval of the request submitted to the Obama-Biden Transition Team and the 111th Congress.

While I believe the heart of the Obama Administration is with us, as always, we must begin by telling others who the Navajo People are, and how we live, that Navajoland is the largest among Native nations, equal in size to the New England states of Connecticut, Rhode Island, Massachusetts and Vermont. We need them to know that within the vast space of our homeland there are too few employers for our people, thousands of miles of rough dirt roads that are traveled daily and inadequate means of communication. As other Americans deal with the national financial crisis in their ways, more than half of our families still heat their homes with wood they cut themselves, drink water hauled in barrels in pickup trucks, while many of our students do their homework each night by the light of kerosene and gas lanterns. Our people's wealth is not measured by what's in a savings or retirement account, but by what's in their sheep corral or held in a border town pawn shop. Still, our people need an income, a home and a vehicle, and most struggle as best they can to make their payments. Ironically, the Navajo Nation is at the geographic centre of the fastest-growing region of the United States. We are at the very crossroads of Albuquerque to the east and Las Vegas to the west, Denver to the north and Phoenix to the south. We are a corridor for energy, for food products, for manufactured goods, and for national defense. Railroad cars and interstate highways carry untold cargo and passengers along our boundaries. Truck stops, depots and train stations just beyond our reach to realize any benefit are laden with prosperity meant for others. We are encircled by more national parks and tourist destinations than anyplace else in the country.

No place and no people are more deserving of the help an economic stimulus program could provide than Navajos. In the past, when American farmers received federal subsidies, Navajos received federal live-stock reduction that dispirited every family. When we see American financial institutions and auto-makers receive multi-billion dollar federal bailouts to fix problems of their own making, Navajos recall a federal law that halted home repairs and the slightest development for 40 years, and another that forced 10,000 of our most traditional people to relocate from their homes to resolve a problem they did not cause.

Source: Extracted from 'State of the Navajo nation address' by president Joe Shirley, JR. Presented to the 21st Navajo Nation Council, January 26, 2009 (pp. 2–3); http://opvp.org/cms/kunde/rts/opvporg/docs/622850067–01-30–2009-09–22-53.pdf.

Indigenous cosmologies and acculturation

The content of Box 5.4 raises the point that indigenous peoples have many and diverse origin narratives, also known as cosmologies. These seek to explain the existence of the universe, our relationship to and purpose in it and what will become of us (Kaholokula, 2007). Cosmologies answer the questions:

- Who am I?
- Where do I fit in?
- Where am I going?
- What are the important things to do?

For many Europeans of the old world, these questions were answered through Judeo-Christian beliefs in one God, who created heaven and earth and all that is between, including humankind. This dominant cultural narrative has come to displace or at least alter indigenous cosmologies.

Consideration of the cosmologies of indigenous peoples is crucial for developing understandings of indigenous worldviews. These cosmologies are central to the psychologies of indigenous peoples. For the indigenous Polynesian peoples of the Pacific, questions regarding who, where and what are also answered within the framework of cosmological and historical precedent. Such precedents explain and position Pacific peoples as tribal, island or village beings, who explore lives together before returning to Hawaiki, the place of ancestors, upon death. They prescribe relationships such as those with the land, sky and sea and to the flora and fauna found therein. Kinship relationships carry responsibilities that are also prescribed. The firstborn is obligated to care for younger siblings, and younger siblings carry a responsibility to support and respond positively to the guidance and care of older siblings (Ritchie & Ritchie, 1985, p.189). Among the Maori people of New Zealand, it is accepted that one's ancestors remain as an ongoing presence and influence in one's life (Box 5.6).

Cosmologies are modified across generations, always in parallel with the modern world, and serve to structure human existence, providing ways of knowing, understanding, relating, valuing and being. They are also a basis for responding to, and resisting, colonization and associated processes of acculturation (Box 5.7). Such cosmologies offer

---

BOX 5.6   Ancestor worship

Fundamentally, ancestor worship refers to the belief in, and often the propitiation of, the spirits of the dead. These dead are not, however, merely generalized ghosts. Instead, there is the belief that the spirits of one's dead kinsmen are of special concern. Thus, Bradbury insists that we should confine ancestor worship to those instances in which there is a genealogical relationship between the spirits and the living. The involvement of these spirits in human life differs from one society to another. Ancestor worship can be classified in terms of the degree to which the ancestors involve themselves with their descendants. One such classification has been suggested by Swanson and a modified version of it will be adopted here. The activity of the ancestors is of course at its weakest when this religious type is totally absent. The next level is otiose ancestor worship, in which the ancestors are believed to exist and are aware of the activities of their living descendants but refrain from acting in the lives of those descendants. Active ancestor worship exists when the ancestors are involved in the lives of their descendants but do so on a largely capricious basis – for example, compliance or failure to comply to kinship obligations is not linked to rewards or punishments from the ancestors. The strongest form of ancestor worship, supportive ancestor worship, obtains when the ancestors involve themselves in the lives of their descendants and reward or punish for fulfilling, or failure to fulfill kinship obligations.

Source: Sheils (1975, p. 428).

BOX 5.7   Acculturation

'Acculturation' is a general term used to describe processes by which a particular culture, or a minority group, comes to adopt the cultural knowledge, practices and language of another culture – often that of a dominant group. Acculturation is central to processes of colonization in that indigenous peoples are assimilated, to varying degrees of totality, into the settler society and are expected to adopt the values and practices of this new culture. Acculturation occurs through ongoing contact between the groups and involves a process of resocialization and learning (Chapters 2 and 3). Ideally, cultures should be in dialogue with each other, sharing understandings and enhancing options for addressing complex social issues. Unfortunately, contact usually involves domination of one culture over another. Dominant groups can often function with little or no understanding of minority and indigenous cultures with whom they share a society.

'Enculturation' refers to the process of adaption by which people learn the values, norms and requirements of the surrounding culture and as a result are able to function within that culture (Grusec & Hastings, 2007). This process shapes who each of us becomes and is associated with the cultivation of 'acceptable' and 'functional' members of a cultural group. It is thought to occur through both conscious and unconscious means. The term 'inculturation' is often used interchangeably with 'acculturation' and 'socialization'.

Despite the efforts of the dominant groups to pacify local populations, indigenous groups are not simply passive in the acculturation process. Minority groups can and do act strategically in their interactions with dominant groups (Lewin, 1948). Strategies undertaken by minority groups in response to acculturation include assimilation, integration, separation and marginalization (Rudmin, 2003). Members of indigenous groups may differ in their responses: some may attempt to assimilate fully into the dominant culture; others may defy assimilation and defend their own culture; others may attempt a bicultural weaving together of the two cultures; and others may attempt to live in both worlds. An emphasis on these strategies reflects how indigenous groups do not necessarily give up their strong traditional identities through the process of acculturation (cf. Berry, 1986). We discuss these concepts further in Chapter 7 and in relation to immigration.

---

alternative identities and knowledge to those being imposed by a settler society. Cosmologies shape the practices and relationships of people across the health centre, school and housing facility, and beyond, in our opening scenario.

Indigenous voices in psychology

It seems appropriate to reflect on the role of psychology in processes of colonization and on the inclusion of indigenous voices in the discipline as a means of challenging the colonizing tendencies of our discipline. So-called Western or North American psychology has been criticized for its colonizing tendencies, culture boundedness and culture blindness (Gergen, Gulerce, Lock & Misra, 1996; Sinha & Kao, 1997). The uncritical application of Western psychological technologies of psychological assessment, education and therapy in different cultural contexts can be interpreted as an example of symbolic colonization. Eurocentric assumptions, such as the independent and autonomous self, and other values and norms have been used to assess the lives and mental health of groups who may not share these assumptions and norms. As Nsamenang (in Allwood & Berry, 2006a) writes: "Psychology is much more an intellectual arm of Europe's civilizing mission and much less a universal science of human behavior" (p. 258). One might think of the Borg in *Star Trek*, who travel the universe seeking to assimilate other species and cultures into their collective. Their catchphrase is "Resistance is futile. Your distinctiveness will be added to our own. ... Your culture will be adapted to service ours." The Borg collective can operate as a metaphor for processes of symbolic colonization that are far too evident in the discipline of psychology. In most countries, psychologists are trained in the current dominant Western tradition. Indigenous psychologists must 'unlearn' the tradition imposed from outside their cultures as part of developing locally relevant versions of psychology. The quote from the Borg collective also invokes a tension we have experienced when writing this chapter. On the one hand, we want to showcase the importance of indigenous psychologies for the social psychology of everyday lives. In doing this, we also do not seek simply to assimilate ideas and insights from indigenous groups into the Western tradition of psychology. Indigenous psychologies remain distinct in their own right. Resistance is far from futile. The situation in psychology shows signs of change with the recognition of indigenous psychologies in areas such as cultural psychology (Valsiner, 2009) and the proliferation of courses across many new world universities.

Until recently, the discipline that came closest to exploring the psychologies of indigenous peoples was social anthropology. This discipline engages communities at the level of everyday life, typically employing ethnographic and naturalistic forms of enquiry. Research explores local customs, economic and political organization, law and conflict resolution, patterns of consumption and exchange, kinship and family structures, gender relations, childrearing and socialization, religion and so on. Social anthropologists are also interested in the role of meanings, ambiguities and contradictions of everyday life, patterns of sociality, violence and conflict, and the underlying logics of social behaviour. The research products of social anthropology are often detail-rich and layered descriptions of complex community life. Many scholars within this tradition look first at customs and then seek to understand the negotiations and motives that lead to various practices.

Indigenous psychologists – that is, those psychologists who are indigenous and committed to developing a psychology of and for their own communities – have adopted similar approaches. For example, Lyndon (1983, p. 188), a Maori woman situated and versed in the customs of her own indigenous community and trained in the methods of Western psychology, explored the Maori customs of *tapu* (prohibitions), *mate maori* (culturally induced sicknesses) and *makutu* (culturally based curses) and their relevance to the diagnosis of mental illness among the Maori. In a similar fashion, Durie (1999, p. 190) proposed a model for understanding Maori social behaviour based on customary encounter rituals. He described nine domains, broad conceptual zones, within which distinctive psychological activities occur. These are the domains of space, time, reciprocity or circularity, mind and earth, safety, metaphor, authority and generosity, interconnectedness and synchronicity. Such models of health often inform the development of health centres such as the one in the opening scenario and provide a basis for combining medical (emphasizing the repair of bodies) and traditional healing practices (also emphasizing spirituality, connectedness and local cosmologies) with education, housing and economic development initiatives (emphasizing the social determinants of health discussed in Chapter 8).

Durie's indigenous psychology model, while firmly emerging from within the Maori world, is not unlike psychologies developed by other indigenous psychologists in locations such as Hawaii and the Philippines (Box 5.8). Another example worth exploring is the work of the Hawaiian psychologist Rezentes (1996, p. 191), who synthesizes traditional Hawaiian concepts and practices with contemporary issues and approaches to build culturally relevant therapy and healing efforts for individuals and families of Hawaiian descent and heritage.

Filipino psychologists Virgilio G. Enriquez and Rogelia Pe-Pua have both been firm advocates of indigenous psychologies in the Philippines since the 1970s. Their work is part of a broader effort to represent *emic* ways of seeing and giving voice to indigenous realities and psychologies. Such work draws on both emic and *etic* approaches to knowledge production (Chapter 4) in contemporary indigenous communities. Enriquez (1993) discuss two forms of indigenization in the context of the discipline of psychology. The first involves indigenization from the outside and the second indigenization from the inside (cf. Berry, 1999). The outside, or etic approach, involves indigenous psychologists taking existing insights, methods and approaches from outside the culture or society and adapting these for use in local contexts. External ideas are integrated into existing cultural frames so as to be made more applicable to local settings. This often occurs in the adaptation and translation of psychological tests and other practices developed in the European countries and the United States for use in other countries. This practice is associated with cross-cultural

BOX 5.8   Interesting study (methodology)

Pe-Pua (2006) provides a useful overview of the development of indigenous psychological research in the Philippines and of how associated local methods can be adapted across indigenous psychologies emerging in other locations. Pe-Pua's work involves the application of specific cultural concepts to psychological research. It emerges from a movement towards developing Filipino psychology during the 1970s (Enriquez, 1993). This movement sought to explore local people's experiences and actions from an indigenous perspective, as part of an attempt to decolonize psychology in the country. Many Filipino psychologists used local knowledge and cultural concepts to guide the development of research and theoretical understandings. The concept of shared identity, or *Kapwa*, became central to Filipino social psychology because it refers to practices through which Filipinos treat other people as fellow human beings. This concept shapes the way indigenous research is conducted. Much of this work involved adapting interview, focus group and participant-observation methods and refining these techniques to meet the cultural needs and practices of Filipinos. The methodological approach is ethnographic in nature and involves practices such as 'dropping in' on participants when 'in the neighbourhood' or 'passing by'. This meets with cultural requirements of building relationships and trust over time through frequent visits, or *Pagdalaw-dalaw*. As relationships develop between researchers and participants, more 'formal' methods such as interviews and group discussions are employed. In discussing the indigenous interview, Pe-Pua refers to the Filipino cultural practice of *Pagtatanong-tanong*, which can be translated as 'asking questions'. In daily life, *Pagtatanong-tanong* involves people spending hours exchanging ideas and chatting. This practice is the basis for an indigenous interview that is participatory in nature in that research participants have input into the structure of the conversation. Questions can be asked by both parties during the interview. This is consistent with the cultural concept of *Kapwa* in that research participants are engaged in open dialogue as fellow human beings with equal status as the researcher, rather than as the 'subjects' of research (Chapter 4). In a Western methodological sense we might say that *Pagtatanong-tanong* interviews are unstructured interviews (see Flick, 2009). However, it is more accurate to describe these as culturally structured interviews designed in response to local cultural practices. Pe-Pua sees the development of indigenous methods as part of the refinement of psychological research globally. Indigenous Filipino methods have been applied to research outside of the Philippines, with Korean, Hawaiian and Japanese participants, with some success. Modifications need to be made to such methods when they are used with different cultural groups. However, the principles of sharing, equal status and open dialogue remain. Important are efforts to facilitate research participants having input into the focus of research and the framing of issues and concerns.

psychology. The emic, or 'insider', approach involves developing insights, methods and approaches from within a culture by drawing on indigenous knowledge, as in the examples referred to above. Some indigenous psychologies have drawn heavily on historical and religious texts for underlying philosophical bases, including Chinese use of Confucian classics and Buddhism, Indian use of Hinduism and Western use of Descartes (Kim, Yang & Hwang, 2006b). This emic approach is evident, for instance, in the work of Pe-Pua (2006), which offers an alternative to individualistic models of the self, which have come to dominate Western psychology. Alternative conceptions of the self are based on local cultural knowledge and often place more emphasis on relationships and contexts than the Western notion of the self-contained individual (Chapter 4).

Ideally, the relationship between emic and etic approaches is symbiotic. Increased insight can come from a combined approach that draws on insights from both the inside and outside (Berry, 1999). In fact, in introducing these terms to psychology, Pike (1967) saw these approaches as overlapping or being shaded by each other. Both have value in allowing the foregrounding of indigenous and universalist perspectives in a research project. The emic approach allows for the development of local concepts and insights that might be missed by outsiders. The etic approach allows for comparisons and dialogues across cultures. Thus, both etic and emic approaches can be used together to add depth and diversity in perspective to a study. Sinha (1996) contends that indigenization is a process of bringing imported understandings into conversation with locally derived understandings. This process can happen when structures within the society can produce and disseminate local knowledge, when psychology is used to address social issues, or when new theories and methodologies that are based in the local frame of knowledge and worldviews are developed and reflect local realities and lived experiences.

In short, anthropologists have historically been an indigenous community's first encounter with agents of Western institutions of higher learning. As noted in Chapter 2, many psychologists no longer assume the universal applicability of Western psychological concepts. Since the crisis in social psychology in the 1970s, increased effort has been made to develop psychologies that are localized, relevant to people's everyday lives and in concert with the connections and relationships that people have, rather than psychologies that defend the dominant Western individualist stream of social psychology. More localized or embedded psychologies are not necessarily directly related to specific indigenous peoples. Some relate to nation-states (Adair, 1999), some to religious philosophies such as Buddhism (Sugamura, Haruki & Koshikawa, 2007), some to ethnic or racially defined groups such as African Americans (Jones, 2004) and some to locales such as cosmopolitan India (Sinha, 1996). Such approaches emphasize the development of diverse understandings of human action in the context of localized and culturally, historically and politically enmeshed practices.

Indigenous psychologies and the global discipline

Local traditions of psychology have existed, in one sense, alongside the inception and growth of modern psychology. It is only during recent times that indigenous psychologies have begun to gain greater currency in the discipline, in particular since the publication of Kim and Berry's (1993) seminal book. Their edited collection showcased different indigenous psychologies and introduced general issues concerning the place of such psychologies within the global discipline. These discussions have been continued in more recent collections (Allwood & Berry, 2006a; Kim, Yang & Hwang, 2006b), which illustrate substantial developments in this diverse and complex field. In this chapter, we offer a general overview of the ways indigenous knowledge and processes of indigenization can inform the development of social psychology around the world. We cannot hope to cover all such psychologies, and thus we provide only an introduction to core issues and insights. Our stance is that there are a range of indigenous psychologies around the world that offer much to inform the reconstruction of a relevant and culturally anchored social psychology. Indigenous psychologies are coherent systems in their own right, and the relationship with social psychology needs to be one of dialogue, rather than one of assimilation. We respect the stance of many indigenous scholars who converse with the broader international discipline of psychology while maintaining their autonomy and distinctiveness. It should become apparent that indigenous psychologies offer much more than simply the study of 'exotic native peoples' or people living in so-called developing countries.

Cross-cultural psychology emerged from a recognition that assumed universal psychological processes may not operate equally across different cultures (Cole, 1998). Cross-cultural psychology continues to produce some interesting insights into cultural variations. However, it is limited by the tendency to treat culture (Box 5.9) as yet another independent variable upon which comparisons can be made across groups in terms of unidimensional cultural constructs such as individualism versus collectivism. Cultural psychology (Chapter 7) is moving beyond this early preoccupation and is beginning to engage more fully with the richness of indigenous psychologies. The latter are viewed as cultural psychologies in their own right (Valsiner, 2009) that talk to the mainstream global discipline but remain focused on local needs. This conversation contributes new insights into how certain groups of people think, understand themselves and perceive the world, and why they tend to conduct their everyday lives in particular ways (Chakkarath, 2005).

Indigenous psychologies often emerge from an engagement with the everyday life practices and ways of knowing of the groups developing these psychologies. Local ways of being and conducting life and relationships stem from indigenous cosmologies, from ancient precedents, from knowledge derived over generations of living in place, with each other and with newcomers. These include ways of

---

BOX 5.9   Culture and psychology

Valsiner (2009) provides a useful review of cultural psychology and the relationship of this broad subdisciplinary area to indigenous psychologies. In the process, he notes that *"Culture* is in some sense a magical word – positive in connotations but hard to pinpoint in any science that attempts to use it as a core term" (p. 6). It is a concept that has been in play within psychology for more than 100 years, but which has not been as prominent as it could have been due to its slippery nature. The concept is increasingly prominent as psychologists attempt to respond to the diverse needs of different peoples, including indigenous and immigrant groups who experience the world differently and whose lives are often regulated by different norms and shared practices. Here we see the emergence of a particular orientation towards culture as a dynamic symbolic system and set of social practices shared by particular group of people. Culture is often conceptualized as an all-encompassing way of life, or a consensus that contains the specific rituals, beliefs, habits, institutions and language of a group. This perspective can, however, lead to the glossing over of complexities and inconsistencies in a given culture. As Tanner (1997) states, coherence is often given to cultures by researchers from an outsider perspective. Cultures are often more incoherent to those living within them, who often experience more fluidity, contradiction and change, particularly when different groups come into contact with each other and take on new practices and beliefs. "In an age of global travel and communication, local communities are seldom 'pure' or untouched by other cultures. A certain level of hybridity emerges" (Dueck, Ting and Cutiongco, 2007, p. 68). This can add further layers of complexity to issues of indigenization and the orientations members of particular communities wish to develop.

---

experiencing, understanding and making meaning in the world. Historically described as superstitious, folkways (e.g. Shortland, 1980) are ways of knowing that are entwined with and shape what Sumner (1907) considered to be the patterns of conventional behaviour in a society, norms that apply to everyday matters. These include the conventions and habits learned from childhood and are in effect psychologies that span centuries and emerge from the engagement of people in their everyday lives, most often in the absence of psychologists. Because such practices are embedded in culture and place, the nature of an indigenous psychology is more visible when contrasts or clashes occur between interacting people, perspectives or worldviews; otherwise, it is simply that which is taken for granted on a day-to-day basis.

Indigenous psychologies legitimate traditional knowledge and allow us to bring new perspectives and concepts to bear on a raft of social psychological phenomena that occur in everyday life. Mkhize (2004) defined indigenous psychologies "as forms of knowledge that arise out of the social and cultural realities of the people concerned. They are not imposed from the outside. They also investigate mundane (everyday) rather than experimental (laboratory) behaviours" (pp. 4–6). However, Mkhize also suggested that this definition may be too narrow, and that cultures are not static and impenetrable.

Therefore, we need to clarify processes and practices of indigenization as these evolve over time and through social transformation.

Review exercise

Think about a cultural group to which you belong:

■ Does this group have a 'recognized' psychology?
  – If so, what are the core assumptions of this psychology and how does it relate to the broader discipline?
  – If not, why do you think this is?

Indigenous psychologies are highly relevant to the social psychology of everyday life because they are grounded in the daily realities and lives of diverse groups of people. These approaches are particularly useful as they are often built from the bottom up, growing out of the need to explain local phenomena (Allwood & Berry, 2006a, 2007). Central to these psychologies is the idea that human experience and actions are shaped within a range of social, historical and cultural contexts. Broadly speaking, the discipline of social psychology in North America and Europe is also one such context. As a result, Western social psychology is more applicable to Western societies, and other psychologies are more applicable to the particular groups developing them. Allwood and Berry (2006b) note that:

indigenous psychologies may be described as a set of approaches to understanding human behaviour within the cultural contexts in which they have developed and are currently displayed. They can also be seen as attempts to root psychological research in the conceptual systems that are indigenous to a culture, including the philosophical, theological, and scientific ideas that are part of the historical and contemporary lives of people and their institutions. (p. 214)

Indigenous psychologies offer a means of reinvigorating the global discipline of social psychology. The development of indigenous psychologies allows for the diversity of human life and being to be brought to the fore, and for us to move beyond the limited cultural view of the dominant American–European perspective. After all, there is more to see and learn about human beings than Western psychology is able to show us. As Kuo-Shu Yang (in Allwood & Berry, 2006a, p. 250) notes, indigenous psychologies, or at least those emerging in non-Western countries, constitute attempts to redress the global dominance of North American-inspired Western psychology. These indigenous psychologies represent efforts to develop locally based understandings of people's everyday actions and experiences.

The continued development of indigenous psychologies involves the refinement and application of local knowledge. In pursuit of this, some confusion may arise in terms of historically located knowledge systems and the development of a modern psychological system. Both are interrelated in that the modern system incorporates and refines traditional concepts and insights. Although drawing on traditional knowledge, contemporary indigenous psychologies are distinct from such knowledge (Allwood & Berry, 2006a). For example, in various indigenous psychologies located in Asia the Buddhist notion of the interconnected self can be used to develop an alternative to the Cartesian notion of individuals. As we will show later in this chapter, this alternative notion of the self can also be used to challenge or relativize core elements of the dominant North American tradition. The development of distinct conceptualizations in psychology can be seen as part of a process of indigenizing psychology. Further, the use of indigenous resources need not be totally relativized to local settings. Many indigenous ideas, such as a more holistic understanding of what it means to be human, can also be applied in other settings and to improve global understandings. Reflecting on the general outcome of their survey of different indigenous psychologists, Allwood and Berry (2006a) note, "Somewhat more than half of the contributors discussed the possibilities of developing a more universal psychology via a comparative integration of the different IPs [indigenous psychologies]" (p. 265). While an integrated social psychology may be informed by different indigenous psychologies from around the world, it also needs to recognize its local anchorage points from which any interpretation is constructed.

As some countries have experienced the suppression of their cultures through colonization, they will differ from countries that have not experienced such trauma in the ways in which indigenous psychology develops. Sociopolitical and historical contexts shape indigenous psychologies, and these differences should not be lost when we consider the place of different approaches in the global discipline of psychology. Dueck, Ting and Cutiongco (2007) note that just as it would be a mistake to homogenize culture as a monolithic whole rather than a pluralistic space, we need to avoid trying to produce one coherent discipline. Just as we need to recognize the pluralist character of our global community and ethnic diversity, we might also recognize multiple psychologies that relate to local identities.

It is important at this point in our discussion to acknowledge that Western psychology is also made up of a number of indigenous psychologies. Dueck, Ting and Cutiongco (2007) propose that "North Americans would do well to examine and recognize the indigeneity of their own psychology" (p. 55). This is an important point because it challenges the idea that Western psychology is somehow non-indigenous and thereby universally relevant. What we are left with is the realization that, despite their ubiquity, Western psychologies are also particular cultural interpretations, or indeed comprise a cluster of local ways of viewing people and the human condition (Box 5.10).

In brief, indigenous psychologies often arise in colonial settings as part of a broader process of decolonization. Indigenous scholars have advanced the idea that Western social psychology is as culturally located as any other psychology and is therefore an indigenous psychology that has colonized other cultures and regions (see contributions to Allwood & Berry, 2006a). This is a direct challenge to the individualistic stream in social psychology that asserts objectivity and neutrality as normative goals (see Chapters 1 and 4). Critiques of the relevance of many Western theories to the psychology of indigenous groups around the world can be read as central to a process of developing a more relevant and responsive social psychology of everyday life. In other words, we can see the relationship between dominant and minoritized groups (Box 5.11) being played out in our own discipline. For example, in Chapter 2 we explored how the structure of the intergroup experiments of Sherif and colleagues was in effect the product of culturally located power relations.

BOX 5.10   Indigenous psychology and the crisis in social psychology

The rise in prominence of indigenous psychologies since the 1970s can be linked to the crisis in social psychology (Chapter 2) and to calls for the development of historically located approaches that offer responses to diverse needs in the real world. Fourth world psychologists were also raising concerns regarding such issues prior to the 1970s. As Uichol Kim and Young-Shin Park (in Allwood & Berry, 2006a) note:

The limitations of psychological theories came to be recognized by third world scholars in the early 1970s, who began to question the validity and generalizability of western psychology. Similar criticisms emerged in Europe, which resulted in the creation of numerous critical psychology European associations and journals. (p. 249)

Moghaddam (1987) notes that from the 1960s European social psychologists such as Henri Tajfel and Serge Moscovici worked to re-establish European psychologies that were distinct from the dominant individualistic and North American approach (Allwood & Berry, 2006a). Although these psychologists sought to develop a more inclusive social psychology, the voices of non-European indigenous psychologists remained less prominent, in part due to the emphasis the latter place on practice rather than academic writing in many parts of the world. Both collectivist-oriented social psychologists and indigenous psychologists agree that psychology needs to be responsive to social injustices (Chapter 9), economic conditions that undermine the health of communities (Chapter 8), the complexities of knowledge production in daily life (Chapter 3) and increased global diversity and displacement (see Chapter 7).

BOX 5.11   Minority group influence in social psychology

In explaining what a minority group is, scholars often invoke inequities in power between minority and dominant groups. In many respects this conceptualization is preferable to a simple distinction in terms of group size because historically many minority groups have actually been numerically superior to dominant groups that are often referred to as the majority. Based on the work of Feagin (1984), we might propose that minority groups contain five elements. First, they experience discrimination and subordination. Second, they have cultural characteristics and practices or physical traits that distinguish them from a dominant group that often disapproves of minority group behaviour. Third, they share a sense of identity, suffering and displacement. Fourth, their social status is determined by rules about who belongs and who does not belong, and such rules are often determined by the dominant group. Fifth, despite being the numerical majority they are subjugated to the rules and culture of a dominant group that sets the rules of the game in the society and monopolizes resources.

It is important not to assume that minority groups have no influence on the dominant group or culture. Social psychology contains a mass of research into minority group influence. As is explored in Chapter 4, Serge Moscovici (1981, 1994) has spent a career studying the collective construction of knowledge among different groups of people and how knowledge is appropriated and changed over time and through daily use (for a recent account of Moscovici's work and the production of knowledge, see Jovchelovitch, 2007). Moscovici investigated minority influence and how the ideas and practices of small groups can influence larger groups. He proposed that if majority influence were as all-encompassing as some social psychologists had suggested, then people would likely all think the same way. He pointed to how small groups of like-minded people have grown into larger groupings in which their ideas have become mainstream. Examples include major religions and even communism.

The concept of minority group influence can be used to understand the development of indigenous psychologies. The development of indigenous psychologies is in part an attempt to expand and diversify the dominant Euro-American tradition of Western psychology (Allwood & Berry, 2006a). Attempts are being made to make the discipline more relevant to diverse social, historical and cultural contexts through the integration of indigenous psychologies into the broader discipline. This is a process of de-centring the individualistic stream of Western social psychology. In short, one goal of indigenous psychologies is to have a minority influence on the broader discipline and its future development – participation on one's own terms.

The development of many indigenous social psychologies has been closely associated with processes of decolonization and with assisting minority groups to find a voice and gain access to resources for self-determination (Allwood & Berry, 2006a). Dissatisfaction with individualistic strands of Western psychology has led indigenous psychologists to look outside and to the edges of the discipline in order to begin solving the pressing problems of their own communities (Henry Kao in Allwood & Berry, 2006a). The following section explores processes of colonization and decolonization with reference to psychological testing.

Decolonizing global psychology

The circumstances of many indigenous peoples appear to be improving in specific locations around the world. However, basic human rights continue to be violated in other locations (Dean & Levi, 2003). A key process in ensuring more positive futures for indigenous peoples is decolonization (Box 5.12). Decolonization is a process of recovery, re-establishment of culture and legitimacy and the assertion of rights – it is anchored in indigenous ways of knowing, being and doing. This process includes the preservation and expansion of language and culture, access to land rights, control over resources and autonomy. Writing about research practice, Smith (1999) suggests that decolonization requires that scholars be aware of and work to redress processes of colonialism. "For researchers one of the levels is having a more critical understanding of the underlying assumptions, motivations, and values which informs research practices" (p. 20). Issues of power and privilege are exposed in taken-for-granted processes of knowledge production, and there are calls for different methodologies and approaches that will ensure that "research with indigenous peoples can be more respectful, ethical, sympathetic, and useful" (p. 9). Along similar lines, Martin (2003) writes that indigenous research "is culturally safe and culturally respectful research that is comprised of three principles: resistance as an emancipatory imperative, political integrity in Indigenous research and privileging Indigenous voices in Indigenous research" (p. 205). She goes further to state that indigenous research is both reactive and about opposition; it is about valuing the strength of being Aboriginal and "viewing anything Western as 'other', alongside and among Western worldviews and realities" (p. 205).

BOX 5.12   Decolonization

The decolonization project has significant implications for psychology: it means rethinking how psychology does business. It does not simply require the proliferation of multiple local ethnic psychologies or research methodologies. Although such a proliferation is useful in many respects, decolonization also requires examinations of issues of power and privilege in modes of practice and the machinery of knowledge production (Sonn, 2006). This can include:

- Research and action strategies that privilege the lived experiences of individuals and their communities
- Valuing different forms of knowledge, ways of knowing, and ensuring that in practice (i.e. praxis) we work against oppression and exclusion
- Promoting everyday practices that recognize our embeddedness in sociopolitical realities as part of the process of working for change at individual, interpersonal and institutional levels

Here we use the example of psychological testing to explore the implications of indigenization and decolonization. The psychological test is a particularly prominent technology in our discipline of Western psychology that has been employed with colonial tendencies. Concern about the theory and practice of assessment and testing in culturally diverse settings is not new (Jones, 1996; Kearins, 1999). There are many cogent and thorough reviews of the problems of assessment and testing in general with cultural groups (Anastasi & Urbana, 1997; Groth-Marnat, 1997). The first set of arguments revolves around the appropriateness of standardized tests and the extent to which they misrepresent the actual abilities of the person being tested (Anastasi & Urbana, 1997). A number of issues are conflated in this area, including the relevance of the attributes being assessed to different cultural groups, the interpretation of the attributes by different cultural groups, the omission of potentially relevant cultural attributes, the modalities used to assess the attributes (verbal, nonverbal), cultural taboos in the exploration of certain attributes, the intra-psychic versus public expression of attributes, the validity of comparisons of attributes across cultural and other differentiating boundaries (e.g. gender) and the sociohistorical, cultural and political climate of both the micro (assessment) and the macro (societal) setting (Box 5.13).

The consequences of poor assessment in general can be profound. At the school level, the consequences for indigenous children may include overrepresentation in 'remedial' classes. Mike and Anna, from the opening scenario, may be kept back at school. This is not because of a problem that they have personally. It is due to the

BOX 5.13   Culture-free, culture-fair and culture-specific tests

Attempts to deal with the problems of assessment and testing gave rise to the development of so-called culture-free tests (Jones, 1996). Culture-free tests have, however, proven impossible, because they could not be separated from the culture in which they were developed. Similarly, the movement towards culture-fair tests was confounded by the fact that they measured only the transcultural aspects of the phenomena being tested (Suzuki, Ponterotto & Meller, 2001). It was found that despite best efforts these tests again tended, inevitably, to favour the culture in which they were developed. The final turn was towards culturally specific tests, and this has also been a mixed bag. The concepts being tested may not be culturally relevant, and, generally speaking, the results of indigenization add nothing to our understanding of cultural difference beyond the mere observation (Lindsey, 1998). A further, broad set of issues are the contextual or circumstantial factors that affect performance in assessment. There is ample evidence that the modes of administration, including the cultural identity of the tester and the physical location of the assessment, can have an impact on the assessment outcomes (Padilla, 2001). Very rarely, if at all, are members of cultural minorities involved in the development, conceptualization and validation of assessment tools and processes (Jones, 1996).

problems psychologists often have with using tests inappropriately. This will inevitably have knock-on effects on self-worth, feelings of marginalization and alienation and ultimately on retention, which has been related to health outcomes in later life (SGRGSP, 2007). This type of overrepresentation can contribute to stereotyping (Chapter 4) and the pathologizing of indigenous people as problematic students (Padilla, 2001). Similarly, poor assessment practices may lead to the provision of a basis for disadvantageous comparison and lower expectations from indigenous people themselves (stereotype threat), leading to self-fulfilling prophesies with respect to their performance and self-evaluations (Lindsey, 1998). Lidz (2001) summed it up nicely when she observed that "assessment has proven benign and malignant" (p. 523). To paraphrase Holland (cited in Brown, 2001, p. 35), there is only one thing worse than being poorly assessed, and that is to be poorly assessed and indigenous.

Assessment practices are still on the whole in the thrall of the dominant traditions, and "little has been done to shake up the assessment community despite the development of alternative practices" (Suzuki, Ponterotto & Meller, 2001, p. 666). Gone (2007) provides an impassioned plea for us to "reimagine wellness" in the interests of creating services that "collaboratively engage and competently incorporate local conceptualizations of emotional experience and expression, prevailing communicative norms, cultural notions of disorder and its treatment and implicit meanings of personhood, social relations and spirituality" (p. 298). Decolonizing assessment practices involves foregrounding the importance of cultural competence. As a foundation for good assessment practice, cultural competence provides the capacity to analyse, reflect on and, if necessary, name the monocultural tendencies of many service providers (Riggs, 2004). Culturally competent practice is a dynamic reflexive and reflective process of engagement that requires us to step away from the traditional role of objective mirror on people's life world (Lidz, 2001). Without it any assessment regime will be fatally flawed. No technology, technique or framework can overcome the absence of cultural competence. Without it assessments will be reproductive not transformative, disabling not enabling, disempowering not empowering. It is clear that the lack of cultural competence in past practice has been a contributing factor to the overall failure of systems of care, including assessment, for indigenous people (Garvey, 2007).

On the basis of this discussion, there are two complementary elements to the reflective process of engaging with indigenous communities as culturally competent practitioners. The first is a commitment to indigenous terms of reference. Indigenous terms of reference place indigenous people at the centre of the interaction or process that impacts them (Garvey, 2007; Oxenham, 2000). The second is a commitment to a critical examination of 'whiteness' (Chapter 7). Both are crucial forms of perspective taking that position practitioners in relation to indigenous people. Both promote decolonizing practice (Sherwood & Edwards, 2006). The reproduction of Western dominance in practice should no longer be tolerated as a form of secondary colonization (Green, Sonn & Matsebula, 2007; McCabe, 2007).

This dual lens is an imperative element and component of the processes of deconstructing colonizing Western psychological practices in the interests of decolonizing practices. Both strive to move the practitioner towards cultural competence as a necessary precursor to working *with* rather than *on* (Chapter 4) indigenous people (Danzinger, 2006). Typically, the education of non-indigenous practitioners does not adequately address the relationships between culture and the sociocultural, historical, political and cultural realities of indigenous people. This issue can be addressed by working *with* people, and this has important ramifications for decolonization.

Next we take the topic of decolonizing psychology further by displacing the Cartesian notion of the independent self (Chapter 4), which has informed social psychological theory and research for several centuries. This independent self limits our understanding of people and everyday life. A key link to the present section is that indigenous psychologies do not have to be modelled on the physical sciences or adopt quantitative methods such as testing (Dueck, Ting and Cutiongco, 2007).

Interconnected selves

Another way of decolonizing psychology is fundamentally to rethink the core subject of the discipline – the self. This section presents an account of notions of interconnected selves that are informed by various indigenous psychologies. The emphasis placed on interconnected selves is important because it offers a more pluralistic understanding of who people are and what it means to be human. Danzinger (2006) provides further comment on the link between the growth in indigenous psychology and the limitations of the Cartesian-oriented Western psychology based on individualistic notions of the self (Chapter 4). He notes that dialogue between Western psychology and different indigenous psychologies is important for the refinement of the individualistic focus that dominates the discipline in many countries. It is useful to note that 'interconnected', 'interdependent' and 'dialogical' selves, often promoted within Asian (Kim & Park, cited in Allwood & Berry, 2006a) and other indigenous psychologies (Mikulas, 2007), are not unique to indigenous peoples. As is recognized by proponents of the collectivist stream of social psychology (Chapters 2 and 3), we are all interconnected and interdependent beings. This way of conceptualizing the self takes us beyond a dichotomous view of subject–object relations and into the domain of interobjective relations (Chapter 3).

A core element of notions of the interconnected self is that the human life is woven into relationships and situations and is not independent of context (Box 5.14). Community narratives discussed in Chapters 3 and 4 exemplify the interconnected character of the self in that our own stories are often based in collective tales. Notions of an interconnected self are evident in a raft of cultures and are far more complex and diverse then we could hope to do justice to here. Our task is to provide an alternative view to the self-contained independent individual that dominates social psychology at present.

According to notions of the interconnected self, human beings are much more than fixed personality-based entities residing within the heads of individuals (Mikulas, 2007). This assertion is counter to the current cultural emphasis in many Western countries on individuals as separate inner beings. Indigenous psychologies informed by Buddhism draw on the notion of 'dependent origination', or the idea that everything is interlinked and stems from dependence on something else. Mikulas (2007) advances the idea that the feeling of being separate from the social world and environment, and of having independent self-entities, is a particular Western construction. It is important not to get lost at the personal level and focus only on our individuality. People need to consider the broader contexts shaping their lives, including the social networks within which they are situated. From this perspective, rather than being detached observers of social life, we are submerged in the sea of daily life. The self is an

BOX 5.14   Interesting study

Uichol Kim and Young-Shin Park (in Allwood & Berry, 2006a) refer to *Chong*, the Korean concept for "affectionate attachment for a person, place, and thing" (p. 250). This concept is useful in expanding our understandings of the material basis of daily life and the importance of people, place and objects in self-construction (Chapters 3 and 6). *Chong*, and other such Asian concepts, bring into question notions of the independent or disconnected Western individual and emphasize the relational nature of human beings and our identities. Who we are is connected to the places we inhabit, the things we use and the people we interact with. As Kim and Park note, Korean, Chinese and Japanese words for 'human being' translate into English as 'being between'. In other words, it is what happens between human beings that makes us human.

ongoing project, which owes its existence to the lifeworlds within which one is embedded. It follows that if we are to understand people we must understand these connections and contexts, and how one element affects other elements:

our understanding of even a simple event must depend on all sorts of complex relationships, because everything in the universe is related to everything else in some way. One can understand nothing in isolated pieces. The parts are meaningful in their relations to the whole, just as individual musical instruments are to an orchestra. Understanding parts requires us to investigate the whole. (Peng, Spencer-Rodgers & Nian, 2006, p. 255)

In focusing on human lives as complex wholes, we need to study more than the various elements or parts of a person's life. We need to study the relationships between interconnected parts making up the whole person. To understand people we must understand the groups to which they belong and how these groups relate to other groups. For example, Bob from the chapter scenario is a sentient being in his own right (Box 5.15). Yet, to understand him and his health, we need also to engage with processes of colonization, the cosmology of the indigenous group to which he belongs and the broader relationships and historical developments surrounding the health centre and his life.

BOX 5.15   Individuals and groups

A key tension that emerges with this orientation to the interdependent self is the threat of losing the individual to the social context or group. It is important to retain the uniqueness of each human being. None of us is totally reducible to the contexts of our life or the relationships within which we engage. Humanistic psychologists have noted for some time that people are always more than the social categories according to which we theorize them and their lives (Chapter 11). People can act in unanticipated ways within the restraints of their lifeworlds (Valsiner, 2009). This raises the classic tension between structure and agency in the social sciences. What is clear is that each person is solely the product neither of his or her culture nor of his or her own individuality or traits. Recently, Howarth (2009) noted that social psychologists need to be wary about essentializing racial categories onto actual people because the lives of individuals and the daily practices they engage in are often more complex and varied than such categories can account for. This is an important observation that reminds us that it is necessary to avoid stereotyping people (Chapter 4). People can give up an invitation to fit in with their communities and cultures from time to time. The critical humanist perspective outlined in Chapter 10 takes the view that both the social and the personal are woven into a dynamic relationship. Such thinking is also reflected in many Asian psychologies that assert autonomy within life webs, and how one's own actions can affect and be affected by other people linked into our webs (Yang, 2006). A key point here is that we are not passive objects shaped from the outside through processes of socialization. We are active participants in the daily rituals and practices that shape who we are and who we are to become. We can play with, revise and extend these very shared practices and in the process ourselves (Goffman, 1959).

In considering the Chinese self, Yang (2006, p. 345) articulates the important point that the self does not necessarily cause an individual's actions. A person's actions in a particular situation can be seen as being the self, regardless of the causes for particular acts. In this way, each situation is associated with an expressed self. It is through the locating of the self in relationships and situations that a person's actions have influence on others. According to Yang (2006):

the self is a cobweb connected to many other people, each of whom is also a web. The cobweb is a dynamic field in which the person, as an action-taker pursuing everyday life and adjusting to the environment, has to think and do things affecting not only the self, but also those people linked to the web. Many actions may result in reshaping the web and all other webs associated with it. A person's deliberation and choice of action reflect that person's self. (p. 345)

From this perspective, because we affect and shape each other we need to learn to live harmoniously together and accept that we can grow into one another (Figure 5.1). Processes of self-refinement and adjustment to the environment are ongoing and in turn shape the environment and everyday life.

Figure 5.1. Illustration of the cobweb self

Review exercise

Draw a spider web. Now put in the names of family members, friends and colleagues. You might also put in places you feel at home and your prized possessions. Consider the following questions:

- What selves are linked to these elements in your web?
- What do these reflect about you?
- What sort of relationships enact the links between the 'I' at the centre of the web and the various 'me's out on the strands?

Ideas regarding the social and interconnected nature of human beings have been evident in the collectivist stream of Western social psychology for some time (James, 1890; Cooley, 1902; Mead, 1932). The Chinese conceptualization of the self as is reflected in the metaphor of the cobweb resembles aspects of some Western conceptualizations in social psychology which emphasize a holistic perspective (Billig, 2008). As Hermans (2001) writes:

The dialogical self is "social", not in the sense that a self-contained individual enters into social interactions with other outside people, but in the sense that other people occupy positions in a multivoiced self. The self is not only "here" but also "there", and, owing to the power of imagination, the person can act as if he or she were the other and the other were him- or herself. (p. 250)

The dialogical self is evident in how people can experience themselves as a mother or father through their relationships with their children. A key to notions of the dialogical self is continuity and discontinuity, in that what is experienced as 'mine' is often experienced in terms of continuity between partner, children and friends, whereas discontinuity in experience can occur when there is tension between the self as father, for instance, and as employee who cannot spend time with his children due to work commitments. Such situations raise discontinuity in experiences of the self as a coherent whole (Box 5.16).

Hermans (2001) proposed that self and culture are mutually constituting, and that, therefore, it is possible to study cultures in selves and people in cultures. This is possible because individuals are not self-contained and are in fact participating in, and developing through, culture in concert with others. At the same time culture is not simply an abstract set of concepts or practices. Culture is a field of human action and meaning making. It is through culture that we construct and make sense of the world and ourselves.

Theories of interconnected, cobweb and dialogical selves allow us to explore more fully the interwoven nature of self and collectives in everyday life. These connections are of increasing interest to social

---

BOX 5.16   'I' and 'me' in the dialogical self (Hermans, 2001)

In addition to the work of the Russian novelist Bakhtin, the concept of the dialogical self draws heavily on the work of William James (1890) (see Chapter 2) and his distinction between *I* and *me*. The *I* is the self as knower and a sense of personal identity and continuity over time. At least in the West, this *I* is experienced as being distinct from other people. This *I* exercises personal volition in processing experience and rejecting unwanted thoughts. The *me* is the self as known or as seen and experienced by others. According to James, we all have as many selves as there are people who recognize us. The *me* extends to one's possessions and relationships, and as such extends out beyond the mind and body to parents, partner, children, friends, house, reputation, creative products and so forth. The notion of *me* in the world contrasts with the Cartesian self in that who we are exists in the environment and not simply in our minds. It is a view of the self that provides the basis for contemporary notions of the dialogical self and that is compatible with many indigenous notions of self emerging from around the world (Chung-Fang, 2006). What we get from notions of interconnected selves is the idea of unity in experience and multiplicity in manifestations of ourselves across different situations and social interactions. According to James (1890), the *I* organizes the various aspects of the *me* into a conscious whole experienced as a coherent self. This stance is compatible with the Chinese idea that there are as many selves as there are situations.

---

psychologists, which reflects a shift beyond the focus on how individuals behave in group settings (see Chapter 2) that is reflected in the Asch (1952) studies on conformity and work on bystander apathy (Cherry, 1995). This focus has been extended more recently to how groups behave within individuals. For example, Liu and Liu (1999) explore interconnectedness as a dynamic value emerging from Confucian philosophy and increasingly central to Chinese psychology because it allows for a focus on complex relations and contradictions. Interconnectedness enables a focus on not only the self within the society, but the society within the self. A goal of psychological research becomes to increase our awareness of our embeddedness in the lives of others and ability to support each other. This focus on the collective within the individual reflects that assumption "that social categories to which people perceive themselves to belong have a profound impact on their psychological functioning" (Hermans, 2001, p. 261). A collective focus also necessitates a shift from viewing culture as an abstract system out in the world and external to the self to viewing culture as something inside and central to the self. This is a logical extension of notions of socialization, which we have been discussing throughout this book. In a sense, culture provides many of the fibres that make up the strands in our self-cobwebs. The pattern of the webs and links is influenced by norms, values and shared narratives of the groups we live among and grow from. The focus becomes how people and cultures evolve and grow within the dialogical exchanges of everyday life. It is important to note here that notions of the dialogical self are not restricted to verbal dialogue and encompass other shared social practices and community participations, such as body language (Hermans, 2001). We often are engaged in dialogue without noticing it. An approach based on the cobweb self transcends the individualistic and collectivist dualism because the collective is seen as being central to the creation of the individual. Concurrently, individuals and their voices or actions make up the dialogue through which cultures are constructed.

Taking these ideas further, we might add that just as there are multiple voices in individuals so can there be multiple cultures in a person. Think, for example, of social identities, such as black British, and what happens when a black British youth learns Kung Fu. In a sense, elements of African, British and Chinese culture become woven into the person's sense of self. The central point here is that cultural identities are often fluid, dialectical and hybrid when manifest in daily practices (Howarth, 2009). Aspects of different cultures can be brought into dialogue, and new identities and practices may emerge as a result (Box 5.15). These processes of hybridization can become intensified through access to mass media (Chapter 11), which expose us to a broader range of beliefs, practices and other people with whom we may interact. Further, we might extend our discussion of interconnected selves to interconnected communities. After all, people can reside in more than one ethnic space, depending on the context. Such issues are taken up in the following two chapters in relation to how groups share particular places and issues surrounding immigration, and in relation to notions of place-based identities (Cuba & Hummon, 1993) and social identity theory (Tajfel & Turner, 1979). In the context of the present chapter, it is important that indigenous psychologies are developed to provide concepts and insights rich enough to aid us in investigating such complex, social and global processes of human interaction and self-development (Hermans, 2001). This also necessitates investigations of the pain and disruption that can occur for individuals and groups who become caught between worlds and cultures.

Chapter summary

In many respects indigenous psychologies remain marginalized in the discipline of psychology. We have not to date come across a chapter on this topic in another social psychology textbook. This omission reflects a missed opportunity. Engagements with indigenous psychologies enable us to extend social psychological engagements with human diversity. Such psychologies provide insights into how people think and act within different historical and cultural contexts. Indigenous psychologies are having a minority group influence by encouraging social psychologists to deal with diversity in more complex and relevant ways. This is necessary because everyday life is a diverse and complex place. Complexities need to be reflected in a responsive social psychology. Indigenous psychologies should be recognized as a core part of the social psychology landscape. Scholars can draw upon insights from these psychologies to expand and pluralize the discipline and to ensure responsiveness to the diverse ways of being and needs of the world's population. In this chapter, we have attempted to open the door to these diverse psychological realities. The references cited in this chapter provide valuable resources for you to explore these emerging approaches further.

We have noted that discussions about indigenous peoples are often engaged in with reference to processes of colonization and acculturation that often rupture existing ways of life and connections of people to places and their shared identities. Despite hardship, many indigenous peoples survive and flourish today. A range of unique psychological understandings and frameworks are offered as moves are made to decolonize areas of psychology. As part of this process, indigenization can occur from the inside and the outside of a community. The insider, or emic, approach involves developing methods and approaches from within one's own culture and local knowledge. The outside, or etic, approach involves indigenous psychologists drawing on existing insights, methods and approaches developed outside the community culture and appropriating and refining these for local use. Both approaches provide insight and a means of extending the discipline of social psychology and ensuring increased utility across a range of cultural settings. Part of the process of decolonizing psychology also involves rethinking the core notion of the self as an independent entity and replacing it with notions of the interconnected self, which reflect the complexities of being in everyday life.

It is crucial to acknowledge that many of the issues and concerns raised by indigenous psychologists, such as the orientation of social psychology and the need to respond to the particularities of groups and diverse life situations, are shared by many social psychologists in Europe and North America. Indigenous psychologies from around the world are compatible with the collectivist stream of Western social psychology outlined in Chapters 2 and 3. There are also similarities in calls for responsiveness, relevance and attention to contexts. There are also differences in emphasis, orientation and language. While recognizing the differences, we do not wish to be misread as advocating a rigid distinction between all Anglo-American-inspired psychology and indigenous psychologies. In the end, all psychologies are based on cultural knowledge and local histories.

A key point of contrast between prominent variants of the dominant individualistic stream of social psychology in the West and indigenous psychologies relates to context. The individualistic stream seeks to develop theory and insights that transcend historical and cultural contexts. Kim, Yang and Hwang (2006b) draw on the work of Albert Bandura when they reflect on the limitations of the individualistic stream of North American psychology and the emphasis on developing context-free theory:

Existing psychological theories are not universal since they have eliminated the very qualities that allow people to understand, predict, and control their environment. Bandura (1999) points out that "it is ironic that a science of human functioning should strip people of the very capabilities that make them unique in their power to shape their environment and their own destiny" (p. 5)

Conversely, indigenous psychologies seek to embrace those very contexts and to explore the lives of people as they are enmeshed by, shape and are shaped by these contexts. This orientation towards people in context has been called for around the world (Kim, Yang & Hwang, 2006a). Ensuring a diverse range of theories, themes and concerns is put forward as a way to drive the discipline beyond the agendas of dominant cultures. Such a broadening of the discipline is aimed at inclusion, rather than exclusion, and opening dialogue across cultures regarding social psychological issues. However, a key complicating factor is that this dialogue cannot be based in the social psychology of any one culture, and, therefore, much work is yet to be done on establishing the basis for discussion. As we saw in Chapter 4, from the work of Bartlett (1932), it is important to be vigilant in such exchanges in order to ensure that in translating the approaches and insights from one culture to another we are aware of how our own cultural standpoint influences the meanings we make and of our blind spots. This is why open and ongoing dialogue across social psychologies from around the world is crucial for the further development of the discipline. It is important that we strive towards understanding people from their own cultural and historical frames of reference as much as possible. This is, in part, why the voices of indigenous scholars are included in this chapter.

Finally, we can have multiple psychologies within social psychology. There is diversity in the world, and we need to embrace it if we are to understand everyday life.

Review exercise

Consider your own country of residence and answer the following questions:

- Who are the indigenous people and what is their history?
- Have processes of colonization occurred and, if so, what have been the consequences?
- Do these groups still control the legal and social structures that govern everyday life?
- What is the status of these groups in society?

6 Social psychology and place

Core questions to consider while reading this chapter

- What are activity settings?
- Can you outline an example of an arts-based intervention?
- How are community gardens linked to health?
- How is desegregation played out in physical spaces?
- What is environmental psychology?
- How are material objects related to place-based identities?
- What is neighbourhood renewal?
- What are place-based identities?
- How is social inclusion related to place?

Chapter scenario

It is a noisy lunchtime in the food court. The place is packed with shoppers on a rainy mid-winter day. A well-dressed woman sits at a table as her two grandchildren gleefully devour their fries. With the children occupied, the grandmother scans the scene around her. The table next to her has recently been vacated. Despite her distaste for the tainted food, she relishes the relative sense of space offered the empty neighbouring table. Shoppers pause momentarily with their plates but then settle for a freshly wiped table to eat from. The children's bickering about who has the best new plastic toy brings her back to her own table. Then, the grandmother senses movement close by and looks up as the aroma of her latte is momentarily overpowered by musty sweat. The neighbouring table now has a lank-haired occupant dressed in a heavy coat, hunched over and hungrily ladling the cast-off food. Horrified, the grandmother scans the food hall, her eyes homing in on a well-built woman in a uniform. As soon as the woman turns round she beckons her. With a knowing look, the security guard walks over and asks, "Is there anything I can do for you?" "I should hope so!" replies the grandmother. She turns to point to the neighbouring table: "Do you see what she is doing? It's disgusting! What are people like her doing in here?" The musty homeless woman is already getting up from her chair and gathering her rucksack. "I'm going, shame to waste it though," she mutters, glancing at what is left of the food. The security guard walks with the woman towards the exit and, once they are out of the grandmother's earshot, says, "Hey Susan, you'd better not hang round, especially when it's so busy – sorry mate." Susan replies, "So I'll just go outside and catch pneumonia then?" The security guard sighs and continues, "Look, I know I've turned a blind eye in the past, but we've got this new manager, and I'll lose my job if people like her back there complain too much." Susan lowers her head and says nothing. The security guard stops and seems lost in thought. Susan pulls her stained coat closer as she approaches the glass doors that separate the air-conditioned comfort of the mall from the driving rain outside.

This scenario invokes a setting in which people from different walks of life come into contact with each other. It is set in a shopping mall food court because such places are ubiquitous in daily life. These places are designed to appear to be public spaces that any person can occupy. However, they are private spaces specifically created to foster economic activity. Legitimate inhabitants in such places are the shoppers. Anyone who fails to engage sufficiently in economic activity or who in any way offends other people participating in consumptive practices is less likely to be tolerated. This is why Susan can be escorted from the premises. The scenario reflects how the spaces many people frequent in daily life are highly textured and regulated in terms of function, who belongs and what behaviour is deemed to be appropriate. Social scientists have referred to this process of removing 'undesirable' people as being central to the 'Disneyfication' of urban space (Amster, 2003). Disneyfication describes the way in which the public face of cities is increasingly transformed to reflect a Disney theme park, which appears clean and pristine on the outside, but which hides the dirt, exclusion and exploitation within.

Situations such as that depicted in the scenario highlight how cities have very few indoor public spaces where citizens, including homeless people, are free to spend a cold winter's day. The spaces of a modern city are not uniform and equitable, but reflect a complex social landscape overlaid with rules and meanings (Lees, 2004). These places also invoke complex relations between stakeholders, which can alert us to how people negotiate the regulation of the landscapes of everyday life and social participation (Hodgetts et al., 2008). Place-based interactions are central to social psychology. The security guard faces cognitive dissonance (Box 6.1): her personal inclination is towards allowing Susan to stay, while her job requires her to escort Susan from the building. In the past, the guard has allowed Susan to stay. Today, she has no choice but to conform to, and enforce, the rules or risk losing her own position in the space, and in mainstream society at large.

Everyday spaces are therefore sites for tensions between control and regulation, freedom and resistance. Although the idea of heavily regulated public spaces is unappealing, there is some public consensus for the need to regulate offensive behaviour so that the spaces we share remain appealing for the majority of citizens (Mitchell, 2003). However, it is unclear whether scavenging leftover food, panhandling or muttering to lampposts is behaviour that ought to be regulated. What is offensive and what can be tolerated in a public space are questions that are endlessly renegotiated. Although some regulation is unavoidable, completely sanitized public places are not necessarily a way to build an inclusive sense of belonging or community in place.

BOX 6.1   Cognitive dissonance

Cognitive dissonance is the experience of tension stemming from holding two contradictory thoughts simultaneously (Festinger, 1957). The experience is particularly intense when our actions contradict our self-concept. In this case, the security guard removes Susan, the homeless women, from the mall. This action contradicts the security guard's self-image as a caring person who wants to allow Susan to stay.

Review exercise

Think for a moment about particular activities that are or are not regulated (e.g. littering, skateboarding, drunkenness, driving noisy cars).

- Are regulations for such activities enforced fairly across all individuals or groups?

We began with a scenario featuring the experience of a homeless woman because it raises key issues to be explored in this chapter, including the social regulation of bodies in different spaces, inclusion and exclusion, interpersonal and group interactions, identity, belonging and social roles. These are all topics of concern for social psychologists grappling with the complexities of increasingly diverse societies. Our overall aim is to convey an approach to social psychology that takes into consideration the places in which everyday life occurs. The key take-home message here is that places are woven into human relations, and our lives into places. Places are more than backdrops for social life, for we all live somewhere, often move between different places on a daily basis, and encounter and interact with others in various settings. Places are where we include or exclude others, and are ourselves accepted or rejected from time to time. In the twenty-first century, many of our activities, movements and interactions are no longer bound by proximity, or a single physical setting. Lives are often conducted across physical and virtual, or representational, spaces provided by various transportation, media and communication technologies. In this context, the social psychology of place has become more complex and multilayered. Social psychologists increasingly consider the dynamics of place because healthy development and supportive social relationships are associated with a sense of belonging some*where*, be it a home, a neighbourhood, a sports club, a beach or a social networking site.

Chapter overview

The remainder of this chapter explores issues surrounding the social psychology of place, in nine sections. The first section explores insights from environmental psychology that can enrich our social psychology of place. The second considers the relationship between self and place, and the concept of place-based identities. The third takes up how people develop a sense of home and belonging. The fourth section documents how people exist across various places, which they weave together into a lifeworld. The fifth section explores the exclusion of some people from public places and the threat this poses to their sense of belonging and self. The sixth section extends the focus of the fifth by considering links between media or representational settings and physical settings. The seventh considers the importance of developing place-based identities within communities in relation to social cohesion and health. Section eight provides examples of place-based strategies used in psychology to address social problems, build community and enhance health. A general discussion and review exercise concludes the chapter. The mains chapter themes are:

- Links between self and place
- Issues of inclusion and exclusion
- Initiatives to foster place affiliations and healthy communities

Environmental psychology and the social psychology of place

Much has been written about place both within psychology and across the social sciences in the past few decades. It is useful at this point to specify what we mean by 'place'. The word 'place' has many meanings and is used both as a verb and as a noun to refer to a dwelling, position, status or somewhere to be. As the Oxford online dictionary states, place defines "A particular portion of space. A portion of space occupied by a person or thing. A proper or natural position (he is out of his place; take your places). Situation, circumstances (put yourself in my place)." Although geographic locations are readily identifiable, social scientists have been engaged in ongoing debates that extend understandings of place beyond the demarcation of a particular area to identifying the characteristics of a place or what is located in a place. Current definitions include physical, social, relational or cultural processes occurring in a place. This means place is also about context, and that means there is a lot to consider. As Rodman (1993) states, "The creation of place is at once so simple ... and so complex. Any experience of place weaves together space, built form, behaviour, and ideas, at individual and collective levels. And it does so within particular social, economic, political and historical contexts" (p. 123).

De Certeau (1984) proposes two perspectives on 'the city', which are useful in our discussion of place. The first is rather top-down and involves a kind of bird's-eye view from the vantage point of planners, officials, manages and policymakers. From this perspective, psychologists look at the design of places, such as malls and food courts. This approach is also associated with the development of laws and policies on appropriate behaviour and on who belongs and who does not belong in particular places. Efforts are directed at the creation of environments to serve particular purposes, such as shopping and eating. The second perspective is more from the bottom up in that the primary focus is on how people construct their own spaces and on how they understand the physical and social world around them. Psychologists are increasingly interested in the social relations that occur in neighbourhoods, bars, beaches, parks, streets, food courts, malls and houses. In this context, we might concern ourselves with Susan's experiences of displacement from the food court. Of course these two perspectives overlap when, for example, psychologists work on community renewal projects that foster healthy living environments and then lobby authorities to make sure that homeless people are allowed to frequent local civic spaces.

Throughout this book we have noted the limitations of the tendency of psychologists to focus on the individual or small-group actions, as if people exist in a physical vacuum. Coinciding with the crisis in social psychology in the 1970s, environmental psychologists argued that traditional views of mind and behaviour and subject–object relations evident in the individualistic stream of social psychology (see Chapter 2) were too narrow and failed to account for the environmental influences on human action. Environmental psychology developed via the combination of an internalistic focus (on attitudes, cognitions, mental representations and perceptions, and how people impact the environment) and an externalistic focus (on material contexts and the influence of physical environments on people). The field is increasingly diverse and encompasses both physiologically and socially oriented psychologies. For example, a recent issue of the *Journal of Environmental Psychology* (2008, 28[2]) included a wide range of topics: the relationship between perceptions of risk and preparedness for a natural disaster, links between the individual characteristics of adolescents and neighbourhood conditions, the place of social capital in studies of place and health, the function of religious belief in evaluations of a sacred place, and whether eye movements differ across different photographs. These wide-ranging topics reflect how environmental psychology has developed into an interdisciplinary field of study concerned with interrelationships between people and environments. It includes the application of psychological knowledge to understanding how human behaviour and experiences are affected by environments, while also examining how people affect and shape their environments. Environmental psychology includes a focus on physiological issues, such as environmental cues used by individuals to navigate their way through the world, and more social psychologically oriented concerns, such as the intergroup relations that occur in particular places.

Although referring primarily to research into race relations, Dixon and Durrheim (2004) make a number of observations relevant to the development of a social psychology of place. They propose that, until relatively recently, psychologists have approached place in three primary ways. The first approach is to view place as simply a backdrop for, and as having limited impact on, behaviour and social interactions. An example is research that takes people out of the contexts of their daily lives and into experimental settings that are considered inert in terms of extraneous variables. This approach tends to downplay the significance of place in psychological processes. In the second approach, specific settings or places are compared for their impact on behaviour and social relations. Researchers might compare the attitudes of people in towns and people in cities regarding topics such as homelessness or immigration. The town and city settings are contrasted as convenient sites for demographic and psychological factors apparent in the respective populations. Third, particular places are approached as either facilitating or inhibiting specific behaviour or interactions. Here psychologists might focus on group size effects on people's willingness to intervene to help a person in need (bystander apathy, see Chapter 2) or conduct research into the effects of open-plan office spaces on morale or cooperation in the workplace (Box 6.2).

Our view is that these three approaches are useful, but do not comprise the full extent of social psychologically oriented work on place. Social psychologists are increasingly interested in the processes through which people mould and construct their physical worlds at both individual and collective levels. A core concept in advancing this agenda is that of place-based identities. In exploring this concept, the following section offers a social psychological perspective on people and place. For now, it is useful to realise that current theory and research on place constitutes an effort to explore the ways in which people invest aesthetic, moral and personal meanings in different settings and in the process weave themselves into place. It is increasingly realized that place-based psychological research can be helpful for making sense of the actions and experiences of people in the context of their daily lives. A focus on place raises issues around the politics of human interaction and can aid us in understanding the complexities of social situations, particularly those in which people from diverse backgrounds are living together in a particular environment. This is an increasingly important issue in today's multicultural societies.

BOX 6.2   Activity settings

Altman (1993) proposed that social relationships are embedded in specific physical environments or activity settings. This work highlights how people and environments are 'mutually defining' in that they shape and give meaning to each other. Activity settings are observable manifestations of social ecologies and cultural practices. Activity settings include both the features of the physical environment and subjective features, including rules, meanings, values and so forth, which shape what people do there (O'Donnell, Tharp & Wilson, 1993). This concept is useful for psychologists who want to acknowledge the settings in which particular human actions occur and the impact of the environment on shaping what people do and do not do in different settings. Activity settings can be used as a flexible concept that allows psychologists to consider how people both shape and are shaped through the actions they engage in within particular settings. Simple acts reproduce social norms regarding appropriate behaviour. For example, yelling and stamping in support of a team at a sports event is appropriate behaviour. However, we would soon be told to leave if we did the same in a church during a funeral service. Such a reverential space is evident when people kneel in a church. Over time these actions help define what is appropriate and inappropriate behaviour for that place. The idea that everyday actions contribute to the meaning of a place is increasingly evident in social psychology. A social psychology of interpersonal relations needs to consider acceptable and unacceptable behaviour in particular settings. This is necessary because people adjust their actions and, as we will argue in the following section, their very sense of self according to the places they find themselves in.

Place-based identities

Central to social psychology are issues of personal and collective identity. These processes are clearly linked to experiences of place. Writing on place-based identities constitutes an attempt to account for the influence of the places we move through, dwell in and call our own in the development of our sense of self. It involves the rethinking of a somewhat static 'attributes'-oriented perspective on identity (discussed in Chapter 3) and the adoption instead of a more fluid notion of identity construction as occurring through ongoing social interactions.

From a social psychological perspective, place identities are thought to arise because places, as bounded locales imbued with personal, social, and cultural meanings, provide a significant framework in which identity is constructed, maintained, and transformed. Like people, things, and activities, places are an integral part of the social world of everyday life, as such, they become important mechanisms through which identity is defined and situated. (Cuba & Hummon, 1993, p. 112)

Place-based identities are forged through intimate understandings of settings, including bodily placement and social interactions, providing a sense of 'insider' status. Charleston's (2009) study of English football grounds illustrates that the home team's stadium offers a strong sense of continuity, belonging and ownership for fans in their connection to the place and their social relationships in this space. The identity of the football fans is reinscribed during each match by the rituals taking place, the camaraderie and the material objects, such as clothing, banners and signs.

Many people develop 'a sense of place' in which memories are associated with particular locations, providing a sense of connection, history and shared activity. Such associations (Box 6.3) are cultivated through positive experiences and the enactment of relationships (Hernández, Hidalgo, Salazar-Laplace & Hess, 2007; Pretty, Chipuer & Bramston, 2003). Social psychologists have noted that place associations are central to place-based identities throughout our lives (Twigger-Ross & Uzzell, 1996). This is evident in how people often tell others where they are from when telling them who they are. They might say I am from England (country), London (city) or Brockley (suburb), depending on the context of the conversation. All these scales of place tell the listener something about the speaker and how they see themselves. Physical environments often contribute to people's sense of self-efficacy and distinctiveness. Such references to places are also linked to particular groups and associated with prestige or stigma, culture, religion, ethnicity and social class. Places themselves have histories that transcend individual speakers. Places are associated with particular groups, and in the process develop identities of their own. Broken windows, rubbish and graffiti say a lot about an area, as do manicured lawns, water features and the absence of graffiti. As noted in Chapter 2, the relationship between place, people and identity is dialogical (Twigger-Ross & Uzzell, 1996).

The term 'place attachment' refers to an association process by which a person who experiences positive experiences in a specific place can develop an affective bond with the place (Korpela, Ylen, Tyrvainen & Silvennoinen, 2009). Particular places can leave strong memories, and there can be an effect even if we can return to such places only in our thoughts. Nonetheless, the places we return to frequently in the course of our everyday lives can create particularly strong place attachments. People's positive place attachments are considered to have a crucial and enduring role in maintaining psychological and physical health. Regular access to favourite places is important for the restoration of our emotions and the self (Hartig & Staats, 2003; Korpela, Ylen, Tyrvainen & Silvennoinen, 2008). Being in favourite places provides benefits such as relaxation, weakening the hold of worries and random thoughts, increasing positive emotions, alleviating negative emotions and providing the space to think through problems and recollect our focus and attention. Restorative favourite spaces can be everyday natural or physical spaces, although in most studies natural environments (including forests, beaches, waterways, parks and gardens) are cited as having the greatest restorative functions. In a longitudinal study in Finland by Korpela and colleagues (2009), respondents' most frequent and enduring favourite place selection was allotment gardens, because these provided a stable restorative effect, as opposed to the impact of more remote natural settings visited less often.

BOX 6.3   Place associations

Place associations manifest in experiences of close, local relationships with people and, by extension, places in which interactions occur (Pretty, Chipuer & Bramston, 2003). Place associations signify long-term bonds between people and their homes and communities. These attachments are not static, but can change (Eacott & Sonn, 2006). If people fail to make changes in their environment that provide support for their desired identities and goals, then attachment may erode (Brown & Perkins, 1992). Many people have memories of particular events and places with which they feel particular affiliations.

- Do you remember a particular setting from childhood with fondness or nostalgia?
- Who was there and what were you doing?
- When do you share this memory with others?
- How do you feel when you talk about the memory?

Central to this book is the proposition that human beings are much more than fixed personality-based entities residing within the bodies of individuals who display predictable attitudes and behaviour. Reflecting this proposition, Mikulas (2007) recently combined psychological aspects of historical Buddhism and Western psychology to promote a more comprehensive view of what it means to be a person. This view is compatible with the concept of place-based identity. Central to Buddhism is the notion of 'dependent origination', or that everything is interlinked, stemming from dependence on something else. Such an assertion does not necessitate the dismissal of individuality, personal autonomy or human agency. Rather, it is to propose that people are interwoven into lifeworlds that exist within social structures. People are influenced by other people, institutions and physical environments at a fundamental level. We can experience such influences directly in a sense of obligation, as in our understandings of what is right and wrong in particular places and situations. This stance is evident in the work of social psychologists such as James (1892/1984), Cooley (1902), Mead (1934), Fuller (1990) Billig (1996), Musolf (2003), and Hermans and Hermans-Konopka (2009), who propose that the self is an ongoing project and can shift in orientation across different contexts and interactions. You, as a person, can change with circumstances, adjust and grow. We come to know ourselves through our engagements in the world. Generally, the self can be experienced through one's internal voice, body, clothing and possessions, habits, places (home), friends and family.

Through daily life, people occupy the world physically and psychologically, as embodied beings whose social practices give meaning to places and situations. The self manifests in our actions, bodily displays, the things we collect and the places we frequent. Psychological (mental) and psychological (material) dimensions are interwoven in the doing of daily life (de Certeau, 1997). The places we dwell in and the things we collect become part of us, and crystallize aspects of who we are, want to be and show to others. This orientation to the self situates human existence within material and social contexts. A core idea advanced by Mikulas (2007) is that people's feeling of being separate from their environments, and of having independent self-entities, is a particular historically situated Western construction. Contemporary psychology is a discipline that has individuals with their thoughts and actions as its focus, yet it is important not to get lost at the personal level and focus only on our individuality. Our understandings of people can be extended if we consider the broader contexts shaping their lives, including the social networks they are situated within and the places in which they reside.

A sense of home, things and place

The domestic home provides a useful illustration of the intimate relations between self and place, evident in a sense of belonging, familiarity, comfort and even self-regulation. Place-based identities are often anchored in the home setting as the place that (hopefully) meets our most basic psychological needs and provides us with continuity and a 'haven' or retreat from the public realm. The decorating of a house textures the environment as a reflection of the inhabitants' tastes, and the display of personal objects such as family portraits can symbolize what is important to these people. Many people strive to create places for themselves where they feel at home. What are often treated as the internal dimensions of the self are frequently manifest in the display of objects. Hurdley (2006) explored the objects people display in their homes as aspects of their identities. Mantelpieces were seen as warranting investigation, as they have traditionally functioned as a focal point for family or living rooms in the United Kingdom. People in the study talked about their objects as if they represented their character and the relationships they hold dear.

Review exercise

Consider your own house or apartment.

- Are photographs of fun events in your family history displayed?
- Are there objects you and other family members have collected that remind you of particular people and places?

Households are often full of such objects that reflect the lives of inhabitants stretching beyond the four walls and through time and space.

Our homes, and particularly our living rooms, have both public and private functions (Rechavi, 2009) that are vital for our relationships to the places which we dwell in and which anchor aspects of the self. The furniture and objects in our domestic domain offer comfort, and personal objects such as photos enable us to restore and reaffirm the self. These personal objects communicate aspects of the self to the people we live with or invite into our home as guests. A hotel room may have more comfortable furniture than we can afford at home, but it lacks the expression of self and identity that is part of making a home. As people accumulate objects in the home, they accumulate *being* (Noble, 2004). Objects such as photographs, books, souvenirs, artwork and ornaments offer proof of being, and the memory and recognition of events.

Personal things are invested with history and tradition, and often crystallize connections with other people and places. The retelling of the significance of an object invokes a nexus of meaning and relationships that interweave people's lives and exceed the materiality of the object, invoking shared relations. The meaning of these objects should not be seen as fixed or static. The accounts people give of objects depends on the aspects of self they wish to display and communicate and on the nature of the interactions they are engaged in at the time. For many people a home is more than simply a place to dwell, reside or take care of basic needs such as food and shelter. A home is also felt and woven into a person's very sense of belonging, refuge and self (Mallett, 2004). If people are fortunate, a home is where they can realize their responsibilities towards others, and more fully negotiate the direction of their lives. This raises the point that not everyone has access to a home in the form of a private domestic dwelling. Many citizens rent an apartment, are homeless like Susan or live in institutions. However, a sense of home (Box 6.4) is still crucial to the mental health of such people.

Although having a safe, secure and comfortable house or dwelling is important to our material and psychological well-being, the concept of home refers to a much greater variety of possible scales, locations and settings (Manzo, 2003). People can refer to a city or a country as home, and their sense of attachment at this scale may become more apparent if they relocate to a less familiar place for a time. For many people their place of dwelling is only one of a range of settings where they experience aspects of home. The study of English football fans by Charleston (2009) referred to earlier in this chapter argues that the ways in which these fans experienced their home team stadium bore many similarities to experiences of a typical home space. Fans viewed the stadium as a place for important social interactions with like-minded people, a place of escape, happiness and self-expression, and a place to experience a strong sense of togetherness and belonging. Although most respondents in the study said the stadium was as important as their home space, only 1 per cent stated they were "more at home" while in the stadium. Accordingly, Charleston argues that there are both similarities and distinct subtle differences between different notions of home as a dwelling and more symbolic secondary home spaces such as a country or a stadium. Although we may experience many different place attachments over the course of our lives, at a particular point in time we generally have only one place where we feel *most* 'at home'. Rather than becoming too entrapped in trying to classify the concept of home, Charleston suggests we need to increase our understanding of the symbolic essence of home. A broad understanding of what is required for most people to feel at home can help us to improve the various private and public spaces people dwell in as they live out their daily lives.

BOX 6.4   Consequences of a sense of home for mental health

Wright and Kloos (2007) found that for people living with mental illness, the physical qualities and aesthetics of their dwelling, or being able to construct a sense of home in an attractive and tidy place, were crucial in developing a sense of place. In turn, such a sense of place is important for good mental health outcomes and adaption to community life. These authors found that neighbourhood-level factors, or the social environment beyond the front door, were also strong predictors of reduced psychiatric symptoms and increased adaptive functioning among these citizens. Factors such as traffic flows, sidewalks, street lighting, amenities and opportunities for social interaction and cultivating a sense of belonging appear to be crucial in promoting place-based identities and wellness. "Supported housing models that facilitate recovery and community participation for persons with serious mental illness have been shown to have a positive influence on overall psychosocial well-being across various domains" (Wright & Kloos, 2007, p. 80).

We hope to have convinced you that identities are not evident simply in the heads or verbal accounts of people. Identities are also evident in people's actions, daily practices, things and the places they frequent or call home. Links between people, places and things do not relate simply to personal identities. These links are also evident among groups. For instance, Snell and Hodgetts (2007) explored the function of a bar in the production of a place-based identity by a group of heavy metal fans. They illustrated how shared practices such as dressing a certain way, decorating the bar for gigs and dancing in a mosh pit were central to the reaffirmation of a shared identity within the group that was anchored in a sense of ownership of the bar. This was evident in the decorations in the bar, which included various skulls, disfigured dolls' heads, coffins, skeletons, axes and photographs of prominent musicians (see Figure 6.1). This work exemplifies the interconnected nature of relational and spatial dimensions of everyday life and identity construction. These dimensions are important because we are all embodied beings who live in a material world and who reaffirm relationships through participation in shared activities and the display of affiliation.

The combination of things, bodies and shared practices in a particular place reminded heavy metal fans who they were and wanted to be. References to such participative acts as patrons going into and decorating the bar before a gig convey notions of pride, caring and belonging. Mirroring such patron statements, the bar's proprietors referred to a widespread 'sense of belonging to 6ft' among patrons, many of whom had become 'part of the furniture' or 'one of the fixtures'. Describing participants as part of the furniture reflects how identities and community membership can merge with physical spaces. There appeared to be a reciprocal relationship between collective activities and the venue, which was manifested in a congruence or synergy between bar

Figure 6.1. Photograph of the bar 6ft Under supplied by David Snell

symbolism and patron attire. The bar's logo is a dagger. This symbol has come to represent the community. Several patrons and staff have tattooed the dagger onto their bodies as an expression of their belonging to the bar and commitment to the community. The ways in which patrons adorned the bar, and in turn their own bodies, with metaller symbols reflect how people, places, symbols and objects can come to represent each other, and reflect the intersection of subject, object and place (Snell & Hodgetts, 2007). In short, metaller symbols transform the physical space of the bar into a communal environment congruent with a shared place-based identity. These practices epitomize how people and environments can be 'mutually defining' in that they shape and give meaning to each other.

Weaving places together into a lifeworld

In the previous section, we focused on processes of inclusion and the formation of place-based identities in particular settings. However, few people spend their lives in one place. Individuals move around and as a result develop a sense of self that spans particular locations. People can also manifest different selves in different settings. This is an important consideration because, although we advocate a focus on the places within which daily life is conducted, it is important not to adopt a view that fixes people in particular places (Dixon, Levine & McAuley, 2006). Mobility is central to understanding the role of place in everyday life. This is particularly the case for people who are often moved along or displaced, such as Susan in the scenario that opened this chapter. These citizens often live their lives between sites such as malls, parks, public toilets and libraries. This raises concerns central to social psychology regarding how people cope with or adapt to being excluded from particular places and the social practices occurring there.

Review exercise

Note the places you go over the course of a typical week. Now think about the roles you engage in and the people you interact with in each of these places. Looking across these settings think about how you would describe your life to someone else. The point is that we live our lives across a range of settings and that different aspects of who we are come to the fore in different locations.

In exploring the relationship between a person's sense of self, material objects and place, Hodgetts and colleagues (2009) illustrate how a homeless man associates particular objects with particular places and particular identities. Brett stated that he had "different sides to his life", which he located in specific places. One side is reflected in Brett's photographs of quiet places within the Auckland Central Business District, including a bookstore. In this place, Brett experienced life as a 'normal person' or reader who hoped to pick up a good book. Another side is reflected in his photographs of public toilets in the central city, where he sees himself as a "druggie". Returning to the toilets to take the photographs was an ordeal, as Brett felt the physical urge to use drugs again. Brett's reaction reflects the depth of connection between the location and a sense of self as a druggie. This identification threatened to engulf Brett simply by his being in a place that was normalized for him as a site for drug use. He stated, "Just being there triggers my addictive side. The place has a strong pull on me and I'm better off away from there." Another side is reflected in photographs he produced of coastal bays he walked to from Auckland city as a way to escape his drug use and 'street life'. Brett's account reveals processes through which the identity of a place can be shaped by the practices that occur there. For example, drug use textures a public toilet as a place to be a druggie, whereas escaping into a book is associated with the quiet space of a bookstore. In visiting different places, Brett literally weaves himself into locations and an existence as a hermit, druggie or normal citizen. Different places exemplify different facets of his life or selves and render tangible different habits and practices of escapism enacted through the use of particular places and associated material objects, including needles and books. Consequently, the way Brett sees himself is not simply contained within his body or psyche. For Brett, aspects of the self manifest in the places he goes, the practices he engages in and the things he uses.

Despite associating different versions of himself with different locations and practices, Brett maintained a core sense of self as he moved across different places. He established a sense of continuity and connection through the use of portable objects. Hodgetts and colleagues found that Brett's MP3 player allowed him to construct a space from which to weave the different places he frequented together and to constitute a geographically located life. Brett created a mobile home out of sound, which he used to transit the city. As he walked, Brett was engulfed within a sound cave emanating from his MP3 player. This allowed him to transcend the immediate physical environment and to cultivate a sense of security, privacy, dwelling and familiarity. The routine of listening provided him with a sense of home on the move. Brett's use of the player suggests that communications technologies have contributed to dissolving the separation between public and private spaces, people, things and places. As noted in Chapter 10, social psychologists (García-Montes, Caballero-Muñoz & Pérez-Álvarez, 2006) have observed how the users of distinct public and private spaces negotiate the intersection or fusion of these spaces smoothly and skilfully. Similarly, Thibaud (2003) proposed that a 'sonic bridge' enables domiciled listeners to move seamlessly from the domestic realm to the street. This occurs when one gets up in the morning and prepares for university while listening to an iPod or similar device. When it comes time to leave one can take the music and to some extent the sense of a private morning routine with oneself when stepping out into the street, grabbing a coffee, stepping onto a bus and going into the library to study before class. These places are stitched together into a daily routine.

To this point, we have attended to some of the ways in which identities, whether personal or collective, are constructed in the world and are reflected in accounts of affiliation with particular places, the social relationships occurring in these places and the collection or display of meaningful objects. People often texture their places to reflect personal and more communal qualities, interests and styles. Thus, places can come to stand for and communicate something about the people who inhabit them. Human affiliation with particular places is often intensely emotional, and is cultivated through a history of engaging in particular activities that occur there. This is evident when people associate different places with different activities and selves. However, not everyone is afforded comparable opportunities to develop a sense of belonging and place-based identity throughout the different phases of his or her life. In the following section we consider issues of segregation and exclusion.

Place-based segregation and exclusion

As a consequence of continued globalization and urbanization, major metropolitan areas have become sites for an increasing convergence and cohabitation of people from diverse groups. In response to these changes, social psychologists have utilized the study of everyday life to provide understanding of the ways in which different groups cohabit and of the politics and history of intergroup relations in specific shared spaces. Struggles over inclusion and exclusion involve the social regulation of place where belonging is not necessarily guaranteed and discrimination can become legitimated. As our cities become more crowded and diverse, a key issue to explore is how people from different groups might live together in the same place. This section focuses on such issues.

The social psychology of desegregation offers some insights for exploring the issues surrounding cohabitation. This field includes the early efforts of figures such as Gordon Allport (1954), who sought to understand the formation and maintenance of attitudes shaping racial integration. Allport advocated for more inclusive interactions between social groups in shared environments. Early work was conducted in accord with Allport's contact hypothesis, which proposed that with increased contact between groups racial prejudices would be reduced and as a result a more tolerant society would develop. There are common processes here with those outlined in the classic Sherif boys camp studies outlined in Chapter 2 of this book. Intergroup integration and cohesion, and a reduction in conflict, are often facilitated by engagements in cooperative ventures or the identification and pursuit of common goals of importance to people in both groups (Brewer, 1996). Allport's seminal work encouraged psychologists to theorize and intervene to enhance the conditions under which contact can produce harmony between social groups.

Social psychologists have demonstrated the benefits of intergroup contact for reducing racial stereotypes and anxieties and for increasing empathy and inclusion felt across groups. If people from different groups spend time together in ideal situations, 'they' can become 'we'. The grandmother in the scenario for this chapter might become more tolerant towards homeless people if she spent time with these fellow citizens. As Dixon and colleagues (2008) note:

Since the early decades of the last century, social psychologists have accumulated a wealth of data on the psychological benefits of racial contact and desegregation, including a reduction in race stereotypes and anxiety, an increase in positive interracial emotions such as liking and empathy, and a heightened tendency to form inclusive identities in which "they" become "we". (p. 2)

Evidence suggests that harmony is much less likely when desegregation is conducted in situations where cooperation and mutual goals are absent. For example, prejudices are more likely to persist in situations where one group has the power to set the agenda and limited dialogue is occurring between groups. In such cases, the benefits of desegregation are unlikely to be realized. Instead, desegregation may even exacerbate and produce further tensions and anxiety between groups (Brewer, 1996).

Despite the efforts of social psychologists, segregation remains a feature of daily life for many people. Overt markers of the segregation of races in daily life such as 'whites only' signs may have been removed from restaurants, movie theatres, public facilities and schools in many countries; however, more subtle practices still exist. For example, immigrant and minority groups are often forced to reside in 'less desirable' locations. More affluent citizens can retreat into walled suburbs or compounds to avoid contact with groups perceived to be different. "Like other forms of segregation, then, micro-ecological segregation involves the production of social spaces that create, maintain and signify racial separation" (Dixon et al., 2008, p. 4). In response, social psychologists, including Dixon and colleagues (2008), have explored issues of racial segregation by focusing on the local practices through which broader intergroup relations are patterned and reproduced. These authors draw on the concept of place-based identities to propose that desegregation can change relations both between self and other and between self and place (Box 6.5). They show how the inclusion of another group of people can generate

---

BOX 6.5   Re-segregation at the beach

Dixon and Durrheim (2003) investigated relations between white and black South Africans on beaches in coastal Natal. The beaches in the study had historically been whites only and a prime site for family vacations among members of this racial group. Relaxing, watching others and enjoying the sun were activities associated with the good life, a sense of belonging and 'being' relaxed. The whites' privileged access to exclusive and uncrowded beach space was overturned by the 1989 repeal of South African beach Apartheid. Since then, the beaches have become more crowded, and whites are expected to share the space with black citizens. Dixon and Durrheim conducted an in-depth study to explore how the process of desegregation was actually going, and whether there was any evidence that sharing the beach space was leading to greater racial harmony. The research was based on a sequence of ninety-nine maps compiled during the peak holiday periods of 1999 and 2001.

Photographs were used to map the movement of racial groups on the beach over time (Figures 6.2 and 6.3). Their analysis revealed that a process of re-segregation was occurring on the beach. The maps documented racial isolation patterns, dispersal between groups and a temporal process of segregation in beach occupancy. As black beach-goers entered areas and increased in density, white beach-goers moved to other areas or left the beach. Such patterning was based on a sequence of events over the course of the day. White South Africans entered and occupied the beach early in the day. As black South Africans entered the beach later in the day, the whites moved into clusters and to different areas. Once the density of black South Africans increased sufficiently, the whites exited the beach. The authors point out that it is dangerous to base our inferences of intergroup relations on such maps or observations of space alone. It is also important to engage with actors in the space and gain a deeper appreciation of their interactions. Durrheim and Dixon (2005) interviewed beach-goers to explore their interpretations of the migration patterns at the beach. Interviewees from different groups employed different explanatory models for the clustering patterns. This in-depth qualitative research revealed that attempts at desegregation in the local setting were associated with a loss of place and self for white South Africans (Dixon & Durrheim, 2004). This participant group explained the patterns in terms of 'crowding', 'invasion' and 'displacement'. The accounts of white South Africans coalesced around a nostalgic tale of loss of place and anxiety about family safety reflected in their fears of the black beach-goers now present in a previously white domain. Conversely, black South Africans explained the patterns in terms of white flight and racism.

Figure 6.2. Photograph of a beach in South Africa provided by Professor John Dixon

Figure 6.3. Map showing racial clustering on a South African beach provided by Professor John Dixon

feelings of dislocation for the groups that previously had privileged access to a place. Although desegregation is justifiable on the basis of equity, the broader impacts of desegregation tend to challenge existing experiences of local subjectivity.

The work of Dixon and colleagues (2003, 2004) highlights broader issues around the creation and disruption of place-based identity. These authors provide clear insights into the ways in which institutional-level processes of desegregation can be obstructed by practices of re-segregation. Regardless of policy changes, segregation and exclusion can be reinscribed in the mundane practices occurring in daily settings. These findings appear applicable to contexts beyond South Africa. For example, Billig and Churchman (2003) found that a new housing development in the United Kingdom could invoke negative meanings for both new and existing residents when they were from different groups. The co-locating of different ethnic and socioeconomic groups in this case appears to have had a negative impact on perceptions of place. In the absence of supported integration, these groups opted to separate themselves through stereotyping members of the out-group and resisting opportunities for interactions with members of the other group. Accordingly, the groups defined 'our space' in opposition to 'their space'. Again, we see that intergroup relations have an important role in people's sense of place. Such work highlights barriers to desegregation and the need to consider the continuing resistance by dominant groups to such change and the impact of everyday practices. As noted in Chapter 5, immigrant groups often face struggles when resettling in new cities. Newcomers struggle to assert their identities on a place, and when they do so often find that majority-group perceptions associate the places they come to live in with stigma rather than renewal.

Representational and physical spaces

Tensions around who belongs have been taken up in research to reveal that people can feel, or be seen by others as being, out of place. It is likely that when escorted from the mall Susan experiences a sense of being out of place. Although experienced locally in a very intimate way, such processes of exclusion do not occur in a vacuum, or solely in the local setting. Rather, they are influenced by wider processes of meaning-making in society. These processes include storytelling institutions such as the mass media, which constitute representational spaces in everyday life, and can promote exclusionary practices or challenge discrimination (Chamberlain & Hodgetts, 2008). Further, people's impressions of groups they have little to do with personally are frequently constructed via media portrayals, and through the accounts from other people they do interact with (see Chapter 10). Traditional news, entertainment and web-based media are primary sources of taken-for-granted frameworks for understanding social concerns. Such repertoires are central to the definition of social issues and the legitimization of specific approaches to addressing these issues. It is impossible to have first-hand knowledge of every possible social issue, setting or situation. Thus, people also draw on broader explanations for social issues and what might be done about particular issues, and to decide who belongs or does not belong in particular settings.

Review exercise

Think for a moment about a recent news story in your country regarding immigration.

- Were the people from another country depicted as belonging in your community, or were they portrayed as being out of place?

If you have not come across such stories in the media do a search of news websites for stories on immigration. Consider the characterization of immigrant people and where they do or do not belong.

The pervasive presence of the media in daily life, discussed in Chapter 11, highlights the connections between physical spaces such as food courts and libraries and the representational spaces constructed by the media. It also raises a point discussed by Livingstone (2007a, 2007b), that people can occupy physical and representational spaces simultaneously. These issues are discussed by Hodgetts and colleagues (2008) in their investigation of links between the representational space offered by newspaper portrayals of homeless men's use of a public library and the lived interactions in the space of the library. This research was conducted in response to an article in the local newspaper that raised concerns about the appropriateness of the presence of homeless men in the city library. The item promoted exclusion of homeless men by emphasizing the danger and deviancy these men supposedly represented for housed citizens. Hodgetts and colleagues reported subsequent fieldwork in which they interviewed homeless men, library staff and patrons. They worked with journalists on follow-up articles foregrounding the positive function of the library in homeless men's lives, and challenged news narratives that advocated the exclusion of the homeless from prime public spaces. The result was a two-page feature article that introduced the opinions of homeless men, librarians and NGO staff on the issue and challenged the assumption that these men were dangerous. This involved publicizing the broader functions of libraries in homeless men's lives, and included comments by domiciled patrons who were more compassionate towards the homeless men. The article also dispelled the myth that these men had any involvement in violent incidents. Homeless men identified a public library as a space for safety and social participation, or to engage in conversations from a life predominantly lived alone in marginal spaces, such as under bridges. These men reiterated that the library allowed them to engage in academic pursuits and provided a space to move beyond the stigma of a homeless identity. Participants raised the importance of relationships and interactions with library staff in supporting a sense of belonging, respite and refuge amongst homeless men. Calls to exclude homeless men from the library were subsequently dropped.

The library study exemplifies how social psychology is about more than observing and documenting interactions occurring in particular settings. It is also about getting involved and improving situations for people facing social exclusion from public places. These psychologists demonstrate that there are possibilities to promote the inclusion of homeless people in prime spaces through media advocacy work. This study also exemplifies the action research process outlined in Chapter 1. It involved theorizing, planning, engaging and revising an understanding, followed by more planning and engagement.

To recap, studies of social exclusion and place foreground the importance of cohabitation in public spaces and the important human need to feel that we belong in the spaces we encounter in our daily lives. The opportunities for and barriers to successful cohabitation exist within a broader symbolic and political context, which is textured by tensions between various understandings of appropriate behaviour or legitimate actions. In considering these tensions, we should not focus solely on local interactions occurring in particular physical settings. It is also necessary to consider encounters occurring via media technologies and associated links between news media constructions of people, social issues and the concrete spaces of lived politics. For example, scrutiny of the rights of homeless people or immigrants to be somewhere, and of their status as citizens, is not evident only in a local setting such as a library, food court or particular neighbourhood. Such scrutiny extends to more distant forums, including media deliberations. What is of core importance to the present discussion is that a sense of belonging is a sentiment cultivated through everyday activities, including the use of spaces such as libraries and food courts. Being asked to leave a place can disrupt a person's sense of belonging and identity as a legitimate community member and citizen. To address such concerns, the social psychology of place needs to promote inclusion and the cultivation of healthy place-based identities. We expand on this issue in the following sections.

Place-based identity and social inclusion

Efforts to promote place-based identities have implications for social inclusion and health. Of particular interest in such place-based projects are the links between neighbourhood design, physical features, identity, participation and health. The concept of social capital (Box 6.6) and its implications for health are attracting increasing attention in social psychology.

In reviewing literature in this area, Wood and Giles-Corti (2008) propose that the existence of social capital is predictive of a range of positive physical and psychological health outcomes. These authors propose that where we live (physical settings) can enhance social capital by providing opportunities for positive interactions, or it can undermine social capital by isolating individuals through processes of fear and disengagement. Their review supports the idea that neighbourhoods high in social capital are more resilient and can respond better to disruption. This is supported by the early work of Marie Jahoda and colleagues in the 1930s, discussed in Chapter 2. Wood and Giles-Corti (2008) emphasize that it is important not to ignore the physical dimensions of place when considering such issues as links between the cultivation of social capital and health. Some environments are simply more conducive to building social ties because they have shops nearby, the climate enables one to dwell outside in public parks or there is sufficient lighting for people to feel comfortable walking at night. The positive features of a place can add up to generate more opportunities for social interaction. In most cases, having a environment that encourages people to be outside and to walk and interact in public spaces leads to a greater sense of safety, participation and place, which in turn increases people's propensity

BOX 6.6   Social capital

Social capital is often theorized as a communal resource that can buffer groups facing adversity against threats to their health. Social capital refers to the various bonds that hold communities together, and is more likely to be present wherever there is a sense of belonging and support, trust, shared goals, social networks and group affiliation. It is evident in volunteerism and civic participation. "Social capital consists of the stock of active connections among people: the trust, mutual understanding, and shared values and behaviours that bind the members of human networks and communities and make cooperative action possible" (Cohen & Prusak, 2001, p. 4).

to engage with their communities. The availability of spaces that provide opportunities for building social capital is crucial in developing place-based identities and healthy communities. If a physical setting lacks the elements required for building social capital, people may develop a sense of alienation rather than place identification.

Tangibly, aspects of the physical environment impact on opportunities for social interaction and recreation and the formation of support networks. Less tangibly, perceptions of social isolation and inclusion, personal safety and friendliness are potentially influenced by the interchange between social capital and people's physical environments. (Wood & Giles-Corti, 2008, p. 161)

This statement invokes the need to ensure adequate infrastructure to sustain a community and encourage participation. Positive aspects of a physical environment can enhance a shared sense of belonging and place, which in turn sustains networks that can be drawn upon as resources for supporting such infrastructure over the longer term.

Recently, social psychologists have considered the influence of area-oriented interventions on promoting health for local residents (O'Dwyer, Baum, Kavanagh & MacDougall, 2007; Putland, 2008). They have considered how the health of local people can be improved by changing something about the places where they live. Beyond the physical environment and factors such as air pollution, water quality or insulation in homes, such work also focuses on the provision of health services, the education and economic status of local residents, levels of social capital and opportunities for social participation, place-based identities and area reputation. In working to build social ties and lobby for changes in the physical environment, the ultimate aim is to create environments that are supportive for residents and allow people to live healthy lives (Box 6.7).

The cultivation of positive place-based identities in which people experience affiliation with the local setting is associated with the willingness to get involved for the communal good. Conversely, a negative or disassociated sense of place has negative implications for self-worth, self-efficacy and willingness to participate in community life. Generating a sense of ownership and care is an important facilitator for the resident mobilization required for successful place-based change efforts (Nowell et al., 2006). In the absence of a positive place-based identity, residents are more likely simply to opt out and not take responsibility for their environment. Opting out provides a means for people to cope with the stigma of negative associations between a place and the people who dwell there. Opting out and disassociating from the place in which one lives can be a psychological strategy that enables one to define oneself as being different and not like other people who live in that place (Proshansky, Fabian & Kaminoff, 1995).

These findings are supported by related research on poverty and social inclusion. Wells and Harris (2007) explored psychological distress

BOX 6.7   Neighbourhood renewal

Nowell, Berkowitz, Deacon & Foster-Fishman (2006) discuss the tradition of neighbourhood renewal that underlies much contemporary work on place-based initiatives to improve people's physical environments in order to foster mutual support and health. Such efforts are based on the premise that the qualities of a place have an impact on the well-being of residents. Place is seen as a social determinant of health (Putland, 2008). Success with such initiatives is more likely if the strategies psychologists employ are based on in-depth understandings of community settings and the everyday experiences and needs of people living within these places. As Nowell and colleagues (2006) explain:

[such] research on neighborhood effects has examined the relationships between broad, aggregate, characteristics of neighborhoods (e.g. SES [socioeconomic status], homeownership, crime rates) and an array of outcomes for youth and adults in areas such as delinquency, educational achievement, and employment, focusing on answering whether and when neighborhood contexts are significant predictors of individual health and well-being. (p. 30)

The meanings local residents assign to place and their sense of identity are linked to their willingness to engage in projects aimed at improving the environment and strengthening community ties. To illustrate this point, Nowell and colleagues sought to build an understanding of the relationships between the physical features of a specific US neighbourhood and the experiences of residents. A core theme to emerge from the research was how the physical environment contained markers for participants' personal histories. For example, public places such as parks were identified by residents as being important resources that enabled them to enact enduring relationships in the community. Such public spaces were used to convey messages about community values, history and identity. For example, monuments to the town's history as a stop on the Underground Railroad were used to invoke the fair-mindedness of the community and how it contained good people who showed respect and generosity towards others. Physical conditions in the neighbourhood were also related to the willingness of locals to engage in community life. Neglected areas tended to encourage more neglect, or even antisocial behaviour and crime such as tagging or vandalism. Conversely, the upkeep of areas was associated with people exhibiting pride in the environment and increased willingness or motivation for greater numbers of residents also to do their bit for the community. Thus, well-maintained and cared-for environments tend to increase community participation.

among women moving from inadequate housing to new houses. The study found that social withdrawal was a mediating factor in the link between housing quality and psychological distress. Poor housing can lead to social withdrawal and in the process contribute to a reduction in social supports crucial for psychological wellness. A young person may not want to take friends home due to stigma and embarrassment. "A reluctance to invite guests to one's home may lead occupants to severely limit their social networking opportunities. Thus, socially withdrawing may lead to a break-down of existent social networks, a hindering of future social networks, and a subsequent increase in psychological distress" (Wells & Harris, 2007, p. 70). Such situations raise considerable barriers to efforts at using community engagement strategies for renewal in distressed neighbourhoods: "That is, before residents can work together as a neighborhood, they must at the very least be willing and able to recognize themselves as a neighborhood, and identify strongly enough with the neighborhood to commit their time and energy toward improving it" (Nowell et al., 2006).

It is, however, important that neighbourhood renewal initiatives do not rely solely on a deficit view of poorer neighbourhoods. Although improvements in amenities and aesthetics can offer some benefits for low-income neighbourhoods, these can sometimes come at the cost of disrupting the social capital and community ties that exist despite (and often as a result of) the challenges faced by the residents. Recent trends in social housing policy are drawing criticism from researchers due to their destruction of sense of place and community. Manzo, Kleit and Couch (2008) conducted an in-depth study of the impact of the US HOPE VI programme, which has the seemingly worthy goal of replacing 'pockets of poverty' with mixed estates of market-rate and subsidized housing. In their study, Manzo, Kleit and Couch (2008) found that the tenants of the so-called public housing ghettos expressed a surprisingly strong sense of connection with their community. This was partly attributed to the need for supportive relationships between neighbours facing similar economic hardships, which meant that informal exchanges of food or the sharing of transport and household items were a more common practice. In more affluent neighbourhoods, residents can more consistently supply the needs of their households and may thus have less reason to interact. Poorer neighbourhoods do indeed suffer stigma, yet there was little evidence to suggest that poorer people would not continue to be stigmatized when living in mixed neighbourhoods. Moreover, there are many social and economic costs associated with forced relocation, including the time it takes to rebuild informal supportive networks, which may be much harder in the mixed-income housing estates. While the decision to demolish public housing may provide some fiscal benefits, Manzo, Kleit and Couch (2008) argue that such policies have "imposed the cost of relocation, redevelopment and displacement on the poor" (p. 1874). Although poorer communities may lack the aesthetics and facilities of more affluent areas, it does not necessarily follow that the socioeconomic poverty in such neighbourhoods extends to a poverty of sense of place or community.

Initiatives for cultivating place affiliations and wellness

Despite the obstacles and complexities discussed in the previous section, programmes designed to promote health by cultivating social capital and place-based identities among residents have shown considerable success. Place-based interventions have worked best when "there was a change or difference in the physical environment; funding was adequate; there was good leadership and partnership with communities; there were appropriate and well-designed programmes; political support was firm; the objectives did not change over the course of the programme; and the size of the area was appropriate to the particular inequality" (O'Dwyer et al., 2007, p. 329). If, for example, local health issues relate to the social isolation of elderly people, then locally focused initiatives may be most appropriate. Conversely, neighbourhood-focused efforts to address poverty can be ineffective if the cause of local poverty is related to restructuring or to policies at a regional or national level. Such situations require a broader focus that links the local with the national scale.

Building a commitment to a community can be done through projects involving residents working together. Handbooks on how to conduct such work are readily available. For example, Kuppers (2007) draws on twenty-three years of experience in this field to present an account of various strategies for using arts projects for promoting community experiences to audiences both within and beyond local settings in order to achieve social change (Box 6.8). Such projects

---

BOX 6.8   Art-iculating place meanings

The Community Arts Network (Western Australia) (CANWA) is an agency that uses culture, arts and arts practices to promote community participation in planning and community-building activities. Community arts include a range of visual, theatre and textual art forms. Community "arts are not only end products but provide a medium through which community members engage in the joint identification and production of images, symbols, and other resources that indexes their visions and aspirations for their community" (Sonn, Drew & Kasat, 2002, p. 12). Many of CANWA's projects have involved communities in rural or remote areas of Western Australia, and emphasis has also been placed on promoting indigenous self-determination. In one project, after an initial consultation period with community members (which involved scoping out community resources), an artist was commissioned to work with community members in drawing their aspirations. In that particular community there was a concern about invisibility as well as a need to articulate a shared identity, something many felt was an implicit, taken-for-granted and undervalued collective resource. Workshops aimed at teaching people about community arts and the connections between arts and community identity provided an opportunity for community members to explore what their community meant to them and how those meanings could be externalized to represent the community. This workshop resulted in the articulation of place-derived meanings that were in turn externalized onto 'bush poles'. These bush poles captured the fact that the community stretches from the sea to bushlands. The images etched into the poles included sea creatures, landscape and other symbols. The poles were used as an entry statement to the community and as an attraction for those passing through, and the process for creating them served to strengthen collective identity.

are used to build networks, raise public awareness, increase cross-cultural understanding and contribute to a sense of control and self-determination among communities under pressure (Putland, 2008).

Initiatives can focus on beautification and physical change, as well as targeting aspects of the environment with which residents affiliate. Small-scale community-based projects can have a larger significance than one might initially expect in terms of motivating participation in community renewal and of building commitment, relationships and capacity. This has been a consistent finding with the use of community gardens to promote social networks and health for some time (Armstrong, 2000). Community gardens often constitute efforts to promote healthy communities through group participation in a shared project. They provide community bonds, food and recreational opportunities in a neighbourhood. In practical terms, such gardens can address some of the costs of healthy food in the present time of rising food, fuel and transport costs. Gardens can provide local food supplies, much like they did during conflicts and depressions. There are also less food-oriented, but still very practical, social benefits. Caring for a garden conveys a sense of belonging to, and respect for, a neighbourhood (Robbins, Polderman & Birkenholtz, 2001). Thriving gardens act as identity markers for a thriving neighbourhood, and the existence of social connections and capital. Gardening is a fundamental means of texturing one's environment (Gross & Lane, 2007). Beyond the obvious therapeutic and dietary benefits for individuals, community gardens can increase community satisfaction and a sense of belonging (Box 6.9).

The existence of communal gardens is associated with limited local vandalism and an increased sense of belonging and positive attitudes towards the neighbourhood. "This was usually evidenced by improvements in the maintenance of other properties in the neighbourhood, reduced littering and increased pride in a neighbourhood" (Armstrong, 2000, p. 324). Gardens also appear to provide a mechanism for facilitating social networks and contribute to further grassroots organizing and capacity to work cooperatively towards shared goals. "Community gardens involve the main characteristics that have been described as important for health promotion in minority communities; these are social support, an emphasis on informal networks, and community organizing through 'multiple

BOX 6.9   Community gardens

A useful site for information on community gardens is the American Community Gardening Association (http://www.communitygarden.org).

change tactics'" (Armstrong, 2000, p. 324). Gardens are about building a sense of pride and place and identity, and they contribute to the improved health of a community, including that of vulnerable residents such as those experiencing mental health difficulties, as has been demonstrated by Wright and Kloos(2007).

Chapter summary

In studying everyday life, social psychologists have demonstrated a renewed interest in place and the ways in which human relations are played out in physical and representational environments. After all, human beings are always located somewhere. Experiences of place draw together behaviour, thoughts, perceptions, physical form and personal and collective history. Places are simultaneously social, political, historical, collective and personal. Our locatedness is central to understanding the social practices through which we inhabit our worlds, materially and symbolically. Social psychologists increasingly approach place as more than simply the backdrop for psychological processes. Places shape, and are shaped by, our sense of self and relationships with others in profound ways. We might say that who people are is fundamentally emplaced. Correspondingly, being denied connections to places is associated with a sense of dislocation and loss of self and can result in mental health concerns.

A focus on place, and on the objects displayed in particular settings, provides insights into human identity as more than a fixed personality-based entity located solely in the head of an individual. In this chapter, we have considered how places exhibit aspects of the identities of people who dwell there and are often communally constructed through the actions of people who go and reside there. Although we may experience places as individuals, the nature of that experience is frequently a consequence of collective activities, affiliations and the uneven distribution of resources at the national and global scales. Babies born in a poor neighbourhood are likely to have very different experiences of life than those born in middle-class suburbs within the same society.

People do not usually live in only one place. Even a person with agoraphobia is likely to occupy different rooms and may possibly surf the Internet. Most of us live our lives across a range of settings, and in interactions with different people. Nonetheless, people from lower socioeconomic status backgrounds have fewer options in terms of the spaces they can occupy and their mobility across different places. As we discuss in Chapter 11, a range of media devices, including mobile phones and MP3 players, allow us to weave different spaces together and to experience a sense of coherence and a world that is manageable. It is when we come into contact with people who are different from us in shared spaces that tension and conflict can arise. This chapter has foregrounded issues of concern for social psychologists regarding the co-location of people from diverse groups in the same places. Evidence suggests that the corresponding contacts can lead to positive intergroup relations. However, this relies on ensuring adequate support systems and the employment of procedures to ensure dialogue between groups, and must be done in consultation with these groups.

Highlighting links between place, health and social cohesion, psychologists have developed neighbourhood renewal and community arts projects as a means of fostering social capital and a sense of place among local inhabitants. Many of these interventions are deceptively simple and involve providing opportunities for people to build social networks by working together on shared projects. One example is community gardens, which have the potential to grow social capital. As discussed in Chapter 10, such efforts reflect a positive orientation in psychology that aims to build capacity within communities in order to foster growth and cooperation to pro-social ends. Of central concern is the cultivation of a physical and social environment within which people can support, trust and cooperate with one another. Outcomes include increased self-efficacy and civic participation.

In this book, you are presented with a range of social psychological issues and processes that have a bearing on individuals and groups of people in contemporary societies. The various issues discussed do not operate in isolation from each other. These issues overlap and are interconnected to comprise a whole that exceeds the sum of its parts. Trying to comprehend the full dimensions of everyday life can be quite daunting. One way to create some kind of overview and draw all the seemingly disparate parts together is to concentrate on particular places. Focusing on specific geographical settings allows us to examine the dynamics and processes that occur in the messiness of 'everyday life', where nature, culture, history and intergroup relations occur at once in a type of synthesis. This process works the other way too. The aim is not to generalize to all places and situations. Rather, it is to understand the mechanisms and processes surrounding contemporary issues in the environments in which they occur. In this way, human action is not simply the product of social rules, norms and values or the influence of institutions. Rather we are woven into, and emerge out of, such social phenomena that texture the very places we inhabit or are removed from on a daily basis. Who we are is often profoundly interconnected with the places we have been and now live our lives across. Herein resides the usefulness of the concept of place-based identities in explaining aspects of the fundamental locatedness of everyday life. People belong somewhere, and social psychology needs to consider this in order to develop ways of enhancing health and social support, be it through neighbourhood renewal or community gardens. The places we live are associated with our social status, affiliations with others and material circumstances, and are linked to our health. The types of places we have access to and dwell in, and the extent to which we have control over some of their positive or negative impacts, affects our quality of life and can increase or decrease our lifespan. Recent social psychological research highlights that it is important that we feel a sense of inclusion and connection as we move in and across the spaces in which we live our lives. As will be discussed in Chapter 7, feeling connected to places and establishing a sense of belonging are of particular importance for people who have moved from familiar to unfamiliar settings due to migration.

Review exercise

With a classmate consider the place-based affiliations and identities you both hold.

■ What is similar and different about these locations and your sense of place?

Now consider the particular things located in these settings and perhaps the practices you engage in there.

■ How do these things and practices texture particular places to feel safe and familiar?
■ Who belongs and who does not belong in these settings?

Think of a place in your city or town that you avoid or in which you feel unsafe.

■ What is it about the place that makes you feel unsafe?
■ Is it the physical setting, events that occur there, the other people who are there, or a combination of these?
■ What could be done to make you feel safe in this setting?

These are useful exercises because the places we frequent and dwell in are where we find ourselves, develop and interact with others. Reflecting on these spaces is a means of considering who we are, where we go and what we do on a daily basis.

7 Immigration, acculturation and settlement

Core questions to consider while reading this chapter

- What is culture shock?
- How does acculturation help us understand relocation and settlement?
- What are some of the key criticisms of acculturation models?
- What is the connection between power and social identity, and how is this relevant to immigration and settlement?
- Why is the concept of contact zones important in understanding human migration?

Chapter scenario

Celine has been in Australia about two years, Johan arrived eighteen months ago, and Mervyn has lived in Australia about two years as well. Celine, Johan and Mervyn are all relieved at being in Australia; they express a sense of freedom and safety. But they also speak of the painful realities of remaking lives and communities in a new country. One day Celine, who lived in Liberia, left home for work in her clothing and jewellery export and import business, leaving one of her younger children with her mother. That was the day of a military coup. Celine had to flee for safety, as did her husband. They both ended up in refugee camps across the border, and eventually arrived in Australia (three years later), where she was reunited with some of her children. Celine spent her first six months learning English, her third language. She knows enough now to be able to work. But life has been difficult: the people are different, the climate is different, the streets are quiet and people are not outside in the streets like in her home country.

For years Celine believed that her one child, the one who had stayed with her mother, had been killed. It was not until a few years ago that she found out that both her mother and her son were alive and living in a refugee camp in a country neighbouring Liberia. For her, being employed in a low-paid position as an aged care worker in a nursing home in Australia is about accumulating resources so that she can be reunited with the rest of her family. This she expresses as being physically in Australia and psychologically in another place: you feel split between making a living and providing for the children, on the one hand, and yearning to be reunited with those who were left behind, on the other. Celine speaks about everyday experiences of being treated differently and being bullied by others at her workplace – about racism. She does not want this to be part of the story told here because, in her view, no one will be able to do anything about it and she does not want to make trouble or risk losing her job.

Mervyn and Johan also tell stories of how grateful they are to be in Australia. But mixed in with these is talk about how difficult it was to find work and the implications of unemployment for family life. Johan's children ask why he does not go to work like other parents. For him, not being able to find employment has meant losing status in his family; it has contributed to conflicts and tensions within the family. He feels helpless. Not being able to participate in the labour market has numerous implications for engaging in social, cultural and everyday activities for a person and his or her family. Although Johan wanted to work, he could not find work. As happens to many others immigrants, his qualifications were not recognized in the host country. Many refugees have no documents of proof for qualifications obtained in their home country, and some have limited written and oral communication skills.

At the other end of the employment and settlement spectrum, Mervyn managed with help, over time, to start a small business. But he had to close it down because people vandalized the shop on several occasions and left threats of violence against him. He was unwelcome, misrecognized, not the sort of person they wanted in their town.

The scenario at the beginning of this chapter contains the stories of three people who have been granted asylum in Australia. These conversations about settlement experiences took place at a migrant resource centre. The centre provides settlement services and other resources to immigrants and recently arrived humanitarian entrants. The conversations capture various challenges and issues associated with remaking lives in a new country where you may or may not be welcomed, where your qualifications may or may not be recognized, where the language spoken is different and where you have little family or social support.

■ How do we understand the challenges for those who are dislocated?

■ What are the implications of dislocation for identity and community construction?

■ What are the social, cultural and psychological processes involved in the remaking of community connections in new contexts?

These questions are central to the social psychology of everyday life and this chapter, which provides an overview of theoretical and empirical work that is relevant to understanding transition and settlement experiences for those who have been displaced. The following sections pursue the questions posed above by reviewing literature relevant to understanding the cultural, social and psychological dynamics of relocation and settlement processes and intergroup relations. We draw out the point from Chapter 2 that social psychologists need to consider historical and socioeconomic contexts when they seek to understand social psychological phenomena. We also draw on issues of everyday experience and knowledge production from Chapter 3, and acculturation and the self from Chapter 5.

Immigration is a central process that contributes to the cultural diversification of nation-states. Throughout human history, groups of people have moved voluntarily or have been displaced, often losing a sense of belonging. These people are usually required to adapt to the social settings and norms of other groups. Central to the displacement and the subsequent transition and settlement is the threat to culture and identity. Displacement and dislocation usually mean a disruption of taken-for-granted social and support systems, cultural rules, rituals, symbols and meanings that are central to identity construction and personhood. The recognition of migration as an intense and at times deeply problematic process is reflected by Bhabha (1994), who notes, "It is from those who have suffered the sentence of history – subjugation, domination, diaspora, displacement – that we learn our most enduring lessons for living and thinking" (p. 172).

Displacement and dislocation are particularly distressing for migrants who experience racism and marginalization in the new country. For other people (perhaps children and more fortunate migrants), shifting into a new culture can also include positive elements. For those able to maintain a strong sense of self, being in a new culture provides an opportunity to experience cultural hybridization and perhaps escape from some of the constraining aspects of their home culture. Thus, aside from the negative experiences, migration can provide different opportunities for identity and community construction. Many migrants move to have a better chance at securing opportunities and resources for current and future generations. Migration is seldom solely a good or a bad experience. Instead it creates a complex and deeply felt mix of emotions. An incomplete list includes a sense of grief, loneliness, unfamiliarity and loss of status, but also discovery, possibility, hope and renewal.

Chapter overview

This chapter does not offer an exhaustive review of theory and research regarding immigration and settlement. Rather, we provide a brief overview of different frameworks and ways in which people have understood the issues of immigration, settlement and intergroup relations. Our focus is on culture shock (Oberg, 1960) because this continues to be prominent in informing policy and practice in the areas of immigrant settlement. We then explore work in the area of acculturation (introduced in Chapter 5; Redfield, Linton & Herskovits, 1936), which has been central to the development of a social psychology of immigration. Social identity theory (Tajfel, 1982) is also considered, because of its relevance to understanding identity dynamics in the context of intergroup relations. We suggest that this work has been usefully integrated to offer a relational understanding of immigration, settlement and intergroup relations. This work is also extended with reference to a critical sociopolitical framework that more explicitly deals with history, colonial relations and collective memory. These notions are central to illuminating the complex ways in which identities and settlement challenges are negotiated. However, before we consider these topics, it is important to distinguish among the different circumstances and motives that lead to relocation. This is useful because these have significant implications for the transition, acculturation and settlement processes and outcomes. Thus, this chapter considers:

- Transition and settlement processes
- Acculturation and identity formation
- Power and community-building

Types of movement

Individuals and groups leave their home territory or country for many different reasons and under diverse circumstances. In some circumstances groups are displaced because countries or territories are invaded or because of development projects, and there is often little or no choice in the dislocation (Castles, 2002, 2003; UNHCR, 2006, 2007). Whatever the reasons for movement, there are key factors that make the experiences very different for groups in different territories or countries. These factors are permanency, voluntariness and mobility of groups in a particular context (Segall, Dasen, Berry & Poortinga, 1999). These reasons for movement are used to categorize new groups in the host society, be they immigrants, sojourners, refugees or asylum seekers (Box 7.1).

Some migrants move to escape violence and conflict, and they may have traumatic memories or have continuing concern for and guilt about leaving other family and friends behind. For example, internal armed conflict and activities serving powerful economic interests in Colombia have left many people displaced who end up as refugees and often homeless in other cities in that country (Sapica Rodríguez, Tovar Guerra, Galindo Villareal & Vidales Bohorquez, 2009). Some refugees have stated intentions of returning to their home territory or country when circumstances improve. For others there is the realization they may never go back. Sometimes people make a decision to move because of the political climate of their country. Such people could be considered fortunate (compared with those left behind) in having the financial or other resources to come as immigrants (Box 7.2).

BOX 7.1   Immigrants, sojourners, refugees and asylum seekers

Immigrants are people who have made a relatively free choice to relocate from one country, region or area to another. Theirs is seen as a permanent decision to make their home in a new place. Sojourners are people who make a sustained, but time-limited visit to live in another country. For example, the Peace Corps, international students and embassy staff can be considered sojourners. More recently, those entering countries as 'guest workers' on specific limited-time visa categories can be considered in this category too. Refugees and asylum seekers are people who have been forced to move from their home countries for various reasons. We know of refugees from war, natural disasters, persecution and so on (see UNHCR, 2006). Development projects such as the building of dams, roads and luxury housing can also lead to people being forcibly displaced. Often ethnic minorities and indigenous people bear the highest costs and suffer most, whereas companies, business developers, entrepreneurs and upper- and middle-class people are more likely to benefit or profit from the new facilities and infrastructure provided (Castles, 2003).

BOX 7.2   Statistical overview of asylum seekers in different regions of the world

To help put things into perspective, we provide a brief statistical overview of the claims for asylum in different regions. A report by the UNHCR (2008) indicates that in 2008 there were an estimated 383,000 asylum seekers across fifty-one European countries. Although this is an increase of 12 per cent from the previous year, it is way below the 623,000 applications for asylum recorded across those countries in 2001 (for a breakdown, see UNHCR, 2009). In North America there were an estimated 86,000 asylum seeker applications, with 49,000 in the Unites States. In Australia there were 4,700 claims for asylum in 2008, and this is far below the 13,100 claims observed in 2000. Japan (1,600 claims) and the Korean Republic (360 claims) have recorded increases in applications, mostly from people from Myanmar. (For a more detailed breakdown of the origins of asylum seeker applications and the variations within different regions and over time, see http://www. unhcr.org/statistics/STATISTICS/49c796572.pdf.)

As we discussed in Chapter 5, First Nations peoples and indigenous groups represent another situation in which issues of cultural transition and domination must be considered. For many cultures around the world the colonization experience has seen indigenous people dominated by groups who have come from the outside. Often their way of life, religion, food supplies and land have been threatened. In their simplest sense, colonial relationships can be understood as unequal political and economic relationships that favour one group to the detriment of another group (or groups).

From a social psychological perspective, the experiences of transition and settlement are complex and have been theorized by authors from different disciplines. Central to this theorizing are the issues of identity negotiation and community reconstruction following displacement, transition and settlement. Deaux (2000) referred to her work with Hispanic immigrants and emphasized that essentially "immigration involves leaving one domain in which identity has been enacted and supported, and coming to a new domain in which identity must be resituated and often redefined" (p. 429). It is to these issues that we now turn as a means of making sense of the experiences and changes faced in the everyday lives of people such as Celine, Johan and Mervyn. One common experience of such people is culture shock.

Review exercise

If your own family has moved in recent generations to another country or to a distinctly different region within a country, consider the reasons for the move and the associated positive and negative experiences. If your family has lived in the same place for a considerable period of time, perhaps talk to other people (neighbours, friends, international students) who have had the experience of moving to a new place and culture.

Culture shock and models of adjustment

This section provides an overview of some of the models that have been used to understand the social and psychological dimensions of transition and settlement processes. These models are associated with the notion of culture shock, which is often used to inform policy work and can be used to guide interventions with sojourners and with students who relocate to study in new countries. After all, there is usually only a short-term focus on the experiences of those making adjustments to new social and cultural contexts and environments.

Displacement, relocation and settlement present a variety of issues, such as culture shock, unfamiliarity with a new location, losing social ties and support, and changing diets (Box 7.3). Oberg (1960) coined the term 'culture shock' to refer to the process of cross-cultural relocation (Bochner, 1982; Furnham & Bochner, 1986). The experience is profound and brings into focus deeply internalized, tacit and taken-for-granted practices, routines and knowledge. As we noted in Chapters 3 and 4, it is through these social psychological phenomena that we construct and come to understand our everyday lives. This can be as basic as the familiar symbol on a building that reminds you where to turn to go to a particular venue or the memory of the mountain that defines the physical environment in your town and serves as a marker to let you know where you are. Oberg observed that culture shock is precipitated by the anxiety that results from losing all our familiar signs and symbols of social intercourse. These symbols include multiple ways that people orient themselves to specific situations in daily life. Relocation can lead to mild disorientation, which results from a lack of familiarity with the new environment (Furnham, 1990). Some have reported more severe impacts, such as psychological and physical health problems, arising from relocation and settlement challenges (Furnham & Bochner, 1986).

Review exercise

Imagine you are in an airport lounge, sitting next to a person from a different country. The person asks you to describe your culture in approximately 200 words.

- Is this a relatively easy or difficult task?
- What does this say about your acknowledgement and awareness of your cultural identity?
- Is your culture shaped by any other culture?
- Are particular places, people, practices or objects important to you? Why?
- Now that you have described your culture, describe your mother's culture. Is it similar to yours? How is it different?

Keep this exercise in mind and make some notes. You can revisit what you have written as you read this book.

Stage models have been put forward to capture the relocation settlement process (e.g. Furnham & Bochner, 1986; Markovizky & Samid, 2008). These models view relocation and settlement as cyclical and ongoing processes that vary from person to person. The culture shock concept also has an associated stage model (Figure 7.1). The typical phases of the culture shock model represent a U-shaped curve and are characterized by different emotional and

BOX 7.3   Experiences of transition

Over the past few years three of the authors of this book (Chris, Linda and Neil) have been researching people's experiences of transition. Some of this work has considered internal migration (e.g. indigenous footballers moving from rural and remote locations to cities to join football clubs); other work has involved the movement of people from one country to another. Consistent across this work has been the way in which people describe some of their initial experiences following the move to a new place. The accounts of experiences often refer to the changes in the physical landscape, increased traffic, different road rules, different smells, the noise of the city and the different languages spoken. This is captured in the following excerpts:

Melbourne is a lot different to (hometown). It's always on the go. The trams and the hook turns in the city. I remember one of the first times I drove into the city I nearly hit a tram. I didn't see it. You do get used to it. It's all so compact whereas (hometown) is all spread out over so much land up the coast (male relocating from country to city). (Campbell, 2009, p. 120)

Traffic is a big one. I still haven't adapted to the traffic. Just the culture down here, you have to change everything. Like (hometown) is easy going, do whatever you want whereas in Melbourne you've got to watch your step and everything you do. (Campbell, 2009, p. 119)

Both these extracts capture how transition is about gaining new tacit knowledge and learning how things are done around here (see Chapter 3). With this process can come feelings of difference and exclusion, as well as shared understanding and inclusion. The second quotation also suggests that children often adapt more quickly than adults. Children have a fairly literal way of being in the world, and they perhaps have a less entrenched sense of habits and customs. Certainly, children seem to find it easier to learn a new language or to find nonverbal ways to communicate.

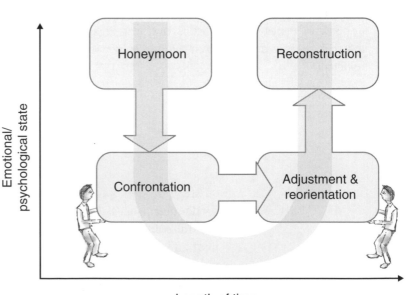

Figure 7.1. U-shaped model of culture shock

BOX 7.4   The issue with linear models

Psychologists have a fascination with stage models. Piaget's (1929, 1977) model of cognitive development and Erikson's (1963) model of social development are to a greater or lesser degree subject to the criticisms made of the culture shock model and settlement process described above. People's experiences are not necessarily as linear, unidirectional and contained as the models depict. Everyday life is much messier than any linear model could fully capture. Although these models identify the different stages and how these might occur in a linear pattern, they do not tell us about the arrows. How do people move between the different stages? Surely this is just as interesting as the stages themselves? In summary, the models are all better understood as starting points for discussion, and as one small part in the dialogue about the complexity of everyday social life.

psychological reactions. The phases include the honeymoon stage, the confrontation stage, the adjustment and reorientation stage and the reconstruction stage. It must be noted that these stages of adjustment are not entirely linear. Some new arrivals never reach particular stages, and others move back and forth between particular stages. The meanings of settlement and adjustment differ for different people across the different stages of settlement, for forced and voluntary immigrants and for different members of a family. For example, Crawshaw (2006) found that for refugees in the earlier stages of settlement, safety and freedom experienced in the new country played a key role in their evaluation of the settlement experience. For refugees and immigrants at a later stage, isolation and separation from the home country and community may texture the settlement experience, and this may well be compounded by how the receiving community responds to the newcomers (Box 7.4).

The different phases and settlement challenges for migrants must be considered within the broader social-cultural context in which people begin to reconstruct identities and communities. Think back to the scenario and how adjusting to a new culture is not simply an internal and individual process for Celine, Mervyn and Johan. Their experiences, in terms of adjusting to a new cultural setting, are hampered or helped by the actions of the people they interact with, by labour market and employment situations, by the policy frameworks that establish the validity of their qualifications and by the (un)availability of language classes or other training they might need. Although many migrants have common challenges and perhaps even stages related to their internal psychological processes, their experiences also depend on a wide range of societal factors.

To understand the importance of context and how factors such as race, the economy, policy changes and the timing of the migration can converge to create a range of experiences and situations, we could delve further into the different experiences of Mervyn, Johan and Celine as they attempt to settle in Australia. Mervyn could not find a job because his qualifications as a graphic design artist were not recognized, and there was an oversupply of qualified Australians when he arrived in the country. Mervyn attended a job-seekers seminar at his local social welfare office. From what he could understand from the discussion and the lengthy and unintelligible application form, it seemed that he was ineligible for a benefit. So he had few options in terms of broadening his social contacts or activities outside the home. This meant he was not learning a lot of English or meeting potential customers for freelance work. Perhaps you remember from the opening scenario what happened when Mervyn tried to open up his own shop. Johan was an optician; however, before he could secure employment in his field he needed to complete further training, sit exams and apply for registration – all of which cost time and money. One of Johan's children was experiencing post-traumatic stress and problems at school. The local health authority had just cut back on services for special needs children due to budget constraints. Johan and his wife found it difficult to navigate the health system and find the support they needed to assist their child. Celine found a job, but her wages barely covered the cost of her rent, which left her very little money to send back to family at home or to save for her son's future education. Celine had been an independent and successful businesswoman in her home country, and she was feeling increasingly demoralized by the racial taunts from one of her managers and other workers. A co-worker made a mistake with a resident's medication but deflected the blame onto Celine, stating that her poor English skills meant she had mis-read the instructions. Celine needed the job, so she preferred to put up with the humiliation rather than lodge a complaint. After all, most of the staff still seemed to stick together and view her as an outsider.

Not all migrants have such difficult experiences. Perhaps the extended scenario seems a little gloomy, but the point is to remind us that migrants are not dealing only with the emotional and psycho-logical effects of dislocation and disorientation; migrants also experi-ence many practical everyday life constraints in trying to rebuild their lives. They often find that they are at the back of the queue when it comes to obtaining and maintaining jobs (especially dur-ing a recession), and their unfamiliarity with cultural systems in the new society means they often miss out on opportunities and benefits that locals tend to take for granted. It is apparent that some migrants do exceptionally well in the host community. These migrants may over time surpass locally born people in terms of wealth and status, in part due to a strong work ethic (often born out of the necessity of their situation). Yet such success stories occur less often among migrants who are refugees or belong to marginalized groups. The successful migrants would most likely have had class or educational advantages (cultural capital) in their country of origin had they not decided to move or been forced to flee.

Despite the variety of experiences, many migrants do have some common experiences, and the concepts discussed in this chapter can help to explain aspects of such shared experiences. The culture shock model may be more relevant to understanding the dynamics of immigration, dislocation and settlement in the earlier phases of transition – in the first two to four years and during re-entry follow-ing movement back to their country of origin. Although it provides a starting point, the concept of culture shock has been criticized for being deficit oriented and for pathologizing what can be construed as normal responses to what are in essence very challenging events (Markovizky & Samid, 2008). The situations that many migrants find themselves in frequently contain multiple challenges, and their culture shock is not the result solely of a lack of cultural appreci-ation or adjustment. We take up this idea of the deficit approach in Chapter 8.

Review exercise

Think back to a situation in which you experienced culture shock. Perhaps you are a migrant and can reflect on your experiences of transition. If not, you could think of other situations in which you have felt out of place in a cultural sense. This could be when you travelled to a foreign country, began a long-term relationship with a person from a distinctly different culture or started high school or university. Many people experience a culture shock when they get their first 'real job' or start a new job in a large and unfamiliar organization (or alternatively when they suddenly lose their job). Ask yourself the following questions:

- What were the most disorienting factors for you?
- Did you notice any distinct changes, or stages, over time as you adjusted to your new situation? For example, did you progress through feeling mostly curious and excited at first, to perhaps being overwhelmed, feeling isolated, and then later beginning to feel more confident? Perhaps you experienced only some of these things, or felt them in a different order.
- Were there any particular people or resources that helped to smooth the transition? What would have happened if you had not received such support, but were instead bullied or ostracized?
- Once you had been in your new cultural setting for a while and it had become more familiar, were there any particular events or situations that triggered the feelings of culture shock again?

Proponents of the model, such as Markovizky and Samid (2008), whose research findings support the U-curve model of social adjustment, argue that different responses at different times in the settlement process can be viewed as normative assimilation stages. They also suggest that viewing the model in this way may make it easier for those adjusting to cope with the challenges of settlement and that it may help inform the development of programmes aimed at assisting with the settlement process. Accepting that aspects of the migration experience follow some type of pattern can provide the incentive for policymakers and agencies to put initiatives in place to support the common issues faced when migrants arrive and start to build their new lives.

Acculturation and adaptation

The culture shock model reflects a recognition of some of the issues and social psychological reactions people experience in the earlier phases of settlement. Other researchers have gone further to theorize the challenges that follow when two or more cultures come into continuous first-hand contact. Anthropologists Redfield, Linton and Herskovits (1936) produced a memorandum of the study of acculturation in which they defined it as "those phenomena which result when groups of individuals having different cultures come into continuous first-hand contact, with subsequent changes in the original cultural patterns of either or both groups" (p. 149). This idea can be explicated further to distinguish between psychological acculturation and sociocultural acculturation (Graves, 1967).

There is a significant body of work in different disciplines, mostly anthropology and sociology and more recently cross-cultural psychology, exploring acculturation. This work often considers the issues from the perspective of those with the least power in the situation – for example, immigrants, ethnic minorities, indigenous people or refugees. It is often those who are newly arrived who have to make the largest adjustments in order to live in a new community (Box 7.5). If you are not such a person yourself, can you imagine what it might be like to lose all that is familiar and precious to you? As the definition of acculturation suggests, the receiving community also has to make adjustments; however, much of the research has been concerned with the changes that those in less powerful positions have to make. Throughout history, there have been instances when a large influx of migrants has meant that the migrants have had more power, which has allowed them to reshape and redefine aspects of the receiving country. In many cases, indigenous groups have lost power and resources to the migrants. Colonization occurs when migrants come in sufficient strength and numbers to dominate and exploit the host community (as was discussed in Chapter 5).

Berry and colleagues (1984, 1989, 1997, 2001, 2006) have been prominent in developing psychological perspectives that can contribute to our understanding of immigration and the dynamics of immigration, settlement and acculturation in pluralistic societies. As noted earlier, immigration and colonizing practices continue to contribute to the cultural diversification of many countries. In these countries many communities come to live together, but there are stark differences in power (economic, political and cultural). These differences are often reflected in the way in which different communities are described in the literature as ethnic minority, non-dominant, dominant, mainstream or illegal aliens (Segall et al., 1999) (Box 7.6). Berry (1997, 2001)

BOX 7.5 Settlement experience reflecting the process of acculturation

The following is a quotation from a male migrant, aged eighteen, from southern Sudan:

The cultural differences they will fade away, some years only after you come to this country... Now before, when they first came, they use to fight a lot (the parents and teenagers), but now they are changing. Even when we go to their parties, before they would fight and be bad people, but now things have changed. They can sort out their own problems, they want their parents to know what is going on, there are also many people now working. They use to say Sudanese were bad on television, what they are doing here, but we only come in '99, this is when Sudanese first started coming. ... So I think in some years there has been big change. (Crawshaw, 2006, p. 39)

BOX 7.6   Categorizing people moving

Acculturation processes can be complicated by the ways in which receiving communities manage immigrants and refugees. Mansouri, Leach and Traies (2006) showed that different categories of visa affected the acculturation and settlement experiences of temporary protection visa holders in Australia. Those who were uncertain about their future were less focused on community-making and more concentrated on achieving permanent visas and thereby stability and security. Those in more secure visa categories (permanent protection visa) could engage more with community and identity practices related to cultural maintenance. For these refugees, this claimant period is a phase in the relocation process and presents a specific set of acculturation challenges. Marginalization, or even separation as a strategy, may become prominent only at another phase of the refugee settlement and adaptation process (Berry, Phinney, Sam & Vedder, 2006).

---

has argued that there are two key issues of intercultural contact that have shaped inquiry into this area; these are the degree of contact and participation and the manifested cultural maintenance. We discuss these issues briefly in Chapters 6 and 11; in the current context, these key issues refer to how immigrants make decisions about their contact with the host society and the retention of their culture of origin. Simultaneously, people in the receiving community deal with different questions and acculturation issues, including making decisions about how they want to deal with the newcomers.

In Berry's (1997, 2001) formulation, questions about cultural maintenance and participation define an 'intercultural contact space' in which people from different groups construct perspectives on whether acculturation is appropriate. These perspectives are cultivated within a broader social, cultural, political and historical context. They can emphasize assimilation, integration, separatism or marginalization. In this model of acculturation, migrants who adopt an assimilation orientation are likely to denounce their culture of origin and embrace the dominant culture. Those who favour integration seek to maintain their home culture but also to participate in the dominant culture. Separatism means maintaining the culture of origin and having minimal contact with the dominant culture. Marginalization means having little interest in the culture of origin or the dominant culture. Research shows that some contact experiences (often those involving oppression) can result in extremely negative outcomes for individuals and communities, and that in some situations groups can resist these oppressive experiences and protect their members. These resistive and protective actions have been written about as community resilience (Sonn & Fisher, 1998). We discuss this concept in Chapter 10. The literature in the area of acculturation suggests that those who are rooted in their home culture report better social and psychological well-being than those who are not (Berry et al., 2006; La Fromboise, Coleman & Gerton, 1993). In the process of acculturation, at best people become enriched because of relocation and contact; at worst they become disintegrated and marginalized. It can be argued that the theoretical model of acculturation implies that integration is the preferred option; thus it operates from an unstated ideological position. The finding by Berry and colleagues (2006) that people with a strong home culture are more resilient is perhaps not so surprising, given the importance of the ways in which we reaffirm our identity and sense of self through the cultural practices and material objects we surround ourselves with in our homes (see Chapter 9). As discussed in Chapter 8, the private space of the home is an important sphere where we build and maintain our sense of self (assuming that we have a secure home).

Different theoretical perspectives and concepts can be used to understand the experiences of dislocation, transition and settlement as reflected in the stories of Celine, Johan and Mervyn. The culture shock notion highlights the initial challenges of uprooting, and the acculturation models bring into focus the ways in which cultures are renegotiated as part of the settlement process. Some of the focus is on the individual-level changes, but these changes must be understood within the broader social, cultural, historical and political context. There is also a need to consider the dynamic ways in which people reconstruct histories and communities in new contexts.

The important role of informal and formal social and support networks in the settlement process cannot be overestimated (Box 7.7). Immigrant communities often construct settings within their own communities that provide social support and access to social networks, which are central to acculturation, identity negotiation and settlement (Deaux, 2000; Keel & Drew, 2004; Sonn, 2002). These

BOX 7.7   Interesting study

In a recent study on refugee settlement, McMichael (2002) reported that religion provided an anchor to Somali women who had settled in Australia. She took on the role of participant-observer, seeking to understand the ways in which women negotiated everyday life in Australia. McMichael showed that the women, who were mostly Muslim, engaged in daily religious practices (prayer) and displayed symbols of religious significance in their homes. These symbols and practices provided much-needed routines and stability in the women's lives in an otherwise unstable world. Furthermore, these practices were central to engaging with other women and constructing new social relationships and identities in the Australian context. Deaux (2000) termed the processes of identity resituation and redefinition 'remooring' – to describe the ways in which "people connect identity to a system of supports in the new environment" (p. 429).

settings may include social and youth groups, religious organizations, sports clubs and other settings in which people can meaningfully participate in activities, take on social roles and construct
stories about the home and new community that are central to identity-making process.

Hopefully, by now you are somewhat convinced that strategies of
acculturation, and specifically identity negotiations, take place within
a broader social, political and cultural context. Castles (2003) has
argued that this includes the context of globalization. Globalization
has increased the movement of people and the spread of cultural
diversity. In contemporary developed societies, many of us experience or have contact with many different cultures and places around
the world. Our grandparents and great-grandparents may not have
had such diverse cultural experiences, unless they travelled for work
or to fight in wars, and communication technologies in their time
were limited, so it was expensive and more difficult to contact people
in other parts of the world. Yet globalization can also lead to a form
of cultural backlash whereby people feel overwhelmed or that their
own cultural norms and status are being undermined. In response,
they may become unsympathetic (and even aggressive) towards other
cultures and retrench to a static and insular cultural position. The
rise of Neo-Nazism in parts of the world, and especially in Europe,
is a grim reminder that some people find it difficult to share their
countries and cultural lives with 'foreigners', especially in situations
in which the migrants are seen to be taking jobs and changing the
culture of the host country too much.

Although globalization is, according to some critics, leading to
an increasing convergence or cultural sameness, there are still distinct differences in the ways dominant and migrant cultures interact,
overlap and integrate in different parts of the world. In some countries, population policies may require that communities assimilate;
in other places there are policies of multiculturalism. Assimilation is
based on the assumption that groups are better off if they are absorbed
into the mainstream. Multiculturalism, on the other hand, values the
diversity of the new groups, but recognizes that to benefit and participate fully groups must also learn the culture of the host community. There are challenges associated with both options. However, it is
generally recognized that assimilationist policies can be detrimental
to the well-being of ethnocultural communities. We return to socioeconomic and policy issues shortly. For now it is important to consider briefly some of the limits of Berry's approach to acculturation.

Although Berry's work has been influential, it has come under
scrutiny because it often seems to oversimplify individual and community responses. Berry (2001) has warned that studies of acculturation must consider a range of individual and contextual factors to

understand the phenomenon, but efforts seem to have been hampered by the fact that social psychological studies have largely relied on survey designs and psychometric approaches that have inherent measurement problems – as we saw in Chapter 5 in the discussion of psychometric testing and assessment with indigenous people (Rudmin, 2006). Furthermore, the survey-dominated orientation has meant that the nature and roles of group-specific settings and social, cultural and material resources in negotiating the challenges implicit in intergroup relations have been overlooked. The ways in which receiving communities act to include or exclude the newcomers are often not given sufficient attention (Fisher & Sonn, 2002, 2008; Sonn & Fisher, 2005).

Celine is hampered in seeking justice in her employment situation even though her workplace has anti-discrimination policies, as there are subtle ways such policies can be undermined for people who are seen to be different and less deserving of justice. In Chapter 9, we discuss inclusion and exclusion of different groups of people with respect to social justice. Many people are excluded from the moral community for reasons that are related to their perceived racial or ethnic identity. King and Mai (2009) have discussed the complex ways in which Albanian immigrants' settlement in Italy is compromised by hostile discourses that construct them in a negative way as criminals, prostitutes and uncivilized people, while at the same time they are negotiating changing relationships with their homeland. The broader context has significant implications for settlement and belonging.

To this end, researchers have argued that the acculturation models can be expanded by paying closer attention to issues of identity construction and reconstruction, which are a central part of the transition and settlement process. Identity and culture are central to intergroup relations (Deaux, 2000; Tadmor & Tetlock, 2006). However, it seems that, although attention has been given to developing more complex understandings, the focus remains on interpsychic processes of restructuring in the light of acculturation and group relations (Tadmor & Tetlock, 2006). The following section draws on social identity theory to address some of the limitations of Berry's approach.

Social identity theory and acculturation

For many immigrants, the voluntary and involuntary learning of a new culture is crucial, because so much of what we do on a daily basis in everyday settings is regulated and informed by systems of meaning that are culturally and historically bound. Culture is central to

identity and identity negotiation. Culture-making and identity negotiation are about collective and shared understandings and practices
(Geertz, 1973; Valsiner, 2009). These are also political processes to
the extent that meanings are constructed within a broader context of
power relations. To understand this complex process, Colic-Peisker
and Walker (2003) offer a framework that brings together acculturation theory with social identity theory. Social identity theory,
originally developed by Henri Tajfel (Box 7.8), is relevant to understanding immigration dynamics and intergroup relations because
it is concerned with understanding the complex ways in which

BOX 7.8   Henri Tajfel

Henri Tajfel was born on 22 June 1919 in Poland and died on 3 May 1982 in the United Kingdom. Tajfel
served in the French army during the Second World War and spent most of the war experiencing the hospitality of German prisoner of war camps. His hosts never discovered his Jewish ancestry. His immediate
family and most of his friends did not survive. The loss of loved ones and the experience of pretending to
be a member of another ethnic group in order to survive influenced Tajfel's subsequent work on intergroup
dynamics. Tajfel worked for several years for organizations, including the United Nations, addressing the
needs of concentration camp survivors and war orphans. He also began studying psychology and obtained
a degree in 1954.

   As a social psychologist Tajfel worked on topics such as prejudice and nationalism at Oxford University
and is arguably best known for his social identity theory (developed in collaboration with John Turner) and
time at the University of Bristol (Tajfel & Turner, 1979). Social identity theory was developed to provide a
psychological framework for understanding discrimination between social groups. The theory presents four
core elements. First, people often place themselves and others into categories, such as rugby player or Brit, as
a way of inferring things about the people who belong to such groups (*categorization*). Second, people often
associate with certain groups as a means of increasing their self-esteem or elevating their sense of positive
qualities (*identification*). Third, people often compare their own groups with other groups in a manner that
favours their own groups (*social comparison*). Fourth, people often desire an identity that is distinguishable
from, and compares favourably with, other groups (*psychological distinctiveness*). This theory sets out general psychological processes through which people come to understand themselves in relation to people
thought to be different from themselves, and attempts to explain discriminatory actions as people encounter each other in everyday life.

   Tajfel offered the theory as a means of understanding how psychological dynamics operate in broader
societal and historical contexts in relation to the lives of those who were displaced during the Second World
War and immigrants in the United Kingdom. In the 1970s, Tajfel strongly criticized experimental social psychology for de-contextualizing our understanding of social psychological phenomena, including identity construction. Tajfel's first-hand experiences of hatred towards his own ethnic group helped him to understand
that his fate as a person was tied to his social group membership and that the Holocaust was most certainly
not the product of intrapsychic phenomena. Rather, psychosocial processes operating within specific social,
cultural and historical contexts contribute to such historical events.

social identities are constructed within contexts of dominance and subjugation.

For Tajfel (1981, 1982; see Billig, 2002) identity is fluid and contextual; it is tied to social, structural and broader arrangements, and to threats to the perceived legitimacy and stability of social structures (Colic-Peisker & Walker, 2003). Social identity theory is concerned with understanding the process involved in maintaining or changing group memberships. The basis of the theory is the idea that people want to maintain a positive self-concept and that this can be achieved by belonging to groups with high status. Thus, people engage in social comparison processes to evaluate self and others on some dimension that is valued, typically a dimension determined by the dominant cultural group. If a group is negatively valued, group members may seek to move away from the group or they may seek to change the negatively valued aspects of the group. For instance, one could think of the different ways in which ethnic minority and racial groups are represented (or not) in the media in different contexts (see Chapter 11), as well as what standards and knowledge are used to decide what is valued and what is not valued in a particular society.

Those in positions of non-dominance may respond to social exclusion and minoritization[1] in many different ways. Strategies outlined by Tajfel (1981) include assimilation, which involves rejecting a minority status. They also include passing, or the masking of a 'true' group membership and social identity and the appearance of moving into a new group. For example, in South Africa under the Apartheid system (a form of institutional racism or internal colonialism) many people were classified according to racial groups using arbitrary criteria such as skin hue, hair texture and other physical markers. In that context, racial group membership afforded people certain privileges; the higher in the hierarchy, the greater the privilege. In response, people sometimes tried to pass from one racial group to another, typically the next one above in the system, to gain access to privilege. It was seldom the case that people passed from white to black or white to coloured, unless the law dictated that they do so. Such cases occurred only if people previously considered white committed a crime by marrying outside their racial group. In so doing, they lost their status as a white person.

In Tajfel's framework, accommodation means a group's attempts to compete on its own terms to gain material and other resources that are valued by the majority while retaining its ethnic identity. This strategy is reflected in the political slogan "Black is beautiful," which was used by the US civil rights movement in the 1960s and 1970s. Internalization means acceptance of a minority status, and it often takes place when groups see no alternatives to an existing system, and when the existing system is perceived as more legitimate. This is similar to Hussein

Bulhan's (1985) notion of capitulation, where communities come to see themselves in the terms of the dominant group. This is currently a major area of interest in Australia, where researchers are taking a closer look at internalized racism among Aboriginal Australians (Paradies, Harris & Anderson, 2008). In some ways the negotiations outlined in Tajfel's social psychology of minorities are similar to Berry's acculturation attitudes, but they differ in that social identity theory focuses on identity dynamics within a context of domination and subordination – that is, within a context of oppression and colonization. If we relate Tajfel's framework to Johan's children, whereas one child might attempt to stay within the immigrant group with minimal interaction with the broader society (accommodation), another might internalize her minority status (internalization), and the third child might learn to see herself as the dominant group sees her (capitulation).

Social identity theory, acculturation and economics

Work on acculturation and social identity theory has been integrated and extended by connecting it with human capital theory (Colic-Peisker & Walker, 2003). This work explains migration using an economic model. In this view, "people migrate to places where their human capital – formal education and training, as well as their other 'value-adding' features – will attract higher profits, that is, where they can better 'sell themselves' on the labour market" (p. 339). Colic-Peisker and Walker claim this approach allows one to consider internal group dynamics because it moves the focus away from artificially homogenized ethno-cultural communities. The focus shifts to analyses of identity-making and social comparison processes and of acculturation strategies among people with different socioeconomic backgrounds, who may or may not belong to the same ethnic or migrant groups. Consequently, this approach recognizes the agency of migrant groups, whose members often strive to be active participants in the settlement process. This is an important standpoint given the centrality of economics in migration–settlement dynamics and the role that human capital (Box 7.9) plays in the dynamics of acceptance and rejection in the new country.

Despite the active strategizing of migrants, Colic-Peisker and Walker (2003) reported the ongoing difficulties of the acculturation and identity reconstruction processes for a Bosnian refugee community. This situation is complicated by the fact that unemployment and welfare dependency are high among the community, despite their efforts to invest in the labour market. As with the refugees mentioned in the scenario for this chapter, labour market participation

---

BOX 7.9   Human capital

Human capital refers to those skills, resources, attributes such as language, values, history and education that are valued and shared by the dominant cultural community (Hage, 1998). Further, the dominant cultural community determines what is valued and on whose terms. To this end, human capital is also about power and the distribution of power within a society (Lareau & Weininger, 2003).

---

is often made difficult because of underemployment (i.e. working too few hours or working in a job well below the migrant's ability or skills), particular skills deficits (i.e. language skills or cultural comprehension), a lack of opportunities to train and the cultural biases of employers. In a different project, Colic-Peisker and Tilbury (2007) also reported challenges in gaining employment for humanitarian entrants. Refugees fail to gain employment because they are seen to lack skills and qualifications, are excluded for not having Australian work experience and are often viewed as having a different work culture. These systemic barriers and under- or unemployment are potentially problematic because of the importance of employment to mental health and participation more broadly in civic life. Without employment, migrants miss an opportunity to build social networks in the workplace, and they consequently also lack the income to cover the costs associated with leisure and entertainment, which constitute other ways of engaging civically. Many unemployed migrants do participate in voluntary work or community activities, as a way to ensure they build social networks and a greater understanding of the host community. However, it remains difficult for them to deal with even the minimal costs of such activities (i.e. transport) in addition to the costs of settlement.

Identity (re)construction and community-making are an ongoing and integral part of the settlement process (Deaux, 2000). Migrants experience a loss of familiar roles, relationships, status and practices, and so resettlement involves finding a new way of operating in the new context. Clearly, the extent of the changes migrants face depends on the degree of difference between the culture of the place of origin and the new context. Accordingly, identity- and community-making represent a particular and embedded kind of dialogical process in search of a renegotiated cobweb self (see Chapter 5). The migration experience can sever many strands of the cobweb a person has built in his or her life thus far. The process of rebuilding parts of the cobweb often accompanies resettlement.

Although acculturation involves learning about the new culture, it is importantly also about developing opportunities for meaningful engagement in mediating structures (schools, social clubs, employment) and social settings – in the context of everyday life in the broader society. As noted earlier, this aspect is often overlooked in the work on acculturation. What are the social settings created by the host society or other migrants (who have been in the host country for a longer period and may thus be more acculturated) that provide opportunities for meaningful social engagement? This question is central to acculturation, in particular for people attempting to reacquire meaningful social roles that are central to social identity construction (Reynolds, 2006). Colic-Peisker and Walker (2003) wrote the following about acculturation: "This process includes getting citizenship of the host country, finding employment, furthering one's education, establishing formal and informal social networks, developing a feeling of 'territorial belonging', all the way to finding a favourite television channel and a sports team" (p. 355). We consider the general social psychological processes related to such settlement experiences (Box 7.10) in relation to the construction of place-based identities in Chapter 6.

Acculturation is not necessarily a smooth and predictable process of shifting from being foreign to being familiar. It can be much more complex. As migrants become more familiar in their host country, they can become more foreign in their country of origin. Yet they can also find new ways to weave aspects of their home country identity into

---

BOX 7.10   Resettlement experience

As mentioned in the text, migrants can offer support to each other, and such support is frequently a key to resettlement. The experience of one of the authors of this book is drawn on to explain this further. Ottilie emigrated as a child from the Netherlands to New Zealand in 1969. Like many other immigrants, her family struggled with the unfamiliar language and culture, and with the severing of family ties. Other Dutch migrants who had been in New Zealand for longer and understood the local culture and some of the typical 'slip-ups' for new migrants were instrumental in helping the family to settle. These more experienced migrants became the family's support network, not just for learning about the new country, but also for providing an expatriate community with whom they could socialize and where they could practise aspects of Dutch language and culture. This social network became the backbone for the family not only to acculturate, but also to form a hybrid Dutch–Kiwi identity. The family were no longer Dutch, but neither were they 'normal' Kiwis. They had a new identity. This new identity was very apparent every time the family went back home to the Netherlands; they realized with each successive trip that they no longer fitted in there. Instead, the Dutch–Kiwiness had evolved as its own hybrid cultural identity. Culturally oriented activities and groups are very important for many migrants. Dutch culture is different from New Zealand culture, but due to the common Western cultural origins there is also a lot of common ground. Migrants from cultures that are very different from the receiving culture are likely to experience more difficulties and discrimination. Resettlement is also a lot harder for the first wave of migrants into a host community that has not received migrants (in significant numbers) from the country before. Such issues of cultural difference are often faced by refugees, and can make their adjustment even more difficult.

their identity-making in a new place (Box 7.11). Not all migrants have the same experience outlined in Ottilie's example. Some may not be encouraged to practise aspects of their culture in the new community and may be forced to 'forget' where they came from. This was the case for many migrants to New Zealand in the 1950s and 1960s. Many were expected to lose their 'differences' or other cultural markers in order to fit into the dominant New Zealand culture. During the large-scale post-Second World War migrations to New Zealand, there seemed to be a widespread view that migrants (and other citizens in New Zealand) should adopt the dominant Pakeha[2] New Zealand culture of the time and make English their primary, if not sole, language. The perhaps well-intentioned belief behind this was that it was all too taxing, especially for children, to contain more than one language and cultural identity at a time. Maori, the indigenous people of New Zealand, had suffered similarly in terms of being expected to relinquish their distinct culture and language, but for much longer and much more severely (see Chapter 5). Although Pakeha culture still dominates, it is more common today for New Zealand schools and society in general to view having more than one cultural identity as a positive dimension that enhances a person's development and the community more widely.

The examples above and work by researchers such as Colic-Peisker and Walker (2003) illustrate the necessity and utility of combing concepts such as acculturation, identity construction and economic theory to develop relational and contextualized ways of understanding the complex social psychological processes through which refugee and immigrant communities negotiate lives in transition.

BOX 7.11   Immigration and home making

There are several studies that consider power relations (and in particular for marginalized or previously colonized groups) in relation to identity- and community-making. For example, Espiritu (2003) explored Filipino immigration to the United States. She offered a transnational framework and the notion of homemaking to examine the ways in which generations of Filipinos in the United States negotiate belonging and identity. For her, homemaking provided a metaphor that could be read at different levels of analysis, including interpersonal, national and international, within a framework that placed immigrant community-making within the context of globalization. Espiritu argued that the history of colonialism plays a significant role in the settlement experience of Filipinos, and that identity- and community-making involves both literal and symbolic ties with the home community. She illustrates how memories of place, history and country of origin play a significant role in the community formation and personal identity-making processes. She wrote that in "immigrant communities, the remembered homeland takes on a special significance: not only does it form a lifeline to the home country and a basis for group identity in a new often alien and oppressive context, but it is also a base on which immigrants construct community and home life and which they stake their personal and sociocultural claims on their adoptive country" (p. 14).

There are other developments informed by critical approaches in which authors have raised questions about some of the underlying assumptions that inform knowledge production in psychology (see Chapter 4), including the core notions of culture, identity and self (see Chapter 4; Aveling & Gillespie, 2008), that inform acculturation research. Others have emphasized the need to examine the implications of histories of colonialism for settlement (see Bhatia, 2007; Bhatia & Ram, 2001; Grosfoguel & Georas, 2000).

Developments in various disciplines have focused on challenging the dominant ways in which psychology and other disciplines have produced knowledge and the implications of that knowledge, in this case regarding settlement, for different groups in a society. As noted in previous chapters of this book, one core issue that continues to be problematic is psychology's tendency not to examine the historical, cultural and socioeconomic influences from which we operate (e.g. Gergen, 1985; Holdstock, 2000; Martín-Baró, 1995; Montero, 2007; Parker, 2005; Sinha, 1997). In this book we have foregrounded the ideas of psychologists who emphasize the importance of such disciplinary self-awareness or reflexivity. As the example of psychological testing exemplifies in Chapter 5, we need to be critical of uncritical applications of Western-centred theories and methods in intercultural contexts (Sinha, 1997; Nsamenang, 2006). The criticism extends to the uncritical assumption that cultures are bounded and homogeneous; Western culture, in particular individualism, remains the implicit standard for comparison, and there is an underlying essentialism that informs the research that focuses upon cultures. Some of these criticisms are reflected in the burgeoning of indigenous psychologies around the globe (Chapter 5). In addition, some writers (e.g. Quijano, 2000; Smith, 1999) have argued for decolonization, showing how knowledge and knowledge production processes have been used to name and construct cultures and identities as the 'other' and to justify the oppression of those who have been othered. For Smith (1999) and others (Reyes Cruz, 2006) knowledge and knowledge production is not a neutral activity; it is a political process infused with power relations. We will now turn to these critical approaches to consider what they offer in terms of understanding the challenges of immigration and intergroup dynamics.

Within this broader critique of mainstream knowledge production, some authors have argued for critical approaches to understand the complexities of immigration and the challenges of settlement processes. Central to these arguments is the call for researchers to:

- Move from essentialist and bounded understandings of the notions of culture and identity
- Give attention to histories of colonization and oppression in dynamics of identity- and community-making

These are central themes in this book and in our approach to the social psychology of everyday lives. They are explored further in the following section.

Review exercise

People have many social identities; some are acquired (e.g. dentist, dancer) and some are ascribed (e.g. ethnicity, gender). To get you started with the material below, which relates to social categories and identities, respond to the following questions. These questions are designed to get you to clarify your own social identities. Take your time to think about these and then write your responses on a separate piece of paper.

- What are some of your social group memberships?
- What does it mean to be a member of those groups?
- What are the disadvantages of a particular social identity?
- What is a privilege associated with a particular social identity?
- In what ways is your group identity defined in relation to other groups? In particular, think about the way you do or do not fit within dominant groupings.
- If you think you do fit into a dominant group, are there any comparisons you make between yourself and people not in this dominant group that confirm your identity?

  For example, does seeing older people (such as parents, grandparents or senior citizens on the bus or in the doctor's surgery) serve some type of conscious or subconscious process to confirm that you are young, hip and trendy? Have you ever been surprised to discover that such older people were young, hip and trendy once?

Deterritorialized understandings of culture and identity

It is widely accepted that culture is a rather slippery and difficult concept to define. Rather than use the term 'culture' in a traditional sense of cultivating taste, style and appreciation of the 'finer things' in life (Kroeber & Kluckhohn, 1952), we refer more to shared patterns of understanding and daily practices that are engaged in by groups of people, which is a definition more in line with the processual approach to culture put forward by Geertz (1973). Culture provides a way of differentiating among groups of people and how they often conduct their everyday lives. This brings us within the domain of cultural psychology as envisioned by Valsiner (2009). To study a living culture, its patterns and variations, we need to study everyday life and the associated practices engaged in by group members, as well as the material artefacts or objects they produce.

Social psychologists have noted that such research should also include artefacts produced for consumption by particular social groups, such as television programmes and other media products (Chamberlain & Hodgetts, 2008). Such a research orientation is important because "[c]ultural objects are thus everywhere – in our private domains of homes (including the homes themselves), and in public: in the streets, town squares, and so on. They are both stationary (temples, monuments, etc.) and moving (busses, trains, airplanes, etc.)" (Valsiner, 2009, p. 23). In relation to immigration, social psychologists even explore the daily interactions of people from different cultures and how patterns of conducting life are transferred and adapted across groups. This is central to understandings of acculturation and raises issues regarding adaptation and cultural change.

The very notion of a unified and stable culture has become problematic in psychology. Various authors (Espiritu, 2003; Hermans & Kempen, 1998) draw on the work of global systems theorists (see Quijano, 2000) to argue that historical and contemporary global changes (economic, political, military, demographic) require the understanding of cultural changes in broader terms. Cultures can be fluid, variable and dynamic. The authors noted above argue that conceptualizing culture as bounded, essentialized and fixed can no longer be sustained; neither can the practice that treats culture as a dichotomous variable. This practice occurs when we assume universal differences between East and West or individualistic and collectivistic cultures and treat these as independent variables in cross-cultural research. This conceptualization oversimplifies and homogenizes groups (Espiritu, 2003; Hermans & Kempen, 1993, 1998; Holdstock, 2000; Shweder, 1990). This is a paradox that often emerges when we make arguments about population groups and try to apply these arguments to what happens in individual lives. Group patterns are not always reproduced in personal lives. There are plenty of individualistic people in collectivist cultures and community-oriented people in more individualistic cultures. Further, cultures are often in contact, and cultures can influence each other over time. These interactions are increasingly prevalent in everyday life in multicultural societies.

Essentialist practices can also have the function of othering particular cultures against a static, unnamed culture – typically Western culture – and this can lead to the separatism of particular non-dominant groups. Although this is in some sense justifiable (why should Western culture rule?), it can also lead to the isolation of non-dominant groups and an entrenchment of cultural divisions. Another possibility (which is perhaps more progressive) is a situation in which non-dominant groups are able to engage with the dominant culture in mutually respectful ways, so that in time the dominant culture becomes enriched and pluralistic. This pluralistic possibility also acknowledges that what we call Western culture is not a stable, immutable and homogeneous reality; it is also constantly changing, in part due to the influence of non-dominant cultural groups. Consequently, there is a need for a deterritorialized understanding of culture, one that gives attention to global and interconnected systems of communication and relationships, which we explore further in Chapter 11. Through these systems, including new communication technologies and mass media, cultures interact and interpenetrate and become more complex (Box 7.12).

A deterritorialized understanding of culture means that we give greater consideration to the zones of contact, which is where cultures meet and interact; instead of comparing countries and cultures, we can look at processes in the contact zone. The idea of a contact zone, often located in daily life, is a spatial and metaphorical notion referring to a place where separate people or groups come together (Somerville & Perkins, 2003). This is a zone where various groups cross borders into a different space, where our own and other group identities come into interaction. In this space there is negotiation of identities and practices. Somerville and Perkins (2003) use the notion of hybridization, a dynamic of intercultural processes that can lead to a recombination of existing cultural practices and the formation of new practices, which challenges the idea of homogeneous cultures. That is, cultures interact and fuse, and out of these new understandings, practices and forms can be created for the development of shared cultural identities.

BOX 7.12   **Immigration and technology**

Espiritu (2003), in her study on Filipinos in the United States, has argued that bounded notions of culture and community are limited because they do not allow for the networks and linkages that immigrant communities maintain across national boundaries through new communication technologies and other sources of communication. Naverette and Huerta (2006) maintain that the Internet has provided an important infrastructure for community interaction. They show that online immigrant community organization influences the life of community members in both the receiving and home community. For these immigrants the memories that they hold of the home community and the connections with family play an important role in building community in the new country. These memories are constructed around what life was like in the home country and are renewed and reinvigorated by literally and figuratively crossing boundaries – that is, visiting the home country and interacting via communication networks. This relates directly to notions of the double articulation of space, discussed in Chapter 11.

Taking a more complex and dynamic view of culture also has implications for understanding self and identity. In Chapters 3 and 5 we introduced notions of the dialogical self (Box 7.13). This concept is important in understanding contact zones and settlement. To recap, Hermans and Kempen (1998; Hermans, 2008) offer the notion of the dialogical self to theorize self and identity within this framework of complexity. From this viewpoint, self and identity can be conceived "as a dynamic multiplicity of different and even contrasting positions of voices that allow mutual dialogical relationships" (p. 1118). There are characterizing features of the dialogical self. First, the dialogical self is multivoiced; the self shifts depending on the salience of differing identities. That is, one can be an educator, athlete, parent, member of an ethnic group, and these identities dominate under different circumstances. Second, the self is not an intrapsychic phenomenon, but a relational concept as it extends to the social world. A person's sense of self is developed on the basis of the positions of others and is the embodiment of the social context localized in time and space. Voice is conceptualized not just as the voice of the individual, but

---

BOX 7.13   The dialogical self and immigrant lives

Drawing on the dialogical self as a framework, Ali (2008) explored the ways in which second-generation women who are Muslim negotiate belonging and identity in Australia. The women she interviewed positioned themselves as Muslim, female, Australian and Turkish during the course of the interview. Ali illustrated the complexity, multiplicity and contradictory nature of these identities as the women take and reshape themselves in relation to the dominant identity position. For instance, when the Australian Muslim identity was dominant, the majority of the participants explained being both a Muslim and an Australian as compatible.

The women took on cultural values that they associated with living in Australia, such as having a career or understanding and blending into the Australian way of life, for example by attending social functions. However, at times their stories demonstrated the contradictory and complex nature of being an Australian Muslim, in particular in instances when their Australianness started fragmenting when race, religious and cultural discourses arose. When each woman's identity as a Muslim was dominant, the participant expressed being different from the norm due to her cultural and religious beliefs towards chastity. Such beliefs were not considered oppressive, but rather expressed as a positive marker of her identity. However, when gender equality discourses arose, the women expressed parental expectation of their daughters relative to their sons as being unfair and unequal.

The complex and seemingly paradoxical nature of the dialogical self has important ramifications for the social psychology of everyday life. Everyday life takes us to places and spaces where the complex interplay of selves in community is evident. Social psychologists must relinquish the desire to identify and focus exclusively on understanding the immutable self in favour of grappling with the complex, dynamic and fluid dialogical, interconnected and cobwebbed self.

also as the voices of institutions, groups and surrounding discourses (Hermans, 2001). The concept allows us to relate contact between people and across different cultural groups to the hybrid nature of daily life, and to the senses of self and place that people construct there (see Chapter 6).

Histories of colonialism and oppression: Race and power

The argument for more dynamic and contextual understandings and analyses of culture and identity is welcomed, and is in concert with the arguments offered, by some cultural psychologists (Greenfield, 1997; Shweder, 1990; Valsiner, 2009). Although the dialogical self offers a more relational understanding of identity, it often leaves the historical and current conditions of domination and power implicit (Bhatia & Ram, 2001). Other scholars (Bhatia & Ram, 2001; Hermans, 2001; van Meijl, 2006; Tappan, 2005) have extended the notion of the dialogical self by incorporating the concept of power into their examinations of identity construction and community-making. For example, Bhatia and Ram (2001; Sonn & Lewis, 2009) suggest that the literature in colonial and postcolonial studies, which concerns itself in part with effects of colonization, may offer a more nuanced and critical framework for acculturation and intergroup research.

Critical and postcolonial theorists examine the ideological cornerstones of colonialism, including race, class, gender and culture, and contemporary asymmetrical power relationships between countries by examining identity- and community-making in postcolonial contexts (Grosfoguel & Georas, 2000; Fanon, 1967; Moane, 2003; Okazaki, David & Abelmann, 2008) (Box 7.14). Ideology is a central

---

BOX 7.14   Frantz Fanon

Frantz Fanon is often cited in anticolonial and postcolonial writing. He was born in Martinique (a French colony) in 1925 and left in 1943 for France to fight in the Second World War. He stayed in France and studied psychiatry and medicine. Fanon wrote political essays during this time, and before he left France to return home he wrote several influential pieces about the effects of racism and colonization. Fanon's work elaborates experiences of being a black academic in a 'whitened' world. In particular, he offers insight into the dynamics of colonialism, and his work is central to the psychology of oppression and liberation. Key works include *Black Skin, White Masks*, published in 1952, and *The Wretched of the Earth*, published in 1961. Hussein Bulhan reviewed Fanon's contribution and published a wonderful book titled *Frantz Fanon and the Psychology of Oppression* in 1985.

notion for critical perspectives and comprises "stories, narratives, discourses, as well as practices which construct subject positions for both rulers and ruled" (Foster, 2004, pp. 1–7). Consequently, from a critical perspective there is a focus on challenging ideologies, dominant narratives and resources for identity that are oppressive and engaging in processes of reconstruction in order to promote opportunities to self-determine identities and futures (Freire, 1970/1993; Watts & Serrano-Garcia, 2003). For Bhatia and Ram (2001) understanding the multiple ways in which communities and individuals may respond to new and changing contexts should include attending to issues of the memory, history, knowledge production and politics of both the immigrant and the receiving community, including examining the various stories and discourses that are created in response to and by incoming refugee and immigrant communities. We frequently celebrate the exotic and interesting new foods that migrants bring into receiving communities; why not experience some of their different stories and viewpoints as well? Of course, we can still also appreciate and celebrate our own cuisine and culture. Deepening our experience of our own culture and deepening our experience of other cultures do not need to be mutually exclusive, either-or processes. There is nothing wrong with also really enjoying our meat and potatoes, or whatever else is our traditional fare (animal rights arguments aside).

A key concept in studies of colonialism and postcolonialism is the notion of power (see Box 7.13). In this approach, power is viewed as relational. Power is produced in and through cultural means such as discourses that inform our understandings of ourselves and others. Because of histories of colonialism and ongoing dynamics of oppression and resistance, power is differentially distributed, and unequal access to resources for living can manifest in everyday interactions (Bulhan, 1985; Mama, 1995). There is a concern with understanding how individuals and communities create meanings and construct identities within the opportunities and constraints provided by the new context following dislocation. The challenge, then, from a perspective that acknowledges the role of power is not only to consider cultural learning and how individuals and communities are absorbed into society (Espiritu, 2003; see also Verkuyten, 2005) (Box 7.15); it

BOX 7.15   Interesting studies

For a more extensive review of the social psychological literature pertaining to ethnicity and identity construction, see Verkuyten's (2005) *The Social Psychology of Ethnic Identity*. We also recommend Bhatia's (2007) *American Karma: Race, Culture and Identity in the Indian Diaspora*.

is also about examining the complex dynamics of identity- and community-making as actions that involve resistance, struggle and liberation within a broader social, historical, political and global context.

Lewis (2008; Sonn & Lewis, 2009) examined the significance of notions of race, culture and ethnicity in the identity negotiations of South African women living in Western Australia. Lewis argued that current acculturation models, although valuable to a point, often failed to consider structural and contextual issues of politics, historical relations of power and patterns of privilege and race relations in both the country of origin and the host country, which shape acculturation and identity formation (Bhatia, 2002; Bhatia & Ram, 2001; Fijac & Sonn, 2004; Hook, 2003; Sonn & Fisher, 2003; Verkuyten, 2005). Lewis explored the experiences of women who are the descendants of people who grew up as coloured during the Apartheid era in South Africa and who now live in Australia. During the Apartheid era and prior to this period, life was organized according to the notion of race; the population was organized according to a racial hierarchy, with life opportunities and privilege assigned by racial group membership. For those lumped together into the heterogeneous 'coloured community', the racial classification meant exclusion and subordination. Skin colour, other physical characteristics and racial designation influenced every aspect of life; they were central to social identity development. Emigration to Australia, the United Kingdom, New Zealand, the Netherlands, Canada and other countries meant this community brought their own cultural conceptions of their identities, along with the historical legacy of Apartheid, to a sociopolitical context with different ideological constructions of race and ethnicity.

Lewis (2008) reported that the women renegotiated the notion of 'colouredness' and that this notion itself was not homogeneous and essentialist. Instead, it was contingent and fluid, and participants used a range of historical, political and social resources in making meaning of, and situating the cultural marker of, being coloured in the process of constructing their identities. The women's knowledge of their country of origin's history of slavery and colonialism and their awareness and life experiences under Apartheid shaped their construction of ancestry. These understandings in turn influenced how they understood culture as it related to this community. For the women, culture meant multiplicity, ambivalence and contradiction. For some it meant that their identity consisted of a mixed culture made up of many heritages, for others it signified ambivalence about what can be claimed given the multiple cultural foundations, and for some it meant contradictory things reflected in practices by which one lives or feelings of belonging and exclusion. The women used different categories for identification apart from the notion 'coloured'.

These categories included black, mixed race, South African, South African-born Australian, woman and person. These markers took on meaning within a complex historical, sociopolitical and contextual matrix. Importantly, although the women have increased freedoms for identity construction and belonging in the Australian context, there are also external constraints on these freedoms, which impact the identity choices they have available to them. Central here are the ways in which others see, categorize and relate to them in daily life. These limitations on the women's freedoms for self-determination can be viewed within the wider context of social relations of power and privilege, and how these are connected with dynamics of race, in particular the operations of whiteness in the Australian context or similar Anglophone contexts such as the United Kingdom or United States.

In Australia, the United States, and other postcolonial settings, whiteness as a metaphor for core culture hegemony (Box 7.16) can be used to understand the ways in which non-white, non-European immigrants are often racialized or othered and how this plays out in the acculturation and community-making processes (Frankenberg, 1993; Green, Sonn & Matsebula, 2007; Hage, 1998). Racialization

---

BOX 7.16   Examining whiteness activity

Tannoch-Bland (1998) wrote that racism is dialectical: there are those who are disadvantaged by it and those who benefit from it. White race privilege is taken for granted and reproduced in everyday institutions. Privilege refers to a variety of situations that disproportionately benefit white people, ranging from being in control of the economic and political systems to more simple forms such as being able to buy cosmetics suitable for white skin and watching television programmes and news media that are representative of white people (MacIntosh, 1992; Tannoch-Bland, 1998). Tannoch-Bland (1998) provides some forty examples of the kinds of invisible privilege and unearned benefits associated with whiteness. We have selected ten for illustrative purposes.

- *I can be reasonably confident that in most workplaces my race will be in the majority, and in any case that I will not feel isolated as the only, often token, member of my race.*
- *When I am told about the country's history or about 'civilization', I am shown that people of my colour made it what it is.*
- *I can send my children to school in unironed uniforms without it reflecting on their race.*
- *I can dress down, or get drunk in public, without reinforcing negative stereotypes about my race.*
- *When I speak in public my race is not on trial.*
- *When I am late, my lateness is not seen as a reflection of my race.*
- *When I win a job or a scholarship, I am not suspected of doing so because of my race rather than my merit.*
- *When I need legal or medical help, my race does not work against me.*
- *I expect that neighbours will be neutral or friendly to me.*
- *From among the people of my race, I can choose from a wide range of professional role models. (pp. 34–36)*

pertains to social psychological processes in which social relations are structured by the ways in which human characteristics have been made significant in defining and differentiating social groups (Miles, cited by Stevens, Swart & Franchi, 2006). Racialization takes place in different ways, including through the use of social practices. The sense of belonging for many of these non-white and non-European immigrants is regulated by seemingly innocuous questions about where they are from or where their parents are from. These practices have been part of mundane or everyday racism (Essed, 1991) and work to affectively regulate social belonging (Noble, 2005). For example, think of typical introductions between the dominant population in a country and migrants (who may be clearly different because they are black, are Muslim, or speak with a strong accent, for example) and of the tendency for such conversations to start with questions about where such 'different' people are from and what they are doing in the new country. Such introductions may continue even when migrants have been in the new country twenty years or more. Such seemingly innocuous practices are part of a broader system that normalizes whiteness as 'Australian' or 'American' and leaves as 'other' those who do not fit those representations. The others are questioned as legitimate citizens, as is the extent to which they can ever fully belong (Noble, 2005). A significant body of work has documented similar dynamics in various countries with colonial histories (Green, Sonn & Matsebula, 2007; Winant, 2004). For example, in a Puerto Rican study on identity construction, Godreau, Reyes Cruz, Franco Ortiz and Cuadrado (2008) detail the practices of blanqueamiento, or whitening, to show how black history is marginalized in national identity construction.

Everyday racism and practices of othering impact acculturation and bring into focus how ideologies of race play out in settlement and identity construction processes as well as in processes regulating belonging and citizenship. For instance, in work with South African immigrants, the ideological meaning of the label 'coloured', which symbolized a position on a racial hierarchy in South Africa, is disrupted through immigration. Sonn (1996) explains how most of the participants did not identify with the label as they did in South Africa. Instead, they elected to identify through their national identity, South African. Despite rejecting the 'coloured' label by describing its negative connotations, participants still internalized aspects of the negative stereotypes associated with the label and coloured status. Fisher and Sonn (2003) explain that the participants' ambivalence towards the 'coloured' identity label indicated a mixture of accepting, rejecting and co-opting imposed identity labels and that these equivocal ways of responding to the imposed identity labels need to be understood within the larger sociohistorical context of racialized oppression and the creation and perpetuation of myths about racial superiority and inferiority. Using a personal anecdote of an experience of racialization, Sonn (2006) illustrates how the label 'coloured' was disrupted in the Australian context, where he was positioned as black. He explained this shift in racial identity positioning in relation to Australia's particular history of race relations. Sonn demonstrated the continuous role of race and racism in Australia, where he was constructed as the other against an unnamed, taken-for-granted white dominant culture. The narratives of this cultural group position the identities of people who differ from this ideal of whiteness, namely migrants from different ethnic and racial backgrounds, as the other. Sonn's work illustrates how the supremacy of whiteness has followed those historically classified as coloured from their country of origin. In South Africa, coloured people were positioned as inferior to white people but as superior to black people. In Australia, where there is a different racial formation, coloured people are also othered, but in accordance with the discourses and meanings of race in that country. In an autoethnographic piece along similar lines, Reyes Cruz (2006) illustrates the role of memory and racialization in identity negotiation. In brief, such work illustrates how racialization has implications for acculturation and belonging and will impact everyday lives in everyday settings (Box 7.17).

BOX 7.17   Qualifying whiteness

It is crucial to note that it is not our intention to homogenize white people and neglect the social class, geographical and gender complexities held within such a categorization. If we take one of these strands, social class, we can acknowledge the range of research showing distinct cultures associated with socioeconomic status in society. The work of sociologists such as Bourdieu, for instance, points to the ingrained distinctions that exist between economically dominant French people and their fellow citizens of lesser economic means. These distinctions in perspective, taste and dress mark differences in everyday cultural practice and being. What renders the picture even more complex is mobility between such groups. Such shifts require a person to resocialize into the new group in order to pass as someone who belongs. To state the obvious, not all people with the same skin pigmentation think or act alike. However, in many contexts being white is associated with advantage.

Chapter summary

As we return to the scenario that was used to open this chapter, it is evident that different frameworks may be relevant to making sense of the challenges that confront people who are remaking their lives in a new place following dislocation. The issue of forced migration is a major humanitarian concern. It means dislocation and disruption to taken-for-granted ways of living and sources of support. It also means being afforded opportunities to remake lives in a new, often unfamiliar and often hostile environment. For those mentioned in the scenario and millions of people who have been forced to move, it often means separation from family and extended networks and the long wait to be reunited with family members. Once people arrive and have been granted refugee status or some other relevant visa, there is the challenge of remaking lives and communities.

The models that have been developed in psychology attest to the challenging nature of transition and settlement, let alone involuntary settlement. The culture shock model highlights some of the short-term and immediate settlement needs and challenges. This model takes a clinical perspective on the experiences, and notes the range of social, interpersonal and formal supports and resources that may be useful to assist with the settlement process. The acculturation models that have been offered are concerned with understanding the core challenges that immigrants and receiving communities negotiate. They involve cultural negotiations and are reflected in individual- and group-level perceptions and outcomes. For instance, immigrants and refugees who come to Australia with their own histories, experiences and worldviews will make important decisions about how much engagement they want to have with the host community. For the receiving community there are similar decisions, but they are the ones with the power to set limits and boundaries for the newcomers, to decide how to engage with newcomers and how newcomers should be managed. The process of acculturation is ongoing, and the acculturation model that has been developed is complex. However, the way in which this model has been applied in social psychological research has fallen victim to particular strategies of inquiry, problematic assumptions about culture and an emphasis on minority assimilation. Hermans and Kempen (1998), for example, question the way in which culture is equated with nation, and also how culture is treated as something that is bounded and unified. Others critique the essentialism and reification that come with the methodological approaches used in acculturation research (Bhatia & Ram, 2001; Espiritu, 2003). It is imperative to understand the basic assumptions that inform psychological work in the area of intercultural relations. The very processes of constructing self and others, including the practices of naming and describing cultures in essentialist ways, can contribute to racialization.

Developments concerned with reformulating understandings of culture and intercultural relations within global systems theory have been helpful in shifting understandings from dichotomies to more dynamic understandings that consider the interconnectedness of countries around the globe. However, as this area of inquiry shows, resources, networks and knowledge production systems are not distributed equitably. Writing in colonial and postcolonial studies brings into focus the notion of power and emphasizes histories of colonialism and ongoing geopolitical struggles that are important to consider in immigration and settlement processes. In this orientation the notions of race and culture, which are produced through symbolic means, are examined to reveal the complex ways in which social and political processes mediate acculturation and identity construction. That is, how are social exclusion and inclusion achieved in everyday contexts through seemingly mundane practices that regulate belonging? This approach means that we need to consider the political nature of intergroup relations and to understand the dynamics of oppression and resistance and the implications for identity negotiation. The focus put forward in this chapter also means that we need to understand culture as meaning-making and daily practice in the context of power relations. Therefore, the very process of knowledge production and constructing understandings of self and other becomes a site for social psychology theory, research and action.

Review exercise

As noted in this chapter culture and identity are played out in complex ways in everyday life. The following questions are designed to encourage you to relate these complexities to your own life.

- Do you identify yourself in terms of a specific culture or cultures?
- Does this identification change in specific contexts or when you are interacting with particular people?
- Is there one culture you identify with predominantly?
- How might your current sense of identity be challenged if you emigrated to another country?

Notes

1. We use this term here because, aside from being a numerical minority, ethnic and indigenous groups are often constructed as inferior clusters of lesser beings through political processes controlled by other and dominant groups.
2. The word 'Pakeha' was originally used by Maori to refer to the dominant settler society (many of whom were British, Scottish or Irish) who arrived in New Zealand during the early stages of colonization. Today it is used to refer to people born in New Zealand who are of European descent.

8 Understanding health and illness

Core questions to consider while reading this chapter

- What are the five variants of health psychology and how do these differ?
- How would you explain the biopsychosocial model of health?
- Can positive social relationships protect people from the negative health consequences of stress?
- What is the role of social stratification in work-related health outcomes?
- Can you explain individual and collectivist health promotion?
- What is healthism?
- How is health political?

Chapter scenario

Picture this scene – a young woman, Nicky, is at the supermarket with baby Emma and four-year-old Mark. As she walks down the aisles, she compares her shopping list with the advertised specials, attempting to make healthy purchases, and noting that the large bottle of soft drink that her child wants is cheaper than milk. Nicky notices that each aisle ends with a 'specials' display: potato chips, chocolate, cakes, beer, wine – no fresh vegetables or fruit. While they wait at the checkout, Mark begins picking up packets of sweets, asking whether he can have them. Mark's protests begin to escalate as a result of his mother's negative response.

By the time it is their turn at the checkout, the tempers of mother and both children are wearing thin. Nicky is noticeably embarrassed by the disapproving looks at her and her snivelling children from another customer and the checkout operator. Groceries are put on the counter and, as they are checked through, Nicky anxiously watches the total climb. She realizes that the total might be more than the balance of her bank account, and wonders which would be more embarrassing: to tell the checkout operator that she can't take everything on the counter after all, or to take the chance and risk her cash card being declined. Feeling flustered, she decides on the former and says she will have to leave the last few items. Unfortunately, among the early items were several bags of sweets Mark put on the counter unnoticed while Nicky was bending to unload the trolley; as a result Nicky will have to leave behind most of the fruit she had intended to buy.

Nicky hurries to catch the first of two buses she needs to take in order to get home before nightfall. She catches her reflection in a shop window, and pulls a face as she passes a hand over her tummy, still showing her 'baby weight'. Next to the shop window is an advertisement for a recreation centre membership special that is still more than her electricity budget for the year. It is cold out, and they need to keep the heater going at home in an attempt to take some of the damp off the air. While waiting for the bus, Nicky reflects on what it might be like to live in a neighbourhood with its own supermarket and recreational facilities. Almost home now, she takes a wide path away from the youths on the corner wearing gang 'colours' and hurries inside her flat. As she collapses, exhausted, on the couch, she is too tired to get up and wipe the damp from the walls and windows of the apartment. Eventually, she finds the energy to get up because she knows that if she does not reduce the moisture, Mark will have another asthma attack. She tells herself that things will get easier when Emma sleeps through the night and she gets her degree and is able to move to a better place.

Social psychologists are increasingly interested in the cumulative effects of daily living situations on the health of people such as Nicky and her family. This scenario raises the complexity of health and the range of factors influencing the likelihood and incidence of illness in their lives. Nicky is concerned to promote her family's health by obtaining healthy food and working to obtain an education and well-paying job in order to improve their living conditions. A key message from the scenario is that a rounded social psychology of health and illness must encompass a broad approach to health promotion that considers individual, relational and societal factors as these evolve within everyday life.

As you read this chapter, consider the likely health consequences of stress associated with having to travel long distances with children in tow to acquire the basic necessities of life. You should also think about the health consequences of Nicky having to raise children in a damp dwelling and with limited social support. We could not hope to cover all the issues, theories and research relevant to the social psychology of health and illness. What this chapter provides is an introduction to the field and some core dimensions pertinent to individual and collectivist approaches to understanding health and illness in the context of everyday life.

Chapter overview

This chapter provides an account of issues related to health and illness that are relevant to the social psychology of everyday life. We explore social cognitive models of health that reflect the individual-oriented stream of social psychology. We also explore more collectivist-oriented work that investigates and seeks to address the impact of socioeconomic status on health. Particular emphasis is placed on social determinants of health. This emphasis reflects efforts within psychology to move beyond notions of personal responsibility for health and to consider broader contexts that shape the daily realities and health of many citizens. This broader focus is important because the places people live and dwell in can have beneficial or harmful effects on their health. Attention is given to health promotion initiatives to address health inequalities, such as resource redistribution, that are informed by ideas about place (Chapter 6), discrimination (Chapter 7), social justice (Chapter 9) and community resilience (Chapter 10). In sum, this chapter covers the following key topics:

■ Individualistic orientations to health and illness
■ Collectivist orientations to health and illness
■ Links between psychological processes, social structures and physical health

Health and illness

In this section, we explore some of the complexities reflected in understandings of health and illness. Across cultures there are a range of frameworks for making sense of health and illness (Helman, 2000; Kleinman, Eisenberg & Good, 2006). We note that for many members of the public and health professionals, health and illness represent two sides of a coin and encompass a range of biological, relational and situational considerations (Hodgetts & Chamberlain, 2000).

The word 'health' comes from the Anglo-Saxon word meaning 'whole' and 'holy'. Health is often conceptualized as a 'normal' state of biological and social functioning. It denotes a situation in which everything is working as it should. Yet there is more to health than such an objective, physical state. Health is more than an absence of disease or bodily malfunction. Health can also be conceptualized as a functional process (Radley & Billig, 1996). People diagnosed with various diseases can still rightly describe themselves as being healthy because they are physically able to do what they want to do. Health is a physical, psychological, relational, environmental, economic and inherently social phenomenon, which includes people's ability to participate fully in social life (World Health Organization, 1986). According to indigenous scholars such as Mason Durie (2004), health requires an integrated and supported life that encompasses environmental considerations, family, cultural participation, spirituality, societal processes, biological functioning and personal behaviour. From this perspective, health initiatives can focus on individual factors, social processes and environmental and societal contexts (Williamson & Carr, 2009).

According to the World Health Organization (1986), health is a resource that is cultivated and preserved over time through the conduct of everyday life. Health allows Nicky to look after her children and get the shopping done. In this way, health is not an end in itself. Health allows people to do the things they want to do, meet their obligations, care for others and respond to the demands of everyday life (Williamson & Carr, 2009). Health does not stop with individuals, because people with health are able to engage in activities, often caring for and supporting other people, family, community and society at large. People often describe being healthy as when they have energy, are fit and happy and feel as if they belong (Williamson & Carr, 2009). In this way, health is associated with getting on with daily life and with when one's body and mind seem to be in sync with one's situation in life.

Psychologists are often more preoccupied with illness than with health. We know more about the incidence of disease and experiences of illness than we do about health. Renewed interest in humanistic and positive psychology (discussed in Chapter 10) appears to signal some movement towards a focus on health. For now, the prominence of a focus on illness requires us to consider what we mean by this concept.

Illness is often constructed as a deviation from a 'normal' state of health, wholeness and balance. Here illness is seen as a state of abnormality, disorder, disequilibrium and even badness and evil. You might have heard people talk about killer bugs invading the body and threatening people's lives. Table 8.1 (adapted from Marks et al., 2000) presents some of the prominent explanations of illness evident in contemporary Western-oriented societies, which are reflected in the cultural patterning of sickness and care (Helman, 2000; Kleinman,

Table 8.1. Examples of approaches to illness

Idea	Primary causes	Primary solutions	Social psychology
Biomedical	Bodily malfunctions, physical injuries, genetic problems, hormone levels	Pharmaceuticals, vitamins, herbs, surgery, manipulation of muscles and joints	Individual
Psychological	Personality defects, abnormal development, anxiety	Talk, meditation, relaxation, hypnosis	Individual
Relational	Abuse, exclusion, exploitation, stigma, harassment, conflict	Repair relations, conflict resolution, legal protections	Collectivist
Socioenvironmental	Social determinants: political domination, economic hardship, pollution	Social transformation, removing or mitigating environmental hazards	Collectivist
Spiritual/moral	Demons, planetary movements, ethical transgressions, lifestyle, magic, evil	Confession, ritual, behaviour change, magic, talismans, positive affirmation	Individual & collectivist
Biopsychosocial	Attempts to combine previous ideas	Attempt to combine previous ideas	Individual & collectivist

Eisenberg & Good, 2006). This is not an exhaustive list. It simply provides an overview of some of the key ideas about the causes of and solutions for illness that permeate everyday life in many societies. These understandings span different ethnic and subcultural groups. We have also related these ideas to the individual and collectivist streams of social psychology introduced in Chapters 1 and 2.

Different ideas about illness overlap. For instance, when considering the everyday life of someone like Nicky, social psychologists need to think about individual aspects (such as diet and exercise) and how these aspects might relate to social, relational and economic factors (such as the neighbourhood setting and what type of housing Nicky can afford). A broad focus is important because many people experience economic instability, unhealthy environments and limited opportunities for civic participation. The unrelenting worry about providing their families with the basics in life means such individuals tend to be sicker and to die earlier than more affluent citizens (Wilkinson & Marmot, 2003). We will return to the issue of social stratification later in this chapter. For now it is useful to consider the focus and orientation of health psychology.

Health psychology

In part, and as a response to the complexities of illness and its centrality to human existence, the field of health psychology emerged from clinical and social psychology as a specialism in its own right. Marks and colleagues, Evans and Willig (2000) define health psychology as "an interdisciplinary field concerned with the application of psychological knowledge and techniques to health, illness and health care" (p. 8). Health psychologists work, often as part of multidisciplinary teams, in a raft of medical, public health and community settings. They are involved in rehabilitation, paediatrics, oncology, dentistry, social policy, organizational development and a range of grass-roots programmes in community settings. This diversity of roles is reflected in the variants of clinical, public, organizational, community and critical health psychology that have emerged (Table 8.2). These variants span the distinction drawn throughout this book between individualistic and collectivist approaches to social psychology.

Considerable effort in health psychology has been focused on developing individual-focused interventions based on sociocognitive and behavioural models of human thought and action (Lyons & Chamberlain, 2006). We will explore some of these models shortly. For now, it is useful to note that the assumed primary causes of illness according to such models are individual health-related choices and behaviours (Box 8.1). Today, community, public and to some extent organizational health psychologists are paying increasing attention to collective action and efforts to change the contexts in which people live and work (Raphael, 2003). These psychologists see the primary cause of illness not as personal behaviour choices, but as life circumstances and relationships in society. Increased emphasis is being placed on

Table 8.2. Selected variants of health psychology

Clinical	Predominantly involves work in hospitals and clinics. Psychologists inform medical practices with psychological insights into pain management and patient adjustment. A core focus is on developing procedures to ensure mistakes in medical treatment are minimized. These psychologists treat individuals and help families adjust to chronic illness.
Public	Takes place in the field of health promotion and involves a core focus beyond the hospital ward or consulting room. Health outcomes are associated more fully with broader socioeconomic and political processes. These psychologists attempt to prevent illness and to treat society.
Community	Also involves health promotion, but tends to focus more on local community action and collective responses to adversity. In the process, the aim is to strengthen community supports as a means of preventing illness and building coalitions for social change. These psychologists promote people's participation in efforts to identify and address health needs.
Organizational	Draws on all three of the previous approaches and applies psychological knowledge to workplaces in an attempt to foster healthy work practices and environments. It often involves the use of employee assistance programmes to help people cope with work stress. Emphasis is placed on issues such as work–life balance.
Critical	An initially academically oriented approach that enhances the development of public and community health psychologies. Increasing emphasis is placed on the application of theory to addressing health concerns. These psychologists draw upon notions of social justice and investigate how social injustices can contribute to illness.

Note: Most health psychologists draw upon more than one of these variants. This categorization is adapted from Marks (2002).

BOX 8.1   Interesting study

There is often a mismatch between theory and practice in the health field. For instance, Easterling, Gallagher and Lodwick (2003) asked community groups to identity the causes of and solutions to illness. Respondents often referred to "issues such as poverty, racism, lack of jobs, crime, environmental quality, and the social pressures associated with population growth and community conflict" (p. 204). Many people share an understanding of the broad range of factors contributing to health and illness. Similarly, when canvassed about the causes of illness and how illness should be addressed, 90 per cent of public health professionals identified the social conditions noted by Easterling and colleagues (see Wallack, 2003). When asked where their work was focused, 90 per cent of professionals identified individual behaviour change and personal interventions.

---

issues such as social justice and the need for social transformation to ensure equity in health (Chamberlain & Murray, 2009; Hodgetts & Chamberlain, 2006b; Marks, 2008; Murray & Campbell, 2003; Murray & Poland, 2006; Navarro, 2004; Rappaport & Seidman, 2000). Such work extends from a focus on individuals to explorations of people in context, and is in keeping with the overall orientation of this book. Later in this chapter, we will discuss the collectivist approach, which attempts to prevent or reduce the negative consequences of societal arrangements, injustices, power and politics. This requires psychologists to work collaboratively *with* people within community and work contexts (Chapters 1, 4 and 5) in an effort to cultivate social conditions in which people can be healthy (Campbell & Murray, 2004). In the process, increased emphasis is placed on links between individual, community and societal levels of health. This broad focus is often associated with the biopsychosocial model of health (Engel, 1977).

Biopsychosocial model and stress

Health professionals and the general public are increasingly aware of the interrelationship between psychological, physical and social aspects of health and illness. Recognition of the need for a broad focus on all these aspects is evident in Engel's (1977) formulation of the biopsychosocial model of health. This model draws on systems theory to postulate the dynamic and dialogical interactions across various levels of the human lifeworld. These levels span the biochemical and sociopolitical domains (Crossley, 2000). The model was welcomed in health psychology because it foregrounds the importance of psychological factors in the study of illness. As Kazarian and Evans (2001) note:

The biopsychosocial model assumes that individual susceptibility to disease and patterns of subjective experiences of illness and recovery are affected interactively by psychological factors, the immune system,

*stress and social support, and quality of helper–helpee relationship. ... Psychosocial factors include person-
ality, coping skills, and lifestyle. (p. 9)*

Within this formulation, adverse psychosocial factors such as stress and fatigue are related to physical conditions such as heart disease, migraines, ulcers, anxiety, depression and reduced life expectancy. The model provides a framework for psychologists to begin to understand how illness can result from the daily stressors experienced by Nicky as she attempts to gain an education and care for her child on her own and with limited finances. It has been influential as a framework for integrating the person into his or her environment (Chapters 3 and 6) (Whitbourne, 2007).

Stress (Box 8.2) and ways of coping with its negative effects have been areas of particular interest for health psychologists (Lyons & Chamberlain, 2006). Stress often arises from everyday life: arguments with flatmates or family members, financial problems, meeting work and study commitments and so forth (Holmes & Rahe, 1967). These fairly minor, but frequent, sources of stress appear to be an important contributor to ill-health (Bolger, DeLongis, Kessler & Schilling, 1989). Although far from conclusive, research supports the existence of a link between chronic stress, a weakened immune system and vulnerability to physical illness (Herbert & Cohen, 1993; Robles, Glaser & Kiecolt-Glaser, 2005). Financial and job strains, neighbourhood stress and the demands of caring for others without adequate support have been designated chronic stress exposure and as increasing a person's risk of a range of physical and mental health conditions (Chandola, Brunner & Marmot, 2006; Steptoe, O'Donnell, Marmot & Wardle, 2008).

According to Lazarus and Folkman's (1984) model of stress and coping (Box 8.3), how we appraise the situation will determine how

---

BOX 8.2   What do we mean by 'stress'?

One common conceptualization is that environmental stimuli invoke a psychological and physiological reaction in people that we experience as stress. Here the focus is on the external or circumstantial causes of stress, including events in everyday life such as the illness of a loved one, shifting countries or conflict at work. Stressors lead to the experience of stress as a physiological state of arousal and sense of being challenged or even being unable to deal with events or tasks. Sometimes these challenges can be viewed with excitement and operate as motivators. A great sense of achievement can follow if the challenge is overcome (i.e. doing well in your exams). We might say that stress involves a series of dynamic transactions between people and circumstances. It occurs when there is a gap between perceived demands placed on us by circumstances and our perceptions of our ability to respond to, handle or control events (Timms, Graham & Caltabiano, 2007; see our discussion of the Whitehall Study later in this chapter).

we experience stress and what coping strategies we employ. This appraisal and coping process occurs against a background of social determinants, such as the resources we have available to us and our ability to exert some control over the situation. Individuals are more likely to appraise events as being less stressful when they have social support (Cohen & Wills, 1985).

There is mounting evidence of links between psychological factors, life circumstances and conditions such as coronary heart disease (Pressman & Cohen, 2005; Skodova et al., 2008; Steptoe, Wardle & Marmot, 2005). That is, there appear to be complex links between one's socioeconomic status (education, ethnicity, social class, occupational status and financial situation), psychological factors (levels of anxiety, optimism, stress and social support), behaviours such as smoking and physical illness. For example, positive affect (happiness) and social support (Box 8.4) have been associated with practices such as confiding in others, active coping strategies and maintaining social ties. These practices appear to act as buffers, partially protecting people from adverse life situations and stressors (Steptoe et al., 2008). The stress-buffer model (Cohen & Wills, 1985) posits that strong social ties can buffer people from stressful situations. This in part occurs by the diminishing of potentially harmful physiological responses to stress.

Experimental studies have demonstrated that cardiovascular reactivity to stressful stimuli (increased heart rate) in laboratory settings is diminished when participants are not alone and are accompanied by a supportive stranger or friend (Lepore, 1998; O'Donovan & Hughes, 2008). We noted in Chapter 2 how such effects of social ties in buffering people against the effects of deprivation and life stress

BOX 8.3   A person coping

On a personal level, coping strategies for stress can be categorized as problem focused or emotion focused (Lazarus & Folkman, 1984). Nicky may choose to cope with pressure prior to final examinations by asking a relative to care for her children so that she can study. This would be an example of problem-focused coping because it involves an effort to change the stressful situation. Alternatively, Nicky might talk to a close friend about the stress she is experiencing or have a night on the town. This would probably do nothing to change the stressful situation (and possibly would make it worse), but it might change her appraisal of the situation and provide release from the emotional distress. A third possibility is proactive coping. This involves preventing the stressful situation from occurring in the first place or intervening as soon as possible. In this case, Nicky would plan her commitments at the beginning of the semester, being sure to study throughout the semester and to save a portion of her income (thereby reducing her need to work in paid employment as the examination period approaches). Of course, this planning could be upset by other situational factors, such as her children getting sick or Nicky being evicted from the apartment.

BOX 8.4   Social support

Social support is a complex concept encompassing both the size and quality, in terms of active function, of one's social network. As noted in Chapters 3 and 5, such networks are foundational to a person's function and very being. Social support involves emotional reassurances, intimacy and the manifestation of these elements in everyday life (Lakey & Cohen, 2000). As we learned from social psychological research in the 1930s (Jahoda, Lazarsfeld & Zeisel, 1933/1972) some people are better able to handle stressful events than others. They are hardier. As we will see in Chapter 10, such hardiness can be shared and used as a basis for building community networks, support systems and resilience.

were also noted by Jahoda and colleagues (1933) during the Great Depression. Gender has been found to play a role in these processes, in that women are often socialized to make more use of and draw upon relationships as resources for health (Kawachi & Berkman, 2001; Reevy & Maslach, 2001). Further, research suggests that due to their greater degree of access to social support networks, women are more likely to experience positive growth or change following traumatic or highly challenging life events (Swickert & Hittner, 2009). This reflects the point made in Chapter 3 regarding disruption to the routine of everyday life that can come with challenging events, including illness. People can grow from such experiences and are more likely to do so if they can draw upon supportive relationships.

The degree of social support available to Nicky is an important factor in her coping with stress. Social integration and associated

Review exercise

It is likely that you have experienced some major life events that have been significant sources of stress.

- How did you cope?
- What personal and relational resources did you draw upon?

Now think about the more mundane sources of stress in your life. These are also important and can have a cumulative effect on your health.

access to close family members, friends, supportive workmates and support groups can have a major effect on physical and psychological well-being (Cohen, Underwood & Gottlieb, 2000). Equally, working or living in unsupportive environments is bad for psychological and physical health. Discussion of social support and health is associated with research into the broader concept of social capital. The term 'social capital' appears to have been used first by Hanifin in 1916.

Social capital has a positive association with health (Hyyppa & Maki, 2003). Just as access to money, property and financial resources can be referred to as financial capital, social capital refers to access to social resources, such as networks of friends, family members and others who can provide social support. In Chapter 6, social capital is defined as comprising the social bonds that underpin our lives at the individual and collective level. The people we form supportive relationships with may encourage us to take care of ourselves or engage in healthy behaviours with us, such as having fun, eating well and exercising. The concept has long been recognized as being central to the lived experiences of coping with health risks (Adger, 2003). Social capital can facilitate security and resilience (see Chapter 10).

Let us take this notion of transactions between people and their health-preserving consequences a little further in relation to notions of dialogue developed throughout this book (see Chapter 3). If, as we have been arguing, people are interdependent, then stress and people's reactions do not simply reside in independent individuals. We need to look at the physical environment, social relationships and how stress emerges through and resides within people's daily social interactions and encounters. Social psychologists have explored issues such as the nature of people's relationships and social support. In fact, our very appraisals of the stressor can be negotiated through dialogue with others (Gottlieb & Wagner, 1991). This is particularly relevant insofar as communities under pressure can experience and respond to societal stress together (Jahoda, Lazarsfeld & Zeisel, 1933/1972).

The biopsychosocial model is useful for highlighting important links between individual, relational and societal factors in health and illness (Box 8.5). This model also situates individuals and groups within a broader set of sociopolitical relationships shaping their everyday lives (Chapter 3). Steptoe and colleagues (2008) note that "[h]appier individuals do not experience lower levels of chronic adversity in their lives, but have greater protective resources that enable them to handle problems flexibly and effectively, together with better mental health" (p. 223). This reflects the association of positive affect with greater social connections and rewarding relationships – resources for helping people cope with adversity and associated life stressors. Having others to rely upon and feeling loved helps us to remain positive, to cope with illness and to remain healthy. High levels of optimism allow cancer patients to rally resources and cope with diagnosis and treatment (David, Montgomery & Bovbjerg, 2006).

Despite adopting a biopsychosocial perspective and being aware of the importance of social determinants of health, psychologists have tended to limit their attention to individual behaviour in causing or responding to illness (Lyons & Chamberlain, 2006). This involves the

---

BOX 8.5 Criticisms of the biopsychosocial model of health

The biopsychosocial model has been subject to useful criticisms. For instance, Gordon (1988) argues that the biopsychological model still equates the individual with responsibility for health and simply adds variables such as stress to a Western medical equation. Of particular note is the failure of the model to explain just how biological, psychological and situational factors impact health (Ogden, 1997). The model carries the assumption of a holistic approach in asserting unity across mind, spirit and body. What is promoted is a perspective on the whole individual. This is somewhat limited in that it can sideline the material and social world and associated influences on illness that reside outside of the individual. For instance, a stress management programme can relieve some of the symptoms of stress by teaching an individual to cope. However, the causes of stress may remain in place and symptoms will likely return unless changes are made to the material and social environment. Spatial and geographical life situations, particularly those associated with poverty, are significant stressors for many people (see Chapter 6). Living in damp or noisy conditions, a lack of privacy and a sense of place, and feeling unsafe in one's neighbourhood are all important social determinants of health (Wilkinson & Marmot, 2003). Social determinants of health are discussed in detail later in this chapter. In brief, this term refers to social factors and material conditions that can influence human health, such as crime, the affordability of housing and the availability of nutritious food.

---

study of why people make the choices they do and why they engage in healthy and unhealthy behaviours. In the following section, we explore prominent social cognition models that have been developed to explain the health-related behaviour of individuals. This orientation towards behaviour is important because personal actions clearly affect our health, such as when we consume too much alcohol or smoke cigarettes as a means of coping with life stressors. However, this approach provides only a limited perspective on personal health-related actions in everyday life. As well as investigating coping strategies, psychologists increasingly work to remove stressors and other risk factors for illness from the environment.

Considering health-related knowledge and behaviour

Since the 1950s, a number of social cognitive models have been proposed to explain the health-related choices individuals make. All focus on the beliefs that individuals have towards health issues and how these beliefs can shape their behaviour. According to these models, intentions to change the behaviour and a sense of efficacy in being able to change the behaviour are the primary predictors of actual behaviour (Conner & Norman, 2005). Unfortunately, meta-analyses show that intentions are not as predictive of behaviour as these models imply (Webb & Sheeran, 2006). To a large extent, behaviour change is explained by factors such as environmental circumstances, peer pressure, gender and social identity (Kiran-Esen, 2003). Social cognitive models of health remain relevant because they are widely used to inform a raft of health promotion initiatives. A lot of time and money continue to be spent on applying these models in attempts to encourage people like Nicky to give up smoking (Ajzen, 1991; McMillan, Higgins & Conner, 2005; Mielewczyk & Willig, 2007). In fact, one of the models discussed below was developed specifically to address smoking behaviour.

Nicky has, of course, seen the media campaigns designed to discourage smoking: the television advertisements and the warnings on cigarette packets. She is aware of the severe health risks that smoking poses to her and her children. However, many people she knows smoke, including all her close family members. Her grandfather, who is seventy years old, has smoked two packs a day since he was fifteen, and although he coughs a lot, he has not developed any smoking-related diseases. Sometimes Nicky wonders whether maybe there is a gene in her family, yet to be discovered, that protects them. After all, if there are genes that make it more likely that you will develop a disease, then why not genes that can protect you? Nicky is experiencing optimistic bias – unrealistic optimism about the likelihood that something negative will happen to oneself, despite wider evidence. Her perceived susceptibility is low. On the other hand, she is aware of the statistics around smoking and health, in regards to not only mortality, but also potential pain, distress and reduced quality of life if one survives a smoking-related disease. Perceived severity is high. From time to time Nicky does think about quitting; apart from the health issues, smoking is expensive and inconvenient (there are fewer and fewer places where people can smoke, and at university and her part-time job smoking means standing outside, regardless of the weather). Nicky is concerned about the effect on her children both from second-hand smoke (she tries not to smoke around them, but it is harder now that Mark is running around) and from the children modelling smoking behaviour. She is sure she read somewhere that the children of smokers are far more likely to smoke. But a cigarette with a cup of coffee at the end of a long day is so nice! Nicky has tried to quit once before: it made her bad-tempered (she had a major fight with her ex-partner), and she could not stop coughing or eating and put on three kilograms. So Nicky can see both benefits and barriers to giving up. Finally, although she sees the warnings every time she takes out her cigarette packet, they somehow don't seem very real or at least very urgent. Nicky is young; she thinks she has plenty of time to give up, and no one else she knows seems interested in giving up at the moment. Maybe it could be a New Year's resolution? Nicky's cues to action are currently weak.

A key sociocognitive model is the health belief model (Figure 8.1), which was developed by Rosenstock (1966), who built on the work

---

Review exercise

- How likely do you think it is that Nicky will give up smoking? Why?
- Are there factors that might help Nicky make this change in lifestyle?

Such questions lead to the development of social cognitive models of health.

---

of Hochbaum (1958) and others. This model sought to explain the experiences of people like Nicky, and to inform the development of interventions designed to assist people to change unhealthy habits. According to this model, health behaviours are based on four factors:

1. Perceived susceptibility to a health threat: Nicky's perception of how likely it is that she will become ill.
2. Perceived seriousness of a health threat: how ill Nicky thinks she could become.
3. Benefits of and barriers to undertaking particular health behaviours: the advantages and disadvantages of Nicky's engaging in a particular behaviour.
4. Cues to action: the influence of external factors, such as media campaigns or her friends' behaviour, on Nicky's actions.

Another sociocognitive model, the protection motivation theory of health, adds the component of *self-efficacy*, or the belief that one is able to achieve a desired goal or change (Bandura, 1977; Condiotte, 1981) to the health belief model. Unless people believe they can successfully change their behaviour in the long term, they are unlikely

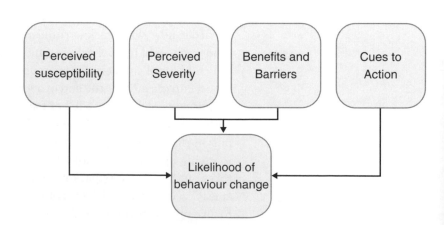

Figure 8.1. Health belief model

to attempt to change their behaviour (Janz, Champion & Strecher, 2002). This addition theoretically explains the situation in which Nicky believes she is susceptible to illness, considers the threat to be severe, believes the benefits of changing the behaviour would outweigh the costs and has sufficient cues to action, and yet, despite all of this, does not engage in behaviour change by giving up smoking because she does not believe that she will be successful in giving up smoking.

Adding yet another sociocognitive variable to the mix, the theory of reasoned action incorporates Nicky's *attitudes* towards health behaviour and the role of subjective norms. These attitudes refer to beliefs about the outcome of a behaviour (or behaviour change) and the evaluation of those outcomes. For example, Nicky might believe that giving up smoking would result in significant health benefits. Perceptions of how others would react to the behaviour, and motivation to comply with their desires, reflect subjective norms. For example, if the norm among Nicky's close friends is not to smoke and if Nicky believes these friends will approve of her giving up, then according to this theory, the likelihood of her giving up is increased. These two elements combine to form the intention to give up (or not), and then the appropriate behaviour.

Yet another model, the stages of change model (Figure 8.2), was developed by Prochaska (1983) to incorporate insights from previous models, and specifically in relation to the smoking behaviour of

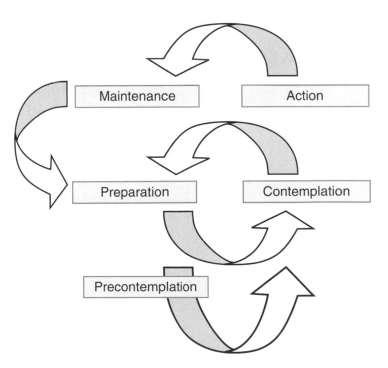

Figure 8.2. Spiral model of behaviour change

people like Nicky. This model is often referred to as the *spiral model of change* and consists of five stages: precontemplation, contemplation, preparation, action, maintenance. Prochaska and DiClemente argue that before behaviour change occurs, a person such as Nicky is engaged in the behaviour largely unreflectively (just enjoying smoking, for example); this is the precontemplative stage. If Nicky then begins to think about behaviour change, she has entered the contemplative stage. This may be followed by preparation, for example setting a date to give up and buying a nicotine substitute such as chewing gum. The fourth stage is action, which is then, hopefully, followed by maintenance. The model is frequently depicted as a spiral, showing that individuals may not necessarily achieve long-term maintenance because they return to one of the earlier stages instead.

Limitations of social cognitive models of health behaviour change

Psychologists draw on these sociocognitive models in an attempt to explain the health-related choices of individuals, and in order to change their health-related behaviours. Much of this work is firmly focused on individuals who are thought to behave in a thoughtful, predictable and rational manner. This assumption is not shared by all psychologists. Some have questioned the assumption that people are rational actors who consistently make reasoned health choices based primarily on stable attitudes and personal cognitions (Ingham, 1993; Stam, 2006). People are also contradictory and impulsive. Personal beliefs about health issues can vary across contexts. This makes it difficult to measure and predict health-related cognitions and behaviours in the manner that social cognitive models attempt. Some have gone so far as to argue that health behaviours, as theorized solely through such models, do not exist (Mielewczyk & Willig, 2007) (Box 8.6).

Social cognitive models are limited by a Cartesian understanding of people and their knowledge of health (see Chapter 4). These models focus on abstract mental representations located in the heads of individuals, and seek to explain how these representations shape individual behaviour in the world. Thoughts and actions are treated as distinct variables within causal pathways, and little is said about how these variables are connected causally. The associated narrowing of health decisions to mechanistic individual choices neglects the fact that health behaviours tend to emerge from contexts of ongoing social interaction. A decision to use a condom is usually necessary only when one person is having sex with another person (Mielewczyk & Willig, 2007). A major problem with these models is they offer little in terms of addressing the social and interactive

BOX 8.6 Criticisms of social cognitive models of health

Criticisms of social cognitive models of health have used the metaphor of old clothes that are constantly being refashioned with new buttons and features in an attempt to explain the causes of health-related behaviour patterns (Mielewczyk & Willig, 2007). The refinement of these models through the inclusion of additional variables is like

individuals trying to squeeze into clothes they first wore when they were very much younger (and, presumably, thinner)...[and] since the results of such attempts would be far from comfortable even if success were somehow to be achieved, the "old clothes" which the SCMs [social cognitive models] represented could be sent to the jumble and some new ones purchased. (Mielewczyk & Willig, 2007, p. 812)

Rather than change their attire, many psychologists have focused on expanding the waistbands of health behaviour models. The addition of more variables has not dramatically increased the explanatory power of social cognitive models or their relevance to the realities of daily life. Simply adding variables to these models does nothing to address the underlying assumptions regarding individuals, and reminds us of Gordon Allport's (1968) observation that the preoccupation with technical refinement can lead psychologists to lose sight of the real world and what people are actually like (see Chapter 3).

nature of many health decisions and the broader socioeconomic factors, such as poverty and unemployment, that frequently limit the options available to individuals.

Clearly, it is important for psychologists to explore why people behave in certain ways that can have either negative or enhancing consequences for their health. After all, smoking, drinking too much alcohol or consuming a poor diet can kill you, or at least hasten your demise. Nonetheless, there is a need for a shift from a focus on social cognitive models and their constant technical refinement to a focus on developing new approaches that attend to the actual social practices within which people are embedded in everyday life (Box 8.7). This shift adds new and contextually informed insights to help understand health-related behaviours.

As noted in Chapters 2 and 3, the investigation of everyday life provides a basis for developing our understandings of why people act the way they do in particular settings (Fry et al., 2008; Laurier, McKie & Goodwin, 2000). For example, the meaning of having a cigarette can vary across a single day, depending on whether one is getting up and ready for work, taking a break at work or having a drink at a bar on the way home from work. In order to understand the reasons a person smokes, we need to study the actual situations and practices within which people's actions are embedded (Mielewczyk & Willig, 2007). This involves looking at the interconnectedness of activities within specific settings and daily life. For instance, smoking is not necessarily an isolated 'behaviour', in that it might also involve taking a break

---

BOX 8.7   Interesting study

Fry, Grogan, Gough and Conner (2008) explored the social dimensions of youth smoking by drawing on the experiences of sixteen- to twenty-four-year-old smokers and nonsmokers. These authors found that the desire to smoke cannot be reduced to addiction or intentions alone. Cigarettes are social objects (see Chapters 3 and 6) that have complex functions within the everyday lives of young people. Smoking is often relational and a daily practice that is used as a 'social tool' in attempts to control the perceptions other people have of one's self (see Chapter 7 and the discussion of social identity theory). Smoking is woven into the conduct of daily lives. "One of the major aspects of social life that our young participants identified as being an obstacle to stopping smoking was the fact that so much of everyday life is conducted with peers" (Fry et al., 2008, p. 775). These authors note that it may be time to move beyond social cognition theory-driven approaches to smoking cessation and to focus more on the complexities of smoking within the contexts of everyday life, relationships and the actual meanings the act of smoking has for people.

---

with colleagues, getting to know others or calming down after realizing that you have just had unprotected sex and may have contracted a life-threatening disease. What it means to smoke may be very different in each context. A focus on context and everyday practice also allows us to explain why it is easier to remain smoke free in some situations than in others. You might really need a cigarette to calm yourself down after having unprotected sex. Further,

if having a cigarette with a close friend is experienced as a way of establishing a sense of community and connection, it may be possible to replace it with another practice which captures similar meanings (e.g. linking arms when walking down the street; sharing a bowl of ice-cream or a bottle of wine; verbalizing feelings of warmth and connection). ... The important thing to bear in mind is that the "target behaviour" for this type of health promotion work would not be "smoking" ... as such, but rather more specific and contextualized practices such as "sharing a cigarette with my friend". (Mielewczyk & Willig, 2007, p. 830)

In pointing to the limits of social cognitive models of health behaviour, we are not suggesting that psychologists should simply abandon any attempt to promote personal healthy practices. Social cognitive models have provided a useful focus in terms of establishing what people can do for their health. However, there are a range of interrelated factors that impact our health and are not under direct personal control. Social cognitive models cannot account for these factors. It is time to turn our attention to the links between the health of individuals and the broader societal contexts and relationships that are integral to their lives (Fry et al., 2008). Many psychologists are calling for a reorientation away from the refinement and application of social cognitive models of behaviour towards more inductive work that seeks to understand unhealthy behaviour and promote healthy practices in the context of everyday life (Marks,

2008; Mielewczyk & Willig, 2007; Murray & Campbell, 2003). This requires us to understand broader sociopolitical processes, such as colonization (Chapter 5), that impact the health of different groups of people differently. After all, health-related behaviours occur in sociopolitical contexts, as does illness. Any effective health psychology will need to engage with the politics of health (Bunton, 2006). This takes us into the domain of social determinants of health.

Social determinants of health

Survival and health are determined by a range of interrelated factors, from the state of the physical environment, to social stability, access to food and shelter, social status, the availability of economic resources, access to health care and education, community cohesion, family and hereditary factors, migration and events such as wars, famines and natural disasters (Hofrichter, 2003; Wilkinson & Marmot, 2003; Williamson & Carr, 2009). The health of a population is shaped by processes of social justice and power that are in turn shaped by historical, financial, environmental and political factors. No one controls all these factors that shape their lives and health.

Social psychologists need to explore the interrelated impact on health of social context, work and environment, personal lifestyle actions, biological makeup and community and social networks. People exist in interactions with others, and health is fundamentally relational in nature (Cornish, 2004). Individuals reside at the centre of a set of layers of interaction related to social structures, politics, hereditary factors and lifestyles. Factors such as community networks are related to other factors such as work, biology and lifestyle. Let us consider Nicky as the person in the middle. Nicky is in a low-paid part-time job that is stressful in that she has limited control over the pace of her work and has to juggle paid employment with university study and parenting. In terms of lifestyle she smokes and exists on an unhealthy diet. Biology may exert an influence on her health. Community settings are also important in that Nicky's neighborhood is rife with crime, and her apartment is damp and noisy. Moreover, Nicky lacks the close community relations that can buffer people against the impacts of other factors on health. As a result, her risk of illness is increased (Box 8.8).

Identifying links between social deprivation and illness is hardly groundbreaking. Early epidemiological work allied to the public health movements of the nineteenth century documented the health impacts of adverse living conditions (Chadwick, 1842). It is well established that lower socioeconomic status (SES) is a precursor to illness, rather than a consequence of it (Wilkinson, 1996). Carroll,

BOX 8.8   Social determinants of health

Social determinants of health pervade the social environment we live in together. Specifically, they include such things as relative poverty or deprivation (particularly in early life), stress, social exclusion, adverse work conditions, substandard housing, unemployment, poor education and social fragmentation (Wilkinson & Marmot, 2003). An important question for this book is: Why should social psychologists involve themselves in addressing social determinants of health? One answer is that social determinants are unfair, unnecessary and preventable. Recognizing this, the World Health Organization operates on the basis of human rights and the principle of equity (see Meier, 2007). This means that "access to life-saving or health-promoting interventions should not be denied for unfair reasons, including those with economic or social roots" (http://www.who.int/about/agenda).

Davey Smith and Bennett (2002) note that "SES-health differentials are not a transitory phenomenon, but are evident throughout history; those in more favorable circumstances appear always to have enjoyed better health than those in less favorable circumstances" (p. 140). The relationship between socioeconomic status and health is continuous or a gradient, and appears to involve both material conditions and psychological factors. For almost every ailment, as one descends the SES ladder morbidity and mortality increase. It is evident that these differences cannot be reduced to the 'unhealthy' behaviour patterns of lower-SES groups. Throughout history, unhealthy behaviours such as alcohol abuse have been equally prevalent among affluent groups. Yet their advantage in good health remained (Carroll, Davey Smith and Bennett, 2002). This is not to ignore the contemporary situation, where smoking is more common among lower-SES than higher-SES groups, and thereby contributes to higher rates of cancer among lower-SES groups. We are proposing that smoking and other health-related behaviours do not, on their own, account for the persistence of an SES-based gradient in health. "While statistically controlling for such behaviours may attenuate SES-health gradients, it in no way abolishes them" (Carroll, Davey Smith and Bennett, 2002, p. 147). These authors propose that "[i]f SES-health gradients are not, for the most part, attributable to variations in unhealthy behaviour, the major influences must reside in the broader fabric of people's lives" (p. 147). Possible explanations lie in cumulative exposure to adversity and a range of health hazards across the lifespan, both material (damp housing and inadequate income) and psychological (stigma and social exclusion) in nature. Life stressors that make people overly worried and anxious and reduce their sense of control and coping can potentially be as harmful to their health as smoking and having a poor diet.

People like Mark often lead more health-averse lives. This is not just because of their personal choices. It is also because of the options in life they are left with and the consequences of the choices made by other people and institutions (Box 8.9). Nonetheless, negative health outcomes are not certain. Members of lower-SES communities who have social capital, live in more cohesive societies with adequate social programmes and have opportunities to exercise some control over their destiny are less likely to get sick and die early (Wilkinson, 1996).

Research suggests that inequitable social arrangements impact people not only physically, but also psychologically, through their experiences of stigma, stress, loneliness, low self-esteem, powerlessness and poor-quality social relations (Bolam, Hodgetts, Chamberlain, Murphy & Gleeson, 2003). This is reflected in discussions of the role of social capital, social support and networks in health (Wilkinson & Marmot, 2003). Despite emphasizing the importance of personal

---

BOX 8.9   The role of social determinants in Mark's life

Consider the future life course for Nicky's son Mark. This is useful for illustrating the importance of a broad focus on how a range of factors contribute to people's health status over the course of their lives. Mark's health and his performance at school are already compromised by his asthma due to his damp living conditions. His future depends to some extent on the sacrifices Nicky is making to gain an education in order to raise the family's SES profile, although this upward shift depends on her actually gaining a job once she completes her degree. The harsher realities of single parenting are softened by government assistance, but not totally alleviated. The high costs of housing mean the family end up living in a lower-SES neighbourhood, which increases the risk of family members becoming victims of violence and crime. The local children and teenagers Mark will likely form friendships with come from less privileged backgrounds, have fewer educational opportunities and are less likely to aspire to well-paid professions. The manual and semi-skilled occupations that are predominant sources of employment for lower-SES neighbourhoods have traditionally been associated with exposure to hazardous substances, a higher risk of workplace accidents and insecure working arrangements and income levels. Having to rent a house means the family may be forced to move more frequently, which can disrupt Mark's schooling and his friendships with other children. Mark may experience fewer positive psychological rewards than his peers from more affluent backgrounds. Skip forward. Living as a single mother, Nicky never had sufficient income to pay for Mark's orthodontic treatments, so as an adult he has ongoing dental problems. Due to the cost, Mark often delays dental treatment and ends up with toothache, unable to perform his job as a forklift driver at the recycling centre. This contributes to an erratic work history. As a retired person, Mark is less likely to have adequate resources to cover the costs of living and his medical needs. Mark dies ten years earlier than the national average for men. This scenario of Mark's life path shows how the clustering of personal actions and contextual factors within the context of a person's daily life holds the key to understanding health and illness.

experience and psychosocial processes in health inequalities, we would not want to draw attention away from the physical and structural determinants of such inequalities. Both quantitative and qualitative research indicates that social support and networks do not alleviate material hardship, even though such interpersonal supports can buffer people against the severity of material hardship (Cattell, 2001). Advocates of both 'materialist' and 'psychosocial' approaches to health inequalities now acknowledge the importance of material conditions, such as not having to sleep on a wet and cold concrete doorstep, and experiences, such as being stigmatized or fearing assault for being homeless (Hodgetts, Chamberlain & Radley, 2007). Due to the socially exclusionary nature of life experienced by people living in hardship, such people often face barriers to accessing basic physical necessities such as a warm dwelling and adequate food, as well as psychological resources for good health, including support networks, respite from stress and a sense of belonging, self-esteem and hope.

Work and health

Work is a social determinant of health that has been investigated by psychologists for some time (Poelmans, O'Driscoll & Beham, 2005) and that highlights the importance of social stratification for health (Box 8.10). Work is an activity that most of us will spend a large portion of our lives doing. Due to this time factor alone, work has the potential to have a major impact on our lives, including on our health. In addition, work itself appears to be an important health issue for many people (Wilkinson & Marmot, 2003). Recent research found that one in seven women and one in ten men with no previous mental health difficulties reported being stressed at work and suffering clinical depression or anxiety by

---

BOX 8.10   Social stratification

Social stratification refers to patterns of social relations or relationships that are stable, recurring and usually transgenerational. These relationships reflect the ways in which individuals or groups are ranked according to power, status and prestige. Groupings are generally based on SES, ethnicity, age, gender and sexuality. Social stratification is often played out in the workplace. For example, women from minority backgrounds are more likely to be employed in lower-paid part-time jobs, typically with fewer benefits, less security and more risks of illness.

the age of thirty-two (Melchior, Caspi, Milne, Danese, Poulton & Moffitt, 2007).

A study often cited as an exemplar of connections between work, social stratification and illness is Marmot and colleague's 'Whitehall Study' of 17,000 civil servants working in UK government offices in Whitehall. Each employee was categorized in terms of the hierarchy of employment grades in the civil service. Even after controlling for smoking, cholesterol, glucose tolerance, blood pressure and height, the death rate from heart disease was four times greater for lower-grade staff than for senior office staff. Differences were attributed to social stratification in the workplace.

Explanations for the impact of social stratification on health include increased daily hassles and stress, which in turn contribute to strained social relations, reduced social support and limited control or opportunity for self-efficacy among lower-SES groups (Carroll, Davey Smith and Bennett, 2002). This would support the view that material and psychosocial factors interact in contributing to health inequalities. If Nicky graduates and then ends up getting a job at the lower level of an institution like Whitehall, she will face these issues.

Work–life balance has become a key focus for labour relations in recent years. Work-related stress costs billions of dollars via illnesses, lowered productivity, absenteeism and the cost of sick leave (Poelmans, O'Driscoll & Beham, 2005). People working night shifts, overtime or irregular hours and those who have high work-related stress or pressure report more ill-health, whereas those who are more extroverted, are self-employed or have work decision-making ability or use a variety of skills in their work report better health (Ettner, 2001). Therefore, the manner in which work is conducted can be a source of stress and attendant ill-health. Fordist and Taylorist job designs, which were developed and popularized over the course of the twentieth century, involve separating tasks so that each worker performs a very small number of activities, minimizing skill requirements, and in turn leading to the minimization of required knowledge. For employers, this has the advantage that employees require little training and are easily replaced, and that standardized processes provide minimal variation in products. These job designs may be visualized most easily as factory assembly lines, but the adoption of these principles has become increasingly widespread. George Ritzer (1995) suggests that the success of the fast-food company McDonald's is the result of the dissemination of Fordist principles of work design and de-skilling. In this sense, a McDonald's (Box 8.11) outlet is one big assembly line dedicated to delivering a range of standardized, production-line food.

BOX 8.11   McDonaldization

McDonaldization is "the process by which the principles of the fast-food restaurant are coming to dominate more and more sectors of American society as well as of the rest of the world" (Ritzer, 1995, p. 1). The term 'McJobs' refers to low-paid, dead-end positions into which increasingly large numbers of young people are channelled. McJobs epitomize de-skilling and the exercise of managerial control alongside the use of new technologies of control and surveillance. The technologies that allow this include:

- Tracking individuals (CCTV, face recognition, swipe cards and computer logins)
- Tracking things, including inventory and stock (barcodes, integrated alarms)
- Recording activity (sales, phone calls, use of electronic tills or registers)

In the face of these developments, workers become more and more constrained, and stress from potentially constant supervision and monitoring is increased. However, according to Du Gay (1996), as employees lose respect for their employers, new and subversive forms of resistance to the pressure of the panopticon can arise, including:

- 'Work to rule': performing exactly what is required, as and when required; stopping work exactly at the designated time; refusing flexibility
- Maximizing use of sick leave
- Pilfering of nonmaterial resources (ideas, computer time)
- Using company resources for oneself

Promoting health by focusing on people and contexts

Health promotion involves a range of initiatives at the individual, community and population levels that are designed to protect, prolong and increase the quality of human life and health. Activities can vary widely and include the cleanup of toxic sites, insulating houses, smoking cessation programmes, public housing and graduated taxation systems. We present two mutually enhancing approaches to health promotion that reflect a key theme in this book (Prilleltensky & Prilleltensky, 2006). The first focuses on individual behaviour change and the second on collective action. Both are necessary in the development of a relevant social psychology of health and illness. Given what we know from the biopsychosocial orientation and stress-buffering research, individual-level health promotion needs to be woven in with more broadly focused initiatives for building social networks that can protect people's health. We also need to remove health hazards and stressors from the contexts of everyday life.

Promoting individual health

The behaviour change approach to health promotion focuses primarily on individual actions and the consequences of these for health. This approach refers to efforts made to encourage people to reduce unhealthy behaviours (smoking) and increase healthy behaviours (physical exercise). It involves raising awareness about health risks and informing people about how to live healthy lives (Box 8.12). It is then up to individuals to choose to look after their own health. This approach often involves targeting individual health behaviours relating to issues such as HIV/AIDS, coronary heart disease and smoking en masse. Such interventions, for example in relation to coronary heart disease, often combine media campaigns informing the public about the dangers of unhealthy eating with face-to-face community initiatives such as encouraging local shops to provide healthy food (DiMatteo & Martin, 2002; Farquhar et al., 1990).

Health information is increasingly demanded by 'health consumers' who are no longer content to rely upon curative approaches to disease (Hodgetts, Bolam & Stephens, 2005). People often seek information to guide their efforts to prevent a range of illnesses and to manage their own health. Associated recommendations for healthy living are now central to everyday life, contributing to the construction of health beliefs and health care policies in many Western countries (Hodgetts & Chamberlain, 2003). Access to health information is useful in helping people manage their own health. Information can encourage people to seek professional assistance and improve their understanding of information given to them by health professionals. With the advent of the Internet, many people have access to a huge amount of information; they also write about experiences of illness and share insights with others. Communities are built around people with specific ailments communicating online (Hodgetts &

BOX 8.12   Examples of simple health promotion interventions

Promoting the health of individuals through targeting specific behaviours such as physical activity and stress reduction does not have to be complex. For example, supportive relationships can effectively increase physical activity. Cholewa and Irwin (2008) demonstrated how a peer buddy system assisted the adoption of personal activity regimes among university students. Waltman and colleagues (2009) found that the health of patients with coronary artery disease could be improved by an intervention in which they forgave someone who had caused them ongoing stress. The forgiveness decreased their anger and the strain on their hearts. This simple intervention also reminds us of the fundamentally transactional and relational nature of an individual's physical health.

Chamberlain, 2006b). This information is of varying quality and accuracy, and may not always be health enhancing. For example, particularly worrying are websites, often described as social support sites, that normalize and even promote behaviour generally construed as negative, including anorexia and self-harm (Mulveen & Hepworth, 2006). Such information is increasingly part of the symbolic landscape into which official information campaigns are injected (Chapter 11) and within which people are seeking to manage their health (Hodgetts & Chamberlain, 2006b).

Despite the potential health-enhancing benefits of practices such as taking regular exercise and consuming a balanced diet, critics point to the problematic effects of unacknowledged assumptions and values that underlie lifestyle-oriented health promotion initiatives. Social psychologists have critiqued the pervasive individualistic morality evident in the behaviour change approach to health promotion (Hodgetts, Bolam & Stephens, 2005). One common basis of criticism is that the moral code of self-reliance for health can contribute to victim blaming. This has been associated with intolerance of those who, due to an apparent lack of self-discipline and personal weakness, do not engage in the prescribed health-enhancing practices or become ill. Much has been written over the past two decades about the rise of healthism (Box 8.13) and the individualization of health concerns, often through behaviour-oriented health promotion messages (Crossley, 2000).

BOX 8.13   Healthism

The term 'healthism' was initially used by Crawford (1980) to describe a new form of health consciousness in American society and the rise of individually focused preventive practices. It can be argued that healthism promotes individual choice as the primary source of health and associates the prevention of illness with personal choices, willpower or the alleviation of barriers to behaviour change. Thus, a morality of health containing specific norms and values that emphasize an individual's obligation to be concerned with his or her health is promoted. To be healthy is to live a balanced and controlled existence, to demonstrate vigilance and self-restraint, and to ensure the avoidance of risks such as smoking, eating unhealthy food and misusing drugs. Davey-Smith (2004) explores the origins of healthism and the focus on personal morality with respect to health in the Eugenics movement of the 1920s and Nazi Germany. He points out that smoking and lifestyle are indeed important health concerns, but can also hide wider issues. Individualistic approaches distract us from the economic and political inequalities and patterns of ill-health. Referring to a Jewish physician's perspective during the Nazi regime, Davey Smith writes:

Martin Gumpert ... considered the lifestyle campaigns to be a cover up for the fact that health in Nazi Germany deteriorated dramatically. Gumpert proclaimed that the "abstinent Hitler, who from conviction never takes a drop of alcohol ... now drives the people at whose head he stands into fatal alcoholism". (p. 3)

Times are changing. There is a shift in individual behaviour change-oriented health promotion away from psychologists relying primarily on social cognitive models for explanation and then applying these to programmes that are administered to target groups. There is increased recognition of the complexity and contextually specific nature of health promotion interventions, which requires collaborations with target groups (Schaalma & Kok, 2009). This reflects a shift to action research processes (see Chapter 1) in which various stakeholders are involved in the identification of health needs and the design, implementation and evaluation of programmes (Minkler & Wallerstein, 2002). Guidelines for behavioural change at the individual, community and populations levels developed in the United Kingdom by the National Institute for Health and Clinical Excellence (NICE) reflect such developments (Kelly & Abraham, 2009) (Box 8.14). The guidelines emphasize the need for careful planning of interventions in a manner informed by local and national contexts that involves working in collaboration with the people whose behaviour is being targeted and ensuring that their needs are being met (Yardley & Moss-Morris, 2009). Aro and Absetz (2009) provide a compelling example of why it is important to look at individual, community and national factors when planning behaviour change. These authors refer to the importance of physical activity, specifically cycling, and the need for cyclists to wear helmets (Kakefuda, Stallones & Gibbs, 2008). They note that personal engagement in such physical activity is made more likely if the surrounding context, including environmental resources and policy changes, supports the behavioural change to take up cycling. "Without a bicycle…, skills for riding it, bicycle lanes, and a safe neighbourhood, biking as a physical activity may not be attractive or sustainable" (Aro & Absetz, 2009, p. 125). Here we see that factors outside of the social cognitive models of behaviour change are important for people engaging in physical activities such as cycling. The infrastructure needs to be put in place for people to be healthy. This takes us into the arena of collective action-oriented health promotion, which is often driven by communities for themselves.

BOX 8.14   Designing behavioural change interventions

For further guidance on the orientation, design and implementation of behavioural change interventions, go to http://www.nice.org.uk/PH006. The focus of these guidelines is personal change to improve personal health en masse through targeting the community and population levels. They include guidance for designing, costing and implementing programmes.

Promoting collective health

Substantive evidence suggests that individual behaviour patterns have a smaller impact on the health of a population than many people assume, when compared with socioeconomic conditions that expose people to a raft of risk factors (Williamson & Carr, 2009). A relevant social psychology of health and illness has to address the inequalities in resources and health status that are prevalent within and across societies, and that are due in most part to societal structures (Marks, 2008). This involves developing strategies for challenging social inequalities and re-politicizing health (Murray, Nelson, Poland, Maticka-Tyndale & Ferris, 2004). Bambra, Fox and Scott-Samuel (2005) argue that "an awareness of the political nature of health will lead to a more effective health promotion strategy and more evidence-based health promotion practice" (p. 1). This requires attending to the ways in which social contexts, processes such as colonization, and the distribution of resources and control can damage the health of particular groups in society.

Reflecting the early work of collectivist-oriented social psychologists (Chapter 2), Campbell and Murray (2004) propose that an effective health psychology must highlight and contest power imbalances in society and processes that lead to health inequalities. We must acknowledge that many of the factors that impact negatively on health exist beyond the control of individuals and local communities, and as a result beyond the regulation of social groups who have the poorest health. This takes us into the realm of collective action as a basis for health promotion. It requires us to get political and obtain resources that can lift people out of poverty and support the development of communities. Fostering healthy communities

involves reducing levels of educational failure, reducing insecurity and unemployment and improving housing standards. Societies that enable all citizens to play a full and useful role in the social, economic and cultural life of their society will be healthier than those where people face insecurity, exclusion and deprivation. (Wilkinson & Marmot, 2003, p. 11)

The collective action approach to health promotion attempts to address economic, environmental and social factors associated with illness (Beaglehole, Bonita, Horton, Adams & McKee, 2004; Meier, 2007; Minkler & Wallerstein, 2002; Eng & Blanchard, 2007). The health of individuals is addressed by targeting the everyday contexts within which their lives are played out. Graduated taxation systems that fund welfare services and universal health care are examples of such interventions (Box 8.15). As noted in Chapter 2, early social psychologists engaged in labour reform and social justice attempted to address health inequalities by improving the options people have

BOX 8.15   Addressing social determinants of health

Successful initiatives to address social determinants of health include strengthening individuals' knowledge and capacity to act to preserve their health, strengthening communities, improving access to essential services, and encouraging macroeconomic and cultural change. Such macro-level changes are achievable through income maintenance policies that provide adequate financial support for those who fall into poverty, increased access to education and training to prevent poverty in the longer term, and the development of more equitable policies for taxation and income distribution (Scrambler & Higgs, 1999). Wilkinson and Marmot (2003) state:

Through policies on taxes, benefits, employment, education, economic management, and many other areas of activity, no government can avoid having a major impact on the distribution of income. The indisputable evidence of the effects of such policies on rates of death and disease imposes a public duty to eliminate absolute poverty and reduce material inequalities. (p. 17)

According to these authors this requires:

1. Minimum income guarantees and access to services
2. Interventions to reduce poverty and social exclusion
3. Protection for vulnerable groups
4. Public health policies, including affordable housing
5. Reducing social stratification in work, education and family welfare
6. Equity and fairness

in life, and consequently reducing their likelihood of illness and an early death (Flournoy & Yen, 2004). The effectiveness of such efforts becomes apparent when we look at them historically. Most improvements in morbidity and mortality rates in the industrialized world during the 1800s resulted from increased safety requirements for work and home, good sanitation, child labour reforms, protection for workers and the distribution of vaccines throughout the population (Hofrichter, 2003). Further improvements in health in many developed nations occurred during the period between the 1940s and 1960s, when we invested in social services and infrastructure (Casswell, 2001). Since then, the most important factor eroding the health of the world's population has been inequalities in resource distribution and increased insecurity and deteriorating work conditions (Wilkinson & Marmot, 2003).

Many interventions to address social determinants of health come from progressive governments. Others are initiated by specific community groups. Putland (2008) points out that the arts are useful in building social capital, inclusion and community development from the bottom up (Chapter 6). Considerable resources are now allocated to such community-based initiatives aimed at building social capital (Box 8.16) by networking existing organizations

BOX 8.16   Social capital is also shaped beyond the local setting

Social capital is not just determined locally. It is also shaped at a societal level through the mass media (Chapter 11). Wallack (2003) provides an illustration of this:

In the summer of 1999 the East Coast was suffering through a terrible heat wave, and deaths were mounting. ... New York City sagged under the oppressive weight of the heat, and city officials were struggling to address the crisis. The apparent cause of death for those who died was the physical effects of the heat. However, the underlying cause simply may have been fear and isolation, and in part the consequences of not being connected to a broader community. One news report related the observations of emergency workers, who said "an alarming number of city residents without air-conditioning keep their windows shut because they fear becoming victims of crime, and instead became patients". Of course, these deaths were not random occurrences; those most likely to die were isolated, disconnected, and likely to live in high homicide areas. (pp. 594–595)

This example highlights how people's behaviour can be affected by their perceptions of the health risks of their environments. Opening a window to cool down may not be as straightforward as one might think in a community with low social capital. We also see how institutions such as the media matter in how they frame health, how they identify concerns and what solutions they offer. The media also matter because they can be used to build civic participation and cultural capital through the cultivation of a public commitment to social change, and thereby enable elderly community members to feel that they can open their windows (Chapter 11). Part of this might involve a shift from the 'bad news is good news' or 'if it bleeds it leads' mentality that can contribute to a socially isolating siege mentality.

and fostering the development of new ones (Campbell & Murray, 2004; Hyyppa & Maki, 2003). When working collectively to address health concerns, a group can generate leaders and strengthen the bonds that bind a community (Gallagher, Easterling & Lodwick, 2003). Such initiatives involve cultivating social cohesion and strengthening communities so that developing communities can take control of their own health through civic participation (Campbell & Jovchelovitch, 2000). Factors indicating the presence of social capital have been noted throughout this chapter and include friendship, trust, strong supportive networks and a respect for and sense of mutual obligation towards others. These features have a major bearing on health and can buffer people against the adverse affects of relative deprivation, although only to a point (Wilkinson & Marmot, 2003, p. 22).

We have noted throughout this book that social psychology involves a dialogical process of adapting to change in partnership with stakeholders, rather than 'training' or 'resourcing' groups. We know from the history of our discipline (Chapter 2) that psychologists can work alongside community members to clarify and address community concerns and in so doing ensure that there is genuine participation from stakeholders (Box 8.17). Guareschi

---

BOX 8.17   Interesting study

Gooptu and Bandyopadhyay (2007) explore the ways in which a development intervention contributed to the collective acts of sex workers in Kolkata who challenged their exploitation and ostracism. This involved a shift in perspective among the women from seeing themselves as passive victims to seeing themselves as social actors with collective rights and the capacity to act. The transition to action involved the establishment of a health project with an egalitarian organizational structure and the use of a dialogical approach to education (see Chapter 1). The researchers also worked with group members to establish norms of political activism within the group to challenge inequalities and discrimination and to assert their human rights as citizens. The shift in attitudes and social identity allowed the women to reposition themselves in society and challenge the discrimination they faced. The women are now in a better position to protect themselves from health risks such as contracting HIV/AIDS.

---

and Jovchelovitch (2004) discuss some of the limitations of collectivist-oriented participative health promotion in Brazil. They refer to work on various forms of participation, including manipulative and passive forms that are often cultivated through processes of consultation and the use of material incentives. These strategies for participation exclude community members from any real power in terms of decision-making. The agenda for what is healthy and the boundaries of intervention have been set elsewhere, often by government agencies or not-for-profit organizations. Material and symbolic contexts that provide limited opportunities for oppressed people actually to pursue their goals and interests (rather than those of development professionals) undermine efforts at social change. Participation in such contexts can simply become a hollow exercise.

What becomes crucial for effective collectivist approaches is an empowerment orientation to participation (Box 8.18). Empowerment is the process by which disadvantaged people are supported in working collectively towards social inclusion. Central to helping this to happen is encouraging people to say what it is they want

---

BOX 8.18   Participation

Participation involves "processes that enable individuals and groups in the community to contribute to debate and decision-making about a particular activity. In relation to community health, this means opportunities for community members to participate in planning, implementing, managing and evaluating community health services, and identifying health issues and ways of addressing them" (Australian Community Health Association, 1991, p. x).

and then to find ways of making this happen. Psychologists following the principle of collective action must find common interests between people and strengthen these 'constituencies of interests'. Action research (see Chapter 1) provides one mechanism for involving people as fully as possible in setting priorities for, designing, conducting, assessing and revising health promotion initiatives. Notions of social justice outlined in Chapter 9 must guide our actions to such ends (Box 8.18).

Finally, individual and collectivist approaches to health promotion are compatible (Prilleltensky & Prilleltensky, 2006). Tobacco control initiatives in many countries ban the promotion of cigarettes and restrict who is able to purchase them. Such societal-level initiatives can be linked with education initiatives and investment in programmes to help individual smokers kick the habit. Focusing on individuals, groups and sociopolitical realities is necessary in effecting long-term transgenerational change for health. For instance, access to education is crucial for providing increased life opportunities for lower-SES children and improving their health today and later in life. Unfortunately, many families need such children to work in order to help support them. Therefore, to be effective any effort to increase participation in education must address the economic needs of the family. One effective strategy for fostering participation in education in South America is to pay families a wage for having their children attend school (Carr, 2003). More work is emerging from this perspective, and researchers are beginning to unpack the psychological processes underlying collective action (Box 8.19).

BOX 8.19   Psychological mechanisms and collective action

Van Zomeren, Spears and Leach (2008) explore some of the psychological mechanisms underlying collective action. Two studies – a field study with people participating in a protest, and a follow-up experiment with university students – are reported by the authors to demonstrate the importance of group identity and perceptions of group efficacy as influences on collective action among people coping with disadvantage. Tendencies towards collective action appear to increase in situations in which group identity becomes relevant to the group members and they become angry or frustrated with how they are being treated and recognize their disadvantage. When group identity is not as relevant, or when group members are not in situations in which their disadvantage is brought to the fore, their tendency towards collective action appears to be more dependent on perceptions of efficacy and whether collective action is likely actually to benefit the group. These findings suggest that raising people's collective identification with the group and their sense that the action will be successful would likely increase their willingness to participate in collective action to address social disadvantage.

Chapter summary

Social psychology has produced considerable insights into processes of health and illness. This knowledge has contributed to the development of health psychology as a specific field of research and practice. This chapter has explored what we know about health and illness through individualistic and collectivist approaches, and the tension between these approaches in the discipline. In the process, we have considered different understandings of illness and how these foreground the interwoven nature of individual, relational and societal factors in health. A social psychology of health and illness that considers this broad range of factors is better equipped to address the everyday health needs of people from a range of backgrounds. It is crucial for ensuring equitable access to health for all.

There are clear socioeconomic gradients in health in most countries that are often related to, but are not reducible to, the actions of individuals at the bottom of the heap. The existence of these gradients alerts us to the importance of links between material circumstances and social relations and their impact on physical and mental health. Factors in people's lives such as relative deprivation, social exclusion, adverse working conditions, discrimination, poor housing, unemployment and limited education are things that we can do something about. These are things we should do something about, because they are unjust. However, when considering social determinants of health we need to remind ourselves that contextual factors are not all-determining. Those living modest lives do not always become sicker and die earlier than their more affluent counterparts. Perceptions of belonging, inclusion and access to social support can buffer people against some of the effects of social inequalities. As noted by social psychologists since the 1930s (see Chapter 2), individuals in cohesive communities tend to be hardier and better prepared to weather adverse conditions. In this we can see the importance of the quality of our social relations and the importance of sharing a life together. Health is relational, and people can be supported in helping each other (Chapter 10). One key is ensuring access to adequate food, shelter, education and employment. Beyond material solutions there is also a need for social psychological solutions that involve the promotion of civic participation, a sense of control and social capital among groups in society who are more vulnerable to illness. In addressing social capital, we cannot assume that all the answers lie in local settings. Community climates are also influenced by decisions that occur beyond the borders of a local community. We also need to address issues of power in society and the distribution of resources.

Issues of power, inclusion and the quality of social relations are critical determinants of the health of the population. Adversarial societies in which people care more for themselves than others are less conducive to health than more egalitarian societies in which we can count on the support of others when dealing with adversity and attempting to maintain our health. Adversarial societies are also more stressful for the majority of citizens. Stress is one useful concept for psychologists to explore links between individuals and societal structures that can either support or undermine their health. Responses to stress span efforts to teach people to cope with adversity to removing stressors (where possible) from the settings in which people conduct their lives and work. In some occupations, such as fire-fighting, stress is a part of the territory. However, its impact can be minimized by ensuring adequate 'down time' and collegial and supportive workplace relations.

Although useful in making us cognisant of the role of personal actions in the maintenance of health and onset of illness, social cognitive models of health behaviour do not provide a complete picture. This is, in part, because health-related knowledge and action is far more complex and embedded in the practices of everyday life than social cognitive models suggest. If we are to develop the most efficient means possible of supporting people in living healthy lives, then the contexts in which particular acts such as smoking take place become crucial foci. The approach to understanding human beings and everyday life that is developed throughout this book enables us to appreciate more contextually situated understandings of health and illness. The focus on daily life allows us to consider a broader range of factors leading to specific health-related actions such as smoking. These include opportunities for experiencing connection and sharing with others, stress release and the need simply to take time out and relax for a while. In short, to address health-related actions such as smoking we have to address the broader range of factors within which the practice of smoking is embedded.

For some, our getting involved in social change for health might be evidence for a lack of objectivity (see Chapter 1). Here we return to core ideas from liberation social psychology (Chapters 1–3). In developing liberation social psychology, Ignacio Martín-Baró proposed that involvement constituted an ethical choice rather than bias (Lykes, 2000). Involvement can be based on compassion and reason. We can care about others and deduce from the mass of existing literature that ensuring health for all requires social justice and change. We can work towards these ends. This involves a continued focus on illness and the ways in which existing problems can be addressed now so that they do not affect future generations. We also need to move beyond the primary focus of psychology on illness to a psychology of health. Such a shift involves complementing the current focus on health problems with a focus on strengths and capacities. This is precisely what we do in Chapter 10.

Review exercise

- Why are social psychologists interested in health?
- When was the last time you tried to stop an unhealthy behaviour or started a new healthy behaviour? Were you successful for more than a few weeks? Why/why not?
- How have your perceptions of what constitutes 'health' been formed? (You might like to think back to Chapter 3, on knowledge.)
- What does social capital mean to you?

9 Social justice in everyday life

Core questions to consider while reading this chapter

- Why is justice so central to people's everyday experiences?
- If justice is so central, why is it so hard to define?
- Why are some people afforded fair treatment and others excluded from considerations of fairness?
- Are people concerned more with the distribution of resources or the processes by which the distribution was determined?

Chapter scenario

It is late at night in an inner-city nightspot. A young couple leave a well-known nightclub laughing and holding one another. They look around for a cab. The queue at the taxi rank is 100 metres long. The groan to each other. This city is notorious for long delays during peak time. Resignedly they join the queue. Forty-five minutes later they reach the head of the queue and enter a taxi. They are tired and in no mood for a chat. Their driver, however, thinks otherwise: "Hey, how are you? Where you goin'?" They indicate their destination and the driver pulls away from the curb. The driver chats incessantly. He is a former refugee from Afghanistan, he says. Ian was in mandatory custody for five years. Prior to coming to Australia he had trained as an engineer. "No work here for me," Ian says, with just a hint of resentment. "There is a shortage of engineers in Australia but they won't recognize my qualifications. First they lock me up... then they won't let me work. Five years! My father and brother are still there, you know. I worry. If I had stayed, I would be dead. I come here... locked up. Pah, five years. But it's OK. I like to drive a taxi." His passengers make noncommittal sounds indicating agreement, looking at each other and raising their eyebrows, preferring silence. They don't really care to hear his story.

As they leave the city they pass an open area. There are several Aboriginal people sitting together under a streetlamp. Ian erupts, startling his passengers, "You see that? Those people there. That's what makes me angry. I had nothing when I came here. I worked, made something of myself. In Australia, if you want, you can be someone... you know? Next year I sit my exams... I will be an engineer again. These guys, just sit, drink, do nothing. The government give them money to just sit. They drink, they fight, they hit their kids." He glances in his mirror at the park dwellers. "I read in the paper that up north everyone in those communities is abusing their kids. They get millions, for just sitting around – abuse their kids. I say take their money, just give it back when they look after their kids, stop messing with them. The government was right to do that in the Northern Territory. Take that lot too and send them back home to the bush." His male passenger leans over to his partner and whispers, "And you can go with them mate, you and your refugee mates! Queue jumpers." The driver gives no indication that he heard the exchange, but the rest of the trip is completed in silence. The following morning the passenger is listening to the news on the radio. He calls to his partner in the shower, "Some taxi driver got beaten up last night just up the road. Maybe it was that bloke from last night. Serves him right, wouldn't shut up... should have stayed in his own country." She laughs.

On the face of it this scenario speaks to the issue of racism and discrimination, which we have discussed in previous chapters. It also speaks to what has been referred to as a foundational principle of social life, justice. Ian, the taxi driver, has left his country of origin to escape persecution under an oppressive regime. He and his family have been relentlessly hunted, and some of them have been killed, for their beliefs and ethnic identity. In accordance with international law Ian sought refuge overseas, only to be imprisoned for a lengthy period. His detention is widely believed to be unjust and a clear violation of international human rights law. Thousands of asylum seekers are detained by governments, sometimes for several years in detention centres where conditions are harsh. Ian is one of the lucky ones. In time his application for refugee status proved successful and he was released into the community on a temporary protection visa. However, Ian cannot find work in his profession of engineering.

One would expect the general population of a supposedly tolerant and accepting society to rise up against the unjust treatment of refugees, demanding that they be treated humanely and with compassion (and, incidentally, in accordance with international law). However, with the exception of a hardy band of protesters, there is no widespread public condemnation of the government's action. Why? The procedures and policies that govern the treatment of refugees would not be tolerated if they were applied to 'ordinary' citizens of the country. One explanation that will be elaborated in this chapter is that refugees have been situated outside the moral envelope, or scope of justice (Opotow, 1990), of society. The same is true of the Indigenous Australians sitting in the park. If people are placed outside our scope of justice, the normative standards of justice simply do not apply and they can be treated unjustly with impunity (Opotow, 2001), as six million Jews, gypsies, homosexuals and disabled people found during the Nazi regime.

The application of different procedures, policies and processes to manage refugees is a clear violation of the principles of procedural fairness – the fairness of procedures by which outcomes are determined (Lind & Tyler, 1988). The quarantining of welfare and other payments to Aboriginal Australians in 2007 was also a differential application of policy that included the suspension of the Racial Discrimination Act (NTER, 2008). Welfare payments to Aboriginal families in remote communities were withheld on the grounds that money was being used to purchase alcohol, rather than food, and that children were at significant risk of neglect as a result. Payments were distributed in the form of food vouchers that could be redeemed at the local community store. These policies applied to all families, even those in which there was no evidence of abuse or neglect (Altman & Hinkson, 2007). White Australians were not subjected to the same provisions, even though the matters that acted as the catalyst for the policy are certainly evident in all sectors of society. Actions against white Australians might not have been tolerated. Procedural unfairness is often a powerful predictor of people's affective responses to their circumstances. If perceptions of procedurally unjust treatment persist, extreme responses can result. These include mass murder, as witnessed in a number of school massacres in the United States, or violence turned inwards, as seen in the rising suicide rate in Aboriginal communities.

The observation by Ian, the taxi driver, that Aboriginal Australians receive 'sitting around money' speaks to the issue of distributive justice, or the fairness of the way resources are distributed. Most resources are finite, meaning that there will always be losers when they are distributed. In many colonial contexts, the perception that indigenous people receive a disproportionately large share of the pie is widespread and divisive. Again, our response to perceived distributive unfairness can be profound.

Chapter overview

This chapter is presented in eight sections. The first section explores the importance of social justice in everyday life. The second presents an initial conceptualization of social justice that allows us to move forward in exploring pertinent social psychological processes. It is also necessary, in the third section, to consider the history of social psychological work on social justice. A key focus of work in psychology is on equity theory and distributive justice. We consider this work in the fourth section. It is in the fifth section that we focus on the issue of procedural fairness. The sixth section picks up a key theme of this book and issue for research on social justice: relational concerns and issues of social identity. Relational concerns are extended in the subsequent section in relation to the concept of scope of justice. We conclude with a summary section that reviews key issues from across the previous sections. The key ideas explored in the chapter are:

- The complexity of justice as a social construct
- Distributive and procedural fairness
- Scope of justice and moral envelope

The importance of justice in everyday life

Justice matters. People are concerned about fairness (Brosnan, 2006; Bierhoff & Rohmann, 2006; Miedema, van den Bos & Vermunt, 2006). Justice has occupied the hearts and minds of philosophers and social thinkers since time immemorial. Aristotle, Socrates, Hobbes, Locke all located justice at the heart of the social world. It has been argued that no sociopolitical system can afford to ignore the principles of justice. As Goode notes, "Almost any theory of society is likely to be a theory about justice as well" (cited in Törnblom, 1992, p. 177). The legitimacy of all social institutions fundamentally rests on the perception that they strive for just outcomes for citizens (Blader & Tyler, 2003; Okimoto & Tyler, 2007; Sutton et al., 2008; Tyler, 2004; Wenzel, 2006). For Rawls (1971), perhaps the most influential contemporary justice theorist, justice is the "first virtue of social institutions, as truth is to systems of thought" (p. 3). Justice is undoubtedly at the heart of our social world.

Social psychologists have studied justice for decades. In this chapter we review the literature and theories derived from these efforts. We conclude that the contemplation of justice pervades our everyday lives, not just in matters such as those described in the chapter opening scenario, but in our everyday interactions with family and friends as well as the organizations and institutions that impact our lives. In this respect justice provides a vital lens for understanding everyday life.

In Chapter 3 we said that everyday life is a slippery concept. So too is social justice. We noted that in everyday life events come along that challenge and disrupt our daily routines. Social justice, or more precisely social injustice in its many forms, represents one such disruption. The imperative for social justice demands that people re-story their lives in a climate in which everyday life is not secure or comfortable.

Notwithstanding the pervasive nature of justice in everyday life, its study has been problematic in social psychology. The study of social justice is rooted in the contested nature of social psychology itself, which we discussed in Chapter 2. It is also rooted in the problematic nature of justice itself. Sampson (1981, 1983) rather succinctly summarized the social psychology of justice as being overly individualistic in orientation and the product of the withdrawal of social psychologists from active engagements with the social world (Box 9.1). He referred to such research as falling foul of the truncated subjectivism, abstracted individualism and uncritical positivism that were at the heart of the critical turn during the 1970s and 1980s. Traditional psychological discourses about justice were captured by the rise of experimentalism (Rosnow, 1981), and this reduced our capacity to view justice through a multifaceted lens. The nature of Western democratic society also positioned social psychologists in

BOX 9.1   Brief critical interlude

Sampson (1981, 1983, 1986, 2000) is an influential author in the area of social justice who has an interesting turn of phrase. By "truncated subjectivism" he meant we truncate or shrink our gaze only to intrapsychic, subjective experiences. "Abstracted individualism" refers to the fact, as we saw in Chapter 2, that experimental psychologists removed (abstracted) people from the real world to the laboratory, and by referring to "uncritical positivism" Sampson was criticizing those from the experimental tradition who did not question the limits and constraints of the method. Yes, we know that Sampson's words are perilously close to jargon (as we discussed in Chapter 2), but he is, after all, an esteemed figure in the area, so we have cut him some slack!

North America in particular to view justice as primarily about the distribution of resources. European social psychologists were also historically aligned with the experimental tradition, despite the excellent example of earlier social psychologists working on pressing social issues (Hepburn, 2003). The shifting focus of our disciplinary gaze from marginalized, oppressed and disenfranchised groups positioned the social psychology of justice to emerge in the particular, some would say peculiar, way that it did. This chapter presents a pathway back to relevance in pursuit of a social psychology of justice that is intimately and directly concerned with social issues in everyday life.

A perusal of contemporary library databases yields literally thousands of scholarly papers in the social psychological literature on justice. There are any number of edited texts on the topic (Bierhoff, Cohen & Greenberg, 1986; Cohen, 1986; Folger, 1984; Lerner & Lerner, 1981; Greenberg & Cohen, 1982; Messick & Cook, 1983; Steensma & Vermunt, 1991; Vermunt & Steensma, 1991). Surprisingly, though, with the exception of Sampson's (1981) seminal critique, there are very few authored books devoted to the social psychological understanding of justice in contemporary society (see, e.g., Tyler, Boeckmann, Smith & Huo, 1997). More surprisingly, and of concern, is that an examination of the index of most introductory texts in social psychology yields virtually no reference to social justice (Box 9.2). Our concern is that the centrality of social justice is not foregrounded and the discussion of justice is piecemeal, rather than being fully integrated into social psychology (Baumeister & Bushman, 2009; Breckler, Olson & Wiggins, 2006; Brehm, Kassin & Fein, 2005; Carr, 2003; Hewstone, Stroebe & Jonas, 2008; Kenrick, Neuberg & Cialdini, 2007; McKnight & Sutton, 1994; Schneider, Gruman & Coutts, 2005; Vaughan & Hogg, 2008). And therein lies a central concern about the social psychology of justice.

BOX 9.2   Social justice in social psychology textbooks

Vaughan and Hogg (2008) index social: anthropology, categorization, change belief system, cognition, comparison theory, compensation, constructionism, creativity, decision schemes, development, dilemmas, distance, exchange theory, facilitation, group, identity theory, impact theory, inference, influence, isolation, judgement, learning theory, loafing, markers in speech, matching, mobility, modelling, ostracism, personal attraction, power, protest, psychology, representations, support networks and transition schemes (pp. 479–480). So much for social justice being a central tenet of social life. To be fair, these authors do mention distributive justice in terms of leadership evaluations, group unrest, game theory, social exchange theory and attribution. It is also noteworthy that neither of two recent and popular texts on critical social psychology (Tuffin, 2004; Hepburn, 2003) indexes social justice or justice. They do, of course, as do most texts, discuss issues of social justice. Yet this discussion is limited by the failure to articulate an operational definition of social justice.

Making sense of justice

Defining justice is a difficult task. Prilleltensky and Nelson (2002; Nelson & Prilleltensky, 2005) defined social justice as the "fair and equitable allocation of bargaining powers, resources, and burdens in society" (2005, p. 189). Many circumstances evoke the contemplation of (in)justice. Poverty, homelessness, oppression, marginalization, the glass ceiling for women in the workplace, the lack of appropriate services for people with disabilities, health inequalities for indigenous people, the treatment of refugees, the social exclusion of young people, your lecturer giving you a bad grade on an assignment and so on. However, these things are not injustice; they are at best the manifestations of injustice.

Unfortunately, social justice has become a kind of rhetorical hiccough, an involuntary expiration of breath whenever a situation smacks of unfairness. One of the authors of this book delivers an upper-level undergraduate class on the social psychology of justice. Each semester he asks students in the first class, "What is social justice?" Everyone has an answer of sorts, "Umm, equality for everyone.…Ahh…everybody should get a fair share of the resources.…Everyone gets what they deserve.…Err.…Umm."

Review exercise

Take a few moments to jot down your answer to the question: What is social justice?

Generally speaking, in response to the question students focus on the distributional aspects of justice (distributive fairness). A few will touch on the way that distributions are made (procedural fairness), some will allude to the fact that some people do not receive fair treatment (scope of justice), some may even tangentially indicate that there is an unequal distribution of burdens and costs in society (macro/micro justice), and others may point to the fact that people must be held accountable for acting unjustly (retributive and restorative justice). Few name all these aspects of justice, nor do they grapple with the definitional complexity in any systematic way. They are not alone (Box 9.3).

One of the most interesting perspectives on justice to emerge in recent years is the view that justice is a social construction (Sampson 1981, 1983, 1986). We touched on the idea of social construction in Chapter 4. Sampson (1981) referred to justice as "part of a conversation taking place between people" (p. 107) and as having a "negotiated quality" (p. 111). According to the social constructionist perspective, people give meaning to and interpret the world. Views of justice are constructed through everyday discourse, including conversations, narratives, explanations, excuses, myths, reasons, plans, gossip, anecdotes, jokes and so on (Cvetkovich & Earle, 1992, 1994). The narratives of justice are incomplete if they are not located in the particular sociohistorical, political, cultural and social context in which justice judgements are being made. Markovsky (1991), in describing a social constructionist approach to justice, said, "[A]ssume there is no true or essential justice beyond its socially constructed meanings. Then explain the causes and consequences of those meanings" (p. 33). In this sense what we come to know about social justice can be construed as an item of assertoric knowledge (Polkinghorne, 1983). As we discussed in Chapter 4, assertoric knowledge is knowledge that we assert to the community of interest, making it available for debate, a truly discursive construct. This is consistent with Cherry's (1995) observation (see Chapter 2) that theory itself is historically embedded. What justice is taken to be depends on cultural factors and

---

BOX 9.3   Interesting survey

In a recent study in New Zealand (Maxim Institute, 2006), 258 men and women responded in an online survey to the question "What is justice?" More than half of the respondents answered that social justice was about equality, expressed as equal distribution, equal treatment, equal rights and equal opportunities. Other key themes that emerged emphasized the importance of tolerance and responsibility and the importance of the legislature in enacting social justice. Reis (1984) wrote that although he was confident it was possible to predict people's justice-related behaviour very well, "we [have] yet to understand the entity of justice itself," and any attempt to define justice "is a hopeless and pompous task" (p. 38).

BOX 9.4   Seeking a definition of social justice

This exposition begs the question as to whether it is realistic to try to define justice in the absolute sense. In the social psychological sense we argue that it is not. An unknown, though clearly experienced justice researcher said, "Justice is like a greased pig, it yells loudly, but is hard to catch" (cited in Törnblom, 1992, p. 177). This is, in our view, as good a definition of social justice as any. Some authors have concluded that social justice means different things to different people in different circumstances (Törnblom, 1992). We can live with that too.

---

social relationships. It is not necessarily a universally applicable set of criteria of relevance to all people in all times. We need constantly to negotiate the meaning of social justice and its application in everyday life. The social constructionist view of justice challenges us to view justice from a variety of perspectives and attempt to understand its consequences for a diverse range of people, such as those we looked at in the opening scenario (Box 9.4).

The notion of social justice as a social construction fits well with the overarching goals for this book. We see people situated in everyday life, as actors and producers. We see the mutuality of everyday interaction. The shared narratives and norms are a taken-for-granted part of our everyday lives. People are constructed individually and collectively in everyday practices (Chapter 3). These practices tell us about who and what we are. Our everyday lives are co-constructed with the others in our social realm. This is illustrated in Chapter 3 by the example of the executive strolling home who encounters a homeless man. The encounter with the man changes the nature of the evening for the executive from one of enjoyment and abandonment to one of concern. Surprisingly, there has been little research that examines the construction of social justice (Dixon & Wetherell, 2004). An important point for this chapter is that social justice needs to be reinvested with the social in the context of everyday life.

Historical ruminations on social justice in psychology

Contemporary perspectives on justice in social psychology have their roots in some of the earliest conceptualizations of social behaviour that still resonate today. These include relative deprivation (Stouffer, Suchman, De Vinney, Star & Williams, 1949), cognitive dissonance (Festinger, 1957), balance theory (Heider, 1946), social exchange theory (Blau, 1964; Homans, 1961; Thibaut & Walker, 1959) and attribution theory (Heider, 1958; Jones & Davis, 1965; Kelley, 1971). Each in its way has advanced our understanding of social justice (Box 9.5). Yet each has its genesis in the individualistic stream of social psychology during the ascendancy of social cognition (Rosnow, 1981).

There is considerable evidence that people often strive for equilibrium or balance in their lives. When people feel 'balanced', they are more likely to be content. If, on the other hand, we feel out of balance, this disequilibrium has been found to cause feeling of anxiety and distress. Two theories have been advanced by social psychologists to explain this phenomenon: balance theory (Heider, 1946) and cognitive dissonance theory (Festinger, 1957–1968). These are known as cognitive consistency theories, and although they are most commonly discussed in relation to attitude formation, they have been influential in the development of our understanding of justice.

The fundamental premise of balance theory (Heider, 1946) is that people prefer harmony, consistency and balance in their interactions with others and in relation to events in their social worlds (Box 9.6). In the typical social psychological style of the time, much of the work was expressed metaphorically through a mathematical model, the P-O-X triad. In this formulation P is the person, O is a person or object and X is information about the person or object. Just to confuse some readers for a moment, if you (P) support the government (O), you support capital punishment (X), and the government supports capital punishment,

---

BOX 9.5 Social psychological theory and social justice

Think about your everyday experiences.

- Do you find that you compare yourself with others around you?
- Do you wistfully sneak a peek at the essay of the student next to you and, upon finding she has a high distinction to your credit, feel a frisson of resentment or even anger?
- After all, didn't you work hard, and don't you know that she did not?

We all compare ourselves with others. Social comparison has a long tradition in social psychology (Festinger, 1954; Stouffer, Suchman, De Vinney, Star & Williams, 1949).

Relative deprivation refers to the sense that we are deprived relative to others with whom we compare ourselves. For example, in a study of promotional opportunities in the armed services, Stouffer and colleagues (1949) found that servicemen with better education and better promotional opportunities were less satisfied with their position than their less educated counterparts. Why? Stouffer and colleagues concluded that better-educated soldiers had a greater expectation of success when they compared themselves with their counterparts in civilian life. In other words, these soldiers felt relatively deprived. Relative deprivation has both experimental and intuitive support. Researchers also draw the distinction between egoistic relative deprivation (comparisons with individuals) and fraternal relative deprivation (comparison with groups or the collective) (Callan, Ellard, Shead & Hodgins, 2008).

BOX 9.6   Heider 'the scientist'

Heider is an anomaly in a discipline that prided itself on adherence to the experimental and scientific tradition. Apparently, he published no research studies, supervised little research and wrote only sporadically (Hewstone, Stroebe & Jonas, 2008). His writing, however, was hugely influential, including balance theory and another important social psychological construct, attribution (Hewstone, Stroebe & Jonas, 2008).

then the triad is balanced. If, on the other hand, you do not support the government and do not support capital punishment, but the government does, then the triad will unbalanced. Let us relate this to our opening scenario in an attempt to bring some clarity. If you (P) support the government (O) and you support the mandatory detention of refugees (X), then the triad will be balanced. The same is true if you support the policies to quarantine welfare payments to Aboriginal people.

Cognitive dissonance (Festinger, 1957) stems from the notion that as part of the appraisal processes through which people make sense of the world, they evaluate their own cognitions (or ideas). If two or more ideas are consistent, then they are in harmony or balance. The relationship between them is consonant. If the two are inconsistent, then the relationship between them is dissonant. This elegant and simple notion, like balance theory, has been an influential thread permeating a range of topics in social psychology, including justice. According to Festinger, cognitive dissonance is an aversive state that people try to reduce or avoid. Two mechanisms are proposed for reducing the distress caused by cognitive dissonance. We can either change the way we think about things or change the way we act in the world. This proposition became the cornerstone of research into equity theory, the dominant expression of research into social justice throughout the 1970s.

A parallel stream of social psychological consciousness emerged at around the same time as balance and cognitive dissonance theories. This parallel stream was to shape the future of social psychological research into justice for almost three decades. Social exchange theory was premised on the widely held view that people were social animals largely concerned with maximizing their rewards and minimizing the costs of their interactions with others (Blau, 1964; Crosby & Gonzalez-Intal, 1984; Homans, 1961; Thibaut & Kelley, 1959). Social exchange theories were concerned with the principles that govern the distribution or allocation of goods and took their inspiration from earlier theories discussed above: social comparisons, relative deprivation, dissonance theory and balance theory (Greenberg & Cohen, 1982; Folger, 1984; Törnblom, 1992). Human beings were seen as hedonistic, in pursuit of pleasure over pain, and as utility maximizers (Peters & van den Bos, 2008) determined to maximize their gains and minimize the costs of their social interactions (Box 9.7).

BOX 9.7   Interesting aside

Thibaut was influential in the developing obsession in social psychology with distributive fairness, derived from his (and others') work on social exchange. For thirty years distributive fairness dominated the research into the social psychology of justice. However, Thibaut earned redemption when in 1975 he published the classic text with Walker on procedural fairness, which was largely responsible for turning the tide towards more productive and wide-ranging explorations of social justice in psychology.

There is utility in the core propositions of exchange theory. Think of a situation in which you have been rewarded for your behaviour. Were you more inclined to continue to do what you were rewarded for? Imagine that the reward is withdrawn. Would you be likely to "display the emotional activity we call anger" (Homans, 1961, p. 75) (Box 9.8)? Your answer, notwithstanding the tortured language, at a superficial level is probably yes. However, the stimulus-response view of human behaviour has now been largely (but not entirely) debunked in social psychology as the prime motivator of human behaviour, though many behavioural psychologists continue to ply a lucrative trade in clinical practice.

Attribution theory also has a long (though often unstated) history in the social psychology of justice. As we saw in Chapter 4 attribution theory derived from the work of Heider (1958), Jones and Davis (1965) and Kelley (1971) in particular. Attribution theory is

BOX 9.8   The language of the time

The language used in Homans' day was interesting. Language is important. Not only is the language used to describe the psychological mechanisms for such social interactions grounded temporally; it also clearly locates human action in the realm of behavioural economics. Homans (1961) extended five propositions that explained exchange in social relations, and they are worth quoting here:

1. *If in the past the occurrence of a particular stimulus situation has been the occasion on which a man's activity has been rewarded, then the more similar the present stimulus situation is to the past one, the more likely he is to emit the activity or some similar.*

2. *The more often within a given period of time a man's activity rewards the activity of another, the more often the other will emit the activity.*

3. *The more valuable to a man a unit of activity another gives him, the more often he will emit activity rewarded by the activity of the other.*

4. *The more often a man has in the recent past received a rewarding activity from another, the less valuable any further unit of activity becomes to him.*

5. *The more to a man's disadvantage the rule of distributive justice fails of realisation, the more likely he is to display the emotional activity we call anger. (pp. 52–75)*

fundamentally concerned with how we 'attribute' causality in our interpretation of events in our everyday life. The crucial distinction is between internal (or dispositional) attributions and external (or situational) attributions. Attribution is a process of social inference about our own and others' behaviour (McKnight & Sutton, 1994). Ian, the taxi driver, has a choice when he observes the Aboriginal people in the park. He can decide that they find themselves in the park because they are lazy, shiftless, drunken layabouts (a dispositional attribution), or he can see them as the victims of a system that fails to provide adequate services and support to a disenfranchised minority (a situational attribution). It is not that simple, however, and the theory has been elaborated in a number of ways. Jones and Davis (1965) extended Heider's analogy of people as naive theorists (or scientists) searching for the underlying causes for the behaviour they observe by suggesting that people also make inferences from the behaviour they observe to the underlying dispositions of the actors (correspondent inference). This, of course, links back to the ideas of cognitive consistency and balance discussed earlier in this chapter. If we can identify a disposition that explains a specific behaviour, then it appears more predictable and stable – and we like that. Kelley (1971) went on to propose his covariation model of attribution, in which attributions (internal or external) are based on three types (or sources) of information: consistency, distinctiveness and consensus. But, as we saw, it becomes even more complicated. Gardner and colleagues (1981) identified at least eight attributional biases (causality, disposition, actor observer, consensus information, self-serving, just world, self-attribution, and emotion) based on cultural, individual and emotional differences that they claimed undermine the idea of attribution as a rational choice. Later work focused on attributional style, or locus of control. Rotter (1966) developed a locus of control scale to determine whether people are internally or externally controlled. The scale has been used in literally hundreds of studies, and of course reworked and revamped in a variety of ways.

Attribution theory remains influential in the social psychology of justice. Cohen (1982), who provided perhaps the most comprehensive treatment of the role of attributions in justice, said that "perceptions of justice are based fundamentally on attributions of cause and responsibility" (p. 119). He also noted that at the time few of the major theories of justice foregrounded attribution theory, although a careful reading of the work clearly demonstrated that attributions were at the heart of reactions to injustice. In Chapter 4 we saw how a belief in a just world impacts our reactions to the plight of others. Manuel is unemployed because he lacks skills and a work ethic. The Aboriginal people in the park are there because they are drunk and lazy. In both cases they 'get what they deserve'. Belief in a just world as an attributional bias can have profound consequences. As we will see later in this chapter, these kinds of dispositional attributions may lead to people like Manuel and the Aboriginals in the park being denied the right to fair treatment. If people make internal attributions for social issues such as poverty and unemployment (that people are poor through lack of effort, poor financial skills or lack of ability), then they are likely to see the outcomes as more just than those who attribute social issues to external causes (low wage parity, prejudice and discrimination) (Ng & Allen, 2005).

Numerous studies attest to the importance of attribution in justice judgements. Attribution theory adds much to our understanding of justice judgements in such diverse settings as attributions to God for unjust health outcomes (Pargament & Hahn, 1986); understanding legal processes (Lloyd-Bostock, 1991); providing public assistance to the poor (Skitka & Tetlock, 1993); student perceptions of fairness in the classroom (Chory, 2007; Dalbert & Maes, 2002); adolescent perceptions of fairness in family conflict (Fondacaro et al., 2006); unjust treatment by friends and partners (Mikula, 2003); worker layoffs (Barclay, Skarlicki & Pugh, 2005); coping with life stress (Montada, 1991); individual and collective attribution in cross-cultural settings (Chiu & Hong, 1992, 2007).

All the theories discussed in this section were developed in the days of psychology as science; they were largely, though not entirely, devoid of consideration of the social context and were intrapsychic in nature. This means that they are subject to many of the criticisms of social psychology of the time. Critical psychologists have argued that these and other social theories are too prescriptive and formulaic (Tuffin, 2004). We think, however, that to discard these incomplete, but nevertheless insightful, observations about the human experience would be largely unhelpful (Dixon & Wetherell, 2004). They provide part of the picture we need to paint of social justice in everyday life. However, we need more complex and contextual models if we are to engage with social justice in a more meaningful way.

Review exercise

Think of a time when you were treated unjustly. This need not be traumatic, as most of us experience minor injustices on a frequent basis.

- How did you feel?
- What were the processes underlying this?
- How does your experience fit with exchange theories?
- What are the core concepts of social justice relevant to your experience?

At this point, it may seem as if we have come a long way from any clear understanding of social justice. However, social psychology was moving inexorably towards the noughties (twenty-first century). It is improbable that we could have arrived at recent conceptualizations of social justice without the journey of the past hundred years. The next iteration in pursuit of the psychology of social justice was as historically, theoretically, socially and culturally inevitable as it was ultimately misleading. We are talking here about the turn to equity theory and a focus on distributive justice.

Equity theory and distributive justice

The first of the explicitly justice-related theories of social interaction emerged in the mid-1960s with the work of Adams (1963, 1965, 1976). With his theory of inequity he was concerned with specifying the proportionality of inputs (sic) and outputs (sic) in exchange relationships, so this is, of course, a social exchange theory. The basic premise was that people engage in a kind of mental algebra when evaluating their relationships. If inputs and outputs are proportional, then the relationship is equitable. If they are not, then the relationship is inequitable. Harking back to balance and cognitive dissonance, we anticipate, as Adams hypothesized, that those in inequitable relationships will experience distress. The research evidence for this proposition soon mounted, spawning one of the most prolific avenues for research in social psychology.

Perhaps the most influential incarnation of equity theory was developed by Walster and her colleagues (Hatfield, Walster & Berscheid, 1976; Waltser, Berscheid & Walster, 1973, 1976) (Box 9.9). Their work focused on examining the dynamics of close relationships from the equity viewpoint. They adopted as their starting point the proposition discussed earlier that people are essentially self-interested and will attempt, all things being equal, to maximize their rewards and minimize their costs in any interaction. The intellectual roots in the earlier work are clear: the imperative towards cognitive consistency or balance or consonance, individuals as self-interested utility maximizers, and the affective consequences of imbalance.

Overwhelmingly, by the yardstick of productive research of the time, equity theory was a success (Box 9.10). As early as 1976 Adams was predicting great things for his theory, noting that the annual growth rate in publications (and new authors taking up the theory) was indicative of the growing influence of the approach to understanding social interactions and that the theory had a "well articulated structure, being parsimoniously elegant, and having increased predictive range. These are characteristics which bode well for progress" (Adams & Freedman, 1976, p. 44). He spoke perhaps four years too soon. By the early 1980s, in concert with the critical turn in social

---

BOX 9.9   Propositions underlying equity theory

Here are the propositions espoused by Walster, Berscheid and Walster (1976). You can see how they are in essence derivations from Homans' earlier ideas.

- *Proposition I: Individuals will try to maximize their outcomes.*
- *Proposition IIA: Groups can maximize their rewards by evolving accepted systems for equitably apportioning rewards and cost among members.*
- *Proposition IIB: Groups will generally reward members who treat others equitably and generally punish (increase the costs for) members who treat others inequitably.*
- *Proposition III: When individuals find themselves participating in inequitable relationships, they become distressed. The more inequitable the relationship, the more distress individuals feel.*
- *Proposition IV: Individuals who discover they are in an inequitable relationship attempt to eliminate their distress by restoring equity. The greater the inequity that exists, the more distress they feel, and the harder they try to restore equity. (pp. 2–6)*

BOX 9.10   An equity theory-based experiment

Much of the research based in equity theory focused on the consequences of inequity. Let us describe a typical experiment exploring equity. Imagine you are a first-year psychology student (sound familiar?). You are recruited, along with most of your first-year class, to participate in a study by your professor. On entering the laboratory, you are informed that you are to be paid to undertake a proofreading task for your professor. For completing this task you will be paid fifty cents an hour. You duly sit at the desk and work diligently for an hour or so. At the end of that time the professor returns. "Thank you," he says (he would almost certainly have been male in those days). "Unfortunately, I do not have as much research funding as I thought. I can only afford to pay you twenty-five cents an hour for the work." You would then have been required to complete a questionnaire that asked, among other things, how angry, resentful and satisfied you were. But here's the thing: Other participants were paid what they expected to be paid, and some were paid more than they expected. How would you feel?

---

psychology, as we will see below, cracks began to appear in the equity theory façade. Nevertheless, at the time a myriad studies attested to Adams and Freedman's assertion.

The results from experiments such as that described in Box 9.10 generally supported the idea that people in inequitable relationship experience distress. Such studies show that people experience distress when they receive less than they feel they deserve (underbenefited) and interestingly also when they get more than they deserve (overbenefited). Those who are underbenefited feel anger, resentment and dissatisfaction. This is also referred to as disadvantageous inequity aversion or undercompensation (Brosnan, 2006; Bierhoff & Rohmann, 2006), whereas those who are overbenefited feel anxiety and guilt, also known as advantageous inequity aversion or overcompensation (Brosnan, 2006; Bierhoff & Rohmann, 2006). The results also supported the earlier findings that people will try to restore equity (balance). They do this by attempting to restore *psychological* equity, by changing the way they think about events, or by attempting to restore *actual* equity, by changing the way they act.

Another clear manifestation of the social psychology of the time was the energy directed towards specifying the cognitive algebra that people used to make equity judgements. In his original formulation of equity theory, Adams (1965) suggested that:

$$O_a/I_a = O_b/I_b,$$

where O_a and O_b are the outcomes of each participant, and I_a and I_b are their inputs or contributions.

An equitable relationship will be indicated when the proportion of inputs to outcomes for participant a is equal to the proportion of inputs to outcomes for participant b. The extent to which the proportionality of inputs to outcomes differs is a measure of inequity in the relationship. This formula was soon revised (Hatfield, Walster & Berscheid, 1976):

$$\frac{(O_a - I_a)}{|I_a|} = \frac{(O_b - I_b)}{|I_b|}.$$

In this revised formula, $(O_a - I_a)$ represents the net gain. The denominator is the absolute value of the inputs for each participant. You don't need to know this stuff. The point here is to illustrate the thinking in social psychology at the time. The rise and rise of equity theory was framing considerations of justice and injustice in a particular way. Research in equity theory adhered to, and from our perusal of the literature exceeded, the standards for excellent experimentation. And recall that during this period psychologists were still researching in pursuit of the universal truths of human behaviour, which could best be viewed through the most reliable and valid lens for revealing immutable truth, the experiment. The criticisms outlined in Chapter 1 came later. And even when they were voiced, they were dismissed for many years as the ranting of a radical and disaffected fringe.

The cascading demise of equity theory was succinctly summarized by Furby (1986, pp. 155–164) with reference to the huge array of potential inputs and outcomes meaning that choices had to be made. Equity theory did not explain how people choose from the

BOX 9.11   What have we learned about the social psychology of justice?

That social justice is an interpersonal activity involving the pursuit of self-interest, which is best exemplified by the proportionality of inputs and outcomes and is largely acontextual. By the mid-1980s the worm had turned for equity theory, and criticisms emerged. Far from being the grand theory of social behaviour, equity theory was exposed as a partial account of human interaction. One of the most important criticisms to emerge questioned the focus on equity as the "sovereign principle of distributive justice" (Deutsch, 1983, p. 307). There were at least two more principles that as a result of the dominance of equity had been relatively neglected: equality and need. Although these two criteria for understanding distributive fairness are relatively self-evident, Reis (1984) threw the multidimensional cat among the justice pigeons when he argued that there were at least seventeen criteria for justice judgements, with equity, equality and need among them. Another criticism that struck at the heart of equity theory challenged the very foundation established by Adams in 1965. Inputs and outcomes are only one source of the sense of injustice (Folger, 1984). For example, as we will see below, placing someone outside our moral envelope can have a huge impact on our sense of injustice. These and other criticisms were the first inkling that justice judgements may be more than merely intrapsychic maths problems. This was in hindsight a watershed moment that was not fully appreciated until the crisis in social psychology kicked in fully.

huge constellation of potential inputs and outcomes. The choice of inputs and outcomes also reflects a sociological naivety in not accounting for differences in the situations in life in which people find themselves, which can limit their options and choices. Equity research was also caught up in the crisis in social psychology and criticisms of experimentalism, as described in Chapter 2. "In the artificially simple world of the laboratory, people are denied access to a myriad of 'irrelevant' pieces of information and provided with only that information relevant to equity theory" (Furby, 1986, p. 160). Attempts to quantify equity theory through the development of cognitive algebraic formulae were also found wanting (Farkas & Anderson, 1979; Harris, 1976; Moschetti, 1979). Finally, equity theory ignored what was emerging as a crucial determinant of perceived fairness or unfairness, procedural justice.

Does this imply that distributive justice is dead in the water? No. Subsequent work has attested to the importance of distributive justice (Mellers & Baron, 1993; Steensma & Vermunt, 1991; Vermunt & Steensma, 1991). When we position distributive fairness as only one of many potential sites for the exploration of justice, accept its historical and cultural embeddedness, and relinquish the intrapsychic inference of much of the earlier work, then the renaissance of distributive justice can point the way to an enhanced understanding of the complexity of justice in our everyday lives. For example, Gamliel and Peer (2006) examined how the way a similar situation

---

BOX 9.12   Some novel explorations of distributive justice

One particularly intriguing line of enquiry is exemplified in the work of Brosnan (2006), who provides a fascinating account of equity in animals. Chimpanzees, capuchin monkeys, wolves, coyotes and domestic dogs all display displeasure when they experience underbenefit, or what Brosnan refers to as disadvantageous inequity or undercompensation. Brosnan provides the delightful example of Nancy, a capuchin monkey, throwing a tantrum when Winnie gets a (much preferred) grape rather than the usual cucumber (p. 155). In another novel application, Callan and colleagues (2008) explored relative deprivation as a framework for understanding gambling behaviour. Even brainwaves rate a mention in contemporary literature on allocation behaviour. In a study of allocation behaviour using the ultimatum game (where one participant offers a split of a given sum and the other accepts or rejects the offer), Tabibnia, Satpute and Lieberman (2008, p. 340) measured the 'reward centres' of the brain, including the ventral striatum, amygdala, ventromedial prefrontal cortex, the orbitofrontal cortex and the midbrain dopamine regions. They found that fair offers did indeed lead to stimulation of the reward centres. In a study of international aid work, Carr (2003) examined inequity as a predictor of productivity. He compared the inputs and outputs of local and expatriate workers based on salary inequities and related this to demotivation on the part of local workers. Such work is stimulating considerable debate about the roots of allocation behaviour (Bierhoff & Rohmann, 2006; Chen & Santos, 2006; Watson & Platt, 2006).

---

for allocation is framed as either positive or negative impacts perceptions of fairness judgements. Peters, van den Bos and Karremans (2008) extended our understanding of what it means to be overbenefited in allocations. They found that people are concerned with the tension between the hedonic principle (pleasure at getting an advantage) and concern for doing the right thing (equity principle of proportional reward). This tension was found to be especially strong if the disadvantaged person was a friend.

The next phase: A turn to process, procedural fairness and justice

The acknowledgement of limitations in equity theory prompted social psychologists to turn their gaze to procedural justice. Thibaut and Walker (1975) raised the flag with their now classic text *Procedural Justice: A Psychological Analysis* (Box 9.13). Interestingly, this early work on procedural fairness also subscribed to the view of humans as instrumentally self-interested and selfish (Tyler, 1994). Procedural justice was conceptualized as a subsidiary construct to distributive fairness, which may have contributed to its relative neglect until some time later (Lind & Tyler, 1988; Tyler, Boeckmann, Smith &

BOX 9.13   Early work on procedural fairness

Thibaut and Walker's (1975) work focused on the adjudicatory procedures in courtroom settings. These authors were also interested in Rawls's (1971) notion of the veil of ignorance. The veil of ignorance (or original position) is a rhetorical device proposed by Rawls to explore the standards of justice that ought to obtain in contemporary society. What standard of justice would you choose if you did not know whether you were a slave or a slave owner? Rawls's premise is that people would choose the principle that endows the greatest benefit on the most disadvantaged. The focus on the Rawlsian notion of the original position alerts us to the fact the Thibaut and Walker were still in pursuit of universal truth, the universal standards of justice against which we can judge and be judged.

Huo, 1997). Procedures were only necessary when an allocation was in dispute.

From a series of experimental studies, Thibaut and Walker (1975) provide insights into the issue of objective versus subjective justice: "The conclusion suggested is that the position of interested parties in front of the veil of ignorance created conceptions of a just procedural system that are distinctly different from the conception created in the original position" (p. 116). This is an important observation. No one makes justice judgements in everyday life behind a veil of ignorance. Certainly, judgements are made in the absence of complete information, but not in the original position. Thibaut and Walker were on the cusp in social psychology. However, the discipline on the whole had not yet made the inferential leap to social constructionism in research on social justice. They were seeking the elusive universal standard of justice, a Holy Grail in social psychological research.

The second enduring aspect of procedural justice emerging from the work of Thibaut and Walker (1975) was the identification of two important aspects of control: decision control versus process control (Box 9.14). Decision control refers to the power to make a decision, and process control is concerned with the power to influence the processes by which decisions are made. This idea has shaped much subsequent procedural justice research and theory (Lind & Tyler, 1988, p. 36).

So, although the original conceptualizations of procedural justice were flawed, Thibaut and Walker (1975) have nevertheless been credited with providing the impetus for what is now an impressive body of literature on procedural justice in a number of areas (Lind & Tyler, 1988; Tyler et al., 1997). The literature on procedural fairness has burgeoned over the past twenty years. Research has demonstrated the robustness of procedural justice over a number of domains, including the legal, community, organizational and political (Tyler et al.,

---

BOX 9.14   An illustration of decision and process control

Ian, the taxi driver from the opening scenario, belongs to a local community action group. His membership allows him to interact with a range of Australians of different ethnic origins and provides a means of building neighbourhood cohesion and a sense of place (Chapter 6). The group has been agitating with the local authorities for several months over the use of the land recently left vacant when a school was closed (that's a whole other story). The group favours developing an open space community reserve. Other groups have been advocating for a shopping centre or the development of a sporting complex, and one group has been proposing a light industrial area. After some debate, the council decides to engage in a community consultation exercise to determine public support for the range of options. They hire a social psychologist to work with a community reference group to decide on the best strategy for engaging the community. Workshops are held; focus groups explore the issues, and a community survey ranks the options. The community survey finds that the open space community reserve is the most preferred option. After several weeks of deliberation, the council opts for another alternative. Ian feels angry, resentful and betrayed. One of the reasons Ian feels this way is related to the mistaken belief that his group (indeed, the community as a whole) had decision control, when in fact they did not. At best they had a measure of process control endowed by the consultation process. Local councils have a statutory obligation to make such decisions. As elected officials decision control was always vested with them. The consultation process was simply one source of information to help guide the decision-making. Economic, political and other drivers were perhaps equally if not more important to the decision. There is also the question of the process itself. Was it fair? The social psychology of procedural fairness has a great deal to say about such events, as does work on forms of community participation (Chapter 8).

1997). The results suggest that procedural justice effects are remarkably robust across time, circumstance and culture. The discovery of robust effects led Tyler and his colleagues (1988, 1997) to conclude that procedural justice is 'ubiquitous'. This clever choice of word is a deliberate one. The authors do not claim that procedural justice is universal. Rather, it does appear to be evident in most domains in which it has been researched (Gonzalez & Tyler, 2008; Okimoto & Tyler, 2007; Tyler, 2000, 2004, 2006, 2007; Tyler & Wakslak, 2004). It does appear to be ubiquitously evident, but it means different things to different people in different circumstances (Törnblom, 1992). This is a big claim; however, no compelling evidence appears to have arisen in the intervening period to challenge their assertion.

A number of criteria, or 'rules', have been proposed as predicting perceptions of procedural fairness (Lind & Tyler, 1988; Tyler, 1989, 1994; Tyler & Lind, 1992). Although these have been identified as potentially relevant in a range of settings, they by no means constitute an exhaustive list. Nevertheless, they do suggest a number of critical elements derived from the procedural justice literature that, to greater or lesser extent, seem to impact perceptions of procedural fairness.

1. *Knowledge of procedures*: in order to evaluate a policy or decision people will need to be aware of how it was made
2. *Perceptions of fair process:* the extent to which procedures are consistent with perceptions of what constitutes a fair process
3. *Voice:* people's perception of their opportunity to present their views

Lane (1988) identified four criteria for assessing procedural fairness:

1. *Recognition of personal rights:* procedures should respect the rights and dignity of those subject to them
2. *Ease of operation:* procedures should be efficient and quick
3. *Shared values:* procedures will be evaluated according to the extent that decision-makers are seen to hold common values and beliefs
4. *Fair decisions:* procedures will be evaluated in terms of whether they result in fair decisions.

An individual motivated by self-interest underpins the early models of procedural justice. The role of procedural factors was to improve outcomes or relationships. This traditional approach to the justice motive characterizes justice concerns as "an attempt, tempered with realism, to pursue self-interest" (Tyler, 1994, p. 858). In this respect, in procedural justice, procedures were considered instrumental to outcomes.

There is considerable overlap between the criteria for procedural justice outlined by Lind and Tyler (1988) and Leventhal's (1980) rules of procedural justice:

1. *Consistency*: For a procedure to be fair it must be applied consistently across people and across time.
2. *Bias suppression*: It must be ensured that the decision-makers are unbiased.
3. *Accuracy of information*: Procedural fairness will be enhanced if the procedures ensure that decisions are based on accurate information.
4. *Correctability*: Fairness of procedures will be judged by the extent to which they contain provisions for correcting bad decisions (appeals etc.).
5. *Representativeness*: The procedures should represent the interests of all relevant subgroups that may be influenced by the decision.
6. *Ethicality*: The procedure should be seen to conform to a standard of moral and ethical behaviour.

Relational concerns and social identity

An important question at this point is whether people are purely instrumental. That is, are they concerned solely with the end game, the final outcome? Does Ian, the taxi driver, simply take his pay packet at the end of the week regardless of how he is treated at work? As research on procedural justice unfolded it became clear that there was a more complex dynamic between procedures and outcomes. At one level, procedures are certainly instrumental. People do indeed evaluate procedures while keeping one eye on the outcomes. The other eye needs to be kept on another, deeper relationship. People are social beings. It transpires that just as social exchange theories such as equity say something about how people manage their interactions with others, so procedures say something about their role and position in the social group. An alternative to the purely instrumental interpretation of procedural justice became evident. People are willing to temper unfettered self-interest in pursuit of outcomes in order to ensure that relationships are maintained in the social group. This alternative explanation is known as the group value or relational model of procedural fairness (Lind & Tyler, 1988; Tyler, 1994) (Box 9.15).

According to Tyler and colleagues, by virtue of their desire to belong to social groups, with the long-term maintenance of relationships with people, authorities and institutions, people will moderate their assessment of immediate self-interested outcomes. Procedures are judged by what they say about how a person is viewed by the person implementing the procedures (Tyler & Lind, 1992). In this respect they are non-instrumental. Experiences are evaluated in terms of what they say about connectedness to the group, and reactions will be assessed against relationship concerns (such as respect for rights and dignity) rather than what they say about the likelihood of favourable outcomes (Tyler & Lind, 1992). Procedural matters are seen to mirror overarching group values and beliefs about the treatment of others.

A number of studies attest to the importance of relational concerns (Lind & Tyler, 1988; Tyler, 1989, 1994). Resource motives appear to be predictive of distributive justice, whereas relational

---

BOX 9.15   Three relational concerns for justice: neutrality, trust and standing

1. *Neutrality* refers to the extent to which people believe authorities have created a level playing field (Tyler, 1989, p. 831). People are concerned that decision-makers are honest and unbiased and that they make decisions on objective grounds using accurate information not influenced by opinion (Tyler & Lind, 1992; Tyler, 1994).
2. *Trust* is concerned with the overall intentions of the authorities, the extent to which they intend to treat people in a fair and reasonable fashion. Trust also refers to providing opportunities for people to be heard (Tyler, 1994). According to Tyler (1994), to be trustworthy, the authorities must exhibit benevolent intentions.
3. *Standing* refers to a person's perception of his or her status in the group. Rude or dismissive treatment leads people to conclude that they have low status within the group. Standing is a function of the extent to which people feel they have been treated politely, with dignity, in a way that respects rights, values and opinions (Tyler & Lind, 1992; Tyler, 1989, 1994).

matters (standing, neutrality and trust) influence both distributive and procedural concerns (Tyler, 1994). For example, in a study by one of the authors of this book examining trust and confidence in local authorities (Drew, Bishop & Syme, 2002), the local authorities had cut down a sixty-year-old tree on a residential curb side without community consultation. Residents were understandably upset. The residents' evaluations of the outcome (distributive fairness) was best understood in terms of the resource or instrumental factors. The residents' issues related to standing, neutrality and trust not only predicted their concern about the outcome; they were also related to perceptions about the fairness (or in this case, the unfairness) of the procedures that the council used.

Blader and Tyler (2003) have argued that little research has explored the criteria for procedural fairness, and in that regard it has proven fruitless. That is an overstatement. There is significant research on the criteria for procedural fairness (Muller, Kals & Maes, 2008). What is true, however, is that the emphasis has shifted from a focus on the criteria per se to research on a more sophisticated understanding of relational concerns[1] in procedural fairness. This has proven crucial to our understanding of the relationship between social justice concerns and social identity. For Ian, his detention in a refugee centre for five years, the failure to recognize his qualifications and his current position as a taxi driver all say something to him about how he is seen by the wider community. This has important ramifications for how he sees himself in society and his social identity. We examined this in depth in Chapters 4 and 5.

Review exercise

Go to back to Chapter 7 and review our account of social identity theory in the context of the present discussion of procedural fairness and social justice.

- How might you apply social identity theory to research procedural fairness?

In an attempt to shift the focus from criteria per se to a more sophisticated understanding of the relationship between perceptions of procedural fairness and social identity, Blader and Tyler (2003) proposed a four-factor model of procedural fairness (Box 9.16). They were concerned with the quality of treatment and the quality of decisions. In a direct derivation from the relational model, the four-component model suggests that people are concerned with *procedural function*, which they recast as concern about the quality of the decision and the quality of the treatment received, and *procedural source*,

BOX 9.16   Four-factor model of procedural fairness

According to Blader and Tyler (2003, p. 749) procedural justice is seen to be a function of:

1. Formal decision-making quality – rules, policies and practices
2. Informal decision-making quality – the performance of the representatives of the system
3. Formal treatment quality – how we are treated by the system
4. Informal treatment quality – how we are treated by the representatives of the system

which refers to the source of information about the procedures. One source is, in effect, a system, meaning the organization implementing the procedure as reflected in the rules, policies and practices. The other is the person implementing the procedures on behalf of the system. Clearly, these two sources have an interrelated yet distinct impact on the experience of procedural fairness.

Arguably the most important and durable finding to emerge on procedural fairness is that perceptions of procedural fairness enhance trust and confidence in people and authoritative institutions (Lind & Tyler, 1988; Tyler, 1984, 1994; Tyler & Degoey, 1995; Tyler, Rasinski & Griffin, 1986; Tyler, Rasinski & McGraw, 1985). Trust and confidence is important to the legitimacy of authoritative structures (Blader & Tyler, 2003; Greenberg & Cohen, 1982; Okimoto & Tyler, 2007; Sutton et al., 2008; Tyler, 1992, 2004; Wenzel, 2006). In a climate where trust in authoritative institutions is uniformly low, attending to procedural fairness is fundamentally important. This also brings us back to a key point raised earlier. Almost all the recent research points to the relationship between procedural fairness and social identity, confirming the earlier proposition by Tyler and his colleagues about the importance of the relational model. Perceptions of procedural fairness tell us something about our standing and status in the group. This relationship has been found in a variety of recent work, including work on procedural variations by the United States Supreme Court (Skitka, 2002), procedural practices to enhance the legitimacy of the police (Tyler, 2004), monetary compensation (Okimoto & Tyler, 2007), the relationship between procedural fairness and heavy drinking (Kouvonen et al., 2008), multiculturalism (Tyler, 2000), management and governance of community organizations (Weiner, Alexander & Shortell, 2002), the role of the media (Ramirez, 2008), police profiling of racial groups (Tyler & Wakslak, 2004), restorative justice and shaming (Tyler, 2006, 2007), school bullying (Morrison, 2006), political enfranchisement (Gonzalez & Tyler, 2008), leadership accuracy and bias (De Cremer, 2004), and morality and procedural fairness (Skitka & Mullen, 2002). Social identity is important, and the social

> ### BOX 9.17   The importance of personal identity and morals
>
> There are two areas where the procedural imperative does not seem as strong. Skitka and colleagues (2002, 2004) elaborated the social justice model to include personal identity as an important determinant of justice judgements. Other have also referenced the self as part of the justice matrix (Miedemam, van den Bos & Vermunt, 2006). In the value protection model it is argued that people will alter their perceptions of procedural fairness if the outcomes threaten deeply held moral values (such as those relating to abortion, civil rights or refugees). This moral mandate (Skitka, 2002, p. 589) appears to supersede procedural effects. Tyler (2000) noted that people with a strong link to groups (such as cultural groups within the larger society) are not as strongly influenced by procedural fairness as a determinant of trust.

psychology of justice plays a key role in how people make judgements about their place and status in the group. The importance of social identity in this regard is further elaborated in Chapter 7 in relation to place affiliations or people's sense of belonging to particular locations (Box 9.17).

The foregoing discussion of justice provides a more complex picture of justice than most of us routinely conceive of in our everyday lives. It has problematized justice from a rhetorical hiccough to a sophisticated matrix of interpretive possibilities. Justice is a social construction arising within particular circumstances. It has both distributive and procedural components, all of which provide us with a critical lens through which to view and interpret our experiences and the experiences of others.

The scope of justice: Who is in and who is out?

Another important question at this point in our discussion is: Who (or what) is deserving of just treatment? This question raises another crucial element to the social psychological justice equation. This is known as the scope of justice (Opotow, 1990, 1994, 2001, 2008). Without a full appreciation of the implications of this concept, our capacity to understand the function of social justice in everyday life will be markedly diminished.

We have argued that concern for social justice is ubiquitous (if not universal). Justice is at the heart of a functional society. Justice is a basic right. Earlier we asserted that social justice was part of human social currency. But were we being a little hasty? When we think about social justice we assume that all people are entitled to justice (whether they receive it or not is another matter and grist for the social psychological research mill). You might ask yourself whether this is always the case. Think for a moment about your boundaries for justice. Who or what in your world is deserving of fair treatment? Are all people deserving? What about rapists and murderers? Ahh ... what about Adolph Hitler? What about non-humans like snakes and rats? Hmm ... what about dolphins and whales? OK, then ... what about mosquitoes, lice and bedbugs? We all have a boundary within which we afford justice. Anyone or anything outside that boundary does not deserve to be treated fairly. Sometimes the boundary is very simple to define. Few of us would agonize over the decision to squash a mosquito as it buzzed in our ear at night. However, most of us would baulk at the idea of killing someone because they spilled a drink on us at a restaurant. What about the rights of an unborn fetus? If you agree that the fetus deserves fair treatment, when does humanity kick in? At the moment of conception? Six weeks? Nine weeks? Suddenly the boundary setting becomes a little more complex. Few of us would agree that children should be forced to work in the mines from the age of eight. But it was not that long ago that children were indeed chattels that could be exploited with impunity. In some nation-states children still are exploited in this way. Clearly, not only do we have boundaries, but these boundaries are fluid. The boundaries for just treatment are historically, socially, culturally, politically determined.

Until recently, social psychological research on justice assumed that justice is a reciprocal relationship. This led many social psychologists to think about social justice from a certain point of view. Justice was always a point of departure from fair treatment. However, it is clear that if we expect, or feel entitled to, just treatment and fail to receive it, we will react accordingly. If, on the other hand, we do not expect to be treated justly and indeed we are not, then our reaction will be very different. This is the domain of moral inclusion/ exclusion, or the scope of justice. The social psychological literature, in general, assumes moral inclusion (Opotow, 1990).

It is easy to find examples in everyday life where justice is denied. Your local council authorizes a light industrial area in your community without consulting residents; you are denied a deserved promotion; you are unjustly accused of messing up your brother's room. What of cases where not only is justice denied, but it is not seen to be due? If justice is due but denied the consequences can be profound for those unjustly treated. When justice is not only denied but not seen to be due the consequences can be unfathomable and unspeakably dire. Witness Hitler's treatment of Jews, gypsies and the disabled during the Second World War. Placing these people outside the scope of justice enabled death camps and gas chambers to operate at capacity for several years, until six million people had been exterminated.

There are other examples from history: Rwanda, former Yugoslavia and so on. The American Civil War has been analysed as a case study of moral exclusion (Opotow, 2008), as has the internment of Japanese American citizens during the Second World War (Nagata, 1990). Did you know that prior to a referendum conferring citizenship rights in 1967, Aboriginal people in Australia were classified under the Flora and Fauna Act? Colonizers hunted them for sport, just as modern day hunters stalk deer.

There is no question that the scope of justice is vital to understanding the experience of injustice in everyday life. We argue that there are a myriad circumstances in everyday life in which people, groups and even organizations are positioned outside the scope of justice. In many cases this is purposeful activity to enable the suspension of the normal standards of justice that ought to apply.

Review exercise

Go back and read the opening scenario again. Refugees are a good case study for our discussion of the scope of justice.

- Are refugees detained in your country without being afforded the same rights as those enjoyed by citizens?
- Are refugees positioned insider our outside the scope of justice?
- What are the consequences of such positioning?

Frighteningly, it turns out that it is not that difficult to position people outside the scope of justice.

People outside our scope of justice are seen to be undeserving. When we place 'others' outside our scope of justice we legitimize our failure to treat them according to the same standards of justice we afford to those within our scope of justice. When others are positioned outside, mistreatment or overt violations of the standards of justice that apply to those within our scope of justice do not invoke the same levels of guilt, anger or outrage (Opotow, 1993). Those outside the scope of justice may be perceived as "nonentities, expendable, undeserving" (Opotow, 1993, p. 72).

BOX 9.18   Moral exclusion and injustice

Opotow (1990) identified three criteria by which we define membership in our moral community:

1. *Believing that considerations of fairness apply to another;*
2. *A willingness to allocate a share of community resources to another;*
3. *A willingness to make sacrifices to foster another's wellbeing. (p. 4)*

Scope of justice is a simple, logical and morally compelling idea that is attended by complex ethical, philosophical and practical questions. Some we touched on above:

■ Who is in, and who is out?
■ How do moral communities develop?
■ How are they maintained?
■ What purpose do they serve?
■ How do we promote exclusion? How do the excluded respond to unjust treatment?

All these questions continue to trouble social psychologists.

In essence, the process of exclusion revolves around the idea of delegitimization (Box 9.19). Delegitimization allows a dominant group to position a person or group outside the scope of justice (Bandura, 1990). Rhetorical practices include:

■ Moral justifications (such as the legitimacy of killing 'the enemy' in combat)
■ Euphemistic labelling (where inhumane acts are sanitized by labelling; killing is called 'wasting' and terrorists call themselves 'freedom fighters')
■ Advantageous comparisons (by comparing our behaviour with other, more destructive or inhumane behaviour of others)
■ Displacing and diffusing responsibility (concentration camp commandants arguing they were simply following orders)
■ Disregarding and distorting harmful consequences of dehumanizing and blaming the victim – practices that serve to delegitimize 'other' people (Bandura, 1990).

BOX 9.19   Interesting study

In the United States Opotow (2008) proposed a typology of inclusion for explaining the treatment of former slaves that spans self-, instrumental, obstructed and institutionalized inclusion.

■ *Self-inclusion* occurred when former slaves sought full participation in post-Civil War society. This involved engaging in core institutional settings such as schools and churches.
■ *Instrumental inclusion* occurred when former slaves gained suffrage, despite fear and anxiety among members of mainstream white society.
■ *Obstructed inclusion* occurred when access to the resources for full inclusion, including land ownership, were denied to former slaves.
■ *Institutionalized exclusion* took form in direct violence against former slaves by groups such as the Ku Klux Klan and impediments to voting, including educational requirements.

Such practices are evident elsewhere. In Australia the *White Australia* policy prevented migration, led to the mandatory detention of refugees, enabled the categorization of Aboriginal people with the flora and fauna and sanctioned the forced removal of Aboriginal children from families. All this served exclusionary agendas. Nevertheless, the identification of these mechanisms provides an opportunity for exploring and understanding social justice as exclusionary practice.

A crucial site for inclusionary or exclusionary practices is the media. The role of the media in everyday life is discussed at length in Chapter 11. In the social psychology of justice it has a particular role in the promulgation of just or unjust perceptions of people, groups, organizations and even societies. After all, the media constructs and is constructed by and in society. It both reflects and creates social 'reality'. There is considerable evidence that the media is a voice in the dialogues through which many people are socialized. The views we take of particular groups are often anchored in media representations of these groups, particularly when we have limited direct contact with them (Chamberlain & Hodgetts, 2008). Media accounts of the actions of refugees serve to marginalize them and position them as less deserving by dehumanizing them (Esses, Veenvliet, Hodson & Mihic, 2008). Interestingly, Esses and colleagues (2008) link the media representations of refugees to procedural fairness by suggesting that delegitimizing claims are based on creating the perception that refugees have somehow violated procedural fairness in their attempts to gain sanctuary. In Australia the positioning of refugees by the media served the government agenda to gain public support for exclusionary policies.

It is clear that, like other aspects of social justice, moral inclusion is socially, culturally and personally defined, and once defined maintained by the processes of delegitimization (Opotow, 1990). The internment of Japanese Americans during the Second World War is a classic case of moral exclusion (Nagata, 1990). More than 90 per cent of Japanese Americans were interned during the war, whereas German and Italian Americans were not. The Japanese were apparently outside the scope of justice, although the German and Italians were not. In her analysis Nagata (1990) concluded that the Germans were not excluded because of their racial similarity, the large size of the subpopulation and its consequential political influence. Those who had been interned belatedly received compensation for their internment, which Nagata attributed to the changed boundaries of the moral community, associated with such things as the changing perceptions of ethnic groups and increasing Asianization of American society. In a similar vein, DeWind (1990) analysed the exclusion of Haitian refugees from the American government's scope of justice.

Chapter summary

So where does this leave us with respect to understanding social justice in everyday life? Some key issues emerge. First, justice is a complex and contested construct. There is a long tradition of social psychological research in the area that has been largely rooted in the experimental tradition. This has limited both the conception and application of social psychological understandings of justice to everyday life. We must find avenues for knowledge transfer. The insights from the social psychological literature offer much to ameliorate the second issue – the oversimplification of justice in the public domain. Justice is invoked often but seldom unpacked with any depth or sophistication. Justice indeed "yells loudly, but is hard to catch". However, we cannot simply transfer knowledge; we must do so critically, and we must do so discursively as part of the production of social knowledge and practices.

The experimental tradition in social psychology continues apace, and many of the studies referred to in this chapter are either experimental or derivations from experimental thought. Caution is urged in the interpretation. If, however, we accept the outcomes from research as items of assertoric knowledge rather than expressions of immutable or universal truth, they become available as part of the debate about what might really be going on in the world. Dixon and Wetherell (2004), in one of the few discursive explorations of social justice, invoked Sampson's vocabularies of justice in their analysis of the social construction of justice in the division of family labour. These authors note that a view of what constituted fairness in domestic arrangements was an active co-construction between the parties. This harks back to what we argued in the introduction, that people actively create in order to make sense of what is happening around them (Jovchelovitch, 2007). That construction serves some purpose and is strategic in the determination of who gets what and under what circumstances. Power differentials are important (Dixon & Wetherell, 2004). They also remind us that discursively, justice is perceived and accomplished in the doing. As social psychologists we can contribute to the doing. Crucially, Dixon and Wetherell (2004) seek rapprochement between the traditional psychological accounts of social justice and the burgeoning discursive accounts of justice in practice (Box 9.20).

It seems unlikely that the experimentally oriented social psychologists will cease their pursuit of 'truth' as they understand it, nor indeed should they. Critical social psychologists, on the other hand, face a perhaps more compelling challenge. The experimentalists have at least risen to the challenge of exploring the depth and complexity of social justice. Critical social psychologists have not elaborated justice as a social construction (with a few notable exceptions), nor have they unpacked the workings of justice in everyday life. The ideas and concepts from the literature we have reviewed in this chapter provide a network of concepts that sensitize the research to the complexity of issues (Dixon & Wetherell, 2004). As

BOX 9.20   Interesting study

Linda Skitka (2009) provides an interesting and provocative insight into the historical movements in social justice research outlined in this chapter. She observes that the social psychology of justice has evolved through three worldviews that have underpinned research: *Homo economicus*, *Homo socialis* and *Homo moralis*. The early work derived from balance, cognitive dissonance and exchange theories, culminating in the variety of equity formulations, is characteristic of the self-interested *Homo economicus* driven by cost benefits in an attempt to maximize outcomes. The interest in and burgeoning of research into procedural justice from the mid-1970s saw the emergence of *Homo socialis* and a focus on processes for understanding and responding to injustice. The obvious manifestations of this are interactional and relational perspectives of justice as concern for the maintenance and development of social arrangements and social identities. According to Skitka, the recent turn is a renewed interest in the moral imperative for justice. *Homo moralis* asks what 'ought' to be or what 'should' be just (p. 102). Interestingly, this final conception brings us full circle back to the underlying philosophical notions of justice. *Homo moralis* also has a keen interest in the scope of justice. And here is where things get a little provocative. For the most part, the various *Homo justices* have been largely viewed as competing views of the person. Skitka proposes a contingent model of justice, arguing that the *Homo hat* they wear will depend on the context or circumstances within which they are making justice judgements. We have argued throughout this book that the world is infinitely more complex than we often give it credit for, so we are comfortable with Skitka's view of people in their pursuit of justice. What do you think?

social psychologists we can bring the network of concepts to the conversation alongside, but not privileged in relation to, everyday knowledge. The concepts presented in this chapter can add significantly to our capacity to reflect on the workings of justice in everyday life as part of the ongoing conversation through which social psychology is constituted as a discipline.

What, then, can we take to everyday life with us? One obvious point is that we can take complexity. The variety of lenses that we have elaborated in this chapter, such as the distinctions between distributive and procedural justice and the importance of scope of justice concerns, provide a multidimensional frame of reference that may inform the discourse on social justice. It seems clear that matters of social identity are important too. The link between perceptions of procedural fairness and social identity seems robust and ought to be part of the ongoing conversation. The link to the legitimacy of social institutions and structures seems fundamentally unassailable but will find unique expression in different domains, depending on history, culture and place, to name a few. That people are excluded from the scope of justice is unarguable. The point here is not to be prescriptive but to be alert and to bring complexity to the conversation.

In opening this chapter we located social justice as a social construction, and it is to this that we must inevitably return. Our understanding of justice must be located within a social, historical, political, cultural context. In everyday life we traverse many substantive domains (Wicker, 1989). We are imbedded in many places that are constructed by and give meaning to our lives. In these domains we may encounter injustice. At home we may not feel that our partner is shouldering his or her share of the domestic duties (Dixon & Wetherell, 2004), our dog may be impounded by the local authorities for barking, our boss may promote someone we feel is less deserving than we are, and a police officer may impose fines for speeding when we are adamant that we were within the limit. At the broader systemic level people are still homeless, Aboriginal people are still incarcerated at a much higher rate than non-indigenous people, refugees continue to be detained, and people from diverse cultural backgrounds experience racism and exclusion.

As social psychologists we can participate in the construction of everyday life and everyday understandings. The constellation of concepts and ideas about social justice that have emerged in the past few decades provide the opportunity for the creation of rhetorics around social justice that have hitherto been largely unavailable in everyday life (Throgmorton, 1990). These rhetorics become resources that have been underutilized. A quintessential problematic of discourse analysis is the tension between principle and practice (Tuffin, 2004). Discourses are inherently reproductive of the status quo. This has been repeatedly demonstrated in the literature on race, gender and sexual politics, to name a few (Dixon & Wetherell, 2004; Tuffin, 2004). It is clear also that the interpretive community of traditional social psychological discourses has been largely absent from the public discourses, yet has enormous transformative potential. The concepts are compelling, logical and simple. The challenge is to contribute them to the public discourses in ways that enhance the possibility for the creation of new discourses and interpretive communities – new ways to talk (Drew, 2005). The concepts and ideas from the psychological understandings of justice identify clear points of demarcation and argumentation regarding allocation and distribution, process and procedure, inclusion and exclusion. They are an interpretive frame, and as such are potential sites of practical intervention and change. They are also inherently social and reposition social justice outside the individual so that the reproductive imperative towards victim blaming is ameliorated. The social psychology of justice explicitly examines the role of the collective and of social systems in the creation and maintenance of social injustice. We favour the idea of "fracturing" and "disrupting" common (reproductive) constructions (Tuffin, 2004, p. 154).

Our approach to social psychology and everyday life necessitates the combination of theoretical, substantive and transformative work. We must enhance our theoretical understanding, including our understanding of the work of experimental social psychologists (and psychologists of all shapes and sizes); we must locate and understand social justice in multiple substantive domains; and we must strive for transformation in everyday life. The last means, of course, that we must eschew the apolitical tendencies of social psychology in favour of active engagement in the complexity of everyday life. This can be achieved in at least three ways, as suggested by Willig (1999): by exploring, exposing and critiquing the reproductive discourses that construct injustice, by empowering through active participation the creation of alternative discourses and constructions in everyday life and by contributing to the social reform processes by engaging fully in public policy debate.

The experience of justice or injustice is at the heart of everyday life. The discourses we create provide the possibility of being active agents in the creation of social change in pursuit of social justice. In the discursive realm we may be able to engage our taxi driver to understand the processes of exclusion that find him driving a taxi rather than designing bridges. We could talk to him about the systemic processes excluding Aboriginal people from our scope of justice, and how that may be a better explanation for why they are living in the park than individual vilification and victim blaming. Had we done this, the Aboriginal people might not live there, and Ian might not have been beaten up.

Review exercise

- Why is justice so difficult to define?
- What are some of the conceptual precursors of contemporary models of social justice?
- What is the difference between distributive and procedural fairness?
- What are the possible consequences of placing someone (or a group) outside our scope of justice?
- What are some of the mechanisms or processes that may be invoked to position someone (or a group) outside our scope of justice?

Note

1. There is also a debate in the literature regarding the distinction between relational concerns in procedural fairness and interactional justice (Greenberg, 1993; Wenzel, 2006). In essence they refer to the same underlying issue of the impact of justice concerns on social identity.

10 Pro-social behaviour and critical humanism

Core questions to consider while reading this chapter

- What is altruism?
- What is humanistic psychology?
- How does the inverse care law relate to positive psychology?
- What do social psychologists mean by human dignity?
- What is critical humanism?
- What do we mean by community resilience?

Chapter scenario

Grey Street is in an inner-city suburb. It is a good place to live because it houses a close-knit community with a tradition of neighbours looking out for one another. Employment has been generally good in the city, and most people have always had jobs and have a strong sense of place. Recently, things have begun to change. Redundancies have come as a result of economic decline in the region. There are fewer financial resources for community projects. However, due to the close-knit nature of the community, people are helping each other through a productive community garden and the sharing of resources. Neighbours know they can count on one another – and they do. As a result, the impact of the economic downturn is not as severe as it might have been without such supports. Carol has lived in Grey Street all her life. She has run a small local cafe with her husband Arthur for the past forty years. Unfortunately, Arthur's health is not what it used to be. He is now confined to his bed for most of the day, fighting a chronic illness.

Carol and their youngest daughter are coping with the support of neighbours and friends who help with the cafe and Arthur's care. Mick and Phillip, a retired couple from next door, also help out with jobs around the yard. Though saddened by Arthur's illness, Carol is also gaining a sense of satisfaction and maintaining a sense of connection to the neighbourhood through the support of others and through being able to care for Arthur at home. Carol has also been volunteering for thirty years at Street Wise, a charity serving the needs of lower-socioeconomic-status people in a neighbouring suburb. On this particular morning she is working at a drop-in centre where people in need can come in for a free breakfast. Carol is well known and liked by the regulars. She has coordinated local businesses in supplying food and contributing to the charity's overheads. On this particular day, Carol meets a newcomer who seems somewhat distraught. Neville is new to the city and life on the streets. Carol knows that he is vulnerable and requires mentoring in order to survive. While she is talking to Neville about his predicament, she spots Tom, a regular who has survived on the streets for more than twenty years. He has also thrived and developed into something of a local celebrity. Tom has a history of taking newbies under his wing and agrees to look out for Neville.

This scenario raises the importance of looking at strengths and capacities within and among people and how these are shaped by, and in turn shape, daily lives. We can see examples of what psychologists refer to as pro-social behaviour, altruism, social support, resilience and competence. The scenario reflects the types of selfless acts of giving and volunteering that occur every day in communities. These pro-social phenomena can be cultivated in environments of caring and compassion, as well as through tragedies, mistakes and hard lessons. We know that the negative effects of economic hardship can be buffered by the existence of supportive social networks (Chapter 8) that can be drawn upon as resources in times of need.

The work of many founding figures in social psychology, such as William James, George Mead, Marie Jahoda, and Kurt Lewin (Chapter 2), reflects a humanistic tendency to consider the potential and abilities of people like those in the opening scenario. These early scholars were interested in the positive aspects of our lives together. This chapter discusses ways in which more recent psychologists have thought about, researched and worked to enhance positive dimensions of everyday life and how we can grow these capacities and in the process improve people's lives. A focus on such positive phenomena is important because as a discipline we can get overly pessimistic if we focus only on problems. There is much that is good about everyday life.

Chapter overview

A starting point for the chapter is pro-social behaviour and the importance of kind acts to human existence. We then turn to the humanistic tradition and its development as a means of ensuring a focus on the good and potential in people. Humanistic psychology conceptualizes people in relational, historic, economic and social contexts that are central to much of what we have had to say so far in this book. The approach foregrounds issues of self-reliance, self-determination and self-help. We then consider the recent popularity of positive psychology as an application of strength-based work, primarily in clinical psychology. Positive psychology is presented as a newer version of humanism. Both humanist and positive psychologies have been accused of self-centredness and of focusing too much on the ability of individuals to transcend the world and do great things, while neglecting structural restraints. In pointing out limitations in these approaches we propose a critical humanist approach that recognizes humanistic psychology's focus on strengths and combines this recognition with a societal focus on resilience in the face of socioeconomic hardship and political intolerance. This approach looks both within the person and at settings for strengths and resources. It involves drawing on early humanist traditions and ensuring that social psychologists do not lose sight of social and political realities, and how power relations can shape people's lives. This repoliticizing of the field is also necessary if we are to take useful contributions into people's lives and ensure social justice. After all, criticality emerges when we address injustices requiring people to be resilient and support one another. In summary, this chapter emphasizes:

- Pro-social behaviour and resilience as central concepts for social psychology
- Humanistic and positive psychologies and the emphasis on human potential
- Critical humanism as a contemporary orientation in social psychology

Pro-social behaviour (altruism)

When we attend to social psychological phenomena such as prejudice and social exclusion, it is easy to forget that our communities are often frequented by acts of kindness, love, caring and sharing. We might forget that social psychologists have also paid particular attention to the pro-social actions of individuals and groups (Mastain, 2007). This focus is central to understanding our everyday lives together. Sometimes, simple acts of giving, sharing and volunteering can enable people to achieve more than simply coping with adversity (Mattis et al., 2009). People can be supported in growing into creative and helpful human beings (Monroe, 1996; Post, Underwood,

Schloss & Hurlbut, 2002). Social psychologists explore pro-social behaviour and altruism at personal, communal and societal levels. Psychologists consider the ways these levels are interconnected. For example, recent literature on place (Chapter 6) emphasizes the benefits of integrating people facing hardship into established communities from which they can draw social support (Chapter 8).

In 1851, Auguste Comte (1973) introduced the term 'altruism' (Box 10.1) as part of an explanation for moral acts and the efforts of human beings to assist others. He referred to the selflessness of 'living for others'. Altruism is often used with reference to unselfish behaviour that helps others grow and develop or alleviates suffering (Post et al., 2002). It is associated with key figures such as Jesus Christ, the prophet Muhammad, Martin Luther King and Mother Theresa. Concern for other people's welfare is central to philanthropic and humanitarian efforts and is seen as important in many societies. Altruism is also central to the Hindu, Buddhist, Islamic and Christian belief systems (Christopher & Hickinbottom, 2008).

In psychology, the concept of altruism was brought to the fore in theory and research arising from the Kitty Genovese case (Chapter 2) and subsequent study of bystanders' willingness (or unwillingness) to render assistance to others (Latane & Darley, 1970). Following Comte (1973), some psychologists propose that true altruism contains no self-interest and represents a sort of pure form of self-sacrifice and selflessness (Mastain, 2007). By some means, if a person gains something while helping another person, then this tarnishes the act and invalidates it as being altruistic. This stance seems overly restrictive. Taking a more pragmatic stance, Batson (1991) conceptualized altruism in terms of motivation as an intention to help and increase the welfare of another person. Altruism is not simply about feeling empathy towards or concern for the welfare of others. It is about acting on such concerns and rendering assistance without an expectation that the person giving will be rewarded or recognized personally for acting. This may involve self-sacrifice, but often we do not have to give up much to help others (Batson, 1994). People can gain rewards such as a sense of satisfaction for having done a good thing and a sense of self as a good person (Mastain, 2007). The key is

BOX 10.1   Altruism

'Altruism' and 'pro-social behaviour' are terms used by psychologists with reference to the actions of human beings that help other people. The Altruism International site provides a useful resource for further information: http://www.altruists.org/about/altruism/

that the primary motivation for the kind act is not self-interest, but rather helping another person (Batson, 1994).

Linking back to the point made in Chapters 2 and 4, there are as many amateur social psychologists as there are people in the world (Box 10.2). Human beings have a capacity to speculate about and reflect on social phenomena, including pro-social behaviour. Recently, Mastain (2007) investigated how a group of participants made sense of their own altruism, documenting how people are often motivated to be altruistic because it makes them feel good and because they are concerned for the welfare of others. To explain participants' motivations for altruism, Mastain drew upon corresponding 'egoistic' and 'reciprocity' academic explanations for altruism. Freud (1920, in Strachey, 1955) proposed that people are never truly selfless, as all acts of altruism are, at their core, driven by egoism. This egoistic explanation posits that people are motivated to act altruistically out of the sense of self-worth they can experience from helping others. Another important motivating factor for altruism appears to be reciprocity based on a person's previous experiences of having benefited from the altruistic actions of others (cf. Mattis et al., 2009). Clearly, these motivations are not necessarily incompatible, in that we can feel good about ourselves while contributing to the welfare of other people. According to Mastain (2007), ego-oriented motivations appear to be associated more strongly with 'planned altruism' such

---

BOX 10.2   Interesting study

Mattis and colleagues (2009) explored what motivated forty people living on a low-income housing estate to act altruistically. These authors note that contemporary research on urban communities under pressure tends to highlight deficits, including family disruption, violence, distress and a lack of social capital. The picture painted of the relationships at play in such settings is overly bleak. The research was conducted in accord with the notions of community partnership building and participation discussed in Chapters 1, 4 and 8 of this book. The authors established four general motivation categories. First, *needs-centred motives* involved a desire to respond to the emotional, physical, material and specific needs of an individual and of particular social groups. Second, *norms-based motives* involved the enactment of specific relational-oriented religious, faith and ideological beliefs about the importance of helping others and acting selflessly. Third, *abstract motives* represented a form of humanism and a sense of the sanctity of all human life. This orientation was associated with particular self-characterizations of a caring person. Fourth, *sociopolitical factors*, including personal experiences of poverty and experiences of discrimination, were linked to an appreciation of the value of human life. Many altruistic acts were linked to efforts to support people and buffer them from the ravages of social deprivation (Chapter 8). The authors illustrate how everyday life in the community is punctuated by both mundane and extraordinary acts of altruism. Mattis and colleagues note that through such pro-social acts social capital and community resilience can be cultivated (Chapters 6, 8 and 10).

as volunteering, because the sense of accomplishment would likely sustain the activity over time. Spontaneous acts may be motivated more directly by a sense of the importance of increasing the welfare of another person.

If one's primary goal is to help others, then the act can be conceptualized as altruism. When Mick and Phillip help out at Carol's house they do so in an attempt to enhance the family's welfare and in the process can feel good about themselves. They are being good neighbours. There are often multiple factors at play in such altruistic acts.

Helping others is good for one's self-esteem and is often a manifestation of a sense of moral obligations and social norms (Post et al., 2002), which is often reflected in shared narratives (Mattis et al., 2009) and which can validate a sense of self as a good person. Enhancing self-esteem is recognized in research on social identity theory (Tajfel & Turner, 1979) as a key motivation for identifying with particular social groups (Rubin & Hewstone, 1998). We discussed social identity theory in Chapter 6. This theory is relevant to our discussion of pro-social behaviour because much of people's sense of self comes from how they perceive others to see them (Cooley, 1902). Groups give us a sense of place in the world and expectations for pro-social actions. Human beings identify themselves as being interconnected within groups and as a result often behave in the interest of these groups (Stone, 2008). This is the basis for the health benefits of social networks discussed in Chapter 8 and for our very being, which is negotiated over time through daily practices and actions in relation to others (see discussions of the dialogical self in Chapters 3, 5 and 7).

Much of the theory and research into social identity and intergroup relations focuses on conflict. In Chapters 5–7 we explored processes of colonization, immigration and the politics of place and re-segregation. However, there is more to interactions between groups than conflict, and pro-social behaviour is not simply restricted to interactions within our own social groups (Stone, 2008). This raises issues of the self and the other considered in Chapters 3 and 4.

Aristotle proposed that a sense of likeness to another person is associated with empathy and recognition of the possibility that one might find oneself in a similar situation of need. This sense of relatedness has been associated with an increased likelihood of rendering aid. In Chapter 8, we noted that people are more likely to act for the collective good when their shared social identities are brought to the fore and they experience an 'us-ness' (van Zomeren, Spears & Leach, 2008). It has been posited that, owing to psychological processes of attachment to others with whom one shares a social identity (Batson, 1991), individuals are more likely to help others who are members of their own families or social groups. The influence of a sense of attachment is not a guarantee that a person will always help some people over others. It is important not to lose sight of the fact that pro-social acts also cross group boundaries, such as when people give to international aid agencies or local charities. Mastain (2007) found that "all of the altruists in this study helped individuals who were different from them physically, socially, racially and/or socio-economically. ... [I]t was the universal human commonality they perceived in the other that motivated them to help, and a sense of attachment that compelled them help" (p. 93) (Box 10.3). A universal and inclusive orientation towards humanity has been identified as a core element in the psychology of altruistic people (Monroe, 1996). We might say this is an identity of self as a global citizen interconnected to all other citizens. Mattis and colleagues (2009) also found that people were willing to act altruistically towards people different from themselves (cf. Stone, 2008).

Our discussion of pro-social behaviour leads to a discussion of how kind acts might alter the social landscape for the better. Social transformation does not have to be top-down or involve great events such as the overthrow of a government – though in some cases this is warranted (Chapters 1 and 8). Change can be gradual and cumulative, and based on simple pro-social acts in everyday life. Seemingly small actions conducted each day can have much bigger consequences in maintaining supportive social structures and the common good by

---

BOX 10.3   Interesting study

Stone (2008) provides an insightful commentary on possible genetic and evolutionary components of pro-social behaviour. He outlines how neo-Darwinian theories of pro-social behaviour associate pro-social acts with kin selection and reciprocity. Such acts are reduced to a means for ensuring the continuation of one's genetic stock. Stone concludes that these theories paint an overly limited picture of human pro-social practices that cannot explain altruistic acts towards strangers. These acts are part of what makes humans unique and can be explained with reference to the evolutionary complexities of human morality, thought and culture. These social aspects can be used to explain why human beings can also act altruistically towards strangers and feel sympathy towards people who are not members of their own families. In doing so, people acting in a pro-social manner are not doing so simply in self-interest. Stone (2008) notes:

Literally hundreds of studies by behavioral economists employing the Ultimatum, Dictator and Public Goods games have demonstrated beyond any doubt that humans often care about the welfare of non-intimates, they have a refined sense of justice, and they will often expend their own resources in one-shot games to punish "free riders" and those who harm anonymous and innocent strangers. ... The selfish hypothesis advanced by orthodox neo-Darwinians simply does not hold up to empirical scrutiny. (p. 147)

Other scholars, including Monroe (1996), have challenged the common view that people are motivated primarily by self-interest.

BOX 10.4   Structuration

In addressing the traditional dichotomy between personal action/agency and social systems, Anthony Giddens (1986) proposed the theory of structuration. This theory attempts to transcend boundaries between micro and macro systems and to explore the ways in which individual actions can reproduce social systems. The focus goes beyond the individual actor and society to explore how social practices give order to everyday life. Human action is neither free of nor simply the exercise of social influences. Our existence is the product of social structures and human agency. Giddens proposed that human action takes place in the contexts of existing social structures, including social norms. It is through collective personal actions or human agency that social structures evolve. Structure/restraint and agency/human autonomy are locked in a dialogical relationship and each reproduces the other through shared practices that reproduce moral codes, traditions, institutions. To some degree, we all feel obliged to act in specific ways according to the particular settings we find ourselves in. However, we can misbehave from time to time and give up the invitation to fit in.

---

cultivating trust, civic engagements and social capital (Mattis et al., 2009). These elements of a healthy community can buffer people against negative events and contribute to the development of a sense of belonging, shared purpose and place-based identities (Chapter 6). Here, we might invoke the concept of structuration (Box 10.4), which was developed to account for the ways in which daily practices are central to the cultivation and reproduction of humane social systems. Mastain (2007) writes, "By better understanding the experience of altruism, my hope is that we will be able to more effectively foster it in ourselves and others" (p. 63).

Pro-social behaviour (volunteering)

Societies often value some behaviours, such as helping others, sharing and volunteerism, because these actions contribute to the well-being of people and broader functioning of society. People's willingness to assist others without payment is often referred to as volunteerism. This phenomenon is often used as a key indicator of social capital (Chapter 6) and the health of a community. Volunteers include missionaries or aid workers engaged in development projects, rescue workers searching for a lost boat, people working in a food bank and those teaching young people how to read and write. People who devote their time and energy to helping others, in what is often termed 'community service' or 'charity work', constitute a gift economy that is foundational to modern society. People often (but not always) volunteer for altruistic reasons and contribute to the social and economic health of a society. Many social benefits come from volunteering, and thus contribute to building social capital and cohesion in a community (cf. Mattis et al., 2009). Volunteerism is associated with increased trust and reciprocity. Economic benefits include a reduced pressure on private philanthropic funds and local and central government budgets (because the work is done for free). Volunteer work also improves the health of individuals and communities and has the potential to reduce costs to society (for example in health care, welfare and justice areas).

Review exercise

Take a moment to think about people in your community.

- Do people take time to help others? If, so what distinguishes those who help from those who are less likely to render assistance?
- Has anyone come to your aid or the aid of someone you know in a time of distress?
- What situational factors (e.g. number of other people present and attributes of the setting) might encourage or discourage people from helping?

These are the sorts of question that guide psychological research into pro-social behaviour

There is a strong body of research that has examined people's motivations for volunteering. Stukas, Daly and Clary (2006) suggested that motivations for volunteering can be organized in to seven functions and goals:

- *Values*: to express humanitarian values
- *Career*: to explore careers
- *Understanding*: to gain understanding of the world
- *Enhancement*: to feel important and to build esteem and networks
- *Protective*: to provide distraction from personal concerns
- *Social*: to satisfy expectations
- *Community concern*: to satisfy an obligation to community

Other researchers have developed similar schemes for understanding the diverse motivations for volunteering. For example, Dolnicar and Randle (2007) developed schema to capture some of the diversity of motivations among volunteers. Accordingly, they proposed three categories of volunteers. First, *classic volunteers* are motivated to do something worthwhile for another person and gain personal satisfaction in the process. Second, *dedicated volunteers* emphasize donating time because of personal connections with an organization. Third, *niche volunteers* are motivated by care for the welfare of others and personal satisfaction and a range of more specific motivations such as

'This is what my mother always did, so I am carrying on the tradition.' Rehberg (2005) reported similar findings in his study of motivations for volunteering among young adults in Switzerland. His groups included those who volunteer to achieve something positive for others, those who are seeking new experiences and those who seek personal rewards and satisfaction. This research points to similar motivations, but suggests that motivations can also vary according to age, gender, race and social class, which are all social structural phenomena influencing our experiences and motivations for volunteering.

One key concept explaining why people volunteer to assist others or act altruistically and give to others is social norms (Post et al., 2002). People can be socialized into helping others based on such social norms as:

- *Fairness*: belief that people deserve assistance and support
- *Equity*: treating all people with dignity
- *Obligations*: duty to assist others
- *Justice and morality*: notion that helping is the right thing to do
- *Reciprocity*: doing for others what you might expect them to do for you

The existence of such norms in a culture will not dictate who will (or will not) act in an altruistic manner in particular situations. However, it does increase the likelihood of altruistic acts within a population. Altruism can also be encouraged through the rewarding of altruistic acts and the modelling of pro-social behaviour. This is evident in, for example, the awarding of a Nobel Prize to Mother Theresa, whereby others have been encouraged to model their own efforts on the good mother's selfless acts. As noted in Chapter 3, through processes of social learning human beings can learn from observing others. People may also model altruistic behaviour from role models to whom they feel attached (Mikulincer, Shaver, Gillath & Nitzberg, 2005). It is likely that Carol, from the opening scenario, learned about the need to help others by observing the behaviour of likeminded folk in the Grey Street community (Box 10.5).

There are also negative aspects of volunteerism (Box 10.6). Vigoda-Gadot (2006) explores the abuse of altruistic people who voluntarily invest extra time and effort in the workplace above the formal requirements of their employment. Volunteering can result from

BOX 10.5   Selfish volunteers

A recent phenomenon has been the rise of the selfish volunteers. Selfish volunteers are motivated not by altruism, but by a desire to build personal credibility in the interests of opening up future opportunities and enhancing their curriculum vitae (CV).

BOX 10.6 Negative aspects of volunteerism

Dambisa Moyo, an African economist, in her book *Dead Aid* (2008) argues persuasively that international aid since the 1960s has been overwhelmingly detrimental to the very people it was meant to assist. She points to sixty billion dollars in aid that has been poured into producing little tangible benefit in areas such as poverty reduction. The primary outcomes in her view are entrenched corruption and aid dependence. She advocates the cessation of all international aid to Africa within five years. Although we do not necessarily agree with this conclusion, the book is compelling reading.

coercion by colleagues and managerial manipulation. Pressure to work extra unpaid hours and take on extra tasks is all too common in many organizations and a key source of work stress (Chapter 8). Overreliance on volunteers in the provision of social services can also lead to the exploitation of the good will of community members. In societies where status is associated with financial recognition, not paying people for community work can undermine the status of such work. An overreliance on volunteerism and philanthropy can lead to a fairly ad hoc approach to addressing social needs. There is perhaps more chance that certain groups will be overlooked because their needs do not fit within the scope, agendas or resources of the volunteering agencies. Imposing volunteer assistance on a person in need can undermine his or her self-esteem and be 'soul destroying'. Volunteerism can also detract from social norms of self-reliance and autonomy in many cultures (Fisher, Nadler & De Paulo, 1983).

Finally, volunteering does not have to occur face to face (Cravens, 2007). For example, the Internet has lots of shareware (e.g. Linux) created by people and given away to others to overcome glitches in commercial software. Virtual volunteers also help others build their pages on social networking sites such as Facebook and Bebo (Chapter 11), translate texts for circulation among cultures and facilitate self-help groups for people living with a range of ailments or life challenges.

Now that we have explored pro-social behaviours, it is necessary to explore traditions within psychology that have investigated positive human action and potential.

Humanistic psychology

During the 1950s and 1960s, the tendency to focus on pro-social aspects of human behaviour and human potential to act justly in the world came to the fore in the form of humanistic psychology

(Schneider, Bugental & Pierson, 2001; Wertz, 1998). This tradition bridges psychology and the humanities. Proponents believe in the dignity of people in all their complexities, and that this orientation should be the focal point of our discipline. Humanistic psychology is committed to the study of the whole person in the ecological context of his or her life. The person exists beyond the sum of the parts that can be associated with him or her. In other words, we cannot reduce people to psychological factors because who we are often extends beyond such base elements.

The rise of humanistic psychology was, in part, a response to the dominance of behavioural approaches that decompartmentalize aspects of individuals and their lives (see Chapter 2) and all but ignore human dignity, agency, autonomy and creativity (Wertz, 1998). Whereas behavioural psychologists emphasize that people are products of their environments, humanists emphasize that environments are important, but are not determining of human growth or character. There is more to people than their experiences and the forces that come into play in their lives. Humanists argued against the behaviourist notion that psychological enquiry should be restricted to directly observable behaviour (see Chapter 2). Such a behavioural perspective can leave us with a situation in which a social psychological phenomenon that cannot be reliably measured does not exist. Such a stance can minimize the human condition and leave us with a caricature, rather than a portrait, of human experience and action (see Chapter 2). Humanists also saw a need to move beyond the behavioural focus on how stimuli determine behaviour to how people perceive or come to understand stimuli and their own actions in the context of their everyday lives (Wertz, 1998). Rather than try to study behaviour by separating elements of a person's life into variables to be examined under laboratory conductions, humanists sought to explore patterns in people's lives in the context of their histories and lived circumstances (Box 10.7). As a result, psychology was extended into the study of history and literature.

BOX 10.7   Postulates for humanistic psychology

Bugental (1964) put forward five postulates for humanistic psychology:

1. It is impossible to reduce human beings to component parts. Reductionism provides an incomplete picture.
2. Within each person is a uniquely human quality.
3. Central to consciousness is a self-awareness that is related to one's relationship with others.
4. People can make choices, and do so in the context of responsibilities and restraints.
5. People are intentional beings. We are creative and seek understanding from experience.

Reflecting the value placed on the potential of human beings, research is often conducted *with* people whose behaviour is being studied. As discussed in Chapter 4 this is preferable to conducting research *on* people. Humanists conduct research with people because emphasis is placed on self-perceptions and the meanings people attach to their experiences and events in their lives. Like indigenous psychologists (Chapter 5), humanists propose that the whole person is best studied in the contexts in which he or she lives and interacts. From a humanist perspective, what comes first is a person's status as a human being and then we might worry about how he or she is labelled and what roles or status the person might have in society (Rogers, 1972).

Here, we might reconsider the core point made across several chapters and reiterate that people live somewhere, engage in different places, exist in groups and cultures, and are affected by issues of social justice and encounters with people who are different from themselves. People are individual and collective, social and intra-psychic, and thus humans are connected, interwoven beings who come to understand themselves and others through dialogue and engagement. Our discussion of the interconnected, dialogical self in Chapters 3, 5 and 7 is relevant here. People rarely live in social isolation away from all other people. Thus, in order to understand a person we need to understand his or her social networks without reducing individuals to such networks. In this regard, humanistic psychology can be aligned with the concept of the dialogical or interconnected self, which we have placed at the centre of our understandings of everyday life. Humanistic psychology developed out of a long-standing tradition in European philosophy that bore many similarities to traditions across different cultures, including Hindu and Buddhist philosophies. Such humanistic underpinnings were reintroduced to North American psychology in the 1950s (Schneider, Bugental & Pierson, 2001).

Humanistic psychologists view human beings as possessing the potential to self-regulate and assert some agency over their lives (Schneider, Bugental & Pierson, 2001) (Box 10.8). This extends to all citizens, including homeless people like Tom from the opening scenario, who can develop the capacity for choice and creativity, caring for others (Neville), sharing responsibility and trust. Humanists acknowledge that forces in society can enhance or undermine this human capacity for good and caring. Homeless people may end up competing for scarce resources, rather than cooperating with one another. Human growth needs to be supported by social and institutional developments that enable people to flourish. Humanists emphasize the need for social structures to support human development, and, if necessary, psychologists should work to change social

---

BOX 10.8   The Association of Humanistic Psychology

In 1962 the Association of Humanistic Psychology (AHP) was founded as a global community. AHP core values are:

- A belief in human potential and commitment to fostering the potential of all people
- A belief that change is inevitable because life is a process
- The valuing of the intuitive and spiritual dimensions of human lives
- A commitment to ecological integrity
- The recognition of and commitment to addressing problems affecting the world

See http://www.ahpweb.org.

---

structures that are coercive and unjust and that undermine human growth. Thus, humanistic psychologists have explored issues of social justice at least since Carl Rogers (1951).

In the 1950s, Abraham Maslow set out an early positive focus for psychology arguing for the need to focus on human potential, rather than just problems or deficiencies. This reflects a core idea in humanistic psychology that human beings are innately good and that social problems result from unjust social structures that frustrate our propensity for caring and goodness. From this perspective, we might explore Carol's lifeworld with her, attending to the ways in which people in her life support one another to meet the demands of life and grow. Carol could provide invaluable information on the social significance of mundane acts such as cleaning the neighbour's windows. This is what is promoted is a 'nonpathologizing' understanding of people, which focuses on health rather than illness (Clay, 2002). The focus is on uniquely human qualities such as hope, creativity, love, health, being and meaning. Maslow (1943, 1970, 1979) believed that people can understand their own behaviour and work to realize their potential (Box 10.9). He proposed that certain material and social needs had to be met before human growth and potential could be obtained. Maslow discussed the need for social justice, freedom and fairness as contextual preconditions for positive human growth.

Humanistic psychology has not gone unchallenged. For example, Prilleltensky (1992) is sympathetic to the humanistic tradition but raises a number of criticisms applicable both to humanistic psychology and to the newer manifestation of such ideas in positive psychology. Although humanists have written about the need to consider ecological factors, there is a tendency to focus on individuals. A humanistic perspective can lead to the promotion of self-absorption and narcissism. The problem emerges in relation to the core idea

BOX 10.9   Self-actualization and the hierarchy of needs

Humanistic psychology is associated with the work of Carl Rogers and Abraham Maslow, who brought us such concepts as self-actualization and the hierarchy of needs (Schneider, Bugental & Pierson, 2001). The term 'self-actualization' was brought to the fore in psychology as a key component of Maslow's hierarchy of needs. In this hierarchy, self-actualization is presented as the highest level of development achieved by human beings who reach their full potential. Maslow (1943) considered self-actualization to be a desire towards self-fulfilment and reaching one's potential. It is a process of becoming what one is able to become. Self-actualization can be conceptualized as a drive towards psychological healthiness. Maslow was clear that self-actualization did not determine a person's life. It provided motivation and drive to achieve ambitions and develop personal capacities. Qualities of an actualized person include independence, deep relationships, humour, autonomy and resilience.

Work on self-actualization reflects the focus of humanists on growth rather than deficits that inhibit growth. In discussing inhibiting factors, Maslow invokes a hierarchy of needs that requires people to meet lower-level basic needs such as food and shelter before personal development is possible. People grow up through Maslow's hierarchy, achieving specific needs and reaching the peak of self-actualization. At the base of the hierarchy are *physiological needs*, such as water and food, and basic functions such as gaining rest. On achieving these needs, people can move to fulfil *safety needs* and gain a sense of comfort, shelter, security and employment. Once this is achieved, people can move on to the level of *belongingness and love needs*. This level includes strong affiliations with others, a sense of belonging and sexual intimacy. *Esteem needs* revolve around gaining recognition of one's achievements, competence and respect. Meeting all of these needs is a precursor for a person to reach self-actualization.

It should be noted that Maslow's work is somewhat culturally specific in that the person is presented as a Western individual who is striving the make the best of his or her self and to be independent. As noted in Chapters 3 and 5, many cultures value interdependence. Wahba and Bridgewell (1976) questioned the existence of a hierarchy that people must progress through. Human needs may be nonhierarchical, in that a homeless man like Tom still requires love and acceptance despite often lacking food and shelter. The hierarchy of needs also has no provision for assessing how people's needs might change as society changes. This reveals an underlying assumption of universal applicability, which was identified as a problem during the crisis in social psychology.

of humanistic psychology that individuals can transcend circumstances. In focusing on individual strengths, humanistic psychology may reaffirm the status quo and neglect the need for social change as a means of fostering human growth. The idea that if we change individuals then social change will follow is also problematic (Maslow, 1971). This assumes that events such as conflicts are interpersonal in nature, rather than often systemic and economic in nature. "Attitudinal changes are given much more consideration than power redistribution" (Prilleltensky, 1992, p. 321). This quotation reminds us of a scene from the movie *The Life of Brian*, in which a man is being crucified while he sings, "Always look on the bright side of life." According to Prilleltensky, the focus on the ability of individuals to overcome adversity can serve to obscure the extent to which we are products of our environments, and although some can do exceedingly well in the face of hardship, many people remain trapped in poverty. Change is not solely up to, or predicated on, the individual. Social structures, such as restricted access to education and histories of oppression, can act as barriers to personal transformation. This is exemplified in the work of Freire, which is discussed later in this chapter.

Notwithstanding the criticisms of humanistic psychology, it does set the stage for emergent themes in critical humanism. In many ways, the criticisms of humanism demonstrate the limitations of psychology in the 1950s. With the emerging dominance of the positioning of psychology as a physical rather than a social science aligned with the humanities (see Chapter 2), it is remarkable that humanism not only survived, but flourished in the 1960s and 1970s.

Positive psychology

We now enter a discussion of positive psychology, having covered the basic tenets of humanistic psychology and the associated limitations of this approach. These limitations remain largely relevant to the newer movement in positive psychology (Becker & Marecek, 2008; Christopher, Richardson & Slife, 2008). Positive psychology can be read as the latest manifestation of humanistic psychology, rather than a radically new step in the discipline of psychology (Linley & Joseph, 2004; Robbins, 2008). We support the focus on positive aspects of life and people's strengths that are central to both approaches. Therefore, it is useful to spend some time on positive psychology before outlining our own orientation towards critical humanism (Box 10.10).

Positive psychology focuses on positive dimensions of human experience and action, including how people make a life that

---

BOX 10.10   Main points so far

The main points we want to communicate at this stage in the chapter are:

1. Humanistic psychology has a long history shaped by the broader discipline and the desire of many psychologists to challenge the dominance of behaviourism.
2. Although traditional humanistic psychology does consider individuals, it does not begin and end with individuals. The self-actualized individual is one with a high sense of social connectedness and responsibility.
3. More recently, positive psychology has emerged out of clinical psychology in an attempt to reimagine humanistic psychology. Positive psychology is not really taking the discipline in a radical new direction.

encompasses hope, courage, future expectations, spirituality, responsibility, optimism, creativity, talent and ability, civic engagement. What is offered is a "vision of the good life" based on empirical evidence (Seligman & Csikszentmihalyi, 2000, p. 5). It is proposed that psychology has more to offer than simply providing insights into individual problems, crises and how people survive in the face of adversity. The discipline can also be extended to produce knowledge of life in more benign conditions and of how people can be supported in reaching their potential. Seligman and Csikszentmihalyi (2000) assert that positive psychology should extend beyond an understanding of how people cope with adversity, to considering the everyday situations that foster growth and potential. These authors set out a number of individual and group levels that encompass different institutional settings:

The field of positive psychology at the subjective level is about valued subjective experience: well-being, contentment, and satisfaction (in the past); hope and optimism (for the future); and flow and happiness (in the present). At the individual level, it is about positive individual traits: the capacity for love and vocation, courage, interpersonal skill, aesthetic sensibility, perseverance, forgiveness, originality, future mindedness, spirituality, high talent, and wisdom. At the group level, it is about the civic virtues and the institutions that move individuals toward better citizenship: responsibility, nurturance, altruism, civility, moderation, tolerance, and work ethic. (Seligman & Csikszentmihalyi, 2000, p. 5)

Core goals of positive psychology are to identity and measure universal positive traits across cultures, promote positive experiences and cultivate more positive communities and institutions that are equipped to promote human growth and happiness (Seligman, 1998a, 1998b). Topics explored by Martin Seligman, one of the core proponents of positive psychology, and colleagues range from personal strengths (Peterson & Seligman, 2004), to learning to be optimistic (Seligman, 1998a), fulfilment and happiness (Seligman, 2002), well-being (Diener & Seligman, 2004) and positive organizations that foster human growth (Peterson & Seligman, 2003).

Review exercise

The public in many countries have an appetite for positive psychology. Books, DVDs and websites are full of self-help information. Examples include motivational materials and advice on how to develop one's self-confidence, self-coaching, emotional healing, alleviating worry, transforming one's life, learning to love oneself – much of which is focused on the individual. Next time you are in the local mall, take a visit to the book store to confirm the range of self-help advice on offer. The existence of this material may remind you of the point made in Chapter 3 regarding how psychological knowledge not only documents events in everyday life, but is circulated back into public dialogue. You may also want to consider the contexts within which these individual-oriented qualities and processes are produced.

Leading positive psychologists have differentiated their approach from humanistic psychology by proposing that the latter is unscientific and narcissistic. The main criticism of humanistic psychology forwarded by Seligman and Csikszentmihalyi (2000) is that humanistic psychology is unscientific in that it relies overly on qualitative, rather than quantitative, methods. However, Friedman (2008) noted that it is difficult to maintain a strict methodological distinction between humanistic and positive psychology because qualitative and quantitative methods are used in both traditions.

In a reply to Seligman and Csikszentmihalyi (2000), Bohart and Greening (2001) correct some factual errors regarding the limitations of humanistic psychology proposed by Seligman and Csikszentmihalyi in an attempt to establish distinctions between humanistic and positive psychologies. Emerging from this process was the importance positive psychologists placed on 'scientific' methods as opposed to more qualitative and interpretive approaches, which were more in keeping with humanistic psychology. This exchange reproduced the tension in the discipline noted in Chapters 1 and 2 between versions of psychology as a physical and a social science. In the process, Bohart and Greening reiterate elements of humanistic psychology, including the focus on cultivating positive social interactions between groups, which are important for social psychology (cf. Prilleltensky, 1992), and the work of critical humanists. Bohart and Greening note the narrow reading of humanistic psychology presented by Seligman and Csikszentmihalyi (2000):

Neither the theory or practice of humanistic psychology is narrowly focused on the narcissistic self or on individual fulfillment. A careful reading of Carl Rogers and Abraham Maslow would find that their conceptions of self-actualization include responsibility toward others (Maslow's list of actualized people, presented as exemplars of his theory, were mostly people with a heightened sense of social responsibility). (Bohart & Greening, 2001, p. 81)

Humanistic psychologists have worked on problems such as the reduction of violence and conflict and have promoted social justice for decades. Humanistic psychology values alternative cultural understandings and attempts to engage in dialogue through which equity can be fostered. In the same issue of *American Psychologist*, Shapiro (2001) notes that positive psychology is grounded in the humanistic tradition, but has neglected the breadth of research and action conducted by humanists and the broader tradition dating back to antiquity and evident in the long-standing philosophies of humanism, Buddhism, Christianity and Islam.

Even psychologists sympathetic to the orientation of positive psychology have raised various criticisms of the approach, including the focus on individuals from a Western and culturally specific vantage point, the overreliance on methods modelled on the physical sciences and the focus on flourishing elites to the detriment of people living in adversity (Becker & Marecek, 2008; Christopher, Richardson & Slife, 2008; Christopher & Hickinbottom, 2008). Christopher, Richardson and Slife (2008) propose that more work needs to be done on what exactly the 'good life' comprises for people in different cultural contexts. They highlight the culturally located nature of constructs such as happiness and propose that more work needs to be done from a range of cultural perspectives, rather than assuming the universality of human experiences of happiness and the good life (Becker & Marecek, 2008). This line of criticism is extended by Christopher and Hickinbottom (2008), who argue that positive psychology needs to account for its own cultural locatedness and engage with indigenous and cultural perspectives to reflect different contexts (see Chapter 5). This is particularly important because positive psychology is centrally about enhancing the development of the self (Christopher & Hickinbottom, 2008). Christopher and Campbell (2008) have noted that positive psychology requires a more dialogical and socially embedded understanding of the self than that of the Cartesian individual (see Chapter 4) currently informing the approach. This is crucial because if the self lies within the individual, then happiness and growth also lie inside the person and well-being is marked by autonomy and self-expressiveness (Becker & Marecek, 2008; Christopher & Hickinbottom, 2008). Throughout this book we have been arguing that the self extends out into the world, is relational and interconnected. Consequently, growth, self-development and being a good healthy person involve other people in a profound way, and are manifest in daily practices (including pro-social behaviour), objects (from which we derive pleasure) and places (which can be developed to foster community and growth).

Moreover, unlike mainstream positive psychology, many cultural and moral traditions, both non-Western and Western (e.g., Buddhism, Hinduism, communitarian social thought, transpersonal psychology), define their sense of identity in terms of belonging to wider communal and/or spiritual realities. (Christopher, Richardson & Slife, 2008, p. 557)

It is evident from our discussion of pro-social behaviour that a person's satisfaction with life, growth and happiness can come from helping others, and not just himself or herself (Christopher & Hickinbottom, 2008).

Overall, the similarities in focus between humanistic and positive psychologies that have evolved in the North American context appear to outweigh the differences (Linley & Joseph, 2004). What we see in contemporary debates between proponents of each approach is a feud between kinsfolk. Both humanistic and positive psychologies are part of the same essential trajectory in the discipline that focuses on human potential, what is good about life and how we can shape institutions and everyday contexts so as to maximize the potential for people to flourish (Robbins, 2008). One gets a sense from the positive psychology movement, and the focus on people who are doing well in society, that there is a risk of reproducing the inverse care law (Box 10.11). Social psychologists also need to consider how social structures can be changed in order to ensure equality of opportunity for all people to experience positive lives and happiness. As we noted in Chapter 9, our search for justice should include moral inclusion through the enactment of procedural fairness.

BOX 10.11   Inverse care law

The term 'inverse care law' was coined in 1971 by Julian Tudor Hart (1971), a UK physician. According to this law, the availability of medical care varies inversely with the actual needs of particular population groups. People of higher socioeconomic status (SES), who tend to be healthier, tend to consume more resources and attention from the medical profession. Conversely, people of lower SES, who tend to be sicker and die earlier, consume fewer resources and attract less attention from the medical profession. The original article was published in the *Lancet* and can be found at http://www.sochealth.co.uk/history/inversecare.htm.

We are not suggesting that positive psychologists should not conduct studies of people who are doing well and realizing their potential. This is a useful focus, but one that should not come at the expense of shifting attention or resources away from people who are less fortunate and in more need of our attention.

Critical humanism

Critical humanism draws insights from currents from within both humanistic and positive psychology. These currents are engaged in social critique and action at collective as well as personal levels. As noted by Wertz (1998), some variants of humanistic psychology have engaged in emancipatory politics or the critique of prevailing social trends, and have engaged proactively in the development of institutional practices and policies that support human dignity, growth, mutual understanding and social development. Critical humanism involves moderating the emphasis placed on personal choice and action by positive psychologists with consideration of the influence of life chances and resources for supporting such action. Some time ago, Prilleltensky (1992) noted, "An improved understanding of the long-term effects of noxious psychological environments on the individual will help humanistic psychologists realize the need to invest considerable efforts at social change" (p. 322). Growing up and living with adversity can wound people both emotionally and physically. It hurts, and can require considerable effort, support, and capacity for people to grow and enable growth in others. A more adequate positively oriented psychology should attend to sociopolitical and economic contexts that foster or undermine human potential and health (see Chapters 6 and 8) and to how injustices (Chapter 9) can be addressed (Becker & Marecek, 2008). Central to critical humanism is the concept of resilience outlined in the following sections. For now, let us consider critical humanism by drawing on the work of Paulo Freire.

Contemporary work in social psychology (and liberation social and community psychology) in the area of community development is informed by Freire's (1970/1993) work on critical consciousness-raising and community-based action research approaches to social transformation (Carlson, Engebretson & Chamberlain, 2006). Working from the broader humanist perspective in philosophy, Freire focused on fostering the autonomy, creativity, freedom and choices available to illiterate peasants living under repressive regimes in Brazil and other Latin American countries. Freire developed an approach to education that conceptualized teachers and learners as co-constructors of knowledge. He shifted power relations in education from a didactic approach to a conversational approach involving the mutual exploration of topics. This egalitarian orientation saw insights and knowledge as the product of joint introspection and exploration fostered through dialogue with the people being studied (Hodgetts, Chamberlain & Groot, in press). This reflects the humanistic belief in participants' own experiences and ability to grow and act autonomously.

Becker and Marecek (2008) point to the work of Paulo Freire as illustrating how the growth of subordinate groups can be fostered and lead to the development of strengths, dignity and collective action. Knowledge of one's oppression can lead to pro-active and collective coping with adversity and social transformation (Chapter 1). Freire (1970/1993) outlined three levels of understanding and engagement with reality that members of marginalized groups can be guided through to such ends. At the *magical-conforming* level people are restrained by feelings of inferiority and helplessness. They see the status quo as natural and therefore do not question or challenge it. Their adaptation to adversity allows them to survive, but their passivity contributes to continued oppression. At the *naïve-reforming* level, people focus on the corrupt nature of the status quo. However, instead of challenging the status quo and injustice, they engage in in-fighting and blaming peers for the situations in which they find themselves. The *critical-action* level involves people reflecting on the ways in which values and assumptions shape their understandings of their situations and actions. People become aware of their own role in accepting or challenging the status quo. At this level, collective action is more likely and civic engagement can occur. In helping illiterate peasants acquire sociopolitical literacy and move through these levels of consciousness, Freire attended to their daily practices as a site for the reproduction of social injustices. He used techniques such as drawing exercises to link such practices and emotional experiences to broader processes of oppression and to encourage reflection and dialogue. Through these techniques, alternative understandings were cultivated as a basis for enhancing capacity to change and improve the world. Freire emphasized that such social change requires a combination of insights from actual experiences and daily life along with more abstract academic understandings of the social processes shaping such lives.

Freire's approach to social transformation has informed the work of a range of areas of psychology. For example, liberation social psychology emphasizes a commitment to an ethics of compassion and the development of knowledge in partnership with communities aimed at transforming oppressive social realities (Martín-Baró, 1994; Montero, 2007; Montero & Sonn, 2009). Freire's focus on participatory knowledge production and conscientization has informed the work of change-oriented researchers who used methods such as photovoice (Box 10.12) (Hodgetts, Chamberlain & Groot, in press).

Critical humanism focuses on issues of social cohesion, inclusion, support and action. It supports human beings and communities and their self-worth because all are thought to have dignity and rights and to be deserving of respect and equity. Critical humanists work

BOX 10.12 Interesting study

Wang and Burris (1994), for example, used Freire's work in developing the photovoice methodology to assess the needs and strengths of rural Chinese women. This research drew upon auto-photography, where people take photographs of their lives and participate in follow-up photo-elicitation interviews and workshops to discuss their photographs. Photographs, drawings and stories were elicited from the women as a way of identifying local resources and raising community concerns, identifying underlying influences and working through possible courses of action based on the strengths of the group to address these concerns. Photovoice enhanced participant reflexivity and contributed to participants' knowledge of, and efforts to enhance, their own lives. Photo-elicitation interviews based upon photographs allowed participants to show as well as to tell the researchers about their experiences of life. The approach provides opportunities for participants to have more substantially engaged interactions with researchers that contribute to revealing deeper and richer information about lives than often comes from traditional one-off semi-structured interviews. This work has a long tradition in humanistic psychology, where the arts are used as a medium for encouraging dialogue, reflection and conflict resolution (Estrella & Forinash, 2007). In many respects, such work is about drawing out local potential and developing strengths in local settings in order to effect change at a broader societal level.

BOX 10.13 Dignity

Foundational to critical humanism is the concept of dignity. Jacobson (2007) provides a useful review of the complex concept of dignity, distinguishing human dignity and social dignity. This distinction is crucial in distinguishing positive psychologies from the critical humanistic approach advocated in this chapter. Jacobson notes that for Immanuel Kant dignity was an element of people as sentient beings based in our capacity for moral freedom and rationality. Bestowing dignity on a person is to bestow rights and obligations, often as a citizen. This links directly to the idea of moral inclusion discussed in Chapter 9. If people are positioned outside the scope of justice it allows others to deny them rights, obligations, citizenship and thereby dignity. As we saw, the consequences can be catastrophic.

Human dignity follows Kant and advocates the inalienable valuing of people by virtue of their humanity and is manifest in persons and groups as moral agents. It is not contingent of contextual factors because "all human beings are equal and thus as individuals should be treated with certain minimum levels of decency and respect" (Jacobson, 2007, p. 294). This provides a basis for notions of social justice and procedural fairness as outlined in Chapter 9.

Social dignity stems from the recognition that human dignity is contingent and contextually situated. We can earn, give and experience social dignity in different settings. Social dignity has two intertwined aspects. First, dignity-of-self is a form of self-confidence or decorum that a person can hold as an autonomous being. One can be a dignified person. This approach is linked to Cooley's (1902) looking-glass self in that what it means to be dignified is socially constructed through interactions with others and how we see others perceiving us and our actions. This raises the second aspect of social dignity. Dignity-in-relation is a process through which we reflect value towards others through our actions and language at particular times and in particular places. This might be when we pay respect to a person holding a particular rank or status such as a judge or doctor. It must be earned through good deeds, achievements and service to others. Just as social dignity can be earned through good deeds it can be violated and lost through antisocial acts. Through discrimination and the denial of human rights, dignity can be taken from people. Those acting in a discriminatory manner are also undermining their own dignity.

to ensure that the dignity (Box 10.13) of others is respected and that barriers to people living a dignified existence are removed. They also focus on issues and are concerned with generative psychology (Moghaddam, 1987), a psychology that is not only about describing and documenting social life, but also about social transformation (Chapter 1). A key aim of this orientation and of our book as a whole is to assist people and communities to become more resilient.

Resilience in the face of adversity

Resilience is a multidimensional and complex concept that can manifest differently for different people as they respond to challenging situations (Prince, 2008). At its base, resilience is about how people not only survive, but can live rewarding lives despite facing adversity. A central question for work on resilience is what it is that allows some people to succumb to adversity or trauma while others survive and may even thrive. A key point emerging from this work is how people access resources to support their own growth and the growth of other people around them. Therefore, to study resilience psychologists look at what is available and how people draw on constellations of resources to sustain themselves and grow. Psychologists can also work with people to look for ways to enhance their resilience (Box 10.14). This includes findings ways to identity resources, to cultivate capacities, and to remove barriers to growth. Resilience has been referred to as 'bounce-backability' or, as Fuller, McGraw and Goodyear (1999) saw it, the ability to bungee jump through life.

BOX 10.14   Supplies for resilience

Caplan (1964) discussed protective factors that mediate stress (Chapter 8). He referred to these as types of supplies that people have available to them. Physical supplies include food and shelter. Psychosocial supplies refer to interpersonal networks of support. Sociocultural supplies relate to culture and social structures. Those with greater supplies generally are better able to deal with adversity.

The importance of resilience as a factor in enabling people to survive and adapt to adverse circumstances is a mainstay of social psychology (Chapter 2). Researchers have highlighted various protective factors that buffer people against corrosive environments such as poverty (Bonanno, 2005). Resilience can fluctuate over the life course and across contexts, such as when a person is homeless or housed (Williams, Lindsey, Kurtz & Jarvis, 2001). Thus, resilience is not a fixed attribute solely located within, and determined by, an individual. It comprises relational processes that can either enable or undermine the ability of people to respond and adapt to risks as they are confronted by these in the course of their lives. Resilience includes receiving assistance and giving it to others. It includes various combinations of tenacity, self-sufficiency, resourcefulness, locus of control, problem-solving, humour, persistence, mentoring, accepting assistance from others, pride and cooperation (Bonanno, 2005). The psychological foundations for resilience include self-belief, acceptance and a sense of belonging (Prince, 2008). At a material and activity level, resilience involves people having strategies for accessing resources, including food and shelter, and being embedded in active social networks from which assistance can be gained from others (Box 10.15).

BOX 10.15   Resilience

In researching children who thrive in adversity and exhibit resilience, psychologists have identified a cluster of interrelated elements, including personal characteristics and resources in the environment (Cicchetti & Garmezy, 1993; Reed-Victor & Stronge, 2002). Personal factors include:

- *Extraversion*: willingness to seek assistance and ability to make friends
- *Agreeability*: helpful and cooperative towards others
- *Emotional stability*: confident, with a positive self-image
- *Conscientiousness*: persistent and goal oriented
- *Experiential*: open to learning and engages actively in problem-solving

These personal factors are not necessarily individualistic in that they rely on interactions and relationships with other people. For example, young people often learn well together when supporting each other.

Broadening the focus, Reed-Victor and Stronge (2002) identify more overtly ecological factors crucial for individuals. These include:

- *Opportunities*: having avenues for developing interests and talents, and the existence of support services
- *Interpersonal supports*: caring relationships with peers and adults providing recognition of achievements and encouragement
- *Structure environment*: encompassing consistent and shared values, clear and appropriate expectations, mentoring in decision-making, goal setting, and completing tasks

These ecological factors stem from family, school and community sources of nurturing and care. They bestow social dignity on a child and allow the child to develop a dignified life. Children from such supportive environments can grow into positive adults.

Clinical psychologists tend to look at resilience as a personal capacity to overcome adversity. Social psychologists need to add the social dimensions of having access to resources and relationships that not only support us in surviving, but also make growth possible (Box 10.16). For social psychologists, resilience is fundamentally relational and is often negotiated in interactions between people, rather than simply being the property of any one person. We can share and, in the process, grow resilience. Sharing strengths with others does not reduce them in ourselves. Resilience is something that we can give away and still retain, because giving it away increases the likelihood that others will be there to support us. Social psychologists need to look at people's daily practices and survival strategies in order to see them being resilient. If we define resilience too tightly as the property of a person we might miss the relational dimensions that are essential to people's efforts to help one another (Unger, 2008).

From a study of young people from around the world, Unger (2008) proposed that resilience involves a process of juggling several

BOX 10.16   Interesting study

Kidd and Davidson (2007) worked with homeless youth in New York and Toronto to document their accounts of survival and resilience as linked to the self, others and daily practices. In the process, these authors point to the wide range of lives and survival strategies (practices) among homeless youth. This diversity is important. 'The homeless' are not a homogeneous group in terms of origins, self-identification, affiliations with street culture, daily practice or aspirations. Resilience requires each person to learn to survive and, for some, to cooperate and live with other 'streeties'. In order to make their own place on the street, homeless people must adapt to societal meaning systems and attempts by officials to regulate homeless bodies in public places. Resilience also involves adapting one's strategies in response to events such as the loss of a friend or being moved along from a favoured begging spot by police.

balls, all of which rely on or are related to one another. Many of these balls resemble the 'external factors' often associated with psychological research and include identity, positive relationships, agency or some power and control over one's life, social justice or being treated fairly, access to basic material resources such as education, cultural adherence and cohesion in a humanistic sense, involving spirituality. Figure 10.1 provides a diagrammatic representation of a person juggling social and personal elements of resilience.

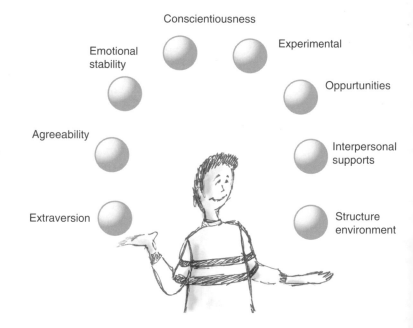

Figure 10.1. Resilience as an act of juggling multiple dimensions

Review exercise

- Consider some of the things you do that might enhance your own resilience.
- Now think about how your actions might enhance the resilience of others.

The concept of resilience is useful in focusing research and interventions towards personal strengths. Both humanistic and positive psychology tend to focus on individual-level resilience and flourishing (cf. Robbins, 2008; Fuller, McGraw & Goodyear, 1999). Collective aspects of resilience also need consideration (Bonanno, 2005; Sonn & Fisher, 1998). After all, "Resilience is the dynamic process of adaption despite adversity" (Reed-Victor & Stronge, 2002, p. 160). It involves personal strength and contextual elements such as supportive others and life chances – phenomena often labelled as 'protective factors', which are generally associated with the environment outside the individual. Gunnestad (2006) provided a grouping of protective factors that includes networks of support, individual abilities and skills, and meanings, values and faith, which he views as existential support.

Throughout this book we have promoted a fundamentally social notion of the self. The conceptualization of the interconnected self leads us to perceive what are often treated as individual protective factors as fundamentally relational. These factors are part of a person, as are the relationships and interactions in that person's cobweb self (Chapter 5). This orientation towards resilience as an interpersonal and collective resource is central to the concepts of dialogue and socialization emphasized in Chapters 2 and 5. As with the notions of the looking-glass self, dialogical selves and the interconnected self, who people are is a reflection of whom they interact with. Protective factors shape the self over time and can build up our resilience. If mentored and supported by another homeless person (e.g. Tom from the scenario) a homeless individual (e.g. Neville) can be socialized into street life and can incorporate the lessons and strategies of other homeless people into his or her very being. People can draw experiences and resources into themselves. From this perspective, we can see community resilience in individuals. In short, resilience encompasses the range of factors and processes in people, communities and settings that can buffer people against risks such as poverty, discrimination and homelessness and allow them to survive in the face of adversity.

Community resilience

Many people develop strengths, skills and resources through their integration into communities. As noted in Chapter 6, it is necessary to research resilience at a communal level, as people exist somewhere, and often in concert with the aspirations and efforts of others. Although the literature on individual resilience has burgeoned, community resilience is still relatively poorly conceptualized. One area where there has been some excellent work is in communities experiencing natural disasters, unemployment and environmental planning (Norris, Stevens, Pfefferbaum, Wyche & Pfefferbaum, 2008; Pooley, Cohen & O'Connor, 2006). Communities can exist under continued or cyclical threat of natural disaster, such as those in cyclone or hurricane zones. Pooley and colleagues (2006) note that community resilience is more than simply the capacity to bounce back. Resilient communities accept and embrace change as an opportunity for positive growth. Some factors that contribute to the capacity to grow are assets and skills, indicators of community sustainability such as the harmonization of people and nature and community competence (Pooley, Breen, Pike, Cohen & Drew, 2007). Norris and colleagues (2008) offered a similar view, defining resilience as *"a process linking a set of adaptative capacities to a positive trajectory of functioning and adaptation after a disturbance"* (pp. 130–131, italics in original). These authors propose that communities must have economic resources to attend to areas of need, community members must be meaningfully engaged and have access to forms of social capital, community members must have access to information and communication networks, and communities must be competent in the sense that they have the capacity for collective action and decision-making.

Work in psychology on community resilience can be traced back to ideas of hardiness (Jahoda, Lazarsfeld & Zeisel, 1933/1972) and community competence (Cottrell, 1976; Iscoe, 1974). Competent communities (Box 10.17), much like resilient individuals, have the aptitude and resourcefulness to cope positively with adversity (Sonn & Fisher, 1998). Competent communities have many attributes that link individual and collective capacities. The interconnectedness of people and social structures has been emphasized throughout the book and is probably familiar to you now as a central thesis in our conceptualization of the dialogical and place-based identities (see Chapters 3, 5 and 6). Resilient communities provide opportunities for group members to experience stability, security, belongingness and psychological connectedness (Sonn & Fisher, 1998). Community resilience has also been linked to the idea of vital communities. Vital communities are those in which there is collaboration, a sense of collective efficacy (empowerment or liberation), a sense of belonging and a recognition that events impact not only the individual, but also the collective (or community). Interestingly, vital communities also have internal governance structures, both formal and informal, that enable them to mobilize to counter external threats. This is an expression of

BOX 10.17   Competent communities

From the work of Cottrell (1976) and Iscoe (1974) it can be proposed that competent communities have many of the following elements:

- *Commitment:* community members value the community as something worth sustaining and enhancing.
- *Awareness:* community members are aware of their own interests and how these interests relate to wider community interests.
- *Articulateness:* community members are able to express their views.
- *Communication skills:* community members are able to listen to the views of others.
- *Conflict:* community members have the ability to manage conflict and work positively to maintain relationships.
- *Participation:* community members actively engage in community affairs and work towards meeting the community's goals.
- *Ability to manage relations with society at large:* community members are able to manage their relationships with the wider society and manage threats posed by the wider system.
- *Mechanisms to facilitate interaction and decision-making:* the community has developed mechanisms to effectively manage the decision-making process.

community as collective political power advocated by many indigenous psychologists (see Chapter 5). This idea of collective efficacy is central to resilience.

Ethnic, and other social minority, communities are often represented as lacking in competence and not having much in the way of resilience (Chapters 5, 7 and 11). Instead, they are described as disorganized, damaged and unable to offer sufficient social and psychological resources for members to cope with adversity. Sonn and Fisher (1998) contest that the cultural yardstick used to measure efficacy and functionality of adaptations to social contexts by minority communities is usually based on the cultural values and norms of the (white) middle class. Although some responses may take on the appearance of being negative or self-destructive (e.g. substance misuse), the resilient and resourceful ways in which these groups respond should not be overlooked. Community membership as an essential determinant of well-being can act as an antidote to alienation and psychosocial stressors (Chapter 8): Sonn and Fisher (1998) note that groups facing social marginalization and external pressures do not simply give in to oppressive systems. These groups often develop alternative social spaces and ways to resist oppression. In the process they can build a sense of community.

Rather than simply approaching marginalized groups as victims of oppression and social inequalities, we might consider strategies through which groups work to construct alternative settings, meanings and ways of being (cf. Mattis et al., 2009). This has been construed as a positive direction, taking a strengths-based approach as opposed to the more traditional deficit-focused position. These settings can be everyday settings such as social, sports, collectors and performing arts clubs (see Chapter 7 for the role of support and other support settings in the migrant relocation and settlement experience). As is discussed in Chapter 6, having healthy environments to be in and having access to public spaces is essential to psychological, social and community well-being (Box 10.18).

In brief, resilience cannot be separated from other concepts such as dignity, social justice and social transformation (Prilleltensky & Prilleltensky, 2005). This assertion is in accord with our notion of critical humanism. What we require is a way of thinking about community resilience and the benefits for individual and groups. Kimhi and Shamai (2004) propose that work on community resilience can be placed into three main streams. The first focuses on resistance to adversity and how communities respond to and absorb adversity. The second focuses on the ability of communities to recover from adversity and the speed at which recovery is achieved. The third explores creativity in the community, which allows the group not only to recover but also to grow and improve people's lives. Central to all these streams is a focus on positive responses to adversity and the role of social psychological (mutual support, leadership, culture) and material (economic support and institutions) factors in how communities overcome adversity (Box 10.19).

BOX 10.18   Importance of community resilience

Kimhi and Shamai (2004) investigated the influence of perceptions of community resilience among 741 adults affected by the Israeli withdrawal from Lebanon. Of the four groups of respondents, three lived close to the Lebanon–Israel boarder and were directly exposed to the terror of the war. The final group functioned as a control group. This group was made up of people from central Israel not directly exposed to the conflict. Questionnaires administered directly following the Israeli withdrawal measured stress effects, community resilience and life satisfaction. Over time the war impacted those living in the vicinity by diminishing their perceptions of community resilience. Yet the authors also found that community resilience served as a partial mediator between living with a constant threat, life satisfaction and stress. Such findings support the view that (perhaps unsurprisingly) a sense of community resilience is important in helping groups cope with adversity created by war and terror.

BOX 10.19   The dark side of community resilience, vitality and competence

Audrey Armour is a Canadian authority on social impact assessment (the social consequences of planned community change). Some years ago she presented a public lecture that highlighted some differences between social and physical scientists in their approach to working with vital, competent or resilient communities. As part of her work, Armour was involved with determining the site of waste facilities (rubbish dumps). Needless to say, there is a great deal of community resistance to placing such facilities, or LULUs (locally unwanted land uses), in their backyard, otherwise known as NIMBYism (not-in-my-back-yard). As part of the process, Armour identified several alternative sites for the dump then assessed each community to determine how well it might cope with the facility. Some communities were resilient or vital, and some were devitalized and lacking resilience. Clearly the resilient and vital communities had a greater capacity to cope with the waste facility, but they also had the collective political power to resist the proposition to place the facility in their locale. The devitalized communities clearly had less capacity to advocate on their own behalf, and therefore there was likely to be less conflict if the decision was made to place the facility in such a community. Armour asked the audience, "Where would you place the facility?"

■ How would you (the reader) answer this question of where the facility should be placed – in the resilient or less resilient communities?

You should not be surprised that physical scientists (engineers, construction designers etc.) all voted for a quiet life and supported locating the facility in a devitalized community. The social scientists, on the other hand, wanted the facility placed in a vital community.

Chapter summary

Although being attentive to the problems people face is crucial, social psychologists also need to consider the strengths and resilience of the people with whom we work. This latter focus opens up a space for social psychologists to consider individual- and collective-oriented responses to adversity situated in everyday life. With this focus comes attention to the ways in which adversity can undermine this capacity and the need to work towards both personal and social transformation in unison. In the process, we can turn back to the tradition of humanistic psychology that has influenced the growth of community and more recently positive psychology. These traditions bring practices of everyday life such as giving, helping and volunteering to the fore. They enable us to explore what it means to be human and to contribute in a positive way to society.

Social psychologists are increasingly attentive to the pro-social actions of individuals and groups, which include sharing and volunteering, and which people often take for granted, noticing only when they are needed and absent. Such actions can be seen as mechanisms through which we can make each other more resilient and able to thrive in a range of settings. We are used to valuing the efforts of exceptional human beings such as Muhammad, Mother Theresa, Martin Luther King and Jesus. However, we should not lose sight of the fact that helping behaviour is foundational to most societies and more prevalent then we might initially think. It is particularly important not to forget positive actions when studying psychology and when being confronted with the horrors of violence and prejudice. The motives for human action, such as whether helping behaviour is at its core either fully selfish or altruistic, can be endlessly debated. We take the view that everyday acts of helping, which may seem unremarkable, are essential for individual and community health, well-being and growth. The reproduction and growth of human societies depend on this. What is clear is that such actions are foundational to the reproduction and growth of humane societies based on norms of equity, fairness, the obligation to help, social justice and reciprocity. Such societies are more resilient and the citizens suffer less from illness and live longer lives on average than societies where pro-social behaviour has been displaced by antisocial and selfish behaviour. What is crucial here is the idea that we can actually foster pro-social behaviour through simple acts of kindness, which add up to a mode that promotes social support and capital. Societies can change for the better.

Humanistic traditions in psychology value the dignity of all people and emphasize the need to explore the experiences and understandings within their everyday social contexts. What is particularly interesting is the emphasis placed on something intangible yet distinctly human and good about all people. As we noted in Chapter 2, not everything that counts can be counted or measured. An emphasis on people being more than their environment allows social psychologists to avoid the reductionism of behaviourism and to focus on human potential and growth. Positive psychology has picked up on the emphasis on people's capabilities and potential, and it is developing yet another variant of psychology based on this theme. Clearly a balanced social psychology needs to engage with such traditions and look, along with their proponents, beyond social problems to explore human creativity and exceptional functioning. The good life is worth taking notice of. However, this should not detract from the importance of adversity as a restraining reality for many citizens today. Violence and conflict still plague our world and can undermine or efforts to grow and thrive and act in a humane manner towards others. Social psychologists continue to combine a focus on the positive with concerns regarding the negative aspects of daily life.

In this chapter, we have noted that resilience is a complex social psychological phenomenon that takes on a different shape for different people and communities. Despite requiring recognition of the diversity of communities, the concept of resilience allows psychologists to investigate both adversity and human potential at the same time. Resilience can be explored at the level of the individual, but only in the context of the community and social relations. This is because resilience is inherently relational, and a person's ability to thrive and grow is generally enmeshed in the lives and actions of other people. It is enacted and grown through problem-solving, mentoring, help, giving and cooperation. Even hardiness, and a belief in one's abilities, needs reaffirmation from others from time to time. It is through social interactions that people can form communities and grow or undermine each other's resilience. Supportive communities in which we can gain a sense of place and belonging make it much easier for people to be resilient. The shared experiences, the meanings of those experiences and appreciations of reality contribute to a sense of solidarity and connectedness. We can come to understand resilience better through the dialogical process we have advocated throughout this book. Just as people in a community come to understand and act in the world through dialogue and the exploration of the interconnected self, we as social psychologists are also interconnected. Our pursuit of understanding complex ideas such as resilience must become part of the community dialogue about the concept. As we saw in Chapter 5, it is important to understand that not only are people in community, but community is in people.

In brief, although humanistic traditions in psychology have much to offer social psychology, these must be tempered by the need to maintain a focus beyond the individual and to consider social structures that can prevent some people from reaching their potential. This is where the importance of developing a critical humanism comes in. Critical humanism is an orientation that allows us to tie this positive strengths-based focus to the reality of oppression and hardship faced by many people in society today. Critical humanism builds upon elements of humanistic and positive psychologies that respond to the need for collective action to ensure the development of environments that serve the needs of all people in an equitable and humane manner. The core of critical humanism is guided by the notion that all people have dignity and should be treated in a socially just manner. What are promoted are efforts to build social inclusion and support.

Review exercise

- What is meant by self-actualization?
- Can you think of two instances of altruism?
- What are five key elements of resilience?
- What is the relationship between culture and resilience?

11 Media and daily practice

Core questions to consider while reading this chapter

- Why should social psychologists study the media?
- In what ways do psychologists work with the media?
- Do violent media games cause violence in society?
- Why is it useful to consider media *influences* rather than media *effects*?
- Can civic participation be enhanced through media use?
- What can children's bedrooms tell us about media use in everyday life?
- How are media involved in identity construction?

Chapter scenario

Like many first-world families, the Grays' house contains a range of media, from the radio in the garage, favoured haunt for grandpa Tom, to the big screen television used by grandma to watch cartoons with five-year-old Nathan, to the Internet computers in the rooms of sixteen-year-old Sally and fifteen-year-old Richard. The newspaper is delivered daily, and William and Michelle (the parents) have monthly subscriptions to *House and Garden* and *Time Magazine*. On this particular evening, the local football team is playing at the stadium. Grandpa has taken Sally to the game. The rest of the family watches the telecast. The two teams have a long-standing rivalry, and some fans have been prone to violence. The home team is ahead by one goal when a fight breaks out between groups of fans in the southern stand. The violence quickly spreads when police attempt to intervene. The crowd turns on the officers, and in the ensuing clash at least a dozen people are seriously injured. Family members at home are following the events with horror via the television broadcast. They are concerned for the safety of Grandpa and Sally. The coverage is focusing on the southern stand, and they cannot see the northern stand where their family members were sitting. Just when they are getting really worried, the telephone rings. It is Sally calling on her mobile to say that they are being ushered out of the stand by officials as the violence spreads. The noise is overwhelming, and Sally says, "I'll call back once we are out of the ground." Richard suggests that they log on to the stand's website and follow the family members' progress via a webcam. After some switching between cameras, they are able to track the progress of Grandpa and Sally out of the ground and to safety. In the ensuing days, news media reconstruct the events of the night, drawing on news footage and snippets from portable recording devices, including digital recorders and mobile phones. The family continues to make sense of the events, comparing the first-hand experiences of those at the game with the mediated experiences of other family members, and those being worked through further via news reports.

Violence at public events is all too common and is regularly brought into our homes via media reports. The scenario raises issues central to this chapter regarding the pervasiveness of a range of media in everyday settings, and how people can keep up with events or in touch at a distance using media devices. As a result, distinctions between what is happening out there (at the sports arena) and in here (our homes) are being redrawn (Silverstone, 2007). Combined, media technologies can be used to create an information-rich environment, or media nexus, from within which people can engage with events outside the domestic dwelling. Media objects and the worlds they bring into our home are an integral part of daily life. They enable the Grays to keep tabs on the events at the stadium, thus extending tangible links between family members out from the domestic dwelling and across to the stadium and beyond into the media nexus. Psychologists explore aspects of the nexus created across various media forms as a source of shared experience that people all use to understand the world and our place in it.

In the living room of your home there are likely comfortable chairs, family memorabilia and a range of media technologies from a telephone, radio, books and magazines to a television, DVD player/digital recorder, iPod and perhaps a networked computer. These devices are mobile and can be moved or relocated around the house, shifting from communal to more personal devices as family members seek privacy in media consumption or respond to different tastes in film, musical or gaming content. Such practices open up a range of issues that need to be explored in this chapter, regarding human relations, identity, time and space.

The presence of media devices in daily life has invoked concerns regarding the possible negative effects of exposure to media violence and broader issues around reduced civic participation, and positively focused issues regarding the use of media to build and maintain social ties. Many social psychologists have been preoccupied with issues of measuring negative, and sometimes pro-social, media effects (Comstock & Scharrer, 2005; Doyle, 2004; Giles, 2003). Others have worked to generate understandings of people's use of media in everyday life (Chamberlain & Hodgetts, 2008; Livingstone, 2007a, 2007b). This reveals a tension in the discipline around what the media does to individuals and what people do with media. The emphasis in this chapter is on considering relationships and social practices surrounding media use in everyday life. This is not to deny any negative influence of media use in some instances. Rather, it is to temper the dominance of the traditional focus in social psychology on the negative effects of media with a perspective that includes a broader consideration of social practices associated with media use in daily life. We consider some of the ways in which people engage with media and each other using communications technologies, and thereby promote a social psychology of media that attends to media-based practices as and where they occur.

Chapter overview

The first section considers the prevalence of media in society today. The second outlines what we mean by the term 'media'. The third section explores some of the ways psychologists work with the media; the fourth considers efforts to document patterns in the representation of minority groups, and strategies for cultivating equitable news depictions. It is in the fifth section that we consider traditional psychological research into the effects of media on citizens. This leads to a discussion in section six of cultivation analysis as an approach to researching media effects by drawing on 'real' media content from daily life. The seventh section briefly considers the tendency in effects research within psychology to blame the media for causing a raft of social ills. Limitations in such work raise the need to look also at what people do with media content and devices in everyday contexts. The eighth section considers the integration of new technology into daily life and how this can alter common social practices. The focus on what people do with media technologies in daily life is continued in the next section, through a discussion of the role of media in fostering community across online and offline spaces. The chapter is concluded with a general discussion providing an overview of social psychology, the media and everyday life. The key themes covered in the chapter are:

- The range of media pervading everyday life
- Issues of media influence
- Consequences of daily use of media devices

The complex and ubiquitous nature of media

Why should social psychologists concern themselves with media? The short answer is reflected in the scenario used to open this chapter. Media are both pervasive and fascinating; media pervade our everyday lives and captivate our attention in a variety of ways. If you consider your own engagements with various forms of media over the past twenty-four hours, the extent of your media interactions may possibly surprise you. Very few people in contemporary societies would not have interacted extensively with media over that time period. Our daily lives are punctuated with mediated experiences – communications via telephone, email or chat rooms and engagements with television, radio, magazines, newspapers, websites, digital games, billboards, packaging and advertising.

Review exercise

On your computer or phone or with a pen and paper, slate, or rock and chisel make a list of the media you currently use. Now compare your list with a list of media your parents and grandparents grew up with. In considering your lists and preparing for the content of this chapter, consider the following questions:

- What trends do you see across these lists?
- Where are the media listed typically located?
- Which media are in your home, and where are these situated?
- Do people use different media in different ways in different places?

On the face of it, the pervasiveness of media in daily life is a recent and dramatic shift in social life. This seems true in the sense of the seemingly increased ease of access to technology for many, but not all, citizens. However, media have been part of people's lives for millennia. People have used a range of media and communications technologies from cave painting, to roads, to sculpture and carving, to radio and the Internet. We will return to the broad conceptualization of the term 'media' shortly. For now, it is important to note that communication via such technologies has been central to the coordination of societies for a long time (McQuail, 2002). We might say that the functions of media have become more complex and contested through the ages (Box 11.1), as citizens move from being the receivers of information from societal elites to acting as producers and redistributors of information.

BOX 11.1   Historical periods in the development of media technologies

McQuail (1992) set out four primary periods for the growth of media in Western society. We have adapted these and added a fifth period:

- *Antiquity*: the first period stems from cave painting, sculpture and theatre up until the advent of the printing press. With the possible exception of ancient Greece, and a few privileged male citizens, this was the period of increased direct control of information and media.

- *Renaissance*: the second period arose with the advent of printing and lasted up until the mid-seventeenth century. This period saw increased challenges to established power among elites epitomized by the religious conflicts of the Reformation. The advent of the printing press raised issues regarding the rights of people to publish their own concerns, self-governance and tolerance for different beliefs. The period saw increased efforts by Church and state to reassert control over public utterances. Foundations were being laid for more open communication system.

- *Industrial Revolution*: the third period stems from the early industrial age and lasts to the mid-nineteenth century. This period saw the emergence of modern nation-states and was associated with increased use of pamphlets, books, newsletters and so on. There was a period of increased conflict over the control of information, and emphasis on the need for open channels of communication. This period saw the rise of mass education and literacy, the establishment of libraries and improvements in the postal service.

- *Modern*: the fourth period saw the rise of the modern mass media. Prior to this period, mediated communication had become dominated by print media, and in particular newspapers and magazines. Although still important, such media have been supplemented by film and broadcasting. Media such as television have taken on the role of primary public informers and sources of news.

- *Contemporary*: this period includes a continuation of earlier media technologies and the uptake of digital technologies. These include web-based forms that allow for ease of information sharing and for audiences to become producers of media content that can be shared globally. Issues surrounding the existence of information-rich and information-poor people remain. However, there is greater potential for people to produce as well as consume media content. Television is being replaced by computer-based forums that combine content from personal experience and professional outlets to create a media nexus within which public knowledge is increasingly negotiated.

Contemporary engagements with media are not simple. Media technologies from a number of generations are folded together in daily life and offer a range of options for gaining information, expressing oneself and interacting with others. We interact with different media in many different ways, many of which are raised by our scenario, where family members attempt to communicate with others, maintain familial ties, gain information on events and sustain a sense of self as someone who is concerned about others. Media provide shared experiences through which notions of life and death, relationships and the events of the day are constructed and revised. Daily media consumption rituals provide people with access to ready-made stories that can be used to navigate the pleasures and dilemmas of everyday life. In addition, new segments of information are (re)framed in relation to previous exchanges, as people construct symbolic meanings based on the interaction of interpersonal and mediated spheres (Hodgetts & Chamberlain, 2006a; Hodgetts, Chamberlain, Scammell et al., 2007). In fact, in today's mediated world, media provide much more than a miscellany of information: they can operate to reaffirm our trust or distrust of people and institutions, and to highlight developments and uncertainties about our world. Media extend well beyond the screen and the page into daily conversations and interactions between citizens that may also occur at a distance via Skype, email or a mobile phone (Silverstone, 2007).

Review exercise

Consider what you use various media for.

- Is it entertainment, gathering information or simply passing the time?
- Do media provide you with a means of engaging with or avoiding interactions with other people?

These are core concerns for social psychologists.

Although readers, viewers, posters and bloggers are offered (and increasingly offer) glimpses of almost every issue and concern of life today, they do not have to engage directly with specific media content for it to enter their lives; they often learn about such things in discussions with friends, partners and colleagues in which media accounts are discussed and reworked. Media are primary sources of taken-for-granted frameworks for understanding the ongoing issues of life. Therefore, media are central to the definition of these issues and the legitimation of approaches to addressing them. This is referred to as agenda-setting (Giles, 2003). In short, media are implicated in processes through which common knowledge is created in everyday life (see Chapter 4). Media are essentially a set of key social processes that surround us in a variety of ways, with considerable potential to impact who we are and what we do (Hodgetts & Chamberlain, 2006a) or our socialization (Chapters 2 and 3).

What do we mean by 'the media'?

A major issue in media research is to determine the scope of the term 'media'. Mass communication media, such as television, newspapers and magazines, are an obvious category of media that attracts a good deal of attention. The content of this media category varies substantially, including formats such as news, current affairs, drama, documentary, soaps, advertising, reality shows, docudrama and so forth. It has become common to identify 'new media' and information and communication technologies as a separate and different category, covering web content (including that provided by mainstream media such as newspapers, television and radio), blogs and wikis, mobile telephones, Internet messaging, digital gaming and social networking spaces such as MySpace and Facebook (Chamberlain & Hodgetts, 2008). Of course, the degree to which these media are considered new is time dependent and generational, and it is salient to recall comments about how the introduction of television would change everything. Clearly, television is now a mainstream medium that has contributed to the evolution of daily rituals. However, the introduction of this medium did not produce the enormous social changes in newspaper readership and movie attendance that were predicted in advance (Curran & Seaton, 2003). In addition, it can be difficult to find a criterion, other than the recency of its appearance, by which to distinguish much of this new media from mass communication media as defined above.

Review exercise

According to communications theorists such as Denis McQuail (2002) media also include roads and rivers, because these are channels used for the passage of information and communications.

- Do you agree that roads and rivers should be included in a conceptualization of media?
- If not, why not?
- If so, how might we research such 'media'?

Apart from all this, but intimately connected with it, is another group of media that include such things as films, books, theatre, comics and manga, and art in all its forms. While we may attempt to categorize media in these ways, we need to recognize that many of these forms interrelate and interpenetrate: the same piece of artwork can be involved across many formats for advertising, promotion and branding; the same news report may appear simultaneously on television, radio, websites, blogs and mobile phones; the same advertisement may appear across newspaper, magazine, billboard, television, bulk-mailing and new media forums (Curran & Seaton, 2003). We live a good deal of our lives through a media nexus that provides much of the social fabric for daily life today. The weaving of a media nexus across various technologies invokes notions of media convergence and cross-fertilization (Box 11.2).

Although social psychologists have studied all of these media forms at some time and for some purpose, the bulk of research in

---

BOX 11.2   Media convergence and cross-fertilization

Media convergence is a process by which various media forms, such as computers, can now screen television programmes and films and can be used to download music. One can also read comic books online and download texts onto a mobile phone. Convergence also relates to media cross-fertilization whereby a comic book character such as the Hulk now appears in a movie and video game, and his growl can be used as the ring tone on one's mobile phone.

---

psychology has tended to focus on the mass communication forms of print and broadcast media (Chamberlain & Hodgetts, 2008). The introduction of computer-based media has seen some redirection of this focus (Doyle, 2004). However, rather than attempt to classify media, we should consider that it is more appropriate simply to utilize whatever media form is relevant to answer the questions that the researcher has in mind. Thus, questions about television violence will sustain a focus on television, questions about anonymity in Internet messaging spaces will ensure a focus on that space, and questions about identity in relation to mobile phone use will require a focus on that technology. Questions that ask about 'the media' are obviously much more problematic and will require some rationale for a focus. Social psychological research requires us to make some assumptions about the nature of media and how they can be investigated. Later in this chapter we consider what would happen if we changed our focus from 'the media' to everyday life, as the domain where media are done and the domain where media practices are performed. This requires a social focus and a shift from media-centricity (cf. Silverstone, 1999). It involves starting research with a focus on the social practices of people, and then investigating the media they use to conduct their everyday lives – which may include coping with illness, making and maintaining relationships, sustaining their identities as citizens. In responding to this, we turn back to discuss the issues we see as central for media research in psychology. This raises questions around how psychologists engage and work with media.

Psychologists working with the media

Since before the inception of social psychology as a discipline, there has been considerable academic and public concern about the influence of publicly circulated messages on society, groups and individuals (Curran & Seaton, 2003). This concern in part stems from the ways in which media circumvent traditional professional, community, political and religious networks to enable communication directly with and between people. These concerns have been of interest

BOX 11.3   Division of Media Psychology

One significant occurrence that highlights the persistent interest many psychologists have in the media is the founding of APA's 46th Division of Media Psychology in 1985. This division encompasses a diverse array of activities, including translating psychological research into accessible materials for public consumption, consulting with media producers on the production of educational materials (children's TV), hosting TV and radio shows, developing new communications technology and researching the effects of media on 'vulnerable' members of society. As described at http://www.apa.org/divisions/div46:

Media Psychology focuses on the roles psychologists play in various aspects of the media, including, but not limited to, radio, television, film, video, newsprint, magazines, and newer technologies. It seeks to promote research into the impact of media on human behaviour; to facilitate interaction between psychology and media representatives; to enrich the teaching, training, and practice of media psychology; and to prepare psychologists to interpret psychological research to the lay public and to other professionals.

You might like to visit the division's website and explore the range of work being done by division members working with the media.

to psychologists for some time. For example, since the 1920s psychologists have participated in radio shows and written newspaper columns in their efforts to educate the public about psychological issues and processes (Kutner, 1997). Public interest in psychological processes, from relational dynamics to the manifestation of various disorders, has occupied talk shows, dramatic depictions, news and documentaries (Schwartz, 1999). The extent of the involvement of psychologists is reflected in the establishment of the Division of Media Psychology within the APA (Box 11.3).

Increasingly, psychologists are called upon to engage in writing and producing media material in addition to consulting, advising, advocating for and treating individuals via radio, television and the Internet (Kutner, 1997). Here are six roles that psychologists adopt in relation to the media. There are more roles (Schwartz, 1999); this list simply showcases the range of work engaged in by psychologists:

- *Media celebrities* such as Dr. Phil offer advice and expose the public en masse to psychological insight.
- *Expert sources* emerge when disaster strikes and offer insight into human experiences of catastrophe. Psychologists also produce self-help or 'pop-psych' books for public consumption. Such popular material focuses on a positive orientation to life and on personal growth (see Chapter 10).
- *Romantic historians* are experts who testify about the good old days before television and video games, when the family played together and ate together, and call for families to participate in television- or computer-free days.
- *Producers* design programmes and websites aimed at promoting positive human interaction, social skills, pro-social behaviour and health education. One of the explicit goals of *Sesame*

Street was to teach children to recognize their own and other people's emotions and to respond accordingly in socially responsible ways.

■ *Psycho-engineers* work in the field of human factors, designing communications systems that are more user-friendly and accessible, including those for people with disabilities.

■ *Researcher* is perhaps the most prominent role for psychologists. This role overlaps with that of expert sources and producers because psychology is a research-based and practice-oriented discipline. Some researchers explore the content of media representations and its potential influence on various groups. This work often explores the underrepresentation of minority groups and the incidence of stereotypical depictions of groups such as the disabled, the elderly and those experiencing mental illness.

Let us consider the researcher role briefly, and how it can lead to psychologists appearing as expert sources and shaping media content in a manner that promotes understanding between social groups. Psychologists are increasingly involved in using the media to cultivate understanding and social inclusion. This necessitates a variety of activities, ranging from lobbying media producers in order to promote local concerns through to designing web-based interventions for community development (Hodgetts & Chamberlain, 2007). Psychologists often work to ensure the inclusion of marginalized groups in society, and in the process challenge stereotypical depictions of such citizens (Box 11.4).

Work on social inclusion is core business for social psychologists because people often come to know others through media engagements. The media provide an "unremitting exposure to the discourse of strangers" (Frosh, 2006, p. 266), as we are caught up through media in witnessing stories, events and episodes at which we are not present. Frosh suggests that such witnessing has important consequences for people, intertwining the impersonal and the personal in this imaginative engagement (we know about 'the imagined lives of strangers' only through media engagement). The media achieves this, he argues, by situating the direct personal presence within an impersonal framework of "indifferent social relations" (p. 280) and

---

BOX 11.4   Interesting study

Veno and van den Eynde (2007) illustrated the importance of media advocacy for working towards the inclusion of socially marginalized groups. Their study discusses the actions of politicians and media professionals in marginalizing bikers. Consideration was given to the cultivation of a moral panic leading to the social exclusion of outlaw motorcycle clubs in Australia and the authors' media advocacy work aimed at challenging such exclusionary practices and changing public perceptions. Such action research exemplifies what can be done to effect social change using the media to distribute alternative public narratives and alternative characterizations of a particular community.

thereby creating a civil equivalence between strangers that allows them to be morally involved. As Frosh expresses it, contemporary media witnessed, on a daily basis, "extends and replenishes our ability to imagine what it might be like to be someone else – wherever they might be – and to care about them because we can care about anyone" (p. 282). Issues regarding what social psychologists can do to foster social justice and fairness in the representation of minority groups are discussed in more detail in the following section.

Using media to challenge discrimination and to promote intergroup understanding

In his social identity theory, which we discussed in Chapter 7, Tajfel (1981) proposes that people maintain self-esteem as members of a particular social group through comparisons with members of other social groups that reflect favourably on their own groups. Negative depictions of minority groups in news media can function as a prevalent source of social comparisons for members of majority groups, who are addressed as the audience for reports about others. This influence relies on audience members assuming that depictions are accurate. Without actual experience or sources of alternative information, audience members are more likely to rely on media representations (Comstock & Scharrer, 2005). This issue becomes particularly important when we consider the ways in which mainstream media have tended historically to present stereotypical (Chapter 4) images of minority groups (Chamberlain & Hodgetts, 2008).

Traditional social psychological work on the influence of majority perspectives on minority groups (Chapter 5) includes analyses of news content because the media are now central to intergroup relations and identity formation. Media often operate to fix boundaries of identity formation between groups (Anderson, 1983). As Pietikäinen (2003) writes:

For any group, let alone a minority, news coverage is a means of gaining wider attention for their agenda, of making their voices heard, and of possibly making a difference on issues important to them. News is also a highly controlled forum of ideas and voices. It not only gives room for the flow of ideas and information, but it may also inhibit this flow. (p. 583)

Whose views are privileged and whose views are restrained in news reports reveals a lot about wider power relations in a society (Hodgetts, Cullen & Radley, 2005). Such symbolic power – the power to name and define a group or issue – is often linked to economic and social privilege, which enables dominant group assumptions to impact the lives of minority groups (Box 11.5). It is important

BOX 11.5   Racism and the media in South Africa

Ratele and Duncan (2004) considered the racializing that occurred through South African newspapers during the 1990s. This work is related to our discussion of stereotyping and new racism in Chapter 4. They report that overt racism declined during this period. However, covert racism was evident in a shift from depictions of the barbaric, child-like savage to the almost exclusive depiction of black men in trouble and committing crimes. Correspondingly, coverage did not explore the causes of the inequalities shaping the lives of these men and their communities, in terms of the legacy of Apartheid in causing poverty and unemployment. Rather inequities were displaced by a focus on individual behaviour and traits. "Naturalising inequality and blaming the victims is a strategy that refers to the media's tendency to report on racial patterns of socio-economic inequality without attempting to examine the structural causes of such inequality" (Ratele & Duncan, 2004, p. 79). According to news reports, what is required is personal change rather than social and structural change, and as a result the status quo is not challenged. Reports naturalized images of black people as being prone to crime, violence and educational failure. Related reports tended to depersonalize the death of a black person by concentrating on aggregate numbers without details of the histories or families of those who died. Conversely, the deaths of white people were deeply personalized to invoke sympathy in the audience. Ratele and Duncan (2004) go on to outline ways of challenging such negative and racialized media portrayals:

- The first is simply to try to ignore such images of your group. However, this is a limited strategy and one that does not effect change in representations.
- A second strategy is to appropriate the images, making them one's own and then altering their meaning. This is evident in satirical sitcoms and art activism in South Africa.
- It also links to the third strategy, in which marginalized groups gain resources to produce counter-images by producing their own media. This extends to training racial group members as journalists.

to investigate these processes because "it is through these various media that our relations with others, both neighbours and strangers, are facilitated or, indeed, denied. Relations are created and sustained. Prejudices likewise" (Silverstone & Georgiou, 2005, p. 434).

Acting to ensure that prejudices are not dominating news images of minority groups requires an approach to conceptualizing news production as comprising more than a closed system engaged in only by politically powerful groups (Cottle & Rai, 2006; Hodgetts & Rua, 2008). Such thinking has contributed to a situation where representatives of marginalized communities often see news media and journalists as 'the enemy', to be avoided unless one wants 'to get burnt' (Snell & Hodgetts, 2008). It is important not to become overly pessimistic with regard to the influence of political elites on the openness of news processes. As well as subverting the free flow of information, lobbying can be used to open up deliberations regarding social issues. This is reflected in the library example discussed in Chapter 6, where Hodgetts and colleagues (2008) engaged in media advocacy work to challenge media representations of homeless men who were depicted as not being suitable patrons for a local library. As Cottle and Rai (2006) note, "Simply put, there is more going on in the communication of news than the manipulation of news agendas by powerful strategic interests or the circulation of powerful semiotic codes and agendas" (p. 164).

News media offer more than dominant or stigmatizing representations of the other. Silverstone (2007) has recently drawn on the concept of the Mediapolis to explain the presence of media in civic life today. This involves an extension of the ancient Greek *polis*, the shared civic space where political communication occurred. The Mediapolis is thus a forum reproducing civic engagements in a technologically mediated form. It is a shared space in which contemporary public debates are held:

Contemporary media... reproduce, though of course in an intensely technologically mediated form, the discursive and judgmental space of the polis. Like the polis this mediated space is often, indeed mostly, elitist and exclusive. Like the polis it depends on visibility and appearance in the media. ... Increasingly what passes for public life in contemporary societies takes place, more or less exclusively, on the screen. (Silverstone, 2007, pp. 29–31)

Silverstone's Mediapolis invokes an image of citizens engaged via media in a regulated, but pluralistic symbolic space where controversy can take shape and be worked through. Importantly, the Mediapolis is seen as extending beyond the screen or page into face-to-face conversations and interactions between citizens. Aspects of news media coverage can be said to be dialogical in the sense outlined in Chapter 3. Media are part of the conversations and social interactions through which the self and others are constructed. A significant aspect of the concept of the Mediapolis is that it maintains a notion of communicative restraint in terms of the activities of majority groups, and the potential for extending civic participation via news media through the inclusion of less powerful voices.

In brief, because media constitute a sphere within which the concerns of contemporary life are played out, and where shared ideas are forged and circulated, psychologists have given considerable attention to media depictions of a range of social issues (Chamberlain & Hodgetts, 2008). Content-focused research can reveal aspects of media power, particularly in terms of how media representations and stories are framed. Social psychologists involved in research with marginalized and minority groups can find themselves working to address the symbolic power involved in naming and defining social issues – issues that often arise from the marginalization of the voices of those most affected (Hodgetts & Chamberlain, 2006b). This often involves framing and supplying information that meets journalists' needs and work constraints while staying faithful to the hopes and aspirations of the marginalized and minority groups. News media have the capacity to pause and reflect on the ways in which events have been covered or people have been characterized (Hodgetts et al., 2008).

Review exercise

Perhaps now is a good time to take a break from reading this chapter and check out resources on the web for media advocacy. We have found the following sites particularly useful:

■ http://www.marininstitute.org/action_packs/media_advocacy.htm
■ http://www.who.int/tobacco/policy/media_advocacy/en/

Considering media effects, or what media do to people

One reason for the focus on possible negative effects of media on individuals is that psychology has evolved as primarily a problem-driven discipline that responds to broader concerns in society. In the previous section, we proposed a role for media in promoting stereotypes of minority groups (Chapter 7). In this sense, we are concerned about the potential influence of media images on public understandings. However, it is a big step to move from analyses of existing media representations to asserting a direct impact of such representations on people's behaviour towards others in daily life. As discussed in Chapter 4, this is to step from studying prejudicial thoughts to studying discriminatory actions.

Concerns with the possible negative and corrupting effects of media on young people have preoccupied scholars for millennia and motivated social psychological research for more than a century (Cantril & Allport, 1935; Lazarsfeld & Merton, 1948; Tarde, 1910). The ancient Greeks were concerned about the corrupting influence of dramatic plays and sculpture on the youth of the day. More recently, there have been US Senate committee hearings on the impacts of comic books in the 1940s, rap music in the 1980s and 1990s, and digital games this decade. 'Violent', 'graphic', 'rude', 'zany' and 'unsophisticated' comic books were associated anecdotally with every social ill from the rise of delinquency, poor literacy and moral decay to 'mass idiocy' (Hajdu, 2008). The fact that comics were enjoyable and provided a basis for young people to negotiate social relations with peers was ignored. Comic book scares highlight how fears regarding the negative impact of media on youth resurface with each new generation and technology. Attention has shifted from comics, radio, film and television to include digital games (Box 11.6).

BOX 11.6   **Psychology and the promotion of concerns regarding media effects**

News media have numerous reports in which psychologists raise concerns regarding the impact of media on violence and antisocial behaviour. Such material is often circulated to media via press releases and websites, such as Science Daily, that showcase research. A recent example is 'Psychologists Explore Public Policy and Effects of Media Violence on Children' (ScienceDaily, 27 Dec. 2007; http://www.sciencedaily.com). This article proposes that:

Although hundreds of studies link media violence to aggression in children and adolescents, most public policy attempts to reduce children's media violence exposure in the U.S. have failed. Efforts to restrict children's access to violent video games have been struck down by the courts as infringing on children's First Amendment rights.

The news story goes on to showcase a review of the literature on the effects of media violence on children that highlights the absence of effective policy responses to shield children from the 'risk'. The article cites the three psychologists who authored the review and who propose that media effects are cumulative and not necessarily always as dramatic as the Columbine High School massacre. The rhetorical inference here is that the school shooting was the result of exposure to media violence. Professor Anderson is cited as stating:

This confusion about equating media violence with extreme atrocities allows people to think that there are no effects on them because we all know that we've watched lots of media violence and never gone on a shooting rampage, but that's not where we should look for the effects. The effects are more subtle. In order to do something seriously violent, one must have multiple risk factors for aggression – media violence is only one risk factor, and it's not the largest one. It's also not the smallest.

Various policy initiatives are suggested for protecting children:

1. A public forum could be created for presenting research findings, discussing solutions and translating science into policy.
2. A mandatory ratings system for all media, including games, movies, music and television, could be developed.
3. Media literacy standards could be introduced into school curricula.
4. Paediatricians could be trained to support parents with information on media effects.

Injecting another perspective into the controversy over media effects, Kutner and Olson (2008) provide a comprehensive review of, and empirical research into, possible links between violent video games and violent behaviour, finding scant evidence for such a link: "After all, millions of children and adults play these games, yet the world has not been reduced to chaos and anarchy" (p. 18). This is not to say that some children who spend considerable time playing these games, like those who spend too much time reading books, may not be influenced in their actions in adverse ways. Interestingly, Kutner and Olson note a dramatic rise in violent video gaming during a period in which violent crime rates were dropping in the United States. These authors note, "Violent video game play is extremely common, and violent crime is extremely rare" (p. 66). When violence does occur perpetrators are more likely to have impoverished backgrounds and histories of family violence and substance misuse. In this context gaming behaviour is unlikely to be the primary precipitating factor.

It is common for textbooks in social psychology to spend considerable time exploring the intricacies of laboratory research into media effects without mentioning competing explanations such as poverty. We began this section with a critical take on the existence of media effects in order to foreshadow competing explanations for violence in society, including poverty and social deprivation. We opt to use the term 'influences' rather than 'effects' when considering what the media might do to people. The remainder of this chapter presents an overview of selected ideas from experimental research into media effects and influences, the function of media technologies in everyday life and how people use various technologies to engage with others, often in positive ways. The notion of influences denotes a more complex set of relations whereby people engage with various media across a range of social settings and with other people over time.

Review exercise

Those of you who play digital games might pause for a moment and think about whether your play involves aggression against victims or engagements with scenarios and explorations of game worlds.

- Are you rehearsing to kill people?
- Are you aware that the characters in the game are not real?
- Do violent games also contain opportunities to help one another?

These are important questions that have not been taken up until recently in psychological studies of media effects. They invoke a social context and the broader motives and experiences of people who game that experiments exclude due to the limitations of experimental designs. For now, it is important to note that not all psychologists support the view that violent media content causes violent behaviour. Nonetheless, the existence and centrality of such effects is a core assumption underpinning experimental studies in social psychology.

Effects research in experimental social psychology surged during the 1960s, and focused on measuring short-term and usually negative reactions from exposing research 'subjects' (usually undergraduate students) to specific media stimuli (Giles, 2003). Traditional effects research focuses on the use of single issues such as violence or pornography as depicted in single media forms and responded to by individuals. Such studies cannot account for the ways in which the Grays interact with various media forms and content areas, sometimes simultaneously. Regardless of such limitations, experimental studies have raised some interesting questions regarding how people might learn from media content, and perhaps model behaviours displayed on our screens. This raises social learning theory as a central theoretical model that has informed many media experiments (Box 11.7). In essence, social learning theory emerged from behaviourism and proposes that people can learn by observing the actions of others. Bandura (2001) points out that theory in psychology has tended to focus on learning from the implications of one's own actions. Learning is explored as a consequence of direct experience, where one can also observe the implications of the actions of other human beings. Such a focus on direct experience neglects how insights into human behaviour, thinking and values can be "gained from the extensive modeling in the symbolic environment of the mass media" (p. 271). People may imitate the actions of others depicted on television or in digital games, for instance, if they think that they will be rewarded for doing so or to avoid punishment.

BOX 11.7   Bobo doll studies

In a series of classic studies, Bandura and colleagues exposed children to situations in which a research confederate beat a Bobo doll (Bandura, Ross & Ross, 1961, 1963). The inflatable Bobo doll is about the same size as a small child. The experiments involved sixty-six children, aged three to six years, in an experimental group and twenty-four children matched in terms of age and gender in the control group. Each child took part in the experiment individually so as to avoid influences from other children. Each child and an adult model were brought into a playroom. In the experimental condition, the model subsequently hit the Bobo doll using a mallet. The child was then taken into another room in which another adult model played with other toys and ignored the Bobo doll. Each child was then taken into a third room containing a number of toys. He or she was allowed to play with the desirable toys for only a short period before being told that the toys were reserved for other children but that there were toys in the next room that he or she could play with. The child was then left alone in the final room for twenty minutes with the toys, which included a Bobo doll, mallet, dart gun, paper and crayons, and balls. The child was observed from behind a one-way mirror. Children exposed to the aggressive model were much more inclined to behave in a physically aggressive manner. Boys were also more likely to behave violently than girls. Bandura and colleagues reached the conclusion that in seeing an adult behave violently, children could learn that such behaviour is more acceptable, and thus could be more likely to behave violently themselves. In the 1963 study, Bandura found that video-modelled aggression was less influential than in-person modelling by adults who were physically present, but still influential. In a later study Bandura found that when behaviour viewed via video was punished or rewarded the child was less or more likely to imitate the behaviour, respectively. The conclusion reached was that showing the consequences of a violent act had an impact on children's levels of aggression. On the basis of such results, we might surmise that if violence is presented in the media as a legitimate way to resolve personal conflicts, people learn that it is socially acceptable to use violence to achieve one's goals.

In a standard contemporary media experiment, Bushman and Anderson (2002) rated the attributions of aggression to story characters after playing either violent or nonviolent video games, finding more aggressive responses from those who had played violent games. Similarly, Anderson, Carnagey and Eubanks (2003) reported that college students who listened to a violent song felt more hostile and held more aggressive thoughts than those who listened to a similar, but nonviolent song. Such studies reflect the common practice of exploring individual reactions to media stimuli under controlled conditions. Clearly, people often consume media with friends, family and even strangers (e.g. at a concert). When recently taking interpersonal dimensions into account for a revised social cognitive model of mass communication, Bandura (2001) writes:

People are socially situated in interpersonal networks. When media influences lead viewers to discuss and negotiate matters of import with others in their lives, the media set in motion transactional experiences that further shape the course of change. This is another socially mediated process through which symbolic communications exert their effect. (p. 286)

BOX 11.8   Two-step flow model of communication

The two-step flow model of communication postulates that media information first reaches opinion leaders, who are individuals who attend to attend to media sources and emerging trends in society. These leaders then pass on their interpretations of the messages to other people in the community. They exert a personal influence on the flow of ideas from the media to the public.

Such shifts reflect how the field is still developing and becoming increasingly complex and varied. Psychologists are also rediscovering insights from previous generations – in this case, Katz and Lazarsfeld's (1955) two-step flow model of communication (Box 11.8). This model explores the influence of interpersonal networks on the flow of ideas from media throughout society. Schneider, Gruman and Coutts (2005) provide a detailed review of recent developments in effects research in social psychology. These authors argue strongly for the existence of overwhelming evidence for the direct impact of negative media content on human behaviour.

Cultivation theory and the shift from laboratory to everyday life

From the previous section it should be clear that we are not totally convinced that experimental studies provide all the necessary evidence to conclude that violent media images cause violence in society. What such studies do show is short-term student reactions to 'media' stimuli under controlled conditions. Experiments are not the only way in which social psychologists investigate media influences. Research such as cultivation analysis offers further insights into the influences of media on public understandings. Cultivation theory (Box 11.9) is arguably the most relevant approach to media effects in terms of providing insights into the opening scenario for this chapter because it considers the cumulative impact of audience exposure to violent depictions in the media.

BOX 11.9   Cultivation theory

The term 'cultivation' is used to describe "the independent contributions television viewing makes to viewer conceptions of social reality" (Gerbner, Gross, Morgan & Signorielli, 1994, p. 23).

BOX 11.10   Cultural indicators project

The Cultural Indicators project in the United States tracked major themes in television coverage from the 1960s to the 1990s. Studies explored common, overarching and stable patterns in television content across genres. Questionnaires with items reflecting these patterns were administered to samples of the public. Any patterns across media content and public responses were taken as evidence of television's contribution to the construction of social reality. This project demonstrated differences between rates of violence on television and statistical facts regarding the actual incidence of violence in society. Results suggest that television coverage overestimates the level of violence in society. This demonstrated cultivation effect is referred to as the 'mean world syndrome'. Heavy viewers perceive a higher incidence of violence and aggression in the world than there is in reality. Those witnessing violent incidents, like the Grays, may become fearful of attending public events over time because they come to assume a higher level or risk of violence than is actually the case.

Cultivation analysis focuses the cumulative impact of the 'symbolic environment' created across media forms in fostering a climate of fear among the general population. Cultivation theory proposes that over time the sheer amount of violence and crime depicted in the media cultivates fear among the general population and the perception that the world is more violent then it is in actuality (Gerbner et al., 1994). This approach was developed to move research beyond behaviourally oriented models guiding effects experiments. It initiated an exploration of the influence of media, as a 'symbolic environment', on socialization (Chapters 2 and 3) and how people come to perceive the world over time (Chapter 4). Proponents assert that television, for instance, is instrumental in cultivating a selective view of society, and in shaping the beliefs and values of the public (Box 11.10). Heavy viewers of television are said to adopt a distorted view of the world that reflects the programmes they are exposed too.

Cultivation analysis was established to explore some of the consequences of growing up in a media-saturated world. The approach is concerned with questions such as how the media might increase the general level of fear in a society due to the amount of violent images broadcast. Gerbner and colleagues (1994) make a number of interesting points that reflect the way in which they have extended psychological studies of media effects:

- Cultivation analysis was developed in an attempt to overcome some of the criticisms of effects experiments in regard to the artificial nature of such studies and the ecological validity of findings. Rather than constructing images for one-off experiments and measuring immediate effects, effort was made to actually analyse real media images and to explore their impact on actual viewer perspectives over an extended period of time. If effects occur over time then it follows that research needs to be longitudinal.
- The key to cultivation analysis is the idea that "[e]xposure to the total pattern rather than only to specific genres or programmes is what accounts for the historically new and distinct

consequences of living with television: the cultivation of shared conceptions of reality among otherwise diverse publics" (Gerbner et al., 1994, p. 18). The focus is on long-term patterns of exposure on various subcultures.

- There is no control group from which to compare the impact of television. We are all born into the existing symbolic environment. "Neither the before and after exposure" model, nor the notion of "predispositions as intervening variables, so important in traditional effects studies, apply in the context of cultivation analysis. Television enters life in infancy; there is no 'before exposure condition'" (Gerbner et al., 1994, p. 37). Thus, television is involved in the development of personal predispositions that mediate the communication process (our personal beliefs and values are already mediated).

- Media effects are multidirectional. There is an interaction between public opinion and media perspectives. Here we can see a shift from a one-way transmission model of communication to a more complex understanding. As Gerbner and colleagues (1994) write, "Thus, television neither simply 'creates' nor 'reflects' images, opinions, and beliefs. Rather, it is an integral aspect of a dynamic process" (p. 23).

- Cultivation is seen as a gravitational process whereby over time the norms of dominant groups controlling the media colonize those of minority groups, bringing them into closer orbit. People from different subcultural groups are socialized in the norms and values of dominant groups, which are emphasized in the media. This is the process of *mainstreaming*, in which diversity in society is diminished and people come to think more alike due to our interactions with television.

Cultivation research highlights the need to be careful about jumping to causal conclusions based on the results of correlational research. Cultivation research relies on making causal inferences on the basis of weak correlations between the quantitative content analysis of television programmes and viewer opinion surveys. Not all researchers accept the existence of such effects, and some question the conclusion that the mean world syndrome would be a bad thing if it did exist. Felson (1996) proposed that the mean world syndrome would prevent people from putting themselves in dangerous situations and thus protect them from violence. The assumption that violent content leads to violent crime has also been questioned. Messner (1986) found that in cities with high levels of television viewing there were lower levels of violent and nonviolent crime. These authors drew on the *routine activity approach* to explain this trend. According to the routine activity approach, if routine activities or daily practices reduce the likelihood of perpetrators of crime and victims coming into contact with each other, then the frequency of crime will be reduced.

The tendency to blame the media for social ills

One of the major agendas in media research within psychology remains the establishment of media effects on the basis of the assumption that people are rational actors making rational choices about how to be and what to do. This leads researchers to conceive of media as an environmental variable that can be assessed for its effects on people's behaviour, and it works to sustain a dominant focus on media effects in much psychological research. In fact, one of the major objectives of the Media Psychology Division of the American Psychological Association is stated as being to "[s]upport research on the effects of media on the public, and the effectiveness of media in transmitting psychological information" (www.apa.org/divisions/div46). Media are viewed here quite simply as information transmitters (able to be employed more or less effectively) and as causing effects on receivers of this information. Media forms are viewed as sites for behaviour and social interaction, and the research remains largely underpinned by behavioural stimulus–response models (Chapter 2) and assumptions that the transmission of knowledge will lead to behavioural change. Thus, we find many psychologists commenting on, and contributing to, moral panics around the effects of violence in televised images, heavy metal music or digital gaming (e.g. Anderson, Berkowitz et al., 2003; Bartholow, Bushman & Sestir, 2006), or about why some women are susceptible to media portrayals that 'cause' young women to become anxious about body weight and lead to disordered eating (e.g. Bessenoff, 2006). Even with the move to examine new media, which is more obviously interactive in nature, much psychological research has remained effects-oriented (e.g. Joinson, 2003). As Buckingham (2002) notes, as for mass media, most research into new media has tended to be "preoccupied with the search for evidence of negative effects; and much of it has been based on implicitly behaviourist assumptions" (p. 79).

The jury is still out on the issue of direct media effects on behaviour and processes by which media influences take shape in everyday life. There is much work still to be done in this area. The tendency to position media as the main cause of a raft of social problems is now regularly questioned within the discipline. For example, in a keynote address to the APA, Fischoff (1999) generated controversy by challenging the tendency of psychologists to blame the media for violence in society while ignoring issues such as poverty and discrimination. When referring to the use of examples such as school killings, Fischoff (1999) noted that despite more than 1,000 separate studies and more than fifty years of effort psychologists were no closer to predicting such massacres. He proposed:

To argue that because subjects in a lab situation displayed desensitization to violence we can safely predict that non-quiche-eating real men, watching sexually violent films in real theaters or in real homes are more likely to acquit a real-life rapist in a real jury setting is a psychologically huge and untested leap of faith. (p. 2)

Fischoff (1999) was referring to the *fundamedia attribution error*, which involves blaming media rather than material circumstances for social problems. It is proposed that psychologists should look at society for answers and not just the media, which play a role, but are not the sole factor at play. Media are said to foster certain values and perspectives, rather than dictating behaviour. Any influence is likely to occur through far more complex and uncertain processes than has been proposed in psychological research to date (Chamberlain & Hodgetts, 2008).

Regardless of the media form investigated, proving media effects has always been difficult and contentious (Thomsen, 2007). As Couldry (2004, p. 117) has argued, proving a clear causal pathway between media images, a person's consumption patterns and changes in a person's behaviour is highly problematic. Statistically significant relationships between media viewing and changes in audience understandings, beliefs, intentions and behaviours have been difficult to establish (e.g. Signorielli & Morgan, 1990), and when carefully conducted research does find effects (e.g. Terry-Mcelrath et al., 2007), they turn out to be very small. However, notions of 'media effects' remain widespread in social psychology and in everyday talk about media. As Couldry (2004) argues, media effects are actually "hard to avoid if you start from the text itself: Outside literary approaches, why else study the detailed structure of a media text as your primary research focus unless you can plausibly claim that those details *make a difference* to wider social processes?" (p. 17, italics in original). The tendency to accept the existence of direct media effects among some social psychologist is interesting because it persists despite contrary evidence. Such errors in thinking might be partially explained by the notion of belief perseverance (Box 11.11), whereby people often maintain beliefs even when presented with evidence that contradicts these beliefs (Ross, Lepper & Hubbard, 1975). In the process, they tend to ignore, give little weight to or discredit evidence that challenges the belief in powerful media effects on violent behaviour. This can be seen in reactions to researchers who question the 'commonsense' belief that media content causes violent behaviour.

BOX 11.11   Belief perseverance

Belief perseverance describes how a person comes to believe something and then sticks to this belief and is likely to keep believing it. This can occur despite the person being presented with information that challenges the belief.

Considering uses, or what people do with media

The opening scenario for this chapter reflects the importance of media in raising anxieties regarding what might be happening to loved ones, the use of media to track events as they emerge and the increased capacity of news organizations to report live from events and ease or exacerbate the fears of loved ones. These functions raise the importance of the ways in which media are used by people. Uses and gratifications research was developed in an attempt to create a plural conceptualization of audience members and their engagements with media. Katz's (1959) often cited statement signalled a shift in orientation from 'what the media do to people', evident in the previous section, to 'what people do with the media', evident in this and the following sections. Researchers investigate people's actual uses of media to satisfy their own needs, establish influences on the development of needs and motives for media use, and establish the consequences of seeking to satisfy needs. According to this tradition, any influence of media is mediated in accordance with the functions media use serve within people's everyday lives. Audiences are said to produce differentiated interpretations from and uses for media content in accordance with the gratification of personal needs, interests and goals (Livingstone, 1998). Research primarily explores what people use media products for (e.g. gaining up-to-date information) and what people gain from viewing (e.g. better knowledge of contemporary events).

Despite the useful reorientation away from the ways media stimuli might impact unsuspecting members of the pubic, the uses approach is not without limitations. This approach has been criticized for being too individualistic in focusing on personal uniqueness to the detriment of interpersonal and sociostructural considerations, including material circumstances that influence patterns of media use (Livingstone, 1998). Audience uses are explored as the product of the cognitive processes of independent individuals (Chapter 4). This can lead to the assumption that audience members are not influenced by previous media consumption or other people when making sense of media materials. Media consumption is often a social event, and personal needs are cultivated through social interactions. As noted throughout this book, people are fundamentally interdependent (Chapters 4 and 5). In short, people's use of media in daily life is more complex and varied than a focus on personal needs can explain (Box 11.12). Social psychologists need to know how media are used to guide people's views, as well as how mundane daily practices allow people to escape, dismiss and even challenge dominant worldviews often circulated via the media (Livingstone, 2007a).

BOX 11.12   Human agency and media use

Many psychologists have become more open to associating personal agency in media use and sense-making with information and communications technologies (Contarello & Sarrica, 2007; McMillan & Morrison, 2006) rather than with older media forms such as television (Giles, 2003). However, all forms of media are interactive and involve agency on the part of those watching, reading, calling, writing and posting. People use, and do things with, all media forms. For example, O'Sullivan (2005) explored the presentation of self through calls to a tabloid radio show, a sensationalist media format that serves a number of identity functions for citizens around the world. O'Sullivan illustrates how callers can actively appropriate this medium as a forum for interpersonal communication and, in the process, gain a sense of self as a member of a community of listeners rather than as a socially isolated individual. In this study, participants often considered their calls to the show to involve displays for friends and family. Calls were taped by many callers or a family member so that the successful performance could be relived and shared with friends and family who might have missed the call. This illustrates some of the complexities of relations that are commonly associated with information and communications technologies, but also appear in research on the use of older forms of media, in this case radio.

When investigating media uses, we need to realize that the role of media in society is much more complex than the mere transfer of specific information into the minds of individuals (Rice & Atkin, 2001); media provide shared spaces for engaging in collective practices through which identities can be nurtured and developed, belonging and participation can be fostered, supportive networks can be maintained and a sense of trust and belonging can be cultivated or undermined (Silverstone, 2007). However, in emphasizing the importance of media within our daily lives, we must be careful not to become media-centric (Silverstone, 1999). This can be avoided by not falling into the trap of overasserting the role of media as a factor in the construction of public understandings and human action. We can also balance the focus on what media might do to people with a focus on what people do with, and around, media as technologies that are woven into the very fabric of social life today. This involves seeing media as being embedded in the social practices that make up daily life (Couldry, 2004), rather than as external influences that come from outside daily life and do bad things to people.

It is useful for us to consider what happens when people begin to use media technologies. This involves considering how media devices are integrated into existing social relations and practices, such as interactions with friends, colleagues, family and institutions. In taking up such issues, social psychologists have explored how people's engagements with others via media go well beyond the technologies (Livingstone, 2007a, 2007b). Media content and practices live on and infiltrate our face-to-face discussions and social engagements, such as when people discuss the latest content on YouTube (Box 11.13). At a straightforward level, media can give people something to talk about, and even provide opportunities to talk to others. It has been argued that youth engaged in digital gaming create new virtual spaces of interaction (e.g. Beavis & Charles, 2007) and engage with each other in the playground about their gaming experiences (Livingstone & Bovill, 2001). The key point is that various media are woven into the very fabric of daily life and can support and generate further social interactions.

What is proposed here is a broader outlook on media that draws on the notion that, rather than simply 'impacting' people in everyday life, media devices are absorbed into social life and become part of the dynamics of daily practice (Chamberlain & Hodgetts, 2008). That is, many of the activities we engaged in before the technology, such as catching up with friends after school, continue but may be transformed from face-to-face to web-based encounters on social networking sites. These virtual catch-ups are similar in that they still span from friendship and support to conflict and bullying. Exploring such social psychological processes requires a shift in perspective beyond an exclusive focus on the impact of the Internet on users'

BOX 11.13   Integrating media technologies into everyday life

Social psychologists are increasingly interested in the take-up of media technologies across groups, issues of access and the ways in which media devices are integrated into and completed through daily practice (Katz & Rice, 2002). Social psychologists are coming to the realization that the use of media devices is shaped in and through daily practice, and this use in turn can influence these very practices, contributing to cultural change. For example, García-Montes, Caballero-Muñoz and Pérez-Álvarez (2006) ask:

How does the use of mobile phones affect people's customs and identity?... In our view, there is no doubt that cellphones become incorporated into the practices of individuals within their culture. Otherwise, they would appear as alien and abstruse to potential users. However, recognition of this does not imply that there are no further consequences of technologies for their users. Indeed, it can be said that the emergence of great technological innovations has always brought with it profound social and economic alterations, and even whole new lifestyles. (p. 68)

With this bold assertion, the authors point out that impacts are not homogeneous and psychologists need to consider variations in uptake and use when considering the integration of cell phones into daily life. A pertinent idea here is that media do not simply enter everyday life, our homes, workplaces and social environments; they are *created* there (Chamberlain & Hodgetts, 2008). For example, the meaning and role of the television set, iPod, game consul or stereo in a living room depends on what we do with these technologies and the practices and relationships with which we surround them. In short, media devices are completed in daily life through their use in broader processes of social reproduction in which people and technology can reproduce each other. We can even try out different selves online.

psychological health and participation in social life. Psychologists are focusing on processes of continued human contact through the use of such media (Chamberlain & Hodgetts, 2008). For example, particular attention has been given to the ways media allow people to create and play with new identities from which to engage with others across the globe and different genders (Chapter 3). These online identities can be distinct from dominant modes of being offline or extensions of them; they may last for a single interaction or be maintained for years, such as one's avatar. Here we see the relevance of the work of Cooley (1902) and the notion that we create and construct ourselves through interactions with others and in the context of specific roles. The space provided by the Internet in daily life provides room for the development of a virtual place-based identity as an extension of those discussed in Chapter 6. As Borgida and Stark (2004) note, "[T]he internet may be a new way for people to do old things, as opposed to a transformative technology that has altered basic patterns of social life" (p. 468). When using multiplayer games on the web, people often adopt a new identity, much like when in the 1970s children played dungeons and dragons or those in the 1950s played cowboys and Indians or doctors and nurses. To some extent during such interactions we become who we pretend to be.

Communing across the online/offline divide

The rise of contemporary media continues to raise concerns in some circles regarding the ways in which increased media consumption may undermine traditional social and community ties. Media have been blamed for the demise of social life and undermining community resilience (Chapter 10). Putnam (2000) famously associated increased social isolation and a general decline in civic life with the rise of television, where viewing saps time that could be spent engaging 'productively' with fellow citizens. Social scientists have also considered the role of media in supporting or undermining public deliberations regarding community problems (Rojas et al., 2005). We would assert that it is somewhat simplistic to maintain distinctions between reduced face-to-face and mediated communities, and to associate a supposed drop in civic life with increased media consumption (cf. Hampton, 2001). Since Tarde (1910), psychologists have considered the ways in which public debates via media forums provide resources for face-to-face conversations in which further consideration of issues can occur and courses of action be planed. This work is important because our daily talk regarding issues is often informed by media deliberations, which offer perspectives and resources for making sense of these issues. Research increasingly shows that media often provide spaces for a range of social practices, meetings and interactions beyond the world of virtual friends, movie characters and pop stars (Livingstone & Bovill, 2001). We often watch television together, consuming sports events or concerts with friends and family (Silverstone, 2007). Media-based community activities stretch our meaningful social networks out beyond home locales. Wellman and colleagues (1998) asserted that much of the information, interpersonal resources and social support people access in their daily lives originate from outside local settings. We keep in touch via mobile phones, email and chat rooms. As in instances when callers to talkback radio shows offer support to socially isolated fellow callers, participants in chat rooms and other spaces provided by computer-mediated communications often reach out beyond the screen to meet face to face. Supporting this assertion, Hampton (2001) found that local participation in a suburb wired for broadband computer-mediated communications facilitated neighbourhood recognition, visiting, the maintenance of social ties and collective action. Media can also allow us to establish and maintain intimate relationships (Chapter 3).

When considering the general role of media in community, Silverstone (1999) makes the point that living and engaging with others or communing is the foundation of our humanity (Chapter 3). We now often engage with others via various media. Adding further complexity, Silverstone proposes that to some extent all communities are virtual communities. For Silverstone (1999), "[c]ommunities are lived. But also imagined. ... Ideas of community hover between experience and desire" (p. 97). After all, our sense of belonging and the shared symbols we rely upon to forge communities do not occur in a social or media-proof vacuum. We forge community in face-to-face interactions replete with references to lines in movies and developments in the news. Media often address us as members of specific communities when talking about the opposing team. Thus, media imagine our existence, and we imagine membership of groups when we engage in commonly shared activities such as reading the newspaper, listening to the radio and watching television as discrete individuals consuming common symbols (Anderson, 1983; Tacchi, 1998). It is in such instances that we reform links between self and society.

Review exercise

Reflect on the communities you engage with via the media. These can involve interactions via social networking sites or the friends you text after class. You may participate in 'imagined communities' when watching a national sports event.

- What is similar and different about these communities?
- How do they relate to the conduct of your life online and offline?

Despite the well-documented communal aspects of media use, news reports and parent groups frequently raise concerns regarding how the online participation of youth, for instance, may be occurring at the expense of face-to-face interactions (Box 11.14). Such concerns are understandable but may, in many cases, be misplaced. Recent research indicates that computer-based interactions occur in addition to, rather than instead of, other forms of interaction (Lenhart et al., 2007, 2008; Livingstone & Bober, 2004; Livingstone & Bovill, 2001). Many young people layer modes of communication on top of one another, and have the skill to move seamlessly across a media nexus or communicative landscape (Chamberlain & Hodgetts, 2008). Lenhart and colleagues (2007) found that US teens use media devices that they have at hand, be it landlines, mobile phones, or computers, as well as engaging face to face. The participatory culture (Jenkins, 2006) of youth created through the use of such devices transcends the online and offline divide. Lenhart and colleagues (2007) note that "those who are the most active *online* with social media applications like blogging and social networking also tend to be the most involved with *offline* activities like sports, music, or part-time employment" (p. 9).

Allaying the fears of some parents that their children's computer use will lead to social withdrawal, recent research associates Internet use with increased civic participation. Lenhart and colleagues (2008) explored links between digital gaming and civic participation. Half the research participants reported playing games on the previous day, typically for an hour or more. Ninety-seven per cent of youth played web, computer, consul or portable games that included racing, puzzles, action, strategy and role-playing genres. A majority of these teens (65 per cent) played with others in the same room and 27 per cent with people linked via the Internet. Many played with friends and family as well as people they met online. The authors found that

BOX 11.14   Youth and social participation on/offline

In their recent US survey, Lenhart and colleagues (2007) revealed that social networking and the creation of digital materials is central to the lives of many teenagers. The research showed that 93 per cent of US teens aged twelve to seventeen years participated in the Internet, which has become an important landscape for social interaction and creating shared materials. Blogs, web pages and artistic creations were created by 64 per cent of respondents, and 55 per cent of these teens were present on social network sites such as MySpace and Facebook. Teens use these sites to maintain links with existing friends and family, to make plans for online and offline activities and to meet new people. They also stay informed about social issues through producing or consuming and commenting on blogs. This is what Sally and Richard Gray are doing in their bedrooms each night.

aspects of game-play have a positive relationship with civic outcomes, and include opportunities to simulate political activities, learn about governance, debate issues, form and facilitate guilds or gaming groups (often globally) and help others. Having to learn to cooperate and work as a member of a team to achieve shared objectives in many games can be associated with developing a skill set of relevance to the workplace and community life. Interest in games extends beyond the consul, with players also discussing game-play both via the web and face to face. Further, youth keep in touch with friends while playing games over the web, and engage with each other at school regarding the intricacies of their gaming and associated conventions and groupings. To deprive children of time to game can be seen as a social isolating act (Livingstone & Bovill, 2001).

Review exercise

Think about your own online and offline relationships.

- Do these overlap sometimes while being distinct at other times?

Links between online and offline spaces invoked in the actions of young people are supported by the work of Silverstone (1999), who promoted the idea of a double articulation of space in order to conceptualize the presence of media technologies in daily life. Extending our discussion of place in Chapter 6, we might assert that media technologies provide virtual spaces that are folded into existing spaces for everyday life such as a living room or bedroom. These media or imaginary spaces are also associated with place affiliations and place-based identities. Silverstone (1999, 2007) proposed that research should attend to the weaving of such media spaces into domestic settings. This opens up investigations of the dual purposes as aesthetic objects displayed, for instance, in a youth's bedroom or handbag (in the case of an expensive mobile phone), and modes of transportation that allow people to inhabit or at least survey other worlds and locations beyond the bedroom. Consideration of such media-based practices as interacting at a distance require us to continue conducting social psychological research with a focus beyond the specifics of content of media or audience responses to explore links between our online and offline worlds (Livingstone, 2007a, 2007b) as these are played out across a range of media devices and settings (Box 11.15).

For those of you who read Chapter 6, overlaps between the construction of place-based identities and media use may be starting to surface. Livingstone (2007b) reviewed research into young people's

BOX 11.15   Media use and domesticity

In a recent article considering the work of Roger Silverstone, Livingstone (2007a) raises a number of important observations that we consider central to strengthening and developing social psychology of the media. Livingstone begins by describing a core contemporary domestic space, the living room, and how it is saturated with media technologies, including televisions, stereos, DVD recorders, computers with Internet access and iPods. Those who dwell there might watch a DVD together or cohabitate in silence when plugged into iPods; they might also be dispersed when consuming media in other spaces within this domestic realm. A core issue is that our domestic worlds involve spaces that are simultaneously public and private, individual and shared. To convey how such dwellers are simultaneously located in the particular house and the wider world, Livingstone invokes the metaphor of the time machine in *Doctor Who*, an object that is relatively small on the outside but much larger on the inside. This metaphor applies very well to media technologies such as television, mobile phones and networked computers, which function as portals to wider and often physically distant worlds. The complex use of such media in domestic spaces is increasingly of interest to social psychologists because media devices are situated in everyday environments and caught up in the social relations of everyday living (Chamberlain & Hodgetts, 2008). Livingstone (2007a) notes that these spaces of mundane media consumption demand "that economic and societal processes are to be understood significantly through the messiness of domestic practices in everyday life; if these are tidied away, the relation between macro and micro accounts of power becomes incomprehensible" (p. 17).

use of media in domestic settings that shows that media technologies are used to create personal spaces in the home and a sense of place (Chamberlain & Hodgetts, 2008). Media devices are often treated as personal things, and, as noted in Chapter 6, one's things can become part of oneself. It is likely that many readers of this book would feel lost or out of sorts without their PDA or mobile phone (Box 11.16). Livingstone points out that many of our prized possessions are media objects such as iPods, computers, web pages and games consuls. Links between media and self can be taken further when we consider how people develop in part through the consumption of music, movies, games and practices such as interacting with others via social networking sites. It is through such mediated modes of social interaction that our identities are increasingly formed. As Livingstone (2007b) notes, "Personal ownership of media dramatically increases in the early teenage years, part and parcel of the development of identity" (p. 314). Technologies become a means of creating and enacting identities.

Staying with the issue of links between media use and self-constructions, Bloustien (2007) reports on a longitudinal, ethnographic and cross-cultural project studying marginalized young people's media practices that shows how their use of convergent media forms – music, mobile phones, blogging, websites, the

---

BOX 11.16   Media use beyond the home

Clearly, in daily life media devices are not used solely in domestic settings. For example, mobile phones provide a means of conducting one's life across physical contexts or staying in touch while on the move. We can fold places into one another by using media to take us somewhere else. In the process, traditional distinctions between public and private are brought into question (García-Montes, Caballero-Muñoz & Pérez-Álvarez, 2006). Such devices provide for more fluid interchanges across lifespheres that are increasingly interfolded, such as when we check on a sick child during a break in a conference or take a business call while at the beach with friends. "On accepting a call we receive on a mobile phone, we commit ourselves to being simultaneously in two different places" (García-Montes, Caballero-Muñoz & Pérez-Álvarez, 2006). This separation not only requires the user to negotiate the intersection or fusion of these spaces smoothly and skilfully and is something they prefer to avoid, but it also demands new forms of identity work. We can extend the notion of the double articulation of space offered by media in asserting that people can be in two places at once, sitting at home with family while surveying the surface of the Moon. This involves cognitive flexibility and an ability to seamlessly multitask. This requires a reconsideration of time and space in daily life. This is necessary because we are increasingly conducting our lives across multiple locations simultaneously, such as when watching a movie with friends in our bedroom while surfing the web.

Internet, desktop publishing, digital cameras – brings new forms of agency, networking, collaboration and trust to the fore. Her research shows how youth involvement with these practices provides valuable pathways for identity work, training and social inclusion, not only facilitating a greater sense of belonging to existing social and familial networks, but also providing opportunities to create new experiential and economic communities based on music, the arts and leisure activities. In sum, recent research illustrates how researchers need to consider the offline contexts in which online practices take place if we are to extend our understandings of media in everyday life.

Chapter summary

Due to the centrality of media in daily life, psychologists have studied media influences and been involved in shaping media content for more than 100 years. We have contributed advice columns, written self-improvement books, hosted radio shows, featured as experts on reality TV programmes and evaluated web-based efforts to educate people about a raft of social concerns. Increased recognition of such efforts is reflected in the development of media psychology practice guidelines by the APA (www.apa.org/divisions/div46). Media remain even more relevant to psychological research and practice today because public consumption of various news and entertainment forms is a primary leisure activity. From reading newspapers to listening to the radio or surfing the web, people come to understand what is happening in different communities, what issues they should be concerned about and how these issues should be resolved (Chamberlain & Hodgetts, 2008). Media have been explored as a source of shared experience that we all use to understand the world and our place in it. This raises issues regarding what we are offered and how media content can enhance or undermine our collective lives.

Generations of psychologists have conceptualized the media as a battleground between 'healthy' and 'unhealthy' messages. We have been concerned with the possible effects of 'unhealthy messages' and with developing strategies for using media to promote 'healthy messages'. When reflecting on this preoccupation, Katz's (1959) famous call for a shift in focus from 'what the media do to people' to 'what people do with the media' is highly relevant. Today, we need to consider both media influence on public understandings and related practices as well as how audiences can select, ignore, criticize, accept or appropriate media representations. When investigating such processes we need to realize that the role of media in everyday life is broader than the transfer of specific information. Media provide shared spaces for engaging in collective practices through which belonging and participation can be fostered, supportive networks can be maintained and a sense of trust and belonging can be cultivated (Hodgetts & Chamberlain, 2006b). While emphasizing the centrality of media to our daily lives and such related processes, care is also needed so that we do not become media-centric and make a "fundamedia attribution error" (Fischoff, 1999) by asserting that media are the sole influence on how people make sense of their lives and related practices.

Simply dismissing the potential for negative influences from media use on people would be shortsighted. In this chapter, we have presented a more balanced account than is typically evident in social psychology textbooks, which often assume that laboratory evidence for direct imitation and social learning is sufficient for understanding of the function of many forms of media in society. It is not. Despite the insights such studies provide, we also need to use other methods and ask different questions when considering what people actually do with media in daily life. There is much more to media than information consumption, imitation and emulation. People can share and care via the media, stay in contact and build or maintain social ties and identities that cross the boundaries between representational and physical spaces. At times, people may behave differently online than they do offline. However, this still depends on the human context of an interaction. People can also behave differently at work with colleagues and at home with family members. The point is that media can be approached as providing further spaces for human interactions in everyday life. This perspective enables us to see media as woven into society and daily routines rather than as a negative variable from outside of society that comes along to 'shape' behaviour. This is an orientation that allows us to make more sense of the media-saturated nature of contemporary existence for many people.

Citizens often forge and maintain social ties through the use of various media. We can develop a sense of community through mundane actions such as calling talkback radio, reading local newspapers, deliberating upon sportscasts and accessing various Internet sites. Media are important to geographically and relationally based communities because they provide opportunities for communing with others, sharing and belonging. We might go so far as saying that media are central to the organization of society today (Curran & Seaton, 2003). Media can be used to increase participation in civic life and efforts for social change.

It is important to keep in mind that media do not offer an unproblematic panacea for community (Hodgetts & Chamberlain, 2007). Media can bring us together as well as tear us apart. Media can encourage understanding and support as well as ignorance and discrimination. Media can become central to the promotion of negative relations between communities and the dominance of some over others. The functions of media become overtly political when control over public narratives and characterizations of social groups is denied to some and monopolized by others (Silverstone & Georgiou, 2005). We should be careful not to take such concerns regarding media power to the extent of being overly deterministic. After all, stigmatizing and discriminatory media practices can be resisted, refused and challenged through, for instance, media advocacy work or the use of alternative media (Hodgetts et al., 2008; Veno & van den Eynde, 2007). Maligned groups can give up an invitation to fit in or comply with roles and characterizations prescribed for them by dominant groups via the media.

In sum, everyday life is punctuated with mediated experiences, communications via telephone, email or chat rooms, and engagements with television, radio, magazines, newspapers, websites, digital games, billboards, packaging and advertising. People's engagements with media are not simple: we use the media for such things as communicating with others, maintaining social networks, accessing information, staying informed, sustaining a sense of self and place and gaining pleasure and entertainment. Research into the diffuse and varied ways in which media engagements are undertaken in everyday living enables social psychologists to become even more engaged with the messiness of everyday life and the complexity and fluidity of social psychological processes. The focus is audience centred, exploring what people do with media and how they respond to and use available content and technology.

Review exercise

Ask some people you know about what impact media have on them.

- Do those who watch horror movies or play violent video games see themselves as sociopaths ready to lay waste to those around them?

A common response is that media do not affect them personally, but that they are concerned about the effects on other people. This is commonly referred to as the *third-person effect*.

12 Towards social psychologies of everyday life

Chapter scenario

Mark calls to his partner Jenny, who is in the shower: "Some foreign taxi driver got beaten up last night just up the road. Maybe it was that bloke who dropped us home last night. Serves him right ... should have stayed in his own country." Jenny laughs. The toast pops up, and Mark begins to butter the slices as Jenny emerges from the bathroom. Mark complains, "I feel dreadful. Think it's the flu that's going round." Jenny answers, "Perhaps you should see the doctor today." Mark replies, "Remember those herbal tablets that Mary gave me last time I had a sore throat? They were great. ... I'll take some of those and see how I go." Jenny retorts, "That's just nonsense! That stuff's useless. ... You should see the doctor. You were just overworked last time. The herbs had nothing to do with it." Mark shrugs and goes about preparing breakfast.

Everyday life occurs when you get up in the morning and go about your routine. You might turn on the kettle and put two slices of bread into the toaster. Turning on the radio, you might catch the morning news. Apparently, another taxi driver has been assaulted and killed overnight. You may shake your head in dismay or discuss the event with a loved one. In this context you might think about what we have covered in this book. You have read through a lot of material that can be used to help make sense of such events. Perhaps you are left wondering what it means to understand the outside world through news reports (Chapter 11). You might be concerned about how Mark and Jenny can so easily position the taxi driver outside their scope of justice (Chapter 9). Making sense of the above scenario can be enhanced by consideration of where and how the taxi driver is placed with respect to social justice. Understanding the couple's response in the context of the scope of justice enables us to understand how it is that people may be notionally unsympathetic to the plight of others. Dismissing the plight of other people, as we saw in Chapter 9, is a common element in processes of marginalization in the case of indigenous peoples (Chapter 5), refugees (Chapter 7) and many other groups in society (Chapters 6 and 8). You may also want to consider the procedural fairness of policies, procedures and practices that impact the capacity of the refugee taxi driver introduced in Chapter 7 to remake his life in another country. More sophisticated understandings of such societal problems can lead to the targeting of our efforts towards more appropriate pathways for action. In short, the scenario relates directly to core topics for a social psychology of everyday life that addresses the pervasiveness of media, intergroup relations, social justice, common knowledge and health.

This book foregrounds the need for a social psychology that is vibrant and alive, and that is relevant to people's everyday experiences. Social psychology is not merely an amalgam of academic theoretical abstractions. Rather, it provides a multifaceted lens through which people can make sense of, interpret and actively construct their own lives and the

Chapter overview

This chapter draws out core insights from across the previous chapters and applies these to the experiences of Mark and Jenny as they go about their day. We then return to broader issues regarding the focus and direction of social psychology and the place of this book within the broader discipline. In summary, the chapter covers:

- Combining insights from various chapters
- Theory, research and action
- Developing your own social psychology

lives of people around them. The chapters in this book have presented a crucial, but by no means exhaustive, set of approaches for understanding aspects of people's everyday lived experiences. In the process, we have sought to recast the derisive observation that psychology simply tells people what they already know in a language they do not understand. Social psychologists produce knowledge that can enrich human lives in ways that resonate intuitively with almost anyone.

Putting the pieces of the puzzle together

The construction of common understandings or knowledge is central to everyday life and social psychology. In a sense such knowledge is being negotiated when Mark and William discuss the history of Localville and what needs to be done to make it an even better place to live. Human thought, dialogue and action represent core topics for social psychology and have been taken up across all the chapters of this text. As noted in Chapter 3, knowledge involves personal experience and the appropriation of other people's understandings, often through processes of socialization. The world has already been rendered meaningful by other people, and individuals engage with these existing understandings when making sense of their own lives. Interpretive communities to which Mark and Jenny belong have

shared memories and often tell stories of 'who they are' and 'where they are from' and 'who belongs' (see Chapters 3, 7 and 6, respectively). This orientation does not imply that people are 'cultural dupes' who simply parrot communal explanations in a predictable manner. Each of us often embellishes and builds on shared understandings when creating our own knowledge of the world. This is part of the reason Mark and Jenny can disagree on the usefulness of herbal remedies and the need for Mark to see a doctor (Chapter 8).

Chapter scenario (cont.)

Mark and Jenny live on the housing estate across the road from the indigenous health centre discussed in Chapter 5. The tribal authority is keen to have a range of groups present on the estate and to be as inclusive as possible so that local children grow up interacting with people from a range of backgrounds. Mark and Jenny baby-sit the neighbour's children when Sue and William go out. The couples are good friends, and Mark enjoys learning about local history over a coffee with William. On this particular morning Mark looks out of the window and sees families taking their children to the health centre and school across the road. He sees Sue and William and leans out the window: "Hey, William, the street lights we got the authority to install really make a difference around here, hey? What's next on the agenda, a swimming pool?" William replies, "Could be. It's good how they actually listened to us. We actually get a say in making this place work for us all. I've to get over to the centre, but let's catch up for a beer on Saturday." Mark: "Sounds like a plan. I'll send you a text." Jenny leans past Mark: "Sue we'll get some more work done on the mural while the guys are doing their thing." Sue replies, "Yeah, it'll be great to get that ugly wall covered up with a bit of colour."

The interactions in the scenario above reflect how people can work together to create a safer and healthier place to live. Cooperation and inclusion can lead to the cultivation of an environment in which a range of place affiliations can be held in harmony rather than disharmony (Chapters 6, 8 and 10). The scenario also reveals how people from different backgrounds like Mark and William can develop friendships and work together for the common good, in this case improving the physical and social environment in which they live together. As noted in Chapter 6, what is important for the development of healthy environments is investment in decent street lighting, parks and communal areas for positive social interactions.

We noted in Chapters 6 and 10 that members of communities with social capital who have opportunities to exercise some control over their environments and destiny tend to be healthier. Social support and networks do not alleviate material hardship, even though such interpersonal supports can buffer people against the severity of material hardship. Mark and Sue recognize that things are being done in the community to develop the neighbourhood as a positive place to live and feel safe. This reflects how a range of initiatives engaged in by the tribal authority, in collaboration with the city and local residents, are having a positive impact for people beyond the walls of the clinic and housing estate. In Chapter 8 it was proposed that health promotion involves a range of initiatives at the individual, community and population levels that are designed to protect, prolong and increase the quality of human life. These can span regular checkups, support for educational initiatives, the provision of dry housing, ensuring political representation, efforts at building positive relationships in the community through collaborative projects, and ensuring adequate participation in local decision-making processes (Chapters 6 and 9).

Chapter scenario (cont.)

With breakfast finished, Jenny heads off to work. She has extracted a promise from Mark that he will go to see the doctor. As Jenny walks down the street to catch her commuter bus to work she drops in at her local café to pick up a take-away coffee. The owner, Carol, greets her as an old friend: "How are you this morning?" Jenny replies cheerily, "Can't complain, you know how it is." As Carol prepares Jenny's usual coffee, she chats ceaselessly, recounting her experiences from earlier in the morning. Carol, despite her age, spends every morning before opening the café at Street Wise, a local charity that provides free breakfasts for those in need. "Met a new bloke this morning at the drop-in," says Carol. "Neville. Don't know where he came from but he was dead scared. Came to the right place, though. I put him touch with Tom. You know Tom? Great bloke – looks after all the newbies. That's what I love about the neighbourhood... people look out for each other." As Jenny pays for the coffee, she asks, "How's Arthur?" Carol looks sadly into the distance: "Not good, love. Can't get out of bed anymore. My youngest helps as much as she can, and Mick and Phil from next door are great. Couldn't survive without them."

Having read this book, you should recognize that Carol exemplifies the values we discussed in Chapter 10 associated with positive-oriented psychologies. She strives for a positive worldview despite some deeply concerning issues in her own life and the lives of those around her. You might now empathize with people like Carol at a deeper level, recognizing the intuitive humanism they posses that is inherent in their pro-social behaviour. Carol's commitment to action with Street Wise might remind you of the Freirian concerns with critical consciousness and social transformation. Importantly, readers might respect and admire Carol's resilience in the face of adversity. Not only does Carol display resilience at a personal level; she also appears to be connected to a resilient community. The way Tom, a veteran of the streets, looks after the newbie, Neville, is evidence of a connectedness and a shared desire for 'bouncing back' and positive growth. In one sense, Jenny's purchase of a cup of coffee from Carol is fairly mundane and unremarkable. Yet, if we bring our social psychology of everyday life to the conversation, this exchange also provides an opportunity to understand the lived experiences of both women in a deeper, more compassionate way.

Chapter scenario (cont.)

It is lunchtime. Mark is starving and really needs to get out of the office for a break. He is still not feeling great. Mark heads to the local food court. As he walks towards the food court he passes a job centre. A man is emerging from the doorway. He is dark skinned, and Mark guesses he may be of Asian descent. The man is clean-shaven, well dressed and polite, saying "Excuse me" as he brushes past. Mark is appalled when a man driving by shouts, "Hey, you useless immigrant, why don't you go home and stop trying to steal jobs from us!" Shocked at this incident, Mark lends his sympathy to the man through a knowing glance and walks on. The food hall is packed with shoppers, so Mark takes his lunch to what he hopes will be a quiet corner of the hall. Sitting nearby is a grandmother with her two grandchildren. Mark watches with amused interest as the two rowdy children devour their fries. He enjoys being here at this noisy intersection of so many people as they take a short break from the hustle and bustle of their everyday lives. It seems like a microcosm of society, diverse, colourful and ever changing. Mark's reverie is suddenly disturbed. He turns his attention back to the grandmother, who has summoned a security guard. "Do you see what she is doing?" The grandmother asks in a shrill voice. "It's disgusting! What are people like that doing in here?" She gestures to the lank-haired occupant of an adjoining table who is hungrily shovelling discarded food into her mouth. She is unkempt and dirty. The security guard ushers the homeless women towards the door. As they walk by, Mark hears the guard say, "Hey, Susan, you'd better not hang round, especially when it is so busy – sorry mate." Susan replies as they drift out of earshot, "So I'll just go outside and catch pneumonia then?"

As Mark finishes his salad he thinks about Susan. She did not look at all well. Mark is reminded of Arthur (Carol's partner), the guy who used to run a local restaurant and who has had to retire early due to illness. Arthur is very unwell. However, Arthur has at least some resources at his disposal, including a loving and caring family. It appears that Susan does not have access to such an array of resources. She is unkempt, unwell and unwelcome. Mark reflects on how health and well-being are unequally distributed in society. Health inequalities are as much a social justice issue as they are economic and political issues.

As Mark finishes his salad, he speculates about Susan's place in society. Clearly, the security guard knows Susan. It is possible that her sense of self may be bound up in her regular attendance at the food hall. Moving her on may impact her place-based identity. Mark hopes that he will see Susan here on another day when perhaps it is less busy.

This scene represents the kind of situation and circumstance that ought to be grist for the mill for social psychologists. Social psychologists have a history of researching and responding to such situations as those occurring outside the job centre and in the food court, in which societal tensions and differing attitudes and needs between groups of people bubble to the surface. Yet our solutions and reflections often seem, paradoxically, at once too simplistic and too complex. Our attempts to reduce human behaviour to cause-and-effect relations has led to the nagging belief that it is all too hard. And yet it ought not to be so. The scenarios presented throughout this book provide an authentic setting within which we can tease out the regularities and grapple with the complexities in developing new theoretical understandings and practical solutions.

Review exercise

At this point it might be useful to go back through previous chapters, and in particular Chapters 6, 8 and 10, and review the types of strategy social psychologists use when addressing these issues.

We now know that places are crucial to how people come to understand themselves, their relationships with others and their place in the world. Personal and social identities emerge and are formed across physical places and social spaces, and through daily practices. A sense of self and belonging is often associated with particular activities, such as going to a local pub and participating in a speed dating night with friends. Yet not all people are as welcome in such communal spaces.

Chapter scenario (cont.)

After work Jenny stops by the supermarket to pick up some food for the evening. She resolves to stock up on fresh fruit and vegetables and prepare a healthy meal. Jenny and Mark have been burning the candle at both ends for a while now, and as the events of the morning showed, it is beginning to affect Mike's health. Jenny wonders whether Mike visited the doctor as promised. She waits in the queue to pay for her goods behind a young mother who is clearly flustered. Her child has been noisily demanding sweets and is clearly unhappy when told he can't have them. As the check-out operator totals up the woman's purchases Jenny sees that the child has managed to sneak a bag of sweets onto the counter and that they have been processed unnoticed by the mother, who is anxiously watching the cash register. The young mother suddenly asks the check-out operator to stop processing the goods. Clearly she is worried that she will be unable to pay for all the goods and loads a number of items back into the trolley, pays for the accumulated goods and leaves hurriedly. "Excuse me," Jenny says. "Your child put some sweets." But the young women does not hear Jenny as, clearly embarrassed, she hurries from the shop.

Throughout the book we have proposed that social psychology has much to offer in developing an understanding of the challenges of living in increasingly diverse societies. A complex world demands and deserves complex understandings and solutions. The supermarket queue may seem like one of the most unremarkable situations possible. However, closer inspection reveals the variety of experiences among the people queuing and the overlap and interplay between their lives and situations. We are now acutely aware that the young mother's attempt to buy healthy food is as much a social justice issue related to health inequalities as it is a biological health issue. Her choices (or lack of them) will depend on the social support networks she is linked to. There are many social determinants of health that will impact the young mother's capacity to provide a healthy environment for her son, such as work, lifestyle and community networks. These issues also go to her sense of self as a good mother and competent parent.

Chapter scenario (cont.)

After dinner Mark decides to visit an elderly relative at a nearby aged-care facility, while Jenny heads off to the local football stadium to watch the local team in action. Some of their friends comment regularly on the fact that Jenny is the 'football head' while Mark has never really developed an interest in sports. Mark's aunt is aged, but still mentally alert, and Mark really enjoys the visits. Mark takes some of the fresh fruit as a gift. He joins aunt Mary in the guest room, where staff, residents and family mingle. There is a television in one corner, but the constant chatter drowns it out. Mary is in fine form. "I was on the Internet today," she says proudly. "I love it. I was blogging with Paul [another nephew]. I'll bet you never thought anyone could teach this old dog new tricks, eh?" Mark is surprised and delighted that Mary has found a new way to connect with the world, beyond the somewhat boring and sterile space of the rest home. "See that girl over there?" Mary whispers, suddenly changing the topic. Mark looks over to see a young woman in a carer's uniform. "That's Celine. She's lovely. Came here from Liberia as a refugee. Do you know that before she came here she couldn't speak English at all? You should hear her now – don't know how she does it." As if suspecting she is being spoken about, Celine turns and smiles at Mary, who smiles back at her. "See – she's lovely. But tragic, you know. When she emigrated Celine had to leave her baby behind. How could someone do that? Apparently until recently she thought the child had been killed – awful! Then, out of the blue she discovers that he is alive – and so is her mother. But they are stuck in a camp somewhere. Celine is trying to get them out." Mark looks at Celine's back thoughtfully as she bends over and plumps a pillow for an elderly man by the television. Mark is intrigued by Celine's story. He wonders how people who move from other countries make the transition.

As social psychologists we now know that such transitions involve issues of acculturation and that they emerge through complex sociopolitical processes. We are also acutely aware that people such as Celine may experience significant culture shock as a result of their displacement, relocation and settlement. Another important dimension of Celine's experience, which we now have the concepts to understand at a deeper level, is how she comes to remake her identity. Celine is negotiating an identity in her new life. Social identity theory helps us to understand how Celine is seeking to maintain positive group relations to bolster her self-esteem and her efforts to do so may invoke the processes of assimilation and accommodation or even capitulation. Celine attempts to keep up with events in her home country and the refugee camps. Even so, information is scarce and often out of date. What's more, media technology cannot replace actually being with the people you love, especially if there is little hope of being reunited or if you are worrying about their safety. No matter which angle we take, the processes of race and power for Celine are irrefutable and pervasive.

Chapter scenario (cont.)

As Mike heads home from his visit he can hear the sound of sirens. Something serious has happened. He is able to differentiate fire, ambulance and police sirens in a cacophony of sound signaling trauma of some kind. When Mike arrives home he switches on the television. Mike is horrified to see breaking news of a serious outbreak of violence at the game being attended by Jenny. Anxiously Mike scans the screen in vain for a glimpse of Jenny. He can see smoke, rubbish and crowds milling around the exits out of the sports ground. Mike sees several people being loaded into ambulances while the police usher and marshal the crowd into cordoned areas. He calls Jenny's mobile only to find that the phone is switched off. Mike is feeling panicky and calls some friends. They too are concerned. Their daughter Sally has gone to the game with her grandfather and they have been unable to get in touch. As Mike is speaking, their son Richard suggests logging onto the football ground's website and checking the ground from the webcams in the stands. Before hanging up, Mike asks Richard to keep an eye out for Jenny. Several frantic minutes later Mike receives a call from Richard's mother to say that they have seen Sally and her grandfather on the screen and that Jenny is with them and looks well. At that moment, Mike's mobile rings and the caller ID indicates that Jenny is on the line.

A key social psychological issue invoked by several of the instalments of the chapter scenario so far is media: the news report that Mark listens to, the computer in the nursing home and Celine's use of media to keep tabs on events back home. Media are pervasive in contemporary society. We take much of this for granted. Media provide a site for both understanding and constructing our social world in ways that would seem strange to earlier generations. The old days of simply coming to know the world through the newspapers are gone. The relief people such as the Grays (see Chapter 11) feel at finding their friends and loved ones are safe and well via communications technologies is a direct result of media convergence. The convergence and cross-fertilization of media both complicate and enrich our understandings of how people come to see themselves and their place in the world in relation to events in the world and other people. We have seen our online and offline realities come together. As audience members, we are not simply the receivers of information via the media; we are also purveyors, producers and redistributors of information in an increasingly diverse media-bound technological world. For more than a hundred years social psychologists have explored how public deliberations occurring via media technologies are informed by and inform ongoing face-to-face deliberations.

Media provide information-rich environments (the media nexus discussed in Chapter 11) for people to engage with events in society and other social groups. We can formulate, revise or confirm our understandings of the world through the use of mobile devices, radio, books, magazines, computers and games, and that staple of contemporary wisdom and enlightenment, television. People's lives are punctuated with mediated experiences – communications technologies and interactions with others at a physical distance. Media provide shared experiences. Watching the report about the taxi driver often comes with a sense of awareness of what is going on in our society. It can also enable Mark to maintain his social identity as a citizen who is a member of a group distinct from such immigrants.

The increased capacity of media to enlighten and build relationships as well as to misinform and build tensions between groups has been a key feature of this book. It is an important focus, as media are so ingrained within everyday life. Yet the role of media in society is much more complex than the mere transfer of specific information; media provide shared spaces for engaging in collective practices through which identities can be nurtured and developed, belonging and participation can be fostered, supportive networks can be maintained and a sense of trust and belonging can be cultivated or undermined.

Chapter scenario (cont.)

As Jenny and Mark have a quiet glass of wine together and prepare for bed they reflect on quite a day. Jenny fills Mark in on the events at the football ground. The experience was dramatic and frightening and captures his attention. As Jenny excitedly recounts the dramatic moments, Mark quietly reflects on his own experiences, less momentous, perhaps, though no less profound. Mark is still unsettled and affronted by the treatment received by the polite man who emerged from the job centre. In the past, Mark's father made regular donations to the local refugee support group. Although Mark is not certain whether the man was a refugee or not, the experience of blatant racism prompts Mark to decide to become a volunteer at the job centre. Mark believes that as a student of social psychology he has something to offer in terms of understanding the issues and acting to change a world that creates the circumstances in which such abuse is tolerated. Mark is now on a roll in terms of thinking about social justice issues he sees right on the doorstep of his community. The next day he phones a friend who is working with a local university professor on a large-scale homelessness project. After Mark describes the situation in the food hall, his friend agrees to pass on the story to the professor and get back to him in a few days.

People are often contradictory and can change their perspectives over time or across situations. Mark, like most people, is capable of prejudice towards Ian the taxi driver while also displaying empathy towards Manuel and Celine. There is much work still to be done in extending our understanding of such processes. For now we might propose that people can hold multiple and conflicting perspectives regarding other people and bring these to bear in complex ways when making sense of the events of the day.

Thinking back over the day, Jenny and Mark have concluded, as we might after such events, that it was indeed quite a day. In truth *every* day is quite a day if you think about it. In this book we have argued that we all should think about what the notion of the everyday means and its significance. The everyday can become invisible. This book has been an invitation, or perhaps more of an unashamed exhortation, to become mindful rather than mindless of the everyday world around us. Transformation and positive social change require a mindful reflection on the experiences we have every day, from the seemingly trivial daily actions such as buying a coffee from someone like Carol to the dramatic events at the football ground.

Painting a richer picture

Throughout this book we have emphasized the importance of situations and contexts for understanding human thoughts, actions and ways of being. Human lives, and the very discipline of social psychology that seeks to understand these, are shaped by historical events, such as migration, colonization, politics and social change. To understand people we must understand their places in the world and how the situations people find themselves in are influenced by wider historical, institutional, cultural and sociopolitical contexts. This requires us to get out there and engage with people as they go about their everyday lives and to work with them to make the world a better place. This book has illustrated how social psychology has much to offer in developing an understanding of everyday life and the challenges of living in increasingly diverse societies.

Social psychology has a long history of informing our engagements with the world and the people who inhabit it through research (Chapter 2). Research has provided the basis for making significant contributions in challenging prejudice and alleviating discrimination (Chapters 4, 5 and 9) and improving the health of our fellow citizens (Chapters 2, 8 and 10). Such efforts reflect the emphasis social psychologists often place on the relationship between theory, research and action (Chapters 1 and 4) (Box 12.1). In the process social psychologists enact commitments to critical humanism (Chapter 10), autonomy (Chapter 5), social inclusion (Chapter 7) and equitable social relations (Chapters 8 and 9). Guiding such work is the proposition that human beings have dignity and should be afforded equitable chances in life. This raises the importance of community development (Chapter 6), collectivist health promotion (Chapter 8) and building group resilience (Chapter 10).

A crucial take-home message from this book is that social psychology ought to be indivisible from everyday life. Social psychology provides a shared language for understanding our own lives and the experiences of others. The social psychology of everyday life presented in this book contributes a critical lens that allows us to become part of a global interpretive community. As you can see from the 'day in

---

BOX 12.1   Themes from across the chapters

Key themes to emerge across chapters revolve around linking research and action in order to:

- Explore relationships between people, communities, places and societies
- Promote the application of social psychological insights as a means of preserving and enhancing human dignity
- Facilitate self-determination among groups and the development of effective strategies that ensure collective wellness

To enhance the relevance and effectiveness of such efforts, social psychologists acknowledge the fundamentally historical, social and cultural embedded nature of both the people we engage with and ourselves as researchers.

the life' scenario elaborated throughout this chapter, the theoretical concepts of social psychology allow us to share deeper understandings of people's everyday experiences. This understanding not only enhances knowledge, but also provides clear directions for action in the pursuit of positive social change.

In demonstrating the usefulness of this orientation to social psychology, it is crucial to look back in history as well as towards the future. Some work stands the test of time and can be rediscovered and reinterpreted in different contexts. For example, Chapter 2 covers many ideas from late eighteenth- and early nineteenth-century social psychology that are particularly relevant to the challenges facing society today. In developing our orientation towards everyday life, we found it particularly useful to retain the interdisciplinary and humanistic focus from early social psychologists. Of particular use was the emphasis many of these scholars placed on systematic problem-solving and civic engagement through processes of evaluation, dialogue, self-criticism and revision. We hope that you will take on board the point that what is needed is a social psychology engaged with the complexities of human life that paints portraits and detailed landscapes of everyday life, rather than sketchy caricatures. From reviewing early ideas it became apparent to us that there is room for a range of approaches to the discipline. Social psychology can be a diverse enterprise. The social world is a complex and contradictory place, and we need a range of options for making sense of and improving it. It is essential that we embrace the wide variety of traditions in social psychology and bring them into our current engagements with everyday life.

We hope this book has enhanced your interest in social psychology and begun to answer some of the questions you may have brought with you to the exploration of social psychology. These questions often relate to the relationship between individuals and groups, helping behaviour, the functions of culture in our lives and how people might relate to others from different backgrounds from their own. What is crucial is that you approach the discipline as a vibrant intellectual space. In fact, you might consider developing your own interests and working towards developing your own approach to social psychology. The discipline is open to further possibilities. The best way for you to predict the future is to create it. We hope that you continue efforts to give the social psychology you develop away and make the world a more equitable and healthy place.

In closing, this book is based on the premise that social psychology has much to offer our understanding of everyday life. We go further to propose that a focus on what actually happens in everyday life ought to be the core focus of the discipline if we want to remain relevant and improve the human condition. The social psychology of everyday life presented in this book is very much a reflection of the personal and professional journeys that brought us together as friends and colleagues with shared aspirations to make a difference in society. This book is the fruit of conversations we had about a positive and transformative social psychology. One intention behind this book is that it should provide a catalyst for similar conversations and open up the field for the next generation of social psychologists to take the discipline in new and innovative directions. We hope that you will get on the bus. It is a bus that many societal-oriented social psychologists have been boarding for more than a century. The bus constitutes a continuation of that principled, transformative journey towards a more just and inclusive world.

References

Adair, J. (1999). Indigenisation of psychology: The concept of its practical implementation. *Applied Psychology: An International Review*, 48(4), 403–418.

Adams, J.S. (1963). Toward an understanding of inequity. *Journal of Abnormal Social Psychology*, 67, 422–436.

Adams, J.S. (1965). Inequity in social exchange. In L. Berkowitz (Ed.), *Advances in Experimental Social Psychology*, Vol. 2 (pp. 267–299). New York: Academic Press.

Adams, J.S. & Freedman, S. (1976). Equity theory revisited: Comments and annotated bibliography. In L. Berkowitz & E. Walster (Eds.), *Advances in Experimental Social Psychology*, Vol. 9 (pp. 43–56). New York: Academic Press.

Adger, N. (2003). Social capital, collective action, and adaptation to climate change. *Economic Geography*, 79(4), 387–404.

Ajzen, I. (1991). The theory of planned behavior. *Organizational Behavior and Human Decision Processes*, 50, 179–211.

Ali, L. (2008). Claiming voice: Second generation Muslim women's stories of resistance and liberation. M. Reyes Cruz (Chair), Racism, Coloniality and Representation: Examining Dynamics of Oppression and Liberation in Community Psychology. Symposium conducted at the 2nd International Community Psychology Conference, Lisbon, Portugal.

Allport, G. (1954). *The Nature of Prejudice*. Reading, MA: Addison-Wesley.

Allport, G. (1968). Six decades of social psychology. In S. Lundstedt (Ed.), *Higher Education in Social Psychology* (pp. 9–19). Cleveland: Case Western Reserve Press.

Allport, G. (1985). The historical background of social psychology. In G. Linzey & E. Aronson (Eds.), *The Handbook of Social Psychology* (3rd ed.) (pp. 1–46). New York: Random House.

Allwood, C. & Berry, J. (2006a). Origins and development of indigenous psychologies: An international analysis. *International Journal of Psychology*, 41, 243–268.

Allwood, C. & Berry, J. (2006b). Preface: Special issue on the indigenous psychologies. *International Journal of Psychology*, 41, 241–242.

Allwood, C. & Berry, J. (2007). Origins and development of indigenous psychologies: An international analysis. *International Journal of Psychology*, 41(4), 243–268.

Altman, I. (1993). Challenges and opportunities of a transactional world view: Case study of contemporary Mormon polygamous families. *American Journal of Community Psychology*, 21, 135–163.

Altman, J. & Hinkson, M. (Eds.) (2007). *Coercive Reconciliation: Stabilise, Normalise, Exit Aboriginal Australia*. North Carlton, Australia: Arena.

Amster, R. (2003). Patterns of exclusion: Sanitizing space, criminalizing homelessness. *Social Justice*, 30, 195–221.

Anastasi, A. & Urbana, S. (1997). *Psychological Testing* (7th ed.). New York: Prentice Hall.

Anderson, B. (1983). *Imagined Communities: Reflections on the Origin and Spread of Nationalism.* London: Verso.

Anderson, C., Berkowitz, L., Donnerstein, E., Huesmann, L., Johnson, J., Linz, D., Malamuth, N. & Wartella, E. (2003). The influence of media violence on youth. *Psychological Science in the Public Interest*, 4, 81–110.

Anderson, C., Carnagey, N. & Eubanks, J. (2003). Exposure to violent media: The effects of songs with violent lyrics on aggressive thoughts and feelings. *Journal of Personality & Social Psychology*, 84, 960–971.

Apfelbaum, E. (1986). Prolegomena for a history of social psychology: Some hypotheses concerning its emergence in the 20th century and its raison d'etre. In K. Larsen (Ed.), *Dialectics and Ideology in Psychology* (pp. 3–13). New York: Ablex.

Apfelbaum, E. (2000). Critical reflections on history: Some teaching from the history of social psychology. *Journal of the History of the Behavioral Sciences*, 36, 529–539.

Arrindell, W. & Luteijn, F. (2000). Similarity between intimate partners for personality traits as related to individual levels of satisfaction with life. *Personality and Individual Differences*, 28, 629–637.

Armstrong, D. (2000). A survey of community gardens in upstate New York: Implications for health promotion and community development. *Health & Place*, 6, 319–327.

Aro, A. & Absetz, P. (2009). Editorial: Guidance for professionals in health promotion: Keeping it simple – but not too simple. *Psychology and Health*, 24(2), 125–129.

Aron, A. & Corne, S. (Eds.) (1994). *Writings for a Liberation Psychology: Ignacio Martín-Baró.* Cambridge, MA: Harvard University Press.

Aron, A., Mashek, D., McLaughlin, Volpe, T., Wright, S., Lewandowski, G. & Aron, E. (2004). Including close others in the cognitive structure of self. In M. Baldwin (Ed.), *Interpersonal Cognition* (pp. 206–232). New York: Guilford.

Asch, S. (1952). *Social Psychology.* New York: Prentice Hall.

Asch, S. (1956). Studies of independence and conformity: A minority of one against a unanimous majority. *Psychological Monographs*, 70(9).

Augoustinos, M. & Reynolds, K. (2001). Prejudice, racism, and social psychology. In M. Augoustinos & K. Renolds (Eds.), *Understanding Prejudice, Racism and Social Conflict* (pp. 1–23). London: Sage.

Augoustinos, M. & Walker, I. (1995). *Social Cognition: An Integrated Introduction.* New Delhi: Sage.

Australian Community Health Association (ACHA). (1991). *Manual of Standards for Community Health: Community Health Accreditation and Standards Project.* Sydney: ACHA.

Aveling, E. & Gillespie, A. (2008). Negotiating multiplicity: Adaptive asymmetries within second-generation Turks' 'Society of Mind'. *Journal of Constructivist Psychology*, 21(3), 200–222.

Ayllón, T. & Azrin, N.H. (1968). *The Token Economy: A Motivational System for Therapy and Rehabilitation.* New York: Appleton-Century-Crofts.

Bambra, C., Fox, D. & Scott-Samuel, A. (2005). Towards a politics of health. *Health Promotion International*, 20, 187–193.

Bandura, A. (1988). Organizational application of social cognitive theory. *Australian Journal of Management*, 13, 275–302.

Bandura, A. (1990). Selective activation and disengagement of moral control. *Journal of Social Issues*, 46, 27–46.

Bandura, A. (1997). *Self-Efficacy: The Exercise of Control*. New York: W.H. Freeman.

Bandura, A. (2001). Social cognitive theory of mass communication. *Media Psychology*, 3, 265–299.

Bandura, A., Ross, D. & Ross, S. (1961). Transmission of aggressions through imitation of aggressive models. *Journal of Abnormal and Social Psychology*, 63, 575–582.

Bandura, A., Ross, D. & Ross, S.A. (1963). Imitation of film-mediated aggressive models. *Journal of Abnormal and Social Psychology*, 66, 3–11.

Barclay, L., Skarlicki, D. & Pugh, S. (2005). Exploring the role of emotions in injustice perceptions and retaliation. *Journal of Applied Psychology*, 90, 629–643.

Bartholow, B., Bushman, B. & Sestir, M. (2006). Chronic violent video game exposure and desensitization to violence: Behavioral and event-related brain potential data. *Journal of Experimental Social Psychology*, 42, 532–539.

Bartlett, F.C. (1927). Critical notice of Watson's behaviorism. *Mind*, 36, 77–83.

Bartlett, F.C. (1932). *Remembering: A Study in Experimental and Social Psychology*. Cambridge: Cambridge University Press.

Bartlett, F.C. (1956). Changing scene. British Psychological Society presidential address, March 1951. *British Journal of Psychology*, 47, 81–87.

Bartlett, F.C. (1958). *Thinking: An Experimental and Social Study*. London: Allen & Unwin.

Batson, C. (1991). *The Altruism Question: Toward a Social-Psychological Answer*. Hillsdale, NJ: Erlbaum.

Batson, C. (1994). Why act for the public good? Four answers. *Personality and Social Psychology Bulletin*, 20, 603–610.

Batson, C. & Powell, A. (2003). Altruism and pro-social behavior. In T. Millon & M. Lerner (Eds.), *Handbook of Psychology: Personality and Social Psychology* (pp. 463–484). New York: Wiley.

Baum, W.M. (2004). *Understanding Behaviorism: Behavior, Culture and Evolution*. London: Blackwell.

Baumeister, R. & Bushman, B. (2009). *Social Psychology and Human Nature*. Belmont, CA: Wadsworth.

Baumeister, R. & Leary, M. (1995). The need to belong: Desire for interpersonal attachments as a fundamental human motivation. *Psychological Bulletin*, 117, 497–529.

Bazarova, N. & Walther, J. (2009). Attributions in virtual groups: Distances and behavioral variations in computer-mediated discussions. *Small Group Research*, 40(2), 138–162.

Beaglehole, R., Bonita, R., Hortan, R., Adams, O. & McKee, M. (2004). Public health in the new era: Improving health through collective action. *The Lancet*, 363(9426), 2084–2086.

Beavis, C. & Charles, C. (2007). Would the 'real' girl gamer please stand up? Gender, LAN cafes and the reformulation of the 'girl' gamer. *Gender and Education*, 19, 691–705.

Becker, D. & Marecek, J. (2008). Positive psychology: History in the remaking? *Theory and Psychology*, 18(5), 591–604.

Belk, R. (1988). Possessions and the extended self. *Journal of Consumer Research*, 15, 139–168.

Berger, P.L. & Luckmann, T. (1966). *The Social Construction of Reality*. New York: Doubleday.

Berry, J.W. (1984). Cultural relations in plural societies: Alternatives to segregation and their sociopsychological implications. In N. Miller & M.B. Brewer (Eds.), *Groups in Contact: The Psychology of Desegregation* (pp. 11–27). Orlando: Academic Press.

Berry, J.W. (1986). The acculturation process and refugee behavior. In C.I. Williams & J. Westermeyer (Eds.), *Refugee Mental Health in Resettlement Countries* (pp. 25–38). New York: Hemisphere.

Berry, J.W. (1997). Immigration, acculturation & adaptation. *Applied Psychology & International Review*, 46, 5–34.

Berry, J.W. (1999). Emics and etics: A symbiotic conception. *Culture & Psychology*, 5, 165–171.

Berry, J.W. (2001). A psychology of immigration. *Journal of Social Issues*, 57, 615–631.

Berry, J.W., Kim, U., Power, S., Young, M. & Bujaki, M. (1989). Acculturation attitudes in plural societies. *Applied Psychology: An International Review*, 38, 185–206.

Berry, J.W., Phinney, J.S., Sam, D.L. & Vedder, P. (Eds.) (2006). *Immigrant Youth in Cultural Transition: Acculturation, Identity and Adaptation across National Contexts*. Mahwah, NJ: Lawrence Erlbaum.

Berry, J.W., Poortinga, Y., Seggall, M. & Dasen, P. (2002). *Cross-cultural Psychology: Research and Applications*. Cambridge: Cambridge University Press.

Bessenoff, G. (2006). Can the media affect us? Social comparison, self-discrepancy, and the thin ideal. *Psychology of Women Quarterly*, 30, 239–251.

Bhabha, H. (1994). *On the Location of Culture*. London: Routledge.

Bhatia, S. (2002). Acculturation, dialogical voices and the construction of the diasporic self. *Theory & Psychology*, 12(1), 55–77.

Bhatia, S. (2007). *American Karma: Race, Culture, and Identity in the Indian Diaspora*. New York: New York University Press.

Bhatia, S. & Ram, A. (2001). Rethinking 'acculturation' in relation to diasporic cultures & postcolonial identities. *Human Development*, 44(1), 1–18.

Bierhoff, H., Cohen, R. & Greenberg, J. (Eds.) (1986). *Justice in Social Relations*. New York: Plenum.

Bierhoff, H. & Rohmann, E. (2006). Conditions for establishing a system of fairness: Comment on Brosnan. *Social Justice Research*, 19(2), 194–200.

Bigler, R. & Liben, L. (2007). Developmental intergroup theory: Explaining and reducing children's social stereotyping and prejudice. *Current Directions in Psychological Science*, 16, 162–166.

Billig, M. (1976). *Social Psychology and Intergroup Relations*. London: Academic Press.

Billig, M. (1993). Studying the thinking society: Social representations, rhetoric, and attitudes. In G.M. Breakwell & D.V. Canter (Eds.), *Empirical Approaches to Social Representations* (pp. 39–62). Oxford: Clarendon Press.

Billig, M. (1996). *Arguing and Thinking: A Rhetorical Approach to Psychology*. Cambridge: Cambridge University Press.

Billig, M. (2002). Henri Tajfel's 'Cognitive aspects of prejudice' and the psychology of bigotry. *British Journal of Social Psychology*, 41, 171–188.

Billig, M. (2008). *The Hidden Roots of Critical Psychology*. London: Sage.

Billig, M. & Churchman, A. (2003). Building walls of brick and breaching walls of separation. *Environment and Behavior*, 35, 227–249.

Blader, S. & Tyler, T. (2003). A four component model of procedural justice: Defining the meaning of a 'fair' process. *Personality and Social Psychology Bulletin*, 29, 747–758.

Blau, P. (1964). *Exchange and Power in Social Life.* New York: Wiley.

Block, J. & Funder, D.C. (1986). Social roles and social perception: Individual differences in attribution and 'error'. *Journal of Personality and Social Psychology*, 51, 1200–1207.

Bloemraad, I. & Trost, C. (2008). It's a family affair: Intergenerational mobilization in the spring 2006 protests. *American Behavioral Scientist*, 52, 507–532.

Bloustien, G. (2007). 'Wigging people out': Youth music practice and mediated communities. *Journal of Community and Applied Social Psychology*, 17, 446–462.

Bochner, S. (1982). The social psychology of cross-cultural relations. In S. Bochner (Ed.), *Cultures in Contact: Studies in Cross-cultural Interaction* (pp. 5–44). Oxford: Pergamon.

Bohart, A.C. & Greening, T. (2001). Humanistic psychology and positive psychology. *American Psychologist*, 56(1), 81–82.

Bolam, B., Hodgetts, D., Chamberlain, K., Murphy, S. & Gleeson, K. (2003). 'Just do it': An analysis of accounts of control amongst lower socio-economic status groups. *Critical Public Health*, 13, 15–31.

Bolger, N., DeLongis, A., Kessler, R.C. & Schilling, E.A. (1989). Effects of daily stress and negative mood. *Journal of Personality and Social Psychology*, 57, 808–818.

Bonanno, G.A. (2005). Resilience in the face of potential trauma: Current directions in psychological science. *Journal of the American Psychological Society*, 14(3), 135–138.

Bourdieu, P. (1990). *The Logic of Practice.* Trans. R. Nice. Cambridge: Polity.

Borgida, E. & Stark, E. (2004). New media and politics: Some insights from social and political psychology. *American Behavioral Scientist*, 48, 467–478.

Bornstein, R. (1989). Exposure and affect: Overview and meta-analysis of research, 1968–1987. *Psychological Reports*, 106, 265–289.

Bowman, J. (1995). *The Cambridge Dictionary of American Biography.* Cambridge: Cambridge University Press.

Breckler, S.J., Olson, J.M. & Wiggins, E.C. (2006). *Social Psychology Alive!* Belmont, CA: Wadsworth.

Brehm, S., Kassin, S. & Fein, S. (2005). *Social Psychology* (6th ed.). Boston: Houghton Mifflin.

Brewer, M. (1979). In-group bias in the minimal intergroup situation: A cognitive-motivational analysis. *Psychological Bulletin*, 86, 307–324.

Brewer, M. (1996). When contact is not enough: Social identity and intergroup cooperation. *International Journal of Intercultural Relations*, 20, 291–303.

Briñol, P. & Petty, R.E. (2003). Overt head movements and persuasion: A self-validation analysis. *Journal of Personality and Social Psychology*, 84, 1123–1139.

Brock, A. (2006). *Internalizing the History of Psychology.* New York: New York University Press.

Brosnan, S. (2006). Nonhuman species' reactions to inequity and their implications for fairness. *Social Justice Research*, 19(2), 153–185.

Brown, B.B. & Perkins, D.D. (1992). Disruptions in place attachment. In I. Altman & S.M. Low (Eds.), *Place Attachment* (pp. 214–235). New York: Plenum.

Brown, R. (2001). Australian indigenous mental health. *Australian and New Zealand Journal of Mental Health Nursing*, 10, 33–41.

Bruner, J.S. (1990). *Acts of Meaning*. Cambridge, MA: Harvard University Press.

Buckingham, D. (2002). The electronic generation? Children and new media. In L. Lievrouw & S. Livingstone (Eds.), *The Handbook of New Media* (pp. 77–89). London: Sage.

Bugental, J. (1964). The third force in psychology. *Journal of Humanistic Psychology*, 4, 19–25.

Bulhan, H.A. (1985). *Frantz Fanon and the Psychology of Oppression*. New York: Plenum.

Bunton, R. (2006). Critical health psychology. *Journal of Health Psychology*, 11, 343–345.

Burkitt, I. (2004). The time and space of everyday life. *Cultural Studies*, 18, 211–227.

Burton, M. & Kagan, C. (2005). Liberation social psychology: Learning from Latin America. *Journal of Community and Applied Social Psychology*, 15, 63–78.

Burton, M. & Kagan, C. (2009). Towards a really social psychology: Liberation psychology beyond Latin America. In M. Montero & C.C. Sonn (Eds.), *Psychology of Liberation: Theory and Applications* (pp. 51–72). Peace Psychology Book Series. New York: Springer.

Bushman, B. & Anderson, C. (2002). Violent video games and hostile expectations: A test of the general aggression model. *Personality and Social Psychology Bulletin*, 28, 1679–1686.

Byrne, D. (1971). *The Attraction Paradigm*. New York: Academic Press.

Callan, M., Ellard, N., Shead, N.W. & Hodgins, D. (2008). Gambling as a search for justice: Examining the role of personal relative deprivation in gambling urges and gambling behavior. *Personality and Social Psychology Bulletin*, 34, 1514–1529.

Caltabiano, M., Sarafino, E. & Byrne, D. (2008). *Health Psychology: Biopsychosocial Interactions* (2nd ed.). London: Wiley.

Campbell, C. & Jovchelovitch, S. (2000). Health, community and development: Social psychology and participation. *Journal of Community and Applied Social Psychology*, 10, 255–270.

Campbell, C. & Murray, M. (2004). Community health psychology: promoting analysis and action for social change. *Journal of Health Psychology*, 9, 187–195.

Campbell, E. (2009). Relocation stories: Experiences of indigenous footballers in the AFL. Unpublished Doctor of Psychology thesis, Victoria University, Australia.

Candland, D. (1993). *Feral Children and Clever Animals: Reflections on Human Nature*. New York: Oxford University Press.

Cantril, H. & Allport, G. (1935). *The Psychology of Radio*. New York: Harper.

Caplan, G. (1964). *Principles of Preventative Psychiatry*. London: Tavistock.

Carlson, E., Engebretson, J. & Chamberlain, R. (2006). Photovoice as a social process of critical consciousness. *Qualitative Health Research*, 16(6), 836–852.

Carr, S. (2003). Poverty and justice. In S. Carr & T. Sloan (Eds.), *Poverty and Psychology: From Global Perspective to Local Practice* (pp. 45–68). New York: Kluwer Academic; Plenum.

Carroll, D., Davey-Smith, G. & Bennett, P. (2002). Some observations on health and socio-economic status. In D. Marks (Ed.), *The Health Psychology Reader* (pp. 142–162). London: Sage.

Cartwright, D. (1979). Contemporary social psychology in historical perspective. *Social Psychology Quarterly*, 42(1), 82–93.

Castelli, L., Zogmaister, C. & Tomelleri, S. (2009). The transmission of racial attitudes within the family. *Developmental Psychology*, 45(2), 586–591.

Castles, S. (2002). Migration & community formation under conditions of globalization. *International Migration Review*, 36(4), 1143–1168.

Castles, S. (2003). Towards a sociology of forced migration and social transformation. *Sociology*, 37, 13–34.

Cattell, V. (2001). Poor people, poor places, and poor health: The mediating role of social networks and social capital. *Social Science & Medicine*, 52, 1501–1516.

Chakkarath, P. (2005). Indigenous psychologies. Lessons from Hindu psychology. In W. Friedlmeier, P. Chakkarath & B. Schwarz (Eds.), *Culture and Human Development: The Importance of Cross-Cultural Research to the Social Sciences* (pp. 31–51). Hove, UK: Psychology Press.

Chamberlain, K. & Hodgetts, D. (2008). Social psychology and media: Critical considerations. *Social and Personality Psychology Compass*, 2, 1109–1125.

Chamberlain, K. & Murray, M. (2009). Critical health psychology. In D. Fox, I. Prilleltensky & S. Austen (Eds.), *Critical Psychology: An Introduction* (2nd ed.) (pp. 144–159). London: Sage.

Chandola, T., Brunner, E. & Marmot, M. (2006). Chronic stress at work and the metabolic syndrome: Prospective study. *British Medical Journal*, 332, 521–525.

Charleston, S. (2009). The English football ground as a representation of home. *Journal of Environmental Psychology*, 29(1), 144–150.

Chen, M.K. & Santos, L. (2006). Some thoughts on the adaptive function of inequity aversion: An alternative to Brosnan's social hypothesis. *Social Justice Research*, 19(2), 201–207.

Cherry, F. (1995). *The 'Stubborn Particularities' of Social Psychology*. Routledge: London.

Chiu, C-Y. & Hong, Y.-Y. (1992). The effects of intentionality and validation on individual and collective responsibility attribution among Hong Kong Chinese. *Journal of Psychology*, 126(3), 291–300.

Chiu, C-Y. & Hong, Y.-Y. (2007). Cultural processes: Basic principles. In E. Higgins & A. Kruglankski (Eds.), *Social Psychology: Handbook of Basic Principles* (pp. 783–804). New York: Guilford.

Cholewa, S. & Irwin, J. (2008). Project impact: Brief report on a pilot programme promoting physical activity among university students. *Journal of Health Psychology*, 13, 1207–1212.

Chomsky, N. (1959). Verbal behavior. *Language*, 35, 26–58.

Chory, R. (2007). Enhancing students' perceptions of fairness: The relationship between instructor credibility and classroom justice. *Communication Education*, 56(1), 89–105.

Christopher, J.C. & Campbell, R.L. (2008). An interactivist-hermeneutic metatheory for positive psychology. *Theory and Psychology*, 18(5), 675–697.

Christopher, J.C. & Hickinbottom, S. (2008). Positive psychology, ethnocentrism, and the disguised ideology of individualism. *Theory & Psychology*, 18, 563–589.

Christopher, J.C., Richardson, F.C. & Slife, B.D. (2008). Thinking through positive psychology. *Theory and Psychology*, 18(5), 555–561.

Chung-Fang, Y. (2006). The Chinese conception of the self: Towards a person-making perspective. In U. Kim, K. Yang & K. Hwang (Eds.), *Indigenous and Cultural Psychology: Understanding People in Context* (pp. 327–356). New York: Springer.

Cicchetti, D. & Garmezy, N. (1993). Prospects and promises in the study of resilience. *Development and Psychopathology*, 5, 597–603.

Clausen, J. (1968). *Socialization and Society*. Boston: Little Brown.

Clay, R. (2002). A renaissance for humanistic psychology: The field explores new niches while building on its past. *American Psychological Association Monitor*, 33(8), 42–43.

Cohen, D. & Prusak, L. (2001). *In Good Company: How Social Capital Makes Organizations Work*. Boston: Harvard University Press.

Cohen, R. (1982). Perceiving justice: An attributional perspective. In J. Greenberg & R. Cohen (Eds.), *Equity and Justice in Social Behaviour* (pp. 119–160). New York: Academic Press.

Cohen, R. (Ed.) (1986). *Justice: Views from the Social Sciences*. New York: Plenum.

Cohen, S., Underwood, L.G. & Gottlieb, B.H. (2000). *Social Support Measurement and Intervention: A Guide for Health and Social Scientists*. New York: Oxford University Press.

Cohen, S. & Wills, T. (1985). Stress, social support, and the buffering hypothesis. *Psychological Bulletin*, 98, 310–357.

Cole, M. (1998). *Cultural Psychology: A Once and Future Discipline*. Cambridge, MA: Harvard University Press.

Colic-Peisker, V. & Tilbury, F. (2007). *Refugees and Employment: The Effect of Visible Difference on Discrimination*. Centre for Social and Community Research, Murdoch University, Australia.

Colic-Peisker, V. & Walker, I. (2003). Human capital, acculturation and social identity: Bosnian refugees in Australia. *Journal of Community and Applied Social Psychology*, 13, 337–360.

Collier, G., Minton, H. & Reynolds, G. (1991). *Currents of Thought in American Social Psychology*. New York: Oxford University Press.

Comstock, G. & Scharrer, E. (2005). *The Psychology of Media and Politics*. Burlington, MA: Elsevier Academic.

Comte, A. (1973). *System of Positive Polity*. New York: Ben Franklin.

Condiotte, M. (1981). Self-efficacy and relapse in smoking cessation programs. *Journal of Consulting and Clinical Psychology*, 49, 648–658.

Connell, A. & Russo, N. (1990). *Women in Psychology: A Bio-bibliographic Source Book*. Westport, CT: Greenwood.

Conner, M. & Norman, P. (Eds.) (2005). *Predicting Health Behavior: Research and Practice with Social Cognition Models*. Buckingham, UK: Open University Press.

Conner, S. (2002). Rough magic: Bags. In B. Highmore (Ed.), *The Everyday Life Reader* (pp. 346–351). London: Routledge.

Contarello, A. & Sarrica, M. (2007). ICTs, social thinking and subjective well-being: The Internet and its representation in everyday life. *Computers in Human Behavior*, 23, 1016–1032.

Cooley, C.H. (1902). *Human Nature and the Social Order*. New York: Scribners.

Cornish, F. (2004). Making 'context' concrete: A dialogical approach to the society-health relation. *Journal of Health Psychology*, 9, 281–294.

Cottle, S. & Rai, M. (2006). Between display and deliberation: Analyzing TV news as communicative architecture. *Media, Culture & Society*, 28, 163–189.

Cottrell, L.S. (1976). The competent community. In B.H. Kaplan, R.N. Wilson & A.H. Leighton (Eds.), *Further Explorations in Social Psychiatry* (pp. 195–209). New York: Basic Books.

Couldry, N. (2004). Theorising media as practice. *Social Semiotics*, 14, 115–132.

Cravens, J. (2007). Online volunteering enters middle age – and changes management paradigms. *Nonprofit Quarterly*, Spring. http://www.nonprofit-quarterly.org/content/category/4/29/28/

Crawford, R. (1980). Healthism and the medicalization of everyday life. *International Journal of Health Services*, 10, 365–388.

Crawshaw, E. (2006). Culture and identity: Perceptions of Sudanese Australian refugee youth. Unpublished fourth-year thesis, Victoria University, Australia.

Crosby, F. & Gonzalez-Intal, M. (1984). Relative deprivation and equity theories: Felt injustice and the undeserved benefits of others. In R. Folger (Ed.), *The sense of injustice: Social psychological perspectives* (pp. 141–166). New York: Plenum.

Crossley, M. (2000). *Rethinking Health Psychology*. Buckingham, UK: Open University Press.

Csikszentmihalyi, M. (1997). *Finding Flow: The Psychology of Engagement with Everyday Life*. New York: HarperCollins.

Cuba, L. & Hummon, D. (1993). A place to call home: Identification with dwelling, community and region. *Sociological Quarterly*, 34, 111–131.

Cullen, A. & Hodgetts, D. (2001). Unemployment as illness: An exploration of accounts voiced by the unemployed in Aotearoa/New Zealand. *Analysis of Social Issues and Public Policy*, 1(1), 33–51.

Curran, J. & Seaton, J. (2003). *Power without Responsibility: The Press, Broadcasting, and New Media in Britain*. London: Routledge.

Cvetkovich, G. & Earle, T. (1992). Environmental hazards and the public. *Journal of Social Issues*, 48(4), 1–20.

Cvetkovich, G. & Earle, T. (1994). The construction of justice: A case study of public participation in land management. *Journal of Social Issues*, 50(3), 161–178.

Dalbert, C. & Maes, J. (2002). Belief in a just world as a personal resource in school. In M. Ross & D. Miller (Eds.), *The Justice Motive in Everyday Life* (pp. 365–381). Cambridge: Cambridge University Press.

Danzinger, K. (1990). *Constructing the Subject: Historical Origins of Psychological Research*. Cambridge: Cambridge University Press.

Danzinger, K. (2006). Comment. *International Journal of Psychology*, 41, 269–275.

Darley, J. & Batson, C. (1973). From Jerusalem to Jericho: A study of situational and dispositional variables in helping behavior. *Journal of Personality and Social Psychology*, 27, 100–108.

Davey-Smith, G. (2004). Lifestyle, health, and health promotion in Nazi Germany. *British Medical Journal*, 329, 1424–1425.

David, D., Montgomery, G. & Bovbjerg, D. (2006). Relations between coping responses and optimism-pessimism in predicting anticipatory psychological distress in surgical breast cancer patients. *Personality and Individual Differences*, 40, 203–213.

de Certeau, M. (1984). *The Practice of Everyday Life*. Trans. S. Rendall. Los Angeles: University of California Press.

de Certeau, M. (1997). *Heterologies: Discourse on the Other*. Minneapolis: University of Minnesota Press.

De Cremer, D. (2004). The influence of accuracy as a function of leader's bias: The role of trustworthiness in the psychology of procedural justice. *Personality and Social Psychology Bulletin*, 30, 293–304.

Dean, B. & Levi, J. (2003). *At the Risk of Being Heard: Indigenous Rights, Identity and Postcolonial States*. Ann Arbor: University of Michigan Press.

Deaux, K. (2000). Surveying the landscape of immigration: Social psychological perspectives. *Journal of Community and Applied Social Psychology*, 10, 421–431.

Denham, S., Bassett, H. & Wyatt, T. (2007). The socialization of emotional competence. In J. Grusec & P. Hastings (Eds.), *Handbook of Socialization: Theory and Research* (pp. 614–637). New York: Guilford.

Descartes, R. (1641/1989). *Meditations on First Philosophy*. Dennett: Prometheus.

Deutsch, M. (1983). Current social psychological perspectives on justice. *European Journal of Social Psychology*, 13, 305–319.

DeWind, J. (1990). Alien justice: The exclusion of Haitian refugees. *Journal of Social Issues*, 46(1), 121–132.

Diener, E. & Seligman, M.E.P. (2004). Beyond money: Toward an economy of well-being. *Psychological Science in the Public Interest*, 5(1), 1–31.

DiMatteo, M.R. & Martin, L.R. (2002). *Health Psychology*. Boston: Allyn & Bacon.

Diprose, R. (2005). Community of bodies: From modification to violence. *Journal of Media & Cultural Studies*, 19(3), 381–392.

Dixon, J. & Durrheim, K. (2003). Contact and the ecology of racial division: Some varieties of informal segregation. *British Journal of Social Psychology*, 42, 1–23.

Dixon, J. & Durrheim, K. (2004). Dislocating identity: Desegregation and the transformation of place. *Journal of Environmental Psychology*, 24, 455–473.

Dixon, J., Levine, M. & McAuley, R. (2006). Locating impropriety: Street drinking, moral order, and the ideological dilemma of public space. *Political Psychology*, 27, 187–206.

Dixon, J., Tredoux, C., Durrheim, K., Finchilescu, G. & Clack, B. (2008). 'The inner citadels of the color line': Mapping the micro-ecology of racial segregation in everyday life spaces. *Social and Personality Psychology Compass*, 2, 1–23.

Dixon, J. & Wetherell, M. (2004). On discourse and dirty nappies: Gender, the division of household labour and the social psychology of distributive justice. *Theory and Psychology*, 14, 167–189.

Dolnicar, S. & Randle, M. (2007). What motivates which volunteers? Psychographic heterogeneity among volunteers in Australia. *Voluntas*, 18, 135–155.

Doyle, K. (2004). Introduction: Psychology and the new media. *American Behavioral Scientist*, 48, 371–376.

Drew, N. (2005). Phrenology and the art of community engagement. *Artworks*, 63, 3–6.

Drew, N., Bishop, B. & Syme, G. (2002). Justice and local community change: Towards a substantive theory of justice. *Journal of Community Psychology*, Special Issue, 30(6), 623–634.

Dudgeon, P. & Fielder, J. (2006). Third spaces within tertiary places: Indigenous Australian studies. *Journal of Community and Applied Social Psychology*, 16, 396–409.

Dueck, A., Ting, S.-K. & Cutiongco, R. (2007). Constantine, Babel, and Yankee doodling: Whose indigeneity? Whose psychology? *Pastoral Psychology*, 56, 55–72.

Du Gay, P. (1996). *Consumption and Identity at Work*. London: Sage.

Durie, M. (1999). Marae and implications for a modern Maori psychology: Elsdon Best Memorial Medal Address, Polynesian Society Annual General Meeting. *Journal of the Polynesian Society*, 108(4), 351–366.

Durie, M. (2004). Understanding health and illness: Research at the interface between science and indigenous knowledge. *International Journal of Epidemiology*, 33, 1138–1143.

Durrheim, K. & Dixon, J. (2005). Studying talk and embodied practices: Toward a psychology of materiality of 'race relations'. *Journal of Community & Applied Social Psychology*, 15, 446–460.

Eacott, C. & Sonn, C. (2006). Beyond education and employment: exploring youth experiences of their communities, place attachment and reasons for migration. *Rural Society*, 16, 199–214.

Easterling, D., Gallagher, K.M. & Lodwick, D. (Eds.) (2003). *Promoting Health at the Community Level*. Thousand Oaks, CA: Sage.

Eastwick, P., Finkel, E., Mochon, D. & Ariely, D. (2007). Selective versus unselective romantic desire: Not all reciprocity is created equal. *Psychological Science*, 18, 317–319.

Elms, A. (1975). The crisis of confidence in social psychology. *American Psychologist*, 30, 967–976.

Eng, E. & Blanchard, L. (2007). Action-oriented community diagnosis: A health education tool. *International Quarterly of Community Health Education*, 26, 141–158.

Engel, G.L. (1977). The need for a new medical model: A challenge for biomedicine. *Science*, 196, 129–136.

Enriquez, V. (1993). Developing a Filipino psychology. In U. Kim & J. Berry (Eds.), *Indigenous Psychologies: Research and Experience in Cultural Context* (pp. 152–169). Newbury Park, CA: Sage.

Enriquez, V. (1995). *From Colonial to Liberation Psychology*. Manila: De La Salle University Press.

Erikson, E. (1963). *Childhood and Society*. New York: Norton.

Espiritu, Y.L. (2003). *Home Bound: Filipino Lives across Cultures, Communities and Countries*. Ewing, NJ: University of California Press.

Essed, P. (1991). *Understanding Everyday Racism: An Interdisciplinary Theory*. London: Sage.

Esses, V., Veenvliet, S., Hodson, G. & Mihic, L. (2008). Justice, morality, and the dehumanisation of refugees. *Social Justice Research*, 21(1), 4–25.

Estacio, E.V. (2009). Human exploitation is NOT a Joke – so don't laugh! *Journal of Health Psychology*, 14, 627–637.

Estrella, K. & Forinash, M. (2007). Narrative inquiry and arts-based inquiry: Multinarrative perspectives. *Journal of Humanistic Psychology*, 47, 376–383.

Ettner, S. (2001). Workers' perceptions of how jobs affect health: A social ecological perspective. *Journal of Occupational Psychology*, 6, 101–113.

Faircloth, C., Boylstein, C., Rittman, M., Young, M. & Gubrium, J. (2004). Sudden illness and biographical flow in narratives of stroke recovery. *Sociology of Health and Illness*, 26, 242–261.

Fanon, F. (1967). *Black Skin, White Masks*. New York: Grove Press.

Farkas, A.J. & Anderson, N.H. (1979). Multidimensional input in equity theory. *Journal of Personality and Social Psychology*, 37, 879–896.

Farquhar, J., Fortmann, S., Flora, J., Taylor, C., Haskell, W., Williams, P., Maccoby, N. & Wood, P. (1990). Effects of community-wide education on cardiovascular disease factors: The Stanford five-city project. *Journal of the American Medical Association*, 264, 359–365.

Farr, R.M. (1991). The long past and the short history of social psychology. *European Journal of Social Psychology*, 21, 371–380.

Farr, R.M. (1996). *The Roots of Modern Social Psychology*. Oxford: Blackwell.

Feagin, J. (1984). *Racial and Ethnic Relations* (2nd ed.). New York: Prentice Hall.

Felson, R. (1996). Mass media effects on violent behavior. *Annual Review of Sociology*, 22, 103–128.

Festinger, L. (1954). A theory of social comparison processes. *Human Relations*, 7, 117–140.

Festinger, L. (1957). *The Theory of Cognitive Dissonance*. Stanford, CA: Stanford University Press.

Fijac, B.M. & Sonn, C.C. (2004). Pakistani-Muslim immigrant women in Western Australia: Perceptions of identity and community. *Network*, 16, 18–27.

Finkel, E., Eastwick, P. & Matthews, J. (2007). Speed-dating as an invaluable tool for studying romantic attraction: A methodological primer. *Personal Relations*, 14, 149–166.

Fischoff, S. (1999). Psychology's quixotic quest for the media-violence connection. Invited address to the Annual Convention of the American Psychological Association, Boston, August 21.

Fisher, A.T. & Sonn, C.C. (2002). Psychological sense of community in Australia & the challenges of change. *Journal of Community Psychology*, 30, 597–609.

Fisher, J.D., Nadler, A. & De Paulo, B. (1983). *New Directions in Helping: Recipient Reactions to Aid*. New York: Academic Press.

Fiske, S.T., Cuddy, A., Glick, P. & Xu, J. (2002). A model of (often mixed) stereotype content: Competence and warmth respectively follow from perceived status and competition. *Journal of Personality and Social Psychology*, 82, 878–902.

Fiske, S.T. & Taylor, S.E. (1991). *Social Cognition*. New York: McGraw-Hill.

Flick, U. (1998a). The social construction of individual and public health: Contributions of social representations theory to a social science of health. *Social Science Information*, 37, 639–662.

Flick, U. (Ed.) (1998b). *Psychology of the Social*. Cambridge: Cambridge University Press.

Flick, U. (2000a). Everyday knowledge in the history of social psychology: Styles and traditions of research in Germany, France and the United States. *Journal of the History of the Behavioral Sciences*, 36, 568–573.

Flick, U. (2000b). Qualitative inquiries into social representations of health. *Journal of Health Psychology*, 5(3), 315–324.

Flick, U. (2009). *An Introduction to Qualitative Research* (4th ed.). London: Sage.

Flores-Osario, J.M. (2009). Praxis and liberation in the context of Latin American theory. In M. Montero & C.C. Sonn (Eds.), *Psychology of Liberation: Theory and Applications* (pp. 11–36). Peace Psychology Book Series. New York: Springer.

Flournoy, R. & Yen, I. (2004). *The Influence of Community Factors on Health: An Annotated Bibliography.* Oakland, CA: PolicyLink.

Folger, R. (Ed.) (1984). *The Sense of Injustice: Social Psychological Perspectives.* New York: Plenum.

Fondacaro, M., Brank, E., Stuart, J., Villanueva-Abraham, S., Luescher, J. & McNatt, P. (2006). Identity orientation, voice, and judgements of procedural justice during late adolescence. *Journal of Youth and Adolescence*, 35(6), 987–997.

Foster, D. (2004). Liberation psychology. In K. Ratele, N. Duncan, D. Hook, N. Mkhize, P. Kiguwa & A. Collins (Eds.), *Self, Community and Psychology* (chapter 4, pp. 1–44). Landsdowne, South Africa: University of Cape Town Press.

Frank, A. (1995). *The Wounded Story Teller: Body, Illness and Ethics* (2nd ed.). Chicago: University of Chicago Press.

Frankenberg, R. (1993). *White Women, Race Matters: The Social Construction of Whiteness.* London: Routledge.

Freire, P. (1970/1993). *Pedagogy of the Oppressed.* Harmondsworth, UK: Penguin.

Freud, S. (1923). *The Ego and the ID.* In James Strachey (Gen. Ed.), *The Standard Edition of the Complete Psychological Works of Sigmund Freud*, Vol. 19 (pp. 3–66). New York: W.W. Norton.

Friedman, H. (2008). Humanistic and positive psychology: The methodological and epistemological divide. *Humanistic Psychologist*, 36, 113–126.

Frosh, P. (2006). Telling presences: Witnessing, mass media, and the imagined lives of strangers. *Critical Studies in Media Communication*, 23, 265–284.

Fry, G., Grogan, S., Gough, B. & Conner, M. (2008). Smoking in the lived world: How young people make sense of the social role cigarettes play in their lives. *British Journal of Social Psychology*, 47, 763–780.

Fryer, D. (2008). Some questions about 'The history of community psychology'. *Journal of Community Psychology*, 36, 572–586.

Fuller, A. (1990). *Insight into Value: An Exploration of the Premises of a Phenomenological Psychology.* New York: State University of New York Press.

Fuller, A., McGraw, K. & Goodyear, M. (1999). Bungy-jumping through life: What young people say promotes well-being and resilience. *Australian Journal of Guidance and Counselling*, 9(1), 159–168.

Furby, L. (1986). Psychology and justice. In R. Cohen (Ed.), *Justice: Views from the Social Sciences* (pp. 153–203). New York: Plenum.

Furnham, A.F. (1990). On the move: The psychology of change and transition. In S. Fisher & C.L. Cooper (Eds.), *Expatriate Stress: The Problems of Living Abroad* (pp. 275–304). Chichester, UK: Wiley.

Furnham, A.F. & Bochner, S. (1986). *Culture Shock: Psychological Responses to Unfamiliar Environments.* London: Methuen.

Furnham, A.F. (1988). *Lay Theories: Everyday Understanding of Problems in the Social Sciences.* Oxford: Pergamon.

Gallagher, K., Easterling, D. & Lodwick, D. (2003). Introduction. In D. Easterling, K. Gallagher & D. Lodwick (Eds.), *Promoting Health at the Community Level* (pp. 1–16). London: Sage.

Gamliel, E. & Peer, E. (2006). Positive versus negative framing affects justice judgements. *Social Justice Research*, 19(3), 307–322.

García-Montes, J., Caballero-Muñoz, D. & Pérez-Álvarez, M. (2006). Changes in the self resulting from the use of mobile phones. *Media, Culture & Society*, 28, 67–82.

Garvey, D. (2007). *Indigenous Identity in Contemporary Psychology: Dilemmas, Developments, Directions*. Melbourne: Thomson.

Geertz, C. (1973). *The Interpretation of Cultures: Selected Essays*. New York: Basic Books.

Geismar, H. & Horst, H. (2004). Materializing ethnography. *Journal of Material Culture*, 9, 5–10.

Gerbner, G., Gross, L., Morgan, M. & Signorielli, N. (1994). Growing up with television: The cultivation perspective. In J. Bryant & D. Zillmann (Eds.), *Media Effects: Advances in Theory and Research* (pp. 17–41). Hillsdale, NJ: Lawrence Erlbaum.

Gergen, K.J. (1973). Social psychology as history. *Journal of Personality and Social Psychology*, 26, 309–320.

Gergen, K.J. (1978). Experimentation in social psychology: A reapprasial. *European Journal of Social Psychology*, 8, 507–527.

Gergen, K.J. (1994). *Toward Transformation in Social Knowledge*. Thousand Oaks, CA: Sage.

Gergen, K.J. (1985). The social construction movement in modern psychology. *American Psychologist*, 40, 266–275.

Gergen, K.J., Gulerce, A., Lock, A. & Misra, G. (1996). Psychological science in cultural context. *American Psychologist*, 51, 496–503.

Giddens, A. (1986). *The Constitution of Society: Outline of the Theory of Structuration*. Los Angeles: University of California Press.

Giles, D. (2003). *Media Psychology*. Mahwah, NJ: Lawrence Erlbaum.

Godreau, I.P., Reyes Cruz, M., Franco Ortiz, M. & Cuadrado, S. (2008). The lessons of slavery: Discourses of slavery, mestizaje and blanqueamiento in an elementary school in Puerto Rico. *American Ethnologist*, 35(1), 115–135.

Goffman, E. (1959). *The Presentation of Self in Everyday Life*. Edinburgh: Anchor.

Goffman, E. (1982). *Interaction Ritual: Essays on Face-to-Face Behaviour*. New York: Pantheon.

Gone, J. (2007). 'We never was happy living like a whiteman': Mental health disparities and the postcolonial predicament in American Indian communities. *American Journal of Community Psychology*, 40, 290–300.

Gonzalez, C. & Tyler, T. (2008). The psychology of enfranchisement: Engaging and fostering inclusion of members through voting and decision-making procedures. *Journal of Social Issues*, 64(3), 447–466.

Gooptu, N. & Bandyopadhyay, N. (2007). Rights to stop the wrong: Cultural change and collective mobilization – The case of Kolkata sex workers. *Oxford Development Studies*, 35, 251–271.

Gordon, D. (1988). Tenacious assumptions in Western medicine. In M. Lock & D. Gordon (Eds.), *Biomedicine Examined*. Dordrecht, the Netherlands: Kluwer Academic.

Gorman, M. (1981). Pre-war conformity research in social psychology: The approaches of Floyd H. Allport and Muzafer Sherif. *Journal of the History of the Behavioral Sciences*, 17, 2–14.

Gottlieb, B. & Wagner, F. (1991). Stress and support processes in close relationships. In J. Eckenrode (Ed.), *The Social Context of Coping* (pp. 165–188). New York: Plenum.

Gough, B. & McFadden, M. (2001). *Critical Social Psychology: An Introduction*. Basingstoke, UK: Palgrave.

Graves, T. (1967). Psychological acculturation in a tri-ethnic community. *South-Western Journal of Anthropology*, 23, 337–350.

Green, M.J., Sonn, C.C. & Matsebula, J. (2007). Reviewing whiteness: Theory, research and possibilities. *South African Journal of Psychology*, 37(3), 389–419.

Greenberg, J. (1993). The intellectual adolescence of organizational justice: You've come a long way, maybe. *Social Justice Research*, 6(1), 135–148.

Greenberg, J. & Cohen, R. (Eds.) (1982). *Equity and Justice in Social Behaviour*. New York: Academic Press.

Greenfield, P.M. (1997). Culture as process: Empirical methods for cultural psychology. In J.W. Berry, Y.H. Poortinga & J. Pandey (Eds.), *Handbook of Crosscultural Psychology* (pp. 301–346). Needham Heights, CA: Allyn & Bacon.

Grosfoguel, R. & Georas, C.S. (2000). 'Coloniality of power' and racial dynamics: Notes toward a reinterpretation of Caribbeans in New York City. *Identities*, 7(1), 85–125.

Gross, H. & Lane, N. (2007). Landscapes of the lifespan: Exploring accounts of own gardens and gardening. *Journal of Environmental Psychology*, 27, 225–241.

Groth-Marnat, G. (1997). *Handbook for Psychological Assessment*. New York: Wiley.

Grusec, J. & Hastings, P. (2007). *Handbook of Socialization: Theory and Research*. New York: Guilford.

Guareschi, P. & Jovchelovitch, S. (2004). Participation, health and the development of community resources in southern Brazil. *Journal of Health Psychology*, 9, 311–322.

Gunnestad, A. (2006). Resilience in a crosscultural perspective: How resilience is generated in different cultures. *Journal of Intercultural Communication*, 11, 1.

Hage, G. (1998). *White Nation: Fantasies of White Supremacy in a Multicultural Society*. Sydney: Pluto.

Hajdu, D. (2008). *The Ten-Cent Plague: The Great Comic Book Scare and How It Changed America*. New York: Farrar, Straus and Giroux.

Hampton, K. (2001). Living the wired life in the wired suburb: Netville, localization and civil society. PhD dissertation, Department of Sociology, University of Toronto.

Hanselmann, C. (2001). *Urban Aboriginal People in Western Canada: Realities and Policies*. Alberta: Canadian West Foundation.

Harper, D.J., Wagstaff, G., Newton, J. & Harrison, K. (1990). Lay causal perceptions of Third World poverty and the just world theory. *Social Behaviour*, 21, 393–407.

Harper, D.J. (1996). Accounting for poverty: From attribution to discourse. *Journal of Community and Applied Psychology*, 6, 249–265.

Harris, B. (1983). Telling students about the history of social psychology. *Teaching of Psychology*, 10, 26–28.

Harris, B. (1986). Reviewing 50 years of the psychology of social issues. *Journal of Social Issues*, 42, 1020.

Harris, R.J. (1976). Handling negative inputs: On the plausible equity formulae. *Journal of Experimental Social Psychology*, 12, 194–209.

Hart, J.T. (1971). The inverse care law. *The Lancet*, 297, 405–412.

Hartig, T. & Staats, H. (2003). Guest editors' introduction: Restorative environments. *Journal of Environmental Psychology*, 23, 103–107.

Hatfield, E., Walster, G. & Berscheid, E. (1976). *Equity: Theory and Research*. Boston: Allyn & Bacon.

Heider, F. (1946). Attitudes and cognitive organization. *Journal of Psychology*, 21, 107–112.

Heider, F. (1958). *The Psychology of Interpersonal Relations*. New York: Wiley.

Heider, J. & Skowronski, J. (2007). Improving the predictive validity of the Implicit Association Test. *North American Journal of Psychology*, 9, 53–76.

Helman, C. (2000). *Culture, Health and Illness: An Introduction for Health Professionals*. Boston: Butterworth-Heinemann.

Hepburn, A. (2003). *An Introduction to Critical Social Psychology*. London: Sage.

Herbert, T.B. & Cohen, S. (1993). Stress and immunity in humans. *Psychosomatic Medicine*, 55, 364–379.

Hermans, H.J.M. (2001). Mixing & moving cultures require a dialogical self. *Human Development*, 44, 24–28.

Hermans, H.J.M. & Hermans-Konopka, A. (2009). *Dialogical Self Theory: Positioning and Counter-Positioning in a Globalizing Society*. Cambridge: Cambridge University Press.

Hermans, H.J.M. & Kempen, H.J.G. (1993). *Dialogical Self: Meaning as Movement*. San Diego, CA: Academic Press.

Hermans, H.J.M. & Kempen, H.J.G. (1998). Moving cultures: The perilous problem of cultural dichotomies in a globalizing society. *American Psychologist*, 53, 1111–1120.

Hernández, B., Hidalgo, M., Salazar-Laplace, M. & Hess, S. (2007). Place attachment and place identity in natives and non-natives. *Journal of Environmental Psychology*, 27, 310–319.

Hewstone, M., Stroebe, W. & Jonas, K. (2008). *Introduction to Social Psychology* (4th ed.). London: Blackwell.

Highmore, B. (2002a). *The Everyday Life Reader*. Routledge: London.

Highmore, B. (2002b). *Everyday Life and Cultural Theory: An Introduction*. London: Routledge.

Hochbaum, G.M. (1958). Public participation in medical screening programs: A socio-psychological study. Public Health Service Publication no. 572. Washington, DC: US Government Printing Office.

Hodgetts, D., Bolam, B. & Stephens, C. (2005). Mediation and the construction of contemporary understandings of health and lifestyle. *Journal of Health Psychology*, 10, 123–136.

Hodgetts, D. & Chamberlain, K. (2000). The social negotiation of people's views on the cause of illness. *Journal of Health Psychology*, 5(3), 319–330.

Hodgetts, D. & Chamberlain, K. (2003). Television documentary in New Zealand and the construction of doctors by lower socio-economic groups. *Social Science and Medicine*, 57, 113–124.

Hodgetts, D. & Chamberlain, K. (2006a). Media and health: A continuing concern for health psychology. *Journal of Health Psychology*, 11, 171–174.

Hodgetts, D. & Chamberlain, K. (2006b). Developing a critical media research agenda for health psychology. *Journal of Health Psychology*, 11, 317–327.

Hodgetts, D. & Chamberlain, K. (2007). Community and the media: Considerations for applied social psychology. *Journal of Community and Applied Social Psychology*, 17(6), 411–414.

Hodgetts, D., Chamberlain, K. & Groot, S. (In press). Reflections on the visual in community research and practice. In. P. Reavey (Ed.), *Visual Psychologies: Using and Interpreting Images in Qualitative Research*. London: Routledge.

Hodgetts, D., Chamberlain, K. & Radley, A. (2007). Considering photographs never taken during photo-production project. *Qualitative Research in Psychology*, 4(4), 263–280.

Hodgetts, D., Chamberlain, K., Scammell, M., Nikora, L. & Karapu, R. (2007). Constructing health news: Media production and the possibilities for a civic-oriented journalism. *Health: An Interdisciplinary Journal for the Social Study of Health, Illness and Medicine*, 12, 43–66.

Hodgetts, D., Cullen, A. & Radley, A. (2005). Television characterizations of homeless people in the United Kingdom. *Analyses of Social Issues and Public Policy*, 5(1), 29–48.

Hodgetts, D., Radley, A., Chamberlain, K. & Hodgetts, A. (2007). Health inequalities and homelessness: Considering material, spatial and relational dimensions. *Journal of Health Psychology*, 12(5), 709–725.

Hodgetts, D. & Rua, M. (2008). The social negotiation of risk: Moral panic and men's participation in community life. *Journal of Community and Applied Social Psychology*, 18, 527–542.

Hodgetts, D. & Stolte, O. (2009). Questioning 'black humour': racial exploitation, media and health. *Journal of Health Psychology*, 14(5), 643–646.

Hodgetts, D., Stolte, O., Chamberlain, K., Radley, A., Groot, S., Nikora, L. & Nabalarua, E. (In press). The mobile hermit and the city: Places, objects and sounds for a social psychology of homelessness. *British Journal of Social Psychology*, 48.

Hodgetts, D., Stolte, O., Chamberlain, K., Radley, A., Nikora, L., Nabalarua, E. & Groot, S. (2008). A trip to the library: Homelessness and social inclusion. *Social and Cultural Geography*, 9(8), 933–953.

Hoffman, L. & Thomson, T. (2009). The effect of television viewing on adolescents' civic participation: Political efficacy as mediating mechanism. *Journal of Broadcasting and Electronic Media*, 53(1), 3–21.

Hofrichter, R. (Ed.) (2003). *Health and Social Justice*. Bloomington: Indiana University Press.

Holdstock, L.T. (2000). *Re-examining Psychology: Critical Perspectives & African Insights*. London: Routledge.

Holmes, T.H. & Rahe, R.H. (1967). The social readjustment rating scale. *Journal of Psychosomatic Research*, 11, 213–218.

Homans, G. (1961). *Social Behaviour: Its Elementary Forms*. New York: Harcourt, Brace & World.

Hook, D. (2003). Frantz Fanon & racial identity in post colonial contexts. In K. Ratele & N. Duncan (Eds.), *Social Psychology: Identities & Relationships* (pp. 107–128). Lansdowne: University of Cape Town Press.

Houser, M., Horan, S. & Furler, L. (2007). Predicting relational outcomes: An investigation of thin slice judgments in speed dating. *Human Communication*, 10, 69–81.

Houser, M., Horan, S. & Furler, L. (2008). Dating in the fast lane: How communication predicts speed dating success. *Journal of Social and Personal Relations*, 25, 749–768.

Howarth, C. (2009). 'I hope we won't have to understand racism one day': Researching or reproducing 'race' in social psychological research? *British Journal of Social Psychology*, 48(3), 407–426.

Hughes, L. (2003). *The No-Nonsense Guide to Indigenous Peoples*. Oxford: New Internationalist.

Hurdley, R. (2006). Dismantling mantelpieces: Narrating identities and materializing culture in the home. *Sociology*, 40, 717–733.

Hussain, Z. & Griffiths, M. (2008). Gender swapping and socializing in cyberspace: An exploratory study. *CyberPsychology & Behavior*, 11(1), 47–53.

Hyyppa, M. & Maki, J. (2003). Social participation and health in a community rich in stock of social capital. *Health Education Research*, 18, 770–779.

Ingham, R. (1993). Old bodies in older clothes. *Health Psychology Update*, 14, 31–36.

International Labour Organisation. (2009). Indigenous and tribal peoples' rights in practice: A guide to ILO Convention No. 169. Geneva: Author.

Iscoe, I. (1974). Community psychology and the competent community. *American Psychologist*, 29, 607–613.

Jacobson, N. (2007). Dignity and health: A review. *Social Science & Medicine*, 64, 292–302.

Jahoda, M., Lazarsfeld, P.E. & Zeisel, H. (1933/1972). *Marienthal: The Sociography of an Unemployed Community*. London: Tavistock.

James, W. (1890/1983). *The Principles of Psychology*. With an introduction by G.A. Miller. Cambridge, MA: Harvard University Press.

James, W. (1902). *The Varieties of Religious Experience: A Study of Human Nature*. New York: Longman, Green.

Jamieson, D., Lydon, J. & Zanna, M. (1987). Attitude and activity preference similarity: Differential bases of interpersonal attraction for low and high self-monitors. *Journal of Personality and Social Psychology*, 53, 1052–1060.

Janz, N.K., Champion, V.L. & Strecher, V.J. (2002). The health belief model. In K. Glanz, B.K. Rimer & F.M. Lewis (Eds.), *Health Behavior and Health Education: Theory, Research and Practice* (3rd ed.) (pp. 45–66). San Francisco: Jossey-Bass.

Jenkins, H. (2006). *Fans, Bloggers and Games: Exploring Participatory Culture*. New York: New York University Press.

Jiménez-Domínguez, B. (2009). Ignacio Martín-Baró's social psychology of liberation: Situated knowledge and critical commitment against objectivism. In M. Montero & C.C. Sonn (Eds.), *Psychology of Liberation: Theory and Applications* (pp. 37–50). Peace Psychology Book Series. New York: Springer.

Jodelet, D. (1991). *Madness and Social Representations: Living with the Mad in One French Community*. Berkeley: University of California Press.

Johnson, D.B., Oyama, N., LeMarchand, L. & Wilkens, L. (2004). Native Hawaiians mortality, morbidity, and lifestyle: comparing data from 1982, 1990, and 2000. *Pacific Health Dialogue*, 11(2), 120–130.

Johnson, M. (2004). Hull House. In J. Grossman., A. Keating & J. Reiff (Eds.), *The Encyclopedia of Chicago* (p. 402). Chicago: University of Chicago Press.

Joinson, A.N. (2003). *Understanding the Psychology of Internet Behaviour: Virtual Worlds, Real Lives.* Basingstoke, UK: Palgrave.

Jones, C. (2009). Friendship, romance and possibly more. *Learning Disability Practice*, 12(2), 8–13.

Jones, E. & Davis, K. (1965). From acts to dispositions: The attribution process in person perception. In L. Berkowitz (Ed.), *Advances in Experimental Social Psychology*, Vol. 2 (pp. 219–266). New York: Academic Press.

Jones, E. & Nisbett, R. (1972). The actor and the observer: Divergent perceptions of the causes of behavior. In E. Jones et al. (Eds.), *Attribution: Perceiving the Causes of Behavior* (pp. 79–94). Morristown, NJ: General Learning Press.

Jones, R. (Ed.) (1996). *Handbook for Tests and Measurements for Black Populations*, Vol. 1. Hampton, VA: Cobb and Henry.

Jones, R. (2004). *Black Psychology* (4th ed.). Hampton, VA: Cobb & Henry Press.

Jost, J. & Banaji, M. (1994). The role of stereotyping in system-justification and the production of false consciousness. *British Journal of Social Psychology*, 33, 1–27.

Jovchelovitch, S. (2007). *Knowledge in Context: Representations, Community and Culture*. Hove, UK: Routledge.

Judd, C.M., Blair, I.V. & Chapleau, K.M. (2004). Automatic stereotypes vs. automatic prejudice: Sorting out the possibilities in the Payne (2001) weapon paradigm. *Journal of Experimental Psychology*, 40, 75–81.

Kakefuda, I., Stallones., L. & Gibbs., J. (2008). Readiness for community-based bicycle helmet use programmes: A study using community- and individual-level readiness models. *Journal of Health Psychology*, 13, 639–643.

Kaholokula, J.K. (2007). Colonialism, acculturation, and depression among Kanaka Maoli of Hawai'i. In P. Culbertson, M.N. Agee & C.O. Makasiale (Eds.), *Penina Uliuli: Contemporary Challenges in Mental Health for Pacific Peoples* (pp. 180–195). Honolulu: University of Hawaii Press.

Katz, E. (1959). Mass communication research and the study of popular culture. *Studies in Public Opinion*, 2, 1–6.

Katz, E. & Lazarsfeld, P. (1955). *Personal Influence*. New York: Free Press.

Katz, J. & Rice, R. (2002). *Social Consequences of Internet Use: Access, Involvement and Interaction*. Cambridge, MA: MIT Press.

Kawachi, I. & Berkman, L. (2001). Social ties and mental health. *Journal of Urban Health*, 78, 458–467.

Kazarian, S. & Evans, D. (2001). *Handbook of Cultural Health Psychology*. London: Academic Press.

Kearins, J. (1999). Children and cultural difference. *Indigenous PPH*, 5, 52–60.

Keel, M. & Drew, N.M. (2004). The settlement experiences of refugees from the former Yugoslavia. *Community, Family and Work*, 7, 95–115.

Kelley, H. (1971). *Attribution in Social Interaction*. Morristown, NJ: General Learning Press.

Kelly, M. & Abraham, C. (2009). Editorial. Behavior change: The NICE perspective on the NICE guidance. *Psychology and Health*, 24(2), 131–133.

Kenrick, D., Neuberg, S. & Cialdini, R. (2007). *Social Psychology: Goals in Interaction* (4th ed.). New York: Allyn & Bacon.

Kidd, S. & Davidson, L. (2007). 'You have to adapt because you have no other choice': The stories of strength and resilience of 208 homeless youth in New York City and Toronto. *Journal of Community Psychology*, 35, 219–238.

Kim, U. & Berry, J. (1993). *Indigenous Psychologies: Experience and Research in Cultural Context*. Newbury Park, CA: Sage.

Kim, U., Yang, K. & Hwang, K. (2006a). Contributions to indigenous and cultural psychology: Understanding people in context. In U. Kim., K. Yang & K. Hwang (Eds.), *Indigenous and Cultural Psychology: Understanding People in Context* (pp. 3–25). New York: Springer.

Kim, U., Yang, K. & Hwang, K. (Eds.) (2006b). *Indigenous and Cultural Psychology: Understanding People in Context*. New York: Springer.

Kimhi, S. & Shamai, M. (2004). Community resilience and the impact of stress: Adult response to Israel's withdrawal from Lebanon. *Journal of Community Psychology*, 32, 439–451.

King, R. & Mai, N. (2009). Italophilia meets Albanophobia: Paradoxes of asymmetric assimilation and identity processes among Albanian immigrants in Italy. *Ethnic and Racial Studies*, 32, 117–138.

Kiran-Esen, B. (2003). Examining the adolescents smoking in relation to their peer pressure levels and gender. *Educational Sciences: Theory and Practice*, 3, 167–188.

Kleinman, A., Eisenberg, L. & Good, B. (2006). Culture, illness and care: Clinical lessons from anthropologic and cross-cultural research. *Journal of Life-Long Learning and Psychiatry*, 4, 140–149.

Korpela, K., Ylen, M., Tyrvainen, L. & Silvennoinen, H. (2008). Determinants of restorative experiences in everyday favorite places. *Health & Place*, 14, 636–652.

Korpela, K., Ylen, M., Tyrvainen, L. & Silvennoinen, H. (2009). Stability of self-reported favourite places and place attachment over a 10-month period. *Journal of Environmental Psychology*, 29(1), 95–100.

Kouvonen, A., Kivimaki, M., Elovainio, M., Väänänen, A., De Vogli, R., Heponiemi, T., Linna, A., Pentti, J. & Vahtera, J. (2008). Low organisational justice and heavy drinking: A prospective cohort study. *Occupational and Environmental Medicine*, 65, 44–50.

Kroeber, A. & Kluckhohn, C. (1952). *Culture: A Critical Review of Concepts and Definitions*. Cambridge, MA: Peabody Museum.

Kuppers, P. (2007). *Community Performance: An Introduction*. London: Routledge.

Kurzban, R. & Weeden, J. (2007). Do advertised preferences predict the behavior of speed daters? *Personal Relationships*, 14, 623–632.

Kutner, L. (1997). New roles for psychologists in the mass media. In. S. Kirschner & D. Kirschner (Eds.), *Perspectives on Psychology and the Media* (pp. 173–190). Washington, DC: American Psychological Association.

Kutner, L. & Olson, C. (2008). *Grand Theft Childhood: The Surprising Truth about Violent Video Games and What Parents Can Do*. New York: Simon & Schuster.

La Fromboise, T., Coleman, H. & Gerton, J. (1993). Psychological impact of biculturalism: Evidence and theory. *Psychological Bulletin*, 114, 395–412.

Lakey, B. & Cohen, S. (2000). Social support theory and measurement. In S. Cohen, L. Underwood & B. Gottlieb (Eds.), *Social Support Measurement and Assessment: A Guide for Health and Social Scientists* (pp. 29–52). Oxford: Oxford University Press.

Lane, R. (1988). Procedural goods in a democracy: How one is treated versus what one gets. *Social Justice Research*, 2(3), 177–192.

Langer, E. (1989). Minding matters: The consequences of mindlessness-mindfulness. *Advances in Experimental Social Psychology*, 22, 137–173.

Langlois, J., Kalakanis, L., Rubenstein, A., Larson, A., Hallam, M. & Smoot, M. (2000). Maxims or myths of beauty? A meta-analytic and theoretical review. *Psychological Bulletin*, 126, 390–423.

Lareau, A. & Weininger, E.B. (2003). Cultural capital in educational research: A critical assessment. *Theory and Society*, 32(5–6), 567–606.

Latane, B. & Darley, J. (1970). *The Unresponsive Bystander: Why Doesn't He Help?* New York: Appleton-Century-Crofts.

Laurier, E., McKie, L. & Goodwin, N. (2000). Daily and lifecourse contexts of smoking. *Sociology of Health and Illness*, 22, 289–309.

Lazarsfeld, P. & Merton, R. (1948). Mass Communication, popular taste and organized social action. In L. Bryson (Ed.), *The Communication of Ideas* (pp. 95–118). New York: Harper.

Lazarus, R.S. & Folkman, S. (1984). *Stress, Appraisal and Coping*. New York: Springer.

Leach, C. (2005). Against the notion of a 'new racism'. *Journal of Community and Applied Social Psychology*, 15, 432–445.

Le Bon, G. (1895/1977). *The Crowd*. Middlesex, UK: Penguin.

Lees, L. (2004). *The Emancipatory City? Paradoxes and Possibilities*. London: Sage.

Lenhart, A., Kahne, J., Middaugh, E., Macgill, A., Evans, C. & Vitak, J. (2008). *Teens, Video Games, and Civics*. Washington, DC: PEW/Internet & American Life Project. http://www.pewinternet.org/

Lenhart, A., Madden, M., Macgill, A. & Smith, A. (2007). *Teens and Social Media*. Washington, DC: PEW/Internet & American Life Project. http://www.pewinternet.org/

Lepore, S. (1998). Problems and prospects for the social support-reactivity hypothesis. *Annals of Behavioral Medicine*, 20, 257–269.

Lerner, M. & Lerner, S. (Eds.) (1981). *The Justice Motive in Social Behaviour*. New York: Plenum.

Lerner, M. & Miller, D.T. (1977). Just world research and the attribution process: Looking back and ahead. *Psychological Bulletin*, 85, 1030–1051.

Leventhal, G. (1980). What should be done with equity theory? New approaches to the study of fairness in social relationships. In K. Gergen, M. Greenberg & R. Willis (Eds.), *Social Exchange* (pp. 27–55). New York: Plenum.

Lewin, K. (1935). *A Dynamic Theory of Personality*. New York: McGraw-Hill.

Lewin, K. (1946/1948). Action research and minority problems. In G.W. Lewin (Ed.), *Resolving Social Conflicts* (pp. 201–216). New York: Harper & Row.

Lewin, K. (1948). *Resolving Social Conflicts*. New York: Harper & Row.

Lewis, R.C. (2008). The construction of identity through the dimensions of race & ethnicity: The experience of coloured South African women in Western Australia. Unpublished doctoral dissertation, Edith Cowan University, Perth, Western Australia.

Lidz, C. (2001). Multicultural issues and dynamic assessment. In L. Suzuki, J. Ponterotto & P. Meller (Eds.), *Handbook of Multicultural Assessment* (2nd ed.) (pp. 523–539). San Francisco: Jossey-Bass.

Lind, E. & Tyler, T. (1988). *The Social Psychology of Procedural Fairness*. New York: Plenum.

Lindsey, M. (1998). Culturally competent assessment of African American clients. *Journal of Personality Assessment*, 70(1), 43–53.

Linley, A. & Joseph, S. (Eds.) (2004). *Positive Psychology in Practice*. Hoboken, NJ: Wiley.

Linley, A., Joseph, S., Harrington, S. & Wood, A. (2006). Positive psychology: Past, present, and (possible) future. *Journal of Positive Psychology*, 1, 3–16.

Liu, J. & Liu, S. (1999). Interconnectedness and Asian social psychology. In T. Sugiman, M. Karasawa, J. Liu. & C. Ward (Eds.), *Progress in Asian Social Psychology*, Vol. 2 (pp. 9–31). Seoul: Kyoyook Kwahaksa.

Livingstone, S. (1998). *Making Sense of Television: The Psychology of Audience Interpretation*. London: Routledge.

Livingstone, S. (2007a). On the material and the symbolic: Silverstone's double articulation of research traditions in new media studies. *New Media & Society*, 9, 16–24.

Livingstone, S. (2007b). From family television to bedroom culture: Young people's media at home. In E. Devereux (Ed.), *Media Studies: Various Issues and Debates* (pp. 302–321). London: Sage.

Livingstone, S. & Bober, M. (2004). *UK Children Go Online: Surveying the Experiences of Young People and Their Parents*. London: LSE Research Online. http://eprints.lse.ac.uk/archive/00000395 (accessed 12 November 2007).

Livingstone, S. & Bovill, M. (2001). *Children and Their Changing Media Environment: A European Comparative Study*. Mahwah, NJ: Lawrence Erlbaum.

Lloyd-Bostock, S. (1991). Interactions between law and everyday thinking. In H. Steensma & R. Vermunt (Eds.), *Social Justice in Human Relations*, Vol. 2, *Societal and Psychological Consequences of Justice and Injustice* (pp. 31–48). New York: Plenum.

Lubek, I. (2000). Understanding and using the history of social psychology. *Journal of the History of the Behavioral Sciences*, 36, 319–328.

Lubek, I. & Apfelbaum, E. (2000). A critical gaze and wistful glance at *handbook* histories of social psychology: Did the successive accounts by Gordon Allport and successors historiographically succeed? *Journal of the History of the Behavioral Sciences*, 36, 405–428.

Lykes, M.B. (2000). Possible contributions of a psychology of liberation: Whither health and human rights? In D. Marks (Ed.), *The Health Psychology Reader* (pp. 352–372). London: Sage.

Lyndon, C. (1983). Beliefs in tapu, mate maori, and makutu and the relevance of these beliefs to the diagnosis of mental illness among the Maori. Unpublished masters thesis, University of Auckland, New Zealand.

Lyons, A.C. & Chamberlain, K. (2006). *Health Psychology: A Critical Introduction*. Cambridge: Cambridge University Press.

Mallett, S. (2004). Understanding home: A critical review of the literature. *Sociological Review*, 52, 62–89.

Mama, A. (1995). *Beyond the Masks: Race, Gender, and Subjectivity*. London: Routledge.

Mandler, G. (2007). *A History of Modern Experimental Psychology: From James and Wundt to Cognitive Science*. Cambridge, MA: MIT Press.

Mankowski, E.S. & Rappaport, J. (2000). Narrative concepts and analysis in spiritually-based communities. *Journal of Community Psychology*, 28(5), 479–493.

Manning, R., Levine, M. & Collins, A. (2007). The Kitty Genovese murder and the social psychology of helping: The parable of the 38 witnesses. *American Psychologist*, 62, 555–562.

Mansouri, T., Leach, M. & Traies, S. (2006). Acculturation experiences of Iraqi refugees in Australia: The impact of visa category. *Journal of Intercultural Studies*, 27(4), 393–412.

Manuel, G. & Posluns, M. (1974). *The Fourth World: An Indian Reality*. New York: Free Press.

Manzo, L.C. (2003). Relationships to non-residential places: Towards a reconceptualization of attachment to place. *Journal of Environmental Psychology*, 23, 47–61.

Manzo, L.C., Kleit, R. & Couch, D. (2008). 'Moving three times is like having your house on fire once': The experience of place and impending displacement among public housing residents. *Urban Studies*, 45, 1855–1878.

Markovizky, G. & Samid, Y. (2008). The process of immigrant adjustment: The role of time in determining psychological adjustment. *Journal of Cross-Cultural Psychology*, 39, 782–798.

Markovsky, B. (1991). Prospects for a cognitive-structural justice theory. In R. Vermunt & H. Steensma (Eds.), *Social Justice in Human Relations*, Vol. 1, *Societal and Psychological Origins of Justice* (pp. 33–58). New York: Plenum.

Marks, D. (2002). Editorial essay. Freedom, responsibility and power: Contrasting approaches to health psychology. *Journal of Health Psychology*, 7, 5–19.

Marks, D. (2008). Editorial. The quest for meaningful theory in health psychology. *Journal of Health Psychology*, 13, 977–981.

Marks, D., Murray, M., Evans, B. & Willig, C. (2000). *Health Psychology: Theory, Research and Practice*. London: Sage.

Martin, G. & Pear, J. (2003). *Behavior Modification: What It Is and How to Do It* (7th ed.). Upper Saddle River, NJ: Prentice Hall.

Martin, K.B.M. (2003). Ways of knowing, being and doing: A theoretical framework and methods for indigenous and indigenist research. Voicing dissent: New talents 21C. *Next Generation Australian Studies*, 76, 203–214.

Martín-Baró, I. (1994). Towards a liberation psychology. Trans. A. Aron. In A. Aron & S. Corne (Eds.), *Writings for a Liberation Psychology: Ignacio Martín-Baró* (pp. 17–32). Cambridge, MA: Harvard University Press.

Martinez, M.A. (1995). Discriminations against indigenous peoples E/CN.4/Sub.2/1995/27. United Nations Economic and Social Council Commission on Human Rights. http://www.cwis.org/fwdp/International/untrtst2.txt

Maslow, A. (1943). A theory of human motivation. *Psychological Review*, 50, 370–396.

Maslow, A. (1968). *Toward a Psychology of Being* (2nd ed.). New York: Van Nostrand Reinhold.

Maslow, A. (1970). *Motivation and Personality* (2nd ed.). New York: Harper & Row.

Maslow, A. (1971). *The Farther Reaches of Human Nature*. New York: Penguin.

Maslow, A. (1979). Politics 3. *Journal of Humanistic Psychology*, 17, 5–20.

Mastain, L. (2007). A phenomenological investigation of altruism as experienced by moral exemplars. *Journal of Phenomenological Psychology*, 38, 62–99.

Mattis, J.S., Hammond, W.P., Grayman, N., Bonacci, M., Brennan, W., Cowie, S., Ladyzhenskaya, L. & So, S. (2009). The social production of altruism: Motivations for caring action in a low-income urban community. *American Journal of Community Psychology*, 43, 71–84.

Maxim Institute. (2006). *Perceptions of Social Justice in New Zealand*. http://www.socialjustice.co.nz/social_justice_excerpt.pdf (accessed 15 June 2009).

McCabe, G. (2007). The healing path: A culture and community derived indigenous therapy model. *Psychology: Theory, Research, Practice, Training*, 44(2), 148–160.

McElwee, R.O., Dunning, D., Tan, P.L. & Hollmann, S. (2001). Evaluating others: The role of who we are versus what we think traits mean. *Basic and Applied Social Psychology*, 23, 123–136.

McKnight, J. & Sutton, J. (1994). *Social Psychology*. New York: Prentice Hall.

McMichael, C. (2002). 'Everywhere is Allah': Islam and the everyday life of Somali women in Melbourne, Australia. *Journal of Refugee Studies*, 15(2), 171–188.

McMillan, B., Higgins, A. & Conner, M. (2005). Using an extended theory of planned behaviour to understand smoking amongst schoolchildren. *Addiction Research and Theory*, 13, 293–306.

McMillan, S. & Morrison, M. (2006). Coming of age with the Internet: A qualitative exploration of how the Internet has become an integral part of young people's lives. *New Media & Society*, 8, 73–95.

McPherson, K. & Manuta Tunapee, P. (2005). *The Genocide of Tasmania's Lia Pootah Aboriginal People: A Living Death*. Lindisfarne, Tasmania: Manuta Tunapee Puggaluggalia Publisher.

McQuail, D. (1992). *Media Performance: Mass Communication and the Public Interest*. London: Sage.

McQuail, D. (2002). *McQuail's Reader in Mass Communication Theory*. London: Sage.

Mead, G.H. (1932). *The Philosophy of the Present*. New York: Prometheus Books.

Mead, G.H. (1934). *Mind, Self and Society*. Chicago: University of Chicago Press.

Media Psychology Division 46. (2006). *Media Psychology*. http://www.apa.org/divisions/div46/ (accessed 5 November 2007).

Miedemam, J., van den Bos, K. & Vermunt, R. (2006). The influence of self-threats on fairness judgements and affective measures. *Social Justice Research*, 19(2), 228–253.

Meier, B. (2007). Advancing health rights in a globalized world: Responding to globalization through a collective human right to public health. *Global Health Law, Ethics, and Policy*, Winter, 345–355.

Melchior, M., Caspi, A., Milne, B.J., Danese, A., Poulton, R. & Moffitt, T.E. (2007). Work stress precipitates depression and anxiety in young working women and men. *Psychological Medicine*, 37(8), 1119–1129.

Mellers, B. & Baron, J. (Eds.) (1993). *Psychological Perspectives on Justice: Theory and Applications*. Cambridge: Cambridge University Press.

Messick, D. & Cook, K. (Eds.). (1983). *Equity Theory: Psychological and Sociological Perspectives*. New York: Praeger.

Messner, S. (1986). Television violence and violent crime: An aggregate analysis. *Social Problems*, 33, 218–235.

Mezulis, A.H., Abramson, L.Y., Hyde, J.S. & Hankin, B.L. (2004). Is there a universal positivity bias in attributions? A meta-analytic review of individual, developmental, and cultural differences in self-serving attributional bias. *Psychological Bulletin*, 130, 711–747.

Mielewczyk, F. & Willig, C. (2007). Old clothes and an older look: The case for a radical makeover of health behaviour research. *Theory & Psychology*, 17, 811–837.

Mikula, G. (2003). Testing an attribution-of-blame model of judgements of injustice. *European Journal of Social Psychology*, 33, 793–811.

Mikulas, W. (2007). Buddhism & Western psychology: Fundamentals of integration. *Journal of Consciousness*, 14, 4–49.

Mikulincer, M., Shaver, P.R., Gillath, O. & Nitzberg, R. (2005). Attachment, caregiving, and altruism. *Journal of Personality and Social Psychology*, 89, 817–839.

Milgram, S. (1965). *Obedience*. New York: New York University Film Library.

Milgram, S. (1974). *Obedience to Authority*. New York: Harper & Row.

Miller, D.T. & Ross, M. (1975). Self-serving biases in the attribution of causality: Fact or fiction? *Psychological Bulletin*, 82, 213–225.

Miller, J. (1984). Culture and the development of everyday social explanation. *Journal of Personality and Social Psychology*, 46, 961–978.

Miller, R., Perlman, D. & Brehm, S. (2007). *Intimate Relationships* (5th ed.). New York: McGraw-Hill.

Minkler, M. & Wallerstein, N. (2002). *Community-Based Participatory Research for Health*. San Francisco: Jossey-Bass.

Mishler, E. (1995). Models of narrative analysis: A typology. *Journal of Narrative and Life History*, 5, 87–123.

Mitchell, D. (2003). *The Right to the City: Social Justice and the Fight for Public Space*. London: Guilford.

Mkhize, N. (2004). Psychology: An African perspective. In K. Ratele, N. Duncan, D. Hook, N. Mkhize, P. Kiguwa & A. Collins (Eds.), *Self, Community and Psychology* (pp. 4–1–4–29). Lansdowne, South Africa: University of Cape Town Press.

Moane, G. (2003). Bridging the personal and the political: Practices for a liberation psychology. *American Journal of Community Psychology*, 31, 91–101.

Moane, G. (2009). Reflections on liberation psychology in action in and Irish context. In M. Montero & C.C. Sonn (Eds.), *Psychology of Liberation: Theory and Applications* (pp. 135–154). New York: Springer.

Moghaddam, F.M. (1987). Psychology in the three worlds: As reflected in the crisis in social psychology & the move toward indigenous third world psychology. *American Psychologist*, 42, 912–920.

Monroe, K.R. (1996). *The Heart of Altruism: Reconceptions of a Common Humanity*. Princeton, NJ: Princeton University Press.

Montada, L. (1991). Coping with life stress: Injustice and the question "who is responsible?" In H. Steensma & R. Vermunt (Eds.), *Social Justice in Human Relations*, Vol. 2, *Societal and Psychological Consequences of Justice and Injustice* (pp. 9–30). New York: Plenum.

Montenegro, M. (2002). Ideology and community social psychology: Theoretical considerations and practical implications. *American Journal of Community Psychology*, 30(4), 511–527.

Montero, M. (2006). *Hacer Para Transformar: El Método en la Psicología Comunitaria*. Buenos Aires: Paidós.

Montero, M. (2007). The political psychology of liberation: From politics to ethics & back. *Political Psychology*, 28(5), 517–533.

Montero, M. & Sonn, C.C. (2009). *Psychology of Liberation: Theory and Applications*. Peace Psychology Book Series. New York: Springer.

Moreton-Robinson, A. (2003). I still call Australia home: Indigenous belonging and place in a white postcolonizing society. In S. Ahmed, C. Castañeda, A. Fortier & M. Sheller (Eds.), *Uprootings/Regroundings: Questions of Home and Migration* (pp. 23–40). Oxford: Berg.

Moriarty, T. (1975). Crime, commitment and the responsive bystander: Two field experiments. *Journal of Personality and Social Psychology*, 31, 370–376.

Morrison, B. (2006). School bullying and restorative justice: Toward a theoretical understanding of the role of respect, pride and shame. *Journal of Social Issues*, 62(2), 371–392.

Morry, M. (2007). Relationship satisfaction as a predictor of perceived similarity among cross-sex friends: A test of the attraction-similarity model. *Journal of Social and Personal Relationships*, 24, 117–138.

Moschetti, G. (1979). Calculating equity: Ordinal and ratio criteria. *Social Psychology Quarterly*, 42, 172–176.

Moscovici, S. (1970). Avant-propos. In D. Jodelet, J. Viet & P. Besnard (Eds.), *La Psychologie social: Une discipline en movement* (pp. 5–8). Paris. Mouton.

Moscovici, S. (1972). Society and theory in social psychology. In J. Isreal & H. Tajfel (Eds.), *The Context of Social Psychology: A Critical Assessment*. London: Academic Press.

Moscovici, S. (1981). On social representations. In J. Forgas (Ed.), *Social Cognition: Perspectives on Everyday Understanding* (pp. 181–209). London: Academic Press.

Moscovici, S. (1994). Social representations and pragmatic communication. *Social Science Information*, 33, 163–177.

Moscovici, S. (1998). The history and actuality of social representations. In U. Flick (Ed.), *Psychology of the Social* (pp. 209–248). Boston: Cambridge University Press.

Moyo, D. (2008). *Dead Aid: Why Aid Is Not Working and How There Is a Better Way for Africa*. New York: Farrar, Straus and Giroux.

Muldoon, O., McLaughlin, K. & Trew, K. (2007). Adolescents' perceptions of national identification and socialization: A grounded analysis. *British Journal of Developmental Psychology*, 25, 579–594.

Muller, M., Kals, E. & Maes, J. (2008). Fairness, self interest, and cooperations in a real-life conflict. *Journal of Applied Social Psychology*, 38(3), 684–704.

Mulveen, R. & Hepworth, J. (2006). An interpretative phenomenological analysis of participation in pro-anorexic Internet site and its relationship with disordered eating. *Journal of Health Psychology*, 11(2), 283–296.

Murray, M. & Campbell, C. (2003). Living in a material world: Reflecting assumptions of health psychology. *Journal of Health Psychology*, 8, 231–236.

Murray, M., Nelson, G., Poland, B., Maticka-Tyndale, E. & Ferris, L. (2004). Assumptions and values of community health psychology. *Journal of Health Psychology*, 9, 323–333.

Murray, M. & Poland, B. (2006). Health psychology and social action. *Journal of Health Psychology*, 11, 379–384.

Musolf, G. (2003). *Structure and Agency in Everyday Life: An Introduction to Social Psychology*. New York: Rowman & Littlefield.

Nagata, D. (1990). The Japanese-American internment: Perceptions of moral community, fairness and redress. *Journal of Social Issues*, 46(1), 133–146.

Navarro, V. (2004). *The Political Economy of Social Inequalities: Consequences for Health and Quality of Life*. Amityville, NY: Baywood.

Naverette, C. & Huerta, E. (2006). Building virtual bridges to home: The use of the Internet by transnational communities of immigrants. *International Journal of Communication Law & Policy*, special issue, *Virtual Communities*, Autumn, 1–20.

Nelson, G. & Prilleltensky, I. (Eds.) (2005). *Community Psychology: In Pursuit of Liberation and Well-Being*. Houndmills, UK: Palgrave Macmillan.

Ng, S. & Allen, M. (2005). Perceptions of economic distributive justice: Exploring leading theories. *Social Behavior and Personaility*, 33(5), 435–454.

Nickerson, R. (1998). Confirmation bias: A ubiquitous phenomenon in many guises. *Review of General Psychology*, 2, 175–220.

Noble, G. (2004). Accumulating being. *International Journal of Cultural Studies*, 7, 233–256.

Noble, G. (2005). The discomfort of strangers: Racism, incivility and ontological security in a relaxed and comfortable nation. *Journal of Intercultural Studies*, 26(1), 107–120.

Norris, F.H., Stevens, S.P., Pfefferbaum, B., Wyche, K.F. & Pfefferbaum, R.L. (2008). Community resilience as a metaphor, theory, set of capacities, and strategy for disaster readiness. *American Journal of Community Psychology*, 41, 127–150.

Nowell, B.L., Berkowitz, S.L., Deacon, Z. & Foster-Fishman, P. (2006). Revealing the cues within community places: Stories of identity, history and possibility. *American Journal of Community Psychology*, 37, 29–46.

Nsamenang, A.B. (2006). Human ontogenesis: An indigenous African view on development & intelligence. *International Journal of Psychology*, 41, 293–297.

Oberg, K. (1960). Culture shock: Adjustment to new cultural environments. *Practical Anthropology*, 7, 177–182.

O'Donnell, C., Tharp, R. & Wilson, K. (1993). Activity settings as the unit of analysis: A theoretical basis for community intervention and development. *American Journal of Community Psychology*, 21, 501–520.

O'Donovan, A. & Hughes, B. (2008). Access to social support in life and in the laboratory: Combined impact on cardiovascular reactivity to stress and state anxiety. *Journal of Health Psychology*, 13, 1147–1156.

O'Dwyer, L., Baum, F., Kavanagh, A. & MacDougall, C. (2007). Do area-based interventions to reduce health inequalities work? A systematic review of evidence. *Critical Public Health*, 17(4), 317–335.

Ogden, J. (1997). The rhetoric and reality of psychosocial theories: A challenge to biomedicine. *Journal of Health Psychology*, 2, 21–29.

Okazaki, S., David, E.J.R. & Abelmann, N. (2008). Colonialism & psychology of culture. *Social & Personality Psychology Compass*, 2(1), 90–196.

Okimoto, T. & Tyler, T. (2007). Is compensation enough? Relational concerns in responding to unintended inequity. *Group Processes Intergroup Relations*, 10, 399–420.

Opotow, S. (1990). Moral exclusion and injustice: An introduction. *Journal of Social Issues*, 46(1), 1–20.

Opotow, S. (1993). Animals and the scope of justice. *Journal of Social Issues*, 49(1), 71–85.

Opotow, S. (1994). Predicting protection: Scope of justice and the natural world. *Journal of Social Issues*, 50(3), 49–63.

Opotow, S. (2001). Reconciliation in times of impunity: Challenges for social justice. *Social Justice Research*, 14(2), 149–170.

Opotow, S. (2008). 'Not so much as a place to lay our head ...': Moral inclusion and exclusion in the American Civil War reconstruction. *Social Justice Research*, 21, 26–49.

O'Sullivan, S. (2005). 'The whole nation is listening to you': The presentation of the self on a tabloid talk radio show. *Media, Culture & Society*, 27, 719–738.

Oxenham, D. (2000). Aboriginal terms of reference. In P. Dudgeon, D. Garvey & H. Pickett (Eds.), *Working with Indigenous Australians: A Handbook for Psychologists* (pp. 109–125). Perth, Western Australia: Gunada Press.

Padilla, A. (2001). Issues in culturally appropriate assessment. In L. Suzuki, J. Ponterotto & P. Meller (Eds.), *Handbook of Multicultural Assessment* (2nd ed.) (pp. 5–27). San Francisco: Jossey-Bass.

Paradies, Y., Harris, R. & Anderson, I. (2008). The impact of racism on indigenous health in Australia and Aotearoa: Towards a research agenda. Discussion paper no. 4, Cooperative Research Centre for Aboriginal Health, Darwin.

Paranjpe, A.C. (1998). *Self and Identity in Modern Psychology and Indian Thought.* New York: Springer.

Pargament, K. & Hahn, J. (1986). God and the just world: Causal and coping attributions to God in health situations. *Journal for the Scientific Study of Religion*, 25(2), 193–207.

Parker, I. (1989). *The Crisis in Modern Social Psychology – And How to End It.* London: Routledge.

Parker, I. (1992). *Discourse Dynamics: Critical Analysis for Individual and Social Psychology.* Routledge: London.

Parker, I. (2005). *Qualitative Psychology: Introducing Radical Psychology.* Maidenhead, UK: Open University Press.

Parker, I. (2007). *Revolution in Psychology: Alienation to Emancipation.* London: Pluto.

Payne, B.K. (2001). Prejudice and perception: The role of automatic and controlled processes in misperceiving a weapon. *Journal of Personality and Social Psychology*, 81, 181–192.

Peng, K., Spencer-Rodgers, J. & Nian, Z. (2006). Naïve dialecticism and the Tao of Chinese thought. In U. Kim., K. Yang & K. Hwang (Eds.), *Indigenous and Cultural Psychology: Understanding People in Context* (pp. 247–262). New York: Springer.

Pe-Pua, R. (2006). From decolonizing psychology to the development of a cross-indigenous perspective in methodology: The Philippine experience. In U. Kim., K. Yang & K. Hwang (Eds.), *Indigenous and Cultural Psychology: Understanding People in Context* (pp. 109–137). New York: Springer.

Perloff, R.M. (2008). *The Dynamics of Persuasion.* New York: Lawrence Erlbaum.

Peters, S., van den Bos, K. & Karremans, J. (2008). On the psychology of the advantaged: How people react to being overpaid. *Social Justice Research*, 21, 179–191.

Peters, S. & van den Bos, K. (2008). When fairness is especially important: Reactions to being inequitably paid in communal relationships. *Social Justice Research*, 21, 86–105.

Peterson, C. & Seligman, M.E.P. (2003). Positive organizational studies: Thirteen lessons from positive psychology. In K.S. Cameron, J.E. Dutton & R.E. Quinn (Eds.), *Positive Organizational Scholarship* (pp. 14–28). San Francisco: Berrett-Koehler.

Peterson, C. & Seligman, M.E.P. (2004). *Character Strengths and Virtues: A Handbook and Classification.* Washington, DC: American Psychological Association Press and Oxford University Press.

Piaget, J. (1929). *The Child's Conception of the World.* New York: Harcourt, Brace.

Piaget, J. (1977). *The Development of Thought: Equilibrium of Cognitive Structures.* New York: Viking.

Pietikäinen, S. (2003). Indigenous identity in print: Representations of the Sami in news discourse. *Discourse & Society*, 14, 581–609.

Pike, K. (1967). Etic and emic standpoints for the description of behavior. In D.C. Hildum (Ed.), *Language and Thought: An Enduring Problem in Psychology* (pp. 32–39). Princeton, NJ: Van Nostrand.

Poelmans, S., O'Driscoll, M. & Beham, B. (2005). An overview of international research on the work-family interface. In S. Poelmans (Ed.), *Work and Family: An International Research Perspective* (pp. 3–46). Mahwah, NJ: Lawrence Erlbaum.

Polkinghorne, D. (1983). *Methodology for the Human Sciences: Systems of Inquiry.* Albany: State University of New York Press.

Pooley, A., Breen, L., Pike, L., Cohen, L. & Drew, N. (2007). Critiquing the school community: A qualitative study of children's conceptualizations of their school. *International Journal of Qualitative Studies in Education*, 21, 87–98.

Pooley, J.A., Cohen, L. & O'Connor, M. (2006). Community resilience and its link to individual resilience in the disaster experience of cyclone communities in Northwest Australia. In D. Paton & D. Johnston (Eds.), *Disaster Resilience: An Integrated Approach* (pp. 161–170). Springfield, IL: Charles C. Thomas.

Post, S.G., Underwood, L.G., Schloss, J.P. & Hurlbut, W.B. (Eds.) (2002). *Altruism and Altruistic Love: Science, Philosophy, and Religion in Dialogue.* New York: Oxford University Press.

Potter, J. & Wetherell, M. (1987). *Discourse and Social Psychology: Beyond Attitudes and Behaviour.* London: Sage.

Pratkanis, A. & Aronson, E. (1991). *Age of Propaganda: The Everyday Use and Abuse of Persuasion.* New York: W.H. Freeman.

Prebble, J. (1963). *The Highland Clearances.* Harmondsworth, UK: Penguin.

Pressman, S. & Cohen, S. (2005). Does positive affect influence health? *Psychological Bulletin*, 131, 925–971.

Pretty, G.H., Chipuer, H.M. & Bramston, P. (2003). Sense of place amongst adolescents and adults in two rural Australian towns: The discriminating features of place attachment, sense of community and place dependence in relation to place identity. *Journal of Environmental Psychology*, 23, 273–287.

Prilleltensky, I. (1992). Humanistic psychology, human welfare and the social order. *Journal of Mind and Behavior*, 13, 315–328.

Prilleltensky, I. & Nelson, G. (2002). *Doing Psychology Critically: Making a Difference in Diverse Settings.* London: Palgrave Macmillan.

Prilleltensky, I. & Prilleltensky, O. (2003). Towards a critical health psychology practice. *Journal of Health Psychology*, 8, 197–210.

Prince, L. (2008). Resilience in African American women formerly involved in street prostitution. *ABNF Journal*, 19(1), 31–36.

Prochaska, J. (1983). Stages and processes of self-change of smoking: Toward an integrative model of change. *Journal of Consulting and Clinical Psychology*, 51, 390–395.

Proshansky, H., Fabian, A. & Kaminoff, R. (1995). Place-identity: Physical world socialization of the self. In L. Groat (Ed.), *Readings in Environmental Psychology: Giving Places Meaning* (pp. 87–113). New York: Academic Press.

Purkhardt, C.S. (1993). *Transforming Social Representations: A Social Psychology of Common Sense and Science.* London: Routledge.

Putland, C. (2008). Lost in translation: The question of evidence linking community-based arts and health promotion. *Journal of Health Psychology, 13*, 265–276.

Putnam, R.D. (2000). *Bowling Alone: The Collapse and Survival of American Community*. New York: Simon & Schuster.

Quijano, A. (2000). Coloniality of power and Eurocentrism in Latin America. *International Sociology*, 15(2), 215–232.

Radley, A. (1999). Social realms and the qualities of illness experience. In M. Murray & K. Chamberlain (Eds.), *Qualitative Health Psychology: Theories and Methods* (pp. 16–30). London: Sage.

Radley, A. & Billig, M. (1996). Accounts of health and illness: Dilemmas and representations. *Sociology of Health and Illness*, 18, 220–240.

Ramirez, M. (2008). Procedural perceptions and support for the US Supreme Court. *Political Psychology*, 29(5), 675–698.

Raphael, D. (2003). Toward the future: Policy and community actions to promote population health. In R. Hofrichter (Ed.), *Health and Social Justice: Politics, Ideology and Inequity in the Distribution of Disease* (pp. 453–468). San Francisco: Jossey-Bass; Wiley.

Rappaport, J. (2000). Community narratives: Tales of terror and joy. *American Journal of Community Psychology*, 28, 1–24.

Rappaport, J. & Seidman, E. (Eds.) (2000). *Handbook of Community Psychology*. New York: Kluwer Academic; Plenum.

Ratele, K. & Duncan, N. (2004). *Social Psychology: Identities and Relationships*. Cape Town: University of Cape Town Press.

Rawls, J. (1971). *A Theory of Justice*. Cambridge, MA: Harvard University Press.

Rechavi, T. (2009). A room for living: Private and public aspects in the experience of the living room. *Journal of Environmental Psychology*, 29(1), 133–143.

Redfield, R., Linton, R. & Herskovits, M.L. (1936). Memorandum for the study of acculturation. *American Anthropologist*, 38, 149–152.

Reed-Victor, E. & Stronge, J. (2002). Homeless students and resilience: Staff perspectives on individual and environmental factors. *Journal of Children & Poverty*, 8, 159–183.

Reevy, G. & Maslach, C. (2001). Use of social support: Gender and personality differences. *Sex Roles*, 44, 437–459.

Rehberg, W. (2005). Altruistic individualists: Motivations for international volunteering among young adults in Switzerland. *Voluntas: International Journal of Voluntary and Nonprofit Organizations*, 16, 109–122.

Reicher, S. (2001). Studying psychology studying racism. In M. Augoustinos & K. Reynolds (Eds.), *Understanding Prejudice, Racism and Social Conflict* (pp. 273–298). London: Sage.

Reis, H.T. (1984). The multidimensionality of justice. In R. Folger (Ed.), *The Sense of Injustice: Social Psychological Perspectives* (pp. 25–61). New York: Plenum.

Reyes Cruz, M. (2006). Mis muertos están conmigo [My dead are with me]: An autoethnographic text on racialization, identity and memory. *Qualitative Inquiry*, 12(3), 589–595.

Reynolds, T. (2006). Family & community networks in the (re)making of ethnic identity of Caribbean young people in Britain. *Community, Work & Family*, 9, 273–290.

Rezentes, W.J. (1996). *Ka Lama Kukui: An Introduction to Hawaiian Psychology*. Honolulu: A'ali'i Press.

Rice, R. & Atkin, C. (2001). *Public Communication Campaigns*. London: Sage.

Riggs, D. (2004). Challenging the monoculturalism of psychology: Towards a more socially accountable pedagogy and practice. *Australian Psychologist*, 39(2), 118–126.

Ritchie, J.E. (1992). *Becoming Bicultural*. Wellington: Huia; Daphne Brasell.

Ritchie, J.E. & Ritchie, J. (1985). *E Tipu e Rea: Polynesian Socialization and Psychological Development*. Hamilton: University of Waikato Centre for Māori Studies and Research.

Ritzer, G. (1995). *The McDonaldization of Society: An Investigation into the Changing Character of Contemporary Social Life*. New York: Pine Forge.

Robbins, B.D. (2008). What is the good life? Positive psychology and the renaissance of humanistic psychology. *Humanistic Psychologist*, 36, 96–112.

Robbins, R., Polderman, A. & Birkenholtz, T. (2001). Lawns and toxins: An ecology of the city. *Cities*, 18, 369–380.

Robinson, D. & Groves, J. (1999). *Introducing Philosophy*. Boston: Totem.

Robles, T.F., Glaser, R. & Kiecolt-Glaser, J.K. (2005). Out of balance: A new look at chronic stress, depression and immunity. *Current Directions in Psychological Science*, 14, 111–115.

Rodman, M. (1993). Beyond built form and culture in the anthropological study of residential community spaces. In R. Rotenberg and G. McDonogh (Eds.), *The Cultural Meaning of Urban Space* (pp. 123–138). Westport, CT: Bergin & Garvey.

Rogers, C. (1951). *Client-Centered Therapy*. Boston: Houghton Mifflin.

Rogers, C. (1972). *On Becoming a Person*. Boston: Houghton Mifflin.

Rojas, H., Shah, D., Cho, J., Schmierbach, M., Keum, H. & Gil-De-Zunigga, H. (2005). Media dialogue: Perceiving and addressing community problems. *Mass Communication & Society*, 8(2), 93–110.

Rosenstock, I.M. (1966). Why people use health services. *Milbank Memorial Fund Quarterly*, 44, 94–127.

Rosnow, R. (1981). *Paradigms in Transition: The Methodology of Social Inquiry*. New York: Oxford University Press.

Ross, L. (1977). The intuitive psychologist and his short-comings: Distortions in the attribution process. *Advances in Experimental Social Psychology*, 10, 173–220.

Ross, L., Lepper, M.R. & Hubbard, M. (1975). Perseverance in self-perception and social perception: Biased attributional processes in the debriefing paradigm. *Journal of Personality and Social Psychology*, 32, 880–892.

Rotter, J.B. (1966). Generalized expectancies for internal versus external control reinforcement. *Psychological Monographs*, 80, whole no. 609.

Rubin, M. & Hewstone, M. (1998). Social identity theory's self-esteem hypothesis: A review and some suggestions for clarification. *Personality and Social Psychology Review*, 2, 40–62.

Rudmin, F.W. (2003). Critical history of the acculturation psychology of assimilation, separation, integration, and marginalization. *Review of General Psychology*, 7, 3–37.

Rudmin, F.W. (2006). Debate in science: The case of acculturation. *AnthroGlobe Journal*. http://www.anthroglobe.ca/docs/rudminf_acculturation_061204.pdf (accessed 20 October 2008).

Rusbult, C. & Van Lange, P. (2003). Interdependence, interaction, and relationships. *Annual Review of Psychology*, 54, 351–375.

Rydell, R. & McConnell, A. (2006). Understanding implicit and explicit attitude change: A systems of reasoning analysis. *Journal of Personality and Social Psychology*, 91, 995–1008.

Sampson, E. (1981). Social change and the contexts of justice motivation. In M. Lerner & S. Lerner. (Eds.), *The Justice Motive in Social Behaviour: Adapting to Times of Scarcity and Change* (pp. 97–124). New York: Plenum.

Sampson, E. (1983). *Justice and the Critique of Pure Psychology.* New York: Plenum.

Sampson, E. (1986). Justice ideology and social legitimation: A revised agenda for psychological enquiry. In H. Bierhoff, R. Cohen & J. Greenberg (Eds.), *Justice in Social Relations* (pp. 87–102). New York: Plenum.

Sampson, E. (2000). Reinterpreting individualism and collectivism: Their religious roots and monologic versus dialogic person-other relationship. *American Psychologist*, 55, 1425–1432.

Sapica Rodríguez, S., Tovar Guerra, C., Galindo Villareal, L. & Vidales Bohorquez, R. (2009). Psychological accompaniment: Construction of cultures of peace among a community affected by war. In M. Montero & C.C. Sonn (Eds.), *Psychology of Liberation: Theory and Applications* (pp. 221–235). Peace Psychology Book Series. New York: Springer.

Schaalma, H. & Kok, G. (2009). Decoding health education interventions: The times are a-changin'. *Psychology and Health*, 24(1), 5–9.

Schneider, F., Gruman, J. & Coutts, L. (2005). *Applied Social Psychology: Understanding and Addressing Social and Practical Problems.* London: Sage.

Schneider, K., Bugental, J. & Pierson J. (2001). *The Handbook of Humanistic Psychology: Leading Edges in Theory, Research, and Practice.* London: Sage.

Schwartz, L. (1999). *Psychology and the Media: A Second Look.* Washington, DC: American Psychological Association.

Scrambler, G. & Higgs, P. (1999). Stratification, class and health: Class relations and health inequalities in high modernity. *Sociology*, 33(2), 275–296.

Segall, M.H., Dasen, P.R., Berry, J.W. & Poortinga, Y.H. (1999). *Human Behavior in Global Perspective: An Introduction to Cross-Cultural Psychology* (2nd ed.). Needham Heights, MA: Allyn & Bacon.

Seligman, M. & Csikszentmihalyi, M. (2000). Positive psychology: An introduction. *American Psychologist*, 55, 5–14.

Seligman, M.E.P. (1998a). *Learned Optimism.* New York: Simon & Schuster.

Seligman, M.E.P. (1998b) Message from the president of APA. In *APA Annual Convention Program* (p. xxv). Washington DC: American Psychological Association.

Seligman, M.E.P. (2002). *Authentic Happiness: Using the New Positive Psychology to Realize Your Potential for Lasting Fulfillment.* New York: Free Press.

Shapiro, S.B. (2001). Illogical positivism. *American Psychologist*, 56(1), 82.

Shaw, M. (1974). New Science or no-science? *Contemporary Psychology*, 19, 96–97.

Sheils, D. (1975). Toward a unified theory of ancestor worship: A cross-cultural study. *Social Forces*, 54(2), 427–440.

Sherif, C. (1976). *Orientation in Social Psychology.* New York: Harper & Row.

Sherif, M. (1966). *In Common Predicament: Social Psychology of Intergroup Conflict and Cooperation.* Boston: Houghton Mifflin.

Sheringham, M. (2006). *Everyday Life: Theories and Practices from Surrealism to the Present*. Oxford: Oxford University Press.

Sherwood, J. & Edwards, T. (2006). Decolonisation: A critical step for improving Aboriginal health. *Contemporary Nurse*, 22, 178–190.

Shortland, E. (1980). *Traditions and Superstitions of the New Zealanders*. New York: AMS Press.

Shweder, R.A. (1990). Cultural psychology – what is it? In J.W. Stigler, R.A. Shweder & G. Herdt (Eds.), *Cultural Psychology: Essays on Comparative Human Development* (pp. 1–43). Cambridge: Cambridge University Press.

Signorielli, N. & Morgan, M. (Eds.) (1990). *Cultivation Analysis: New Directions in Media Effects Research*. Newbury Park, CA: Sage.

Silverstone, R. (1999). *Why Study the Media?* London: Sage.

Silverstone, R. (2007). *Media and Morality: On the Rise of the Mediapolis*. Cambridge: Polity.

Silverstone, R. & Georgiou, M. (2005). Editorial introduction. Media and minorities in multicultural Europe. *Journal of Ethnic and Migration Studies*, 31, 433–441.

Simmel, G. (1903). The metropolis and mental life. In K.H. Wolf (Ed. & Trans.), *The Sociology of Georg Simmel* (pp. 409–424). Glencoe, IL: Free Press.

Sinha, D. (1996). Trend towards indigenization of psychology: A historical analysis of the Indian scene. *International Journal of Psychology*, 31(3–4), 4114.

Sinha, D. (1997). Indigenising psychology. In J.W. Berry, Y. Poortinga & J. Pandey (Eds.), *Handbook of Crosscultural Psychology: Theory and Method* (2nd ed.) (pp. 129–169). Needham Heights, MA: Allyn & Bacon.

Sinha, D. & Kao, H.S.R. (1997). The journey to the east: An introduction. In H.S.R. Kao & D. Sinha (Eds.), *Asian Perspectives on Psychology* (pp. 9–22). New Delhi, India: Sage.

Skitka, L. (2002). Do the means always justify the ends, or do the ends sometimes justify the means? A value protection model of justice reasoning. *Personality and Social Psychology Bulletin*, 28, 588–597.

Skitka, L. (2009). Exploring the 'lost and found' of justice theory and research. *Social Justice Research*, 22(1), 98–116.

Skitka, L. & Mullen, E. (2002). Understanding judgements of fairness in a real-world political context: A test of the value protection model of justice reasoning. *Personality and Social Psychology Bulletin*, 28, 1419–1429.

Skitka, L. & Tetlock, P. (1993). Of ants and grasshoppers: The political psychology of allocating public assistance. In B. Mellers & J. Baron (Eds.), *Psychological Perspectives on Justice: Theory and Applications* (pp. 205–233). Cambridge: Cambridge University Press.

Skinner, B. (1945/1984). The operational analysis of psychological terms. *Behavioral and Brain Sciences*, 7, 547–581.

Skodova, Z., Nagyova, I., van Dijk, J., Sudzinova, A., Vargova, H., Studencan, M. & Reijneveld, S. (2008). Socioeconomic differences in psychological factors contributing to coronary heart disease: A review. *Journal of Clinical Psychology in Medical Settings*, 15, 204–213.

Smith, L.T. (1999). *Decolonising Methodologies: Researching & Indigenous Peoples*. Dunedin, New Zealand: University of Otago Press.

Snell, D. & Hodgetts, D. (2007). A heavy metal community of practice. *Journal of Community and Applied Social Psychology*, 17, 430–445.

Somerville, M. & Perkins, T. (2003). Border work in the contact zone: Thinking indigenous/non-indigenous relations spatially. *Journal of Intercultural Studies*, 24(3), 253–266.

Sonn, C.C. (1996). The role of psychological sense of community in the adjustment of 'coloured' South African immigrants. Unpublished PhD dissertation, Victoria University of Technology, Melbourne.

Sonn, C.C. (2002). Immigrant adaptation: Exploring the process through sense of community. In A.T. Fisher, C.C. Sonn & B.J. Bishop (Eds.), *Psychological Sense of Community: Research, Applications & Implications* (pp. 205–222). New York: Kluwer Academic; Plenum.

Sonn, C.C. (2006). Multiple belongings? Reflection on the challenges of reconstructing Apartheid-imposed identities in Australia after immigration. In G. Stevens, V. Franchi & T. Swart (Eds.), *A Race against Time: Psychology and Challenges to Deracialisation in South Africa* (pp. 335–348). Pretoria: University of South Africa Press.

Sonn, C.C., Drew, N. & Kasat, P. (2002). *Conceptualising Community Cultural Development: The Role of Cultural Planning in Community Change*. Perth, WA: Community Arts Network (WA).

Sonn, C.C. & Fisher, A.T. (1998). Sense of community: Community resilient responses to oppression & change. *Journal of Community Psychology*, 26(5), 457–471.

Sonn, C.C. & Fisher, A.T. (2003). Identity and oppression: Differential responses to and in between status. *American Journal of Community Psychology*, 31, 117–128.

Sonn, C.C. & Fisher, A.T. (2005). Immigrant adaptation: Complicating our understanding of responses to intergroup experiences. In G. Nelson & I. Prilleltensky (Eds.), *Community Psychology: In Pursuit of Liberation & Wellbeing* (pp. 348–363). London: Palgrave Macmillan.

Sonn, C.C. & Lewis, R.C. (2009). Immigration and identity: The ongoing struggle for liberation. In M. Montero & C.C. Sonn (Eds.). *Psychology and Liberation: Theory and Applications* (pp. 115–133). Peace Psychology Book Series. New York: Springer.

Stam, H. (2006). Introduction: Reclaiming the social in social psychology. *Theory and Psychology*, 16, 587–595.

Stam, H., Lubek, I. & Radtke, H. (1998). Repopulating social psychology texts: Disembodied 'subjects' and embodied subjectivity. In D. Bayer & J. Shotter (Eds.), *Reconstructing the Psychological Subject: Bodies, Practices and Technologies* (pp. 153–186). London: Sage.

Steele, C. (1997). A threat in the air: How stereotypes shape the intellectual identities and performance of women and African-Americans. *American Psychologist*, 52, 613–629.

Steensma, H. & Vermunt, R. (Eds.) (1991). *Social Justice in Human Relations*, Vol. 2, *Societal and Psychological Consequences of Justice and Injustice*. New York: Plenum.

Steptoe, A., O'Donnell, K., Marmot, M. & Wardle, J. (2008). Positive affect and the psychosocial processes related to health. *British Journal of Social Psychology*, 99, 211–227.

Steptoe, A., Wardle, J. & Marmot, M. (2005). Positive affect and health-related neuroendocrine, cardiovascular, and inflammatory processes. *Proceedings of the National Academy of Sciences* (USA), 102, 6508–6512.

Stevens, G., Swart, T. & Franchi. V. (2006). Changing contexts of race and racism: Problematics, polemics, and perspectives. In G. Stevens, T. Swart & V. Franchi

(Eds.), *A Race against Time: Psychology and Challenges of Deracialisation in South Africa* (pp. 3–27). Pretoria: University of South Africa Press.

Stone, B.L. (2008). The most unique of all unique species. *Society*, 45(2), 146–151.

Stouffer, S., Suchman, E., De Vinney, L., Star, S. & Williams, R. (1949). *The American Soldier: Adjustments During Army Life*, Vol. 1. Princeton, NJ: Princeton University Press.

Strachey, J. (Ed.) (1955). *The Standard Edition of the Complete Psychological Works of Sigmund Freud*. London: Hogarth Press.

Stukas, A.A., Daly, M. & Clary, E.G. (2006). Lessons from research on volunteering for mobilizing adults to volunteer for positive youth development. In E.G. Clary & S.E. Rhodes (Eds.), *Mobilizing Adults for Positive Youth Development: Strategies for Closing the Gap between Beliefs and Behaviors* (pp. 65–82). New York: Springer.

Sugamura, G., Haruki, Y. & Koshikawa, F. (2007). Building more solid bridges between Buddhism and Western psychology. *American Psychologist*, 62(9), 1080–1081.

Sumner, W.G. (1907). *Folkways: A Study of the Sociological Importance of Usages, Manners, Customs, Mores, and Morals*. Boston: Ginn.

Sutton, R., Douglas, K., Wilkin, K., Elder, T., Cole, J. & Stathi, S. (2008). Justice for whom, exactly? Belief in justice for the self and various others. *Personality and Social Psychology Bulletin*, 34, 528–541.

Suzuki, L., Ponterotto, J. & Meller, P. (2001). Multicultural assessment: Trends and directions. In L. Suzuki, J. Ponterotto & P. Meller (Eds.), *Handbook of Multicultural Assessment* (2nd ed.) (pp. 67–99). San Francisco: Jossey-Bass.

Swickert, R. & Hittner, J. (2009). Social support coping mediates the relationship between gender and posttraumatic growth. *Journal of Health Psychology*, 14(3), 387–393.

Tabibnia, G., Satpute, A. & Lieberman, M. (2008). The sunny side of fairness: Preference for fairness activates reward circuitry (and disregarding unfairness activates self-control circuitry). *Psychological Science*, 19(4), 339–347.

Tacchi, J. (1998). Radio texture: Between self and others. In D. Miller (Ed.), *Material Cultures: Why Some Things Matter* (pp. 25–45). Chicago: University of Chicago Press.

Tadmor, T. & Tetlock, P.E. (2006). Biculturalism: A model of the effects of second-culture exposure on acculturation and integrative complexity. *Journal of Cross-Cultural Psychology*, 37, 173–190.

Taft, R. & Day, R. (1988). Psychology in Australia. *Annual Review of Psychology*, 39, 375–400.

Tajfel, H. (1969). Cognitive aspects of prejudice. *Journal of Biosocial Sciences*, Suppl. 1, 173–191.

Tajfel, H. (1972). Experiments in a vacuum. In J. Israel & H. Tajfel (Eds.), *The Context of Social Psychology* (pp. 69–121). London: Academic Press.

Tajfel, H. (1981). *Human Groups and Social Categories*. Cambridge: Cambridge University Press.

Tajfel, H. (1982). Social psychology of intergroup relations. *Annual Review of Psychology*, 33, 1–39.

Tajfel, H. & Turner, J. (1979). An integrative theory of intergroup conflict. In W.G. Austin & S. Worchel (Eds.), *The Social Psychology of Intergroup Relations* (pp. 94–109). Monterey, CA: Brooks-Cole.

Tanner, K. (1997). *Theories of Culture: A New Agenda for Theology*. Minneapolis: Fortress.

Tappan, M.B. (2005). Domination, subordination & the dialogical self: Identity development & the politics of 'ideological becoming'. *Culture & Psychology*, 11(1), 47–75.

Tarde, G. (1910). *L'opinion et la foule* [Opinion and the public]. Paris: Presses Universitaires de France.

Terry-Mcelrath, Y., Wakefield, M., Emery, S., Saffer, H., Szczypka, G., O'Malley, P., Johnston, L., Chaloupka, F. & Flay, B. (2007). State anti-tobacco advertising and smoking outcomes by gender and race/ethnicity. *Ethnicity & Health*, 12, 339–362.

Thibaud, J-P. (2003). The sonic composition of the city. In M. Bull and L. Back (Eds.), *The Auditory Culture Reader* (pp. 329–341). Oxford: Berg.

Thibaut, J. & Kelley, H. (1959). *The Social Psychology of Groups*. New York: Wiley.

Thibaut, J. & Walker, L. (1975). *Procedural Justice: A Psychological Analysis*. Hillsdale, NJ: Erlbaum.

Thomsen, S.R. (2007). Commentary: Searching for media effects. *International Journal of Epidemiology*, 36, 1078–1079.

Throgmorton, J.A. (1991). The rhetorics of policy analysis. *Policy Sciences*, 24(2), 153–179.

Timms, C., Graham, D. & Caltabiano, M. (2007). Perceptions of school administration trustworthiness, teacher burnout/job stress and trust: The contribution of morale and participative decision-making. In A. Glendon, B. Thompson & B. Myers (Eds.), *Advances in Organizational Psychology* (pp. 135–151). Bowen Hills, QLD: Australian Academic Press.

Törnblom, K. (1992). The social psychology of distributive justice. In K. Scherer (Ed.), *Justice: Interdisciplinary Perspectives* (pp. 177–236). Cambridge: Cambridge University Press.

Toulmin, S. & Leary, D. (1985). The cult of empiricism in psychology, and beyond. In S. Koch and D Leary (Eds.), *A Century of Psychology as Science* (pp. 594–617). New York: McGraw-Hill.

Trew, K. (2004). Children and socio-cultural divisions in Northern Ireland. *Journal of Social Issues*, 60, 507–523.

Tuffin, K. (2004). *Understanding Critical Social Psychology*. London: Sage.

Turner, J., Hogg, M., Oakes, P., Reicher, S. & Wetherell, M. (1987). *Rediscovering the Social Group*. Oxford: Blackwell.

Twigger-Ross, C. & Uzzell, D. (1996). Place and identity processes. *Journal of Environmental Psychology*, 16, 205–220.

Tyler, T. (1984). The role of perceived injustice in defendants' evaluations of their courtroom experience. *Law & Society Review*, 18, 51–74.

Tyler, T. (1989). The psychology of procedural justice: A test of the group-value model. *Journal of Personality and Social Psychology*, 57(5), 830–838.

Tyler, T. (1994). Psychological models of the justice motive: Antecedents of procedural and distributive justice. *Journal of Personality and Social Psychology*, 67(5), 850–864.

Tyler, T. (2000). Multiculturalism and the willingness of citizens to defer to legal authorities. *Law and Social Enquiry*, 25(3), 983–1019.

Tyler, T. (2004). Enhancing police legitimacy. *Annals of the American Academy of Political and Social Science*, 593, 84–99.

Tyler, T. (2006). Restorative justice and procedural justice: Dealing with rule breaking. *Journal of Social Issues*, 62(2), 307–326.

Tyler, T., Boeckmann, R., Smith, H. & Huo, Y. (1997). *Social Justice in a Diverse Society*. Boulder, CO: Westview.

Tyler, T. & Degoey, P. (1995). Collective restraint in social dilemmas: Procedural justice and social identification effects on support for authorities. *Journal of Personality and Social Psychology*, 69(3), 482–497.

Tyler, T. & Lind, E.A. (1992). A relational model of authority in groups. *Advances in Experimental Social Psychology*, 25, 115–191.

Tyler, T., Rasinski, K. & Griffin, E. (1986). Alternative images of the citizen. *American Psychologist*, 41, 970–978.

Tyler, T., Rasinski, K. & McGraw, K. (1985) The influence of perceived injustice on support for political authorities. *Journal of Applied Social Psychology*, 15, 700–725.

Tyler, T. & Wakslak, C. (2004). Profiling and police legitimacy: Procedural justice, attributions of motive, and acceptance of police authority. *Criminology*, 42(2), 253–281.

Unger, M. (2008). Hidden Resilience among Youth and Families: Nurturing Contextual Constructions of Positive Development. Faculty of Education Seminar, University of Waikato, 17 November.

Valsiner, J. (2009). Cultural psychology today: Innovations and oversights. *Culture & Psychology*, 15, 5–39.

van Dijk, T. (1992). Discourse and the denial of racism. *Discourse and Society*, 3, 87–118.

Vangelisti, A. & Perlman, D. (2006). *The Cambridge Handbook of Personal Relationships*. Cambridge: Cambridge University Press.

van Meijl, T. (2006). Multiple identifications & the dialogical self: Urban Maori youngsters and the cultural renaissance. *Journal of the Royal Anthropological Institute*, 12, 917–933.

van Zomeren, M., Spears, R. & Leach, C. (2008). Exploring psychological mechanisms of collective action: Does relevance of group identity influence how people cope with collective disadvantage? *British Journal of Social Psychology*, 47, 353–372.

Vaughan, G. & Hogg, M. (2008). *Introduction to Social Psychology*. Frenchs Forest, NSW: Pearson.

Veno, A. & van den Eynde, J. (2007). Moral panic neutralization project: A media-based intervention. *Journal of Community and Applied Social Psychology*, 17, 490–506.

Verkuyten, M. (2005). *The Social Psychology of Ethnic Identity*. Brighton, UK: Psychology Press.

Vermunt, R. & Steensma, H. (Eds.) (1991). *Social Justice in Human Relations*, Vol. 1, *Societal and Psychological Origins of Justice*. New York: Plenum.

Vigoda-Gadot, E. (2006). Compulsory citizenship behavior: Theorizing some dark sides of the good soldier syndrome in organizations. *Journal for the Theory of Social Behaviour*, 36(1), 77–93.

Wagoner, B., Gillespie, A. & Duveen, G. (2007). Bartlett in the digital age. *Psychologist*, 20, 668–669.

Wahba, A. & Bridgewell, L. (1976). Maslow reconsidered: A review of research on the need hierarchy theory. *Organizational Behavior and Human Performance*, 15, 212–240.

Waldram, J., Herring, A. & Kue Young, T. (2006). *Aboriginal Health in Canada: Historical, Cultural, and Epidemiological Perspectives* (2nd ed.). Toronto: University of Toronto Press.

Wallack, L. (2003). The role of the mass media in creating social capital: A new direction for public health. In R. Hofrichter (Ed.), *Health and Social Justice: Politics, Ideology and Inequity in the Distribution of Disease* (pp. 594–625). San Francisco: Jossey-Bass.

Walster, E., Berscheid, E. & Walster, G. (1973). New directions in equity research. *Journal of Personality and Social Psychology*, 25, 151–176.

Walster, E., Berscheid, E. & Walster, G. (1976). New directions in equity research. In L. Berkowitz & E. Walster (Eds.), *Advances in Experimental Social Psychology*, Vol. 9 (pp. 1–42). New York: Academic Press.

Waltman, M., Russell, D., Coyle, C., Enright, R., Holter, A. & Swoboda, M. (2009). The effects of a forgiveness intervention on patients with coronary artery disease. *Psychology and Health*, 24, 11–27.

Wang, C. & Burris, M. (1994). Empowerment through photo novella: Portraits of participation. *Health Education & Behavior*, 21(2), 171–186.

Warr, P. (1987). *Work, Unemployment, and Mental Health.* Oxford: Clarendon Press.

Watson, D., Klohnen, E., Casillas, A., Nus, E., Haig, J. & Berry, D. (2004). Match makers and deal breakers: Analyses of assortative mating in newlywed couples. *Journal of Personality*, 72, 1029–1068.

Watson, J.B. (1925). *Behaviorism.* New York: Norton.

Watson, K. & Platt, M. (2006). Fairness and the neurobiology of social cognition: Commentary on 'Nonhuman species' reactions to inequity and their implications for fairness' by Susan Brosnan. *Social Justice Research*, 19(2), 186–193.

Watts, R.J. & Serrano-Garcia, I. (2003). The quest for a liberating community psychology: An overview. *American Journal of Community Psychology*, 31, 73–78.

Webb, T. & Sheeran, P. (2006). Does changing behavioural intentions engender behavior change? A meta-analysis of the experimental evidence. *Psychology Bulletin*, 132, 249–268.

Weiner, B., Alexander, J. & Shortell, S. (2002). Management and governance processes in community health coalitions: A procedural justice perspective. *Health Education and Behavior*, 29(6), 737–754.

Wells, N. & Harris, J. (2007). Housing quality, psychological distress, and the mediating role of social withdrawal: A longitudinal study of low-income women. *Journal of Environmental Psychology*, 27, 69–78.

Wenzel, M. (2006). A letter from the tax office: Compliance effects of informational and interpersonal justice. *Social Justice Research*, 19(3), 345–364.

Wertz, F. (1998). The role of the humanistic movement in the history of psychology. *Journal of Humanistic Psychology*, 38, 42–70.

Wetherell, M. (1996). Constructing social identities: The individual/social binary in Henri Tajfel's social psychology. In W. Robinson (Ed.), *Social Groups and Identities: Developing the Legacy of Henri Tajfel* (pp. 269–284). London: Butterworth-Heinemann.

Wetherell, M. (2006). Formulating selves: Social psychology and the study of identity. *Social Psychological Review*, 8, 62–72.

Whitbourne, S.K. (2007). *Adult Development and Aging: Biopsychosocial Perspectives* (3rd ed.). New York: Wiley.

Wicker, A. (1989). Substantive theorising. *American Journal of Community Psychology*, 17(5), 531–547.

Wilkinson, R. (1996). *Unhealthy Societies: The Afflictions of Inequality*. London: Routledge.

Wilkinson, R. & Marmot, M. (2003). *Social Determinants of Health: The Solid Facts* (2nd ed.). Geneva: World Health Organization.

Williams, N., Lindsey, E., Kurtz, D. & Jarvis, S. (2001). From trauma to resiliency: Lessons from former runaway and homeless youth. *Journal of Youth Studies*, 4, 233–253.

Williamson, D. & Carr, J. (2009). Health as a resource for everyday life: Advancing the conceptualization. *Critical Public Health*, 19(1), 107–122.

Willig, C. (1999). *Applied Discourse Analysis*. Buckingham, UK: Open University Press.

Wilson, G., Cousins, J. & Fink, B. (2006). The CQ as a predictor of speed-date outcomes. *Sexual and Relationship Therapy*, 21, 163–169.

Winant, H. (2004). Behind blue eyes: Whiteness and contemporary U.S. racial politics. In M. Fine, L. Weis, L.P. Pruitt & A. Burns (Eds.), *Off White: Readings on Power, Privilege, and Resistance* (2nd ed.) (pp. 3–16). New York: Routledge.

Wong, J. & Tseng, V. (2008). Political socialization in immigrant families: Challenging top-down parental socialization models. *Journal of Ethnic and Migration Studies*, 34, 151–168.

Wood, L. & Giles-Corti, B. (2008). Is there a place for social capital in the psychology of health and place? *Journal of Environmental Psychology*, 28, 154–163.

World Health Organization. (1986). Ottawa Charter for Health Promotion. http://www.who.int/healthpromotion/conferences/previous/ottawa/en/

Wright, P. & Kloos, B. (2007). Housing environment and mental health outcomes: A level of analysis perspective. *Journal of Environmental Psychology*, 27, 79–89.

Wundt, W. (1897). *Outlines of Psychology*. New York: Stechert.

Yang, C.-F. (2006). The Chinese conception of the self. In U. Kim, K.-C. Yang & K.-K. Hwang (Eds.), *Indigenous and Cultural Psychology: Understanding People in Context* (pp. 327–356). New York: Springer.

Yardley, L. & Moss-Morris, R. (2009). Editorial. Current issues and new directions in psychology and health: Introducing the NICE guidance on behaviour change interventions. *Psychology and Health*, 24(2), 119–123.

Yerkes, M. & Pettijohn II, T. (2008). Developmental stability of perceived physical attractiveness from infancy to young adulthood. *Social Behavior and Personality*, 36, 691–692.

Zajonc, R. (1989). Styles of explanation in social psychology. *European Journal of Social Psychology*, 19, 345–368.

Zimbardo, P. (2004). Does psychology make a significant difference in our lives? *American Psychologist*, 59, 339–351.

Zimbardo, P. (2007). *The Lucifer Effect: Understanding How Good People Turn Evil*. New York: Random House.

Zuckerman, M., Miyake, K. & Elkin, C. (1995). Effects of attractiveness and maturity of face and voice on interpersonal impressions. *Journal of Research in Personality*, 29, 253–272.

Author Index

Adair, J., 129
Adams, J.S., 267–70
Adger, N., 227
Ajzen, I., 229
Ali, L., 208
Allport, G., 2, 4, 24, 28, 42, 52, 54–5, 59, 89, 165
Allwood, C., 126, 130, 132–5, 140
Altman, I., 155
Altman, J., 255
Amster, R., 150,
Anastasi, A., 137
Anderson, B., 331, 336, 338, 342, 348
Apfelbaum, E., 7, 26, 41, 53–4, 107
Armstrong, D., 176–7
Aro, A., 243
Aron, A., 41, 72
Arrindell, W., 63
Asch, S., 41–4, 144
Augoustinos, M., 90, 94
Australian Community Health Association, 247
Aveling, E., 204
Ayllón, T., 34

Bambra, C., 244
Bandura, A., 84, 147, 230, 281, 337–8
Barclay, L., 266
Bartholow, B., 342
Bartlett, F.C., 31–4, 84, 86–7, 103, 106, 147
Batson, C., 48, 290–2
Baum, W.M., 33
Baumeister, R., 65, 258
Bazarova, N., 96
Beaglehole, R., 121, 244
Beavis, C., 346
Becker, D., 302, 305, 307
Belk, R., 71
Berger, P.L., 82
Berry, J.W., 25, 125, 127, 129, 133, 193, 194, 195, 196
Bessenoff, G., 342
Bhabha, H., 183
Bhatia, S., 204, 209–11, 215
Bierhoff, H., 256, 258, 269, 271

Bigler, R., 92
Billig, M., 5, 22–4, 35, 37–8, 44, 49, 56, 64, 76, 79, 81, 83–4, 90, 92, 97, 101, 103–4, 143, 158, 168, 199
Blader, S., 256, 276–7
Blau, P., 68, 262–3
Block, J., 94
Bloemraad, I., 66
Bloustien, G., 351
Bochner, S., 187
Bohart, A.C., 304
Bolam, B., 237
Bolger, N., 224
Bonanno, G.A., 310, 313
Borgida, E., 347
Bornstein, R., 63
Bourdieu, P., 73, 214
Bowman, J., 54
Breckler, S.J., 258
Brehm, S., 258
Brewer, M., 84, 88, 165
Briñol, P., 92
Brock, A., 32
Brosnan, S., 256, 269, 271
Brown, B.B., 157
Brown, R., 138
Bruner, J.S., 35, 83–4
Buckingham, D., 342
Bugental, J., 298
Bulhan, H.A., 209–10
Bunton, R., 235
Burkitt, I., 59, 66
Burton, M., 40
Bushman, B., 338
Byrne, D., 63

Callan, M., 262, 271
Caltabiano, M., 73
Campbell, C., 223, 244, 246
Campbell, E., 188
Candland, D., 67
Cantril, H., 334
Caplan, G., 310
Carlson, E., 10, 307
Carr, S., 248, 258, 271
Carroll, D., 235–6, 239

Cartwright, D., 36
Castelli, L., 92–3
Castles, S., 184–5, 196
Cattell, V., 238
Chakkarath, P., 130
Chamberlain, K., 168, 206, 223, 237, 282, 323, 327–8, 331, 333, 343, 346–7, 349, 351, 353
Chandola, T., 224
Charleston, S., 156, 160
Chen, M.K., 271
Cherry, F., 45, 47, 144
Chiu, C-Y., 266
Cholewa, S., 241
Chomsky, N., 84
Chory, R., 266
Christopher, J.C., 67–8, 72, 98, 106–7, 120, 290, 305
Chung-Fang, Y., 144
Cicchetti, D., 311
Clausen, J., 25
Clay, R., 300
Cohen, D., 171
Cohen, R., 226, 258, 265
Cohen, S., 225
Cole, M., 130
Colic-Peisker, V., 198–203
Collier, G., 27, 30–1, 36, 39
Comstock, G., 323, 331
Comte, A., 24, 290
Condiotte, M., 230
Connell, A., 30
Conner, M., 228
Conner, S., 72
Contarello, A., 345
Cooley, C.H., 24–5, 65, 69, 71, 143, 158, 292, 347
Cornish, F., 235
Cottle, S., 332–3
Cottrell, L.S., 314–15
Couldry, N., 343, 345
Cravens, J., 297
Crawford, R., 242
Crawshaw, E., 189, 193
Crosby, F., 66, 263
Crossley, M., 223, 242

Csikszentmihalyi, M., 58, 66
Cuba, L., 145, 156
Cullen, A., 80, 99, 102
Curran, J., 327–8, 354
Cvetkovich, G., 260

Dalbert, C., 266
Danzinger, K., 42, 139
Darley, J., 47
Davey-Smith, G., 242
David, D., 227
de Certeau, M., 153, 158
De Cremer, D., 277
Dean, B., 136
Deaux, K., 186, 197, 201
Denham, S., 68
Descartes, R., 99
Deutsch, M., 270
DeWind, J., 282
Diener, E., 303
DiMatteo, M.R., 241
Diprose, R., 73
Dixon, J., 71, 90, 104, 154, 162,
    165–8, 261, 266, 283, 285
Dolnicar, S., 295
Doyle, K., 327, 328
Drew, N., 276, 285
Du Gay, P., 240
Dudgeon, P., 118
Dueck, A., 119, 122, 131, 133, 139
Durie, M., 127, 220
Durrheim, K., 90, 166

Eacott, C., 157
Easterling, D., 223
Eastwick, P., 62
Elms, A., 43
Eng, E., 244
Engel, G.L., 223
Enriquez, V., 119, 127–8
Erikson, E., 189
Espiritu, Y.L., 203, 206–7, 210, 215
Essed, P., 213
Esses, V., 282
Estacio, E.V., 91
Estrella, K., 10, 308
Ettner, S., 239

Faircloth, C., 60, 74
Farkas, A.J., 270
Farquhar, J., 241
Farr, R.M., 3, 5, 23–4, 36, 39, 42, 98
Feagin, J., 135
Festinger, L., 151, 261–3
Fijac, B.M., 211

Finkel, E., 56, 62–3
Fischoff, S., 342–3, 353
Fisher, A.T., 197, 213
Fisher, J.D., 297
Fiske, S., 86, 89
Flick, U., 55, 98–100, 103–4, 128
Flores-Osario, J.M., 40
Flournoy, R., 245
Folger, R., 258, 263, 270
Fondacaro, M., 266
Foster, D., 210
Frank, A., 74
Frankenberg, R., 212
Freire, P., 9–10, 41, 210, 302, 307–8
Freud, S., 291
Friedman, H., 304
Frosh, P., 330–1
Fry, G., 233–4
Fryer, D., 28, 30
Fuller, A., 72, 158, 310, 313
Furby, L., 269–70
Furnham, A.F., 99, 187

Gallagher, K., 246
Gamliel, E., 270
García-Montes, J., 164, 346, 352
Garvey, D., 138–9
Geertz, C., 198, 205
Geismar, H., 72
Gerbner, G., 339–41
Gergen, K.J., 4–5, 40, 42–4, 72, 98,
    125, 204
Giddens, A., 294
Giles, D., 323, 326, 337, 345
Godreau, I.P., 213
Goffman, E., 67, 141
Gone, J., 138
Gonzalez, C., 273, 277
Gooptu, N., 247
Gordon, D., 228
Gorman, M., 38
Gottlieb, B., 227
Gough, B., 90
Graves, T., 193
Green, M.J., 139, 212–13
Greenberg, J., 263, 277, 286
Greenfield, P.M., 209
Grosfoguel, R., 204, 209
Gross, H., 176
Groth-Marnat, G., 137
Grusec, J., 125
Guareschi, P., 246
Gunnestad, A., 313

Hage, G., 201, 212

Hajdu, D., 334
Hampton, K., 347–8
Hanselmann, C., 115
Harper, D.J., 95, 99
Harris, B., 22, 31
Harris, R.J., 270
Hart, T.J., 306
Hartig, T., 157
Hatfield, E., 66, 267, 269
Heider, F., 56, 64, 84, 93–4, 261–5
Heider, J., 92
Helman, C., 219–20
Hepburn, A., 258–9
Hermans, H.J.M., 65–6, 68, 71,
    143–5, 158, 206, 208–9, 215
Hernández, B., 156
Hewstone, M., 258, 263
Highmore, B., 6, 53
Hochbaum, G.M., 230
Hodgetts, D., 70–2, 74, 91, 151, 163,
    169, 219, 223, 238, 241–2, 307–8,
    326, 330–4, 353–4
Hoffman, L., 69
Hofrichter, R., 235, 245
Holdstock, L.T., 204, 206
Holmes, T.H., 224
Hook, D., 211
Houser, M., 61–3
Howarth, C., 141
Hughes, L., 117, 225
Hurdley, R., 159
Hussain, Z., 69
Hyyppa, M., 227, 246

Ingham, R., 232
International Labour Organization,
    117
Iscoe, I., 314–15

Jacobson, N., 309
Jahoda, M., 5, 28, 30, 171, 226–7,
    288, 314
James, W., 5, 24, 31–2, 58, 65–6, 68,
    70–1, 143–4, 158, 288
Jamieson, D., 64
Janz, N.K., 231
Jenkins, H., 349
Jiménez-Domínguez, B., 41
Jodelet, D., 56
Johnson, D.B., 122
Johnson, M., 29
Joinson, A.N., 342
Jones, C., 65
Jones, E., 94, 262, 264–5
Jones, R., 129, 137

Jost, J., 88
Jovchelovitch, S., 8, 10, 56, 67, 72, 79, 83, 98–101, 106, 107, 135, 283
Judd, C.M., 97

Kaholokula, J.K., 122–3
Kakefuda, I., 243
Katz, E., 339, 344, 353
Katz, J., 346
Kawachi, I., 226
Kazarian, S., 223
Kearins, J., 137
Keel, M., 195
Kelley, H., 66, 262, 264–5
Kelly, M., 243
Kenrick, D., 258
Kidd, S., 312
Kim, U., 128, 130, 134, 140, 147
Kimhi, S., 316
King, R., 197
Kiran-Esen, B., 229
Kleinman, A., 219–20
Korpela, K., 157
Kouvonen, A., 277
Kroeber, A., 205
Kuppers, P., 175
Kurzban, R., 62
Kutner, L., 329, 336

La Fromboise, T., 195
Lakey, B., 226
Lane, R., 274
Langer, E., 85
Langlois, J., 63
Lareau, A., 201
Latane, B., 45–6, 290
Laurier, E., 233
Lazarsfeld, P., 28, 30, 334, 339
Lazarus, R.S., 224–5
Le Bon, G., 5, 27, 45
Leach, C., 90, 194, 248, 292
Lees, L., 151
Lenhart, A., 349
Lepore, S., 225
Lerner, M.J., 95, 258
Leventhal, G., 274
Lewin, K., 2–3, 7, 23, 31, 36, 37, 56, 125, 288
Lewis, R.C., 211
Lidz, C., 138
Lind, E., 255, 271–5, 277
Lindsey, M., 137–8
Linley, A., 58, 302, 305
Liu, J., 144

Livingstone, S., 169, 323, 344–6, 348–9, 351
Lloyd-Bostock, S., 266
Lubek, I., 5, 23, 26–7, 30, 38, 39, 44, 54
Lykes, M.B., 250
Lyndon, C., 127
Lyons, A.C., 74, 222, 224, 227

Mallett, S., 160
Mama, A., 210
Mandler, G., 31, 32, 34
Mankowski, E.S., 107
Manning, R., 45–7
Mansouri, T., 194
Manuel, G., 117
Manzo, L.C., 160, 174
Markovizky, G., 187, 191–2
Markovsky, B., 260
Marks, D., 222–3, 234, 244
Martin, G., 34
Martin, K.B.M., 118, 136
Martín-Baró, I., 5, 8, 41, 204, 250, 308
Martinez, M.A., 116–17
Maslow, A., 58, 300–1, 304
Mastain, L., 289–91, 293–4
Mattis, J.S., 289, 291–5, 316
Maxim Institute, 260
McCabe, G., 139
McElwee, R.O., 96
McKnight, J., 258, 265
McMichael, C., 195
McMillan, B., 229
McMillan, S., 345
McPherson, K., 118
McQuail, D., 324–5, 327
Mead, G.H. 25, 29, 71, 143, 158, 288
Media Psychology Division 45, 342
Meier, B., 236, 244
Melchior, M., 239
Mellers, B., 270
Messick, D., 258
Messner, S., 341
Mezulis, A.H., 96
Miedemam, J., 278
Mielewczyk, F., 229, 232–5
Mikula, G., 266
Mikulas, W., 24, 140, 158
Mikulincer, M., 296
Milgram, S., 4, 36, 44
Miller, D.T., 95–6
Miller, J., 94–5
Miller, R., 62, 65
Minkler, M., 243–4

Mishler, E., 107
Mitchell, D., 151
Mkhize, N., 131
Moane, G., 120, 209
Moghaddam, F.M., 23–4, 134, 309
Monroe, K.R., 289, 293
Montada, L., 266
Montenegro, M., 10
Montero, M., 4, 6, 8, 10, 24, 41, 44, 204, 308
Moreton-Robinson, A., 118
Moriarty, T., 46
Morrison, B., 279
Morry, M., 62
Moschetti, G., 270
Moscovici, S., 55, 99–101, 134–5
Moyo, D., 297
Muldoon, O., 68
Muller, M., 276
Mulveen, R., 242
Murray, M., 223, 235, 244
Musolf, G., 24, 66, 70–1, 158

Nagata, D., 280, 282
Navarro, V., 223
Naverette, C., 207
Nelson, G., 259
Ng, S., 266
Nickerson, R., 85
Noble, G., 159, 213
Norris, F.H., 314
Nowell, B.L., 172–4
Nsamenang, A.B., 126, 204

Oberg, K., 184, 187
O'Donnell, C., 155
O'Donovan, A., 225
O'Dwyer, L., 172, 175
Ogden, J., 228
Okazaki, S., 209
Okimoto, T., 256, 273, 277
Opotow, S., 255, 278–82
O'Sullivan, S., 345
Oxenham, D., 139

Padilla, A., 137–8
Paradies, Y., 200
Paranjpe, A.C., 24
Pargament, K., 266
Parker, I., 4–6, 42, 44, 108, 204
Payne, B.K., 97
Peng, K., 141
Pe-Pua, R., 127–8
Perloff, R.M., 64, 79, 92
Peters, S., 263, 271

Peterson, C., 303
Piaget, J., 103, 189
Pietikäinen, S., 331
Pike, K., 129, 316
Poelmans, S., 238–9
Polkinghorne, D., 82, 260
Pooley, A., 314
Pooley, J.A., 314
Post, S.G., 289–90, 292, 296
Potter, J., 108
Pratkanis, A., 43
Prebble, J., 119
Pressman, S., 225
Pretty, G.H., 156–7
Prilleltensky, I., 240, 248, 259, 300–1, 304, 306, 316
Prince, L., 309–10
Prochaska, J., 231–2
Proshansky, H., 172
Purkhardt, C.S., 101
Putland, C., 172–3, 176, 245
Putnam, R.D., 347

Quijano, A., 204, 206

Radley, A., 73, 220, 238, 331
Ramirez, M., 277
Raphael, D., 222
Rappaport, J., 107–9, 223
Rawls, J., 256, 272
Rechavi, T., 159
Redfield, R., 184, 192
Reed-Victor, E., 311, 313
Reevy, G., 226
Rehberg, W., 296
Reicher, S., 90
Reis, H.T., 260, 270
Reyes Cruz, M., 204, 214
Reynolds, T., 202
Rezentes, W.J., 127
Rice, R., 345
Riggs, D., 138
Ritchie, J., 4, 124
Ritzer, G., 239–40
Robbins, B.D., 302, 306, 313
Robbins, R., 176
Robinson, D., 81
Robles, T.F., 224
Rodman, M., 153
Rogers, C., 58, 299–301, 304
Rojas, H., 347
Rosenstock, I.M., 230
Rosnow, R., 42, 257, 262
Ross, L., 94, 343
Rotter, J.B., 265

Rubin, M., 292
Rudmin, F.W., 125, 197
Rusbult, C., 72
Rydell, R., 92

Sampson, E., 257–8, 260, 283
Sapica Rodríguez, S., 185
Schaalma, H., 243
Schneider, F., 258
Schneider, K., 34, 58, 64, 298–9, 301, 339
Schwartz, L., 329
Scrambler, G., 245
Segall, M.H., 184, 193
Seligman, M.E.P., 303–4
Shapiro, S.B., 304
Sheils, D., 124
Sherif, C., 38
Sherif, M., 38, 44
Sheringham, M., 59
Sherwood, J., 139
Shortland, E., 131
Shweder, R.A., 206, 209
Signorielli, N., 339, 343
Silverstone, R., 61, 322, 326, 328, 332–3, 345, 348, 350–1, 354
Simmel, G., 45, 75
Sinha, D., 125, 129, 204
Skinner, B., 33
Skitka, L., 266, 277–8, 284
Skodova, Z., 225
Smith, L.T., 118, 136, 204
Snell, D., 105, 161–2, 332
Somerville, M., 207
Sonn, C.C., 139, 175, 194–5, 197, 209, 211, 213–14, 313–15
Stam, H., 98, 109, 232
Steele, C., 89
Steensma, H., 258, 270
Steptoe, A., 224–5, 227
Stevens, G., 213
Stone, B.L., 292–3
Stouffer, S. 261–2
Strachey, J., 291
Stukas, A.A., 295
Sugamura, G., 129
Sumner, W.G., 131
Sutton, R., 256, 277
Suzuki, L., 137–8
Swickert, R., 226

Tabibnia, G., 271
Tacchi, J., 348
Tadmor, T., 197
Taft, R., 32

Tajfel, H., 4, 35, 42, 44, 54, 78, 84, 134, 145, 184, 198–200, 292, 331
Tanner, K., 131
Tappan, M.B., 209
Tarde, G., 334, 347
Terry-Mcelrath, Y., 343
Thibaud, J.P., 164
Thibaut, J., 66, 262–4, 271–2
Thomsen, S.R., 343
Throgmorton, J.A., 105, 285
Timms, C., 224
Törnblom, K., 256, 261, 263, 273
Toulmin, S., 44
Trew, K., 68
Tuffin, K., 82, 259, 266, 285
Turner, J., 88
Twigger-Ross, C., 156–7
Tyler, T., 256, 258, 271, 272, 273–4

Unger, M., 311

Valsiner, J., 126, 130–1, 141, 198, 205–06, 209
van Dijk, T., 90
van Meijl, T., 209
van Zomeren, M., 248, 292
Vangelisti, A., 65
Vaughan, G., 258–9
Veno, A., 330, 354
Verkuyten, M., 210–11
Vermunt, R., 258, 270
Vigoda-Gadot, E., 296

Wagoner, B., 32
Wahba, A., 301
Waldram, J., 115
Wallack, L., 223, 246
Walster, E., 66, 267–8
Waltman, M., 241
Wang, C., 308
Warr, P., 102
Watson, D., 64
Watson, J.B., 33–4
Watson, K., 271
Watts, R.J., 210
Webb, T., 229
Weiner, B., 277
Wells, N., 172–3
Wenzel, M., 256, 277, 286
Wertz, F., 298, 306
Wetherell, M., 68, 72, 98, 108
Whitbourne, S.K., 224
Wicker, A., 285

Wilkinson, R., 221, 228, 235–38, 244–46
Williams, N., 310
Williamson, D., 220, 235, 244
Willig, C., 286
Wilson, G., 63

Winant, H., 213
Wong, J., 69
Wood, L., 171–2
World Health Organization, 220, 236
Wright, P., 161, 177
Wundt, W., 24, 31–3, 42–3, 84

Yang, C-F., 24, 66, 128–30, 141–2
Yardley, L., 243

Zajonc, R., 43
Zimbardo, P., 7, 37, 53, 57
Zuckerman, M., 63

Subject Index

Aboriginal, 12–13, 19, 117, 136, 200, 254, 255, 263, 265, 266, 280, 281, 285, 286

Acculturation, 16–17, 116, 123–5, 146, 181, 192–204, 211, 213, 215, 216, 366

Action research, 1, 3, 7–10, 28, 106, 170, 243, 248, 307, 330

Activity settings, 149–55

Advocacy, campaigns and media, 170, 229–30, 241–2, 330, 333–4, 349

Altruism, 18, 287–4, 296

American Community Gardening Association, 176

Ancestor worship, 124

Assertoric knowledge, 82, 260, 283

Assimilation, 103, 120, 125, 130, 192, 194, 199, 215, 366

Association of Humanistic Psychology, 300

Asylum seekers, 184–5, 254

Atomization, 64, 76

Attitudes, 14, 36, 37, 62, 64, 92–4, 108, 158, 165, 231, 363

Attribution, 77, 84, 93–7, 99, 106, 110, 262, 263–6, 338, 343

Behavioural psychology, behaviourism, 2, 13, 23, 31–5, 42, 45–7, 84, 92–6, 115, 154, 222, 228–36, 240–4, 246, 249, 260, 261, 264, 271, 298, 299, 302, 318, 329, 334–40, 342–3, 363

Belief perseverance, 343

Biopsychosocial model of health, 217, 223–8

Bobo doll studies, 338

Buddhism, 24, 128, 129, 140, 158, 304, 305

Bystander apathy, 21, 45–7, 144

Chinese, 66, 72, 119, 128, 140, 142–5, 308

Citizenship, 88, 108, 202, 215, 280, 303, 309

Civic participation, engagement, spaces, 23, 29, 69, 153, 171, 178, 201, 221, 246, 249, 294, 303, 307, 323, 333, 347, 349–50, 354, 371

Clinical Psychology, 289, 302

Cognitive dissonance, 151

Cognitive revolution, 35

Colonialism, 118, 120, 136, 203, 209–11

Colonization, 16, 40, 60, 88, 90, 114–16, 124, 125–6, 133, 135–6, 186, 193, 204, 209, 244, 269

and Indigenous people, 118–21

Community Arts Network (Western Australia) (CANWA), 175

Community Psychology, 44, 307

Community resilience, 19, 30, 117, 194, 219, 287, 291, 313–17, 347

Competent communities, 314–15

Confirmation bias, 77, 85, 96

Conflict , 315

Conformity, 16, 17, 36, 39, 40, 42, 54, 64, 144, 151, 274, 307

Contact zones, 181, 208

Coping, 53, 57, 74, 162, 172, 192, 222, 228, 236, 248, 250, 255, 256, 266, 288, 289, 303, 307, 314–17, 328

Cosmology and Cosmologies, 116, 117, 123–5, 121, 127, 130, 141

Crisis in social psychology, 5, 21, 23, 42–9, 129, 134, 154, 270, 301.

Critical Humanism, 19, 287–319

Critical Psychology, 44, 134

Cultivation Theory, 16, 323, 339–41

Cultural capital, 191, 246

Culture; assessment, colonisation, emic/etic, immigration, psychology, self, social representations, 6, 15, 20, 24, 25, 32, 42, 49, 55, 67, 74, 87, 89, 94, 95, 97, 101, 106, 113, 115, 117, 119–20, 125, 126, 128–9, 133–5, 137–9, 140, 146, 147, 175, 178, 183, 186, 194–204, 205–16, 273, 284, 293, 296, 297, 299, 301, 303, 310, 319, 346, 371

Culture Shock, 68, 181, 184, 186–92, 215, 366

Customs (tapu, mate maori, makutu), rituals, 38, 66, 71, 74, 98, 101, 106, 126–7, 131, 141, 156, 183, 221, 225–7, 346

Desegregation, 2, 149, 165–8

Deterritorialized understandings, 205–9

Dialogical, looking glass, cobweb, interconnected self, 9, 16–17, 20, 25, 49, 68, 73, 114, 116, 127, 133, 139–45, 146, 161, 178, 201, 207–9, 215, 233, 290, 292–3, 299, 305, 309, 313, 319

Digital games, 324, 334, 335, 337, 354

Dignity, Human dignity, 11, 29, 88, 111, 274, 275, 287, 296, 298, 306–11, 316, 318

Discourse, 18, 83, 87, 108–9, 197, 208, 210, 214, 257, 260, 284, 285, 286, 330

Discrimination, 2, 6–7, 14, 61, 88, 90–1, 96, 115, 117, 120, 135, 165, 168, 197–8, 202, 247, 254–5, 266, 291, 309, 331

[Dis]empowerment, 107, 138, 247, 286, 314

Dislocation and Displacement, 6, 16, 17, 118, 134, 135, 153, 167, 168, 174, 177, 183, 184, 186, 191, 195, 210, 214–15, 366

Disneyfication , 150

[dis]stress, 52, 57, 71, 122, 172–4, 183, 170, 219, 222–41, 250, 262, 263, 266–8, 291, 295, 297, 310, 315, 316

Division of Media Psychology (American Psychological Association), 329

Domesticity, domestic spaces, 159–60, 283, 285, 322, 350–2

Embodiment, 109
Encoding information, 86
Enculturation, 16, 113, 119, 125
Environmental Psychology, 149, 152, 153–5
Etic and emic approaches, 127–9, 50
Everyday and common knowledge , 55–7, 77–112, 326
Experimentalism, 34–6, 257, 270
Experiments, Experimental tradition, 4–6, 8–9, 31–44, 46–8, 55, 58, 62, 64, 84, 92–3, 97, 101, 131, 134, 154, 198, 225, 248, 257–8, 262–3, 268–70, 272, 283, 286, 336–7, 340

False consciousness, 38, 50
Feral children, 67
Filial piety, 67
Fourth world, 134, 208
Fundamedia attribution error, 343, 353
Fundamental attribution error, 94, 97

Gender, Gender socialisation , 25, 29, 69, 73, 88, 91, 96, 126, 137, 205, 208, 209, 214, 226, 229, 238, 285, 296, 338, 347
Global discipline of psychology, 129–35
Globalization, 164, 196, 203
Group (inter group) dynamics, 6, 36, 54, 198, 200, 204

Habitus, 73–4
Hawaiian , 121–4, 127–8
Health belief model, 230
Healthism, 217, 242
Health promotion, 176, 217, 218, 219, 222, 229, 234, 240–48, 361, 370
Health psychology, 217, 221–3, 235, 244, 249
Helping behaviour, pro-social acts, 18, 22, 37, 45, 47, 54, 78, 95, 114, 178, 202, 227, 241, 249, 287–319, 329, 371
Home, 8, 56, 65, 68, 91, 119–20, 122–3, 143, 152, 157–62, 164, 173, 182–5, 188–95, 197, 202–3, 207, 285, 322, 346, 348, 351–3

Homeless, Homelessness, 28, 70, 115, 150–4, 160, 163, 165, 169–70, 238, 259, 261, 285, 299, 301, 310, 312, 313, 333, 369
Hull House, 27–9
Human capital, 200–1
Humanistic psychology, humanism, 10, 18–20, 28, 34, 55, 58, 64, 109, 141, 220, 287–319, 362, 370, 371

Identity, 6, 68, 73, 75, 78, 84, 105, 108, 116, 118, 119, 121, 128, 135, 144–5, 152, 156–64, 170–7, 173, 175–205, 208–14, 216, 223, 229, 247–8, 254, 256, 274, 276–8, 284, 292–3, 303, 305, 310, 312, 321, 323, 328, 331, 335, 345–7, 352, 366–7.
Illness, 17, 30, 51, 56, 74–5, 79, 102, 127, 161, 217–51, 288, 300, 318, 328, 363
Immigrants and Immigration, 17, 22, 25, 28, 29, 56, 60, 78, 89, 92, 96, 105, 108, 125, 145, 154, 169–70, 181–216, 292, 367
Indigenous, 3, 4, 6, 12–17, 24, 50, 55, 68, 88–91, 96, 111, 113–47, 175, 185, 186, 188, 193, 197, 203–4, 216, 220, 255, 256, 259, 285, 299, 305, 315, 358, 360.
Indigenous voices in psychology, 12–13, 125–9, 136
Indigenous psychology, 116, 127, 129–35, 139
Inequalities, 17, 31, 43, 61, 99, 175, 238–49, 259, 316, 332–5.
Interdisciplinary, 28–9, 56, 222, 371
Intergroup understanding , 113–47, 181–216, 331–4
Inverse care law, 306

Judgment, 41, 78, 93–5, 110, 260, 266–72, 278, 284

Liberation Social Psychology, 5, 40, 41, 43, 107, 119, 142, 170, 209, 250, 307–8

Maori, 4, 124, 127, 203, 216
Marginalization, 40, 122, 125, 138, 183, 194, 259, 315, 333, 358
Material objects, subject-object relations, 20, 52, 64, 70–3, 98–9, 109, 140, 154, 156,

159–60, 162–4, 177, 195, 205–6, 322, 351
McCarthyism, 39, 50
McDonaldization, 240
Media , 25, 45, 57, 68–71, 85, 91–2, 105, 145, 152, 168–73, 199, 206–7, 215, 229, 241, 246, 282, 321–55, 358, 366–8
Media convergence and cross-fertilization, 327–8
Media effects, 334–41
Media nexus, 322, 325, 327, 349, 367
Mediapolis, 333
Mental health, 2, 30, 34, 56, 102, 122, 126, 160–1, 177, 201, 227, 238, 249
Migration, immigration, 25, 29, 56, 60, 89, 120, 145, 166, 181–216, 235, 281, 292, 369
Mind world dualism, 98–100, 111
Minority group influence, 135
Minoritization, 199
Narrative, 15, 71, 78–9, 84, 77, 103, 106–9, 111, 116–17, 123–4, 140, 144, 169, 210, 214, 260–1, 292, 330, 354

National Institute for Health and Clinical Excellence (NICE), 243
Navajo , 122–3
Neighbourhood renewal , 173–4, 178–9
Norms, 15, 16, 18, 25, 38, 45–7, 68, 79, 84, 87, 98, 105, 109, 110, 125, 126, 131, 138, 144, 155, 178, 183, 196, 231, 242, 247, 261, 291, 292, 294, 296, 297, 315, 318, 341

Objectivity, scientific neutrality, 4–5, 35, 39, 43, 134, 250
Online/Offline divide, 347–52
Organizational , 222

Persuasion, 18, 36, 70
Philippine, Filipino , 79, 88, 102, 119, 122, 127–8, 203, 207
Place-based identities, 68, 145, 155, 156–9, 161–2, 164, 168, 171–5, 202, 294, 347, 350, 363
Positive psychology, 58, 220, 300, 302–6, 313, 317–18
Poverty, 14, 22, 28, 31, 40, 47, 53, 95, 97–9, 117, 122, 172, 175, 223, 228, 236, 244–5, 259, 266, 291, 302, 310, 313, 332, 336, 342

Power , 10, 36, 37, 39, 40, 41, 54, 61,
    100, 107, 108, 119, 97–9, 121,
    134–6, 138, 147, 165, 185, 193,
    201, 203, 204, 209–14, 215, 216,
    223, 235, 237, 238, 244, 247,
    249–50, 272, 283, 289, 301, 307,
    312, 315, 317, 325, 331–3, 354
Praxis, 7–9, 136
Prejudice, 4, 15, 28, 30, 31, 36, 54, 61,
    64, 79, 88–91, 93, 104, 115, 165,
    198, 266, 318, 332, 369, 370
Protection Motivation Theory of
    Health, 230

Racialization, 91, 212–15
Racism, 47, 90–1, 97, 104, 167, 182,
    183, 199, 200, 209, 212–14, 223,
    254, 259, 285, 332, 368
Refugees, 182, 184, 185, 189, 191,
    193–5, 200–3, 210–15, 254–5,
    259, 263, 276, 278, 281, 282,
    285, 358, 366, 369
Representational spaces, 19, 91, 152,
    168–71, 177, 353
Research methods, 4–9, 29–33, 35,
    40–4, 63–4, 84, 105, 127–8,
    139, 146, 204, 304, 308, 353
Resilience, individual and
    community, 6, 30, 115, 117, 194,
    207, 226–7, 288, 289, 291, 301,
    309–19, 347, 362, 370
[re]socialization, 6, 15–16, 25, 58,
    63, 65–70, 75–6, 79, 87, 93, 101,
    125, 126, 141, 144, 313, 326,
    340, 360
Rights: animal, civil, collective,
    homeless, human, land,
    women's, 3, 17, 29, 88, 89,
    118–19, 136, 170, 199, 210,
    235, 236, 247, 254, 260, 274–5,
    278–80, 308–9, 325

Schema, 33, 83–7, 91, 99, 110, 295
Segregation, desegregation,
    re-segregation , 2, 88, 90,
    103–4, 118, 164–68, 292
Self-actualization and the hierarchy
    of needs, 301, 304
Self determination, 8, 111, 117, 135,
    175, 212, 289, 370
Self-efficacy, 120, 156, 172, 178, 230,
    239
Separatism , 194, 206
Settlement, 17, 25, 29, 181–216, 316,
    366
Social capital, 154, 171–2, 174, 178,
    226–7, 237, 245–6, 249, 251,
    291, 294–5, 314, 360
Social Cognition, 6, 11, 79, 83–4, 87,
    97, 100, 106, 232, 261–2, 284
Social constructionism, 15, 82, 98,
    101, 260–1, 272, 278, 283–4
Social determinants (of health), 127,
    219, 221, 225, 227–8, 235–38,
    245, 249, 365
Social Identity Theory, 84, 145, 184,
    197–205, 234, 276, 292, 331, 366
Social inclusion, 8, 11, 29, 41, 61,
    107, 110, 125, 147, 152, 162, 165,
    166, 170–4, 179, 188, 197, 216,
    233, 245, 247, 249, 250, 279,
    281–2, 285, 306, 308, 309,
    319, 330, 333, 352, 360, 370
Social justice, 3, 8, 39–41, 65–6,
    110–11, 118, 197, 219, 222–3,
    235, 244, 248, 250, 253–86, 289,
    299–300, 304, 309, 312, 316,
    318, 331, 358, 363, 365, 369
Social Learning Theory, 84–5, 337
Social participation, 30, 151, 170,
    172, 349
Social Representations Theory, 56,
    100–4, 106, 107, 109, 111

Social stratification, 238
Social support, 29, 30, 173, 176, 179,
    183, 195, 219, 224–7, 237–9,
    242, 249, 288, 290, 318, 348,
    360, 365
Social transformation, change, 2,
    7–10, 26–8, 30, 36, 40–1, 44,
    132, 175, 221–3, 246, 247,
    250, 286, 293, 306–9, 316,
    317, 327, 330, 354, 362,
    369, 370
Society for the Psychological Study
    of Social Issues, 30–1, 39
Sociocultural, 44, 49, 54, 139, 193,
    203, 310
Sojourners, 184–6
Stages of change model, 231
Stress, 57, 71, 190, 219, 223–8,
    236–41, 250, 266, 310, 316
Stereotypes, 54, 79, 84–91, 97, 99,
    103, 110, 112, 120, 138, 165,
    212, 213, 334
Structuration, 294

Theory of Reasoned Action, 231
Two step flow model of
    communication, 339

Unemployment, 30, 31, 81, 82, 89,
    94, 98–102, 104, 182, 200,
    201, 233, 236, 244, 249, 266,
    314, 332

Violence, 47–8, 120, 185, 217–51,
    255, 291, 304, 318, 322–3,
    335–42
Volunteering, 54, 171, 288, 289, 292,
    294–7, 317, 369

Whitehall study, 224, 239
Whiteness, 139, 212–14